New Jersey Employment Law

second edition

ROSEMARY ALITO

Contributors
Vincent N. Avallone
Joel L. Botwick
Dominick J. Bratti
Kevin P. Duffy
(Employment Discrimination)
Anthony Palmisano
Stephen F. Payerle

New Jersey Law Journal Books
Newark, New Jersey
(973) 642-0075

New Jersey Law Journal Books
is the book publishing division of the New Jersey Law Journal,
a publication of American Lawyer Media
For further information about New Jersey Law Journal Books contact:
New Jersey Law Journal
P.O. Box 20081
238 Mulberry St.
Newark, N.J. 07101-6081
(973) 642-0075

Suggested citation form: Alito, *N.J. Employment Law (2d ed.),* §___, at ___ (199__).

NOTE: This book is intended only as a survey of New Jersey employment law, and is not intended to offer advice or counsel. Nor is it intended to serve as a substitute for professional representation. Since the information in this book may not be sufficient in dealing with a client's particular legal problem, and because this area of law constantly changes, lawyers and others using this publication should not rely on it as a substitute for independent research.

References to the male pronoun throughout this book are incidental, and are not meant to infer or imply bias on the part of the author or the publisher.

Library of Congress Catalog Card Number
92 - 71078

International Standard Book Number
1 - 879590 - 26 - 3
Printed in the United States of America

PUBLISHER'S CREDITS: Ed Devine, Judy Davis, Linda Manahan; Desktop Composition by FTK Media, LLC
Notice in section 6-11:1 printed with the permission of the New Jersey Division on Civil Rights.

Preface

As the focus in employment law has shifted from organized bargaining to legislative and administrative rule in order to assure workplace equity, the need has grown for a reference guide that makes sense of these confusing and ever-changing regulations. Since 1992, *New Jersey Employment Law* has filled that vacuum with the exhaustive compendium and intelligent analysis that are essential for lawyers, businesspersons, human resources professionals and laypersons.

In this second edition of her heralded book, Rosemary Alito updates every chapter and adds a chapter on workplace privacy. With this current information, *New Jersey Employment Law* boasts an unparalleled breadth of analysis of the employer-employee relationship. Alito takes each aspect of employment law and thoroughly addresses it with unrivaled clarity, insightfulness and intelligence.

We think Alito has created as thorough a treatment of the subject as one might wish. We are sure you will agree.

— Edgar Devine, Esq.
Editor, *New Jersey Employment Law*

Acknowledgments

It was June 15, 1990 at the swearing-in of a Third Circuit Judge when Rob Steinbaum and I first talked about his plans to publish a book series, and the possibility of my writing on employment law to start it off. My work with Rob and Linda Manahan since then—on the original book, the annual supplements and now this Second Edition—has been one of the most rewarding experiences of my career. I owe tremendous thanks to Rob and Linda for affording me that opportunity and for their judgment, skill and especially patience along the way.

I thank all of the attorneys who have enriched this project, the contributors to the first and second editions, my associates Jim Jacobus, Dawn Marmo, Ilan Simon and Ron Weisenberg, and expecially my partners at McCarter & English, LLP who have provided immeasurable understanding and support to me in this and my other endeavors. I also thank the wonderful staff at McCarter & English, LLP and in particular our research librarians. I give special thanks to my assistant, Carmen Torres, who has been involved since the first word was written and who is simply indispensable.

— Rosemary Alito
February, 1999

About the Author

Rosemary Alito is a partner in McCarter & English, LLP, the largest and one of the oldest firms in the state. Ms. Alito represents management in disputes involving employment law and employee benefit law issues. She counsels on workplace policies, union relations and compliance and defends employers in litigation, including employment discrimination, wrongful termination, harassment and employee benefit plan terminations.

A frequent writer and lecturer on issues of employment law, Ms. Alito is vice chair of the editorial board of the *New Jersey Law Journal*, Secretary of the Association of the Federal Bar of the State of New Jersey and a Fellow of the American Bar Foundation. She serves on the Executive Committee of the Labor and Employment Law Section of the New Jersey State Bar Association. She serves on the Lawyers' Advisory Committee to the United States District Court, and has served on the New Jersey Supreme Court Committee on Women in the Courts, and the New Jersey Model Jury Charge Employment Law Subcommittee. Ms. Alito has taught employment law at the New Jersey Judicial College.

Ms. Alito is an experienced litigator in trials and appeals in both state and federal courts. She has served as lead counsel in the successful defense of class actions under ERISA and the LMRA involving multiple-employer welfare and pension trust funds, and trials of class actions challenging termination of retiree medical benefits. Her litigation experience in discrimination matters ranges from single-plaintiff cases to EEOC actions challenging companywide and nationwide policies.

Ms. Alito graduated in 1974 from Smith College and in 1978 from the Rutgers University School of Law in Newark, where she was a member of the *Law Review*.

Contents

page

Chapter 10
Temporary Disability

Chapter 11

Chapter 1

Employment Contracts Express and Implied

I. INDIVIDUAL CONTRACTS

1-1 The Employment Relationship

It is frequently said that the relation of master and servant is not susceptible to exact definition. As a result, it is normally for the trier of fact to determine, in each case, whether an employer/employee relationship exists.[1] That determination may be significant for a number of reasons, including taxation;[2] coverage under various statutes such as the Workers' Compensation Act, the Law Against Discrimination, and the Unemployment Compensation Law;[3] and liability for torts under the doctrine of *respondeat superior.*[4] The determination of whether

---

1. *See Pelliccioni v. Schuyler Packing Co.*, 140 N.J.Super. 190, 198-99 (App.Div. 1976); *Bennett v. T & F Distributing Co.*, 117 N.J.Super. 439, 441 (App.Div. 1971), *certif. denied*, 60 N.J. 350(1972); *Boudrot v. Taxation Div. Director*, 4 N.J. Tax 268, 270 (Tax Ct. 1982) (determination of employee status "is essentially a factual one, to be reached only after an examination of all the facts and circumstances pertaining to plaintiff's activities and his relationship with the other parties involved in those activities"). Restatement (Second) of Agency, §220 comment c(1958) (Restatement of Agency). *But see* New Jersey Model Jury Charges: Civil §4.21 ("[I]f there are no disputed facts or disputed inferences which may be drawn from undisputed facts concerning the elements of the relationship the judge should determine whether or not there is a master-servant relationship as a matter of law").

2. *See Landwehr v. Taxation Div. Director*, 6 N.J. Tax 66 (Tax Ct. 1983) (plaintiff's business expense deductions found proper on ground that he was an independent contractor, not an employee); *Boudrot v. Taxation Div. Director*, 4 N.J. Tax 268 (Tax Ct. 1982) (same); *Domenick v. Taxation Div. Director*, 176 N.J.Super. 121 (App.Div. 1980) (business expense deductions of employee-salesman disallowed). *See generally* Shenkman and Freedman, *"Employees, Independent Contractors and Similar Relationships in the Close Corporation"*, No. 142 New Jersey Lawyer, p.32 (Sept./Oct. 1991).

3. *See* Chapter 4, §§4-5 and 4-6; Chapter 9; *Wilson v. Kelleher Motor Freight Lines, Inc.*, 12 N.J. 261 (1953) (workers' compensation); *Pukowsky v. Caruso*, 312 N.J. Super. 171, 180 (App. Div. 1998) (holding that independant contractors are not entitled to the protections afforded to employees under the Law Against Discrimination); *Dee v. Excel Wood Products Co.*, 86 N.J.Super. 455 (App. Div.), *certif. denied*, 44 N.J. 586 (1965) (workers' compensation).

4. *See* Chapter 3, §3-18:1.

one is an employee, however, may vary depending upon the context and any applicable statutory provisions. Courts have consistently held, for example, that the remedial purposes of the Unemployment Compensation Law require utilization of a far more expansive definition of employee than at common law.[5] As defined in the *Restatement of Agency*, a "servant" [6] is:

> a person employed to perform services in the affairs of another and who with respect to the physical conduct in the performance of the services is subject to the other's control or right to control.[7]

As used in this context, "control" pertains to the employer's right to regulate the means and manner of performance of a task, as distinguished from the more limited right of one procuring the services of an independent contractor to control the end result:

> Under the control test, "[t]he relation of master and servant exists whenever the employer retains the right to direct the manner in which the business shall be done, as well as the result to be accomplished, or in other words, not only what shall be done, but how it shall be done." ... In contrast to a servant, an independent contractor is defined as "one who, carrying on an independent business, contracts to do a piece of work according to his own methods, and without being subject to the control of his employer as to the means by which the result is to be accomplished, but only as to the result of the work."[8]

It is the right to control that is determinative, not whether the right was in fact exercised.[9]

---

5. *See, e.g., Carpet Remnant Warehouse, Inc. v. Dept. of Labor*, 125 N.J. 567, 581 (1991); *Provident Inst. for Sav. in Jersey City v. Div. of Unemployment Sec.*, 32 N.J. 585, 590 (1960); *Gilchrist v. Div. of Employment Sec.*, 48 N.J.Super. 147, 153 (App.Div. 1957).

6. In *New Jersey Property-Liability Ins. Guaranty Ass'n. v. State*, 195 N.J.Super. 4 (App.Div. 1984), the court noted that although "servant" originally was defined in cases involving the common-law liability of the master to third parties based on the doctrine of *respondeat superior*, it has for modern purposes (in that case, coverage under the Workers' Compensation Act) become synonymous with "employee." *Id.* at 9, n.2.

7. Restatement (Second) of Agency, §220, relied on in *Pelliccioni v. Schuyler Packing Co.*, 140 N.J.Super. 190, 198-99 (App.Div. 1976); *Miklos v. Liberty Coach Co., Inc.*, 48 N.J.Super. 591, 602 (App.Div. 1958).

8. *New Jersey Property-Liability Ins. Guaranty Ass'n. v. State*, 195 N.J.Super. 4, 8-9 (App.Div. 1984), *certif. denied*, 99 N.J. 188 (1984) (workers' compensation case). *See Landwehr v. Taxation Div. Director*, 6 N.J. Tax 66, 70 (Tax Ct. 1983); *Wilson v. Kelleher Motor Freight Lines, Inc.*, 12 N.J. 261, 264 (1953).

9. *Aetna Ins. Co. v. Trans Am. Trucking Serv.*, Inc., 261 N.J. Super. 316, 326-27 (App. Div. 1993) ("Under the 'right to control' test, the exercise of control is not as determinative as the right to control .... The primary factors considered significant when analyzing the right to control include: evidence of the right of control, right of termination, furnishing of equipment, and method of payment"). *Boudrot v. Taxation Div. Director*, 4 N.J. Tax 268, 274 (Tax Ct. 1982); *Johnson v. U.S. Life Ins. Co.*, 74 N.J.Super. 343, 352 (App.Div. 1962) (workers' compensation).

Although control is perhaps the most important factor, it is not the only factor utilized in determining whether an employment relationship exists. The entirety of the circumstances should be considered,[10] including:

(1) whether the employee is engaged in a distinct profession or occupation;

(2) the type of occupation, with reference to whether it is one normally performed by an employee or by a specialist without supervision;

(3) the degree of skill required;

(4) whether the employer supplies instrumentalities, tools and the place of work;

(5) the length of time of employment;

(6) the method of payment;[11]

(7) whether the work is part of the regular business of the employer; and

(8) whether the parties believe they are in the relationship of employer and employee.[12]

While the absence of deductions from pay for social security may have some probative value on the issue of whether an employer-employee relationship exists, neither the

---

10. *See Pelliccioni v. Schuyler Packing Co.*, 140 N.J.Super. 190, 199 (App.Div. 1976) ("While the element of control is generally an important—even the most important—determinant in ascertaining whether a master and servant relationship exists, control is not the be-all and end-all of the inquiry. All of the surrounding circumstances must be considered."); *Boudrot v. Taxation Div. Director*, 4 N.J. Tax at 274 (Tax Ct. 1982) (no single factor is conclusive; "rather the relationship or status is to be ascertained by an overall view of the entire situation and an evaluation of the special facts of each particular case"); *Landwehr v. Taxation Div. Director,* 6 N.J. Tax 66, 68 (Tax Ct. 1983) (same); *Andryishyn v. Ballinger,* 61 N.J.Super. 386, 391 (App.Div. 1960). *Cf. Wilson v. Kelleher Motor Freight Lines, Inc.*, 12 N.J. 261, 264 (1953) (control determinative; workers' compensation case). In *Aetna Ins. Co. v. Trans Am. Trucking Serv., Inc.*, 261 N.J. Super. 316 (App. Div. 1993), a Workers' Compensation case, the Appellate Division looked to both the "right to control" and "relative nature of the work" tests. The relative nature of the work test focuses on whether there is substantial economic dependence by the purported employee upon the purported employer and whether there has been a functional integration of their operations. "In other words, the 'relative nature of the work' is tested by 'whether the work is an integral part of the employer's business and whether the worker furnishes independent business or professional service.'" 261 N.J. Super. at 327. *See generally Peck v. Imedia, Inc.*, 293 N.J. Super. 151, 160-61 (App. Div.) (holding that plaintiff was an independent contractor rather than an employee where she never completed an IRS W-2 form or an INS I-9 form, she did not receive an employee manual, and defendant did not take federal and state withholdings from plaintiff's compensation), *certif. denied,* 147 N.J. 262 (1996); *Dunellen Borough v. F. Montecalvo Constr.*, 273 N.J. Super. 23, 28-29 (App. Div. 1994) (noting that there are situations, including cases involving professional employees where the employer would not normally control the details of the work, where the control test is not dispositive); *Swillings v. Mahendroo*, 262 N.J. Super. 170 (App. Div. 1993) (finding registered nurse performing in-home services was an independent contractor and holding that the analysis applied in making that determination should reflect her professional status).

11. However, mere payment by the hour is not inconsistent with the status of independent contractor. *Dee v. Excel Wood Products Co.*, 86 N.J.Super. 453, 458 (App.Div.), *certif. denied,* 44 N.J. 586 (1965).

making nor the failure to make such deductions is in itself determinative.[13]

In *Pukowsky v. Caruso*,[14] the Appellate Division affirmed the trial court's determination that the plaintiff, a roller skating instructor, was an independent contractor and not an "employee" of the roller skating rink within the meaning of the Law Against Discrimination. Although the Court noted that the Federal courts have set forth a number of tests which employ common-law agency principles to interpret statutes which contain the word "employee," but do not helpfully define the term, the Court did not adopt any particular test.[15] The Court did, however, rely upon the following facts to determine that the plaintiff was an indepensent contractor: the plaintiff recruited students herself, she had sole control over what and how she taught her students, her students paid her directly, plaintiff did not receive any compensation or fringe benefits from the roller skating rink, and she characterized herself as self-employed on her 1993 and 1994 tax returns.[16]

An employment contract, like any other contract, must be sufficiently definite in its terms that the performance to be rendered by each party can be ascertained with reasonable certainty.[17] Thus, in *Jenkins v. Region Nine Housing*, the Appellate Division found that the plaintiff's breach of contract claim was properly dismissed in light of plaintiff's deposition testimony that "no specific term of employment was mentioned at the time of the hiring."[18]

---

12. *Miklos v. Liberty Coach Co., Inc.*, 48 N.J.Super. 591, 602 (App.Div. 1958). In *Landwehr v. Taxation Div. Director*, 6 N.J. Tax 66, 68-69 (Tax Ct. 1983), the eight factors listed for determining employee status under the New Jersey Gross Income Tax were: (1) the relationship the parties believed they created; (2) the extent of control exercisable (regardless of whether exercised) over the manner and method of performance; (3) whether the person providing service undertook substantial costs; (4) whether special training or skill was involved; (5) the duration of the relationship; (6) whether the person providing service assumed a risk of loss; (7) whether the person providing service could be discharged without cause; and (8) the method of payment utilized.

13. *Dee v. Excel Wood Products Co.*, 86 N.J.Super. 453, 459 (App.Div.), *certif. denied*, 44 N.J. 586 (1965). The court stated: "While such deductions may have some probative value on the issue of whether an employment status existed, neither the making nor the failure to make such deductions is dispositive of an issue of this type." *Id.* at 457. The court went on to find that in that case the deductions had been made through inadvertence and without any intention of creating or recognizing an employee status. *Id.* at 457-58. *See Boudrot v. Taxation Div. Director*, 4 N.J. Tax 268, 274-75 (Tax Ct. 1982) (issuance of W-2 not determinative); *Arthur v. St. Peter's Hospital*, 169 N.J.Super. 575, 578 (Law Div. 1979) (dicta).

14. 312 N.J. Super. 171 (App. Div. 1998).

15. *Id.* at 182 (citing *Nationwide Mut. Ins. Co. v. Darden*, 503 U.S. 318, 322-23, 112 S. Ct. 1344, 1348, 117 L. Ed. 2d 581, 589 (1992); *EEOC v. Zippo Manufacturing Co.*, 713 F.2d 32 (3d Cir. 1983); *Frankel v. Bally, Inc.*, 987 F.2d 86, 89-91 (2d Cir. 1993); *Cox v. Master Lock & Co.*, 815 F. Supp. 844, 845 (E.D.Pa.), *aff'd*, 14 F.3d 46 (3d Cir. 1993); *Franz Raymond Eisenhardt & Sons, Inc.*, 732 F. Supp. 521, 528 (D.N.J. 1990); *Carney v. Dexter Shoe Co.*, 701 F. Supp. 1093 (D.N.J. 1988).

16. 312 N.J. Super. 171, 183 (App. Div. 1998).

17. *Friedman v. Tappan Development Corp.*, 22 N.J. 523, 531 (1956).

18. 306 N.J. Super. 258, 263 (App. Div. 1997), *certif. denied*, 153 N.J. 405 (1998). *See also Craffey v. Bergen County Util.*, 315 N.J. Super 345, 351 (App. Div. 1998).

1-2 Lifetime Contracts

Lifetime contracts of employment are disfavored. The burden of proving the existence of same, established in *Savarese v. Pyrene Mfg. Co.*, is exacting.[19]

In *Savarese*, the plaintiff-employee hesitated to play on a company baseball team, and when pressed to do so asked what would happen if he got hurt. A supervisor purportedly replied: "If you get hurt I will take care of you. You will have a foreman's job the rest of your life."[20] The employee did get hurt and he did get terminated 21 years later. The Supreme Court found the alleged oral contract of lifetime employment too indefinite, and too lacking in essential terms to be enforced:

> Agreements of this nature have not been upheld except where it most convincingly appears it was the intent of the parties to enter into such long-range commitments and they must be clearly, specifically and definitely expressed. Only then is it grudgingly conceded that not all such contracts are "so vague and indefinite as to time as to be void and unenforceable because of uncertainty or indefiniteness."[21]

Thus, contracts for lifetime or permanent employment are unenforceable unless (1) the responsibilities assumed and obligations imposed are clearly and unequivocally expressed in the contract itself;[22] and (2) the employee has provided some consideration for the lifetime commitment in addition to services incidental to employment.[23] Moreover, delegation of express authority to enter into such an agreement on behalf of the employer must be demonstrated. Because a contract of employment for life is of an "extraordinary nature, outside the regular

---

19. 9 N.J. 595 (1952). *See, e.g., Alter v. Resorts Int'l, Inc.*, 234 N.J.Super. 409, 416 (Ch.Div. 1989) (even where all elements requisite to enforcement of contract for life are proven, enforcement will not be ordered unless employee's job performance is satisfactory). *But see Rogozinski v. Airstream By Angell*, 152 N.J.Super. 133, 143-44 (Law Div. 1977), *modified on other grounds*, 164 N.J.Super. 465 (App.Div. 1979) (stating that permanent contracts are difficult to prove but not unenforceable or against public policy; apparently construing a "permanent contract" as a contract not to discharge without good cause). *See Scudder v. Media Gen., Inc.*, 1995 WL 495945 (D.N.J. 1995) (reaffirming the continued viability of *Savarese*; rejecting as a matter of law plaintiff's claim that he was promised he could keep his job as long as he wanted it).

20. 9 N.J. at 597.

21. 9 N.J. at 601.

22. Deficiencies noted by the Court in *Savarese* included the failure to specify a future salary and to provide for various contingencies, such as plaintiff becoming disabled from other causes or otherwise rendered incapable of working. *See Pitak v. Bell Atlantic Network Servs., Inc.*, 928 F. Supp. 1354, 1370 (D.N.J. 1996) ("New Jersey law demands specific, concrete evidence of a contract for lifetime employment, and neither 'corporate culture' nor the assurances of relocation in this case are sufficient to demonstrate such contracts."); *see also Friedman v. Tappan Development Corp.*, 22 N.J. 523, 531 (1956); *Piechowski v. Matarese*, 54 N.J.Super. 333, 344-45 (App.Div. 1959).

custom and usage of business, [t]he authority of a corporate officer to enter into such a contract on behalf of his principal cannot arise merely by implication."[24]

But even if all these requirements are satisfied, it would appear that truly lifetime contracts will not be recognized; that contingencies will be read into the contract. Thus, in *Savarese*, the Court quoted as "the prevailing rule" that an otherwise valid permanent employment contract will continue to operate only "as long as the employer remains in the business and has work for the employee, and the employee is able and willing to do his work satisfactorily and does not give good cause for his discharge. ..." [25] The court in *Alter v. Resorts Int'l, Inc.*,[26] in turn, relied on that language as establishing the rule that "lifetime contracts, even where upheld, only preclude a discharge 'without cause.' " [27]

---

23. In *Alter v. Resorts Int'l, Inc.*, 234 N.J.Super. 409, 415 (Ch.Div. 1989), the court refused to enforce an alleged lifetime contract due to lack of specificity and lack of additional consideration. It suggested, however, that lack of additional consideration alone would not be fatal: "Presumably, if the intent is clear and unequivocal, the lack of 'additional consideration' would not be critical." *See also Piechowski v. Matarese*, 54 N.J.Super. at 344 ("One of the devices created by the courts to test whether or not the parties specifically and definitely intended to make a permanent or lifetime contract of employment is whether the employee gave some consideration additional to the mere agreement on his part to render service."); *Eilen v. Tappin's, Inc.*, 16 N.J.Super. 53, 56 (Law Div. 1951) (same); *Obendorfer v. Gitano Group, Inc.*, 838 F. Supp. 950, 953-54 (D.N.J. 1993) ("long range employment contract is enforceable if the intention of the parties to make such a contract is clearly, specifically and definitely expressed, and the intent of the parties may be ascertained from the language employed, from the attendant circumstances, and from the presence of consideration from the employee additional to the services incident to his employment;" Court dismissed claim for lack of specific allegations regarding terms and lack of additional consideration from the employee).

24. *Savarese v. Pyrene Mfg. Co.*, 9 N.J. 595, 603 (1952). *See also Labus v. Navistar Int'l Trans. Corp.*, 740 F.Supp. 1053, 1063 n. 3 (D.N.J. 1990) (affirmative proof of authority of an agent to make oral representations is required only where the representation is "unusual or contrary to the employer's standard procedure"); *Alter v. Resorts Int'l, Inc.*, 234 N.J. Super. at 415-16 (Ch.Div. 1989); *C.B. Snyder Realty Co. v. National Newark & Essex Building Co. of Newark*, 14 N.J. 146, 159 (1953).

25. 9 N.J. at 601 (internal quotation marks omitted). In *Borbely v. Nationwide Mutual Ins. Co.*, the district court commented on the permanent/good cause distinction as follows:

> Although contracts for permanent employment and employment contracts terminable only for cause are often treated as one and the same obligation, *see* [*Savarese*], I have accorded them different treatment for purposes of this matter. The distinction I discern here is that "cause" may be cause on the part of the agent, such as dishonesty or inadequate performance, or cause on Nationwide's part, such as business necessity. In *Savarese*, the court treated contracts for permanent employment and contracts terminable only for cause given by the employee as identical in nature.

547 F. Supp. 959, 970 n. 18 (D.N.J. 1981).

26. 234 N.J.Super. 409, 415 (Ch.Div. 1989).

27. 234 N.J.Super. 409, 416. *See also Rogozinski v. Airstream By Angell*, 152 N.J.Super. 133, 144 (Law Div. 1977), *modified on other grounds*, 164 N.J.Super. 465 (App.Div. 1979) ("As to damages, *Savarese* speaks in terms of a perpetual contract operating 'as long as the employer remains in the business and has work for the employee and the employee is able and willing to do his work satisfactorily and does not give good cause for his discharge.' "). The district court's discussion of *Savarese* and *Alter* in *Scudder v. Media Gen., Inc.*, 1995 WL 495945 (D.N.J. 1995) is in accord: "As a matter of law, therefore, it seems that the best bargain an employee can strike is that he can keep his job for as long as he can satisfactorily perform it."

If that is in fact the law, the exacting standard of *Savarese* may be of no practical import in view of the decisions holding it inapplicable where only an agreement not to terminate without cause is alleged.[28] The distinction was explained by the Supreme Court in *Shebar v. Sanyo Business Systems Corp.* as follows:

> The reason *Savarese* required that a contract for lifetime employment be demonstrated by unmistakably clear signs of the employer's intent was that at the time such contracts were deemed "to be at variance with general usage and sound policy." This is still so today, given the unlikelihood of an employer promising to protect an employee from any termination of employment, and the difficulty of determining the terms and enforcing such an agreement. Indeed, in *Woolley*, the court recognized that such contracts for lifetime employment were extraordinary, and would be enforced only in the face of clear and convincing proof of a precise agreement setting forth all of the terms of the employment relationship, including the duties and responsibilities of both the employer and the employee. However, a lifetime contract that protects an employee from any termination is distinguishable from a promise to discharge only for cause. The latter protects the employee only from arbitrary termination.[29]
>
> * * *
>
> To the extent that plaintiff alleges a contract of life employment, the trial court correctly ruled that this claim was barred by *Savarese*. To the extent that plaintiff alleges a promise of discharge for cause only, plaintiff's breach of contract claim should be analyzed by those contractual principles that apply when the claim is one that an oral employment contract exists.[30]

1-2:1 Employment at a Specific Salary

In *Bernard v. IMI Sys., Inc.*, the Supreme Court held that an offer of employment at an annual salary does not constitute a contract of guaranteed employment

---

28. *See, e.g., First Atlantic Leasing Corp. v. Tracey*, 738 F. Supp. 863, 872 (D.N.J. 1990) (holding that *Savarese* standard of proof applies only to contracts prohibiting all terminations, not to contracts prohibiting only termination without good cause and relying on *Shebar* for that proposition).

29. 111 N.J. at 287. *See Greenwood v. State Police Training Center*, 127 N.J. 500, 509-11 (1992) (contract allowing termination only for good cause protects employee from unreasonable or arbitrary termination; employer must have substantial objective evidence).

for one year.[31] "In the absence of a contrary agreement, an employee is hired at-will, regardless of the way in which the salary is quoted in an offer letter."[32]

> [I]n today's volatile employment market, it is both uncommon and unreasonable to expect employment for one year simply because an offer letter quotes an annual salary. Employees realize that the specification of salary merely determines the method of payment and not the time of employment. A salary or benefit package stated in annual terms does not, standing alone, entitle an employee to year-to-year employment.

Id. at 106.

1-3 Specific Performance

Specific performance is a discretionary remedy resting in equity.[33] It provides extraordinary relief not routinely warranted, but reserved for those cases where the subject of the contract is in some way exceptional; where the services are of such a peculiar character as to be incapable of valuation by a pecuniary standard:[34]

> Generally speaking, breach of contract gives rise to an action for damages. When, but only when, that remedy is inadequate, the injured party may sue in equity.[35]

Because specific performance lies in equity, the party seeking aid of the court must have clean hands:

> [H]is conduct in the matter must have been fair, just, and equitable, not sharp or aiming at unfair advantage. The relief itself

---

30. 111 N.J. at 288. The Court cited the federal district court decision in *Powell v. Fuller Brush Co.*, 15 F.R.D. 239, 242 (D.N.J. 1954), which states: "Our reading of the *Savarese* case discloses no such refusal to recognize or enforce a contract of employment for life, as being the law of the State of New Jersey where this Court is sitting; nor does the case reflect any policy of the law of New Jersey indicating that such contracts are not binding in legal principle, or that they are contrary to public policy, but rather it emphasizes that such contracts are difficult in fact to prove, and that most cases involving such fail for insufficiency of evidence to establish them in fact."

31. *Bernard v. IMI Systems, Inc.*, 131 N.J. 91 (1993) (no guarantee of employment for one year created by letter agreement that: "Your compensation will be at the rate of $80,000 per year"). *See Craffey v. Bergen County Util.*, 315 N.J. Super 345, 351 (App. Div. 1998).

32. 131 N.J. at 96. This opinion overruled *Willis v Wyllys Corp.*, 98 N.J.L. 180 (E. & A. 1922).

33. *Barry M. Dechtman, Inc. v. Sidpaul Corp.*, 89 N.J. 547, 551-52 (1982). *See generally* Dreier and Rowe, *Guidebook to Chancery Practice in New Jersey*, pp. 86-93 (4th ed. 1997).

34. *See Crowe v. DeGioia* (II), 203 N.J.Super. 22, 34 (App.Div. 1985).

35. *Crowe v. DeGioia*, 179 N.J.Super. 36, 41 (App.Div. 1981), *rev'd on other grounds*, 90 N.J. 126 (1982), *on remand*, 203 N.J.Super. 22 (App.Div. 1985).

> must not be harsh or oppressive. In short, it must be very plain that the claim is an equitable one.[36]

The availability of specific performance also depends upon the clarity of the contract: "The oft-stated rule is that the terms of the contract must be definite and certain so that the court may decree with some precision what the defendant must do."[37] However, this test is not a mechanical one. The Supreme Court has stated that uncertainty as to subordinate details of performance need not preclude specific performance unless the uncertainty is "so great as to prevent the existence of a contract."[38]

The general rule has historically been that personal service contracts, including employment contracts, are not specifically enforceable, even when the individual rendering the services possesses a unique talent.[39] That rule precluded enforcement by the principal on the ground that "equity will not make a vain decree."[40] It precluded enforcement by the employee on the basis of (1) the precept of agency law that a principal may revoke his agency at any time, and (2) lack of mutuality of enforcement in view of inability to compel the employee to perform.[41]

Although the denial of specific performance of personal service contracts continues to be referred to as the general rule, exceptions have been made. In *American Ass'n of University Professors, Bloomfield College Chapter v. Bloomfield*

---

36. *Barry M. Dechtman, Inc. v. Sidpaul Corp.*, 89 N.J. 547, 552 (1982), *quoting Stehl v. Sawyer*, 40 N.J. 352, 357 (1963).

37. *Barry M. Dechtman, Inc. v. Sidpaul Corp.*, 89 N.J. 547, 552 (1982). Appropriate extrinsic evidence may be examined to determine the intent of the parties; reasonable certainty of the terms is sufficient. *Barry M. Dechtman, Inc. v. Sidpaul Corp.*, 89 N.J. 547, 552 (1982) "Seeming difficulties of enforcement due to uncertainties attributable to language may vanish in the light of practicalities and a full understanding of the parties' intent." *See Fountain v. Fountain*, 9 N.J. 558, 565 (1952) ("If a promise such as this is capable of being made certain by an objective standard, as, for example, extrinsic facts, it is enforceable.").

38. *Fountain v. Fountain*, 9 N.J. at 566.

39. *Crowe v. DeGioia*, 179 N.J.Super. 36, 41 (App.Div. 1981), *rev'd on other grounds*, 90 N.J. 126 (1982), *on remand*, 203 N.J.Super. 22 (App.Div. 1985); *Sarokhan v. Fair Lawn Memorial Hospital, Inc.*, 83 N.J.Super. 127, 133 (App.Div. 1964). *See generally* 5A *Corbin on Contracts* §1204, pp.398-403 (1964); Dreier and Rowe, *Guidebook to Chancery Practice in New Jersey*, p. 90 (4th ed. 1997) ("Personal service contracts are not generally specifically enforceable, although they may be so enforced under exceptional circumstances." *Citing Endress v. Brookdale Community College* and *American Ass'n of University Professors, Bloomfield College Chapter v. Bloomfield College*, discussed *infra*, at text accompanying nn. 42-48.).

40. *Crowe v. DeGioia*, 179 N.J.Super. at 41; *Sarokhan v. Fair Lawn Memorial Hospital, Inc.*, 83 N.J.Super. at 133 ("Equity will not compel performance of personal services, even where the contract involves a 'star' of unique talent, because equity will not make a vain decree. At most, equity will restrain violation of an express or implied negative covenant, thus precluding the performer from performing for somebody else.").

41. *See Crowe v. DeGioia*, 90 N.J. 126, 133-34 (1982); *Sarokhan v. Fair Lawn Memorial Hospital, Inc.*, 83 N.J.Super. at 133-35. In *Fiedler, Inc. v. Coast Finance Co., Inc.*, 129 N.J. Eq. 161, 166-67 (E. & A. 1941), the Court denied specific performance because of the absence of mutuality: "If the enforcement of the obligation may not be granted to both contracting parties, it should not be enforced against one party." *See* 5A *Corbin on Contracts* §1204, pp. 400-02 (1964).

College,[42] the Appellate Division affirmed an order reinstating tenured faculty members who were found to have been discharged in breach of their employment contracts. The court acknowledged the "general rule" but found that it "is not inflexible and that the power of a court of equity to grant such a remedy depends upon the factual situation involved and the need for that type of remedy in a particular case." [43] More significantly, the two considerations listed by the court as warranting deviation from the "general rule" are factors that may be found in other employment contract controversies: (1) "uncertainty in admeasuring damages because of the indefinite duration of the contract;" [44] and (2) "the importance of the status of plaintiffs in the milieu of the college teaching profession."[45]

A somewhat similar result obtained in *Endress v. Brookdale Community College*, where the Appellate Division upheld the reinstatement of a professor who alleged she had been terminated in breach of her contract.[46] The court acknowledged the "settled law" that "personal service contracts are generally not specifically enforceable," and reiterated its *Bloomfield College* opinion in support of the flexibility of the rule. But unlike the *Bloomfield College* case, *Endress* involved more than a breach of contract claim. The court specifically pointed out that "[a]lthough not clearly articulated below" the trial court was of the view that plaintiff's termination was in violation of her First Amendment rights of free speech and press, and that in such case the remedy of specific performance is appropriate.[47] Of course that begs the question, because if it is a constitutional injury that is being remedied, the traditional rule limiting specific performance for breach of contract is irrelevant. In such a case, the court is not ordering specific performance of a contract; it is voiding a termination and compelling reinstatement. The difference is more than semantics. Thus the basis of the *Bloomfield College* rule and the circumstances in which it will be applied remain somewhat unclear. In particular, it is not apparent from either decision the extent to which the unique nature of a tenured faculty position controlled the outcome, or whether the court's flexibility was instead based upon a more gen-

---

42. 136 N.J.Super. 442 (App.Div. 1975).

43. *American Ass'n of University Professors, Bloomfield College Chapter v. Bloomfield College*, 136 N.J.Super. 442, 448 (App.Div. 1975).

44. 136 N.J.Super. at 448. The court included no explanation of how it reached this conclusion, or why an economist's calculation of the present value of front pay would be inadequate. (*See* Schlei & Grossman, *Employment Discrimination Law*, pp.1434-36 (2d ed 1983), regarding the availability of front pay as an alternative to reinstatement under federal employment discrimination laws).

45. *American Ass'n of University Professors, Bloomfield College Chapter v. Bloomfield College*, 136 N.J.Super. 442, 448 (App.Div. 1975).

46. *Endress v. Brookdale Community College*, 144 N.J.Super. 109 (App.Div. 1976).

47. *Id at* 130-31.

eral erosion of the rule against specific performance of personal service contracts, growing out of the common availability of reinstatement as a remedy under state and federal anti-discrimination laws.[48]

1-4 Statute of Frauds

The New Jersey statute of frauds, which is codified at N.J.S.A. 25:1-5, was amended effective January 5, 1996.[49] The amendment repealed subsection (e) of the statute which previously required agreements that are not to be performed within one year from the making thereof to be in writing. Thus, oral contracts of employment for fixed-terms greater than one year are no longer rendered unenforceable under the statute of frauds.[50]

Despite its amendment, the repealed section of the statute of frauds may be given prospective effect only. Thus, given the six year statute of limitations governing contract claims,[51] the statute of frauds may still be a defense in those cases where the alleged oral contract was breached before the effective date of the amendment.[52]

Prior to the amendment, oral employment contracts which by their terms were incapable of being performed within one year were barred.[53] In *Deevy v. Porter*,[54] a husband and wife entered into an oral contract whereby they were to be employed for a one-year period commencing at a later date, upon their departure for Casablanca. In addition, the husband was to perform and did perform services for the employer in the United States. The Supreme Court found that the parties

---

48. The plaintiff in *Alter v. Resorts Int'l, Inc.*, 234 N.J.Super. 409, 413 (Ch.Div. 1989), sought specific enforcement of an alleged lifetime contract, but resolution of that issue was not necessary in light of the court's other rulings, and no discussion of the question was included.

49. P.L. 1995, c.360, section 8.

50. Oral contracts of employment for life were never barred by the statute of frauds because such contracts are capable of being performed within one year; the employee might die within a year of contract making. *See Loeb v. Peter F. Dasbjerg & Co.*, 22 N.J. 95, 99 (1956) (N.J.S.A. 25:1-5 "inapplicable to an oral agreement bearing no fixed term and possibly performable within one year even though complete performance in that term may be unlikely"); *Shiddell v. Electro Rust-Proofing Corp.*, 34 N.J. Super. 278, 282 (App. Div. 1954) (alleged oral contract for lifetime employment outside the scope of statute of frauds); *Deevy v. Porter*, 11 N.J. 594, 597 (1953). Similarly, a strike settlement agreement that did not specify the time within which it was supposed to be performed was found outside the scope of the statute of frauds. *I.U.E. v. ITT Federal Laboratories*, 232 F. Supp. 873, 879-80 (D.N.J.1964).

51. N.J.S.A. 2A:14-1.

52. *See Jenkins v. Region Nine Housing*, 306 N.J. Super. 258, 263 (App. Div. 1997) (raising, but not deciding issue as to whether the repealed section of the statute of frauds applied to plaintiff's claim for breach of oral contract of employment), *certif. denied*, 153 N.J. 405 (1998).

53. *Kreuzberg v. Computer Services Corp.*, 661 F. Supp. 877, 879 (D.N.J. 1987). *See generally*, 2 *Corbin on Contracts* §447, pp. 555-58 (1964).

54. 11 N.J. 594 (1953).

had bargained for an oral contract that could not be performed within one year, and that, as such, it was unenforceable under the Statute of Frauds.[55] Other fixed-term oral contracts of employment have similarly been barred.[56]

The fact that an oral employment contract for a fixed term not performable in one year may be terminable by operation of law upon death within one year did not remove it from the scope of the Statute.[57] Similarly an otherwise unenforceable fixed-term employment contract was not saved by the employee's retention of the right to quit or by the employer's retention of the right to terminate under specific circumstances such as bankruptcy. The time required for performance was controlling, not whether and when excusable non-performance might occur.[58] In the case of an employment contract, a writing or memorandum did not suffice under the Statute of Frauds prior to the 1995 amendment unless the writing itself contained the essential terms of the agreement, including the salary or other compensation to be paid.[59]

Although there were suggestions that there may be circumstances in which equitable or promissory estoppel might bar application of the Statute of Frauds to an employment contract prior to the 1995 amendment, those circumstances appear to have been neither found nor described in any New Jersey opinion.[60] However, where one party to the agreement had rendered full performance and application of the statute would have resulted in unjust enrichment, a contract otherwise unenforceable was generally enforced.[61]

---

55. *Deevy v. Porter*, 11 N.J. at 599.

56. *See Olympic Junior, Inc. v. David Crystal, Inc.*, 463 F.2d 1141, 1143-44 (3d Cir. 1972) (five-year contract of employment unenforceable under N.J.S.A. 25:1-5(e) because essential elements of contract were not in writing); *Barnes v. P. & D. Mfg. Co.*, 123 N.J.L. 246, 248-50 (E. & A. 1939) (five-year oral contract for services within Statute of Frauds); *Kooba v. Jacobitti*, 59 N.J. Super. 496, 500-501 (App.Div. 1960) (two-year oral employment agreement unenforceable under Statute of Frauds).

57. *See Deevy v. Porter*, 11 N.J. 594, 597 (1953), *citing LaBett v. Heyman Bros., Inc.*, 13 N.J. Misc. 832 (Sup. Ct. 1935), *aff'd*, 117 N.J.L. 115 (E. & A. 1936). *See also* 2 *Corbin on Contracts* §447, pp.555-56 (1964).

58. *See Deevy v. Porter*, 11 N.J. 594, 598-99 (1953).

59. *See Olympic Junior, Inc. v. David Crystal, Inc.*, 463 F.2d 1141, 1144 (3d Cir. 1972).

60. *See generally Kooba v. Jacobitti*, 59 N.J.Super. 496, 500-01 (App.Div. 1960); *Olympic Junior, Inc. v. David Crystal, Inc.*, 463 F.2d at 1144 n.3 (3d Cir. 1972); Robert A. Brazener, *Annotation, Action by Employee in Reliance on Employment Contract Which Violates Statute of Frauds as Rendering Contract Enforceable*, 54 ALR 3d 715 (1974).

61. *See Crowe v. DeGioia (II)*, 203 N.J.Super. 22, 34 (App.Div. 1985) (unwritten agreement to transfer real property enforced where full performance rendered by co-habitant); *Kreuzburg v. Computer Sciences Corp.*, 661 F.Supp. 877, 879-80 (D.N.J. 1987) (exception not applicable to plaintiff's claim for commissions because full performance was not rendered); *Edwards v. Wycoff Electrical Supply Co.*, 42 N.J. Super. 236, 241-42 (App. Div. 1956) (contract partially enforced on unjust enrichment theory).

1-5 Employees Covered by Collective Bargaining Agreements

The principle of exclusive representation expressed in §9(a) of the National Labor Relations Act, 29 U.S.C. §159(a), generally prohibits employers from negotiating individual contracts with employees who are members of a bargaining unit, and pre-empts state law to the contrary on the ground that it would "upset the balance of power between lbor and management expressed in our national labor policy." [62]

But an individual contract properly negotiated while an employee is not represented is not necessarily rendered null or subsumed into the collective agreement if the employee later moves into the bargaining unit.[63] United States Supreme Court and Third Circuit opinions suggest three criteria that must be met for such a contract to remain effective and enforceable under state law: (1) the individual contract must not be inconsistent with the collective bargaining agreement;[64] (2) enforcement of the individual contract must not constitute an unfair labor practice;[65] and (3) interpretation of the individual contract must not be substantially dependent upon interpretation of a collective bargaining agreement.[66] If the contract claim is "substantially dependent upon analysis of the terms of an agreement made between the parties in a labor contract," then any action for enforcement must either be treated as asserting a claim under §301 of the Labor Management Relations Act, 1947,[67] or dismissed as pre-empted by federal labor law.[68] If a dispute can be resolved without interpreting a collective agreement, there is no pre-emption.[69]

---

62. *Teamsters v. Morton*, 377 U.S. 252 (1964). *Accord San Diego Building Trades Council v. Garmon*, 359 U.S. 236 (1959) (state law that infringes upon the NLRB's primary jurisdiction over unfair labor practice charges is pre-empted). It is generally an unfair labor practice for an employer to disregard the bargaining representative by negotiating with individual employees, whether a majority or a minority, with respect to wages, hours, and working conditions. *See Medo Photo Supply Corp. v. NLRB*, 321 U.S. 678, 684 (1944).

63. *See J. I. Case Co. v. NLRB*, 321 U.S. 332, 339 (1944); *see also Caterpillar Inc. v. Williams*, 482 U.S. 386, 396 (1987); *Berda v. CBS, Inc.*, 881 F.2d 20, 24 (3d Cir. 1989); *Malia v. RCA Corp.*, 794 F.2d 909, 912 (3d Cir. 1986), *cert. denied*, 482 U.S. 927 (1987).

64. *See J. I. Case Co. v. NLRB*, 321 U.S. 332, 339 (1944); *see also Mossberg v. Standard Oil Co. of New Jersey*, 98 N.J.Super. 393, 401-02 (Law Div. 1967) (collective bargaining agreement superseded individual contract); *Malia v. RCA Corp.*, 794 F.2d 909, 913 (3d Cir. 1986) ("Nor does LMRA prevent an individual—whether an applicant for new employment or a current employee in a supervisory position—from negotiating for a job in a bargaining unit so long as that employment will be on the terms and conditions set forth in the collective bargaining agreement.").

65. *See id.*; *see generally San Diego Building Trades Council v. Garmon*, 359 U.S. 236 (1959) (state law that infringes upon NLRB's primary jurisdiction over unfair labor charges is pre-empted).

66. *See Caterpillar Inc. v. Williams*, 482 U.S. at 396;

67. 29 U.S.C. §185.

The seminal Supreme Court opinion on the viability of individual contracts with bargaining unit employees is *J. I. Case Co. v. NLRB.*[70] That employer had entered into individual hiring contracts before a bargaining unit was certified, and then refused to bargain about matters covered by those agreements. Although noting that the "purpose of providing by statute for the collective agreement is to supersede the terms of separate agreements of employees," the Court did not adopt a blanket prohibition. Instead, it stated that individual contracts may be entered into if they are "not inconsistent with a collective agreement" and do not amount to an unfair labor practice.[71]

The Court reiterated the *J.I. Case* rule four decades later in *Caterpillar Inc. v. Williams*, where the issue before it was when the defense of federal pre-emption of state law contract claims will support removal.[72] The Court also discussed when an individual contract will be found pre-empted by §301:

> [I]ndividual employment contracts are not inevitably superseded by any subsequent collective agreement covering an individual employee, and claims based upon them may arise under state law. ... [A] plaintiff covered by a collective bargaining agreement is permitted to assert legal rights *independent* of that agreement, including state-law contract rights, so long as the contract relied upon is *not* a collective bargaining agreement.[73]

---

68. *Berda v. CBS, Inc.*, 881 F.2d 20, 23 (3d Cir. 1989), *quoting Allis-Chalmers Corp. v. Lueck*, 471 U.S. 202 (1985). Section 301 provides a federal cause of action for violations of contracts between employees and unions, and has been found to reflect congressional intent that labor contracts be governed by a uniform federal common law. *See Textile Workers Union v. Lincoln Mills*, 353 U.S. 448 (1957); *Allis-Chalmers Corp. v. Lueck*, 471 U.S. 202 (1985).

69. *See Lingle v. Norge Div. of Magic Chef, Inc.*, 486 U.S. 399, 413 (1988). *See also Carrington v. RCA Global Communications, Inc.*, 762 F. Supp. 632 (D.N.J. 1991).

70. 321 U.S. 332 (1944).

71. The question of what constitutes an unfair labor practice under the National Labor Relations Act is beyond the scope of this treatise. *See generally*, Morris, *The Developing Labor Law* p.566 (2d Ed. 1983).

72. Plaintiffs in *Caterpillar* were bargaining unit employees who were promoted into managerial positions, then returned to the bargaining unit, and then ultimately laid off. They claimed that while they were management employees the company made oral and written representations that they could look forward to indefinite and lasting employment, and that they could count on the company to take care of them. They sued for breach of these individual agreements under state law and defendant removed on the ground of complete pre-emption of plaintiffs' claims by §301 of the Labor Management Relations Act, 1947, 29 U.S.C. §185.

73. It is important to note, as the *Caterpillar* Court did, that it did not resolve the validity of the individual contracts or even whether they would ultimately be found pre-empted by §301. *See* 482 U.S. at 399. It held instead that the employer was required to present those issues in the first instance in state court:

> The employer may argue that the individual employment contract has been pre-empted due to the principle of exclusive representation in §9(a) of the National Labor Relations Act (NLRA) ... Or the employer may contend that enforcement of the individual contract arguably would constitute an unfair labor practice under the NLRA, and is therefore pre-empted.

482 U.S. at 397 (citations omitted). *But see* Morris, *The Developing Labor Law*, pp.660-67 (1982-88 supp.).

The Third Circuit applied this rule in *Berda v. CBS, Inc.*[74] At issue in *Berda* were state law contract and tort claims for breach of an alleged oral agreement for "indefinite and lasting employment" entered into before plaintiff became a member of the bargaining unit. The court rejected the employer's contention that the contract was pre-empted by §301 on the ground that it was not substantially dependent upon interpretation of the collective bargaining agreement. No other defenses to enforcement having been raised by the employer, no others were considered. More specifically, as the court noted, it had not been presented with the questions whether (1) the existence of the subsequent collective bargaining agreement constituted a defense under state or federal law; or (2) whether the oral agreement was void as an unfair labor practice.[75] As a consequence, no final determination of the enforceability of the contract was made.

Berda is of particular note in that the individual contract was entered into at the time plaintiff was hired into a bargaining unit position; not, as in *Caterpillar* and other prior cases,[76] at a point when the employee was a management employee with no immediate expectation of entering the bargaining unit. Although that distinction may be irrelevant to the §301 pre-emption test, it is highly significant to labor-management relations and the exclusive representation rights of unions.

II. EMPLOYEE HANDBOOKS

1-6 When is a Handbook a Contract?

The Supreme Court's 1985 opinion in *Woolley v. Hoffmann-LaRoche, Inc.*[77] held for the first time[78] that in appropriate circumstances, representations made in employee handbooks or manuals are enforceable:

> [w]hen an employer of a substantial number of employees circulates a manual that, when fairly read, provides that certain

---

74. 881 F.2d 20 (3d Cir. 1989).

75. 881 F.2d at 26. *See also Malia v. RCA Corp.*, 794 F.2d 909 (3d Cir. 1986).

76. *See, e.g., Malia v. RCA Corp.*, 794 F.2d at 911 (plaintiff alleged that when he accepted promotion into managerial job he was promised he could return to the bargaining unit if he didn't like his new job), *cert. denied*, 482 U.S. 927 (1987).

77. *Woolley v. Hoffmann-LaRoche, Inc.*, 99 N.J. 284, *modified*, 101 N.J. 10 (1985).

78. Because it was a clear break with prior law, *Woolley* is not retroactively applicable: "While it may have had its conceptual origins in antecedent contract law, it involved a novel and unanticipated interpretation and application of that law and, in fact, altered the basic structure of employer/at-will-employee relations." *Grigoletti v. Ortho Pharmaceutical Corp.*, 118 N.J. 89, 116 (1990). *Accord Bimbo v. Burdette Tomlin Memorial Hospital*, 644 F. Supp. 1033, 1039 (D.N.J. 1986). *Kapossy v. McGraw-Hill, Inc.*, 921 F. Supp. 234, 246 (D.N.J. 1996) (*Woolley* applies only to post-1985 handbooks).

> benefits are an incident of the employment (including, especially, job security provisions), the judiciary, instead of "grudgingly" conceding the enforceability of those provisions ... should construe them in accordance with the reasonable expectations of the employees.[79]

Woolley is not an exception to the doctrine of at-will employment, but rather, "a recognition of basic contract principles concerning acceptance of unilateral contracts."[80]

In determining whether a manual is enforceable, courts must look to its meaning and effect and the circumstances under which it was prepared and distributed.[81]

1-6:1 Distribution

To be enforceable under *Woolley*, a manual must have been distributed or generally disseminated to all or to the relevant portion of the workforce. General distribution or dissemination of the terms of a manual is a vital element of a *Woolley* claim because it forms a basis for the legal presumptions that (1) the employer intended to be bound and (2) employees were generally aware of and could have reasonably relied upon the manual's terms.[82]

---

79. *Woolley v. Hoffmann-LaRoche, Inc.*, 99 N.J. at 297-98.

80. *McQuitty v. General Dynamics Corp.*, 204 N.J.Super. 514, 520 (App.Div. 1985); *cf. Shebar v. Sanyo Business Systems Corp.*, 111 N.J. 276, 286 (1988). *See* n. 120 and accompanying text.

81. *Woolley v. Hoffmann-LaRoche, Inc.*, 99 N.J. at 298. *See Nicosia v. Wakefern Food Corp.*, 136 N.J. 401 (1994) (looking to the content and distribution of a manual to determine whether employees reading it would have a reasonable expectation that it was binding); *Witkowski v. Thomas J. Lipton, Inc.*, 136 N.J. 385 (1994) (no categorical test can be applied in determining whether an employment manual when fairly read gives rise to the reasonable expectations of employees that it confers enforceable obligations; relevant factors relate to both the manual's specific provisions and the context of its preparation and distribution). *Cf. Gilbert v. Durand Glass Mfg. Co.*, 258 N.J. Super. 320, 330 (App. Div. 1992).

82. *See Woolley v. Hoffmann-LaRoche, Inc.*, 99 N.J. at 302-04 and n. 10. *But see Grigoletti v. Ortho Pharmaceutical Corp.*, 226 N.J.Super. 518, 527-28 (App.Div. 1988), *rev'd in part and modified in part on other grounds*, 118 N.J. 89 (1990) ("plaintiffs will be required to prove the content and meaning of the provisions of the manual which they have invoked; that the manual constituted a *promise upon which one or both plaintiffs relied*; that the promise was not kept, and that ascertainable damages flowed from the breach.") (Emphasis added.) The extent of distribution of manuals was a factor in finding binding promises in *Witkowski v. Thomas J. Lipton*, Inc., 136 N.J. 385 (1994) (distribution to all employees "indicates that Lipton understood that it would be read and considered by all its employees."); *Nicosia v. Wakefern Food Corp.*, 136 N.J. 401 (1994) (manual distributed to 300 of 1500 non-union employees); *Falco v. Community Medical Center*, 296 N.J. Super. 298, 324 (App. Div. 1997) (stating that the preparation or distribution of the employee handbook are factors to consider in determining the reasonableness of an employee's belief that a handbook created a binding, legally enforceable commitment). *See also Geldreich v. American Cyanamid Co.*, 299 N.J. Super. 478, 484 (App. Div. 1997) (policy memorandum received by plaintiff, but not distributed to the general non-unionized workforce of defendant, met the *Woolley* distribution test because it was not marked "confidential," it was made available for review by employees who sought to review it, and there was widespread awareness of its contents by management).

Thus, where a manual has not been generally distributed, employee claims have been rejected for lack of actual reliance; in effect, the asserted *Woolley* cause is rejected and the claim evaluated under an individual estoppel burden of proof.[83] The distinction was well put by the court in *Labus v. Navistar Int'l Trans. Corp.*, in rejecting a *Woolley* claim based upon a manual neither generally distributed nor relied upon:

> The *Woolley* court found that a presumption of reliance arises and the manual's provisions become binding at the moment the manual is distributed to the general work force. The court noted that, if reliance were not presumed, a strict contractual analysis, requiring bargained-for detriment, would protect the rights of some employees but not others. Following *Toussaint v. Blue Cross & Blue Shield of Michigan*, the court agreed that employees neither had to read the manual, know of its existence, or rely on it to benefit from its provisions any more than employees in a plant that is unionized have to read or rely on a collective bargaining agreement to obtain its benefits.[84]

Similarly, manuals distributed only to supervisory employees, and intended for their use in dealing with subordinates, have been found unenforceable under *Woolley*.[85]

---

83. *See, e.g., House v. Carter-Wallace, Inc.*, 232 N.J. Super. 42, 55 (App. Div.), *certif. denied*, 117 N.J. 154 (1984) ("[a]n employee cannot have a reasonable expectation of job security based on a document which was not distributed to him."); *Labus v. Navistar Int'l Trans. Corp.*, 740 F. Supp. 1053, 1062 (D.N.J. 1990) (plaintiff could not reasonably rely upon promise in a manual he never saw that was distributed to only certain upper-level employees). *See Gilbert v. Durand Glass Mfg. Co., Inc.*, 258 N.J. Super. 320, 330 (App. Div. 1992) (employee need not have known the particulars of a *Woolley* policy; "[i]t is enough that the employee reasonably believes that a particular personnel policy has been established and is applied consistently and uniformly to each employee."). In *Tripodi v. Johnson & Johnson*, 877 F. Supp. 233, 239-40 (D.N.J. 1995), the court found that distribution of a company credo to customers, suppliers and stockholders, as well as to employees, was an indication that it was *not* intended to create binding obligations. "This serves to emphasize the aspirational rather than the contractual nature of the document. Surely, the credo was not a contract with doctors, nurses, patients, mothers and all others that Johnson & Johnson's products and services would be of high quality and sold at reasonable prices." *Id.* at 239.

84. *Labus v. Navistar Int'l Trans. Corp.*, 740 F. Supp. 1053, 1062 (D.N.J. 1990). *Cf. Michota v. Anheuser-Busch, Inc. (Budweiser)*, 755 F.2d 330, 335-36 (3d Cir. 1985) (employees have constructive notice of terms of collective bargaining agreement).

85. *See Ware v. Prudential Ins. Co.*, 220 N.J.Super. 135, 144-47 (App.Div. 1987), *certif. denied*, 113 N.J. 335 (1988) (reasonable expectation of benefits could not be based upon guide distributed only to supervisors—and not to plaintiff—and by its terms directed to the delineation of management responsibilities); *Maietta v. United Parcel Service, Inc.*, 749 F. Supp. 1344, 1362 (D.N.J. 1990), *aff'd without published op.*, 932 F.2d 960 (3d Cir. 1991) (book that served as a "curriculum aid" for "workshop on communication and personnel management skills for full-time management employees," and that was distributed to only senior management, was not a *Woolley* contract).

1-6:2 Legally Binding Language

The job security provisions of the employee handbook enforced in *Woolley* were found by the Supreme Court to be "explicit and clear," and the provisions pertaining to discipline and discharge were comprehensive. These factors appear to have been vital to the Court's determination in that case that the handbook was intended to be binding and should be enforced.[86] Conversely, the provisions of a handbook will not be enforced if the language is such that "no one could reasonably have thought it was intended to create legally binding obligations."[87] As the Appellate Division stated in *Ware v. Prudential Ins. Co.* "If the document was intended to serve as a handbook guaranteeing employee benefits, it would be reasonable to expect that it also would specifically set forth those benefits."[88] But what is found to be too vague or indefinite to constitute a binding promise varies. In *Levinson v. Prentice-Hall, Inc.*, the district court found the following language too vague to constitute a promise of promotion:

> The policy of Prentice-Hall is that all management personnel be supportive of employee efforts both to improve in their present jobs, and to be promoted to jobs of greater responsibility.
>
> Available jobs will be posted on bulletin boards in accordance with Prentice-Hall's policy. Employees who apply will be considered on the basis of their skills and abilities.
>
> Where prior experience in any department has given an employee knowledge and familiarity with the character and procedures which are required in the performance of the higher level job, the department head may give preference to such applicant.[89]

In *Radwan v. Beecham Laboratories*, the Third Circuit found it doubtful that *Woolley* would apply to a manual that contained a non-exclusive list of causes for discipline but lacked any detailed procedures for employee counselling or discipline.[90] In *Falco v. Community Med. Ctr.*, the employee handbook's inclusion of disciplinary guidelines that provided a comprehensive pronouncement of the employer's termination policy was not sufficiently definitive to create an employment contract. The handbook contained a disclaimer and further stated that the guide-

---

86. *Woolley v. Hoffmann-LaRoche, Inc.*, 99 N.J. 284, 306, *modified*, 101 N.J. 10 (1985). *See Kane v. Milikowsky*, 224 N.J. Super. 613, 616 (App. Div. 1988).

87. *Woolley v. Hoffmann-LaRoche, Inc.*, 99 N.J. at 299.

88. *Ware v. Prudential Ins. Co.*, 220 N.J.Super. 135, 146 (App.Div. 1987), *certif. denied*, 113 N.J. 335 (1988).

89. *Levinson v. Prentice-Hall, Inc.*, 1988 WL 76383, p.1 (D.N.J. 1988), *aff'd in part and rev'd in part, on other grounds*, 868 F.2d 558 (3d Cir. 1989).

lines did not prevent the employer from terminating employees with or without cause in its discretion.[91] And in *Maietta v. United Parcel Service, Inc.*, a policy statement that "We Treat Our People Fairly and Without Favoritism" was found unenforceable as an "ideal." [92]

In contrast, in *Preston v. Claridge Hotel & Casino*, the Appellate Division held that a general promise of "maximum job security," combined with a policies manual describing a progressive discipline program, and a warning in the employee manual that certain specific acts of misconduct would be grounds for discharge, constituted a promise not to discharge employees except for good cause. "Having offered these representations as an attractive alternative to collective bargaining," the employer "cannot avoid its obligations on the basis of semantic differences." [93]

---

90. *Radwan v. Beecham Laboratories*, 850 F.2d 147, 151 (3d Cir. 1988) (dicta). In *Witkowski v. Thomas J. Lipton, Inc.*, 136 N.J. 385 (1994), the Supreme Court held that a non-exclusive list of grounds for discharge, coupled with a progressive warning notice system, constituted a promise to discharge employees only in accordance with the manual. However, the statement that a broad program of employee benefits set forth in a more than 100-page manual "will assist you in providing security and protection for your family during your working years and into retirement" was found unsupportive of a claimed protection against discharge without cause. *Brunner v. Abex Corp.*, 661 F. Supp. 1344, 1355 (D.N.J. 1986). *See also Varrallo v. Hammond Inc.*, 94 F.3d 842 (3d Cir. 1996) (employee handbook lacked requisite definiteness and comprehensiveness needed to imply a contract of "for cause" termination); *Marzano v. Computer Science Corp.*, Inc., 91 F.3d 497, 512-13 (3d Cir. 1996) (holding that a two-page memorandum explaining entitlements under the New Jersey Family Leave Act did not create an implied contract of employment); *Rodichok v. Limitorque Corp.*, 1997 WL 392535 (D.N.J. 1997) (employee handbook did not contain language creating an implied contract); *Barone v. Gardner Asphalt Corp.*, 955 F. Supp. 337, 342-43 (D.N.J. 1997) (memorandum entitled "Conditions of Employment" did not create an implied contract); *Monroe v. Host Marriot Services Corp.*, 999 F. Supp. 599 (D.N.J. 1998) (holding that a one-page memorandum entitled "Guarantee of Fair Treatment," which outlined the employer's greivance procedures, was lacking in specificity and explicit terms regarding job security and termination policies, and was therefore not an employment contract).

91. *296 N.J. Super. 298* (App Div. 1997).

92. *Maietta v. United Parcel Service, Inc.*, 749 F.Supp. 1344, 1363 (D.N.J. 1990), *aff'd without published op.*, 932 F.2d 960 (3d Cir. 1991).

93. *Preston v. Claridge Hotel & Casino*, 231 N.J.Super. 81, 86 (App.Div. 1989). "[P]olicy statements cannot as a matter of law create a contractual obligation and abrogate the employment at-will doctrine." *King v. Port Auth.*, 909 F. Supp. 938, 942-43 (D.N.J. 1995), *aff'd*, 106 F.3d 385 (3d Cir. 1996). In *Tripodi v. Johnson & Johnson*, 877 F. Supp. 233 (D.N.J. 1995), the court found that employees could not reasonably understand a one-page company credo to create enforceable obligations, because it contained only generalized statements, did not cover the subject of termination, and did not define impermissible employee conduct. The credo, which provided as follows, was deemed aspirational rather than contractual:

> We are responsible to our employees, the men and women who work with us throughout the world. Everyone must be considered as an individual. We must respect their dignity and recognize their merit. They must have a sense of security in their jobs. Compensation must be fair and adequate, and working conditions clean, orderly and safe. Employees must feel free to make suggestions and complaints. There must be equal opportunity for employment, development and advancement for those qualified. We must provide competent management, and their actions must be just and ethical.

877 F. Supp. At 235.

In *Witkowski v. Thomas J. Lipton*, Inc.,[94] the Court found an issue of fact as to whether a binding promise was created by a manual which contained no specific representation of for-cause termination only, but did contain reference to a "trial period" for new employees, a progression of three warnings and discipline, and nonexclusive list of grounds for immediate discharge. Noting that the overriding consideration in determining whether contractual obligations are created is the reasonable expectations of employees, the Court found that the nonexclusive list of grounds for immediate termination could reasonably lead an employee to conclude that he would not be terminated without either going through the progressive warning system or committing an offense like those listed as grounds for immediate discharge. The Court thus found these job security provisions sufficiently comprehensive and definite to allow a jury to decide whether an implied contract was created.

In appropriate circumstances, the question of whether a document constitutes a *Woolley* contract may be resolved in a motion for summary judgment.[95]

1-6:3 "Just Cause" Provisions

An employment manual that prohibits termination except for just cause protects against "arbitrary discharge."[96] It remains unsettled, however, whether an employer may satisfy this standard by acting in good faith, or whether he must be correct, *i.e.*, that the facts upon which he acted be accurate. One district court opinion adopts the good faith standard, holding that a discharge is not arbitrary if the employer has made a good faith determination having credible support that good cause exists:

> Just cause is ... a fair and honest cause of reason, regulated by good faith on the part of the party exercising the power. A discharge for 'just cause' is one based on facts that (1) are supported by substantial evidence and (2) are reasonably believed by the employer to be true and also (3) is not for any arbitrary, capricious, or illegal reason.[97]

The Appellate Division has indicated that, in at least some circumstances, it will apply that rule. Where an employer specifically reserved to itself the right to de-

---

94. 136 N.J. 385 (1994)

95. *Cf. Giudice v. Drew Chemical Corp.*, 210 N.J.Super. 32, 35 (App.Div.), *certif. granted/remanded and certif. denied*, 104 N.J. 465 (1986), with *Radwan v. Beecham Laboratories*, 850 F.2d 147, 151 (3d Cir. 1988), citing *Ware v. Prudential Ins. Co.*, 220 N.J.Super. 135 (App.Div. 1987), *certif. denied*, 113 N.J. 335 (1988). *Accord Woolley v. Hoffmann-LaRoche, Inc.*, 99 N.J. at 307 (ordinary division of issues between court and jury applies).

cide when grounds for termination existed, the court held that "just cause" did not require that the employer be correct, only that he make a good faith determination with credible support.[98]

1-6:4 Economic Necessity

Absent an express promise to the contrary, employers are assumed to have retained the right to terminate employees for economic reasons, even if the em-

---

96. *Maietta v. United Parcel Service, Inc.*, 749 F. Supp. 1344, 1362 (D.N.J. 1990), *aff'd without published op.*, 932 F.2d 960 (3d Cir. 1991). *See also* cases cited therein: *Shebar v. Sanyo Business Systems Corp.*, 111 N.J. 276, 287 (1988); *Woolley v. Hoffmann-LaRoche, Inc.*, 99 N.J. at 301 n. 2 (interpreting manual as protecting employment only from arbitrary termination); *Linn v. Beneficial Commercial Corp.*, 226 N.J.Super. 74, 79, 80 (App.Div. 1988) (action for wrongful discharge does not generally lie for one whose loss of work is actuated by elimination of the job itself due to legitimate economic or business reasons, and not as a bad faith pretext to arbitrarily terminate the employee). In *Greenwood v. State Police Training Ctr.*, 127 N.J. 500, 509-10 (1992), the Supreme Court defined "good cause" in the context of a regulation permitting the suspension or dismissal of police trainees on that basis. The plaintiff in that case had been dismissed from the police academy due to a fear that his blindness in one eye would cause him harm.

> In the employment context, a rule or contract provision allowing termination only for good cause protects an employee from unreasonable or arbitrary termination ... Courts have found good cause for termination in cases in which the discharge is prompted by a legitimate business concern, ... or in which an employee does not perform the job safely or effectively ....
>
> Conversely, courts have noted that termination would be arbitrary or unreasonable and thus not for good cause if the asserted ground was irrelevant to job performance .... Thus, although the good cause standard eludes precise definition, courts ordinarily uphold findings of good cause when the employee's performance is deficient or when the employee creates a risk of harm to himself or herself or others. An employer must present substantial objective evidence to meet the good-cause standard. The few New Jersey courts that have considered the issue of good-cause dismissals are in accord. *See Alter v. Resorts Int'l*, 234 N.J. Super. 409, 416-17, 560 A.2d 1290 (Ch. Div. 1989) (corporation had good cause for discharge when Casino Control Commission required corporation not to employ person who could not qualify for gaming license); *Rogozinski v. Airstream by Angell*, 152 N.J. Super. 133, 143-44, 377 A.2d 807 (Law Div. 1977) (good cause standard not satisfied when allegations of employee incompetence stemmed from personal animosity and employer lacked clear, specific, and definitive evidence), *modified on other grounds*, 164 N.J. Super. 465, 397 A.2d 334 (App. Div. 1979).

In *Abella v. Barringer Resources, Inc.*, 260 N.J. Super. 92 (Ch. Div. 1992), plaintiff alleged that a statement that he was "terminated for cause" was defamatory. In finding a fact issue on the import of that statement, the court held as follows:

> Typically, the fair and natural import of the statement that a person was 'terminated for cause' is only that the termination was not arbitrary. *See Shebar v. Sanyo Business Sys. Corp.*, 111 N.J. 276, 287, 544 A.2d 377 (1988). On its face, it appears to this court that the statement merely posits that Abella's termination was not arbitrary and that Abella refutes this position and may litigate the matter. The statement neither alleges that Abella was incompetent nor recites the particulars that led to his termination. However, this court is not prepared to hold that the phrase "termination by cause" is defined as a matter of law in all contexts as "a non-arbitrary cessation of employment."

260 N.J. Super. at 99.

97. *Maietta v. United Parcel Service, Inc.*, 749 F.Supp. 1344, 1363 (D.N.J. 1990), *aff'd without published op.*, 932 F.2d 960 (3d Cir. 1991), quoting *Baldwin v. Sisters of Providence, Inc.*, 112 Wash. 2d 127, 769 P.2d 298, 303 (1989).

ployee manual otherwise limits discharges to employee misconduct or poor performance.[99]

> [A]n action for wrongful discharge does not generally lie for one whose loss of work is actuated by elimination of the job itself due to legitimate economic or business reasons, and not as a bad faith pretext to arbitrarily terminate the employee.[100]

However, an economic justification for a layoff may not in itself suffice, where procedural requirements of the manual are at issue[101] , or where the selection of employees to be affected implicates statutory concerns such as compliance with state and federal anti-discrimination laws.

1-6:5 Employees Under Contract

Employees covered by collective bargaining agreements or individual contracts of employment have been found precluded by those contracts from asserting *Woolley* claims. It is considered unreasonable for such employees to rely on an employee manual—rather than their contract—as governing the terms and conditions of employment.[102]

1-7 Clear and Prominent Disclaimers

Creation of an implied contract through an employee manual may be avoided by including a clear and prominent disclaimer, but to be effective the disclaimer must be strong, straightforward, and absolutely clear.[103] It should comply with the Supreme Court's description of same in *Woolley*:

---

98. *Vitale v. Bally's Park Place, Inc.*, 1989 N.J. Super. LEXIS 475 (App. Div. 1989).

99. *See Linn v. Beneficial Commercial Corp.*, 226 N.J.Super. 74, 80 (App. Div. 1988).

100. *Linn v. Beneficial Commercial Corp.*, 226 N.J. Super. 74, 80 (App. Div. 1988); *see Brunner v. Abex Corp.*, 661 F. Supp. 1351, 1355 n.3 (D.N.J. 1986) ("It is hard to conceive that the Supreme Court of New Jersey intended to prevent a company from cutting its work force due to economic factors. The doctrine of commercial impracticability, for instance, allows for contract performance to be excused if the cost of the performance has in fact become so excessive and unreasonable that the failure to excuse performance would result in grave injustice.").

101. *Geldreich v. American Cyanamid Co.*, 299 N.J. Super. 478, 486 (App. Div. 1997) (despite a valid reduction in force, employer required to follow procedure in its personnel policy manual to look for and offer alternative employment with the company for employees before their discharge).

102. *Ware v. Prudential Ins. Co.*, 220 N.J.Super. 135, 143 (App. Div. 1987), *certif. denied*, 113 N.J. 335 (1988). *Cf. McQuitty v. General Dynamics Corp.*, 204 N.J.Super. 514 (App. Div. 1985). *See also Gilbert v. Durand Glass Mfg. Co.*, 258 N.J. Super. 320, 327, 609 A.2d 517 (App. Div. 1992) (noting that the absence of an individual employment contract will affect the "reasonable expectations" of an employee receiving an employee manual).

> All that need be done [to avoid creation of a contract] is the inclusion in a very prominent position of an appropriate statement that there is no promise of any kind by the employer contained in the manual; that regardless of what the manual says or provides, the employer promises nothing and remains free to change wages and all other working conditions without having to consult anyone and without anyone's agreement; and that the employer continues to have the absolute power to fire anyone with or without good cause.[104]

The handbook in *Weber v. LDC/Milton Roy* provided that "the statements (in the handbook) are in no way intended to restrict management's obligation for final interpretation of its policies and procedures." [105] This disclaimer, coupled with the absence of a specific promise of permanent employment or the availability of any termination procedure, led the court to conclude there was no *Woolley* contract.[106] Similarly, the handbook in *Edwards v. Schlumberger-Well Services*

---

103. In *Preston v. Claridge Hotel & Casino*, 231 N.J.Super. 81, 87 (App.Div. 1989), the Appellate Division found the following disclaimer inadequate in view of a prior edition of the handbook that had contained references to "maximum job security":

> It is the policy of the Company that this handbook and the items contained, referred to, or mentioned herein, are not intended to create, nor should be construed to constitute, a contract of employment between the Company and any one or all of its personnel. This handbook and its items are presented only as a matter of information and direction regarding Company policy, benefits and other useful information.

In *Sellitto v. Litton Sys., Inc.*, 881 F. Supp. 932 (D.N.J. 1994), the court found that a disclaimer printed in standard typeface under the heading "Note" was not prominent. It also found that several disclaimers, including the following, were not sufficiently clear:

> SUBJECT: STATEMENT OF EMPLOYMENT RELATIONSHIP
>
> Congratulations on your first day at Airtron-Litton Systems. While we are pleased with your decision to begin employment with our Company, we are also aware that a satisfactory employment relationship exists only with the mutual agreement of both employee and Company. As previously stated in our employment application, the Company recognizes your right to resign at any time for any reason, and retains the right to terminate the employment relationship; at any time for any reason.

The court held that although this statement properly avoided legal terms, it did "not adequately put employees on notice that no matter what is said in the Handbook or Manual, the employer is utterly free to abandon its published procedures and fire an employee without progressive discipline, without cause, and without notice," and did not unmistakably indicate that the discharge provisions of the manual were "utterly without effect in the defendant's workplace." 881 F. Supp. at 939. *See Geldreich v. American Cyanamid Co.*, 299 N.J. Super. 478, 486 (App. Div. 1997) (the "generalized disclaimer" in the personnel policy manual was not sufficient to allow employer to avoid complying with unqualified statements elsewhere in the manual that the company will undertake certain procedures in the event of an involuntary termination due to a reduction in force). *But see Rivera v. Trump Plaza Hotel and Casino*, 305 N.J. Super. 596, 601 (App. Div. 1997) (finding that the disclaimer, signed by each plaintiff, was sufficiently clear and definite).

104. *Woolley v. Hoffmann-LaRoche, Inc.*, 99 N.J. 284, 309, *modified*, 101 N.J. 10 (1985).

105. *Weber v. LDC/Milton Roy*, 42 FEP 1507, 1518 (D.N.J. 1986).

106. *Id.* at 1517-18.

contained a disclaimer that was sufficient to avoid the creation of a *Woolley* contract. The disclaimer, which was titled "Notice of Disclaimer," was prominently located at the front of the handbook and stated that the handbook was not a contract or guarantee of employment.[107]

The effect of a manual also may be limited by entry into individual contracts of employment with particular employees providing that the employment is at will; they have been found to take precedence over the terms of a manual.[108] Some employers also include provisions in employment applications stating that the employment applied for will be at will.[109]

In determining the effectiveness of disclaimers, courts seem to use a common-sense standard based upon the totality of the document, which suggests that employers consider not just the language of the disclaimer, but also its prominence (*e.g.*, Is it in the front of the manual? Is it in bold face? Is it set off from other provisions by a separate heading?) and its effectiveness in light of other provisions of the manual (*e.g.*, Is a disclaimer stating that employment is at will seemingly contradicted by other portions of the manual referring to job security?).[110] In addition, the circumstances attendant to distribution of the manual may impact the interpretation and effectiveness of a disclaimer in an appropriate case.[111]

---

107. 984 F Supp. 264, 284-85 (D.N.J. 1997).

108. *See Ware v. Prudential Ins. Co.*, 220 N.J. Super. 135, 144 (App. Div. 1987), *certif. denied*, 113 N.J. 335 (1988) ("Since an employer may avoid any legally binding effect being given to personnel policies set forth in a policy manual by a unilateral statement in the manual, it follows *a fortiori* that this effect may be avoided by the execution of a written employment contract by which the employee expressly agrees to an at will employment status."); *Radwan v. Beecham Laboratories*, 850 F.2d 147, 150 (3d Cir. 1988) (employee who accepted individual agreement of employment at will could have no reasonable expectation not to be discharged except for cause based on employee manual).

109. Such a provision was found effective in *Radwan v. Beecham Laboratories*, 850 F.2d 147, 150 (3d Cir. 1988), where the Third Circuit stated:

> Here, unlike in *Woolley*, the question of the employee's tenure was specifically dealt with in writing when he was hired, for [plaintiff] agreed that he could be discharged at any time without previous notice. Further, nothing in Radwan's application suggested that Beecham's right to discharge him was dependent upon his conduct or job performance. While this application was not part of the employees manual, we do not understand *Woolley* to require that disclaimers of an intent to bind an employer not to discharge an employee must be in the employees manual and not in an individual agreement.

Id. (citation omitted).

110. Compare, for example, *Preston v. Claridge Hotel & Casino*, 231 N.J.Super. 81, 87 (App.Div. 1989), with *Ware v. Prudential Ins. Co.*, 220 N.J.Super. 135, 144 (App.Div. 1987), and *Weber v. LDC/Milton Roy*, 1 IER 1509, 1510 (D.N.J. 1986). *See Kapossy v. McGraw-Hill, Inc.*, 921 F. Supp. 234, 245-46 (D.N.J. 1996) (disclaimers in regular Roman type under the headings 'ABOUT THIS BOOK" and "ABOUT THIS MANUAL" were not conspicuous); *Jackson v. Georgia-Pacific Corp.*, 296 N.J. Super. 1, 15-16 (App. Div. 1996) (disclaimer's location in the very first paragraph under the heading "Termination of Employment-Salaried Employees" was a significant factor to the court in finding the disclaimer to be effective), *certif. denied*, 149 N.J. 141 (1997).

111. *See Preston v. Claridge Hotel & Casino*, 231 N.J.Super. at 87-88.

1-8 Revocation and Alteration

Where a manual without a disclaimer has been distributed, and a *Woolley* contract created, mere distribution of a subsequent manual with an otherwise effective disclaimer may not be sufficient to revoke any promises made in the first. In *Preston v. Claridge Hotel & Casino*, the Appellate Division held that where the original manual (sans disclaimer) was discussed in an orientation meeting, it was inconsistent with the "basic honesty" required by *Woolley* to introduce a revised manual (with disclaimer) by merely asking employees "to pick up the handbook, read it, and sign the detachable acknowledgement form."[112] Thus, to be certain that revocation or amendment is effective, the announcement and publication of a new or revised manual should be at least as prominent as that of the original manual.[113] Changes should be explained clearly, distributed to all concerned, and acknowledged. To the extent possible, advance notice of the change should be provided. Moreover, all new manuals should clearly and specifically reserve the right of amendment and revocation.[114]

1-9 Arbitration

As wrongful discharge suits proliferate, alternative dispute resolution procedures have become increasingly attractive to employers, and the Appellate Division has enforced contractual agreements to arbitrate employment disputes.[115]

---

112. 231 N.J.Super. 81, 87-88 (App.Div. 1989). Of course, an employee's individual contract to work on an at-will basis is not modified by a subsequent distribution of a policies guide to supervisors. *Ware v. Prudential Ins. Co.*, 220 N.J.Super. 135, 144 (App.Div. 1987), *certif. denied*, 113 N.J. 335 (1988).

113. *See Preston v. The Claridge Hotel and Casino, Ltd.*, 231 N.J. *Super.* at 87-88.

114. This reservation may not be necessary; the analysis in the above-cited cases suggests that the right to amend or revoke the provisions of a manual generally exists notwithstanding its articulation. That is particularly apparent with respect to those manuals that disclaim the intent to create a contract. However, language in *Woolley*, decisions in other jurisdictions, and pre-ERISA decisions in New Jersey applying unilateral contract principles to fringe benefit booklets, suggest articulation of a reserved right of amendment as the most appropriate course. *See generally Stopford v. Boonton Molding Co., Inc.*, 56 N.J. 169 (1970); *Russell v. Princeton Laboratories, Inc.*, 50 N.J. 30 (1967); *Bankey v. Storer Broadcasting Co.*, 432 Mich. 438, 443 N.W. 2d 112 (Mich. 1987). The Court noted in *Woolley*:

> Further problems may result from the employer's explicitly reserved right unilaterally to change the manual. We have no doubt that, generally, changes in such a manual, including changes in terms and conditions of employment, are permitted. We express no opinion, however, on whether or to what extent they are permitted when they adversely affect a binding job security provision.

99 N.J. at 309.

115. *See Fastenberg v. Prudential Ins. Co.*, 309 N.J. Super 415 (App. Div. 1998) (plaintiff required to arbitrate wrongful discharge and defamation claims). *Cf. Young v. Prudential Inc. Co. of Am.*, 297 N.J. Super. 605 (App. Div. 1997), *certif. denied*, 149 N.J. 408 (1997) (interpreting valid arbitration agreement as excluding specific dispute). *See* Mayer, "ADR: An Effective Alternative to Litigation," 123 *N.J.L.J.* 1218 (1989).

The United States District Court for the District of New Jersey has held that when an employee handbook provides for grievance and arbitration of claims thereunder, employees must comply with the procedure specified.[116] Noting that it has long been the rule in New Jersey that an aggrieved employee covered by a collective bargaining agreement must exhaust the remedies provided thereunder before resorting to the court for redress, the court found that principle "no less applicable here where the rights asserted by plaintiff are contained in an employee handbook."[117] As a consequence, the court found that breach of contract claims based upon employee handbooks are barred when an employee has failed to exhaust the grievance procedure.[118] It is important to note, however, that the employee claimed he should have been relieved from compliance because invoking the procedure would have been futile, and that this claim was rejected on the ground that the procedure specified in the manual was found by the court to be "extremely fair and impartial."[119]

III. INFORMAL POLICIES

1-10 Oral "*Woolley*" Claims

Although the Supreme Court has held that a company-wide policy in a *written* employment manual, generally distributed to its employees, may create an enforceable unilateral contract, the court has not yet passed on the issue whether *Woolley* should be extended to orally communicated company-wide policies. The Appellate Division has held that an unwritten company policy of non-termination of managers except for cause would be enforceable under *Woolley* if proven.[120] A plaintiff must show:

> (1) that the oral employment policy contained "an express or implied promise concerning the terms and conditions of employemnt"; (2) that the policy was "a definitive, established, company-wide policy"; (3) that the oral statement of policy by

---

116. *Fregara v. Jet Aviation Business Jets*, 764 F.Supp. 940, 951-53 (D.N.J. 1991).

117. *Id.* at 951, *relying on Jorgensen v. Pennsylvania R.R. Co.*, 25 N.J. 541 (1958).

118. *Id.* at 953 ("To the extent that the grievance procedures outlined in the alleged *Woolley* contract are detrimental to his cause of action, plaintiff cavalierly dismisses them as permissive and non-binding. If the provisions governing job security are binding, then so too is the language concerning utilization of the grievance procedures."). *See Hyman v. Atlantic City Medical Center*, 1998 WL 135249, *13-14 (D.N.J. 1998) (dismissing plaintiff's claim due to her failure to follow the grievance procedures outlined in the Grievance Policy and Proceedures Manual).

119. *Fregara*, 746 F. Supp. at 952. The process included several steps, including review by a company board that included elected, non-supervisory employees. *Id.*

a supervisor constituted an "accurate representation of policy"; and (4) that the supervisor was "authorized to make" the oral statements of policy.[121]

Opinions on this issue have been somewhat mixed. In *Labus v. Navistar Int'l Trans. Corp.*,[122] the United States District Court for the District of New Jersey agreed with the Appellate Division decision in *Shebar*, concluding that "the New Jersey Supreme Court's rationale underlying its recognition of an implied contract from a written employee manual also supports the finding of an implied contract from oral communications from the employer."[123] To the same effect is *Palmer v. Schlott Realtors, Inc.*, where the court denied the employer's motion for summary judgment on plaintiff's claim that a form for conducting performance appraisals proved the existence of an unwritten company policy of non-termination except for good cause.[124] In *Ditzel v. University of Medicine & Dentistry of New Jersey*, the Court concluded that "good evaluations and oral praise alone do not create implied agreements to terminate upon good cause only."[125] In *First Atlantic Leasing Corp. v. Tracey*, the plaintiff claimed to be due severance pay under an informal, unwritten company "policy."[126] The district court avoided the general question, holding that the plaintiff's allegations about the terms of the alleged policy were not specific or clear enough to support his claim.[127] The court had

---

120. *Shebar v. Sanyo Busines Systems Corp.*, 218 N.J. Super. 111 (App. Div. 1987), *aff'd on other grounds*, 111 N.J. 275 (1988):

> The legal question then is whether the holding in *Woolley* was intended by the Supreme Court to be limited to a general employer policy expressed only by way of a manual or handbook or whether it was intended to extend to a definitive, established, company-wide employer policy, however expressed. We conclude that the thrust of the *Woolley* holding and the rationale as well as the public policy on which it is based is directed to the existence of the employer's general policy rather than the form in which it is expressed. The difference between a manual or handbook policy and a policy otherwise expressed presents, in our view, an issue of proof rather than of substance. 218 N.J. Super. at 120.

The Supreme Court found it unnecessary to reach this issue. It found the record did not present a claim "that defendant had established and disseminated a definitive company-wide termination policy, or that plaintiff or any other employee had ever relied on such a policy." *Shebar v. Sanyo Businesss Systems Corp.*, 111 N.J. at 284. *See Gilbert v. Durand Glass Mfg. Co.*, 258 N.J. Super. 320, 328 (App. Div. 1992) (noting that the Supreme Court in *Shebar* found it unnecessary to consider whether to extend *Wooley* to instances where a company has orally communicated an established company-wide policy to its employees). Instead, the court characterized plaintiff's claim as one for breach of a unique, oral promise made specifically to him, and thus subject to normal rules of contract construction. 111 N.J. at 284.

121. *Fisher v. Allied Signal Corp.*, 974F. Supp.797, 808 (D.N.J.1997), relying on *Gilbert v. Durand Glass Manufacturing Co. Inc.*, 258 N.J. Super. 320, 330-31 (App. Div. 1992), and *Ditzel v. UMDNJ*, 962 F. Supp. 595 (D.N.J.1997). *Accord Carney v. Dexter Shoe Co.*, 701 F.Supp. 1093, 1103 (D.N.J. 1988) ("Although [the Appellate Division opinion in] *Shebar* has expanded the ways in which a company can be held to have communicated an expectation of continued employment to its employees, it has not eliminated the need, articulated in *Brunner v. Abex Corp.*, 661 F.Supp. 1351 (D.N.J. 1986)], to show clear and convincing proof of a precise agreement.").

122. 740 F. Supp. 1053 (D.N.J. 1990).

held in *Brunner v. Abex Corp.*,[128] issued before the *Shebar* decision, that "*Woolley* was unmistakably limited, even in its broadest interpretation, to commitments arising out of written communications by the employer to the employee."[129]

1-11 Estoppel

Proof of promissory estoppel consists of four elements: (1) a clear and definite promise by the promisor; (2) made with the expectation that the promisee will rely thereon; (3) actual reliance by the promisee; and (4) incurrence of definite and substantial detriment as a result of the reliance.[130]

---

123. *Labus v. Navistar Int'l Trans. Corp.*, 740 F. Supp. 1053, 1063 (D.N.J. 1990). In *Gilbert v. Durand Glass Mfg. Co.*, 258 N.J. Super. 320, 328, 609 A.2d 517 (App. Div. 1992), another panel of the Appellate Division followed Judge Pressler's analysis in *Shebar*, holding that "the difference between a written policy and a policy otherwise expressed is 'an issue of proof rather than of substance.'" The court enforced the employer's unwritten termination policy and described the standard of proof of both written and oral *Woolley* claims as follows:

> What may be distilled from the *Woolley/Shebar* analysis is that the policy, written or oral, must contain an express or implied promise concerning the terms and conditions of employment. It must also be a "a definitive, established, company-wide employer policy," *Shebar*, 218 N.J. Super. at 120, 526 A.2d 1144; *see also Woolley*, 99 N.J. at 302, 491 A.2d 1257, and the employer's statements must constitute "an accurate representation of policy" which the employer was authorized to make. *Shebar*, 218 N. J. Super. at 121, 526 A.2d 1144. However, "[n]o pre-employment negotiations need take place and the parties' minds need not meet on the subject; nor does it matter that the employee knows nothing of the particulars of the employer's policies and practices or that the employer may change them unilaterally." *Toussaint v. Blue Cross & Blue Shield of Mich.*, 408 Mich. 579, 613, 292 N.W. 2d 880, 892 (1980). It is enough that the employee reasonably believes that a particular personnel policy has been established and is applied consistently and uniformly to each employee. *Id.* Also, the enforceability of such a provision must be construed in accordance with "the reasonable expectations of the employees." *Woolley*, 99 N.J. at 298, 491 A.2d 1257.

258 N.J. Super. at 330. *See Morris v. Siemens Components, Inc.*,1996 WL 294074 (D.N.J. 1996) (alleged statements by a representative of the employer's workers' compensation carrier unenforceable as a matter of law because statements were not statements of plaintiff's employer and therefore could not be accurate representations of policy which the employer was authorized to make). *See also Fischer v. Allied Signal Corp.*, 974 F. Supp. 797 (D.N.J. 1997) (granting summary for employer where plaintiff failed to demonstrate a "definitive, established, company-wide policy" and only presented testimony "concerning what Allied supposedly 'kind of promised'").

124. *Palmer v. Schlott Realtors, Inc.*, 4 IER 1553 (D.N.J. 1989).

125. 962 F. Supp. 595, 607 (D.N.J. 1997).

126. *First Atlantic Leasing Corp. v. Tracey*, 738 F. Supp. 863 (1990).

127. The court relied on a series of cases discussing the requisites to enforcement of alleged written policies. 738 F. Supp. at 878. *See Kane v. Milikowsky*, 224 N.J.Super. 613, 616 (App.Div. 1988) (written memorandum did not comprehensively treat subject of employment termination); *Ware v. Prudential Ins. Co.*, 220 N.J.Super. 135, 146-47 (App.Div. 1987); *certif. denied*, 113 N.J. 335 (1988) (handbook did not specifically set forth alleged employee benefits).

128. 661 F. Supp. 1351 (D.N.J. 1986).

129. *Id.* at 1356.

The related doctrine of equitable estoppel is distinguished by the fact that the promisor has made a representation—through act or speech—that is false. To state a basis for application of an equitable estoppel, a party must demonstrate conduct: (1) amounting to a misrepresentation or concealment of material facts; (2) known to the party allegedly estopped and unknown to the party claiming estoppel; (3) done with the expectation or intention that it will be acted upon by the other party; and (4) relied upon by the other party in such a manner as to change his position for the worse.[131]

Both promissory and equitable estoppel should be reserved for the unusual case, where their application is the only method of avoiding injustice.[132] In keeping with the general rule, application of estoppel in the employment context has been limited; however, no clear rule has emerged. Some decisions suggest that special rules for estoppel obtain in the employment context. Most recent decisions fail to distinguish between equitable and promissory estoppel, treating them interchangeably.

1-11:1 Clear and Definite Representation

To support a claim for equitable or promissory estoppel, the representation or action relied upon must be clear and definite. Where it is not, estoppel has been disallowed. Past practices of the employer are insufficient. In *Linn v. Beneficial Commercial Corp.*,[133] the court rejected plaintiff's claim that his employer was estopped by very non-specific conduct from terminating him: "It cannot fairly be said that an employer commits itself to keep an employee indefinitely by promoting him, asking him to transfer and assisting him with expenses."[134] To the same

130. *Jevic v. Coca-Cola Bottling Co. of N.Y.*, 5 IER 765, 768 (D.N.J. 1990); *Rodichok v. Limitorque Corp.*, 1997 WL 392535 (D.N.J. 1997) (plaintiff failed to present evidence of clear and definite promise or reasonable reliance); *Pitak v. Bell Atlantic Network Servs., Inc.*, 928 F. Supp. 1354, 1367 (D.N.J. 1996) (laid-off employees failed to create issue of fact with respect to existence of clear and definite promise or reliance); *Malaker Corp. v. First Jersey Nat'l Bank*, 163 N.J.Super. 463, 479 (App. Div. 1978).

131. *Jevic v. Coca-Cola Bottling Co. of N.Y.*, 5 IER at 768, relying on *Carlsen v. Masters, Mates & Pilots Pension Plan Trust,* 80 N.J. 334, 339 (1979). As noted in Dreier and Rowe, *Guidebook to Chancery Practice in New Jersey* (4th ed. 1997) at 20, these elements are also the basic elements of legal fraud. *See* Chapter 3, § 3-15. *See generally Pitak*, 928 F. Supp. at 1367 (under *Quigley, Inc. v. Miller Family Farms*, 266 N.J. Super. 283 (App. Div. 1993), elements of equitable estoppel are misrepresentation of material fact, reasonable and justifiable reliance and resulting damages); *Chrisomalis v. Chrisomalis*, 260 N.J. Super. 50, 55-56, 615 A.2d 266 (App. Div. 1992) (matrimonial case; defining equitable estoppel).

132. *See Jevic v. Coca-Cola Bottling Co. of N.Y.*, 5 IER at 769; *Peck v. Imedia, Inc.*, 293 N.J. Super. 151, 165-68 (App. Div.) (allowing plaintiff to proceed to trial on her promissory estoppel claim based on plaintiff's detrimental reliance on defendant's promise of employment that was withdrawn prior to start of work), *certif. denied*, 147 N.J. 262 (1996).

133. 226 N.J.Super. 74 (App. Div. 1988).

134. *Id.* at 80.

effect is *McQuitty v. General Dynamics Corp.*, rejecting performance under an expired collective bargaining agreement as a basis for estoppel.[135] Oral representations of continued employment lacking specificity or definiteness similarly have been rejected as mere "friendly assurances."[136] Oral representations made before or at the time of signing a written agreement are also unenforceable.[137] An alleged offer of employment contingent upon a character verification of the plaintiff was found insufficient,[138] as were statements that becoming a facilitator would accererate carrer growth or enhance promotional opportunities.[139]

1-11:2 Detrimental Reliance

Proof of detrimental reliance is essential to an estoppel.[140] To satisfy this standard in the employment context, something more than the mere rendition of services as an employee must be involved.[141] In *Panzino v. Scott Paper Co.*,[142] plaintiffs unsuccessfully asserted that the following incidents, among other things, constituted actionable detrimental reliance on an alleged promise of job security:

---

135. 204 N.J.Super. 514, 520 (App.Div. 1985).

136. *Carney v. Dexter Shoe Co.*, 701 F.Supp. 1093, 1103 (1988) ("Although *Shebar* has expanded the ways in which a company can be held to have communicated an expectation of continued employment to its employees, it has not eliminated the need, articulated in *Brunner v. Abex Corp.*, 661 F.Supp. 1351 (D.N.J. 1986), to show clear and convincing proof of a precise agreement."). *See Fischer v. Allied Signal Corp.*, 974 F. Supp. 797 (D.N.J. 1997) (statements that becoming a facilitator would enhance plaintiff's career were insufficient to support a claim of promissory estoppel).

137. *See Ware v. Prudential Ins. Co.*, 220 N.J.Super. 135, 144 (App. Div. 1987), *certif. denied*, 113 N.J. 335 (1988) (oral assurances of job security allegedly made at the time of execution of an individual contract for at-will employment are not enforceable); *Jevic v. Coca-Cola Bottling Co. of N.Y.*, 5 IER 765, 768-69 (D.N.J. 1990) (alleged concealment of drug test policy could not form basis of equitable estoppel where signed pre-employment statement disclosed it).

138. *Bonczek v. Carter Wallace, Inc.*, 304 N.J. Super. 593, 600 (App. Div. 1997), *certif. denied,* 153 N.J. 51 (1998).

139. *Fischer v. Allied Signal Corp.*, 974 F. Supp. 797, 809 (D.N.J. 1997).

140. *See, e.g., Carlsen v. Masters, Mates & Pilots Pension Plan Trust*, 80 N.J. 334, 339 (1979); *Jevic v. Coca-Cola BottlingCo. of N.Y.*, 5 IER 765,769 (1990) (requiring detrimental action specifically in reliance on the employer's representation). *See also DeJoy v. Comcast Cable Communications, Inc.*, 968 F. Supp. 963, 991-92 (D.N.J. 1997) (where plaintiff alleged that he declined an offer of employment based on the defendant's alleged promise of continued employment, genuine issue of fact precluded summary judgement on plaintiff's promissory estoppel claim); *McDonald's Corp. v. Miller*, 1994 WL 507822 (D.N.J. Sept. 14, 1994), *aff'd*, 60 F.3d 815 (3d Cir. 1995) (plaintiff applicant for a McDonald's franchise could not reasonably have relied upon conditional promises that he would be granted a franchise).

141. *See Fregara v. Jet Aviation Business Jets*, 764 F.Supp. 940, 948 (D.N.J. 1991); *Jevic v. Coca-Cola Bottling Co. of N.Y.*, 5 IER 765, 769 (1990); *Panzino v. Scott Paper Co.*, 685 F.Supp. 458, 462 (D.N.J. 1988). To the extent *Panzino* recognizes an action for violation of a public policy of equitable estoppel, it has been overruled by *DeVries v. McNeil Consumer Products Co.*, 250 N.J.Super. 159 (App.Div. 1991).

142. 685 F.Supp. 458 (D.N.J. 1988).

> —one plaintiff testified that, had he known he was going to lose his job, he would have immediately sought work elsewhere;
>
> —another plaintiff stated that there was a possibility he would have been hired into a new job earlier if he had applied earlier;
>
> —one plaintiff stated that had he not been told his job was secure, he would have applied for a loan to start a new video business while he was still employed, and the loan would have been granted.[143]

The court's analysis in rejecting these claims as speculative provides a useful guide to the factors which may be considered sufficient to support an estoppel.

> An example of one extreme of this continuum might be the situation in which a plaintiff has sought and received job offers, believing his present job to be in jeopardy, but turns down the new jobs after assurances of continued employment, only to lose the job later. In that instance the actions taken in reliance were obviously detrimental and the harm concrete and certain. At the other extreme might be a situation in which a person says that had he known his job was in jeopardy he would have applied for other jobs, but he can't specify where he might have applied and he doesn't know whether other jobs were available in any event. A recovery in such a situation is obviously inappropriate.[144]

In *Peck v. Imedia, Inc.* and *Jenkins v. Region Nine Housing,* the Appellate Division ruled that the plaintiff in each case should have been permitted to proceed to trial on a claim of promissory estoppel. In *Peck,* the defendant offered plaintiff employment as a Desktop Publishing Manager in Northern New Jersey. The plaintiff, allegedly relying on the offer, gave up her deskop publishing business in Boston, rented her apartment in Boston, found an apartment in New Jersey, and hired a mover. The court held that based on these facts, and because the defendants waited for approximately ten days before informing plaintiff of their decision to rescind the job offer, the plaintiff was entitled to proceed to trial on her claim of promissory estoppel even though the offer of employment would have been at will.[145] Similarly, in *Jenkins*, the court ruled that the promissory estoppel

143. 685 F.Supp. at 461-62.

144. *Panzino v. Scott Paper Co.*, 685 F.Supp. at 462 (internal citation omitted); *see Fregara v. Jet Aviation Business Jets,* 764 F.Supp. 940, 948 (D.N.J. 1991) (plaintiff who was unemployed when he accepted job offer cannot establish that he suffered any detriment; he "did not forego any other job offers as there were none ... all that [he] gave up was his right to be unemployed"); *Jevic v. Coca-Cola Bottling Co. of N.Y.*, 5 IER at 769 (plaintiff's move to N.Y. insufficient in circumstances of that case).

claim of a plaintiff who was discharged after she leased a car in reliance on defendant's offer of employment should not have been dismissed. The plaintiff alleged that she did not have a car before accepting the offer, and could not afford a car but for the promise of employment, which included a car allowance. Furthermore, the job plaintiff performed required her to have a car and the defendant accompanied her to the automobile dealership and participated in the car lease.[146]

IV. RESTRICTIVE COVENANTS

1-12 General Requirements

Although agreements not to compete were at one time flatly outlawed, it has now long been recognized that they have a proper place and are enforceable under appropriate circumstances.[147] Because of important protections New Jersey affords the individual right to pursue one's profession or livelihood, a covenant not to compete incidental to the sale of a business is more freely enforceable than one tied to the termination of employment.[148] Nonetheless, an employee's covenant will be given effect if it is reasonable under all the circumstances of his particular case.[149] A determination of reasonableness generally requires the findings that the agreement: (1) simply protects the legitimate interests of the employer; (2) imposes no undue hardship on the employee; and (3) is not injurious to the public.[150]

---

145. *Peck v. Imedia, Inc.*, 293 N.J. Super 151, 165-68 (App. Div. 1996).

146. *Jenkins v. Region Nine Housing,* 306 N.J. Super. 258, 263-64 (App. Div. 1997).

147. *Solari Industries, Inc. v. Malady,* 55 N.J. 571, 576 (1970). For a general discussion *see* Dreier and Rowe, *Guidebook to Chancery Practice in New Jersey*, pp. 106-109 (4th ed. 1997); Valiulis, *Covenants Not to Compete*, (1985).

148. *Solari Industries, Inc. v. Malady,* 55 N.J. at 571, 576 (1970); *Whitmyer Bros., Inc. v. Doyle,* 58 N.J. 25, 32 (1971). The policy was stated in *Magic Fingers, Inc. v. Robins*, 86 N.J.Super. 236, 238 (Ch.Div. 1965):

> Courts have attributed much strength to the social policy that every man should be free to earn his own living and have also recognized that an employee who is asked to sign a covenant may not have the full freedom to bargain about its terms that exists in other business situations. In other words, contracts of this type—if they are to be enforced—must pass a stricter test than other types of contracts; it is not enough to say the parties signed a document in good faith and are, therefore, bound to respect all of its terms.

See also Rubel & Jensen Corp. v. Rubel, 85 N.J.Super. 27, 35 (App.Div. 1964) (agreement not to use name or solicit customers of property sold as a going business is different from ordinary agreement not to engage in a competitive business); *Hudson Foam Latex Products, Inc. v. Aiken*, 82 N.J.Super. 508, 514 (App.Div. 1964) ("The substantial disparity in bargaining positions between a seller and a buyer, and an employee and an employer, is more than sufficient to warrant a heavier reliance on the terms of a contract in the former instance than in the latter."); *Coskey's T.V. & Radio Sales and Serv., Inc. v. Foti*, 253 N.J. Super. 626, 633 (App. Div. 1992).

These same criteria are utilized to determine the enforceability of "holdover" clauses—contracts that require the assignment of future or post-employment patents.[151] Like the post-employment agreement not to compete, ascertaining the reasonableness of a holdover clause involves balancing competing interests: the inventor's right to enjoy his own creativity and use the general skills and knowledge obtained through prior employment, and the employer's right to protect trade secrets, confidential information, and customer relations.[152]

Restrictive covenants in a contract between employer and employee "are assignable as an incident of the business even if not made by express words." [153]

1-12:1 Legitimate Interests of the Employer

The employer has no legitimate interest in preventing competition as such; that interest would be contrary to the public policy of New Jersey as expressed in the anti-trust laws.[154] However, "the employer has a patently legitimate interest in protecting his trade secrets as well as his confidential business information and he has an equally legitimate interest in protecting his customer relation-

---

149. *See Whitmyer Bros., Inc. v. Doyle*, 58 N.J. 25, 32 (1971); *Solari Industries, Inc. v. Malady*, 55 N.J. 571, 576 (1970); *Karlin v. Weinberg*, 77 N.J. 408, 417 (1978); *A.T. Hudson & Co., Inc. v. Donovan*, 216 N.J.Super. 426, 432 (App.Div. 1987); *Raven v. A. Klein & Co., Inc.*, 195 N.J.Super. 209, 213 (App.Div. 1984) ("restrictive covenants will be enforced to the extent that they are reasonable as to time, area and scope of activity, necessary to protect a legitimate interest of the employer, not unduly burdensome upon the employee, and not injurious to the public interest"); *Platinum Management, Inc. v. Dahms*, 285 N.J. Super. 274, 293 (Law Div. 1995).

150. *See Whitmyer Bros., Inc. v. Doyle*, 58 N.J. at 32-33; *Solari Industries, Inc. v. Malady*, 55 N.J. at 576; *Karlin v. Weinberg*, 77 N.J. at 417; *Chas S. Wood & Co. v. Kane*, 42 N.J.Super. 122, 125 (App.Div. 1956). *Id.* at 293-94. *In Coskey's T.V. & Radio Sales and Serv., Inc. v. Foti*, 253 N.J. Super. 626, 633-34 (App. Div. 1992), the Appellate Division described the *Solari* test of reasonableness: "To be enforceable the covenant must protect a legitimate interest of the employer; it may impose no undue hardship on the employee; and it must not impair the public interest. Even if the covenant is found enforceable, it may be limited in its application concerning its geographical area, its period of enforceability, and its scope of activity." (citations omitted). *See Jiffy Lube Int'l, Inc. v. Weiss Bros., Inc.*, 834 F. Supp. 683, 690 (D.N.J. 1993) (restrictive covenants are enforceable only insofar as they are reasonable under the circumstances, determined by the *Solari* standard: "(1) it must protect a legitimate interest of the employer; (2) it may impose no undue hardship on the employee; (3) it must not impair the public interests").

151. *See Ingersoll Rand Co. v. Ciavatta*, 110 N.J. 609, 627 (1988).

152. *Id.* at 626-27. Employees have a common law duty not to disclose confidential information from a former employer, *see Abalene Exterminating Co., Inc. v. Oser*, 125 N.J. Eq. 329, 332-33 (Ch.Div. 1939), or to reveal the former employer's trade secrets. *See Sun Dial Corp. v. Rideout*, 16 N.J. 252, 259 (1954); Valiulis, *Covenants Not to Compete* §1.5, p.5 (1985) ("Under common law, all employees have a duty not to act in a way that is adverse to the interests of their then current employers").

153. *A. Fink & Sons v. Goldberg*, 101 N.J. Eq. 644, 647 (Ch. 1927); *J. H. Renardo, Inc. v. Sims*, 312 N.J. Super. 195, 201 (Ch. Div. 1998) (quoting *Goldberg*).

154. *See Whitmyer Bros., Inc. v. Doyle*, 58 N.J. 25, 33 (1971); *Raven v. A. Klein & Co., Inc.*, 195 N.J.Super. at 213 (employer not entitled to enforce a restrictive covenant principally directed at lessening competition); *see also Ellis v. Lionikis*, 162 N.J.Super. 579, 585 (App.Div. 1978) (restrictive covenant forfeiture of benefits clause).

ships."[155] Thus, an employer that has paid employees to develop clients and customer relations may, in otherwise proper circumstances, restrain former employees from soliciting those customers.[156]

Matters of general knowledge within the industry, trivial differences in methods of operation, and customer lists generally accessible or compilable are not trade secrets or confidential information warranting protection.[157] Professional skills or expertise developed during the employment are similarly unprotected:

> [A] postemployment restriction on an employee requires special justification which is nonexistent where the harm caused by service to another consists merely in the fact that the new employer becomes a more efficient competitor just as the first employer did through having a competent and efficient employee.[158]

To determine what is a trade secret in this context, the Supreme Court has endorsed the definition found in §757 of the Restatement (First) of Torts,[159] and the six factors listed therein: (1) the extent to which the information is known outside

---

155. *See Whitmyer Bros., Inc. v. Doyle*, 58 N.J. at 33; *A.T. Hudson & Co., Inc. v. Donovan*, 216 N.J. Super. at 433 ("While an employer may not prevent competition as such, he does have a legitimate interest in protecting his customer relationships."); *Raven v. A. Klein & Co., Inc.*, 195 N.J.Super. 209, 214 (App. Div. 1984) (a unique manufacturing technique not generally known throughout the industry is protectable under post-employment restrictive agreement and common law protection afforded to trade secrets).

156. *See Solari Industries, Inc. v. Malady*, 55 N.J. 571 (1970); *A.T. Hudson & Co., Inc. v. Donovan*, 216 N.J.Super. 426, 433-34 (App.Div. 1987); *Platinum Management, Inc. v. Dahms*, 285 N.J. Super. 274, 295-98 (Law Div. 1995) ("[M]isappropriated information need not rise to the level of the usual trade secret, and indeed, may otherwise be publicly available. The key to determining the misuse of the information is the relationship of the parties at the time of disclosure;" customer identities and employee's knowledge of customers protectible, but restrictions as to prospective customers unenforceable). *Cf. Coskey's T.V. & Radio Sales and Serv., Inc. v. Foti*, 253 N.J. Super. 626, 638-39 (App. Div. 1992) (distinguishing *A.T. Hudson & Co. v. Donovan*, 216 N.J. Super. 426 (App. Div. 1987), on the ground that the client contacts in that consulting business were close and on-going, and holding that a preliminary injunction should not have issued against former employee where projects were of discrete duration and universe of customers was finite and well known; in that situation, the former employee's "relationships within the industry were not bought and paid for; they were merely rented during the period of employment"); *Hogan v. Bergen Brunswig Corp.*, 153 N.J.Super. 37 (App. Div. 1977).

157. *See Whitmyer Bros., Inc. v. Doyle*, 58 N.J. at 33-34.

158. *Whitmyer Bros., Inc. v. Doyle*, 58 N.J. at 35, relying on 6A *Corbin on Contracts*, §1394 (internal quotation marks omitted). *See Coskey's T.V. & Radio Sales and Serv., Inc. v. Foti*, 253 N.J. Super. 626, 637 (App. Div. 1992) ("An employer may not prevent an employee from using the general skills in an industry which have been built up over the employee's tenure with the employer"); *Subcarrier Communications, Inc. v. Day*, 299 N.J. Super. 634, 643 (App. Div. 1997) (same); *Raven v. A. Klein & Co., Inc.*, 195 N.J. Super. at 213-14 ("trade secrets or confidential information cannot merely be the facility, skill or experience learned or developed during an employee's tenure with an employer").

159. "b. Definition of trade secret. A trade secret may consist of any formula, pattern, device or compilation of information which is used in one's business, and which gives him an opportunity to obtain an advantage over competitors who do not know or use it. It may be a formula for a chemical compound, a process of manufacturing, treating or preserving materials, a pattern for a machine or other device, or a list of customers." Restatement (First) of Torts §757, comment b (1939), *quoted in Ingersoll Rand Co. v. Ciavatta*, 110 N.J. 609, 636 (1988).

of the business; (2) the extent to which it is known by employees and others involved in the business; (3) efforts made by the owner to guard the secrecy of the information; (4) the value of the information to the business and competitors; (5) the effort or money spent in developing it; and (6) the ease or difficulty others would have in duplicating or acquiring the information.[160]

In *Ingersoll Rand Co. v. Ciavatta*, a holdover clause case, the Supreme Court recognized a protectable interest beyond the traditional interests in trade secrets, confidential information, and customer relations. It had a difficult time articulating a standard, however, leaving definition of this new interest to the vagaries of case-by-case determinations:

> We recognize that employers may have legitimate interests in protecting information that is not a trade secret or proprietary information, but highly specialized, current information not generally known in the industry, created and stimulated by the research environment furnished by the employer, to which the employee has been "exposed" and "enriched" solely due to his employment. We do not attempt to define the exact parameters of that protectable interest. ... We expect courts to narrowly construe this interest, which will be deemed part of the "reasonableness" equation. The line between such information, trade secrets, and the general skills and knowledge of a highly sophisticated employee will be very difficult to draw and the employer will have the burden to do so.[161]

The scope and duration of the agreement are also pertinent in determining whether it exceeds the permissible object of protecting legitimate interests. What is reasonable will vary from case to case depending upon the industry, the nature of the employee's position within the company, and the nature of the restriction involved: "Whether a restraining covenant in such a category is equitable, fair, just and reasonably requisite in respect of time or territory or both in its relation to the parties thereto is essentially an inquiry of fact and not a naked matter of law." [162]

This is well illustrated by the Supreme Court's discussion in *Karlin v. Weinberg* of what duration would be reasonable to protect a physician's legitimate interest in protecting his relationship with patients.[163] The Court determined

160. *Ingersoll Rand Co. v. Ciavatta*, 110 N.J. at 637. *See generally Sun Dial Corp. v. Rideout*, 16 N.J. 252, 257-58 (1954).

161. *Ingersoll Rand Co. v. Ciavatta*, 110 N.J. at 638.

the length of time it would take to demonstrate his continued effectiveness to those patients, and noted that the time required to do that would necessarily vary among specialties depending upon the typical frequency of visits.[164] As a general rule the territory specified in a post-employment restraint may not be greater than that to which the business extends.[165]

1-12:2 Undue Hardship on the Employee

A mere showing of personal inconvenience or financial hardship does not amount to an "undue" hardship sufficient to prevent enforcement of an agreement not to compete.[166] Two factors identified by the Supreme Court as pertinent to this inquiry are: (1) the likelihood of the employee finding work in his field elsewhere; and (2) the reason for the termination of the relationship between the parties to the employment contract.[167]

The first factor—likelihood of the employee finding work elsewhere—may in many cases be related to the scope of the agreement. The broader the geographic area and subject matter coverage of the agreement, and the longer its du-

162. *Chas S. Wood & Co. v. Kane*, 42 N.J.Super. 122, 127 (App. Div. 1956). The court noted that in some earlier cases, extensive territorial areas had been specified: "For illustrations see *Wm. T. Wiegand Glass Co. v. Wiegand*, 105 N.J.Eq. 434 (Ch. 1930), and *Irvington Varnish & Insulator Co. v. Van Norde*, 138 N.J.Eq. 99 (E. & A. 1946), in which the United States was therein enveloped; in *Voices, Inc. v. Metal Tone Mfg. Co.*, [119 N.J.Eq. 324 (Ch. 1936), *aff'd*, 120 N.J.Eq. 618 (E. & A. 1936), *cert. denied*, 300 U.S. 656 (1937)], where the range embraces the United States or its territories; in *A. Hollander & Son, Inc. v. Imperial Fur Blending Corp.*, [2 N.J. 235 (1949)], where the expanse included all states east of the meridian passing through St. Louis, Missouri."

163. *Karlin v. Weinberg*, 77 N.J. 408 (1978).

164. *Karlin v. Weinberg*, 77 N.J. at 423. *See Schuhalter v. Salerno*, 279 N.J. Super. 504 (App. Div.), *cert. denied*, 142 N.J. 454 (1995) (upholding two-year restriction on servicing existing clients); *Raven v. A. Klein & Co.*, Inc., 195 N.J.Super. 209, 216-17 (App.Div. 1984) (restrictive covenant enforced for 18-month period it would have taken to independently develop trade secret, plus an additional 18 months' penalty period in place of an award of development costs); *Hogan v. Bergen Brunswig Corp.*, 153 N.J.Super. 37, 42 (App. Div. 1977) (covenant restricting solicitation of customers in Essex and Union Counties for one-year reasonable as to time and space); *Magic Fingers, Inc. v. Robins*, 86 N.J.Super. 236, 239-40 (Ch.Div. 1965) (restriction of competition with no geographical boundary of doubtful enforceability); *Rubel & Jensen Corp. v. Rubel*, 85 N.J. 27, 35 (App.Div. 1964) (five-year restriction in connection with sale of business not unreasonable); *Hudson Foam Latex Products, Inc. v. Aiken*, 82 N.J.Super. 508, 513 (App.Div. 1964) (one-year restriction not an unreasonable period as a matter of law); *Jiffy Lube Int'l, Inc. v. Weiss Bros., Inc.*, 834 F. Supp. 683, 692 (D.N.J. 1993) (in franchise case, three year restriction on competition found excessive and reduced to the 10 months it would take the franchisor to open a new store in the area).

165. *Rubel & Jensen Corp. v. Rubel*, 85 N.J.Super. 27, 35 (App.Div. 1964); *Hudson Foam Latex Products, Inc. v. Aiken*, 82 N.J.Super. 508, 513 (App.Div. 1964) ("Where the territory specified in a post-employment restraint is greater than that to which the business extends, the restriction is unenforceable.").

166. *See Karlin v. Weinberg*, 77 N.J. 408, 417-18, n.3 (1978).

167. *See id.* at 423; *Platinum Management, Inc. v. Dahms*, 285 N.J. Super. 274, 298-99 (Law Div. 1995) (one-year limitation on the ability to solicit customers not an undue hardship; employee did not have to move, no limitations were placed on his ability to work for competitors so long as he did not exploit customer relations and other confidential information).

ration, the more likely it is to hinder the employee's re-employment. The second factor—cause of termination of the employment relationship—places a high premium on the employer's motives, and seems to operate almost as a "clean hands" requirement. The employee's personal sacrifice and lack of guile, coupled with the involuntary nature of his termination, were significant factors in *Ingersoll Rand Co. v. Ciavatta.*[168] The same analysis was outlined in *Karlin v. Weinberg*:

> Where [the termination of employment] occurs because of a breach of the employment contract by the employer, or because of actions by the employer detrimental to the public interest, enforcement of the covenant may cause hardship on the employee which may fairly be characterized as 'undue' in that the employee has not, by his conduct, contributed to it. On the other hand, where the breach results from the desire of an employee to end his relationship with his employer rather than from any wrongdoing by the employer, a court should be hesitant to find undue hardship on the employee, he in effect having brought that hardship on himself.[169]

1-12:3 Injury to the Public

Like the other two prongs of the reasonableness equation, determination of the extent of injury to the public from any particular restrictive agreement is a fact-intensive inquiry. Factors identified by the courts as pertinent subjects of public concern include (1) the effect of enforcement of the agreement on availability of the goods or services to which it pertains;[170] (2) the effect of non-enforcement on corporate investments in long-term research and development programs;[171] and (3) the effect of enforcement on individual initiative.[172] In this connection, the Supreme Court observed in *Ingersoll Rand Co. v. Ciavatta* that there is a "current debate raging in the scientific community about the effect of secrecy in scientific research arising from increased ties between scientists, commercial en-

---

168. *Ingersoll Rand Co. v. Ciavatta*, 110 N.J. 609 (1988). Although noting that the manner of an employee's departure is not dispositive, the Court found it was a factor that weighed heavily in the employee's favor in that case. He had been fired, and had the idea for his invention while installing a light fixture. He worked on it while he searched for jobs and had to borrow extensively to get his business started. The Court made a point to conclude, in effect, that he had clean hands: "His departure from Ingersoll Rand and subsequent invention and development of his own competing product do not suggest that he purposefully left to develop a competing product on the basis of knowledge he gained from his employment." *Id.* at 642.

169. *Karlin v. Weinberg*, 77 N.J. at 423-24.

terprises, and the government, and the effect of such secrecy on the long term progress of scientific programs and innovations."[173]

1-12:4 Consideration

The employer's offer of employment or continued provision of employment has been found to be sufficient consideration for an otherwise enforceable restrictive agreement.[174] Under that rule an at-will employee who is asked to sign a restrictive agreement some time after the start of his employment would not be heard to argue the agreement was void for lack of consideration; the employer's implicit agreement not to exercise its right to terminate him would be sufficient.[175]

1-13 The Professions: Doctors, Lawyers, and Accountants

Attorneys are prohibited, by Rule 5.6 of the ABA Model Rules of Professional Conduct and Rule 5.6 of the New Jersey Rules of Professional Conduct, from entering into restrictive covenants of any scope:

> A lawyer shall not participate in offering or making: (a) a partnership or employment agreement that restricts the rights of a

---

170. In *Karlin v. Weinberg*, 77 N.J. 408, 424 (1978), the Court, in remanding for a determination of the reasonableness of a restrictive agreement among physicians, instructed the trial court to consider whether enforcement would result in a shortage of physicians in the area, the extent to which patients of the precluded physician would be denied access to his services, and the extent to which new physicians could come into the area to fill any void created. *See A.T. Hudson & Co., Inc. v. Donovan*, 216 N.J.Super. 426, 434 (App. Div. 1987) (no unreasonable injury to public where no showing that clients experienced any real difficulty in locating other consultants capable of rendering similar services; commercial cases different from those involving lawyers, doctors, and accountants). A general assertion that competition from the restricted former employee would keep down the cost of bids on public works because he "had a special reputation for devising less expensive ways to provide desired results" was insufficient to raise a public interest concern for or against enforcement of a restrictive covenant. *Coskey's T.V. & Radio Sales and Serv., Inc. v. Foti*, 253 N.J. Super. 626, 634 (App. Div. 1992). *See Schuhalter v. Salerno*, 279 N.J. Super. 504, 512–13 (App. Div.), *cert. denied*, 142 N.J. 454 (1995), (no injury to the public in enforcing accountants' agreement to either refrain from servicing each other's clients for two years or compensate the other if such service is provided).

171. *See Ingersoll Rand Co. v. Ciavatta*, 110 N.J. 609, 635, 639 (1988).

172. *See id.*

173. *Ingersoll Rand Co. v. Ciavatta*, 110 N.J. at 639-40.

174. *Hogan v. Bergen Brunswig Corp.*, 153 N.J.Super. 37, 43 (App.Div. 1977). *But see* Valiulis, *Covenants Not to Compete*, §1.3 p.3 (1985) (noting problems presented by continued employment as consideration and listing out-of-state cases).

175. *Hogan v. Bergen Brunswig Corp.*, 153 N.J.Super at 43 ("A verbalized threat of immediate discharge in the event the employee does not sign a proposed restrictive covenant is not necessary to constitute the consideration required to support a post-employment contract. Such a consequence can be inferred from conduct.").

> lawyer to practice after termination of the relationship, except an agreement concerning benefits upon retirement...[176]

As a result, it has been held that restrictive agreements that purport to limit the area in which an attorney may practice or the clients he may represent are void *per se* as contrary to public policy.[177] The public policy objective of this rule is protection of the *client's* right to select the attorney of his choice.[178] Thus, even an agreement that does not prohibit competition, but which indirectly restricts the practice of law by making receipt of severance benefits contingent upon non-competition, has been found to violate the Rule.[179] "[E]nsuring client choice is the driving force behind the ethical rule."[180] Thus, even an agreement that imposed financial penalties on voluntary departures from a law firm, whether in competion or not, was found to violate the Rule.[181] Similarly, the Supreme Court has held that an agreement that required partners to forfeit their capital accounts if they withdrew from a firm before age sixty-five for reasons other than death, disability, or judicial appointment, discouraged partners from leaving and becoming competitive with the firm, and therefore violated of R.P.C. 5.6.[182]

Restrictive agreements of physicians are not similarly barred. In *Karlin v. Weinberg*, the Supreme Court found nothing in the nature of the medical profession requiring exemption from the general rule, and thus held restrictive agreements between physicians enforceable to the extent they are reasonable in the circumstances of a particular case.[183] The legitimate interest a physician may seek to protect through such an agreement is his interest in his ongoing relationship with patients.[184]

---

176. *N.J. Rules of Prof. Conduct*, 5.6. The Comment to Rule 5.6(a) of the Model Rules provides in pertinent part: "An agreement restricting the right of partners or associates to practice after leaving a firm not only limits their professional autonomy but also limits the freedom of clients to choose a lawyer. Paragraph (a) prohibits such agreements except for restrictions incident to provisions concerning retirement benefits for service with the firm." *See generally ABA/BNA Lawyer's Manual On Professional Conduct*, pp. 51:1201-1204 (1984).

177. *Jacob v. Norris, McLoughlin & Marcus*, 128 N.J. 10 (1992). *See Karlin v. Weinberg*, 77 N.J. 408, 420 (1978); *Dwyer v. Jung*, 133 N.J.Super. 343 (Ch.Div.), *aff'd o.b.*, 137 N.J.Super. 135 (App.Div. 1975) (restrictive covenants among attorneys are *per se* unreasonable and therefore void as contrary to public policy).

178. *Jacob v. Norris, McLaughlin & Marcus*, 128 N.J. 10, 18 (1992).

179. A restriction on the right to recruit law firm lawyers and paraprofessionals has also been found in violation of the rule. *Id.* at 30-31.

180. *Jacob v. Norris, McLaughlin & Marcus*, 128 N.J. at 26. *Cf. Levin v. Robinson, Wayne & La Sala*, 246 N.J.Super. 167, 193-94 (Law Div. 1990) (dicta).

181. *Katchen v. Wolff & Samson*, 258 N.J. Super. 474, 482 (App. Div.), *certif. denied*, 130 N.J. 599 (1992).

182. *Weiss v. Carpenter, Bennett & Morrissey*, 143 N.J. 420, 444-45 (1996).

183. *See Karlin v. Weinberg*, 77 N.J. 408, 415-17 (1978) (prohibiting practice of dermatology within 10 miles of former employer's office for five years). *See Katchen v. Wolff & Samson*, 258 N.J. Super. 474, 480 (App. Div.), *cert. denied*, 130 N.J. 599 (1992) (financial disincentive provisions may encourage lawyers to give up their clients and thus interfere with the lawyer–client relationship).

Accountants have similarly been held subject to the general rule,[185] as have individuals in other service industries professing especially personal relationships with clients.[186] But, application of the *Solari* analysis in the professional setting may result in different conclusions. In *Mailman, Ross, Toyes, & Shapiro v. Edelson*, the court found that the consensual, fiduciary relationship of accountant and client created a right in the client to repose confidence in the accountant of his choice that should not readily be circumscribed.[187] It thus found that while a former employee-accountant could be barred from soliciting clients of his former employer, the clients had the right unilaterally to continue their confidential business relationship with him.[188]

1-14 Enforcement: The Blue Pencil Doctrine

Prior to the Supreme Court's 1970 opinion in *Solari Industries, Inc. v. Malady*, New Jersey generally adhered to the rule that an unreasonably broad restrictive agreement was void *per se.*[189] The "divisibility" or "selective enforcement" doctrine provided some relief from the all-or-nothing rule, but as noted by the Court in *Solari*, it also led to "tortuous interpretations and incongruous differentiations."[190] Thus, the Court adopted a variation of the "blue pencil" doctrine, thereby permitting total or partial enforcement of noncompetition agreements to the extent reasonable under the circumstances.[191] The availability of this remedy, however, should not impel employers to negotiate or impose overly-broad agreements. If there is credible evidence to sustain a finding that a covenant is deliberately unreasonable or oppressive, the blue pencil doctrine will not be applied: "When an employer, through superior bargain-

184. *See Karlin v. Weinberg*, 77 N.J. at 417.

185. *Mailman, Ross, Toyes, & Shapiro v. Edelson*, 183 N.J.Super. 434 (Ch.Div. 1982). *Schuhalter v. Salerno*, 279 N.J. Super. 504, 509 (App. Div.), *cert. denied*, 142 N.J. 454 (1995), (holding a restrictive agreement between accountants subject to the *Solari* rule and specifically rejecting the assertion that restrictive agreements between professionals are void *per se*).

186. *See A.T. Hudson & Co., Inc. v. Donovan*, 216 N.J.Super. 426 (App.Div. 1987) (two-year restriction on a management consultant enforceable; no showing that other consultants not available to fulfill client needs).

187. 183 N.J.Super. at 444.

188. *Id.* In *Schuhalter v. Salerno*, 279 N.J. Super. 504 (App. Div.), *cert. denied*, 142 N.J. 454 (1995), the Appellate Division applied the rule established in *Solari Indus., Inc. v. Malady*, 55 N.J. 571 (1970), to a restrictive agreement between accounting firm partners upon the dissolution of their partnership. The court upheld, *inter alia*, an agreement that for two years after dissolution, each partner would either refrain from servicing clients designated as belonging to the other, or compensate the other for providing such service.

189. *See Solari Industries, Inc. v. Malady*, 55 N.J. 571, 583 (1970), and cases cited therein.

190. *Solari Industries, Inc. v. Malady*, 55 N.J. at 583.

191. *See Solari Industries, Inc. v. Malady*, 55 N.J. at 585; *Karlin v. Weinberg*, 77 N.J. 408, 420 n.4 (1978).

ing power, extracts a deliberately unreasonable and oppressive non-competitive covenant he is in no just position to seek, and should not receive, equitable relief from the courts."[192]

V. GOOD FAITH AND FAIR DEALING

1-15 Requisites

The covenant of good faith and fair dealing applies to employment contracts just as it does to all other contracts in New Jersey.[193] If an at-will employee enters into a contract with respect to particular aspects of his employment, the covenant of good faith and fair dealing applies to those parts of the employment that are covered by the contract.[194] The covenant also applies to implied contracts of employment contained in employment manuals and other documents that satisfy the requirements of *Woolley.*[195]

The covenant does not apply, however, where the employment relationship is at will and not governed by contract: "In the absence of a contract, there can be no breach of an implied covenant of good faith and fair dealing."[196]

As a consequence, efforts to utilize the covenant to engraft a general good faith requirement on the at-will employment relationship have been consistently rejected by the lower courts.[197] The Supreme Court has not addressed the issue.

Tort damages do not lie for breach of an implied covenant of good faith and fair dealing found in an employment contract.[198]

---

192. *See Solari Industries, Inc. v. Malady,* 55 N.J. at 576, 578-79.

193. *See Nolan v. Control Data Corp.*, 243 N.J.Super. 420, 429 (App.Div. 1990). *See also Palisades Properties, Inc. v. Brunetti,* 44 N.J. 117, 130 (1965); *Borbely v. Nationwide Mutual Ins. Co.*, 547 F.Supp. 959, 973 (D.N.J. 1981). *See also King v. Port Auth.*, 909 F. Supp. 938, 942 (D.N.J. 1995), *aff'd,* 106 F.3d 385 (3d Cir. 1996) ("A cognizable cause of action for breach of the implied duty of good faith and fair dealing in the employment context exists where the employer attempts to deprive the employee of the benefits of the employment agreement without an honest belief that good cause for discharge is in fact present); *Katchen v. Wolff & Samson,* 258 N.J. Super. 474, 482 (App. Div.), *certif. denied,* 130 N.J. 599 (1992) (noting that claim for breach of covenant of good faith and fair dealing with respect to agreement between attorney and law firm could be pursued on remand); *Sellitto v. Litton Sys., Inc.*, 882 F. Supp. 932, 940-41 (D.N.J. 1994) (where plaintiff claimed violation of a manual's progressive discipline procedure, his cause of action, if any, should be for breach of the express terms of the implied contract and not breach of the covenant of good faith and fair dealing).

194. *See Nolan v. Control Data Corp.*, 243 N.J.Super. at 429; *Fregara v. Jet Aviation Business Jets,* 764 F.Supp. 940 (D.N.J. 1991); *King v. Port Auth.*, 909 F. Supp. 938 (D.N.J. 1995); *Peck v. Imedia, Inc.*, 293 N.J. Super. 151, 168 (App. Div.), *certif. denied,* 147 N.J. 262 (1996).

195. *See Noye v. Hoffmann-LaRoche, Inc.*, 238 N.J.Super. 430 (App. Div. 1990) ("It is undoubted that a *Woolley* contract, like any other contract, contains an implied covenant of good faith and fair dealing."); *Jaclin v. Sea-Land Corp.*, 1989 WL 200943 (D.N.J. Aug. 23, 1989) (motion for summary judgment denied on plaintiff's claim for breach of implied covenant of good faith and fair dealing arising out of an employment manual).

The covenant generally requires that:

> neither party shall do anything which will have the effect of destroying or injuring the right of the other party to receive the fruits of the contract. ...[199]

Courts applying this test in the employment context have required a showing of bad faith or unconscionable behavior by the breaching party and lack of privilege for the actions taken.[200] An employee's allegations of reliance on false promises of employment for a reasonable period of time fell "woefully short" of demonstrating the bad faith requisite to a claim of breach of the covenant of good faith and fair dealing.[201] Additionally, the Appellate Division has held that even where an "employee performs the duties contracted for satisfactorily, criminal activity by the employee can justify his discharge for breach of an employment contract."[202] But where a franchisor concealed its intent to eliminate an "exclu-

---

196. *Noye v. Hoffmann-LaRoche, Inc.*, 238 N.J.Super. 430, 434 (App. Div. 1990). *See Mullen v. New Jersey Steel Corp.*, 733 F.Supp. 1534, 1554 n. 19 (D.N.J. 1990); *Brunner v. Abex Corp.*, 661 F.Supp. 1351, 1356 (D.N.J. 1986); *Smith v. Hartford Fire Ins. Co.*, 1985 WL 2828 (E.D. Pa. 1985) (applying New Jersey law); *House v. Carter-Wallace, Inc.*, 232 N.J.Super. 42, 55 (App. Div.), certif. denied, 117 N.J. 154 (1989); *McQuitty v. General Dynamics Corp.*, 204 N.J.Super. 514, 520 (App. Div. 1985). *Bishop v. Okidata, Inc.*, 864 F. Supp. 416, 426 (D.N.J. 1994) (in the absence of a contract, there is no covenant of good faith and fair dealing); *Obendorfer v. The Gitano Group, Inc.*, 838 F. Supp. 950, 954 (D.N.J. 1993) (rejecting claim for breach of the covenant of good faith and fair dealing: "In the absence of a contract there is no implied obligation of good faith and fair dealing"); *Edwards v. Schlumberger-Well Services*, 984 F. Supp. 264, 285 (D.N.J. 1997) (same). *But see Peck v. Imedia Corp.*, 293 N.J. Super. 151, 167-68 (App. Div.) (applying the covenant of good faith and fair dealing to an offer of at-will employment), *certif. denied*, 147 N.J. 262 (1996); *Rivera v. Trump Plaza Hotel & Casino*, 305 N.J. Super. 596, 601 (App. Div. 1997) (stating that "[t]o the extent that empoyment at-will nonetheless implicates a covenant of good faith and fair dealing, there is no evidence that such covenant was breached in this case.").

197. *Labus v. Navistar Int'l Trans. Corp.*, 740 F.Supp. 1053, 1063 (D.N.J. 1990); *Brunner v. Abex Corp.*, 661 F.Supp. 1351, 1356 (D.N.J. 1986); *House v. Carter-Wallace, Inc.*, 232 N.J.Super. 42, 55 (App.Div. 1989); *McQuitty v. General Dynamics Corp.*, 204 N.J.Super. 514 (App. Div. 1985); *Citizens State Bank of New Jersey v. Libertelli*, 215 N.J.Super. 190 (App.Div. 1987). *See Scudder v. Media Gen., Inc.*, 1995 WL 495945, p.*6 (D.N.J. 1995):

> Where there is no contract between the parties, there is nothing into which the Court may imply a term of fair dealing. The doctrine will not create rights or obligations between the parties in a vacuum. It is well settled that the implied term of fair dealing will not work to constrain an employer's discretion to terminate an at-will employee.

198. *Noye v. Hoffmann-LaRoche, Inc.*, 238 N.J.Super. 430, 436 (App. Div. 1990).

199. *Borbely v. Nationwide Mutual Ins. Co.*, 547 F.Supp. 959, 973 (D.N.J. 1981) (citing *Palisades Properties, Inc. v. Brunetti*, 44 N.J. 117, 130 (1965)); *McGarry v. St. Anthony of Padua*, 307 N.J. Super. 525, 533 (App. Div. 1998) (same).

200. *Borbely v. Nationwide Mutual Ins. Co.*, 547 F.Supp. 959, 982 (D.N.J. 1981) (jury charge on breach of implied covenant "should have included an explanation of privilege and a statement on the necessity for finding unconscionable behavior on defendant's part."); *Fregara v. Jet Aviation Business Jets*, 764 F.Supp. 940, 953 (D.N.J. 1991) ("A cause of action for breach of an implied covenant of good faith and fair dealing is also cognizable in an employment context where the employer attempts to deprive the employee of the benefit of the employment agreement without an honest belief that good cause for discharge in fact exists.").

201. *Weber v. LDC/Milton Roy*, 42 FEP 1507 (D.N.J. 1986) (court's analysis assumes applicability of the covenant to the employee manual there at issue).

sive" distributorship to induce the distributor's continued investment of substantial sums of money, the covenant was found breached.[203] In *Feldman v. U.S. Sprint Communications Co.*, the court found that the duty of good faith and fair dealing attached to the employer's compensation plans and prohibited the employer from interfering with the contractual procedure through which employees earned commissions:

> It could not, for example, intentionally delay installation or billing to avoid paying commission. Similarly, where Sprint unintentionally cannot produce timely invoices and therefore creates an income maintenance plan to assist its employees, it cannot use that plan to deny the employees the commissions they have actually earned and should have paid but for its failure to send invoices.[204]

The covenant should not be used, however, to make a different or fairer contract for the parties.[205]

VI. WAIVERS

1-16 Common Practice

It is common practice of many employers to seek a release of claims from employees upon the termination of employment. When a release of state and/or federal statutory claims is sought, special considerations apply, and the various statutes and regulations must be consulted for guidance.[206] However, when only employment contract claims are at issue, traditional contract principles have governed the validity of the release.[207]

---

202. *McGarry v. St. Anthony of Padua*, 307 N.J. Super. 525, 533 (App. Div. 1998).

203. *Bak-A-Lum Corp. of America v. Alcoa Building Products, Inc.*, 69 N.J. 123 (1976).

204. *Feldman v. U.S. Sprint Communications Co.*, 714 F.Supp. 727, 731 (D.N.J. 1989).

205. *See Borbely v. Nationwide Mutual Ins. Co.*, 547 F.Supp. 959, 975 (D.N.J. 1981); *Sellitto v. Litton Sys., Inc.*, 881 F. Supp. 932, 941 (D.N.J. 1994) (court dismissed plaintiff's claim that failure to provide a performance evaluation constituted breach of the covenant of good faith and fair dealing: "As a matter of law, in the absence of proof that the parties intended to contract for a performance evaluation in March 1991 or for Airton's support of plaintiff's management incentives, there can be no breach of an implied covenant of good faith and fair dealing. *See Fregara v. Jet Aviation*, 764 F. Supp. 940, 954, n.8 (D.N.J. 1991) (noting that New Jersey does not recognize cause of action for 'negligent evaluation'").

206. *See, e.g.*, Older Workers Benefit Protection Act, 29 U.S.C. §626 (f)(i)(H); *Coventry v. U.S. Steel Corp.*, 856 F.2d 514, 522-25 (3d Cir. 1988) (special considerations beyond traditional contract principles must be applied in evaluating waivers of ADEA claims; voluntariness depends upon totality of the circumstances). *See* §4-46:3 for discussion of waivers under the Law Against Discrimination. Waiver is an affirmative defense that must be pled by defendant. R.4:5-4.

Waiver, under New Jersey law, involves the intentional relinquishment of a known right, and thus it must be shown that the party charged with the waiver knew of his or her legal rights and deliberately intended to relinquish them.[208]

> Releases of actionable claims may be freely entered into if supported by valuable consideration, and in the absence of fraud, duress, or other compelling circumstances.[209]

1-17 Consideration

A waiver or release, like any other contract, must be supported by valuable consideration:

> 'Consideration involves a detriment incurred by the promisee or a benefit received by the promisor, at the promisor's request.' '[L]egal sufficiency does not depend [, however,] upon the comparative value of the consideration and of what is promised in return.' Rather, the consideration 'must merely be valuable in the sense that it is something bargained for in fact.'[210]

In *Borbely v. Nationwide Mutual Ins. Co.*, the court found that the employer's agreement to waive its rights in agents' policies in New Jersey, not to enforce the agents' non-competition agreements, to provide health insurance for a year, to provide severance benefits in a more desirable manner, and to pay additional commissions on certain policies constituted valuable consideration for the agents' waivers of their right to sue.[211] Additional severance or enhanced pension benefits are commonly the consideration for such agreements.[212]

---

207. *See Shebar v. Sanyo Business Systems Corp.*, 111 N.J. 276, 291-92 (1988); *Mullen v. New Jersey Steel Corp.*, 733 F.Supp. 1534, 1548 (D.N.J. 1990).

208. *Shebar v. Sanyo Business Systems Corp.*, 111 N.J. at 291; *Petrillo v. Bachenberg*, 263 N.J. Super. 472, 479-80 (App. Div. 1993) ("It is fundamental that waiver involves the intentional relinquishment of a known right and, thus, it must be shown that the party charged with the waiver knew of his or her legal rights and deliberately intended to relinquish them.").

209. *See Mullen v. New Jersey Steel Corp.*, 733 F.Supp. at 1548.

210. *Borbely v. Nationwide Mutual Ins. Co.*, 547 F.Supp. 959, 980 (D.N.J. 1981) (citations omitted). *See Petrillo v. Bachenberg*, 263 N.J. Super. 472, 480 (App. Div. 1993) ("Waiver implies an election by the party to dispense with something of value or to forego some advantage which the party might have demanded and insisted upon. It must be supported by either an agreement with adequate consideration, or by such conduct as to estop the waiving party from denying the intent to waive.") (citation omitted)

211. *Id.*

212. *See, e.g., Cirillo v. Arco Chemical Co.*, 862 F.2d 448, 454 (3d Cir. 1988) (enhanced benefits provided for release that included federal statutory discrimination claim).

1-18 Duress

Waivers or releases procured by means of duress are inoperative and void.[213] Duress in this sense requires proof that (1) there was a degree of constraint or danger, either actual or threatened and impending, which in fact coerced the mind of the actor; and (2) that the pressure exerted was wrongful.[214]

> [N]ot all pressure is wrongful, and means in themselves lawful must not be so oppressively used as to constitute, e.g., an abuse of legal remedies. Thus, it is insufficient merely to show that a party's consent was involuntarily given, that his will was overborne; at least in this state, he must show as well that the act or threat is wrongful, "not necessarily in a legal, but in a moral or equitable sense."[215]

The test of voluntariness is a subjective one in the sense that the question is not whether a reasonable man in these circumstances would have felt compulsion, but rather whether the circumstances did in fact overcome the will of the complainant in the case at hand.[216] Whether duress exists in a particular case is generally a question of fact, but what in given circumstances will constitute duress is a matter of law.[217] Moreover, to assert the affirmative defense of duress one must demonstrate that at the time of signing there was no immediate or effective legal remedy available.[218]

The mere fact that an employee facing termination of employment may feel economic or personal pressure to agree to a waiver does not constitute duress. Something more than such a subjective reaction is required, such as "malicious, unconscionable, or outrageous motivation on [the employer's] part which might render the pressure experienced by the [employee] wrongful."[219] That is partic-

---

213. *Rubenstein v. Rubenstein*, 20 N.J. 359, 365 (1956); *Borbely v. Nationwide Mutual Ins. Co.*, 547 F.Supp. 959, 978 (D.N.J. 1981).

214. *Rubenstein v. Rubenstein*, 20 N.J. 359, 366-67 (1956).

215. *Borbely v. Nationwide Mutual Ins. Co.*, 547 F.Supp. 959, 978 (D.N.J. 1981) (citations omitted). *See generally* New Jersey Model Jury Charges: Civil, §4.8 (3d ed. 1990).

216. *See Rubenstein v. Rubenstein*, 20 N.J. at 366-67 ("the tendency of the more recent cases, and the rule comporting with reason and principle, is that any 'unlawful threats' which do 'in fact overcome the will of the person threatened, and induce him to do an act which he would not otherwise have done, and which he was not bound to do, constitute duress.' ")

217. *Borbely v. Nationwide Mutual Ins. Co.*, 547 F.Supp. 959, 978 (D.N.J. 1981), *quoting Wolf v. Marlton Corp.*, 57 N.J.Super. 278 (App.Div. 1959).

218. *See Ross Systems v. Linden Dari-Delite, Inc.*, 35 N.J. 329, 336 (1961) ("adequacy of the remedy is to be tested by a practical standard which takes into consideration the exigencies of the situation in which the victim finds himself").

ularly so where the employee is afforded time to consider his decision and consult an attorney.[220]

1-19 Ratification

Even if a release is not effective when signed, it may be ratified by the acceptance of benefits thereunder.[221] Thus it has been held that the acceptance of benefits under a severance agreement and failure to complain until all checks for same had been delivered constituted a ratification of a release.[222] However, the mere acceptance of severance or other post-employment benefits will not in itself constitute a waiver of claims for wrongful discharge; there must have been an agreement to that effect. Thus, in *Shebar v. Sanyo Business Systems Corp.*, the Supreme Court held that the trial court erred in granting the employer summary judgment on its claim that Mr. Shebar had waived his wrongful discharge claims by accepting pay:

> Nothing in the record suggests that either Sanyo or Shebar had any reasonable expectation that Shebar's acceptance of the checks "unequivocally and decisively expressed his election to forego his legal right to challenge the lawfulness of the termination." Indeed, Shebar expressly denied that he did, asserting that he was never advised by Sanyo, either orally or in writing, that acceptance of the benefits "constituted an agreement or a waiver of my rights or a release of my claims or a termination of Sanyo's obligations to me."[223]

---

219. *Borbely v. Nationwide Mutual Ins. Co.*, 547 F.Supp. 959, 979 (1981). *Cf. Ross Systems v. Linden Dari-Delite, Inc.*, 35 N.J. 329, 335-36 (N.J. 1961) (payment of wrongfully extracted commissions under fear of losing franchise was under business compulsion).

220. *Borbely v. Nationwide Mutual Ins. Co.*, 547 F.Supp. 959, 979 (D.N.J. 1981). *Cf. Coventry v. U.S. Steel Corp.*, 856 F.2d 514, 524-25 (3d Cir. 1988) (discussing impact of availability of counsel in evaluation of voluntariness of waiver of claims under ADEA).

221. *See, e.g., Client's Security Fund v. Allstate Ins. Co.*, 219 N.J. Super. 325, 333-34 (App. Div. 1987); *Clarkson v. Selected Risks Ins. Co.*, 170 N.J. Super. 373, 379-80 (Law Div. 1979); *American Photocopy Equipment Co. v. Ampto, Inc.*, 82 N.J.Super. 531, 538-39 (App. Div.), *certif. denied*, 42 N.J. 291, *cert. denied*, 379 U.S. 842 (1964).

222. *Mullen v. New Jersey Steel Corp.*, 733 F.Supp. 1534 (D.N.J. 1990).

223. *Shebar v. Sanyo Business Systems Corp.*, 111 N.J. 276, 291-92 (1988).

VII. REMEDIES

1-20 Compensatory Damages

Breach of an employment contract gives rise to normal contract damages. Except in limited circumstances discussed in the following sections, tort remedies of emotional distress and punitive damages are not available. "When a wrongful discharge of an employee occurs the measure of damages is usually the employee's salary for the remainder of the employment period." [224] Where the employment was for an indefinite term, or for life, future wages may be awarded for a reasonable period.[225] Thus, in *Preston v. Claridge Hotel & Casino*, the Appellate Division rejected the employer's claim that an award of future wages was improperly based upon speculation and conjecture, finding instead that the jury could reasonably find that it would be two years before plaintiff would obtain a salary equivalent to that which she received prior to termination.[226]

Although an action for violation of an implied employment contract would normally sound in contract, it has been suggested by the Appellate Division that an employee proceeding under *Woolley* may maintain an action in tort "only to the extent they can establish a breach of duty arising out of a *Woolley* contract of employment."[227] "An employee wrongfully discharged in violation of a company policy is not entitled to tort damages."[228]

1-21 Punitive Damages

Punitive damages are traditionally reserved for civil wrongs characterized in torts. They are intended to punish the tortfeasor and prevent him from repeating the subject conduct.[229] To recover punitive damages, a plaintiff must establish

---

224. *Goodman v. London Metals Exchange, Inc.*, 86 N.J. 19, 34 (1981) (discrimination case).

225. *See Preston v. Claridge Hotel & Casino*, 231 N.J.Super. 81, 88 (App. Div. 1989).

226. *Id. See also Potter v. Village Bank of New Jersey*, 225 N.J. Super. 547, 562 (App. Div.), *certif denied*, 113 N.J.352 (1988) (in action for retaliatory discharge employee entitled to recover, *inter alia*, "the amount he or she would have earned from the time of wrongful discharge for a reasonable time until he or she finds new employment, including bonuses and vacation pay, less any unemployment compensation received in the interim"); *Levinson v. Prentice-Hall, Inc.*, 868 F.2d 558, 563 (3d Cir. 1989) (front pay in discrimination case); *Weiss v. Parker Hannifan Corp.*, 747 F.Supp. 1118, 1135 (D.N.J. 1990).

227. *Giudice v. Drew Chemical Corp.*, 210 N.J.Super. 32, 39 (App. Div. 1986).

228. *Gilbert v. Durand Glass Mfg. Co.*, 258 N.J. Super. 320, 332 (App. Div. 1992).

229. *See Sandler v. Lawn-A-Mat Chemical & Equipment Co.*, 141 N.J.Super. 437, 448 (App. Div.), *certif. denied*, 71 N.J. 503 (1976).

"actual malice": intentional wrongdoing, an evil-minded act, or an act accompanied by a wanton and willful disregard of the rights of another.[230]

With rare exceptions, punitive damages are not available for breach of contract, including an employment contract.[231]

> Where the essence of a cause of action is limited to a breach of such a contract, punitive damages are not appropriate regardless of the nature of the conduct constituting the breach. Professor McCormick has expressed this notion in the following fashion: "In actions, however, upon mere private contracts ... *even where the breach is malicious and unjustified*, exemplary damages are not available."[232]

Special relationships warranting deviation from this rule include fiduciaries such as bankers and real estate brokers, public utilities and their customers, and the parties to an agreement to marry.[233] The employer-employee relationship has not been accorded this special status.[234]

The Appellate Division has suggested in dicta that punitive damages may be available for breach of contract in exceptional circumstances: there "may arise a case involving such an aggravated set of facts that punitive damages might be appropriate regardless of the contract form of the action and even though it may be beyond the scope of the recognized exceptions in the adjudicated cases."[235] That issue remains unresolved, however, and the circumstances—if any—that might warrant imposition of punitive damages for breach of contract remain unknown.[236]

---

230. *See id.*

231. *Buckley v. Trenton Savings Fund Society*, 111 N.J. 355, 369-70 (1988). *See generally Gilbert v. Durand Glass Mfg. Co.*, 258 N.J. Super. 320, 332 (App. Div. 1992) ("An employee wrongfully discharged in violation of a company policy is not entitled to tort damages")

232. *See Sandler v. Lawn-A-Mat Chemical & Equipment Co.*, 141 N.J.Super. 437, 449 (App. Div. 1976) (emphasis in original).

233. *See id.* and cases cited therein.

234. *Cf. Kass v. Brown Boveri Corp.*, 199 N.J.Super. 42, 56 (App. Div. 1985).

235. *Sandler v. Lawn-A-Mat Chemical & Equipment Co.*, 141 N.J.Super. at 451. *See Ellmex Construction Co., Inc. v. Republic Ins. Co.*, 202 N.J.Super. 195, 207 (App. Div. 1985), *certif. denied*, 103 N.J. 453 (1986), and cases cited therein.

236. *See, e.g., Ryno v. First Bank of South Jersey*, 208 N.J.Super. 562, 572 (App. Div. 1986) ("even if we assume the questionable proposition that under some circumstances punitive damages could be available in this type of contract action. ..."); *Unifoil Corp. v. Cheque Printers and Encoders Ltd.*, 622 F.Supp. 268, 272 (D.N.J. 1985) ("it is theoretically possible to obtain punitive damages on a contract claim, given sufficiently 'aggravated circumstances' "); *W.A. Wright, Inc. v. KDI Sylvan Pools, Inc.*, 746 F.2d 215, 218 (3d Cir. 1984) (there is no indication in any Supreme Court opinion that it would create an exception to the rule of non-recovery of punitive damages in contract claims for egregious contract breaches).

1-22 Emotional Distress Damages

Damages for emotional distress are ordinarily not recoverable in an action for breach of contract.[237] Such damages will be permitted, however, where (1) the breach was willful and wanton; and (2) the harm was foreseeable when the contract was made.[238] A party to a contract is not responsible for a loss he had no reason to foresee as a probable result of a breach when the contract was made: "to impose liability the defendant must have had reason to foresee the injury at the time the contract was made, not at the time of the breach."[239] Employment contracts are not treated differently. In *Noye v. Hoffmann-LaRoche, Inc.*, the Appellate Division held emotional distress damages unavailable for breach of the implied covenant of good faith and fair dealing to an employment contract, finding it sufficient that the employee be compensated for his expectations under the contract.[240]

1-23 Prejudgment Interest

Prejudgment interest may be awarded on compensatory damages for breach of contract, whether liquidated or not.[241] Whether to award prejudgment interest in a particular case is governed by equitable principles; it is not awarded as of right.[242] Such awards are intended to be compensatory and to indemnify the claimant for the loss of moneys he would have earned had payment not been delayed.[243]

---

237. *See Coyle v. Englander's*, 199 N.J.Super. 212, 219 (App. Div. 1985); *Fiore v. Sears, Roebuck & Co.*, 144 N.J.Super. 74, 77 (Law Div. 1976). *See generally Gilbert v. Durand Glass Mfg. Co.*, 258 N.J. Super. 320, 332 (App. Div. 1992) ("An employee wrongfully discharged in violation of a company policy is not entitled to tort damages").

238. *See Buckley v. Trenton Savings Fund Society*, 111 N.J. 355, 364-65 (1988); *Picogna v. Bd. of Educ. of Tp. of Cherry Hill*, 143 N.J. 391, 397 (1996) ("Under contract laws, recovery is permitted where the breach of contract involves conduct that is both intentional and outrageous and proximately causes severe, foreseeable emotional distress."); *Fiore v. Sears, Roebuck & Co.*, 144 N.J.Super. 74, 76-77 (Law Div. 1976).

239. *Coyle v. Englander's*, 199 N.J.Super. 212, 220 (App. Div. 1985).

240. *Noye v. Hoffmann-LaRoche, Inc.*, 238 N.J.Super. 430, 436-437 (App. Div. 1990).

241. *See Preston v. Claridge Hotel & Casino*, 231 N.J.Super. 81, 88-90 (App. Div. 1989); *W.A. Wright, Inc. v. KDI Sylvan Pools, Inc.*, 746 F.2d 215, 219 (3d Cir. 1984); *Ellmex Construction Co., Inc. v. Republic Ins. Co.*, 202 N.J.Super. 195, 209-13 (App. Div. 1985), *certif. denied*, 103 N.J. 453 (1986); *see generally* Pressler, *Current N.J. Court Rules*, Comment to R.4:42-11 (1999 ed.).

242. *See Bak-A-Lum Corp. of America v. Alcoa Building Products, Inc.*, 69 N.J. 123, 131 (1976).

243. *See Busik v. Levine*, 63 N.J. 351 (1973). Prejudgment interest should not be awarded for lost future wages. *Gilbert v. Durand Glass Mfg. Co.*, 258 N.J. Super. 320, 332 (App. Div. 1992).

Chapter 2

Public Policy Claims

I. INTRODUCTION

2-1 Overview

As an historical rule, state and federal laws did not interfere with an employer's right to discharge at-will employees. They were generally subject to termination at any time—for a good reason, a bad reason, or no reason at all—so long as the discharge was not for a statutorily prohibited reason, such as anti-union animus (violative of §8(a) of the National Labor Relations Act of 1935, 29 U.S.C.A. §158(a))[1] or unlawful discrimination (violative of statutes such as Title VII of the Civil Rights Act of 1964, 42 U.S.C.A. §2000e *et seq.*, or the Civil Rights Acts of 1870 and 1871, now 42 U.S.C.A. §§1981 and 1983).[2]

Until 1980, that was the law in New Jersey—in the absence of a contract, employment was at-will, terminable with or without cause.[3] But in *Pierce v. Ortho Pharmaceutical Corp.*, the Supreme Court created an exception to the traditional rule, holding that "an employee has a cause of action [in tort or contract or both] for wrongful discharge when the discharge is contrary to a clear mandate of public policy."[4] Six years after the *Pierce* decision, and at least in part in reaction to the demotion of a State trooper who had testified about his superiors' wrongdo-

---

1. *See NLRB v. Condensor Corp.*, 128 F.2d 67, 75 (3d Cir. 1942); *NLRB v. Standard Coil Products Co.*, 224 F.2d 465, 470 (1st Cir.), *cert. denied*, 350 U.S. 902 (1955).

2. *Tims v. McNeil Bd. of Educ.*, 452 F.2d 551, 552 (8th Cir. 1971) (42 U.S.C.A. §§1981 and 1983); *Winston v. Smithsonian Science Information Exchange*, 437 F.Supp. 456, 473 (D.D.C. 1977), *aff'd without op.*, 595 F.2d 888 (D.C. Cir. 1979) (42 U.S.C.A. §§1981 and 2000e *et seq.*). New Jersey's anti-discrimination laws are discussed in Chapter 4.

3. *See English v. College of Medicine and Dentistry of N.J.*, 73 N.J. 20, 23 (1977); *Jorgensen v. Pennsylvania R.R. Co.*, 25 N.J. 541, 554 (1958); *Savarese v. Pyrene Mfg. Co.*, 9 N.J. 595, 600-01 (1952). For a detailed history of the "at-will" employment rule and its erosion, *see Bernard v. IMI Sys., Inc.*, 131 N.J. 91 (1993).

4. *Pierce v. Ortho Pharmaceutical Corp.*, 84 N.J. 58, 72 (1980). *Pierce* and its progeny are discussed in detail in Part II, §§2-2 to 2-7.

ing,[5] a statutory cause of action was created.[6] Effective Sept. 5, 1986, the Conscientious Employee Protection Act (CEPA)[7] prohibits retaliation against employee "whistleblowers"—generally individuals who oppose or disclose alleged employer wrongdoing. In addition, a number of even more specific statutes prohibit retaliation with respect to particular employee conduct, such as refusing to perform abortions,[8] reporting suspected child abuse,[9] or assisting the Office of the Ombudsman for the Institutionalized Elderly.[10]

Although the general concept of public policy causes of action has become well established, courts are still struggling with the scope of both the common law and statutory prohibitions, their relationship with each other and other statutes affecting the employment relationship, and the extent of survival of the at-will rule of employment to which they are exceptions.

II. COMMON LAW CLAIMS

2-2 *Pierce*: Public Policy Exception

New Jersey's public policy exception to at-will employment was created by the Supreme Court in *Pierce v. Ortho Pharmaceutical Corp.*:

---

5. As reported in *The Star Ledger* of Newark at the time of CEPA's enactment, the bill first gained public attention during Assembly Labor Committee hearings in June 1986. Sergeant Trent Davis, assigned to a special unit in the Department of Human Services, testified that he had previously been ordered by supervisors to illegally access computer files to obtain confidential information about other employees, and that after he questioned that order, he was constantly harassed by those supervisors. Within hours of giving that testimony, Sgt. Davis was stripped of his authority and reassigned, but when Governor Thomas Kean learned of the incident, Davis was reinstated pending an inquiry by the Department and the Attorney General.

In signing the bill into law, Governor Kean issued a statement explaining the need it was designed to serve:

> It is most unfortunate — but, nevertheless true — that conscientious employees have been subjected to firing, demotion or suspension for calling attention to illegal activity on the part of an employer.
>
> It is just as unfortunate that illegal activities have not been brought to light because of deep-seated fear on the part of an employee that his or her livelihood will be taken away without recourse.

6. *See Potter v. Village Bank of New Jersey*, 225 N.J.Super. 547, 561 (App. Div.), *certif. denied*, 113 N.J. 352 (1988) ("We read this legislative enactment as a codification of public policy established through judicial decisions."); *Fineman v. New Jersey Dep't of Human Servs.*, 272 N.J. Super. 606, 610, 617 (App. Div. 1994) (*Pierce* "furnished the underlay for legislative adoption of CEPA;" "CEPA implemented the Supreme Court's opinion in *Pierce*"), *certif. denied*, 138 N.J. 267 (1994).

7. N.J.S.A. 34:19-1 *et seq*. CEPA is discussed in detail in Part III of this chapter.

8. N.J.S.A. 2A:65A-3.

9. N.J.S.A. 9:6-8.13.

10. N.J.S.A. 52:27G-14. These specific whistleblower statutes are discussed, *infra,* §§2-12 to 2-28.

> [A]n employee has a cause of action [in tort or contract or both] for wrongful discharge when the discharge is contrary to a *clear mandate* of public policy. The sources of public policy include legislation; administrative rules, regulations or decisions; and judicial decisions. In certain instances, a professional code of ethics may contain an expression of public policy. However, not all such sources express a clear mandate of public policy.[11]

The Court observed that the public policy cause of action must be carefully delineated so as not to "interfere with the employer's right to make business decisions and to choose the best personnel for the job."[12] The Court emphasized that "unless an employee-at-will identifies a specific expression of public policy, he may be discharged with or without cause."[13]

The employee-plaintiff in a *Pierce* suit bears the threshold burden of identifying the clear mandate of public policy relied on; if he fails to do so, his complaint will be dismissed or summary judgment entered against him.[14] The plaintiff also bears the burden of proving causation: "that he was in fact discharged in retaliation for taking action in opposition to corporate action which violated a clear mandate of public policy," and not for some other reason.[15] The *Pierce* cause of action is available only against an employer, and is not avaiable against non-em-

11. *Pierce v. Ortho Pharmaceutical Corp.*, 84 N.J. 58, 72 (1980) (emphasis added). The plaintiff in *Pierce* was a medical doctor employed by Ortho Pharmaceutical Corporation and assigned to oversee the development of loperamide, a drug for the treatment of diarrhea. The proposed formulation for loperamide contained saccharin, a chemical that had been the subject of much medical controversy. Dr. Pierce refused to perform research on loperamide, asserting that the work would force her to violate professional medical ethics expressed in the Hippocratic oath statement: "I will prescribe regimen for the good of my patients according to my ability and my judgment and never do harm to anyone." She was terminated because of that dispute.

The Supreme Court held that Dr. Pierce's discharge did not violate any public policy: "As a matter of law, there is no public policy against conducting research on drugs that may be controversial, but potentially beneficial to mankind." *Id.* at 76; *see Hennessey v. Coastal Eagle Point Oil Co.*, 129 N.J. 81, 90-92 (1992) (holding that the New Jersey Constitution may be a source of public policy; opinion also collects cases in which violation of a clear mandate of public policy was alleged).

12. *Pierce v. Ortho Pharmaceutical Corp.,* 84 N.J. at 69.

13. *Id.* at 72; *see Bernard v. IMI Sys., Inc.*, 131 N.J. 91, 97 (1993) ("absent a statute, public policy mandate, or agreement to the contrary, contracts of employment of an indefinite duration are at-will").

14. *Id.* at 73; *Cappiello v. Ragen Precision Industries, Inc.*, 192 N.J.Super. 523, 527 (App. Div. 1984).

15. *House v. Carter-Wallace, Inc.*, 232 N.J.Super. 42, 54 (App. Div.), *certif. denied*, 117 N.J. 154 (1989). For a discussion of the requirement of proof of causation, *see* §2-3:6, *infra*. In *Hennessey v. Coastal Eagle Point Oil Co.*, 129 N.J. 81, 92 (1992), the Supreme Court held that the *Pierce* cause of action is not limited to retaliatory actions or violations of statutory rights; "all we require is that the employee 'point to a clear expression of public policy.' "

ployer individual defendants.[16] The *Pierce* action is also not available to independent contractors; however, "employee" in this context is broadly defined.[17]

2-3 Clear Mandate of Public Policy

In the immediate aftermath of *Pierce*, employers feared and employees hoped that the public policy exception to employment at will would be an expansive one, tantamount to a just-cause or fairness doctrine. Although some early decisions sent mixed signals,[18] and creative sources of public policy have been pursued,[19] the courts have generally declined to extend *Pierce* beyond its terms, requiring in each case identification of an articulated public policy and implication of public—as opposed to merely individual employee—rights. Determination of what constitutes a clear expression of public policy is a question of law for the court,[20] which "the judiciary must define ... in case-by-case determinations."[21]

2-3:1 Retaliation for Refusal to Engage in Illegal Conduct

Retaliation against employees for refusing to engage in conduct that is criminal or otherwise prohibited by law violates the public policies expressed in those laws. This is a longstanding rule, suggested by the Law Division two years be-

---

16. *See O'Lone v. New Jersey Dep't of Corrections*, 313 N.J. Super. 249, 256 (App. Div. 1998). One federal court has issued a contrary ruling, although that decision was issued nearly ten years before the Appellate Division's decision in *O'Lone*. *See Borecki v. Eastern Int'l Mgmt. Corp.*, 694 F. Supp. 47, 57-60 (D.N.J. 1998).

17. In *McDougall v. Weichert*, 144 N.J. 380, 389 (1996), the Supreme Court remanded for trial the issue whether a real estate sales associate who received no salary and was paid commission under an independent contractor agreement was an "employee." The "critical issue is whether the elements of control and dependence coupled with the absence of any employment protection predominate over factors that favor an independent contractor status."

18. For example, in *Crowell v. Transamerica Delaval, Inc.*, 206 N.J.Super. 298 (Law Div. 1984), the court held that the discharge of an employee for allowing a manufacturing defect, after his supervisors had ignored his reports of prior defects, violated the judicially-recognized public policy of "equitable estoppel." At the same time, however, the court refused to recognize a claim for violation of purported public policy that at-will employment be conducted in good faith. *Crowell's* recognition of a *Pierce* action based upon a public policy of equitable estoppel was subsequently overruled by *DeVries v. McNeil Consumer Products Co.*, 250 N.J.Super. 159, 172-73 (App. Div. 1991). *Cf. Reilly v. Prudential Prop. & Cas. Ins. Co.*, 653 F.Supp. 725, 735 (D.N.J. 1987) (summary judgment for defendant on plaintiff's claim based on the public policy of equitable estoppel).

19. *See, e.g.*, *Brunner v. Abex Corp.*, 661 F.Supp. 1351, 1357 (D.N.J. 1986) (unsuccessfully asserting a public policy of encouraging job security).

20. *See Warthen v. Toms River Community Memorial Hospital*, 199 N.J.Super. 18, 24 (App. Div.), *certif. denied*, 101 N.J. 255 (1985) ("identifying the mandate of public policy is a question of law, analogous to interpreting a statute or defining a duty in a negligence case"); *Fineman v. New Jersey Dep't of Human Servs.*, 272 N.J. Super. 606, 620 (App. Div. 1994) (court must determine existence of a clear mandate of public policy and, in doing so, engage in the balancing of competing interests recognized in *Hennessey v. Coastal Eagle Point Oil Co.*, 129 N.J. 81 (1992); "Frequently, a summary judgment motion would be useful in this respect.")

fore *Pierce*, in a case in which an x-ray technician had refused to perform a procedure she contended she was legally precluded from performing.[22] Thus, in *Radwan v. Beecham Laboratories*, the Third Circuit held that discharge of an employee for refusing to plant contraband on a union steward would state a cause of action for wrongful discharge under *Pierce* because it would be in violation of the National Labor Relations Act and state labor policy.[23] To the same effect is *Kalman v. Grand Union Co.*, holding that the discharge of a pharmacist for refusal to close a supermarket pharmacy on a day when the rest of the store was open stated a claim under *Pierce*.[24] The closure would have violated a statute which the court found aimed at protecting the public from drugs, and on that basis "public policy" was found in issue.[25]

---

21. *Pierce v. Ortho Pharmaceutical Corp.*, 84 N.J. 58, 72 (1980). The Supreme Court opinion in *Hennessey v. Coastal Eagle Point Oil Co.*, 129 N.J. 81 (1992), makes this inquiry more difficult. The "clear mandate of public policy" relied upon in that case—the right to privacy under the New Jersey Constitution—is arguably different in kind from virtually all of those previously found supportive of *Pierce* claims, in that it is not clearly set forth in its entirety in any place other than the Court's opinion. Unlike the workers' compensation law in *Lally v. Copygraphics*, 85 N.J. 668 (App. Div. 1980), the pharmacy regulations in *Kalman v. Grand Union Co.*, 183 N.J. Super. 153 (App. Div. 1982), or the Occupational Safety and Health Act in *LePore v. National Tool & Mfg. Co.*, 115 N.J. 226 (1989), *cert. denied*, 493 U.S. 954 (1989), the balancing test and other detailed requirements of *Hennessey* cannot be found by employers (or lawyers) in any place other than the *Hennessey* opinion itself. Thus, while the general foundation of this "clear mandate of public policy" is apparent, its detailed substance was the product of the litigation which alleged it had been violated. *See D'Agostino v. Johnson & Johnson,* 133 N.J. 516, 531 (1993) ("The mere existence of a policy does not mean that it will be invoked. 'A "clear mandate of public policy" must be one that on balance is beneficial to the public. That requires a weighing of the competing interests.") (citations and internal quotatons omitted). The Court similarly drew from a variety of sources to create the public policy at issue in *McDougall v. Weichert*, 144 N.J. 380 (1996), where plaintiff had been terminated at the request of an important client of Weichert who objected to a vote plaintiff cast as a member of the town council. Drawing from bribery and illegal threat provisions of the criminal code, the Court concluded there is a clear mandate of public policy that serves to "protect public officials holding legislative office in the exercise of official duties relating to legislative matters." *Id.* at 398. When actions are taken against such officials in a situation that would create a disqualification under conflict of interest laws (which on their face apply only to the office holders), a clear mandate of public policy is violated.

22. *O'Sullivan v. Mallon*, 160 N.J.Super. 416 (Law Div. 1978). The court denied the employer's motion for summary judgment but deferred final resolution of the legal issue until a more complete factual record was established. It noted as follows:

> This court is of the opinion that the public policy of the State of New Jersey may require that this State adopt the rule established [in California] that an employment at will may not be terminated by an employer in retaliation for an employee's refusal to perform an illegal act. This rule is especially cogent where the subject matter is the administration of medical treatment, an area in which the public has a foremost interest and which is extensively regulated by various state agencies. Such a finding may very well be consistent with the existing New Jersey cases that were not concerned with situations where public policy was involved or was being violated.

Id. at 418.

23. *Radwan v. Beecham Laboratories*, 850 F.2d 147, 151-52 (3d Cir. 1988).

24. *Kalman v. Grand Union Co.*, 183 N.J.Super. 153 (App. Div. 1982).

2-3:2 Retaliation for "Whistleblowing"

Traditional whistleblowing—reporting the improper or illegal activities of supervisors to outside authorities—is clearly protected under *Pierce*.[26] But internal complaints about the activities of co-employees or supervisors are not; "the mere voicing of opposition to corporate policy within a corporation provides an insufficient foundation for assertion of a *Pierce* claim"[27] The rationale for this distinction was succinctly stated in *Giudice v. Drew Chemical Corp.*:

> Private investigation of possible criminal activities of fellow employees does not implicate the same public policy consideration as if plaintiffs had been fired as the result of cooperating with law enforcement officials investigating possible criminal activities of fellow employees.[28]

Presumably, the internal reporting required by CEPA as a predicate to involvement of outside agencies is exempt from this rule.[29]

Employee whistleblowing is now addressed specifically in CEPA. Although the statute provides that it does not abrogate any other causes of action,[30] the Su-

---

25. Plaintiff in *Kalman* also contended that the behavior requested was in violation of his professional code. The fact that the statutory and regulatory scheme coincided with the professional ethics code distinguished this case from *Pierce* (Hippocratic Oath) and *Warthen v. Toms River Community Memorial Hospital*, 199 N.J.Super. 18 (App. Div.) (Code for Nurses), *certif. denied*, 101 N.J. 255 (1985), in which plaintiffs' claims were rejected on the grounds that they implicated only personal moral considerations and not public policy. *Kalman v. Grand Union Co.*, 183 N.J.Super. at 159.

26. *See, e.g., Potter v. Village Bank of New Jersey*, 225 N.J.Super. 547 (App. Div.) (discharge for reporting alleged laundering of drug money to law enforcement officials violated public policy), *certif. denied*, 113 N.J. 352 (1988); *Zamboni v. Stamler*, 847 F.2d 73 (3d Cir.) (retaliation for reporting alleged violation of civil service procedures violated public policy as expressed in subsequently enacted statute protecting civil service whistleblowers, freedom of speech guarantees of the New Jersey and United States constitutions, and state court opinions committed to freedom of speech of public employees), *cert. denied*, 488 U.S. 899 (1988).

27. *House v. Carter-Wallace, Inc.*, 232 N.J.Super. 42, 49 (App. Div.), *certif. denied*, 117 N.J. 154 (1989). *See Young v. Schering Corp.*, 141 N.J. 16, 27 (1995) ("Under [the common law cause of action], however, there must be actual notification to a governmental body of illegal employer conduct."); *Citizens State Bank of New Jersey v. Libertelli*, 215 N.J.Super. 190 (App. Div. 1987) (internal protests of alleged regulatory improprieties of board members did not violate public policy as expressed in New Jersey Banking Act); *Crawford v. West Jersey Health Sys.*, 847 F. Supp. 1232 (D.N.J. 1994) (mere voicing of opposition to corporate policy within a corporation provides an insufficient basis for a *Pierce* claim); *Beck v. Tribert*, 312 N.J. Super. 335, 348-349 (App. Div.), *certif. denied*, 156 N.J. 424 (1998) (plaintiff's pre-termination request to repair allegedly defective crane and hoist mechanism insufficient to establish a *Pierce* claim because plaintiff did not notify a governmental body).

28. *Giudice v. Drew Chemical Corp.*, 210 N.J.Super. 32, 36 (App. Div.), *certif. gr. and remanded and certif. denied*, 104 N.J. 465 (1986); *see Smith v. Ebasco Constructors, Inc.*, 1988 WL 44143, pp.*3-4 (D.N.J. 1988) (internal reporting of extreme cost overruns and delay on publicly-funded project did not implicate public policy). The opinion in *First Atlantic Leasing Corp. v. Tracey*, 738 F.Supp. 863 (D.N.J. 1990), highlighted the issue in its comparison of *Potter* (where a public policy violation was found) and *Libertelli* (where the public policy claim was dismissed). The court stated that "*Potter* and *Libertelli* can also be distinguished on the grounds that *Potter* involved a situation where the improprieties were reported to an outside authority, whereas in *Libertelli*, the plaintiff did not report the violations but simply 'insisted on following sound and lawful banking practices and would not go along with the self-dealing improprieties of board members.' " *Id.* at 872 n. 3.

preme Court has indicated that the enactment of CEPA limits the expansion of the common law claim for violation of New Jersey's public policy favoring employee whistleblowing.[31]

2-3:3 Retaliation for Exercising Personal Rights

In line with the previous cases cited requiring a public interest component in *Pierce* claims,[32] the courts have generally declined to permit claims to proceed where the employee alleges he was retaliated against for exercising a purely personal right or privilege. This requirement is highlighted by the Appellate Division decision in *DeVries v. McNeil Consumer Products Co.*, in which plaintiff alleged that she was terminated because of customer complaints about her adherence to an alleged company policy of distributing expired or nearly-expired drug samples.[33] Plaintiff's claim that this violated a public policy of equitable estoppel was rejected as a matter of law, on the ground that only personal rights were involved:

> We conclude the DeVries discharge did not violate a clear mandate of public policy. Although it may have been unfair, it implicated only the private interests of the parties. DeVries' reinstatement or an award of damages to her for wrongful discharge would not further any public interest or serve to vindicate any identifiable public policy.[34]

To the same effect is the decision in *Alexander v. Kay Finlay Jewelers, Inc.*, that firing an employe for bringing suit over a salary dispute does not violate public policy:

> While plaintiff had a legal right to sue his employer for monies considered to be due him in salary, there can be no question that the company also had a compelling interest to operate its

29. N.J.S.A. 34:19-4. *See* discussion *infra* at §2-9. *See also House v. Carter-Wallace, Inc.*, 232 N.J.Super. 42, 50 (App. Div.) ("Where employees' claims have been recognized based solely on internal complaints, it has been under circumstances where the employees have threatened to report the alleged violation of public policy to outside parties but been terminated before their complaints could be made."), *certif. denied*, 117 N.J. 154 (1989).

30. N.J.S.A. 34:19-8. *See* discussion *infra*, §§2-11.

31. *See Young v. Schering Corp.*, 141 N.J. 16, 27 (1995) ("Because CEPA defines the cause of action and concomitantly requires the waiver of *Pierce* and *LePore*-type claims, it indirectly inhibits the expansion of the common law cause of action … ."); *see also Smith v. Ebasco Constructors, Inc.*, 1988 WL 44143, pp. * 2-3.

32. *See* discussion *supra*, §2-3.

33. *DeVries v. McNeil Consumer Products Co.*, 250 N.J.Super. 159, 170-73 (App. Div. 1991).

34. *Id.* at 172; *see Pitak v. Bell Atlantic Network Servs., Inc.*, 1996 WL 341278, p.*13 (D.N.J. 1996) (*Pierce* claim based on equitable estoppel disallowed).

> business without the harassment of suits by employees dissatisfied with their wages or disgruntled because of a reduction in their salary.[35]

The Supreme Court relied on this analysis in *Erickson v. Marsh & McLennan Co.*, in suggesting that firing an employee because he has hired an attorney to sue the employer does not violate public policy.[36]

Actions taken in furtherance of one's own moral beliefs are similarly unprotected, unless they coincide with an expression of public policy; that is so even if those beliefs are in accord with a professional code of ethics or conduct.[37]

The extent to which employee privacy interests may implicate public policy concerns sufficient to support a *Pierce* claim remains unsettled.[38]

2-3:4 Retaliation Proscribed by Other State and Federal Statutes

(1) Pursuit of Workers' Compensation Benefits.

Even before the Supreme Court decided *Pierce*, the Appellate Division held in *Lally v. Copygraphics* that policy considerations mandate recognition of a private common law action for employees retaliated against for seeking workers' compensation benefits.[39] Such retaliation is prohibited by the New Jersey Workers' Compensation Act, but only penal and administrative remedies are provided for therein.[40] After deciding *Pierce*, the Supreme Court affirmed *per curiam* the Appellate Division decision in *Lally*, holding that (1) a discharge for filing a workers' compensation claim violates the public policy expressed in the statute

---

35. *Alexander v. Kay Finlay Jewelers, Inc.*, 208 N.J.Super. 503, 507 (App. Div.), *certif. denied*, 104 N.J. 466 (1986); *see also Rivera v. Trump Plaza Hotel & Casino*, 305 N.J. Super. 596, 602-603 (App. Div. 1997) (no public policy claim recognized for plaintiffs who were terminated for violating employer's hair-length policy).

36. *Erickson v. Marsh & McLennan Co.*, 117 N.J. 539, 560 (1990) ("[A]n employer has an absolute right to discharge an 'at-will' employee even if that employee has retained a lawyer to protest the employer's actions—provided only that the employer not violate any clear mandate of public policy").

37. *See Pierce v. Ortho Pharmaceutical Corp.*, 84 N.J. 58 (1980); *compare Warthen v. Toms River Community Memorial Hospital*, 199 N.J.Super. 18 (App. Div.) (no public policy was implicated by nurse's refusal to dialyze terminal patient pursuant to her personal moral belief and in accordance with Code for Nurses provision permitting refusal to provide treatment to which one is morally opposed), *certif. denied*, 101 N.J. 255 (1986), with *Kalman v. Grand Union Co.*, 183 N.J.Super. 153 (App. Div. 1982) (employee's refusal to close supermarket pharmacy in violation of statute and code of ethics was protected under *Pierce*). *See also Smith v. Ebasco Constructors, Inc.*, 1988 WL 44143, p. * 3 (D.N.J. 1988) (no public policy implicated by reporting of extreme cost overruns on publicly-funded project, where employee was guided by subjective "perception of his professional and moral obligations to the State of New Jersey and the taxpayers of the State of New Jersey").

38. *See* discussion *supra*, §2-3, n. 21; *Slohoda v. United Parcel Service, Inc.*, 193 N.J.Super. 586 (App. Div. 1984) (case remanded for determination whether discharge for adultery would violate public policy with respect to the invasion of privacy), *later opinion*, 207 N.J.Super. 145 (App. Div.), *certif. denied*, 104 N.J. 400 (1986).

39. *Lally v. Copygraphics*, 173 N.J. Super. 162 (App. Div. 1980), *aff'd*, 85 N.J. 668 (1981).

and (2) the remedies set forth in the statute were not exclusive. Had the Legislature wanted to limit redress to the remedies set forth in the statute, the Court reasoned, it would have said so specifically.[41]

It is not necessary for an employee actually to have filed a workers' compensation claim petition to maintain a cause of action under *Pierce*; attempting to make a claim is sufficient.[42]

(2) Reporting Workplace Hazards

It has similarly been held that a *Pierce* claim will lie for violation of the Occupational Safety and Health Act's (OSH Act) prohibition of retaliation against employees who file complaints with the Occupational Safety and Health Administration (OSHA).[43] Like the Workers' Compensation Act provision at issue in *Lally*, the OSHA retaliation ban does not provide for a private cause of action; its exclusive articulated remedy is an enforcement action by the Secretary of Labor.[44]

---

40. N.J.S.A. 34:15-39.1 and -39.2 provide:

> It shall be unlawful for any employer or his duly authorized agent to discharge or in any other manner discriminate against an employee as to his employment because such employee has claimed or attempted to claim workmen's compensation benefits from such employer, or because he has testified, or is about to testify, in any proceeding under this chapter to which this act is a supplement. For any violation of this act, the employer or agent shall be punished by a fine of not less than $100 nor more than $1,000 or imprisonment for not more than 60 days or both. Any employee so discriminated against shall be restored to his employment and shall be compensated by his employer for any loss of wages arising out of such discrimination; provided, if such employee shall cease to be qualified to perform the duties of his employment he shall not be entitled to such restoration and compensation.
>
> As an alternative to any other sanctions herein or otherwise provided by law, the Commissioner of Labor and Industry may impose a penalty not exceeding $1,000.00 for any violation of this act. He may proceed in a summary manner for the recovery of such penalty, for the use of the State, in any court of competent jurisdiction.

See N.J.A.C. 12:235-11.1 *et seq.*; *Lally v. Copygraphics*, 173 N.J.Super. 162 (App. Div. 1980), *aff'd*, 85 N.J. 668 (1981).

41. *See Lally v. Copygraphics*, 85 N.J. 668, 670-71 (1981). Justice Schreiber dissented. He would have recognized the *Pierce* claim, but limited remedies to those set forth in the statute: "This position is harmonious with the general proposition that where a statute expressly provides for a particular remedy, a court should not read others into it in the absence of clear legislative intent." *Id.* at 676.

42. *See Cerracchio v. Alden Leeds, Inc.*, 223 N.J.Super. 435, 442 (App. Div. 1988).

43. *See LePore v. National Tool & Mfg. Co.*, 115 N.J. 226 (1989) (employee covered by collective bargaining agreement may maintain *Pierce* action for wrongful discharge for reporting health and safety violations to OSHA; neither the OSH Act nor §301 of the Labor Management Relations Act of 1947, 29 U.S.C.A. §185, pre-empt that claim), *aff'g*, 224 N.J.Super. 463 (App. Div. 1988), *cert. denied*, 493 U.S. 954 (1989); *Cerracchio v. Alden Leeds, Inc.*, 223 N.J.Super. 435, 442 (App. Div. 1988) (retaliation against employee for filing OSHA complaint violates New Jersey's public policy favoring safe workplace; New Jersey has demonstrated its agreement with federal policy expressed in OSHA by extending it to public employees).

44. 29 U.S.C.A. §660(c).

(3) Pursuing Employment Discrimination Claims.

In *Velantzas v. Colgate-Palmolive Co.*, the Supreme Court held that a *pro se* plaintiff could maintain a *Pierce* action if she alleged she was "discharged for seeking to establish (by demanding her personnel file) a gender discrimination claim."[45] The Court found that the "public policy of the State of New Jersey should protect those who are in good faith pursuing information relevant to a discriminatory discharge,"[46] and noted that under federal law a retaliatory discharge for pursuing a discrimination claim is itself a discriminatory discharge.[47] The Court did not discuss the LAD's prohibition of retaliation for pursuit of discrimination claims or the relation of the statute to the common law cause of action.[48]

Since that time, however, many decisions have either suggested or explicitly ruled that a *Pierce* claim may not be maintained when the conduct at issue is proscribed by the LAD.[49]

2-3:5 Non-Retaliatory Discharge

Pierce claims have not been recognized for:

1. Terminating an employee to avoid paying him commissions on sales.[50]
2. Terminating an employee in violation of a purported "New Jersey public policy of encouraging job security."[51]
3. Not conducting at-will employment in good faith.[52]
4. "Abusive" discharge.[53]
5. Termination in violation of a preempted statute.[54]

---

45. *Velantzas v. Colgate-Palmolive Co.*, 109 N.J. 189, 192 (1988).

46. *Id.* at 192.

47. *Id.* at 193 n.l.

48. *See* discussion *infra*, §2-6

49. See discussion, *infra*, §2-6:1. For a more complete discussion of the relationship of *Pierce* to statutory causes of action, see *infra.*, §2-6.

50. *Schwartz v. Leasametric, Inc.*, 224 N.J.Super. 21, 30 (App. Div. 1988); *but see* 2A:61A-1 *et seq.*

51. *Brunner v. Abex Corp.*, 661 F.Supp. 1351, 1357 (D.N.J. 1986) (recognizing a public policy of job security would allow plaintiffs to "enter this back door so firmly shut by *Pierce*"); *see also Monroe v. Host Marriot Services Corp.*, 999 F.Supp. 599 (D.N.J. 1998) ("A wrongful discharge claim cannot be made on an alleged breach of employer policies which merely suggest standards set by the employer.").

52. *Crowell v. Transamerica Delaval, Inc.*, 206 N.J.Super. 298, 306-07 (Law Div. 1984), *overruled on other grounds, DeVries v. McNeil Consumer Products Co.*, 250 N.J.Super. 159, 172-73 (App. Div. 1991). *But see* discussion *supra*, Chapter 1, §1-15, regarding applicability of covenant of good faith and fair dealing to employment contracts and employee handbooks.

53. *Carney v. Dexter Shoe Co.*, 701 F.Supp. 1093, 1103 (D.N.J. 1988).

54. *Stehney v. Perry*, 101 F.3d 925, 938-939 (3d Cir. 1996).

The Supreme Court opinion in *Hennessey v. Coastal Eagle Point Oil Co.*, makes clear that the *Pierce* cause of action is not limited to retaliatory discharges, but may be based upon any discharge that violates a clear mandate of public policy. Although it agreed with the Appellate Division that the plaintiff in that case had not been wrongfully discharged, the Court held that the New Jersey Constitution's provisions regarding search and seizure and inalienable rights constitute clear expressions of public policy which in appropriate circumstances may form the basis of a *Pierce* claim.[55]

2-3:6 Causation

An employee asserting a public policy claim bears the burden of proving that the protected activity he engaged in was the actual cause of his discharge or other adverse employment action: "that he was in fact discharged in retaliation for taking action in opposition to corporate action which violates a clear mandate of public policy," and not for some other reason.[56]

The timing of a discharge relative to an employee's engagement in protected activities may support—or defeat—an inference of causation.[57] Assuming there is a genuine issue of fact, the question of causation is normally for the jury.[58]

---

55. *Hennessey v. Coastal Eagle Point Oil Co.*, 129 N.J. 81, 93-99 (1992).

56. *House v. Carter-Wallace, Inc.*, 232 N.J.Super. 42, 54 (App. Div.) (evidence failed to show plaintiff was discharged for his opposition to selling of potentially contaminated batches of toothpaste and not because he was politically unacceptable and not doing a proper job), *certif. denied*, 117 N.J. 154 (1989); *Galante v. Sandoz, Inc.*, 192 N.J.Super. 403 (Law Div. 1983) (plaintiff failed to show that discharge was due to filing workers' compensation claim petition and not for excessive absenteeism), *aff'd*, 196 N.J.Super. 568 (App. Div. 1984), *appeal dismissed*, 103 N.J. 492 (1986); *Mallon v. Prudential Property & Casualty Ins. Co.*, 688 F.Supp. 997 (D.N.J. 1988) (discharge as a consequence of the application of a neutral, written disability policy is not against public policy just because plaintiff had also pursued a workers' compensation claim); *First Atlantic Leasing Corp. v. Tracey*, 738 F.Supp. 863 (D.N.J. 1990) (plaintiff failed to demonstrate he was discharged for reporting alleged improper transactions of bank president rather than for his own involvement in improper real estate transactions).

57. *See Radwan v. Beecham Laboratories*, 850 F.2d 147, 152 (3d Cir. 1988) (a jury might infer from a three-year delay that events were unrelated; however, a knowledgeable employer "might mask its reason for discharging an employee by delaying its action for a protracted period after a dispute"); *House v. Carter-Wallace, Inc.*, 232 N.J. Super. at 51 (because three months passed between employee's internal complaint and discharge, no basis for inferring discharge was to prevent communication of those views to outside parties); *Meacham v. Bell Telephone Laboratories, Inc.*, 1990 WL 299805, p. *9 (D.N.J. 1990) (causal connection may be demonstrated by evidence of circumstances justifying a retaliatory motive, such as protected conduct closely followed by adverse action); *Beck v. Tribert*, 312 N.J. Super. 335, 349 (App. Div.), *certif. denied*, 156 N.J. 424 (1998) (because plaitiff did not contact OSHA until nearly two months after his termination, "there is no basis for inferring that defendants discharged plaintiff in order to prevent him from communicating information about defendants' dangerous workplace to outside parties.").

58. *See Warthen v. Toms River Community Memorial Hospital*, 199 N.J.Super. 18, 25 (App. Div.), *certif denied*, 101 N.J. 255 (1985).

2-4 Other Coverage Issues

Although the *Pierce* opinion refers to discharges in violation of public policy, and most reported opinions have involved terminations, the public policy cause of action is not so limited. All substantial retaliatory actions, described by the Third Circuit as "formal personnel actions that have an effect on either compensation or job rank," are actionable.[59]

In appropriate circumstances, United States citizens residing and working in foreign countries, but employed by New Jersey companies, may maintain *Pierce* actions for retaliatory discharge.[60] Among the factors to be considered in determining whether New Jersey law applies are the extent to which employers located in New Jersey were involved in the alleged improper actions and whether the public policy alleged to have been violated was intended to have extra-territorial reach.[61]

2-5 Statute of Limitations

There is no direct authority as to the limitations period applicable to *Pierce* claims. Many of the same considerations that have fueled debate as to the appropriate limitations periods for the Law Against Discrimination and federal civil rights statutes obtain here,[62] and it is not unlikely that a Supreme Court ruling on that issue will carry over in whole or in part to public policy claims. Absent such a ruling, the limitations period applicable to each *Pierce* claim will depend upon the nature of the injury alleged.

Under N.J.S.A. 2A:14-2, all actions for personal injury must be commenced within two years.[63] Under N.J.S.A. 2A:14-1, a six-year limitations period is applied to actions

> for trespass to real property, for any tortious injury to real or personal property ... [and] for any tortious injury to the rights of another not stated in sections 2A:14-2 [personal injury] and

---

59. *Zamboni v. Stamler*, 847 F.2d 73, 82 (3d Cir.), *cert. denied*, 488 U.S. 899 (1988). *Cf.* N.J.S.A. 34:19-2(d) ("retaliatory action" under Conscientious Employee Protection Act defined as "discharge, suspension or demotion of an employee, or other adverse employment action taken against an employee in the terms and conditions of employment").

60. *D'Agostino v. Johnson & Johnson, Inc.*, 133 N.J. 516 (1993).

61. *Id.* at 531-35, 545.

62. This issue is discussed extensively in Chapter 4, *infra*, §4-56.

63. N.J.S.A. 2A:14-2 provides: "Every action at law for an injury to the person caused by the wrongful act, neglect or default of any person within this state shall be commenced within 2 years next after the cause of any such action shall have accrued."

> 2A:14-3 [slander and libel] ... of this Title, or for recovery upon a contractual claim or liability express or implied ... .

In determining which limitations period is applicable, "it is the nature of the injuries, not the theory of recovery, which is controlling."[64] Where the gravamen of the claim is personal injury, the two-year period governs regardless of the theory of recovery asserted.[65]

Thus, public policy claims for breach of contract should be governed by the six-year period for recovery upon a contractual claim set forth in N.J.S.A. 2A:14-1. Conversely, public policy claims in tort seeking compensation for emotional distress or other personal injury should be subject to the two-year period of N.J.S.A. 2A:14-2.[66] The difficult case is where a "tort" claim for wrongful discharge is alleged and no injury other than the discharge and related loss of wages is involved. The Appellate Division has suggested, however, that the two-year statute of limitaions applies if the plaintiff has the "right" to make a claim for physical and emotional harm, even if no such claim is actually asserted.[67]

2-6 Policy Expressed in Statutes

No definitive rule has yet emerged to determine the circumstances under which an employee may maintain a *Pierce* action for violation of the public policy expressed in the various statutes governing the employment relationship. However, dicta in two Supreme Court opinions[68] suggests that the nature and extent of relief available under the statute will be the determining factor: where the statute

---

64. *Brown v. New Jersey College of Medicine and Dentistry*, 167 N.J.Super. 532, 535 (Law Div. 1979). *Cf. Atlantic City Hospital v. Finkle*, 110 N.J.Super. 435, 438 (Law Div. 1970) (claim for personal injuries on breach of warranty theory governed by two-year statute of limitations).

65. *Burns v. Bethlehem Steel Co.*, 20 N.J. 37, 39-40 (1955); *Carney v. Finn*, 145 N.J.Super. 234, 235-36 (App. Div. 1976); *see also Heavner v. Uniroyal, Inc.*, 118 N.J.Super. 116, 120 (App. Div. 1972), *aff'd*, 63 N.J. 130 (1973) (although plaintiff's action arose out of a sales transaction it was essentially a personal injury action subject to the two-year limitations period); *Labree v. Mobil Oil Corp.*, 300 N.J. Super. 234, 242-244 (App. Div. 1997) (civil actions for retaliatory discharge under the Workers' Compensation Act are governed by two year personal injury statute of limitations). In *Montells v. Haynes*, 133 N.J. 282 (1993), the Supreme Court held that the two-year limitations period of N.J.S.A. 2A:14-2 should govern all actions under the LAD, because the injuries suffered as a consequence of employment discrimination more closely resemble injuries to the person, and because the shorter period comports with the LAD's purposes of efficiency and avoidance of stale claims. However, the two-year period established by *Montells* applies prospectively only, to acts or omissions occurring after the date of the opinion.

66. *See Goncalvez v. Patuto*, 188 N.J.Super. 620 (App. Div. 1983) (claim for emotional distress is subject to two-year limitations period of N.J.S.A. 2A:14-2).

67. *See Labree v. Mobile Oil Corp.*, 300 N.J. Super. 234, 244 (App. Div. 1997).

68. *See Shaner v. Horizon Bancorp.*, 116 N.J. 433 (1989); *Erickson v. Marsh & McLennan Co.*, 117 N.J. 539 (1990).

in question affords all of the relief available in a *Pierce* action, the *Pierce* action will be disallowed.

2-6:1 New Jersey Law Against Discrimination (LAD)

The question whether a plaintiff who is protected by the LAD may forego the LAD remedy and instead institute a *Pierce* action for violation of the strong State public policy against employment discrimination appears reasonably settled. In dicta, the Supreme Court has twice suggested that it is unnecessary to recognize a common law cause of action when the conduct at issue is expressly prohibited by statute. In *Shaner v. Horizon Bancorp*, the Court stated:

> Because the LAD provides a victim of age discrimination with a remedy, it might be unnecessary to recognize or create a *Pierce*-type action to vindicate substantially the same rights and provide similar relief.
>
> * * *
>
> [A] plaintiff in appropriate circumstances could pursue an independent action, such as in *Pierce*, to vindicate particular interests in addition to or aside from those sought to be protected by a LAD action.[69]

A year later, in 1990, in *Erickson v. Marsh & McLennan Co.*, the Court noted that the Appellate Division had ruled that the LAD did not preempt a common law claim for wrongful dischsrge based on sex discrimination.[70] The Court stated of that ruling:

> Because no cross-petition was filed, we do not reach that issue. Rather, we affirm what we recently declared in *Shaner v. Horizon Bancorp.*, 116 N.J. 433 (1989): if LAD creates a remedy, 'it might be unnecessary to recognize or create a *Pierce*-type action to vindicate substantially the same rights and provide similar relief.'[71]

The Appellate Division has subsequently ruled that the LAD "encompass[es] all those claims and damages previously available at common law, rendering unnecessary a separate common law claim for discrimination in employment."[72]

---

69. *Shaner v. Horizon Bancorp.* 116 N.J. 433, 453-454 (1989).

70. *See Erickson v. Marsh & McLennan Co.*, 227 N.J. Super. 78, 84-85 (App. Div. 1988), *aff'd in part, reversed in part*, 117 N.J. 539 (1990).

71. *Erickson v. Marsh & McLennan Co.*, 117 N.J. 539, 561-562 (1990).

Several recent federal decisions have also held that the LAD preempts a common law action under *Pierce*.[73]

The issue whether a *Pierce* action will be permitted for alleged violations of the LAD and other statutes relating to the employment relationship is more than an academic exercise. Particularly significant is the common use of a *Pierce* action to avoid procedural requirements or substantive limitations of a statutory scheme. For example, an employee maintaining a *Pierce* action for violation of the public policy expressed in CEPA would presumably be relieved of that statute's internal exhaustion requirement, as well as its one-year statute of limitations.[74] An employee might similarly avoid the LAD's prohibition of simultaneously asserting a claim in both the Division on Civil Rights and in a civil suit, by pursuing a statutory claim in the DCR and a *Pierce* claim in Superior Court.[75] And an employee might avoid the $10,000 cap on punitive damages set forth in the Family Leave Act merely by foregoing an action under that act in favor of a *Pierce* action for violation of the public policy expressed in that act.[76]

2-6:2 Employee Retirement Income Security Act

Section 510 of the Employee Retirement Income Security Act (ERISA) makes it unlawful to discharge or otherwise discriminate against employees because they have exercised any rights under an employee benefit plan or for the purpose of interfering with their right to attain benefits.[77] A *Pierce* action for violation of

---

72. *Dale v. Boys Scouts of America*, 308 N.J. Super. 516, 542-543 (App. Div.), (citations omitted), *certif. granted*, 156 N.J. 381 (1998); *see also Catalane v. Gilian Instrument Corp.*, 271 N.J. Super. 476, 491-492 (App. Div.) ("[C]ommon law causes of action may not go to the jury when a statutory remedy under the LAD exists."), *certif. denied*, 136 N.J. 298 (1994).

73. *See Lawrence v. National Westminster Bank*, 98 F.3d 61, 73 (3d Cir. 1996) ("Because the sources of public policy [plaintiff] relies on are coterminous with his statutory claims, he cannot advance a separate common law public policy claim."); *Caldwell v. KFC Corp.*, 958 F. Supp. 962, 970 (D.N.J. 1997) (dismissing common law wrongful termination claim for failure to state a claim upon which relief may be granted because LAD supplants that cause of action); *Lynch v. New Deal Delivery Service, Inc.*, 974 F. Supp. 441, 459 (D.N.J. 1997) ("Because [plaintiff] has a viable claim under the NJLAD, the Court concludes that a sex discrimination claim based upon public policy is unnecessary."); *DeJoy v. Comast Cable Communications, Inc.*, 941 F. Supp. 468, 475-476 (D.N.J. 1996) (common law claim for wrongful termination is not viable to the extent it seeks the same remedy available under LAD); *Kapossy v. McGraw-Hill, Inc.*, 921 F. Supp. 234, 249 (D.N.J. 1996) ("*Catalane* holds that the New Jersey legislature, by providing a remedy in the NJLAD, intended to preempt any public policy cause of action based on the same facts which support the discrimination claim."); *Schanzer v. Rutgers University*, 934 F. Supp. 669, 678-679 (D.N.J. 1996) ("As it appears the New Jersey Supreme Court would decline to extend a *Pierce* remedy to victims of employment discrimination on the basis that these individuals are similarly protected by the NJLAD, this court will decline to do so as well."); *Butler v. Sherman, Silverstein & Kohl*, 755 F. Supp. 1259, 1263-1265 (D.N.J. 1990) ("The [New Jersey] Supreme Court does not intend to allow a supplementary cause of action where the NJLAD provides a remedy for the wrong.").

74. *See* discussion *infra*, §§§2-9 and §2-11.

75. *See* discussion *infra*, Chapter 4, §4-53.

76. *See* discussion *infra*, Chapter 6, §6-12.

the public policy expressed in this section (or any other section of ERISA) will not lie, because ERISA broadly pre-empts all state laws (statutory, administrative, and common law) relating to employee benefit plans.[78]

2-6:3 Section 301, Labor Management Relations Act

The New Jersey Supreme Court, the United States Court of Appeals for the Third Circuit, and the United States Supreme Court have all held that in appropriate circumstances, bargaining unit employees may maintain civil suits for wrongful discharge in violation of public policy, thus avoiding the grievance and arbitration procedures of their collective bargaining agreements.[79] Whether a state law wrongful discharge claim will be permitted to proceed depends upon whether its resolution requires interpretation of the collective bargaining agreement. If the claim is based directly on rights created in a collective bargaining agreement, or if its resolution is substantially dependent upon an analysis of the terms of the collective agreement, it will be pre-empted by §301 of the Labor Management Relations Act, 1947.[80] But if the state law claim is properly resolved without reference to the collective bargaining agreement, there is no pre-emption: "it would be inconsistent with congressional intent under [§301] to pre-empt state rules that proscribe conduct, or establish rights and obligations, independent of a labor contract."[81]

---

77. 29 U.S.C.A. §1140.

78. 29 U.S.C.A. §1144(a); *see Ingersoll-Rand Co. v. McClendon*, 498 U.S. 133, 111 S.Ct. 478, 112 L.Ed.2d 474 (1990) (ERISA pre-empts state law claim of wrongful discharge to prevent attainment of rights under benefit plan subject to ERISA). *See generally Shaw v. Delta Air Lines, Inc.*, 463 U.S. 85 (1983) (defining scope of ERISA pre-emption broadly); Bruce, *Pension Claims, Rights & Obligations*, pp. 299-303 (1988). *See also Pane v. RCA Corp.*, 868 F.2d 631, 635 (3d Cir. 1989) (claim of intentional infliction of emotional distress based upon, *inter alia*, alleged retaliation for seeking severance benefits, pre-empted by ERISA); *Yekel v. General Biscuit Brands, Inc.*, 1991 WL 43024, p. *3 (D.N.J. 1991) (plaintiff's claim for alleged wrongful discharge to avoid paying disability benefits, styled as a contract claim under New Jersey common law, pre-empted by ERISA).

79. *See LePore v. National Tool & Mfg. Co.*, 115 N.J. 226 (relying on the United States Supreme Court opinion in *Lingle v. Norge Div. of Magic Chef, Inc.*, 486 U.S. 399 (1988), the Court holds that employees covered by collective bargaining agreements may maintain *Pierce* claims for wrongful discharge in retaliation for reporting safety and health violations), *cert. denied*, 493 U.S. 954 (1989); *Lingle v. Norge Div. of Magic Chef, Inc.*, 486 U.S. 399 (1988) (retaliatory discharge claim not requiring interpretation of collective bargaining agreement not preempted); *Herring v. Prince Macaroni of New Jersey, Inc.*, 799 F.2d 120 (3d Cir. 1986) (plaintiff's public policy claim of discharge in retaliation for filing workers' compensation claim not precluded by fact that plaintiff's employment was governed by collective bargaining agreement).

2-7 Remedies

An action for discharge in violation of public policy will lie in contract or tort or both.[82] The choice affects the nature of damages available.[83]

"An action in contract may be predicated on the breach of an implied provision that an employer will not discharge an employee for refusing to perform an act that violates a clear mandate of public policy."[84] The tort action in these circumstances is "based on the duty of [the] employer not to discharge an employee who

---

80. 29 U.S.C.A. §185. *See Lingle v. Norge Div. of Magic Chef, Inc.*, 486 U.S. 399, 412-13 (1988); *IBEW v. Hechler*, 481 U.S. 851 (1987); *Allis-Chalmers Corp. v. Lueck*, 471 U.S. 202 (1985). In *Allis-Chalmers Corp. v. Lueck*, the Court established the rule that "when resolution of a state-law claim is substantially dependent upon analysis of the terms of an agreement made between the parties in a labor contract, that claim must either be treated as a §301 claim ... or dismissed as pre-empted by federal labor-contract law." *Allis-Chalmers Corp. v. Lueck*, 471 U.S. at 220. The claim asserted in that case was a state law tort claim for bad faith handling of an insurance claim for disability benefits authorized by a collective bargaining agreement. Because it derived from the contract, and was defined by the contractual obligation of good faith, the Court found that it would inevitably involve contract interpretation, and thus was pre-empted. *Id.* at 217-18. "Questions relating to what the parties to a labor agreement agreed, and what legal consequences were intended to flow from breaches of that agreement, must be resolved by reference to uniform federal law, whether such questions arise in the context of a suit for breach of contract or in a suit alleging liability in tort." *Id.* at 211. Also supporting pre-emption was the public policy of preservation of the central role of arbitration in our system of industrial self-government: "A rule that permitted an individual to sidestep available grievance procedures would cause arbitration to lose most of its effectiveness." *Id.* at 220.

In *IBEW v. Hechler*, 481 U.S. 851 (1987), the Court applied the *Allis-Chalmers Corp. v. Lueck* rule to a state-law tort claim that a union breached its duty of care to provide a union member with a safe workplace. *Id.* at 852-53. Because any such duty of care on the part of the Union would have to arise, if at all, from the collective bargaining agreement, the Court found that, as in *Lueck*, "questions of contract interpretation ... underlie any finding of tort liability," and the state law claim was therefore pre-empted. *Id.* at 862.

In *Lingle v. Norge Div. of Magic Chef, Inc.* 486 U.S. 399 (1988), plaintiff had alleged that her discharge was in retaliation for filing a workers' compensation claim. Although her union successfully pursued her claim in grievance proceedings under a "just cause" provision of the applicable collective bargaining agreement, plaintiff additionally asserted a state law tort claim aimed at recovering compensatory and punitive damages. The Court found the tort claim not pre-empted by §301, because neither the elements of plaintiff's claim nor the elements of defendant's defense required interpretation of the terms of the collective bargaining agreement. *Id.* at 407. The fact that similar issues were presented in both proceedings was not determinative:

> ... §301 pre-emption merely ensures that federal law will be the basis for interpreting collective-bargaining agreements, and says nothing about the substantive rights a State may provide to workers when adjudication of those rights does not depend upon the interpretation of such agreements. In other words, even if dispute resolution pursuant to a collective-bargaining agreement, on the one hand, and state law, on the other, would require addressing precisely the same set of facts, as long as the state-law claim can be resolved without interpreting the agreement itself, the claim is "independent" of the agreement for §301 pre-emption purposes.

Id. at 409-10.

81. *Allis-Chalmers Corp. v. Lueck*, 471 U.S. at 212.

82. *See Pierce v. Ortho Pharmaceutical Corp.*, 84 N.J. 58, 72 (1980); *Potter v. Village Bank of New Jersey*, 225 N.J.Super. 547, 561 (App. Div.), *certif. denied*, 113 N.J. 352 (1988).

83. *See Pierce v. Ortho Pharmaceutical Corp.*, 84 N.J. at 72; *Potter v. Village Bank of New Jersey*, 225 N.J.Super. at 550 (retaliatory discharge of employee for blowing whistle on suspected laundering of drug money is an intentional tort that exposed employer to compensatory and punitive damages).

84. *Pierce v. Ortho Pharmaceutical Corp.*, 84 N.J. at 72.

refused to perform an act that is a violation of a clear mandate of public policy."[85] "The tort lay not in the breach of contract but in the violation of valuable social norms—denominated by the court as clear mandates of public policy."[86] Insofar as the action is maintained in tort, punitive damages can be awarded to deter improper conduct in an appropriate case; punitive damages are not available in an action based upon breach of contract.[87] A claim for *per quod* damages based solely upon the spouse's economic loss has been rejected.[88] Similarly, punitive damages may not be awarded the spouse absent conduct by the defendant directed to the spouse.[89]

Compensatory damages for the tort of retaliatory discharge are essentially the same as for other torts; they "are designed to put the injured party in as good a position as he would have been in had the tortious conduct not occurred."[90]

> [A]n at-will employee who has sustained a retaliatory discharge in violation of a clear mandate of public policy is entitled to recover economic and non-economic losses. Such an employee may recover (1) the amount he or she would have earned from the time of wrongful discharge for a reasonable time until he or she finds new employment, including bonuses and vacation pay, less any unemployment compensation received in the interim; (2) expenses associated with finding new employment and mental anguish or emotional distress damages proximately related to the retaliatory discharge; and (3) the replacement value of fringe benefits such as an automobile and insurance for a reasonable time until new employment is obtained.[91]

Damages available in a contract action for wrongful discharge in violation of a public policy should parallel those provided for breach of an individual em-

---

85. *Id.* at 72.

86. *Noye v. Hoffmann-LaRoche, Inc.*, 238 N.J.Super. 430, 433 (App. Div.), *certif. denied*, 122 N.J. 146 (1990); *see Schwartz v. Leasametric, Inc.*, 224 N.J.Super. 21, 28-31 (App. Div. 1988).

87. *See Cappiello v. Ragen Precision Industries, Inc.*, 192 N.J.Super. 523, 527 (App. Div. 1984); *Pierce v. Ortho Pharmaceutical Corp.*, 84 N.J. at 72-73. In accordance with the usual rule, no prejudgment interest will be permitted on punitive damages. *See Cappiello,* 192 N.J.Super. at 532.

88. *Cappiello v. Ragen Precision Industries, Inc.*, 192 N.J.Super. at 532.

89. *Id.* at 532.

90. *Potter v. Village Bank of New Jersey*, 225 N.J.Super. 547, 562 (App. Div.), *certif. denied*, 113 N.J. 352 (1988).

91. *Id.* (citations omitted). *See also* Francis M. Dougherty, Annotation, *Damages Recoverable For Wrongful Discharge of At-Will Employee*, 44 A.L.R. 4th 1131 (1986), cited in *Potter v. Village Bank of New Jersey*, 225 N.J.Super. at 562.

ployment contract and for discharge in violation of a unilateral contract enforceable under *Woolley v. Hoffmann-LaRoche, Inc.*[92]

III. CONSCIENTIOUS EMPLOYEE PROTECTION ACT (CEPA)

2-8 Coverage

The Conscientious Employee Protection Act (CEPA)[93] has been described as one of the most far-reaching whistleblower statutes in the nation.[94] It applies to private sector, state, and local government employees.[95] Attorneys employed as in-house counsel for corporations are "employees" within the scope of CEPA.[96] Designed to protect employee "whistleblowers," the statute makes it unlawful for employers to take adverse employment action against employees who disclose, object to, or refuse to participate in certain actions that the employees reasonably believe are either illegal or in violation of public policy. Thus, employees who erroneously accuse their employers of wrongdoing are normally protected under CEPA so long as their belief is reasonable.[97] However, when a physician refuses to render treatment to patients, he is not protected under CEPA unless his belief is correct.[98] More specifically, CEPA provides:

> An employer shall not take any retaliatory action[99] against an employee because the employee does any of the following:

---

92. *See* discussion in Chapter 1, *supra*, §§1-20 to 1-23.

93. N.J.S.A. 34:19-1 to 34:19-8.

94. *See* Mayer, "N.J.'s Whistleblower Act", 119 *N.J.L.J.* 353 (1987). *See generally* Westman, *Whistleblowing: The Law of Retaliatory Discharge* (1991). CEPA has been described as a "partial codification" of *Pierce v. Ortho Pharmaceutical Corp.*, 84 N.J. 58, 72 (1980), that may establish a broader wrongful discharge cause of action for whistleblowers than *Pierce*. *See Chelly v. Knoll Pharmaceuticals*, 295 N.J. Super. 478, 480 n.1 (App. Div. 1996) (citing *Barratt v. Cushman & Wakefield of N.J., Inc.*, 144 N.J. 16, 26 (1990)).

95. An "employee" within the scope of CEPA is defined as: "any individual who performs services for and under the control and direction of an employer for wages or other remuneration." N.J.S.A. 34:19-2(b). *But see Ballinger v. Delaware River Port Authority*, 311 N.J. Super. 317, 329 (App. Div. 1998) (employees of Delaware River Port Authority, a bistate agency, may not sue DRPA under CEPA).

96. In *Parker v. M & T Chemicals, Inc.*, 236 N.J.Super. 451 (App. Div. 1989), the Appellate Division held that an in-house counsel for a corporation could maintain an action for damages under CEPA consistent with the Code of Professional Responsibility. Significantly, the attorney-plaintiff in that case did not seek reinstatement. *But see Kaman v. Montague Township Committee*, 306 N.J. Super. 291, 301 (App. Div. 1997) (expressing "substantial doubt" that tax assessor was municipal "employee" under CEPA, since only state Director of Division of Taxation can remove assessor from office), *certif. granted*, 156 N.J. 383 (1998); *Casamasino v. City of Jersey City*, 304 N.J. Super 226, 242 (App. Div. 1997), *certif. granted*, 156 N.J. 383 (1998) (tax assessor outside of CEPA's scope because he "enjoys a unique, independent status as tax assessor due to his statutorily created job security.") *certif. granted*, 156 N.J. 383 (1998).

a. Discloses, or threatens to disclose to a supervisor[100] or a public body[101] an activity, policy or practice of the employer[102] or another employer, with whom there is a business relationship,[103] that the employee reasonably believes is in violation of a law, or a rule or regulation promulgated pursuant to law;

b. Provides information to, or testifies before, any public body conducting an investigation, hearing or inquiry into any violation of law, or a rule or regulation promulgated pursuant to law by the employer or another employer, with whom there is a business relationship;[104] or

---

97. *See Mehlman v. Mobil Oil Corp.*, 153 N.J. 163, 193 (1998) ("the objecting employee must have an objectively reasonable belief, at the time of objection or refusal to participate in the employer's offensive activity, that such activity is illegal"; "specific knowlege of the precise source of public policy is not required"); *Regan v. City of New Brunswick*, 305 N.J. Super. 342, 355 (App. Div. 1997) (belief that illegal conduct was occurrring must be objectively reasonable; "plaintiff need not know, to a legal certitude, the precise contours and components of the public policy") (citations and internal quotations omitted); *Blackburn v United Parcel Service, Inc.* 3 F. Supp. 2d 504, 515 (D.N.J. 1998) (CEPA requires that employee hold reasonable belief that illegal conduct was occurring or, at the very least, was imminent); *Falco v. Community Medical Center*, 296 N.J. Super. 298, 310 (App. Div. 1997), *certif. denied*, 153 N.J. 405 (1998); *see also Fineman v. New Jersey Dep't of Human Servs.*, 272 N.J. Super. 606, 610-11 & n.2 (App. Div.) (the belief must be objectively reasonable), *certif. denied*, 138 N.J. 267 (1994); *Abbamont v. Piscataway Twp.*, 138 N.J. 405, 423-24 (1994) (the plaintiff must have a "reasonable, objective" belief); *Haworth v. Deborah Heart & Lung Ctr.*, 271 N.J. Super. 502, 505-506 (App. Div. 1994) (inferring that the employee's belief must be objectively reasonable; finding it unnecessary to reach the issue whether, in that case involving the destruction of blood samples, the employee would have had to prove that his objectively reasonable belief was correct—i.e., that in fact a violation of public policy had occurred).

98. *Fineman v. New Jersey Dep't of Human Servs.*, 272 N.J. Super. 606, 625 (App. Div.), *certif. denied*, 138 N.J. 267 (1994).

99. "Retaliatory action" is defined broadly as "discharge, suspension or demotion of an employee, or other adverse employment action taken against an employee in the terms and conditions of employment." N.J.S.A. 34:19-2d. *Cf. Zamboni v. Stamler*, 847 F.2d 73, 82 (3d Cir.) (retaliation sufficient to maintain a public policy claim under *Pierce v. Ortho Pharmaceutical Corp.*, 84 N.J. 58 (1980) is any "formal personnel actions that have an effect on either compensation or job rank"), *cert. denied*, 488 U.S. 899 (1988).

100. A "supervisor" is "any individual with an employer's organization who has the authority to direct and control the work performance of the affected employee, who has authority to take corrective action regarding the violation of the law, rule or regulation of which the employee complains, or who has been designated by the employer on the notice required under [N.J.S.A. 34:19-7]." N.J.S.A. 34:19-2.d. *See infra,* §2-10 concerning notice.

101. A "public body" means the United States Congress; the State legislature, any popularly-elected local governmental body, or any member or employee thereof; any federal, State or local judiciary (or member or employee thereof); any grand or petit jury; any regulatory, administrative, or public agency or authority (or instrumentality thereof); any law enforcement agency, prosecutorial office, or police or peace officer; any department of an executive branch of government; or any division, board, bureau, office, committee, or commission of any of the foregoing. N.J.S.A. 34:19-2c. *Compare Fioriglio v. City of Atlantic City,* 996 F. Supp. 379, 393 (D.N.J. 1998) (plaintiff's campaign comments criticizing incumbent mayor during plaintiff's unsuccessful bid for mayor's office, constitute statements made to public body) *with Casamasino v City of Jersey City,* 304 N.J. Super. 226, 242 (App. Div. 1997) ("[W]e have some reservations as to whether the tax assessor's public criticism of the mayor's proposed tax revaluation and reassessment methods at a public forum convened for the very purpose of inviting public comment falls within the intendment of CEPA's 'whistle blower' protection."), *certif. granted,* 156 N.J. 383 (1998).

c. Objects to, or refuses to participate[105] in any activity, policy or practice which the employee reasonably believes:

(1) is in violation of a law, or a rule or regulation promulgated pursuant to law;

(2) is fraudulent or criminal; or

(3) is incompatible with a clear mandate of public policy concerning the public health, safety or welfare or protection of the environment.[106]

The Supreme Court has made it clear that CEPA is limited to whistleblowing that serves a public purpose. In *Mehlman v. Mobil Oil Corp.*, the court stated that a "salutary limiting principle [of CEPA] is that the offensive activity must pose a threat of public harm, not merely private harm or harm only to the aggrieved employee."[107] Employee protests which are not reasonable may not be protected under CEPA:

> We do not suggest that CEPA provides protection to an employee only where the least intrusive method is used to object to an employer's practices or procedures. Nevertheless, the statutory scheme cannot be read so broadly as to provide blanket immu-

---

102. It is the employer's affirmative conduct, or complicity in the illegal conduct of employees, that establishes the basis for liability under CEPA. *See Higgins v. Pascack Valley Hospital*, 307 N.J. Super 277, 296-300 (App. Div.) *certif granted*, 156 N.J. 405 (1998); *Bowles v. City of Camden*, 993 F. Supp. 255, 270-271 (D.N.J. 1998). An employee who objects to illegal conduct that is not attributable to the employer, but only to a fellow employee, does not have a claim under CEPA. *See Higgins*, 307 N.J. Super. at 294, 296-297, 299-300; *Demas v. National Westminster Bank*, 313 N.J. Super. 47, 52 (App. Div. 1998). In *Higgins*, the court specifically ruled that the illegal conduct at issue must be "of the employer" or "by the employer," even under N.J.S.A. 34:19-3c, which does not contain such an express limitation. *See Higgins*, 307 N.J. Super. at 293-294.

103. As originally enacted, CEPA pertained only to conduct of the employer. Effective Dec. 29, 1989 it was expanded to include other employers with whom the employee's employer has a business relationship. L.1989, c.220. The stated purpose of the amendment is "to discourage collusion between employers for the purpose of inhibiting disclosure by their employees of violations of law committed by either employer." Assembly Labor Committee, *Statement to Assembly No. 661*, reprinted following N.J.S.A. 34:19-3.

104. This provision applies to reports of such misconduct committed by a partner in the other employer. *See Barratt v. Cushman & Wakefield of N.J., Inc.*, 144 N.J. 120 (1996). A business relationship between two employers must exist at the time of disclosure, not necessasrily when the illegal act occurred. *Id.*

105. Thus, CEPA permits employees to refuse to perform work assigned them, so long as they "reasonably believe" it falls into one of the categories described in N.J.S.A. 34:19-3. That right has been described as extraordinary and contrary to the industrial relations principle of work first, grieve later. Mayer, "N.J.'s Whistleblower Act," 119 *N.J.L.J.* 353 (1987). *See Abbamont v. Piscataway Twp. Bd. of Educ.*, 138 N.J. 405, 424 (1994) (adequate ventilation in a school shop, as outlined in an official safety guide incorporating public health regulations, constituted a clear mandate of public policy concerning the public health, safety or welfare). However, an employee who merely questions and disagrees with his employer's practices and is concerned about their potential legal impact, has not engaged in "whistleblowing" activity protected by CEPA. *See Blackburn v. United Parcel Service, Inc.*, 3 F. Supp. 2d 504, 517 (D.N.J. 1998).

> nity to an employee for assaultive or destructive conduct, however well intended.[108]

CEPA applies only to an employer's actions taken in connection with the employment relationship established between the employer and employee,[109] and thus does not apply to an employer's post-employment negative job references concerning the paintiff.[110]

To state a prima facie case under CEPA, a plaintiff must allege that he was engaged in an activity protected by CEPA, he was subjected to an adverse employment decision, and that there was a casual connection between the two.[111] Some

---

106. N.J.S.A. 34:19-3 (footnotes added). As in a common law action for violation of public policy under *Pierce v. Ortho Pharmaceutical Corp.*, 84 N.J. 58 (1980), the detemination whether a CEPA plaintiff has established the existence of a clear mandate of public policy is an issue of law for the court to decide. *See Mehlman v. Mobil Oil Corp.*, 153 N.J. 163, 187 (1998) ("Its resolution often will implicate a value judgement that must be made by the court, and not by the jury."). The judge in a CEPA action "must first find and enunciate the specific terms of a statute or regulation, or the clear expression of public policy, which would be violated if the facts as alleged are true. When the judge has, as a matter of law, identified such a statute, regulation, or other clear source or expression of public policy, the matter may then go to the jury for determination of any disputed facts, and for a finding as to whether there has been a retaliatory action against the at-will employee for either objecting to or refusing to participate in activity reasonably and objectively believed (1) to violate a statute or regulation, or (2) to be incompatible with a 'clear mandate of public policy.' *Fineman v. New Jersey Dep't of Human Servs.*, 272 N.J. Super. 606, 620 (App. Div.) *certif. denied*, 138 N.J. 267 (1994); *see also Demas v. National Westminster Bank*, 313 N.J. Super. 47, 53 (App. Div. 1998); *Falco v. Community Medical Center*, 296 N.J. Super. 298, 310 (App. Div. 1997), *certif. denied*, 153 N.J. 405 (1998). In determining whether a clear mandate of public policy exists, the court must balance the competing interests of employer, employee, other affected individuals, and the public. *Fineman v. New Jersay Dep't of Human Servs.*, 272 N.J. Super. at 623. Thus, the Appellate Division has held that a physician who refused to treat patients as a protest of understaffing acted improperly; that no clear ethical and legal mandate of public policy requires a physician to refuse to treat patients in distress. *Id.* at 624.

The scope of N.J.S.A. 34:19-3c (3) was broadly construed by the court in *Mehlman,* in which the Supreme Court held that CEPA protects a New Jersey employee who objects to the violation of a clear mandate of public policy that threatens to harm citizens of other states or countries. *See Mehlman v. Mobil Oil Corp.*, 153 N.J. at 196. The Court found a clear mandate of public policy in the guidelines of the Japanese Petroleum Association, an industry association of which Mobil was a member. *See id.* at 176, 192.

107. *Mehlman v. Mobil Oil Corp.* 153 N.J. 163, 188 (1998); *see also Demas v. National Westminster Bank*, 313 N.J. Super. 47, 51, 53-54 (App. Div. 1998) (plaintiff's claim dismissed because plaintiff failed to identify any public, as opposed to private, harm threatened by the conduct at issue); *Littman v. Firestone Tire & Rubber Co.*, 715 F. Supp. 90, 93 (S.D.N.Y. 1989) (reporting another employee's alleged fraud against the employer was not the type of activity [CEPA] was designed to combat, or whose disclosure the statute was designed to protect"); *Smith v. Travelers Mortgage Service*, 699 F. Supp. 1080, 1083 (D.N.J. 1998) (filing of an individual complaint of discrimination with the EEOC is not an activity protected by CEPA because no reporting of a public harm was involved).

108. *Haworth v. Deborah Heart & Lung Ctr.*, 271 N.J. Super. 502, 506 (App. Div. 1994) (CEPA did not protect employee who destroyed blood samples without warning or other written protest of the allegedly improper manner in which they were taken and maintained); *see also Fineman v. New Jersey Dep't of Human Servs.*, 272 N.J. Super. 606, 619 (App. Div.) ("In reviewing at-will employee terminations in a regulated setting [such as a hospital], courts should give consideration to whether the regulatory scheme contains effective alternate means for the employee to voice concern about a perceived policy violation."), *certif. denied*, 138 N.J. 267 (1994).

109. *See Young v. Schering Corp.* 141 N.J. 16, 31-32 (1995).

110. *See Beck v. Tribert*, 312 N.J. Super. 335, 342-345 (App. Div.), *certif. denied*, 156 N.J. 424 (1998).

courts have applied the burden-shifting standards ordinarily applicable to employment discrimination actions when addressing questions under CEPA, although its applicability to CEPA has not formally been addressed by a state court.[112]

2-9 Internal Complaints/Exhaustion

To enjoy the protection of CEPA, an employee who intends to report alleged wrongdoing to a public body must in normal circumstances advise a supervisor, in writing, and give the supervisor a reasonable opportunity to correct the problem.[113] Internal reporting is not required in emergency situations where the employee reasonably fears physical harm or where the employee is reasonably certain that the practice in question is already known to one or more supervisors.[114]

Along with the requirement of making internal complaints before going public comes additional protection for employees. Retaliation against an employee for making internal complaints about his employer's policies does not state a claim for violation of public policy under common law.[115] Under CEPA, in contrast, several types of internal objections involving violations of law or impacting public safety and welfare are protected.[116]

---

111. *See Bowles v. City of Camden*, 993 F. Supp. 255, 262 (D.N.J. 1998). The court in *Bowles* held that, except in rare cases, in which the decision to discharge takes place immediately after the employer discovers the employee's participation in protected conduct, temporal proximity between the protected conduct and the adverse employment action is insufficient to establish the causation element of a CEPA claim. *See id.* at 264.

112. *See Abbamont v. Piscataway Twp. Bd. of Educ.*, 269 N.J. Super. 11, 25 (App. Div. 1993), *aff'd*, 138 N.J. 405 (1994); *Blackburn v. United Parcel Service, Inc.*, 3 F.Supp. 2d 504, 513 (D.N.J. 1998); *Bowles v. City of Camden*, 993 F. Supp. 255, 262 (D.N.J. 1998); *Fioriglio v. City of Atlantic City*, 996 F. Supp. 379, 393 n. 6 (D.N.J. 1998).

113. N.J.S.A. 34:19-4. *See Abbamont v. Piscataway Twp. Bd. of Educ.*, 269 N.J. Super. 11, 22 (App. Div. 1993), *aff'd*, 138 N.J. 405 (1994) (school principal was a "supervisor"; he had authority to direct and control the work of shop instructor; he also had power to take corrective action). An employee who complains to a supervisor under the statute is not required to make further disclosure. *Id.* at 23.

114. N.J.S.A. 34:19-4.

115. *See Young v. Schering Corp.*, 141 N.J. 16, 27 (1995) ("Under [the common law cause of action], however, there must be actual notification to a governmental body of illegal employer conduct."); *House v. Carter-Wallace, Inc.*, 232 N.J.Super. 42, 49 (App. Div.) ("The mere voicing of opposition to corporate policy within a corporation provides an insufficient foundation for assertion of a *Pierce* claim."), *certif. denied*, 117 N.J. 154 (1989); *Citizens State Bank of New Jersey v. Libertelli*, 215 N.J.Super. 190, 194-96 (App. Div. 1987) (internal protests of alleged regulatory improprieties of board members did not violate public policy as expressed in New Jersey Banking Act); *Giudice v. Drew Chemical Corp.*, 210 N.J.Super. 32, 36 (App. Div.) (private investigation of possible criminal activities of fellow employees does not implicate same public policy consideration as if plaintiffs had been fired for cooperating with law enforcement officials), *certif. granted and remanded and certif. denied*, 104 N.J. 465 (1986); *Smith v. Ebasco Constructors, Inc.*, 1988 WL 44143, pp. *3-4 (D.N.J. 1988) (internal reporting of extreme cost overruns and delay on publicly funded project did not implicate public policy).

2-10 Notice

Employers are required to post notices of employees' rights and obligations under CEPA, and to "use other appropriate means to keep their employees so informed."[117] The notice must include the name of a person designated to receive the internal complaint required by N.J.S.A. 34:19-4 to be made before making a report to a public body.[118]

2-11 Procedure

An employee or former employee may maintain a civil action under CEPA in any court of competent jurisdiction.[119] Suit must be commenced within one year.[120] There is a right to trial by jury.[121]

The full panoply of tort damages is available, including injunctive relief;[122] reinstatement of a former employee to the same or equivalent position;[123] rein-

---

116. Employers are specifically prohibited from retaliating against an employee because the employee (1) has disclosed or threatened to disclose to a supervisor an activity, policy or practice that the employee reasonably believes is in violation of a law, or a rule or regulation promulgated pursuant to law; (2) has objected to or refused to participate in any activity, policy or practice which the employee reasonably believes is (a) in violation of a law, or a rule or regulation promulgated pursuant to law, (b) fraudulent, (c) criminal, or (d) incompatible with a clear mandate of public policy concerning the public health, safety or welfare or protection of the environment. N.J.S.A. 34:19-3.

117. N.J.S.A. 34:19-7.

118. N.J.S.A. 34:19-7, -4.

119. N.J.S.A. 34:19-5. Some courts have held that CEPA claims are subject to arbitration under individual agreements to arbitrate. *Young v. Prudential Ins. Co.*, 297 N.J. Super. 605, 615-617 (App. Div.), *certif. denied*, 149 N.J. 408 (1997); *Bleumer v. Parkway Ins. Co.*, 277 N.J. Super. 378, 396-97 (Law Div. 1994). *See generally Gilmer v. Interstate/Johnson Lane Corp.*, 500 U.S. 20 (1991). *Lepore v. National Tool & Manufacturing Co.*, 224 N.J. Super. 463 (App. Div. 1988), *aff'd*, 115 N.J. 226 (1989), *cert. denied*, 493 U.S. 954 (1989), is "confined to claims for arbitration of CEPA claims arising under collective bargaining agreements and does not extend to similar claims arising under private employment agreements." *Bleumer v. Parkway Ins. Co.*, 277 N.J. Super. at 397.

120. N.J.S.A. 34:19-5. Compare this with the longer limitations period available for common law claims for violation of public policy under *Pierce v. Ortho Pharmaceutical Corp.*, 84 N.J. 58 (1980); 2-5, *supra*. In *Keelan v. Bell Communications Research*, 289 N.J. Super. 531, 540-41 (App. Div. 1996), the court found that the limitations period began to run on plaintiff's date of actual discharge and not on the earlier date when he was notified of the discharge. In *Boody v. Township of Cherry Hill*, 997 F. Supp. 562 (D.N.J. 1997), the court held that the statute of limitations starts to run no later than the day on which an employee tenders his resignation. *See id.* at 567-568. The *Boody* court also held that because an employer's representations to a former employee's prospective employers cannot establish the basis for a CEPA claim, such representations cannot constitute a "continuing violation" and toll the limitations period. *See id.*; *see also Beck v. Tribert*, 312 N.J. Super. 335, 342-345 (App. Div.), *certif. denied*, 156 N.J. 424 (1998) (rejecting application of the "continuing violation" doctrine).

121. N.J.S.A. 34:19-5. Although the statute states that "The court may also order.... punitive damages," the Supreme Court has held that punitive damages issues are to be tried to the jury. *Abbamont v. Piscataway Twp. Bd. of Educ.*, 138 N.J. 405, 432 (1994).

122. Issuance of an injunction is discretionary and the normal standard of proof must be satisfied, including proof of irreparable harm. There is no presumption of irreparable harm inherent in a CEPA violation. *Smith v. Travelers Mortgage Services*, 699 F.Supp. 1080, 1085 (D.N.J. 1988).

statement of full fringe benefits and seniority rights; compensation for lost wages and benefits; and punitive damages.[124] A claim for *per quod* damages by the plaintiff's spouse has been rejected. [125] Costs and attorney's fees are available to both employees and employers; however, an employer may not recover costs and fees unless the court, on motion, "determines that [the] action brought by an employee ... was without basis in law or in fact."[126] Employers may also be subject to a civil fine of not more than $1,000 for their first violation of CEPA and not more than $5,000 for each subsequent violation.[127] Such fines are to be paid to the State Treasurer for deposit into the General Fund.[128]

CEPA specifically provides that it does not diminish any rights employees may have under federal or state law or regulation or under any collective bargaining agreement.[129] However, once an action is instituted under CEPA, the employee's rights and remedies under any other contract, collective bargaining agreement, state law, rule or regulation or under the common law will be deemed waived.[130]

---

123. The standards governing reinstatement in actions brought under the Law Against Discrimination also apply to CEPA actions. *See Abbamont v. Piscataway Twp. Bd. of Educ.*, 138 N.J. 405, 418 (1994). In arguing against reinstatement, an employer may not rely upon "animosity between the parties which is solely the product of the employer's violation of CEPA and the employee's efforts to vindicate his or her rights under this legislation." *Abbamont v. Piscatawy Twp. Bd. of Educ.*, 314 N.J. Super. 293, 307 (App. Div. 1998).

124. N.J.S.A. 34:19-5. Punitive damages may be awarded against public entities on CEPA claims. *Abbamont v. Piscataway Twp. Bd. of Educ.*, 138 N.J. 405, 432 (1994). In determining whether an employer is liable for the actions of supervisors under CEPA, the standards established by the Supreme Court in *Lehmann v. Toys 'R' Us, Inc.*, 132 N.J. 587 (1993) (sexual harassment case) apply. *Abbamont*, 138 N.J. at 418. "Therefore, in CEPA actions, 'the employer should be liable for punitive damages only in the event of actual participation by upper management or willful indifference.'" *Id.* at 419. Strict liability applies for relief that is equitable in nature, and "agency principles, which include negligence, should be applied to decide if an employer is liable for compensatory damages that exceed that equitable relief." *Id.* at 417 (citation omitted). *See generally Harrington v. Lauer*, 893 F.Supp. 352 (D.N.J. 1995) (motion to strike plaintiff's compensatory damages claim on the ground that he had been paid full salary while his claim was pending denied; "all remedies available in common-law tort actions are available to a party who prevails under CEPA... Thus, in the event that plaintiff prevails on his CEPA claim, he will not be restricted by the fact that the Board has already compensated him for the full value of his employment contract.")

125. *See Catalane v. Gillian Instrument Corp.*, 271 N.J. Super. 476, 500 (App. Div.), *certif. denied*, 136 N.J. 298 (1994); *Jones v. Jersey City Medical Center*, 20 F. Supp. 2d 770, 773 (D.N.J. 1998).

126. N.J.S.A. 34:19-5, -6. *See Buccinna v. Micheletti*, 311 N.J. Super. 557 (App. Div. 1998) (imposition of costs against plaintiff was inappropriate because there was no evidence of plaintiff's bad faith, and no finding that the suit was either frivolous or without basis in law or fact); Duffy, *201* "New Jersey Counsel Fees Statutes", 127 *N.J.L.J.* 340, 357 (Feb. 7, 1991). An employee who through the exercise of reasonably diligent efforts realizes after filing his complaint that there is no basis in fact or law for his CEPA claim may avoid the imposition of costs and fees by filing a voluntary dismissal within a reasonable time after determining the employer would not be liable for damages. N.J.S.A. 34:19-6. *See Moody v. Township of Marlboro*, 855 F. Supp. 685, 689 (D.N.J. 1994) (awards of attorney's fees under CEPA are "strictly discretionary with the court;" also noting that deterrence is an essential component of any award of reasonable attorney's fees to a plaintiff under CEPA; reducing $175,793.75 fee request to $25,000 in case where jury awarded plaintiff $780), *aff'd.*, 54 F.3d 769 (3d Cir. 1995).

127. N.J.S.A. 34:19-5g.

128. N.J.S.A. 34:19-5g.

In *Young v. Schering Corp.*, the Supreme Court held that the waiver "applies only to those causes of action that require a finding of retaliatory conduct that is actionable under CEPA. The waiver exception does not apply to those causes of action that are substantially independent of the CEPA claim."[131] Thus, it would appear that an employee may maintain a Pierce action for violation of the public policy expressed in CEPA, instead of -- but not in addition to -- an action under CEPA.[132]

The statute suggests that the waiver takes place when a CEPA claim is filed, that is, upon the "institution of an action."[133] However, the Supreme Court in *Young* suggested, albeit in dicta, that the waiver may not be effective until later in the proceedings.[134] The Appellate Division has held that the pleading of a CEPA claim that is unavailable to plaintiff does not constitute a waiver of common law claims under CEPA.[135]

One court has held that the failure to refer specifically to CEPA in a release of claims against the employer may create a fact issue as to the voluntariness of the release.[136]

---

129. N.J.S.A. 34:19-8. *See Maher v. New Jersey Transit Rail Operations, Inc.*, 239 N.J.Super. 213 (App. Div. 1990) (plaintiff's CEPA claim not pre-empted by the Railway Labor Act because Federal Railway Safety Act's limited whistleblower provision related to enforcement of federal rail safety laws, and because resolution of plaintiff's claim did not require interpretation of his collective bargaining agreement), *aff'd in part, rev'd on other grounds*, 125 N.J. 455 (1991). *See generally Abbamont v. Piscataway Twp. Bd. of Educ.*, 238 N.J.Super. 603 (App. Div. 1990), *aff'd* 138 N.J. 405 (1994).

130. N.J.S.A. 34:19-8. CEPA's waiver provision has been described as unique. Westman, *Whistleblowing: The Law of Retaliatory Discharge*, p.69 (1991).

131. *Young v. Schering Corp.*, 141 N.J. 16, 29 (1995); *see also Mehlman v. Mobil Oil Corp.*, 291 N.J. Super. 98, 135-139, 141-143 (App. Div. 1996) (maintenance of CEPA claim constitutes waiver of "prima facie tort" claim because "the finding of retaliatory conduct remains essential in both"; it did not constitute waiver of defamation claim based upon alleged puublication of reasons for discharge), *aff'd*, 153 N.J. 163 (1998); *Falco v. Community Medical Center*, 296 N.J. Super. 298, 318 (App. Div. 1997) ("A claim must have a basis independent of the CEPA claim in order to be exempt from the waiver provision."), *certif. denied*, 153 N.J. 405 (1998); *Flaherty v The Enclave*, 255 N.J. Super. 407, 414 (Law Div. 1992) (institution of a CEPA action does not constitute a waiver of all claims arising out of the employment relationship, only those based upon the same proofs or rights as the CEPA claim); *Boody v. Township of Cherry Hill*, 997 F. Supp. 562, 569 (D.N.J. 1997) (CEPA waiver provision is "substantive" state law that federal court exercising supplemental jurisdiction must apply; state law claims based upon same retaliatory conduct supporting CEPA claims are waived); *Lynch v. New Deal Delivery Service, Inc.*, 974 F. Supp. 441, 456 (D.N.J. 1997) (claim of intentional infliction of emotional distress in conjunction with a retaliatory discharge falls within CEPA's waiver provision).

132. *See Catalane v. Gilian Instrument Corp.*, 271 N.J. Super. 476, 492-493 (App. Div.) (plaintiff's public policy claim alleging that he was dismissed in retaliation for his threats of whistleblowing was barred by his assertion of the same claim under CEPA), *certif. denied*, 136 N.J. 289 (1994). For a more general discussion of *Pierce* actions based upon statutory rights, *see §2-6, supra.*

133. *See* N.J.S.A. 34:19-8; *see also Lynch v. New Deal Delivery Service, Inc.*, 974 F Supp. 441, 456 (D.N.J. 1997); *Flaherty v. The Enclave*, 255 N.J. Super. 407, 414 (Law Div. 1992).

134. *Young v. Schering Corp.*, 141 N.J. at 32 ("[T]he meaning of 'institution of an action' [as used in N.J.S.A. 34:19-8] could conceivably contemplate an election of remedies with restrictions in which the election is not consisdered to have been made until discovery is complete or the time of a pretrial conference contemplated by Rule 4:25-1.").

IV. OTHER RETALIATION

2-12 Civil Service Whistleblowers

The Civil Service Act makes it unlawful for an appointing authority to "take or threaten to take any action against an employee ... in retaliation for an employee's lawful disclosure of information on the violation of any law or rule, governmental mismanagement or abuse of authority."[137] An employee subjected to such retaliation may appeal the action to the Merit System Board,[138] which is authorized to award back pay, benefits, seniority, and reasonable attorneys' fees to an employee as provided by rule.[139] The appeal must be taken within 20 days of the action or the date on which the employee should reasonably have known of its occurrence.[140]

2-13 Reporting Child Abuse

Individuals who in good faith report alleged child abuse or neglect to the Division of Youth and Family Services are specifically protected from retaliatory discharge or any manner of discrimination with respect to "compensation, hire, tenure or terms, conditions or privileges of employment."[141] An employee so aggrieved may file a cause of action in the Family Part of the Chancery Division of the Superior Court, in either the county in which the discrimination occurred or the county of his residence. The statute specifically authorizes the award of "reinstatement of employment with back pay or other legal or equitable relief."[142]

---

135. *See Ballinger v. Delaware River Port Authority*, 311 N.J. Super. 317, 331-332 (App. Div. 1998) (because defendant Delaware River Port Authority was not subject to suit under CEPA, plaintiff's pleading of a CEPA claim did not constitute a waiver of common law claims); *Crusco v Oakland Care Center, Inc.*, 305 N.J. Super. 605, 612-613 (App. Div. 1997) (because plaintiff's claim was barred by the statute of limitations, common law claim was not waived).

136. *See Keelan v. Bell Communications Research*, 289 N.J. Super. 531, 545 (App. Div. 1996).

137. N.J.S.A. 11A:2-24. Employees in the career, senior executive, and unclassified service are covered. N.J.S.A. 11A:2-24.

138. *Cf. Zamboni v. Stamler*, 847 F.2d 73 (3d Cir.), *cert. denied.*, 488 U.S. 899 (1988).

139. N.J.S.A. 11A:2-22. *See* N.J.A.C. 4A:2-1.5.

140. N.J.A.C. 4A:2-5.2.

141. N.J.S.A. 9:6-8.13.

142. *Id.*

2-14 Informing the Casino Control Commission

The Casino Control Act imposes an affirmative obligation on licensees, registrants, persons required to be qualified under the act, and persons employed by a casino service industry licensed pursuant to the act to inform the Casino Control Commission or the Division of Gaming Enforcement of "any action which they believe would constitute a violation" of the act.[143] It further provides that:

> No person who so informs the commission or the division shall be discriminated against by an applicant, licensee or registrant because of the supplying of such information.[144]

Any person who violates the provisions of N.J.S.A. 5:12-80 is guilty of a fourth-degree crime and subject to a term of imprisonment of not more than 18 months or a fine of up to $100,000 or both.[145]

2-15 Informing the Ombudsman for the Institutionalized Elderly

State agencies and facilities are prohibited from taking discriminatory, disciplinary, or retaliatory action against, among others, an employee on account of (1) any communication by him with the Office of the Ombudsman for the Institutionalized Elderly or (2) "any information given or disclosed by him in good faith to aid the office in carrying out its duties and responsibilities."[146] Any person who knowingly or willfully violates that prohibition is guilty of a crime of the fourth degree.[147] Although the Office of Ombudsman for the Institutionalized Elderly is authorized to bring suit in any court of competent jurisdiction to enforce any of the powers enumerated in the act,[148] no remedies for employees subjected to retaliation thereunder are provided.[149]

---

143. N.J.S.A. 5:12-80.g.

144. *Id.*.

145. N.J.S.A. 5:12-112; N.J.S.A. 2C:43-6(a)(4).

146. N.J.S.A. 52:27G-14(a).

147. A crime of the fourth degree carries a fine of up to $7,500 and imprisonment of up to 18 months. N.J.S.A. 2C:43-6(a)(4), -3(b).

148. N.J.S.A. 52:27G-14(c).

149. *See Crusco v. Oakland Care Center, Inc.*, 305 N.J. Super. 605, 616 (App. Div. 1997) ("There is nothing in the [Ombudsman] Act that evinces any legislative intention to create private causes of action for the benefit of persons reporting the conduct or conditions the Act was designed to address."). The court noted in dicta, however, that an employee subject to retaliation in violation of the Ombudsman Act may have a common law wrongful discharge claim. *See id.* at 616-617.

2-16 Reporting Abuse of Vulnerable Adults

The Adult Protective Services Act prohibits employers from taking discriminatory or retaliatory actions against any individual who reports the abuse, neglect, or exploitation of a vulnerable adult to the county protective services provider.[150] A "vulnerable adult" is a person "18 years of age or older who resides in a community setting and who, because of a physical or mental illness, disability or deficiency, lacks sufficient understanding or capacity to make, communicate, or carry out decisions concerning his well-being...."[151] The statute further provides that

> An employer or any other person shall not discharge, demote or reduce the salary of an employee because the employee reported information in good faith pursuant to this act.[152]

A person who violates this section is subject to a fine of up to $1,000.[153]

2-17 Refusing to Perform Abortions

The "Conscience Law"[154] provides that no person shall be required to perform or assist in the performance of an abortion or sterilization, and that:

> The refusal to perform, assist in the performance of, or provide abortion services or sterilization procedures shall not constitute grounds for civil or criminal liability, disciplinary action or discriminatory treatment.[155]

2-18 Exercising Rights Granted by the Right to Know Law

The Right to Know Law prohibits employers from discharging, disciplining, penalizing, or otherwise discriminating against an employee because the employee or his employee representative has exercised a right under that law.[156] Aggrieved employees may pursue an administrative remedy by filing a com-

---

150. N.J.S.A. 52:27D-409a, 409d.

151. N.J.S.A. 52:27D-407.

152. N.J.S.A. 52:27D-409d.

153. *Id.*

154. N.J.S.A. 2A:65A-1 to -4.

155. N.J.S.A. 2A:65A-3. *See Doe v. Bridgeton Hospital Ass'n, Inc.* 71 N.J. 478, 490-91 (1976) (Conscience Law not applicable to non-sectarian, non-profit hospitals), *stay denied*, 429 U.S. 1086, *cert. denied*, 433 U.S. 914 (1977).

156. N.J.S.A. 34:5A-17.

plaint with the Commissioner of Labor, who, upon a finding of cause for the complaint, may refer it to the Office of Administrative Law (OAL) to be conducted as a contested case.[157] No alternative enforcement mechanism is provided in the statute.

2-19 Exercising Rights Under the Worker Health and Safety Act

The Worker Health and Safety Act prohibits employers from discharging, disciplining, or otherwise discriminating against an employee because the employee has filed a complaint, instituted a proceeding, testified, or exercised any right thereunder.[158] An aggrieved employee may file a complaint with the commissioner against the "person" alleged to have committed the violation, but must do so within 180 days of gaining knowledge that the violation occurred.[159]

The act specifically provides that it is not to be deemed "to diminish the rights of any employee under any law, rule or regulation or under any collective negotiation agreement."[160] The Federal Occupational Safety and Health Act ("OSHA") does not pre-empt the Worker Health and Safety Act to the extent it provides a private cause of action for retaliatory discharge, at least in so far as allowing removal to federal court based on "complete pre-emption."[161]

2-20 Exercising Rights Under the Law Against Discrimination

The Law Against Discrimination makes it unlawful:

> For any person to take reprisals against any person because that person has opposed any practices or acts forbidden under this act or because that person has filed a complaint, testified or assisted in any proceeding under this act or to coerce, intimidate, threaten or interfere with any person in the exercise or enjoy-

---

157. Proceedings are to be conducted in accordance with the Administrative Procedure Act. If the Commissioner or the employee introduces evidence that he exercised a right under the Law in the relevant time frame, the burden shifts to the employer to show just cause for the discipline with clear and convincing evidence. N.J.S.A. 34:5A-17. *See* Chapter 4, §§4-49 to 4-51 for a detailed discussion of OAL proceedings under the Law Against Discrimination.

158. N.J.S.A. 34:6A-45. The statute is somewhat unclear in that it refers to the filing of complaints, *etc.* "under or related to this section," and the section refers only to the retaliation. Thus read precisely as written, N.J.S.A. 34:6A-45 prohibits only retaliation for complaining about retaliation. A more logical interpretation would read "act" for "section" in subsection 34:6A-45(a).

159. N.J.S.A. 34:6A-45(b). The court is authorized to restrain violations of that section and to order all appropriate relief, including rehiring or reinstatement of the employee to his former position with back pay.

160. N.J.S.A. 34:6A-45(c).

161. *Kozar v. AT&T*, 923 F. Supp. 67 (D.N.J. 1996).

ment of, or on account of that person having aided or encouraged any other person in the exercise or enjoyment of, any right granted or protected by this act.[162]

2-21 Pursuing Workers' Compensation Benefits

The Workers' Compensation Law makes it unlawful to discharge or discriminate against an employee because he has claimed or attempted to claim workers' compensation benefits or because he has testified in any workers' compensation proceeding.[163]

An employer[164] who violates this section is potentially subject to several sanctions. First, the violation may be prosectuted as a disorderly persons offense, for which the employer may be subject to a fine of between $100 and $1,000, or imprisonment of up to 60 days, or both.[165] Second, an employee may commence an administrative proceeding with the Commissioner of Labor, in which the employee would be entitled to seek reinstatement and lost wages.[166] Third, an employee could elect instead to file a common law action in Superior Court, in which the employee could seek the full range of tort remedies available in such actions, including punitive damages.[167] Fourth, the Commissioner of Labor may impose a penalty not exceeding $1,000 per violation through the institution of a summary proceeding.[168] The employer alone and not the employer's insurance carrier is liable for any penalties.[169]

In order to establish a prima facie case of retaliatory discharge, an employee must show that he made or attempted to make a claim for workers' compensation benefits, and was discharged in retaliation for making that claim.[170] Although the timing of the employee's discharge may be significant, it is not, standing alone, sufficient to establish a prima facie case of retaliatory discharge.[171] An employer may terminate an employee pursuant to the neutral application of the employer's

162. N.J.S.A. 10:5-12(d). *See* discussion in Chapter 4, *infra* §4-26.

163. N.J.S.A. 34:15-39.1. *See also* discussion *supra* at §§2-3:4.

164. The immunities conferred by the Tort Claims Act upon public entities and employees do not apply to claims arising under this section of the Worker's Compensation Law. *See Brook v. April*, 294 N.J. Super. 90, 101 (App. Div. 1996).

165. N.J.S.A. §34:15-39.1.

166. *Id.; Lally v. Copygraphics*, 173 N.J. Super. 162, 178 (App. Div. 1980), *aff'd*, 85 N.J. 668 (1981).

167. *See Lally v. Copygraphics*, 85 N.J. 668, 670 (1981), *aff'g*, 173 N.J. Super. 162, 179-183 (App. Div. 1980); *see also* discussion *supra* at §2-3:4(1). A plaintiff who files a civil action in Superior Court must do so within two years. *See Labree v. Mobil Oil Corp.*, 300 N.J. Super. 234, 244 (App. Div. 1997).

168. N.J.S.A. 34:15-39.2.

169. N.J.S.A. 34:15-39.3.

absenteeism policy, even if a substantial number of those absenses were attributable to a work-related injury.[172]

2-22 Farm Laborers

The Farm Labor Law[173] makes it unlawful for any crew leader to retaliate against any present or prospective seasonal farm worker for exercising "any right secured under the laws and regulations of the State or Federal Government."[174] A rebuttable presumption of retaliation arises if adverse action is taken against a worker within 60 days after an attempt by him to exercise any right under a law or regulation relating to farm labor.[175]

Workers may maintain a civil suit against a crew leader for violation of this section.[176] They may seek reinstatement, back wages, costs, attorney's fees, and "exemplary damages in treble the amount of back wages found due."[177]

2-23 School Employees

The Public School Safety Law requires the filing of a report by any employee who observes or has direct knowledge of any act of violence on school property,[178] and makes it unlawful for any board of education to discharge or in any manner discriminate against an employee because he has fulfilled that obligation.[179]

---

170. *Cerracchio v. Alden Leeds, Inc.*, 223 N.J. Super. 435, 442 (App. Div. 1988); *Galante v. Sandoz, Inc.*, 192 N.J. Super. 403, 407 (Law. Div. 1983), *aff'd,* 196 N.J. Super. 568 (App. Div. 1984), *appeal dismissed,* 103 N.J. 492 (1986); *Morris v. Siemens Components, Inc.*, 928 F. Supp. 486, 493 (D.N.J. 1996); *Kube v. New Penn Motor Express, Inc.*, 865 F. Supp. 221, 230 (D.N.J. 1994). Some courts have applied the burden-shifting analysis set forth in *McDonnell Douglas Corp. v. Green*, 411 U.S. 792, 93 S.Ct. 1817 (1973). Under this approach, once the employee establishes a prima facie case, the employer must set forth a non-retaliatory reason for its actions. *See Morris*, 928 F. Supp. at 493; *Kube*, 865 F. Supp. at 230. For a general discussion of the burden-shifting analysis as used in discrimination and retaliation actions under the Law Against Discrimination, see discussion, *supra*, §§4-32 and 4-34.

171. *Morris v. Siemens Components, Inc.*, 928 F. Supp. 486, 493 (D.N.J. 1986).

172. *Galante v. Sandoz, Inc.*, 192 N.J. Super. 403, 409-411 (Law. Div. 1983), *aff'd,* 196 N.J. Super. 568 (App. Div. 1984), *appeal dismissed,* 103 N.J. 492 (1986).

173. "An act providing for the registration and regulation of farm labor crew leaders, and providing penalties for its violation." N.J.S.A. 34:8A-10, *et seq.*

174. N.J.S.A. 34:8A-10.1. Acts specifically prohibited are termination, suspension, demotion, transfer, or "adverse action."

175. N.J.S.A. 34:8A-10.1. The rights giving rise to the presumption are more particularly described as: "any right secured under the provisions of this act or under the laws and regulations of the State or any agency or political subdivision thereof which establish the rights of persons engaged in farm labor or which establish duties of employers of persons engaged in farm labor."

176. *Id.*

177. *Id. See* Duffy, *201 New Jersey Counsel Fees Statutes*, 127 N.J.L.J. 340, 357 (Feb. 7, 1991).

178. N.J.S.A. 18A:17-46.

The law provides that any employee discriminated against in this manner shall be reinstated and compensated by the board of education for any lost wages.[180] The Commissioner of Education has jurisdiction to hear and determine, without cost to the parties, all controversies and disputes under the school laws, except those governing higher education, or under the rules of the State Board of Education or of the Commissioner.[181] Controversies and disputes concerning the conduct of school elections are not deemed to arise under the school laws.[182]

2-24 Family Leave Act

As discussed in Chapter 6, the Family Leave Act (FLA) makes it unlawful for an employer to discharge or discriminate against an individual[183] for opposing a practice made unlawful by that statute.[184] The FLA also makes it unlawful for a person[185] to discharge or discriminate against an individual because he (1) has filed a charge or instituted a proceeding related to the FLA; (2) has given or is about to give information in connection with an inquiry or proceeding related to a right provided by the FLA; or (3) has testified or is about to testify in an inquiry or proceeding related to a right provided by the FLA.[186]

2-25 Asserting Rights Under the Minimum Wage Law

As discussed in Chapter 8, §§210 through 215, the Minimum Wage Law[187] mandates minimum wages and maximum hours of work, to promote the health and well-being of employees and provide compensation fairly and reasonably commensurate with the value of services rendered.[188] It is a violation of the law and a disorderly persons offense for an employer to discharge or otherwise discriminate against an employee because the employee (1) has made a complaint to his employer, the Commissioner of Labor, the Director, or their representa-

179. N.J.S.A. 18A:17-47.

180. The employee will not be entitled to either reinstatement or compensation if he "shall cease to be qualified to perform the duties of his employment." *Id.*

181. N.J.S.A. 18A:6-9.

182. *Id.*

183. The prohibition is not limited to discrimination against employees, but includes any individual.

184. N.J.S.A. 34:11B-9(b).

185. Again, note the expansive coverage of all persons, not just employers.

186. N.J.S.A. 34:11B-9(c).

187. N.J.S.A. 34:11-56a to 34:11-56a30.

188. N.J.S.A. 34:11-56a; *Council of New Jersey Hairdressers, Inc. v. Male*, 68 N.J.Super. 381, 385 (App. Div. 1961).

tives, that he has not been paid wages in accordance with the Minimum Wage Law; (2) has instituted or is about to institute any proceeding under or related to that law; (3) has testified or is about to testify in any such proceeding; or (4) has served or is about to serve on a wage board.[189]

Employers committing such an offense will be fined,[190] and will be ordered to offer the employee reinstatement, to correct any discriminatory action, and to pay back pay.[191] Administrative penalties may also be imposed.[192]

2-26 Asserting Rights Under the Prevailing Wage Law

The Prevailing Wage Law, discussed in Chapter 8, §216, mandates minimum wage levels on certain public works, designed to ensure that such public employees receive compensation comparable to that enjoyed by union employees in the private sector.[193]

It is a violation of the Prevailing Wage Law and a disorderly persons offense for an employer to discharge or otherwise discriminate against an employee because the employee (1) has made a complaint to the employer, to the public body for which work is being performed, or to the Commissioner of Labor that he has not been paid wages in accordance with that law; (2) has instituted or is about to institute any proceeding under or related to that law; or (3) has testified or is about to testify in any proceeding under the law.[194]

An employer convicted of such a violation will be fined not less than $100, nor more than $1,000.[195] Administrative penalties of up to $250 for the first violation, and up to $500 for each subsequent violation, may also be imposed by the Commissioner.[196]

---

189. N.J.S.A. 34:11-56a24; N.J.A.C. 12:56-1.3. Wage boards are discussed in Chapter 8, *infra,* §§8-5:5 to 8-5:7.

190. N.J.S.A. 34:11-56a24; N.J.A.C. 12:56-1.3. The fine is not less than $100, nor more than $1,000. N.J.S.A. 34:11-56a24 as amended by L.1991, c.205.

191. N.J.S.A. 34:11-56a24.

192. *Id.* For a complete discussion of the administrative penalty provision, added to the Minimum Wage Law in 1991, see Chapter 8, *infra,* §§8-8.

193. N.J.S.A. 34:11-56.25; *Horn v. Serritella Bros., Inc.*, 190 N.J.Super. 280, 283 (App. Div. 1983), quoting *Cipparulo v. Friedland*, 139 N.J.Super. 142, 148 (App. Div. 1976).

194. N.J.S.A. 34:11-56.39.

195. N.J.S.A. 34:11-56.39.

196. *Id.* The administrative penalty provision of the Prevailing Wage Law was added in 1991. L.1991, c.205. It is described in more detail in Chapter 8, *infra,* §8-10:5.

2-27 Attending Court for Jury Service

The Court Organization and Civil Code forbids an employer to "penalize ... threaten, or otherwise coerce" an employee regarding that employment because the employee is required to attend court for jury service.[197] An employer who does so is guilty of a disorderly persons offense.[198] An employee so penalized by an employer may recover economic damages, an order of reinstatement, and a reasonable attorney's fee.[199] The civil action seeking such relief must be commenced within 90 days of the date of the violation or the completion of jury service, whichever is later.[200]

2-28 Lie Detector Test Prohibition

It is a violation of the Code of Criminal Justice and a disorderly persons offense for an employer to influence, request, or require an employee or prospective employee to take a lie detector test as a condition of employment.[201] Employee consent to such a test does not save the employer from statutory violation for requesting the test.[202] More importantly, even where the employer expressly informed its employees that the test was optional, the employer's "supreme bargaining position" and the number of employees at its worksite who took the test created "[c]ompelling psychological factors" making the request effectively a condition of employment.[203] Similarly, the involvement of the police in the investigation does not insulate the employer from liability for requesting employees to take a lie detector test.[204] The employee need not have actually tak-

197. N.J.S.A. 2B:20-17.a.

198. N.J.S.A. 2B:20-17.b.

199. N.J.S.A. 2B:20-17.c.

200. *Id.*

201. N.J.S.A. 2C:40A-1. This section, enacted in 1981, replaced the former N.J.S.A. 2A:170-90.1, which was repealed in the same year.

202. *State v. Community Distributors*, 123 N.J. Super. 589, 596 (Law Div. 1974), *aff'd*, 64 N.J. 479 (1974) (interpreting predecessor statute); *State v. Berkey Photo Inc.*, 150 N.J. Super. 56 (App. Div. 1977) (interpreting predecessor statute).

203. *State v. Community Distributors*, 123 N.J. Super. at 597-98 (interpreting predecessor statute). "By merely 'requesting' the employees to take the test, the employer is in fact offering the employee an ultimatum—either he takes the test or he puts his character in doubt among the management as well as his fellow workers." *Id.* at 598.

204. *State v. Berkey Photo Inc.*, 150 N.J. Super. 56, 60 (App. Div. 1977) (interpreting predecessor statute). The Appellate Division found "unspoken compulsion" in the context of the employer's request that the employees take the test, and cited the fact that the guilty employee took the test as further proof that the test was a condition of employment. *Id.* at 60-61.

en the test in order for the employer to be convicted of influencing the employee to do so.[205]

Under certain conditions, an employer who manufactures, distributes, or dispenses controlled dangerous substances may require a lie detector test of an employee or prospective employee who is or will be directly involved in handling those substances or will have access to those substances.[206] In these circumstances, the test may not cover a period greater than 5 years preceding the test and must be limited to the work of the employee in handling dangerous substances.[207] Information obtained from the test may not be released to any other employer or person.[208] The employee further has a right to legal representation, a copy of the written report of the test upon request, and a right to present to the employer the result of a second, independently administered lie detector test prior to any personnel decision.[209]

---

205. *State v. Vornado, Inc.*, 155 N.J. Super. 354 (App. Div. 1978) (interpreting predecessor statute).

206. N.J.S.A. 2C:40A-1. In *State v. Community Distributors*, 64 N.J. 479, 485 (1974), *aff'g* 123 N.J. Super. 589, 594 (Law Div. 1973), the Supreme Court found no implied exemption for employers dispensing drugs in the predecessor statute, and upheld the predecessor statute against a constitutional due process challenge. In *Engel v. Township of Woodbridge*, 124 N.J. Super. 307 (App. Div. 1973), the court rejected an implied exemption for testing of police officers.

207. N.J.S.A. 2C:40A-1.

208. *Id.*

209. *Id.*

Chapter 3

Workplace Torts

I. INTRODUCTION

3-1 Overview

Tort claims relating to the employment relationship arise in a variety of circumstances: employee claims against other employees, employee claims against their employers, and third-party claims against employers for the acts of their employees. This chapter addresses seven of the torts that are most frequently asserted in the employment context: intentional infliction of emotional distress, negligent infliction of emotional distress, interference with contract, defamation, fraud, negligent misrepresentation, and negligent hiring or retention of employees. This is not intended to be an exhaustive analysis of tort law in general, but rather, of the ways in which these claims affect the employment relationship and the manner in which the courts have dealt with them in that context.

II. INTENTIONAL INFLICTION OF EMOTIONAL DISTRESS

3-2 General Requirements

To establish an independent cause of action for the tort of outrage, increasingly referred to as the intentional infliction of emotional distress, a plaintiff must show: (1) intent to commit the act and the emotional distress resulting therefrom; (2) conduct that is extreme and outrageous; (3) proximate cause; and (4) emotional distress that is "so severe that no reasonable man could be expected to endure it."[1] Although this tort has become an almost routine allegation in discrimination and wrongful discharge litigation, it is the rare employment case in which it is sustained.

3-3 Intent

To maintain an action for intentional infliction of emotional distress, plaintiff must prove that defendant acted intentionally or recklessly. More specifically, it must be shown that either: (1) the defendant intended both to do the act and to produce emotional distress; or (2) the defendant acted recklessly in deliberate disregard of a high degree of probability that emotional distress would follow.[2]

3-4 Extreme or Outrageous Behavior

"The touchstone of this tort is the extreme and uncommon nature of the actor's conduct."[3] To form the basis of an independent claim for intentional infliction of emotional distress, the conduct involved must be "extraordinarily despicable" to an average member of the community.[4] As described in the Restatement:

> It has not been enough that the defendant has acted with an intent which is tortious or even criminal, or that he has intended to inflict emotional distress, or even that his conduct has been char-

---

1. *Buckley v. Trenton Savings Fund Society,* 111 N.J. 355, 366-67, 368 (1988), quoting Restatement (Second) of Torts, §46 Comment j. (1965); *see Taylor v. Metzger,* 152 N.J. 490, 509 (1998). Where a claim of intentional infliction of emotional distress is based upon an alleged false publication, proof of defamation is a prerequisite: "'There is ... a certain symmetry or parallel between claims of emotional distress and defamation that calls for consistent results. Thus, it comports with first amendment protections to deny an emotional-distress claim based on a false publication that engenders no defamation per se.'... To hold otherwise would permit plaintiff to use the tort of negligent infliction of emotional distress to circumvent defenses to the defamation action." *Salek v. Passaic Collegiate School,* 255 N.J. Super. 355, 361 (App. Div. 1992), quoting *Decker v. Princeton Packet, Inc.,* 116 N.J. 418, 432 (1989).

2. *Buckley v. Trenton Savings Fund Society,* 111 N.J. 355, 366 (1988); *Hume v. Bayer,* 178 N.J. Super. 310, 319 (Law Div. 1981) ("Defendant's actions certainly evidence either an intention to inflict emotional distress or a reckless disregard of the fact that such distress was probable"); *Taylor v. Metzger,* 152 N.J. 490, 513 (1998) (intent could be inferred from defendant's reference to plaintiff as a "jungle bunny"); *Meacham v. Bell Telephone Laboratories, Inc.,* 1990 WL 299805, p. *11 (D.N.J. 1990) (no cause of action for psychological and emotional injuries in workplace where alleged "actions were not committed with the intent to cause [plaintiff] emotional harm, as is required to recover for intentional infliction of emotional distress"). The United States District Court for the District of New Jersey has noted that an employee asserting a claim of intentional infliction of emotional distress against his employer must additionally prove he falls within an exception to the exclusive remedy provision of the Workers' Compensation Law. *Bishop v. Okidata, Inc.,* 864 F. Supp. 416, 427 n.10 (D.N.J. 1994) ("In some states, the workman's compensation statute provides the sole remedy of the employee against the employer, regardless of whether the tort was intentional....The New Jersey tort bar, however, contains an exception for 'intentional wrongs.' N.J.S.A. §34:15-8. To recover for an 'intentional wrong,' a plaintiff must show an 'actual intent' or 'subjective desire' to injure. *Millison v. E.I. du Pont de Nemours & Co.,* 101 N.J. 161, 170-73, 501 A.2d 505 (1985).")

3. *Major League Baseball Promotion v. Colour-Tex, Inc.,* 729 F.Supp. 1035, 1054 (D.N.J. 1990).

4. *Cautilli v. GAF Corp.,* 531 F.Supp. 71, 72-73 (E.D. Pa. 1982) (applying New Jersey law). *See Taylor v. Metzger,* 152 N.J. 490, 509 (1998) (conduct must be so outrageous in character, and so extreme in degree, as to go beyond all possible bounds of decency, and to be regarded as atrocious, and utterly intolerable in a civilized community).

> acterized by "malice," or a degree of aggravation which would entitle the plaintiff to punitive damages for another tort. Liability has been found only where the conduct has been so outrageous in character, and so extreme in degree, as to go beyond all possible bounds of decency, and to be regarded as atrocious, and utterly intolerable in a civilized community.[5]

Whether the defendant's conduct reasonably may be regarded as so extreme and outrageous as to justify recovery is for the court to determine in the first instance.[6]

The character of conduct required to state a claim for the intentional infliction of emotional distress is well illustrated by *Hume v. Bayer*,[7] the first New Jersey case in which this cause of action was recognized. The facts as accepted by the court on a motion were the following. Larry Hume had an operation for abdominal pain under the care of the defendant doctor. Although the surgery involved only an appendectomy, Dr. Bayer advised Larry's parents that instead of performing an appendectomy, he had removed "an 8-10 inch section of inflamed and possibly cancerous tissue." Dr. Bayer also advised Larry's parents that their son was suffering from a rare disease and that a test would be run two days later to determine if the excised mass was malignant. Although such a test was never performed, Dr. Bayer later advised that the results were negative.

In finding these facts sufficient to state a claim for intentional infliction of emotional distress, the court relied on the Restatement (Second) of Torts, §46[8] and several illustrative examples of actionable conduct from Prosser, Law of Torts (4th ed. 1971), §12:

> spreading a false rumor that plaintiff's son had hung himself; bringing a mob to plaintiff's door with a threat to lynch him if he did not leave town; and wrapping up a gory dead rat inside of a loaf of bread for a sensitive person to open.[9]

---

5. Restatement (Second) of Torts, §46 comment d.

6. Restatement (Second) of Torts, §46 comment h; *Cox v. Keystone Carbon Co.*, 861 F.2d 390, 395 (3d Cir. 1988).

7. 178 N.J. Super. 310 (Law Div. 1981). Of course, cases prior to *Hume v. Bayer* recognized emotional distress as an element of damages in tort actions involving violation of an underlying duty to which the claim for emotional distress damages could attach. In *Hume*, the intentional infliction of emotional distress was recognized as an independent cause of action. *Cf.*, *Portee v. Jaffee*, 84 N.J. 88 (1980); *Berman v. Allan*, 80 N.J. 421 (1979); *Falzone v. Busch*, 45 N.J. 559 (1965).

8. "[T]he conduct must be so extreme and outrageous 'as to go beyond all possible bounds of decency, and be regarded as atrocious and utterly intolerable in a civilized community.' " *Hume v. Bayer*, 178 N.J. Super. 310, 314 (Law Div. 1981).

9. *Id.* at 315.

The Supreme Court has held that a single but extreme racial epithet made in public by the head of an office to a subordinate employee was sufficient to meet the threshold standard of outrageousness.[10] The Third Circuit has found sufficient a supervisor's repeated threats that he was out to get plaintiff, including sexist metaphors and the berating of plaintiff was sufficient to avoid summary judgment.[11] Other courts have held that adverse employment actions, albeit unfair, discriminatory, unkind or cold-hearted, are in themselves insufficient to state a claim. Adverse employment actions coupled with misleading employer conduct, or even employer misrepresentations, have also been found insufficient.

3-4:1 Misleading Conduct/Misrepresentations

In *Cautilli v. GAF Corp.*,[12] plaintiff alleged that his employer had intentionally inflicted emotional distress upon him by inducing him to stay in his job and forego a search for other employment at a time when the employer knew the part of the business plaintiff worked for was going to be relocated and that as a consequence plaintiff was going to be forced to either leave his job or move. The district court dismissed plaintiff's claim as insufficient as a matter of law, predicting that neither New Jersey nor Pennsylvania courts would "extend this tort to cover an employment contract dispute such as that before us."[13]

Employer misrepresentations were also found insufficient in *Brunner v. Abex Corp.*, [14] where plaintiff alleged that she had been misled about job security and induced to relocate, only to be laid off from employment shortly thereafter.[15]

---

10. *Taylor v. Metzger*, 152 N.J. 490, 509-13 (1998) (country sheriff called plaintiff a "jungle bunny" in the presence of another employee; while the Court specifically disclaimed holding that a single racial slur spoken on the street to a stranger could amount to extreme and outrageous conduct, it found that "a jury could reasonably conclude that the power dynamics of the workplace contribute to the extremity and the outrageousness of defendant's conduct").

11. For discussion of the threshold burdens in other contexts *see Buckley v. Trenton Savings Fund Society*, 111 N.J. 355, 368 (1988) (dishonoring check insufficient); *see also Figured v. Paralegal Technical Services*, 231 N.J. Super. 251 (App. Div.), *certif. granted*, 117 N.J. 118 (1989), *app. denied*, 121 N.J. 666 (1990) (insurance investigation including personal surveillance of plaintiff on two occasions found not to have produced sufficiently severe emotional distress); *Major League Baseball Promotion v. Colour-Tex, Inc.*, 729 F.Supp. 1035, 1055 (D.N.J. 1990) ("Finding legal proceedings instituted against oneself is an instance of emotional distress that is not actionable under this tort, although it may be 'one of the regrettable aggravations of living in today's society.' "). *Subbe-Hirt v. Baccigalupi*, 94 F.3d 111, 113-14 (3d Cir. 1996).

12. 531 F. Supp. 71 (E.D. Pa. 1982).

13. *Cautilli v. GAF Corp.*, 531 F. Supp. 71, 72 (E.D.Pa. 1982). *See Grossman v. Daily Racing Form, Inc.*, 1994 WL 273389 (D.N.J. June 10, 1994) (alleged breach of employment contract and publication announcing plaintiff's retirement and assumption of emeritus position insufficient as a matter of law.)

14. 661 F.Supp. 1351 (D.N.J. 1986).

15. *Brunner v. Abex Corp.*, 661 F. Supp. 1351, 1359 (D.N.J. 1986). Plaintiff took four vacation days to facilitate her move. When she called to request an additional day off, she was told her job had been eliminated and she was being laid off. *Id.* at 1353.

3-4:2 Discriminatory/Unkind/Unfair Conduct

The mere fact that employment actions are discriminatory does not make them outrageous. The plaintiff in *Mucci v. Moonachie Board of Education*[16] alleged that her employer had intentionally inflicted emotional distress upon her by discriminating in the terms and conditions of employment because of her sex, including paying her a lower salary than was paid to a man with lesser responsibilities, demoting her, and promoting the man. In rejecting plaintiff's claim for the intentional infliction of emotional distress, the court found that the conduct alleged did "not begin to approach" the required standard.[17]

Similarly, in *Carney v. Dexter Shoe Co.*,[18] the district court rejected plaintiff's claim that his termination at age 60, after 20 years of work, and without any offer of assistance in finding new employment, stated a claim for intentional infliction of emotional distress. In fact, the court found that when compared with examples in Prosser, Law of Torts,[19] the case had "a complete absence of any facts which could be considered 'extreme and outrageous.' "[20]

---

16. 37 FEP Cases 65 (D.N.J. 1987), *aff'd without op.*, 835 F.2d 284 (3d Cir. 1987).

17. *Id.* at 68.

18. 701 F.Supp. 1093 (D.N.J. 1988).

19. *Id.* at 1104, quoting *Hume v. Bayer*, 178 N.J. Super. 310, 315 (Law Div. 1981).

20. *Carney v. Dexter Shoe Co.*, 701 F.Supp. 1093, 1104 (D.N.J. 1988). *See McNemar v. The Disney Store, Inc.*, 91 F.3d 610 (3d Cir. 1996) (affirming dismissal of HIV-positive plaintiff's claim that his termination constituted intentional infliction of emotional distress; termination of employment, without harassment, is insufficient; here, plaintiff admitted his discharge was handled in a discreet manner), *cert. denied*, 117 S. Ct. 958, 136 L.Ed.2d 845 (1997); *Ditzel v. University of Medicine & Dentistry of New Jersey*, 962 F. Supp. 595, 608 (1997) (a few stray sarcastic remarks are insufficient to state a claim). *Tarino v. Kraft Foodservice, Inc.*, 1996 WL 84680, p.*12-13 (D.N.J. 1996) (alleged references to plaintiff and Italian Americans as "Gumba, Mafioso types, dagos, and wops" insufficient as a matter of law; courts are ill-equipped to punish lack of respect and consideration for one's feelings, given the currency of ethnic slurs, reasonable people must learn to endure them); *Pitak v. Bell Atlantic Network Servs., Inc.*, 1996 WL 341278, p.*18, 928 F.Supp. 1354 (D.N.J. 1996) (employees laid off in reduction in force failed to state a claim: "Courts have been particularly reluctant to allow claims for intentional infliction of emotional distress by discharged employees against their employers"). *See Morris v. Siemens Components, Inc.*, 1996 WL 294074, p*10-11 (D.N.J. 1996) (alleged discriminatory discharge and retaliation for workers' compensation claim insufficient); *King v. Port Auth.*, 909 F. Supp. 938, 943 (D.N.J. 1995), *aff'd*, 106 F.3d 385 (3d Cir. 1996) (plaintiff's allegations of race discrimination and retaliation fail as a matter of law; it is extremely rare for employment-based claims to meet the threshold for intentional infliction of emotional distress); *Selitto v. Litton Syst., Inc.*,881 F. Supp. 932, 941 (D.N.J. 1994) (plaintiff's allegation of termination in violation of an implied contract providing for progressive discipline insufficient as a matter of law: "no jury could reasonably find that such conduct is 'beyond all possible bounds of decency,' 'atrocious,' and 'utterly intolerable in a civilized community'"); *Cf. Bishop v. Okidata, Inc.*, 864 F. Supp. 416, 428 (D.N.J. 1994) (plaintiff survived a motion for summary judgment where she alleged that defendants "engaged in a continuing pattern of harassment," "refused to promote her; made false accusations against her and threatened her with discharge; excluded her from training programs; forced her to return to work two weeks after her cancer surgery, in contravention to her doctor's orders; and refused to allow her to leave work for needed radiation and chemotherapy treatments"). *See generally DeJoy v. Comcast Cable Communications*, 968 F.Supp. 963 (D.N.J. 1997) ("Courts, moreover, have been particularly reluctant to allow claims for intentional infliction of emotional distress by discharged employees against their employers.").

To the same effect is *Borecki v. Eastern Int'l Management Corp.*,[21] where plaintiff alleged he was terminated because of his age and in retaliation for his loyalty to a particular supervisor, despite his contribution to and personal sacrifice for the company. The court rejected those allegations as not sufficiently extreme or outrageous, noting that "courts in this circuit have found some sort of harassing behavior to be necessary in addition to the termination of employment."[22]

3-4:3 Rough Treatment by the Employer

In *Maietta v. United Parcel Service, Inc.*,[23] plaintiff claimed intentional infliction of emotional distress based on an internal integrity investigation that included interviews of him in which a supervisor "raised his voice in a threatening manner," and accusations that he cheated and committed breaches of integrity, which accusations were disclosed to a third party. The district court dismissed his claim, holding that "no reasonable mind" could find these acts sufficient to meet the Restatement standard utilized in New Jersey; *i.e.*, "so outrageous in character, and so extreme in degree, as to go beyond all possible bounds of decency, and to be regarded as atrocious, and utterly intolerable in a civilized community."[24]

An employer's investigation of alleged criminal conduct that included "pitting one employee against another in order to extract testimony," and which was alleged to place employees "in a position with no other alternative but to lie in order to cover themselves," was also found insufficient.[25] Similarly insufficient as a matter of law were the allegations that a supervisor refused to speak to plaintiff on the day before termination, "glared menacingly at her" and yelled at her "with clenched fist" at termination, and refused to allow her a telephone call to arrange transportation home.[26]

---

21. 694 F.Supp. 47 (D.N.J. 1988).

22. *Borecki v. Eastern Int'l Management Corp.*, 694 F.Supp. 47, 61 (D.N.J. 1988). *See also Meacham v. Bell Telephone Laboratories, Inc.*, 1990 WL 299805, p. * 11 (D.N.J. 1990) (alleged age discrimination in salary, demotion, negative evaluation and exclusion from management meetings insufficient); *Brunner v. Abex Corp.*, 661 F. Supp. 1351, 1359 (D.N.J. 1986) (misleading plaintiff as to job security, causing her to begin to relocate, and then terminating her insufficient); *Dondero v. Lenox China*, 5 IER Cases (BNA) 819, 820-21, 1990 WL 86061 (D.N.J. June 19, 1990):

> In general, decisions to terminate an employee have been found to be insufficient to support a claim for this tort ... This court recently found 'that the firing of an employee without a hearing is not so atrocious as to be completely intolerable in a civilized society ... Where the termination decision is accompanied by a showing of harassment on the part of the employer, however, courts have allowed claims for intentional infliction of emotional distress to go to the jury.

23. 749 F.Supp. 1344 (D.N.J. 1990).

24. *Id.* at 1368-69.

25. *Glover v. Canada Dry Bottling Co.*, 1990 WL 43739, p. *6 (D.N.J. 1990).

3-4:4 Harassment/Sexual Harassment

In *Taylor v. Metzger,*[27] the Supreme Court found that a country sherriff's public reference to an employee as a "jungle bunny" was in itself sufficient to state a claim. In *Subbe-Hirt v. Baccigalupi,*[28] the Third Circuit held that a supervisor's repeated threats to get plaintiff, his berating of her and use of sexist metaphors and slurs were sufficint to state a claim. In *Porta v. Rollins Environmental Services (N.J.), Inc.,*[29] the female plaintiff had been subjected to a series of offensive incidents of sexual harassment, including threats, obscenity, and public ridicule.[30] That pattern of behavior was found sufficient to meet the legal threshold and create a question of fact.[31]

---

26. *Moore v. Merrill Lynch, Pierce, Fenner & Smith, Inc.*, 1990 WL 105765, p. *3 (D.N.J. 1990).

27. 152 N.J. 490, 509-13 (1998).

28. 94 F.3d 111, 113-14 (3d Cir. 1996).

29. 654 F.Supp. 1275 (D.N.J. 1987), *aff'd without op.*, 845 F.2d 1014 (3d Cir. 1988).

30. The plaintiff recounted specific details of numerous harassing events leading up to her discharge, all of which she said took place because of her sex. Plaintiff alleged that from her hiring in May of 1980 to her termination in June of 1984, she was subjected to disparaging and offensive comments based on her sex, received threatening and sexually offensive notes, was denied a promotion, was told by a superior that her opinion was not respected because she was a woman, was once "set up" to fail a particular assignment, was subjected to pranks, and was ultimately discharged for refusing to submit to the offensive and hostile work environment. 654 F.Supp. at 1279-80.

31. 654 F. Supp. at 1285. The court relied on *Cory v. Smithkline Beckman Corp.*, 585 F.Supp. 871, 875 (E.D. Pa. 1984) (applying Pennsylvania law; suggesting that acts of harassment which alone are insufficient may become outrageous if repeated). *See Wilson v. Parisi*, 268 N.J. Super. 213, 218-19 (App. Div. 1993) (where sexual harassment meets the standard of *Lehmann v. Toys 'R' Us, Inc.*, 132 N.J. 587 (1993), proof of physical injury is not prerequisite to a victim seeking damages for intentional infliction of emotional distress; "[t]ypically, in a sexual harassment case, especially where the supervisor is the harasser, the victim becomes aware, through his or her sensory perception, of the shocking events 'that do not occur in the daily lives of most people.'"). *See also Bishop v. Okidata*, Inc., 864 F. Supp. 416, 428 (D.N.J. 1994) (summary judgment against plaintiff denied where she alleged "a continuing pattern of harassment;" she contended that defendants "refused to promote her; made false accusations against her and threatened her with discharge; excluded her from training programs; forced her to return to work two weeks after her cancer surgery, in contravention of her doctor's orders; and refused to allow her to leave work for needed radiation and chemotherapy treatments"). Compare *Obendorfer v. The Gitano Group, Inc.*, 838 F. Supp. 950, 954-56 (D.N.J. 1993), where the court found that allegations that employer responded inadequately to complaints of harassment and that supervisor made many disparaging remarks about plaintiff's fiance and demeaning remarks about plaintiff were insufficient to state a claim for the intentional infliction of emotional distress:

> Absent other conduct, these insults, no matter how out of touch they are with today's respect for the equality of women, are still nothing more than verbal assaults all too common in today's rude and inconsiderate social and business interactions. A court is ill-equipped to punish lack of respect and consideration for one's fellow's feelings, and therefore New Jersey has prescribed a heavy burden for one alleging intentional infliction of emotional distress. The court must conclude that these insults, no matter how ill-advised, do not reach the threshold prescribed by the New Jersey courts. A civilized community, by definition, must be able to tolerate some friction between its members without resorting to litigation over every verbal insult, actual or perceived. Thus the conduct here alleged is not "utterly intolerable in a civilized community."

838 F. Supp. at 955.

But minor annoyances or rudeness merely labelled as harassment are insufficient. In *Zamboni v. Stamler*,[32] the Third Circuit rejected plaintiff's claim that his supervisor had "engaged in such constant harassment of him that the workplace became oppressive, resulting in [plaintiff's] development of a painful and chronic spastic colon and psychological and emotional problems," based upon incidents such as discipline and suspension, a fine for improper use of office stationery, orders to turn in his gun and submit to a psychiatric exam, and numerous written reprimands for offenses such as failing to say good morning to his supervisor.[33] While noting "the toll that petty vindictive behavior can wreak on vulnerable employees," the Third Circuit found that conduct did not rise to the level required for the tort of intentional infliction of emotional distress.[34]

3-5 Proximate Cause

To be actionable, the defendant's actions must have been the proximate cause of plaintiff's distress.[35] As applied in this context, proximate cause is more than a factual question of cause and effect; it is a concept utilized "to draw judicial lines beyond which liability will not be extended . . . as an instrument of fairness and policy."[36] The determination of proximate cause has been described by the Supreme Court as being based upon "mixed considerations of logic, common sense, justice, policy and precedent."[37] The Court relies upon the limitations set forth in both Prosser, Law of Torts, and the Restatement (Second) of Torts.

> As a practical matter, legal responsibility must be limited to those causes which are so closely connected with the result and of such significance that the law is justified in imposing liability. Some boundary must be set to liability for the consequences of any act, upon the basis of some social idea of justice or policy.

---

32. 847 F.2d 73 (3rd Cir. 1988), *cert. denied*, 488 U.S. 899 (1988).

33. *Id.* at 76, 80.

34. *Id.* at 80.

35. *Buckley v. Trenton Savings Fund Society*, 111 N.J. 355, 366 (1988).

36. *Caputzal v. The Lindsay Co.*, 48 N.J. 69, 77 (1966). In *Caputzal* the issue was physical injuries allegedly caused by shock. The plaintiff drank coffee made with water filtered through a water softener manufactured, sold and installed by defendants. He later drew more water, which was discolored, and, assuming the water he used to make coffee was similarly impure, he became concerned that he had been poisoned. He then suffered a heart attack. *Caputzal* was relied upon by the Supreme Court in *Buckley v. Trenton Savings Fund Society*, 111 N.J. 355, 366 (1988), in discussing the requirement of proximate cause in a cause of action alleging emotional distress only.

37. *Caputzal v. The Lindsay Co.*, 48 N.J. 69, 77-78 (1966), quoting *Powers v. Standard Oil Co.*, 98 N.J.L. 730, 734 (Sup. Ct. 1923), *aff'd o.b.*, 98 N.J.L. 893 (E. & A. 1923).

> This limitation is sometimes, although rather infrequently, one of the fact of causation. More often it is purely one of policy, of our more or less inadequately expressed ideas of what justice demands, or of administrative possibility and convenience, none of which have any connection with questions of causation at all.[38]
>
> * * *
>
> The actor's conduct may be held not to be a legal cause of harm to another where after the event and looking back from the harm to the actor's negligent conduct, it appears to the court highly extraordinary that it should have brought about the harm.[39]

This nature of proximate cause question—nonliability for a highly extraordinary consequence—is a question of law for the court.[40] It is frequently raised in cases of emotional distress where an individual claims an extreme reaction to conduct to which others may not react at all.[41]

3-6 Severe Emotional Distress

To be actionable, distress must be "so severe that no reasonable man could be expected to endure it."[42] It is for the court to decide in the first instance whether, as a matter of law, the emotional distress alleged is sufficiently severe. It is then for the jury to decide whether the distress alleged and found sufficient has in fact been proven to have occurred.[43]

The New Jersey Supreme Court addressed the question of how severe emotional distress must be to meet this threshold burden in *Buckley v. Trenton Savings Fund Society*. It found insufficient as a matter of law allegations of loss of sleep, aggravation, embarrassment, headaches and nervous tension, especially in view of the fact that the alleged distress appeared not to have interfered with the plaintiff's daily routine.[44] Recent decisions in the employment context suggest

---

38. Prosser, Law of Torts, §30, pp. 240-41, quoted in *Caputzal v. The Lindsay Co.*, 48 N.J. 69, 78 (1966).

39. Restatement (Second) of Torts, §435 (2), quoted in *Caputzal v. The Lindsay Co.*, 48 N.J. 69, 78 (1966).

40. *Caputzal v. The Lindsay Co.*, 48 N.J. 69, 78 (1966).

41. *See, e.g., Decker v. The Princeton Packet*, 116 N.J. 418, 430 (1989); *Major League Baseball Promotion v. Colour-Tex, Inc.*, 729 F.Supp. 1035, 1055 (D.N.J. 1990). In *Caputzal*, the Supreme Court stated that it entirely agreed that: "If the psychic stimulus was not calculated to injure an average person, there is no negligence and no liability for injury suffered by an idiosyncratic plaintiff." 48 N.J. at 77.

42. *See Buckley v. Trenton Savings Fund Society*, 111 N.J. 355, 368 (1988), quoting Restatement (Second) of Torts, §46, comment j. *See King v. Port Authority of New York & New Jersey*, 909 F. Supp. 938, 943 (D.N.J. 1995), *aff'd*, 106 F.3d 385 (3d Cir. 1996); *Morris v. Siemens Components, Inc.*, 1996 WL 294074, p.*10-11 (D.N.J. 1996).

43. *See Buckley v. Trenton Savings Fund Society*, 111 N.J. at 367.

that to be actionable, the distress must have had a demonstrable negative effect on the plaintiff's life or work, and/or the plaintiff must have sought medical or psychiatric treatment for same.

In *Taylor v. Metzger,*[45] the Supreme Court found sufficient threshold proofs that plaintiff sought psychiatric treatment for as long as she could afford it, lived in fear, was treated for anxiety, suffered mood-swings, flashbacks and other symptoms for an extended period and was ultimately diagnosed as having post-traumatic stress disorder.[46] In *Maietta v. United Parcel Service, Inc.*, a terminated employee alleged that after his termination, the sight of a UPS truck gave him the same feeling one has when rejected by love, "where your heart stops and you get sick to your stomach," and that his blood pressure had become uncontrollably high. The court rejected these claims as not involving sufficiently severe distress, making particular note of the lack of interference with plaintiff's ability to work and the fact that he never sought psychiatric treatment.[47] Similarly, in *Weber v. LDC/Milton Roy*, the employee's claim of severe emotional distress was "dismissed out of hand" because he was not examined by a physician or psychiatrist.[48]

---

44. 111 N.J. at 368-69. *See Burbridge v. Paschal*, 239 N.J. Super. 139, 157-58 (App. Div.), *certif. denied*, 122 N.J. 360 (1990) (allegations of emotional distress insufficient where conduct was bothersome and an annoyance, but plaintiffs "were able to live with the problem fairly well"); *Acevedo v. Essex County*, 207 N.J. Super. 579, 586-87 (Law Div. 1985) (emotional distress alleged to have occurred upon viewing son's body exhumed due to misdiagnosed cause of death insufficient in view of lack of permanency); *Sellitto v. Litton Systems, Inc.*, 881 F. Supp. 932, 941 (D.N.J. 1994) (plaintiff's allegations of "loss of sleep, inability to concentrate, loss of appetite, anxiety, nervousness, depression and other assorted debilitating physical and emotional ailments," as well as unspecified "enormous and severe" emotional, physical and financial impact on plaintiff and plaintiff's family, insufficient as a matter of law to establish severe emotional distress; defendant's motion for summary judgment on this claim granted).

45. 152 N.J. 490, 514-15 (1998).

46. "Severe emotional distress means any type of severe and disabling emotional or mental condition which may be generally recognized and diagnosed by professionals trained to do so, including ... posttraumatic stress disorder." *Taylor v. Metzger*, 152 N.J. 490, 515 (1998).

47. 749 F.Supp. 1344, 1369 (D.N.J. 1990), *aff'd without op.*, 932 F.2d 960 (3d Cir. 1991).

48. 1 IER Cases (BNA) 1509, 1520 (D.N.J. 1986). *See Lingar v. Live-In Companions, Inc.*, 300 N.J. Super. 22, 34-35 (App. Div. 1997) (husband and wife who hired a caregiver for the husband failed to demonstrate serious, emotional distress resulting from his abandonment of the invalid husband and theft of the wife's automobile and other items; while plaintiffs "'acutely upset' by reason of the incident, their emotional distress was not 'sufficiently substantial' to result in physical illness or serious psychological sequelae"; accordingly, the trial court correctly dismissed their claim against the caregiver's employer).; *Morgan v. Union County*, 268 N.J. Super. 337, 354 (App. Div. 1993), *certif. denied*, 135 N.J. 468 (1994) ("allegations relating to aggravation, embarrassment, minor headaches, and loss of sleep are not enough to withstand a motion for summary judgment;" plaintiff's claims of such distress relating to alleged constructive discharge dismissed); *Nieves v. Individualized Shirts*, 961 F. Supp. 782, 797 (D.N.J. 1997) (concerns about buying nice clothes for children and understandable frustration and depression over losing a job did not rise to the level of severe emotional distress). *See also Schillaci v. First Fidelity Bank*, 311 N.J. Super. 396, 406-07 (App. Div. 1998) (plaintiff's claims against bank for distress suffered as a result of bank's fraudulent statements about its purported search for cash deposited by plaintiff, which statements allegedly resulted in plaintiff's termination by her employer, properly dismissed for lack of proof of severe emotional distress; "although [plaintiff]was acutely upset by reason of the incident, [her] emotional distress was not sufficiently substantial to result in physical illness or serious psychological sequelae").

3-6:1 Necessity of Expert Testimony

Expert testimony is generally required to support a claim for injury that is either subjective in nature or of the sort that its cause and degree of severity cannot be determined by laymen.[49] It was on this basis that it has been held that an employee's claim for emotional distress in the form of depression, sleep loss, embarrassment, and humiliation as a consequence of adverse employment action must be supported by expert testimony or dismissed.[50]

III. NEGLIGENT INFLICTION OF EMOTIONAL DISTRESS

3-7 Requisites

To establish a claim for negligent infliction of emotional distress, a plaintiff must show: (1) that defendant had a legal duty of care to plaintiff; (2) that the duty was breached; (3) that plaintiff suffered genuine and substantial emotional distress; and (4) that defendant's negligence was the proximate cause of that distress.[51]

Because of the extraordinary nature of conduct required to maintain a claim for the intentional infliction of emotional distress, many plaintiffs seeking recovery for perceived mistreatment in the workplace allege that the same conduct constitutes a negligent as well as an intentional infliction of distress. As discussed *infra* in §56, however, claims that employers or co-employees negligently inflicted emotional distress are barred by the Workers Compensation Act.

3-7:1 Duty/Foreseeability

"A prerequisite to recovery on a negligence theory is a duty owed by defendant to plaintiff."[52] The existence of a duty to plaintiff is measured in terms of foreseeability: "liability should depend on the defendant's foreseeing fright or shock severe enough to cause substantial injury in a person normally constituted." [53]

---

49. *Dondero v. Lenox China*, 5 IER Cases (BNA) 819, 821 (D.N.J. 1990), *citing Kelly v. Borwegan*, 95 N.J. Super. 240, 243-44 (App. Div. 1967), and *Menza v. Diamond Jim's, Inc.*, 145 N.J. Super. 40, 46 (App. Div. 1976).

50. *Dondero v. Lenox China*, 5 IER Cases (BNA) 819, 821, 1990 WL 86061 (D.N.J., June 19, 1990). *Accord Gautam v. De Luca*, 215 N.J. Super. 388, 399 (App. Div.), *certif. denied*, 109 N.J. 39 (1987) ("Even if emotional distress damages were recoverable in legal malpractice actions, such awards would be impermissible in the absence of medical evidence establishing substantial bodily injury or severe and demonstrable psychiatric sequelae proximately caused by the tortfeasor's misconduct."). Compure the discusion of emotional distress damages under the New Jersy Law Against Discrimination, Chapter 4, §4-54:4.

As the Supreme Court has noted, foreseeability takes on special significance in this context:

> While the foreseeability of injurious consequences is a constituent element in a tort action, foreseeability of injury is particularly important in the tort of negligent infliction of emotional harm. This reflects the concern over the genuineness of an injury consisting of emotional distress without consequent physical injury. In these situations, there must be "an especial likelihood of genuine and serious mental distress, arising from special circumstances, which serves as a guarantee that the claim is not spurious." [54]

---

51. *See Decker v. The Princeton Packet*, 116 N.J. 418, 429 (1989). *Cf. Buckley v. Trenton Savings Fund Society*, 111 N.J. 355, 365 (1988). This is the rule applicable where the tortious conduct alleged is directed to the plaintiff, such as would be the case in connection with the common allegation that a negligent discharge or other adverse employment action caused emotional distress. Where the alleged tortious behavior is directed toward a third person, and the plaintiff claiming emotional distress is merely a "bystander," the elements of proof are:

> (1) the death or serious physical injury of another caused by defendant's negligence; (2) a marital or intimate, familial relationship between plaintiff and the injured person; (3) observation of the death or injury at the scene of the accident; and (4) resulting severe emotional distress.

Portee v. Jaffee, 84 N.J. 88, 101 (1980). The concern in both types of claims is that the circumstances be such as to ensure the genuineness of the claim. *See Buckley v. Trenton Savings Fund Society*, 111 N.J. 355, 365-66 (1988); *Frame v. Kothari*, 115 N.J. 638, 642-44 (1989). Where a claim of negligent infliction of emotional distress is based upon an alleged false publication, proof of defamation is a prerequisite: "'There is ... a certain symmetry or parallel between claims of emotional distress and defamation that calls for consistent results. Thus, it comports with first amendment protections to deny an emotional-distress claim based on a false publication that engenders no defamation per se.' ... To hold otherwise would permit plaintiff to use the tort of negligent infliction of emotional distress to circumvent defenses to the defamation action." *Salek v. Passaic Collegiate School*, 255 N.J. Super. 355, 361 (App. Div. 1992), quoting *Decker v. The Princeton Packet, Inc.*, 116 N.J. 418, 432 (1989).

One court has suggested that only in unusual circumstances will a claim not meeting the *Portee v. Jaffee*, 84 N.J. 88 (1980), standard be allowed. *Sellitto v. Litton Sys., Inc.*, 881 F. Supp. 932, 942 (D.N.J. 1994) ("While the New Jersey courts have occasionally upheld a claim for negligent infliction of emotional distress beyond the circumstances outlined in *Portee*, *see e.g. Strachan v. John F. Kennedy Memorial Hospital*, 109 N.J. 523, 538 A.2d 346 (1988) (recognizing parents' suffering resulting from hospital's negligent mishandling of son's corpse); *Giardina v. Bennett*, 111 N.J. 412, 545 A.2d 139 (1988) (parents may recover damages for emotional distress from still birth caused by medical malpractice), 'a constant concern about the genuineness of the claim,' *Buckley v. Trenton Saving Fund Soc'y*, 111 N.J. 355, 365, 544 A.2d 857 (1988), has pervaded judicial analysis. Here [where plaintiff alleged wrongful discharge in violation of a progressive discipline procedure] the circumstances of plaintiff's discharge do not merit an extension of the *Portee* standard.").

52. *Strachan v. John F. Kennedy Memorial Hospital*, 109 N.J. 523, 529 (1988).

53. *Decker v. The Princeton Packet*, 116 N.J. 418, 429 (1989), quoting *Caputzal v. The Lindsay Co.*, 48 N.J. 69, 76 (1966). *See also Major League Baseball Promotion v. Colour-Tex, Inc.*, 729 F.Supp. 1035, 1055 (D.N.J. 1990) (institution of legal proceedings could not foreseeably cause fright or shock severe enough to cause substantial injury in a person normally constituted).

54. *Decker v. The Princeton Packet*, 116 N.J. 418, 429-30 (1989).

Thus, to recover for negligent infliction of emotional distress, it must have been reasonably foreseeable that the tortious conduct alleged would cause genuine and substantial emotional distress or mental harm to average persons.[55]

3-7:2 Genuine and Substantial Distress

To be actionable under a theory of negligent infliction, distress must be "truly genuine and substantial."[56] The test is the same as that employed with respect to the intentional infliction of emotional distress.[57] The threshold question of sufficiency of the distress is a question of law for the court. Sufficiency of distress is determined under an objective standard and is related to the question of foreseeability. If the tortious conduct alleged would not cause severe distress in a reasonable person, any distress alleged in a particular case will be found insufficient as a matter of law.[58]

3-8 Exclusivity of Workers' Compensation

The New Jersey Workers' Compensation Act contains an exclusive remedy provision that bars employees from maintaining civil suits against their employers or co-employees for compensable injuries allegedly sustained by reason of or in the course of their employment, except for intentional wrong.[59] To fall within the intentional wrong exception, the employer must either desire to cause the injury or be "substantially certain" that the injury will result from his actions.[60] In

---

55. *Id.* at 430.

56. *Id.*.

57. *See supra* at §§3-2 to 3-6.

58. Thus, in *Decker v. The Princeton Packet*, 116 N.J. 418, 433 (1989), the Supreme Court held: "We determine also that any emotional distress proximately caused by the publication of such a false obituary is not, as a matter of law, sufficiently substantial to constitute a compensable injury."

59. N.J.S.A. 34:15-8 provides:

> Such agreement [to be covered by Workers' Compensation] shall be a surrender by the parties thereto of their rights to any other method, form or amount of compensation or determination thereof than as provided in this article and an acceptance of all the provisions of this article, and shall bind the employee and for compensation for the employee's death shall bind the employee's personal representatives, surviving spouse and next of kin, as well as the employer, and those conducting the employer's business during bankruptcy or insolvency.
>
> If an injury or death is compensable under this article, a person shall not be liable to anyone at common law or otherwise on account of such injury or death for any act or omission occurring while such person was in the same employ as the person injured or killed, except for intentional wrong.

The "intentional wrong" exception to the exclusivity of workers' compensation is applicable to suits against both employers and co-employees. *Millison v. E.I. du Pont de Nemours & Co.*, 101 N.J. 161, 184-86 (1985).

60. *See Millison v. E.I. du Pont de Nemours & Co.*, 101 N.J. at 177-78 (1985).

describing the substantial certainty standard for determining intent, the Supreme Court stated:

> [T]he dividing line between negligent or reckless conduct on the one hand and intentional wrong on the other must be drawn with caution, so that the statutory framework of the Act is not circumvented simply because a known risk later blossoms into reality. We must demand a virtual certainty.[61]

Thus, all forms of compensable, negligently inflicted personal injuries are remediable exclusively in workers' compensation. Because psychiatric injuries incurred in the workplace are compensable,[62] civil suits by employees for the negligent infliction of emotional distress by their employer or co-employees are barred.[63]

IV. CONTRACTUAL INTERFERENCE

3-9 Requisites

To state a claim for interference with contract or prospective economic advantage, four elements must be proved: (1) a contract or protectable right; (2) interference done intentionally and with malice; (3) causation of a loss by the interference; and (4) damage.[64] Interference with one's trade and employment relationships has long been recognized as an appropriate basis for this tort:

> The law protects a man in the pursuit of his livelihood. True, he cannot complain of every disappointment; others too may further their equal interests, and if the means are fair, the advantage should remain where success has put it. But if the act complained of does not rest upon some legitimate interest or if there is sharp dealing or overreaching or other conduct below

61. *Id* at 178.

62. *See Saunderlin v. E.I. du Pont de Nemours & Co.*, 102 N.J. 402 (1986). *Cf. Cairns v. City of E. Orange*, 267 N.J. Super. 395, 405-06, 631 A.2d 978 (App. Div. 1993) (psychiatric injuries resulting from receipt of a layoff notice are not compensable; "Notification of petitioner's proposed layoff was not peculiar to the employment and did not arise out of the employment.").

63. *See Noye v. Hoffmann-LaRoche Inc.*, 238 N.J. Super. 430, 438 n.5 (App. Div.), *certif. denied*, 122 N.J. 146 (1990); *Ditzel v. University of Medicine & Dentistry of New Jersey*, 962 F. Supp. 595, 608 (D.N.J. 1997) (claims of negligent infliction of emotional distress barred by the Workers' Compensation Act); *Dondero v. Lenox China*, 5 IER Cases 819, 820, 1990 WL 86061 (D.N.J. June 19, 1990); *Cremen v. Harrah's Marina Hotel Casino*, 680 F.Supp. 150, 153 n.2, 155-56 (D.N.J. 1988).

64. *See Printing Mart-Morristown v. Sharp Electronics*, 116 N.J. 739, 751-52 (1989); *Jenkins v. Region Nine Housing Corp.*, 306 N.J. Super. 258, 265 (App. Div. 1997), *certif. denied*, 153 N.J. 405 (1998).

> the behavior of fair men similarly situated, the ensuing loss should be redressed.[65]

A contract need not be enforceable to form the basis of an interference claim.[66]

Claims of interference with the employment relationship are frequently asserted in cases involving wrongful discharge and other employment contract claims, as a means of avoiding the general rule of contract law prohibiting awards of emotional distress and punitive damages for breach of contract. As discussed *infra* in §3-9:5, claims that the employer interfered with its own employment relationship with its employee have been routinely dismissed as artfully pleaded breach of contract claims. Claims that supervisory employees interfered with the employment relationship between their subordinates and their employer have been dismissed by some courts, where it has been established that the actions complained of were within the scope of the supervisor's duties. That question, however, has not been resolved by the Supreme Court, and the precise circumstances (if any) that may warrant allowance of an action for interference against supervisory employees remain in doubt.

3-9:1 Protectable Rights

The Supreme Court has defined a protectable interest as "a relationship with the potential of leading to a profitable contract," and endorsed the following comment to §766B of the Restatement (Second) of Torts (1979):

> The expression, prospective contractual relation, is not used in this Section in a strict, technical sense. It is not necessary that the prospective relation be expected to be reduced to a formal, binding contract. It may include prospective quasi-contractual or other restitutionary rights or even the voluntary conferring of commercial benefits in recognition of a moral obligation.
>
> * * *
>
> Included are interferences with the prospect of obtaining employment or employees, the opportunity of selling or buying land or chattels or services, and any other relations leading to potentially profitable contracts.[67] A protectable prospective eco-

65. *Harris v. Perl*, 41 N.J. 455, 461 (1964).

66. *See id.* at 461 ("it usually is held that contracts which are voidable by reason of the statute of frauds, formal defects, lack of consideration, lack of mutuality, or even uncertainty of terms, still afford a basis for a tort action when the defendant interferes with their performance"); *Louis Kamm, Inc. v. Flink*, 113 N.J.L. 582, 591 (E. & A. 1934).

nomic relation is "more than some vague, general future employment opportunity." *Grossman v. Daily Racing Form, Inc.*, 1994 WL 273389, at *10 (D.N.J. June 10, 1994).

3-9:2 Intent

To be actionable, the interference must have been done intentionally and with "malice."[68] In this context, malice is not used in the literal sense requiring ill will toward the plaintiff.[69] Rather, it requires that the harm have been inflicted intentionally and without justification or excuse.[70] "The interference alleged must be both intentional and legally or ethically improper." [71]

Whether particular conduct is malicious must be determined on a case by case basis, under a standard acknowledged by the Supreme Court as being somewhat amorphous, necessarily flexible, and focused on the defendant's actions in the context of the case.[72]

---

67. *Printing Mart-Morristown v. Sharp Electronics*, 116 N.J. 739, 755 (1989). *See McKowan Lowe & Co. v. Wain*, 1993 WL 302257, *7-8 (D.N.J. Aug. 2, 1993) (extant employment contract is not prerequisite to a claim for tortious contractual interference).

68. *See Printing Mart-Morristown v. Sharp Electronics*, 116 N.J. 739, 751 (1989); *Louis Kamm, Inc. v. Flink*, 113 N.J.L. 582 (E. & A. 1934); *Kopp, Inc. v. United Technologies, Inc.*, 223 N.J. Super. 548, 559 (App. Div. 1988); *Gherardi v. Trenton Board of Educ.*, 53 N.J. Super. 349, 361-62 (App. Div. 1958).

69. *Printing Mart-Morristown v. Sharp Electronics*, 116 N.J. 739, 751 (1989), quoting Restatement (Second) of Torts, Chapter 37 at 5 (introductory note) (1979).

70. *Printing Mart-Morristown v. Sharp Electronics*, 116 N.J. 739, 751 (1989); *Rainier's Dairies v. Raritan Valley Farms, Inc.*, 19 N.J. 552, 563 (1955); *See Labus v. Navistar Int'l Trans. Corp.*, 740 F.Supp. 1053, 1063 (D.N.J. 1990). The New Jersey test for intent is substantially similar to—but not identical to—the Restatement, which refers to an "improper" interference, rather than one with malice. The Restatement defines a *prima facie* case as follows:

> One who intentionally and improperly interferes with another's prospective contractual relation (except a contract to marry) is subject to liability to the other for the pecuniary harm resulting from loss of the benefits of the relation, whether the interference consists of:
>
> (a) inducing or otherwise causing a third person not to enter into or continue the prospective relation or
>
> (b) preventing the other from acquiring or continuing the prospective relation.

Restatement (Second) of Torts, §766B (1979); *Printing Mart-Morristown v. Sharp Electronics*, 116 N.J. 739, 752 (1989).

71. *Labus v. Navistar Int'l Trans. Corp.*, 740 F.Supp. 1053, 1063 (D.N.J. 1990). In *R.A. Intile Realty Co. v. Raho*, 259 N.J. Super. 438, 477 (Law Div. 1992), the court described the standard as follows: "There must be a showing by plaintiff of both interference by defendant and that the conduct of the defendant was unconscionable, that is, that such conduct transgressed generally accepted standards of morality." *See Platinum Management, Inc. v. Dahms*, 285 N.J. Super. 274, 307 (Law Div. 1995) (actual malice was established by company's efforts to increase its business by intentionally seeking out and employing competitor's key sales employees, so it could sell to competitor's existing customers by reason of the customer information they had).

72. *Printing Mart-Morristown v. Sharp Electronics*, 116 N.J. 739, 756-57 (1989). *See Leslie Blau Co. v. Alfieri*, 157 N.J. Super. 173, 186, 204 (App. Div.), *certif. denied sub nom Leslie Blau Co. v. Reitman*, 77 N.J. 510 (1978).

> The essence of the cases in this field is that in adjudging whether what the defendant has done is actionable, i.e., not done in the exercise of an equal or superior right, the ultimate inquiry is whether the conduct was "both injurious and transgressive of generally accepted standards of common morality or of law." In other words, was the interference by defendant "sanctioned by the 'rules of the game.' " There can be no tighter test of liability in this area than that of the common conception of what is right and just dealing under the circumstances. Not only must a defendant's motive and purpose be proper but so also must be the means.[73]

Actions taken in the exercise of equal or superior rights are not wrongful acts and therefore preclude a finding of malice.[74] One exercising a superior right is privileged to interfere.[75] Thus, where one has the legal or contractual right to terminate employment—as in the case of an at-will employee—exercise of that right cannot form the basis of a claim for interference.[76] Similarly, one with a valid business reason for terminating employment has a valid defense to an interference claim.[77]

3-9:3 Causation

The interference must have *caused* the loss of contract or prospective gain.[78] A plaintiff must show that "if there had been no interference, there was a reasonable probability that the victim of the interference would have received the anticipated economic benefits."[79]

---

73. *Printing Mart-Morristown v. Sharp Electronics*, 116 N.J. 739, 757 (1989), quoting *Sustick v. Slatina*, 48 N.J. Super. 134, 144 (App. Div. 1957). In *Labus v. Navistar Int'l Trans. Corp.*, 740 F.Supp. 1053, 1064 (D.N.J. 1990), allegations that a supervisor repeatedly denied requests for additional accounts, reduced the number of existing accounts, and orally attacked the employee in response to his letters requesting a raise given to younger employees, were found sufficient allegations of malice to withstand a motion for summary judgment. The requirement of a tri-partite situation for a claim of interference was not addressed.

74. *See Middlesex Concrete Products & Excavating Corp. v. Carteret Industrial Ass'n*, 37 N.J. 507, 517 (1962); *see also Glasofer Motors v. Osterlund, Inc.*, 180 N.J. Super. 6, 26 (App. Div. 1981); *Sustick v. Slatina*, 48 N.J. Super. 134, 143 (App. Div. 1957).

75. *See O'Connor v. Harms*, 111 N.J. Super. 22, 28-29 (App. Div.), *certif. denied*, 57 N.J. 137 (1970).

76. *See Borbely v. Nationwide Mutual Ins. Co.*, 547 F.Supp. 959, 976 (D.N.J. 1981) (even if employer could be sued for interfering with its own contract with employees, exercise of its right to terminate at will employees in accordance with contract procedure could not form the basis of such a claim).

77. *See Weber v. LDC/Milton Roy*, 1 IER Cases 1509, 1521 (D.N.J. 1986) (supervisory employee who terminated plaintiff to promote employer's sales may or may not have exercised good judgment, but undisputably acted for a proper business purpose).

78. *See Printing Mart-Morristown v. Sharp Electronics*, 116 N.J. 739, 751 (1989).

3-9:4 Damages

The injury to economic advantage caused by the interference must have resulted in damage.[80]

3-9:5 Necessity of a Tri-Partite Relationship

"[I]t is 'fundamental' to a cause of action for tortious interference with a prospective economic relationship that the claim be directed against defendants who are not parties to the relationship."[81] Tortious interference developed under the common law to protect the parties to a contract or prospective contract from outside interference; it was not meant to change the rules governing the contract.[82] "Where a person interferes with the performance of his or her own contract, the liability is governed by principles of contract law."[83] Thus, it has been uniformly held that an employer may not interfere with its relationship with its employees.[84]

---

79. *See Printing Mart-Morristown v. Sharp Electronics*, 116 N.J. 739, 751 (1989), *quoting Leslie Blau Co. v. Alfieri*, 157 N.J. Super. 173, 185-86 (App. Div.), *certif. denied sub nom Leslie Blau Co. v. Reitman*, 77 N.J. 510 (1978). *See Levin v. Kuhn Loeb & Co.*, 174 N.J. Super. 560, 572 (App. Div. 1980) (dicta); *Myers v. Arcadio, Inc.*, 73 N.J. Super. 493, 498 (App. Div. 1962).

80. *See Printing Mart-Morristown v. Sharp Electronics*, 116 N.J. 739, 752 (1989); *Norwood Easthill Assocs. v. Norwood Easthill Watch*, 222 N.J. Super. 378, 384-85 (App. Div. 1988). *See Platinum Management, Inc. v. Dahms*, 285 N.J. Super. 274, 308 (Law Div. 1995) (damages for improper hiring of competitor's key employees for purpose of improperly gaining access to customers measured by an accounting of profits or sales to diverted customers).

81. *Printing Mart-Morristown v. Sharp Electronics*, 116 N.J. 739, 752 (1989); *Custom Communications Eng'g, Inc. v. E.F. Johnson*, 269 N.J. Super. 531, 543 & n.1 (App. Div. 1993) (it is fundamental that a tortious interference claim be directed against defendants who were not parties to the contract; where a person interferes with the performance of his or her own contract, the liability is governed by contract law, not tort law); *Silvestre v. Bell Atlantic Corp.*, 973 F. Supp. 475, 485-86 (D.N.J. 1997) ("tortious interference with contract claim can be waged only against third-party who is not a party to the contractual or economic relationship at issue"), *aff'd*, 156 F.3d 1225 (3d Cir. 1998); *Tarino v. Kraft Foodservice, Inc.*, 1996 WL 84680, p.*11 (D.N.J. 1996) ("Under New Jersey Law, a plaintiff cannot maintain an action for tortious interference where the claim is by one party against the other party to the contract and not against a third party interloper who has interfered with the contractual relationship.'"). *See McKenzie v. Merck & Co.*, 1993 WL 493306, at *4 (D.N.J. Nov. 24, 1993) (granting summary judgment to employer on employee's claim that employer interfered with the employment relationship between employer and employee); *Van Natta Mechanical Corp. v. Di Staulo*, 277 N.J. Super. 175, 182 (App. Div. 1994) ("Fundamental to the cause of action . . . is a requirement that the claim be directed against defendants who are not parties to the relationship. . . . One cannot interfere with one's own economic relationship, since in such an instance the matter is governed by principles of contract law.").

82. *See Id.* at 752-53; *Kopp, Inc. v. United Technologies, Inc.*, 223 N.J. Super. 548, 559 (App. Div. 1988) ("A party cannot be guilty of inducing the breach of its own contract.").

83. *Printing Mart-Morristown v. Sharp Electronics*, 116 N.J. 739, 753 (1989). *See Meacham v. Bell Telephone Laboratories, Inc.*, 1990 WL 299805, p. *11 (D.N.J. 1990) (dismissing employee's claim that employer and supervisory employees interfered with his employment); *Smith v. Ebasco Constructors, Inc.*, 1988 WL 44143, p. *6 (D.N.J. 1988) (employees acting within the scope of their employment are unable to interfere with their employer's contract with another).

Substantial question exists, however, as to whether—and if so when—supervisory employees of a corporation may be found to have interfered with the corporation's employment relationship with other employees. In *Printing Mart-Morristown v. Sharp Electronics*, the Supreme Court set out what it described as two conflicting principles of agency law that inform the question, but reached no resolution. The first principle is that an employee committing a tort is not relieved of liability simply because he acted on behalf of the employer. On the basis of that principle, the Court states, cases have held employees liable for intentional interference even though the employer was a party to the relationship and the employee was acting on behalf of the employer. Three cases were cited: *Kyriazi v. Western Electric Co.*,[85] *Louis Kamm, Inc. v. Flink*,[86] and *Cappiello v. Ragen Precision Industries, Inc.*[87]

The contrasting principle cited by the Court is that an employee cannot be held liable for actions that would otherwise constitute a tort if the employee is exercising a privilege of the principal, or a privilege held by the employee for the protection of the principal's interests, or where the principal owes no duty or less than the normal duty of care to the person harmed.[88] The Court noted that courts in other jurisdictions had relied on this principle in holding privileged the conduct of an employee of a party to an economic relationship when that conduct would otherwise constitute a tortious interference.[89]

In *Kyriazi v. Western Electric Co.*, the district court held, without analysis of the third-party requirement, that plaintiff proved a harassing pattern of conduct by co-workers and supervisors that supported a claim for interference with her employment relationship with Western Electric.[90] None of the cases cited by the court in support of its holding involved a similar scenario of corporate agents interfering with the corporation's contract.[91]

Louis Kamm, Inc. v. Flink involved a real estate brokerage commission and thus is not directly analogous to the typical employment interference claim. Plaintiff was a real estate broker who identified a prospective purchaser of a

---

84. *Cappiello v. Ragen Precision Industries, Inc.*, 192 N.J. Super. 523, 529 (App. Div. 1984); *Tarino v. Kraft Foodservice, Inc.*, 1996 WL 84680, p.*11 (D.N.J. 1996); *Meacham v. Bell Telephone Laboratories, Inc.*, 1990 WL 299805, p. *11 (D.N.J. 1990); *Borecki v. Eastern Int'l Management Corp.*, 694 F.Supp. 47, 56 n.11 (D.N.J. 1988); *Smith v. Ebasco Constructors, Inc.*, 1988 WL 44143, p. * 6 (D.N.J. 1988); *Borbely v. Nationwide Mutual Ins. Co.*, 547 F.Supp. 959, 976 (D.N.J. 1981).

85. 461 F. Supp. 894, 950 (D.N.J. 1978).

86. 113 N.J.L. 582 (E. & A. 1934).

87. 192 N.J. Super. 523, 530 (App. Div. 1984).

88. *Printing Mart-Morristown v. Sharp Electronics*, 116 N.J. 739, 763 (1989).

89. *Id.*

90. 461 F. Supp. 894, 950 (D.N.J. 1978).

building owned by a building and loan association of which defendant Flink was an officer. After plaintiff disclosed the potential purchaser's identity to Flink—under a promise of confidentiality—Flink disclosed it to his brother, also a real estate broker. The brother consummated the sale and was paid the commission, and the court found that those allegations stated a claim for malicious interference with contract.[92] This case is dissimilar from the employer's relationship with another employee in that a fourth party—the prospective purchaser—was involved. Thus, the interfering employee lured a third-party client away from the plaintiff, which in turn resulted in plaintiff's loss of a commission from the interfering employee's employer.

More typical is the situation presented in *Cappiello v. Ragen Precision Industries, Inc.*,[93] where plaintiff alleged that corporate officers caused him to be discharged so they could appropriate sales commissions owed him by the corporate employer. The Appellate Division held that while the corporation could not be guilty of interference with its own contract with plaintiff, the individual defendants, "whom the jury found to have acted out of their own greed to procure plaintiff's commissions for their own economic benefit," could be found responsible on such claim.[94] Although not expressly stated, the apparent basis for that opinion was that the employees, acting outside the scope of their duties and for personal—rather than corporate—motives effectively became third parties to the corporation's employment relationship with plaintiff.[95] However, that rationale is defeated by the court's further holding that the corporate defendant was liable for damages assessed against the individual executives, under a theory of *respondeat superior.*[96] Thus, the rather anomalous result that for the purpose of determining liability, the employees were found to be acting outside the scope of authority, but for the purpose of vicarious liability they were not. The interference with contract claim becomes nothing more than an artifice for the imposition of tort damages for what is in reality a breach of employment contract claim.

---

91. *Id.* at 950 (D.N.J. 1978). *See Brennan v. United Hatters of North America, Local No. 17*, 73 N.J.L. 729 (E. & A. 906) (union interference in employer-employee relationship); *Raymond v. Cregar*, 38 N.J. 472 (1962) (interference by doctors with staff privileges in relationship between hospital and doctor denied reappointment); *Harris v. Perl*, 41 N.J. 455 (1964) (prospective purchaser of real estate interfered with broker's opportunity for commission by misleading her and dealing directly with owner of record); *Kuzma v. Millinery Workers Union, Local 24*, 27 N.J. Super. 579 (App. Div. 1953) (union and members, officers, and agent of union interfered in plaintiff's relationship with employer); *Strollo v. Jersey Central Power & Light*, 20 N.J. Misc. 217 (Sup. Ct. 1942) (utility company and its employees interfered with plaintiff's employment with another company by accusing him of stealing electricity).

92. 113 N.J.L. 582, 594-95 (E. & A. 1934).

93. 192 N.J. Super. 523 (App. Div. 1984).

94. *Cappiello v. Ragen Precision Industries, Inc.*, 192 N.J. Super. 523, 529 (App. Div. 1984).

V. DEFAMATION

3-10 Requisites

For a claim of defamation to be actionable,[97] there must be:

1. A false and defamatory statement concerning the plaintiff.[98]
2. An unprivileged publication (i.e., communication) by the defendant to a third person who actually heard and understood the communication to relate to plaintiff.[99]
3. Fault amounting at least to negligence on the part of the publisher.[100]
4. In the case of slander other than slander *per se*, proof of special harm caused by the publication, *i.e.*, material or pecuniary loss, such as the loss of business or employment[101]

---

95. That analysis was applied by the district court in *Smith v. Ebasco Constructors, Inc.*, 1988 WL 44143, p. * 6 (D.N.J. 1988), holding that employers acting within the scope of their employment are unable to interfere with the employer's relationship with other employees. *See Silvestre v. Bell Atlantic Corp.*, 973 F. Supp. 475, 485-86 (D.N.J. 1997) (dismissing tortious interference claims against co-employees where plaintiff failed to establish they acted outside the scope of their employment); *DeJoy v. Comcast Cable Communications, Inc.*, 968 F. Supp. 963 (D.N.J. 1997) (summary judgment granted to individual employee defendants where plaintiff failed to show they acted outside the scope of their employment); *Pitak v. Bell Atlantic Network Servs., Inc.*, 928 F. Supp. 1354 (D.N.J. 1996) (granting summary judgment to corporate and individual defendants on plaintiffs' claim of interference with contract, on the ground of lack of the necessary tri-partite relationship); *Obendorfer v. The Gitano Group, Inc.*, 838 F. Supp. 950, 956 (D.N.J. 1993) (holding that supervisory employees may interfere with the employment relationships of other employees and the employer only when they are acting outside the scope of their employment). *Cf. Morgan v. Union County*, 268 N.J. Super. 337, 367-68, n.7 (App. Div. 1993), *cert. denied*, 135 N.J. 468 (1994) (noting without explanation that "it is possible for employees to tortiously interfere with the employment relationship between a co-employee and the employer").

96. The court states in support of its application of *respondeat superior* that: "Whether an employee is deprived of his commissions by a sole proprietor or by other corporate employees does not appear to be a fair basis of defining his legal remedies." *Cappiello v. Ragen Precision Industries, Inc.*, 192 N.J. Super. at 531, n.1. Yet, that is the apparent result reached. Because the employer in that case was a corporation acting through agents, it was found liable for tort damages for interference with its own contract. If it had been a sole proprietorship, precedent would have precluded that result.

97. This analysis is limited to private actions and does not address the constitutional and other considerations presented in cases involving public figures. *See, e.g., New York Times v. Sullivan*, 376 U.S. 254 (1964); *Gertz v. Welch*, 418 U.S. 323 (1974).

98. If the statement is made in writing, the defamation is called libel; if made orally, it is called slander.

99. *Printing Mart-Morristown v. Sharp Electronics*, 116 N.J. 739, 768 (1989); *Gnapinski v. Goldyn*, 23 N.J. 243, 253 (1957). The plaintiff need not be specifically named in the defamatory statement. "It is enough that there is such reference to him that those who read or hear the libel reasonably understand the plaintiff to be the person intended." *Dijkstra v. Westerink*, 168 N.J. Super. 128, 133 (App. Div.), *certif. denied*, 81 N.J. 329 (1979). The publication must have been made by the defendant either directly or through some agency relationship. *Abella v. Barringer Resources, Inc.*, 260 N.J. Super. 92, 99-100 (Ch. Div. 1992) (holding that independent auditor did not publish corporation's financial report including statement that officer had been terminated for cause).

100. *Bainhauer v. Manoukian*, 215 N.J. Super. 9, 31 (App. Div. 1987).

Defendant may avoid liability by proving that the defamatory statement was true, or that it was protected by an absolute or qualified privilege. Statements made during the course of a judicial or quasi-judicial proceeding are absolutely privileged, regardless of the defendant's motives or recklessness in publishing the statement. Statements made in the employment context and directed to a business purpose are frequently protected by a qualified, business/occasional privilege. That privilege is applicable when defendant has a legitimate interest in the subject matter of statement and the statement is made in good faith to a person having a corresponding interest or duty in the subject matter.

An employer has a legitimate interest/duty in (a) responding to requests for information made by governmental agencies concerning the reasons for an employee's termination, (b) taking steps to detect the theft of its property by employees and notifying and assisting the police with respect thereto, (c) notifying its employees, supervisors, and union representatives of the discharge of a worker and the essential reasons for that disciplinary action; and (d) responding to requests from prospective employers for information about current or former employees.

Protection of a qualified privilege will be lost if it is abused. A qualified privilege is abused if:

(a) the defendant knew the defamatory statement was false or acted in reckless disregard of whether it was true;

(b) the defamatory statement was not made primarily for the purpose of furthering the protected interest;

(c) the defendant knowingly published the defamatory statement to a person he had no reason to believe had a legitimate interest in the matter; or

(d) the publication contained defamatory matter that was not reasonably necessary to the accomplishment of the purpose for which the occasion was privileged.[102]

Abuse of privilege must be established by clear and convincing evidence.[103]

---

101. *Gnapinsky v. Goldyn*, 23 N.J. 243, 250 (1957); *Leers v. Green*, 24 N.J. 239, 251 (1957); *Monroe v. Host Marriott Services Corp.*, 999 F.Supp. 599, 603 (D.N.J. 1988).

102. *Bainhauer v. Manoukian*, 215 N.J. Super. 9, 42-43 (App. Div. 1987).

103. *Erickson v. Marsh & McLennan Co.*, 117 N.J. 539, 565 (1990).

3-11 Defamatory Meaning

The threshold question in any defamation case is whether the statement at issue is reasonably susceptible of a defamatory meaning.[104] It is a question of law for the court,[105] which must view the statement in context and consider the publication as a whole.[106] Words which are defamatory in one context may not always be so, if their intended meaning is different or if they are communicated in jest.[107] In determining whether words are defamatory, the court must accord them the fair and natural meaning that would be given them by reasonable persons of ordinary intelligence.[108] Only when the words in dispute are capable of both defamatory and nondefamatory meanings is the question of whether they defame for the jury.[109]

> If a published statement is susceptible of one meaning only, and that meaning is defamatory, the statement is libelous as a matter of law. Conversely, if the statement is susceptible of only a non-defamatory meaning, it cannot be considered libelous, justifying dismissal of the action. However, in cases where the statement is capable of being assigned more than one meaning, one of which is defamatory and another not, the question of whether its content is defamatory is one that must be resolved by the trier of fact.[110]

A statement is defamatory if it is false and either (1) injures the reputation of another, (2) exposes him to hatred, contempt, or ridicule, (3) causes him to be shunned or avoided, or (4) subjects him to a loss of the good will, esteem, respect, and confidence entertained toward him by others.[111] As defined in the Restatement (Second) of Torts,

---

104. *Printing Mart-Morristown v. Sharp Electronics*, 116 N.J. 739, 765 (1989); *Decker v. The Princeton Packet*, 116 N.J. 418, 424 (1989); *Romaine v. Kallinger*, 109 N.J. 282, 290 (1988).

105. *Decker v. The Princeton Packet*, 116 N.J. 418, 424 (1989); *Schiavone Construction Co. v. Time, Inc.*, 619 F. Supp. 684, 694 (D.N.J. 1985); *Abella v. Barringer Resources, Inc.*, 260 N.J. Super. 92, 98 (Ch. Div. 1992). *See Salek v. Passaic Collegiate School*, 255 N.J. Super. 355, 359 (App. Div. 1992) (whether a photograph represented a false statement of alleged fact and whether it was reasonably susceptible of a defamatory meaning were issues of law for the court).

106. *Decker v. The Princeton Packet*, 116 N.J. 418, 425 (1989).

107. *See Romaine v. Kallinger*, 109 N.J. 282, 290 (1988); *Abella v. Barringer Resources, Inc.*, 260 N.J. Super. 92, 98 (Ch. Div. 1992); *Walko v. Kean College of New Jersey*, 235 N.J. Super. 139, 147-48 (Law Div. 1988).

108. *Higgins v. Pascack Valley Hospital*, 307 *N.J. Super.* 277 (App. Div.), *certif. granted*, 156 N.J. 405 (1998); *Printing Mart-Morristown v. Sharp Electronics*, 116 N.J. 739, 765 (1989).

109. *Printing Mart-Morristown v. Sharp Electronics*, 116 N.J. 739, 765 (1989); *Decker v. The Princeton Packet*, 116 N.J. 418, 425 (1989).

110. *Romaine v. Kallinger*, 109 N.J. 282, 290-91 (1988) (citations omitted).

> [a] communication is defamatory if it tends so to harm the reputation of another as to lower him in the estimation of the community or to deter third persons from associating or dealing with him.[112]

Words need not impute illegality or immorality to be defamatory; it is "sufficient that the false declaration adversely affect a plaintiff's reputation, business, trade, profession, or office."[113] An allegedly defamatory statement pertaining to a person's trade, profession, or business is actionable if it is made with respect to a matter of significance and importance relating to the manner in which the subject of the statement carries out his trade or business.[114] "Injury to reputation may be either (1) presumed from the nature of the words themselves, or (2) proved by evidence of their consequences."[115]

3-12 Libel

Libel is any printed or *written* defamation of a person, published maliciously and without justification.[116] Unlike slander (except slander *per se*), libel does not require proof of special damages.[117]

A letter charging that an employee had food belonging to the defendant company in his personal bag charges the commission of larceny and thus is libelous on its face.[118] A notice advising co-workers that an employee was discharged for failure to follow company instructions is libelous.[119] The publication of an arti-

---

111. *Decker v. The Princeton Packet*, 116 N.J. 418, 425-26 (1989); *Dairy Stores, Inc. v. Sentinel Pub. Co.*, 104 N.J. 125, 133 (1986); *Lawrence v. Bauer Pub. & Printing Ltd.*, 89 N.J. 451, 459, *cert. denied*, 459 U.S. 999 (1982); *Leers v. Green*, 24 N.J. 239, 251 (1957); *Hall v. Heavey*, 195 N.J. Super. 590, 594 (App. Div. 1984). See *Higgins v. Pascack Valley Hosp.*, 307 N.J. Super. 277, 303 (App. Div.), *certif. granted*, 156 N.J. 405 (1998) (letter stating that plaintiff's claims had been investigated, that to date no substantiation had been found, that therefore there was no reason to continue investigation, but that plaintiff could provide additional information, if any, was not defamatory.)

112. Restatement (Second) of Torts, §559, p.156 (1977). It is the loss of esteem of "any substantial and respectable group, even though it be a minority one." Prosser & Keeton on the Law of Torts, §92, p.577, quoted in *Herrmann v. Newark Morning Ledger Co.*, 49 N.J. Super. 551, 555 (App. Div. 1958). (Herrmann II) *See Herrmann v. Newark Morning Ledger Co.*, 48 N.J. Super. 420, 439-42 (App. Div. 1958) (Herrmann I) (whether the plaintiff was demeaned "in the eyes of a substantial number of respectable people in the community," regardless of whether all so-called "right-thinking" people would agree, an issue for the judge, not the jury, to decide).

113. *Printing Mart-Morristown v. Sharp Electronics*, 116 N.J. 739, 766 (1989) ("New Jersey courts have long held actionable false statements designed to produce an adverse effect on one's business or trade").

114. *See Lutz v. Royal Ins. Co. of America*, 245 N.J. Super. 480, 492-93 (App. Div. 1991).

115. *Leers v. Green*, 24 N.J. 239, 251 (1957); *Neigel v. Seaboard Finance Co.*, 68 N.J. Super. 542, 553 (App. Div. 1961).

116. *Kelly v. Hoffman*, 137 N.J.L. 695, 698-99 (E. & A. 1948); Prosser & Keeton on the Law of Torts, §112, p. 785 (5th ed. 1984).

cle stating that an employee was retiring and assuming an emeritus position was not defamatory.[120]

3-12:1 Slander

At least three categories of false oral statements are generally deemed to be slanderous *per se*, and therefore actionable without proof of special damages. They are words which: (1) charge commission of a crime; (2) affect a person in his business, trade, employment, or office; or (3) impute certain loathsome diseases.[121]

(1) *Criminal Conduct.* The traditional rule is that an unprivileged publication of a false statement imputing to another conduct constituting a criminal offense is slander *per se* if the offense charged is an indictable offense.[122] The modern view is that the imputation of crime should be actionable *per se* only if it involves "a major social disgrace"[123] or "moral turpitude."[124] An accusation of theft or larceny is slander *per se*, regardless of whether the offense is indictable.[125] Where the unavoidable implication of the language used is that such a crime has

---

117. *Leers v. Green*, 24 N.J. 239, 251 (1957). Under the traditional rule, damages were presumed as a matter of substantive law upon a determination that words were libelous. *See, e.g., Herrmann v. Newark Morning Ledger Co.*, 48 N.J. Super. 420, 441, 443-46 (App. Div.), *aff'd on reh.*, 49 N.J. Super. 551 (App. Div. 1958). That is apparently no longer the case. *See Rogozinski v. Airstream By Angell*, 152 N.J. Super. 133, 147 (Law Div. 1977), modified, 164 N.J. Super. 467 (App. Div. 1978) (noting that the United States Supreme Court opinion in *Gertz v. Welch*, 418 U.S. 323 (1974), "apparently denies the court the right to presume damages"). *See* n.218, *infra*.

118. *Jorgensen v. Pennsylvania R.R. Co.*, 25 N.J. 541, 563 (1958).

119. *Ramsdell v. Pennsylvania R.R. Co.*, 79 N.J.L. 379, 381 (Sup. Ct. 1910).

120. *Grossman v. Daily Racing Form, Inc.*, 1994 WL 273389, at *9-10 (D.N.J. June 10, 1994).

121. *Gnapinsky v. Goldyn*, 23 N.J. 243, 250 (1957); *Hall v. Heavey*, 195 N.J. Super. at 595; Restatement (Second) of Torts, §§570 to 574, pp. 186-97. Slander that is not actionable *per se* is governed by the same rules that apply to libel, except that special damages must be proved. Statements imputing another as "anti-Semitic" do not fall within slander: per se, and consequently special damages must be proven. *Ward v. Zelikovsky*, 136 N.J. 516, 538-41 (1994), *rev'g* 263 N.J. Super. 497 (App. Div. 1993).

122. *Sokolay v. Edlin*, 65 N.J. Super. 112, 121 (App. Div. 1961) (pharmacy owner stated he was convinced that plaintiff-employee stole narcotics); *Dijkstra v. Westerink*, 168 N.J. Super. 128, 133 (App. Div.), *certif. denied*, 81 N.J. 329 (1979) (defendant accused of stating that plaintiff attempted to shoot him); Restatement (Second) of Torts, §571 & Comment b, pp. 186-87.

123. Prosser & Keeton on the Law of Torts, §112, p. 789. "The idea toward which the courts obviously have been struggling is that the imputation is to be [slander *per se*] only if it involves a major social disgrace, which might very well be the ultimate test." *Id.*

124. *Hall v. Heavey*, 195 N.J. Super. 590, 595-97 (App. Div. 1984). Prosser, *et al.*, note that most courts require that the crime be one which involves "moral turpitude," which means "inherent baseness or vileness of principle in the human heart." Prosser & Keeton on the Law of Torts, §112, p. 789. Accord Restatement (Second) of Torts, §571 Comment g, pp. 189-90. For example, the accusation that plaintiff beat his mother involves the imputation of moral turpitude. Prosser & Keeton on the Law of Torts, §112, p. 789, citing *Sipp v. Coleman*, 179 F. 997 (C.C.D.N.J. 1910). *But see* discussion in *Schiavone Construction Co. v. Time, Inc.*, 619 F. Supp. 684, 694-95 (D.N.J. 1985).

been committed, the statement is slanderous *per se*.[126] The fact that a crime is not explicitly charged is not dispositive because "the sting of an accusation may be more pervasive when made by insinuation."[127]

Thus, an employer who notified the Unemployment Compensation Commission that an employee was discharged, *inter alia*, because he "had to be continually watched and reminded with respect to collection of monies, ordering parts and supplies, and treatment of customers" was guilty of slander *per se* in that there was "an implication of criminality, although slight."[128]

(2) *Business/Employment*. Words concerning plaintiff in his business, trade, employment, or office, which impute a want of integrity, credit, or common honesty, or charge personal incapacity, if without justification, are slanderous *per se*.[129]

> A statement made in the context of and pertaining to a person's trade, profession or business ... is actionable if the statement is made with reference to "a matter of significance and importance" relating to the manner in which the subject of the statement carries out his trade, profession or business.[130]

Negative evaluations of employee job performance are normally found to be defamatory *per se* under this criterion. Thus, it has been held that an employer's statement of reasons for termination, provided to the Unemployment Compensation Commission, were slanderous *per se* where the employer alleged (a) that one employee was terminated because she was incapable of accomplishing the tasks assigned her, thereby resulting in a dramatic drop in sales, and (b) that another

---

125. *Hall v. Heavey*, 195 N.J. Super. 590, 594-97 (App. Div. 1984) (suggesting that crimes of moral turpitude are slanderous *per se*). This position was previously espoused in *Sipp v. Coleman*, 179 F. 997, 998 (C.C.D.N.J. 1910) (applying New Jersey law); *see Schiavone Construction Co. v. Time, Inc.*, 619 F. Supp. 684, 695 (D.N.J. 1985) ("allegations of criminality are universally considered defamatory *per se*"). Accord Prosser & Keeton on the Law of Torts, §112, p. 789; Restatement (Second) of Torts, §571 Comment d, p. 188.

126. *Sokolay v. Edlin*, 65 N.J. Super. 112, 121-22 (App. Div. 1961) (accusing an employee of responsibility for missing narcotics is tantamount to an accusation of theft); *Jorgensen v. Pennsylvania R.R. Co.*, 25 N.J. 541, 563 (1958) (stating that the plaintiff-employee stole or was in the act of stealing company property is libelous *per se*.)

127. *Molnar v. Star-Ledger*, 193 N.J. Super. 12, 18 (App.Div. 1984), quoting *Lawrence v. Bauer Pub. & Printing Ltd.*, 176 N.J. Super. 378, 389 (App.Div.), *rev'd in part on other grounds and vacated in part on other grounds*, 89 N.J. 451 (1982), *cert. denied*, 459 U.S. 999 (1982).

128. *Rogozinski v. Airstream By Angell*, 152 N.J. Super. 133, 140, 145 (Law Div. 1977), *modified*, 164 N.J. Super. 465 (App. Div. 1979). In *Rogozinski*, the defamation was made in a letter, but the court referred to concepts normally applied to slander *per se*.

129. *Freisinger v. Moore*, 65 N.J.L. 286, 287 (E. & A. 1990); *Kelly v. Hoffman*, 137 N.J.L. at 697 (accusing art dealer of selling copy as an original painting for excessive amount); *Kruse v. Rabe*, 80 N.J.L. 378, 379-80 (E. & A. 1911) (accusing real estate broker of charging exorbitant commissions imputes a lack of integrity); Restatement (Second) of Torts, §573, pp. 191-92.

130. *Lutz v. Royal Ins. Co. of America*, 245 N.J. Super. 480, 492-93 (App. Div. 1991).

employee was dismissed because he antagonized both customers and employees, had to be constantly supervised, and no longer could be depended upon, thereby jeopardizing the company's reputation.[131] Likewise, an employer's statement to co-workers that an employee was discharged for failure to follow company instructions was slander *per se*.[132] A statement that an employee has stolen company property is slander *per se*.[133] The statements that plaintiffs were "ripping off" a client, that they "were not qualified" to do work for which they were bidding, and that they did unreasonably priced inadequate work, were sufficient to withstand a defense motion to dismiss.[134]

Further, statements that an individual was "abusive, vulgar and offensive," and that his behavior in the workplace did not epitomize civilized human behavior are defamatory.[135] And a drug company's failure to defend a nurse employed as a salesperson against a customer's accusations that she had distributed expired medication, coupled with the allegedly false statement that the nurse's action violated company policy, was defamatory.[136] However, a supervisor who asked for an employee's keys and files, offered a recommendation letter, and searched his desk and car for a missing report, did not defame him.[137] The statement that an employee was terminated for cause was not defamatory as a matter of law because "[t]ypically, the fair and natural import of the statement that a person was 'terminated for cause' is only that the termination was not arbitrary."[138] However, because "termination for cause" might not always be construed as a "non-arbitrary cessation of employment," there was a fact question as to whether it was defamatory.[139]

3-12:2 Opinion

With respect to matters of public interest, the Supreme Court has held that only facts can be defamatory; that mere expressions of opinion, which can never be true or false, are not actionable.[140] One Appellate Division decision has predict-

131. *Rogozinski v. Airstream By Angell*, 152 N.J. Super. 133, 140, 145 (Law Div. 1977), *modified on other grounds*, 164 N.J. Super. 465 (App. Div. 1979).

132. *Ramsdell v. Pennsylvania R.R. Co.*, 79 N.J.L. 379, 381 (Sup. Ct. 1910) (libel case in which the court applied slander *per se* terminology).

133. *Sokolay v. Edlin*, 65 N.J. Super. 112, 121-22 (App. Div. 1961).

134. *Printing Mart-Morristown v. Sharp Electronics*, 116 N.J. 739, 766-67 (1989).

135. *Lutz v. Royal Ins. Co. of America*, 245 N.J.Super. 480, 493 (App.Div. 1991).

136. *DeVries v. McNeil Consumer Products Co.*, 250 N.J.Super. 159, 166-67 (App.Div. 1991).

137. *Schwartz v. Leasametric, Inc.*, 224 N.J.Super. 21, 28 (App.Div. 1988).

138. *Abella v. Barringer Resources, Inc.*, 260 N.J. Super. 92, 99 (Ch. Div. 1993).

139. *Id.*

ed that the Supreme Court would not extend that rule to matters not implicating the public interest, such as an evaluation of the job performance of an employee whose work does not impact the public.[141] However, *dicta* in another decision seems to assume that opinions about employees with no apparent public impact would be protected as well.[142] A more recent Appellate Division decision stated broadly that: "Only a statement of fact can be defamatory; mere expression of opinion, which, by their nature, can never be proved true or false, are not actionable, unless they imply the existence of undisclosed facts."[143] Where evaluation of a professional's competency is of public import, it is clear that the opinion privilege will apply.[144]

New Jersey follows the approach of the Restatement (Second) of Torts in determining what is protected opinion and what is fact.[145] This determination is a question of law for the court.[146] Pure opinions entitled to full protection are either (1) statements which provide the underlying factual assumptions of the speaker or (2) statements made where the underlying assumptions are known to the listener.[147] Mixed opinions, which imply the existence of defamatory facts in support of the opinion and otherwise unknown to the listener, are not protected.[148]

---

140. *Kotlikoff v. The Community News*, 89 N.J. 62, 68 (1982). *See Gertz v. Welch*, 418 U.S. 323, 339-40 (1974).

141. *Lutz v. Royal Ins. Co. of America,* 245 N.J. Super. 480, 496 (App. Div. 1991) (statements that plaintiff's behavior in the workplace was "abusive, vulgar and offensive," and that it did not "epitomize civilized human behavior"). *See also Ferraro v. City of Long Branch*, 314 N.J. Super 268 (App. Div.), *certif. denied*, ___ N.J. ___ (1998) (dismissing public employee's defamation claim based upon official's statements that employee's lawsuit was frivolous, holding that official "was merely offering his opinion or adopting as his own the opinion of another, and he did so in response to a public official's allegations as reported in the press"). *See Kotlikoff v. The Community News*, 89 N.J. 62, 69 n.3 (1982) [noting that the American Law Institute takes the position that protection of private opinion is the logical extension of the *Gertz* dictum, Restatement (Second) of Torts, §566, comment c (1977)]. *But see* Note, *Fact and Opinion after Gertz v. Welch: The Evolution of a Privilege*, 34 Rut.L.Rev. 81, 97-99, 126 (Fall 1981).

142. *Schwartz v. Leasametric, Inc.*, 224 N.J.Super. 21, 27-28 (App.Div. 1988).

143. *Higgins v. Pascack Valley Hospital*, 307 N.J. Super. 277, 304 (App. Div.), *certif. granted*, 156 N.J. 405 (1998) (co-employee letters expressing negative opinions of plaintiff not defamatory).

144. *See Nanavati v. Burdette Tomlin Memorial Hospital*, 857 F.2d 96, 106-08 (3d Cir. 1988), *cert. denied*, 489 U.S. 1078 (1989) (physician's comment on another physician's alleged incompetency "contributes to a robust debate on matters of public importance, namely the competence of medical care at a hospital").

145. *See Dairy Stores, Inc. v. Sentinel Pub. Co.*, 104 N.J. 125, (1986); *Kotlikoff v. The Community News*, 89 N.J. 62, 68-69 (1982); *Nanavati v. Burdette Tomlin Memorial Hospital*, 857 F.2d 96, 107 (3d Cir. 1988); *Dunn v. Gannett New York Newspaper, Inc.*, 833 F.2d 446, 452-53 (3d Cir. 1987).

146. *Kotlikoff v. The Community News*, 89 N.J. 62, 67 (1982).

147. *Kotlikoff v. The Community News*, 89 N.J. 62, 68-69(1982); *Nanavati v. Burdette Tomlin Memorial Hospital*, 857 F.2d 96, 107 (3d Cir. 1988), *cert. denied*, 489 U.S. 1078 (1989). *See* Restatement (Second) of Torts, §566.

148. *Kotlikoff v. The Community News*, 89 N.J. at 69. *Nanavati v. Burdette Tomlin Memorial Hospital*, 857 F.2d 96, 107 (3d Cir. 1988), *cert. denied*, 489 U.S. 1078 (1989).

3-12:3 Publication

Because the law of defamation seeks to secure reputation, the defendant must have communicated the defamatory statement to someone other than the person defamed,[149] and that person must have actually heard and understood the communication to relate to the plaintiff.[150] This is referred to as "publication" of the defamatory statement.

Publication can be made to any third person, including a corporate employer's own officers, employees, or agents.[151] An employer's statement of reasons for discharge is published when provided to the plaintiff-employee's collective bargaining agent.[152] An employer's response to an Unemployment Compensation Commission's request for information concerning the reasons for an employee's termination constitutes a publication.[153]

3-13 Privilege

In certain situations, paramount public policy requires that individuals be permitted to speak or write freely without being restrained by the threat of a defamation action.[154] "The reason for holding any occasion privileged is 'common convenience and welfare of society, and it is obvious that no definite line can be

---

149. *Gnapinsky v. Goldyn*, 23 N.J. 243, 252 (1957); Prosser & Keeton on the Law of Torts, §113, p. 797.

150. *Id.* at 253; Prosser & Keeton on the Law of Torts, §113, p. 798.

Where the words are reasonably capable of either an innocent or a defamatory meaning, it is a question of fact for the jury to determine which of the two meanings was understood by third persons. Whereas the court determines whether a communication is capable of a defamatory meaning, the jury determines whether the communication, capable of a defamatory meaning, was so understood by the third persons. *Leers v. Green*, 24 N.J. 239, 253 (1957); *Lawrence v. Bauer Pub. & Printing Ltd.*, 89 N.J. 451, 459, *cert. denied*, 459 U.S. 999 (1982); *Sokolay v. Edlin*, 65 N.J. Super. 112, 122-23 (App. Div. 1961) (whether an employer's accusation that an employee was responsible for missing narcotic is defamatory was a question for the jury); *Herrmann v. Newark Morning Ledger Co.*, 48 N.J. Super. 420, 431 (App.Div.), *aff'd on reh.*, 49 N.J.Super. 551, 554-55 (App.Div. 1958) (the imputation that a labor leader attended a labor convention with improperly-obtained credentials was libelous as a matter of law, no harmless interpretation was reasonable).

"The language in question must be construed according to the fair and natural meaning which will be given it by reasonable persons of ordinary intelligence." *Herrmann v. Newark Morning Ledger Co.*, 48 N.J. Super. at 431; *DeVries v. McNeil Consumer Products Co.*, 250 N.J.Super. 159, 166 (App.Div. 1991).

151. Prosser & Keeton on the Law of Torts, §113, p. 798; *Jerolamon v. Fairleigh Dickinson Univ.*, 199 N.J. Super. 179, 185-86 (App. Div. 1985).

152. *Murphy v. Johns-Manville Products Corp.*, 45 N.J. Super. 478, 489-90 (App. Div.), *certif. denied*, 25 N.J. 55 (1957) (*dicta*).

153. *Rogozinski v. Airstream By Angell*, 152 N.J. Super. 133 (Law Div. 1977), *modified on other grounds*, 164 N.J. Super. 465 (App. Div. 1979).

154. *Fees v. Trow*, 105 N.J. 330, 336 (1987); *Maressa v. New Jersey Monthly*, 89 N.J. 176, 191 *cert. denied*, 459 U.S. 907 (1982); *Swede v. Passaic Daily News*, 30 N.J. 320, 331 (1959); *Rainier's Dairies v. Raritan Valley Farms, Inc.*, 19 N.J. 552, 557-58 (1955); *Sokolay v. Edlin*, 65 N.J. Super. 112, 124 (App. Div. 1961).

so drawn as to mark off with precision those occasions which are privileged, and separate them from those which are not.'"[155]

Privilege is an affirmative defense and must be proved by the defendant.[156] The existence of a privilege is a question of law for the court, subject to the exercise of the jury's traditional function where facts are in dispute.[157] The defendant has the burden of establishing that the occasion was privileged by setting forth a recognized public or private interest that justifies the publication.[158]

The privilege may be absolute or qualified.[159] An absolute privilege affords complete protection, whereas a qualified privilege affords protection only so long as the privilege is not abused.[160] The privileges discussed herein are those most likely to be presented in defamation claims arising in the employment context.

3-13:1 Immunity

Absolute immunity is afforded in judicial and quasi-judicial proceedings. Judges, attorneys, witnesses, parties, and jurors are fully protected against defamation actions based on statements made in those proceedings and having some relation thereto, even if the statements are intentionally defamatory and malicious.[161] Defamatory statements made to other officers or bodies, acting officially but not in judicial or quasi-judicial proceedings, are entitled to only a qualified privilege.[162]

---

155. *Swede v. Passaic Daily News*, 30 N.J. at 331, quoting *Coleman v. Newark Morning Ledger Co.*, 29 N.J. 357, 378 (1959), quoting *Stuart v. Bell*, [1891] 2 Q.B. 341, 346.

156. *Sokolay v. Edlin*, 65 N.J. Super. 112, 124 (App. Div. 1961); *Swede v. Passaic Daily News*, 30 N.J. 320, 332 (1959).

157. *Lutz v. Royal Ins. Co. of America*, 245 N.J. Super. 480, 499 (App. Div. 1991); *Bainhauer v. Manoukian*, 215 N.J. Super. 9, 40 (App. Div. 1987); *Sokolay v. Edlin*, 65 N.J. Super. 112, 124 (App. Div. 1961); Prosser & Keeton on the Law of Torts, §115, p. 835; Restatement (Second) of Torts, §619, p. 316.

158. *Swede v. Passaic Daily News*, 30 N.J. 320, 332 (1959); *Sokolay v. Edlin*, 65 N.J. Super. 112, 124 (App. Div. 1961); *Rogozinski v. Airstream By Angell*, 152 N.J. Super. 133, 154 (Law Div. 1977), *modified on other grounds*, 164 N.J. Super. 465 (App. Div. 1979). One early case suggested that the defendant must also establish that the communication was made under an honest belief as to its truth. *Fahr v. Hayes*, 50 N.J.L. 275, 278 (Sup. Ct. 1888). It is now clear that this second requirement is properly part of plaintiff's case, in establishing the defendant's negligence and/or the defendant's abuse of the privilege. *See Lutz v. Royal Ins. Co. of America*, 245 N.J. Super. 480, 496-98 (App. Div. 1991) (whether statement made in good faith goes to abuse of privilege and is usually a fact question); *Bainhauer v. Manoukian*, 215 N.J. Super. at 40-41 (the so-called good faith test that the judge must apply when determining whether the occasion was privileged is an "objective determination of whether the defamatory statement was on its face an apparently reasonable response to the circumstances").

159. *Fees v. Trow*, 105 N.J. 330, 336 (1987); *Dairy Stores, Inc. v. Sentinel Pub. Co.*, 104 N.J. 125, 136 (1986); *Swede v. Passaic Daily News*, 30 N.J. 320, 332 (1959); *Sokolay v. Edlin*, 65 N.J. Super. 112, 124 (App. Div. 1961); *Neigel v. Seaboard Finance Co.*, 68 N.J. Super. 542, 549 (App. Div. 1961).

160. *Dairy Stores, Inc. v. Sentinel Pub. Co.*, 104 N.J. 125, 136, 148-49 (1986); *Rainier's Dairies v. Raritan Valley Farms, Inc.*, 19 N.J. 552, 558 (1955); *Sokolay v. Edlin*, 65 N.J. Super. 112, 124-25 (App. Div. 1961); *Rogozinski v. Airstream By Angell*, 152 N.J. Super. 133, 154 (Law Div. 1977), *modified on other grounds*, 164 N.J. Super. 465 (App. Div. 1979).

A party to a private litigation is absolutely privileged to publish false and defamatory statements in the institution of or during the course and as a part of a judicial proceeding in which he participates, if the statements have some relation thereto.[163]

Communications to which the privilege does not extend must be so wanting in relation to the subject matter of the controversy that no reasonable person can doubt their irrelevancy and impropriety.[164] Whether the communication has a relation to the lawsuit is a question of law to be decided by the court, and every presumption will be in favor of relevancy or pertinency.[165]

The privilege extends to each and every step in the proceeding; communications made before commencement, but in preparation for a judicial proceeding, may also be protected.[166] Although there is some authority to the contrary, the better view seems to be that information given and informal complaints made to a prosecuting attorney, a magistrate, or other proper official preliminary to a proposed criminal prosecution is to be regarded as an initial step in a judicial proceeding, and so entitled to an absolute, rather than a qualified immunity, regardless of whether the information is followed by a formal complaint.[167] One New Jersey court, however, has held that statements made by an employer in a

---

161. *See Fees v. Trow*, 105 N.J. 330, 336-37 (1987); *Rainier's Dairies v. Raritan Valley Farms, Inc.*, 19 N.J. 552, 558-63 (1955); *DeVivo v. Ascher*, 228 N.J. Super. 453, 457 (App. Div. 1988); *Middlesex Concrete Products & Excavating Corp. v. Carteret Industrial Ass'n*, 68 N.J. Super. 85, 91-92 (App. Div. 1961); *Fenning v. S.G. Holding Corp.*, 47 N.J. Super. 110, 117 (App. Div. 1957); *Rogozinski v. Airstream By Angell*, 152 N.J. Super. 133, 149-50 (Law Div. 1977), *modified on other grounds*, 164 N.J. Super. 465 (App. Div. 1979); Prosser & Keeton on the Law of Torts, §114, pp. 816-20.

162. *See Fenning v. S.G. Holding Corp.*, 47 N.J. Super. 110, 117 (App. Div. 1957). *See Fees v. Trow*, 105 N.J. 330, 337 (1987).

163. *See Thourot v. Hartnett*, 56 N.J. Super. 306, 307-08 (App. Div. 1959); Prosser & Keeton on the Law of Torts, §114, p. 817. *Ruberton v. Gabage*, 280 N.J. Super. 125, 134-35 (App. Div.), *cert. denied*, 142 N.J. 451 (1995) (allegedly defamatory statements by attorney in settlement conference absolutely privileged).

164. *See Thourot v. Hartnett*, 56 N.J. Super. 306, 308 (App. Div. 1959); *Ruberton v. Gabage*, 280 N.J. Super. 125, 134-35 (App. Div.), *cert. denied*, 142 N.J. 451 (1995) (allegedly defamatory statements by attorney in settlement conference absolutely privileged).

165. *See Thourot v. Hartnett*, 56 N.J. Super. 306, 309 (App. Div. 1959); *but cf. Fees v. Trow*, 105 N.J. 330, 337 (1987) (absolute privilege "is provided only in the narrowest of instances").

166. According to the Restatement (Second) of Torts, §587, Comment e, p. 250, communications preliminary to a proposed judicial proceeding are privileged if they have some relation to a proceeding that is "contemplated in good faith and under serious consideration. The bare possibility that the proceeding might be instituted is not to be used as a cloak to provide immunity for defamation when the possibility is not seriously considered." *But see Rogozinski v. Airstream By Angell*, 152 N.J. Super. at 152 (response to request for information from the Unemployment Compensation Commission protected by a qualified privilege only); *Dijkstra v. Westerink*, 168 N.J. Super. 128, 135 (App. Div. 1979), *certif. denied*, 81 N.J. 329 (1979) (absolute privilege inapplicable to statements made before commencement of judicial proceedings; however qualified privilege applied); then *cf. DeVivo v. Ascher*, 228 N.J. Super. 453, 459-60 (App. Div. 1988), *certif. denied*, 114 N.J. 482 (1989) (questioning limitation of absolute privilege to statements made after commencement of proceedings; "the ability of an attorney to communicate freely when a matter is in controversy is just as important in the preliminary negotiating stage as it is on the day the suit papers are filed with the court.").

statutorily-mandated response to an investigatory request of the Unemployment Compensation Commission (UCC), concerning former employees' benefit claims, were not entitled to an absolute privilege because no judicial or quasi-judicial proceedings were pending at that time.[168] Likewise, merely reporting a crime to the police and giving the police a statement during its investigation, all prior to the institution of any judicial proceedings, has been found not to give rise to an absolute privilege.[169]

In addition to judicial proceedings, an absolute privilege has been extended to legislative proceedings;[170] executive communications; situations where the plaintiff has "consented" to the defamation;[171] husband and wife; and certain political broadcasts.[172]

---

167. Prosser & Keeton on the Law of Torts, §114, pp. 819-20; Restatement (Second) of Torts, §587 Comment b, p. 249.

168. *Rogozinski v. Airstream By Angell*, 152 N.J. Super. 133, 150 (Law Div. 1977), *modified on other grounds*, 164 N.J. Super. 465 (App. Div. 1979). That court did, as discussed *infra*, find a qualified privilege. Presumably, had the initial proceedings before the Unemployment Compensation Commission involved "safeguards similar to those of a judicial proceeding, including notice, informal pleading, and hearing," those proceedings, at that stage, might have been deemed *quasi*-judicial and thus absolutely privileged. *Cf. Fenning v. S.G. Holding Corp.*, 47 N.J. Super. 110, 119 (App. Div. 1957) (proceedings before county rent control board involved those safeguards and entitled to absolute privilege).

Rogozinski was decided in 1977. In 1984, the Legislature amended N.J.S.A. 43:21-11(g) to provide that information obtained by the UCC from employers and employees is to be held confidential and shall not be subject to subpoena or admissible in evidence in any civil action or proceeding unrelated to the employee's claim for unemployment benefits. L. 1984, c.24, §8. The N.J. Division of Unemployment and Disability Insurance (Division) has read this amendment to mean that:

> All information you give to the Division is *absolutely* confidential and *privileged*, and *cannot be made the subject matter or basis in any action of slander or libel* in any court in the state.

N.J. Dept. of Labor, *Simplifying New Jersey's Unemployment Compensation & Temporary Disability Benefits Law for Employers*, p. 21 (March 1987) (emphasis added). There is no legislative history pertaining to this aspect of the 1984 amendment. Thus, it is not clear whether the Division's broad reading of the amendment—effectively overruling *Rogozinski*—is correct. This broad reading is consistent with the general rule. *See* 1B CCH *Unemployment Insurance Reports*, §1670, p. 4359-2 (Mar. 18, 1986 rev.) ("In most states the law specifically provides that all letters, reports, communications, etc., either oral or written, from the employer or employee to each other or to the state administrative agency, if made in connection with the requirements of the unemployment compensation law, are absolutely privileged and may not be made the basis for any suit for slander or libel"). As to the binding effect of the Division's reading of the 1984 amendment, consider the Division's caveat that the information contained in its booklet "does not have the force or effect of law, rule or regulation." *Simplifying New Jersey's Unemployment Compensation & Temporary Disability Benefits Law for Employers*, p. 1.

169. *Dijkstra v. Westerink*, 168 N.J. Super. 128, 134 (App. Div.), *certif. denied*, 81 N.J. 329 (1979) (qualified privilege, however, existed). *See Geyer v. Faiella*, 279 N.J. Super. 386, 391-92 (App. Div.), *certif. denied*, 141 N.J. 95 (1995) (initial reports of alleged criminal acts to attorney and to the United States Attorney are entitled to only a qualified and not an absolute privilege).

170. *DeSantis v. Welfare Ass'n*, 237 N.J. Super. 550, 554 (App. Div.), *certif. denied*, 122 N.J. 164 (1990). ("We now adopt the Restatement's formulation of the absolute privilege. We add that as long as the allegedly defamatory matter would not have been published except to inform the legislative body, and the material is relevant to the legislative proceeding, the privilege attaches regardless of whether the material is solicited or subpoenaed and regardless of whether it is given under oath.")

3-13:2 Qualified Privilege

A declarant who makes defamatory statements pursuant to a business or other duty is entitled to a qualified privilege. A communication made bona fide, upon any subject matter in which the defendant has a legitimate interest, or in reference to which the defendant has a duty, is privileged, if made to a person having a corresponding interest or duty. That is so even if the statement contains criminatory matter which, without the privilege, would be actionable.[173] This privilege is "based on the public policy 'that it is essential that true information be given whenever it is reasonably necessary for the protection of one's own interests, the interests of third persons or certain interests of the public.' "[174]

A qualified privilege has been recognized in a variety of circumstances in the employment arena:

— a statement describing the reasons for an employee's discharge, in response to a request for information by the Unemployment Compensation Commission.[175]

— statements to union officials about the reasons for a bargaining-unit employee's discharge.[176]

---

171. Where the plaintiff has "himself invited or instigated the publication of defamatory words," he cannot complain of damage to his reputation. Prosser & Keeton on the Law of Torts, §114, p. 823; *Rogozinski v. Airstream By Angell*, 152 N.J. Super. 133, 151 (Law Div. 1977), *modified on other grounds*, 164 N.J. Super. 465 (App. Div. 1979). It has been held that by applying for unemployment benefits an employee did not invite or instigate from his employer more than a mere statement of the reasons for separation. *Id.* at 152.

172. *See generally* Prosser & Keeton on the Law of Torts, §114, pp. 816, 820-24; *Fees v. Trow*, 105 N.J. 330, 337 (1987); *Burke v. Deiner*, 97 N.J. 465, 474-75 (1984).

173. *Coleman v. Newark Morning Ledger Co.*, 29 N.J. 357, 375 (1959), quoted in *Erickson v. Marsh & McLennan Co.*, 117 N.J. 539, 563 (1990); *Jorgensen v. Pennsylvania R.R. Co.*, 25 N.J. 541, 564 (1958); *King v. Patterson*, 49 N.J.L. 417, 442 (E. & A. 1887); *Bainhauer v. Manoukian*, 215 N.J. Super. 9, 36-37 (App. Div. 1987); *Sokolay v. Edlin*, 65 N.J. Super. 112, 123 (App. Div. 1961); *Rogozinski v. Airstream By Angell*, 152 N.J. Super. 133, 153-54 (Law Div. 1977), *modified on other grounds*, 164 N.J. Super. 465 (App. Div. 1979); Prosser & Keeton on the Law of Torts, §115, pp. 825-27.

Prosser, *et al.*, offer the following formulation:

> [T]he publication is privileged when it is "fairly made by a person in the discharge of some public or private duty, whether legal or moral, or in the conduct of his own affairs, in matters where his interest is concerned."

Prosser & Keeton on the Law of Torts, §115, p.825, *quoting Toogood v. Spyring*, 149 Eng. Rep. 1044 (1834). The *Toogood* formulation has been quoted by the New Jersey courts. *See, e.g., Rogozinski v. Airstream By Angell*, 152 N.J. Super. at 153.

174. *Erickson v. Marsh & McLennan Co.*, 117 N.J. 539, 563 (1990), quoting Introductory Note, Restatement (Second) of Torts, §592A, at 258 (1965). *Williams v. Bell Tel. Lab., Inc.*, 132 N.J. 109, 121 (1993) ("The public policy underlying the qualified privilege recognizes the necessity that true information be given whenever reasonably required for 'the protection of one's own interests, the interests of third persons, or certain interests of third persons, or certain interests of the public.'").

175. *Rogozinski v. Airstream By Angell*, 152 N.J. Super. at 153, 156-57. See n.168, *supra*.

— statements made by one management employee to other management employees who the company believes to have a sufficient interest in the matter.[177]

— publication of routine office performance memoranda, even where critical of employees.[178]

— statements at a grievance proceeding setting forth the grounds for an employee's discharge.[179]

— statements by an employer in response to specific inquiries of a third party regarding the qualifications of a former employee.[180]

— statements by an employer to its employees notifying them of the reasons for a fellow employee's discharge.[181] Indeed, one court has stated that:

"an employer's publication to its employees of the reasons for discharge of a co-worker is not only a proper purpose, but is one of the most fitting occasions for applicaion of a qualified privilege."[182]

— statements made in response to an inquiry as to the trustworthiness of an employee applying for credit.[183]

---

176. *Jorgensen v. Pennsylvania R.R. Co.*, 25 N.J. 541, 564-65 (1958); *Murphy v. Johns-Manville Products Corp.*, 45 N.J. Super. 478, 492-93 (App. Div.), *certif. denied*, 25 N.J. 55 (1957).

177. *Murphy v. Johns-Manville Products Corp.*, 45 N.J. Super. 478, 493 (App. Div.), *certif. denied*, 25 N.J. 55 (1957). In *Murphy*, in accordance with published rules of conduct, the plaintiff was discharged from his employment for the unauthorized removal of three wire brushes and 18 emery cloth sheets from the defendant-company's premises. The chief of plant protection detected the theft and so informed the company's supervisor of industrial relations and the head of plaintiff's department. In accordance with the collective bargaining agreement, the company notified plaintiff's union representative and arranged for a hearing on plaintiff's discharge. After the hearing, the company distributed five copies of the minutes of the meeting to the union and 13 copies to management personnel. The claim for libel rested upon a statement contained in the minutes and a statement in a letter to the union president. The court held that the publication within the defendant-corporation and the union group did not, as a matter of law, exceed the bounds of the qualified privilege. All of the people to whom copies of the minutes were sent had a sufficient interest in the matter. The union had an obligation under the collective bargaining agreement to represent plaintiff's grievance to the union-management committee. 45 N.J. Super. at 492-93.

178. *Monroe v. Host Marriott Services Corp.*, 999 F.Supp. 599, 604-05 (D.N.J. 1998) (memorandum identifying business problems in an effort to rectify them protected).

179. In *Jorgensen v. Pennsylvania R.R. Co.*, 25 N.J. 541 (1958), at grievance hearings held pursuant to the collective bargaining agreement, the defendant-company read into the record a letter setting forth the charge—possession of company property in plaintiff's personal bag—for which plaintiff was discharged. The company also sent the letter to the union chairman who represented plaintiff on the appeal. The court held that these publications did not exceed the scope of the privilege since the union official and other persons who processed the grievance had a sufficient interest, as evidenced by the collective bargaining agreement and the Railway Labor Act, in the matter to justify the publications. 25 N.J. at 564-65.

180. *Erickson v. Marsh & McLennan Co.*, 117 N.J. 539, 562 (1990); *Kass v. Great Coastal Express, Inc.*, 152 N.J. 353 (1998) (qualified privilege extends to an employer who responds in good faith to the specific inquiries of a third party regarding the qualifications of an employee).

— communications with law enforcement authorities for the prevention or detection of crime:[184]

"It is the duty of citizens to give to police or other officers such information as they may have respecting crimes which have been committed, and public policy requires that communications of this kind, at least made in good faith, be protected as privileged."[185]

---

181. *Ramsdell v. Pennsylvania R.R. Co.*, 79 N.J.L. 379, 381 (Sup. Ct. 1910); *Sokolay v. Edlin*, 65 N.J. Super. 112, 124-25 (App. Div. 1961). In *Sokolay*, the court held the employer was privileged in stating, in front of other employees, to plaintiff:

> I am convinced that you are responsible for the missing demerol tablets. I am also going to find out who else is implicated in it with you. Because of this, I have got to let you go.

65 N.J. Super. at 119. *Sokolay* was cited with approval in *Bainhauer v. Manoukian*, 215 N.J. Super. at 39.

In *Ramsdell*, a notice stating that plaintiff had been discharged for failure to issue meal checks according to company instructions was posted in an office frequented by dining car employees. Although libelous *per se*, the statement was privileged because co-employees are entitled to be officially informed of the termination of another employee in their department. *Ramsdell*, 79 N.J.L. at 381.

In *Jorgensen v. Pennsylvania R.R. Co.*, several employees were present when the plaintiff-employee was stopped, his personal bag searched, and he was confronted by the fact that he had company property in his possession. The presence of the co-employees did not defeat the privilege. *Jorgensen*, 25 N.J. at 565.

In *Bainhauer*, the court held that physicians within a hospital have both a public and private duty/interest in speaking out about professional incompetency among other health-care professionals in that hospital and that this privilege extended to communications to other doctors within the hospital. 215 N.J. Super. at 36-40.

The reasoning in *Bainhauer* was followed by the New Jersey Supreme Court opinion in *Fees v. Trow*, 105 N.J. 330 (1987). In *Fees*, the court held that an employee of a state facility for the developmentally disabled was privileged in making a defamatory report to her supervisor concerning another employee's abuse of an adult resident of the facility:

> [W]e harbor no doubt whatsoever that the public interest, self-evident moral considerations, and the nature of her employment would require that one in the position of defendant report to her supervisor any incident of patient abuse.

105 N.J. at 339. In *Gallo v. Princeton Univ.*, 281 N.J. Super. 134, 145-49 (App. Div.), *certif. denied*, 142 N.J. 453 (1995), the court held that Princeton University had a qualified privilege to advise alumni and the public about alleged misuse of University property and the resignations of plaintiff and others in connection therewith. These statements "served Princeton's important interest in preventing damage to its reputation within the University Community which supports its activities." *Id.* at 148. In addition, the University reasonably could have concluded that the University community was entitled to this information, and that the University publications to which statements were made were an appropriate means of communication. *Id.* at 148-49.

182. *Garziano v. E.I. du Pont de Nemours & Co.*, 818 F.2d 380, 392 (5th Cir. 1987). The *Garziano* court noted that this is the law in Mississippi as well as in other jurisdictions. 818 F.2d at 387 & n.10. The court also noted that several courts have held, in light of the national interest in a peaceful and harmonious workplace, that employer-employee communications are absolutely priviledged. 818 F.2d at 388 n 11.

183. *Fahr v. Hayes*, 50 N.J.L. 275, 278-79 (Sup. Ct. 1888); *Krumholz v. TRW, Inc.*, 142 N.J. Super. 80, 88-89 (App. Div.), *certif. denied*, 71 N.J. 532 (1976) (the credit agency's report must be based on reasonable grounds, which will depend upon whether the agency's information was received from reliable sources and whether the agency's investigation and evaluation of such information was reasonable under the circumstances). However, a communication made by a creditor to the debtor's employer solely for the purpose of compelling the debtor to pay is not in itself privileged. *Neigel v. Seaboard Finance Co.*, 68 N.J. Super. 542, 549-51 (App. Div. 1961).

— an employee petition and memorandum accusing plaintiff of disrupting the workplace and making false charges of harassment and assault.[186]

An employer also has a qualified privilege to take reasonable steps to recover stolen property; to discover and prosecute the thief; to warn his servants concerning the conduct of plaintiff or others of questionable character; to consult an attorney for legal advice; to protect against the mismanagement of a concern in which he has an interest.[187]

3-13:3 Abuse of the Qualified Privilege

Protection of a qualified privilege is lost if the plaintiff proves by clear and convincing evidence that the qualified privilege was abused.[188] Abuse of privilege is a jury question,[189] traditionally involving considerations of defendant's malice, motive, reasonable cause, good faith, and the like.[190] The Appellate Division

---

184. *Dairy Stores, Inc. v. Sentinel Pub. Co.*, 104 N.J. 125, 137 (1986); *Williams v. Bell Tel. Lab., Inc.*, 132 N.J. 109, 120 (1993) (employer's report of suspected criminal conduct to prosecutor qualifiedly privileged; "The general rule is that a statement charging a criminal violation, made to a law-enforcement official, is qualifiedly privileged."); *Geyer v. Faiella*, 279 N.J. Super. 386, 391-92 (App. Div.), *certif. denied*, 141 N.J. 95 (1995) (initial reports of alleged criminal acts to attorney and to the United States Attorney are entitled to only a qualified and not an absolute privilege); Prosser & Keeton on the Law of Torts, §115, p.830, quoted in *Rogozinski v. Airstream By Angell*, 152 N.J. Super. 123, 150-51 n.3 (Law Div. 1977), *modified on other grounds*, 164 N.J. Super. 465 (App. Div. 1979).

185. *Dijkstra v. Westerink*, 168 N.J. Super. 128, 135 (App.Div.) *certif. denied*, 81 N.J. 329 (1979), quoting 50 Am.Jur.2d, *Libel and Slander*, §214, p. 726 (1970). Simply put, communications to law enforcement officials by employers, employees or other citizens are qualifiedly privileged. *Rainier's Dairies v. Raritan Valley Farms, Inc.*, 19 N.J. 552, 562 (1955).

186. *Feggans v. Billington*, 1996 WL 330354 (App. Div. 1996).

187. Prosser & Keeton on the Law of Torts, §115, p. 826. For example, in *Sokolay v. Edlin*, 65 N.J. Super. 112 (App. Div. 1961), the owner of a pharmacy advised the employees of his belief that the plaintiff-employee stole demerol tablets and his intention to detect whether anyone else was involved. The owner contacted the state police and assisted its investigation. A qualified privilege was found to exist. Similarly, in *Jorgensen v. Pennsylvania R.R. Co.*, 25 N.J. 541 (1958), an employer who conducted an unannounced spot check of its employees' personal bags was entitled to a qualified privilege even though other employees were present—presumably their bags were going to be checked—when company property was found in the plaintiff-employee's bag and plaintiff was led off to the police department office. *Id.* at 546, 565-66.

188. *Erickson v. Marsh & McLennan Co.*, 117 N.J. 539, 565 (1990); *Kass v. Great Coastal Express, Inc.*, 152 N.J. 353, 356 (1998); *Bainhauer v. Manoukian*, 215 N.J. Super. 9, 41 (App. Div. 1987). The qualified privilege provides the defendant with a rebuttable presumption that he acted properly. *Fees v. Trow*, 105 N.J. 330, 342 (1987); *Sokolay v. Edlin*, 65 N.J. Super. at 127; *Garziano v. E.I. du Pont de Nemours & Co.*, 818 F.2d at 388, 390-91. *See generally* Donald Paul Duffalo, *Annotation, Defamation: Loss of Employer's Qualified Privilege to Publish Employee's Work Record or Qualification*, 24 ALR 4th 144 (1983); Schlei & Grossman, *Employment Discrimination Law*, ch. 23, §7, pp. 767-70 (2d ed. 1983); *Feggans v. Billington*, 1996 WL 330354, pp.*4-5 (App. Div. 1996).

189. *See DeVries v. McNeil Consumer Products Co.*, 250 N.J. Super. 159, 169 (App. Div. 1991); *Bainhauer v. Manoukian*, 215 N.J. Super. 9, 40 (App. Div. 1987). *But see Feggans v. Billington*, 1996 WL 330354, pp.*6-7 (App. Div. 1996) (trial court should have granted summary judgment to defendant employees who sent petition about plaintiff to management and the union).

decision in *Bainhauer v. Manoukian* sets out four ways in which the business/occasional privilege—the qualified privilege most frequently raised in the employment context—may be abused.[191]

First, the privilege is lost if the speaker either knows the matter is false or acts in reckless disregard of its falsity.[192] "Reckless disregard as to truth or falsity exists when there is a high degree of awareness of probable falsity or serious doubt as to the truth of the statement."[193] Recklessness in communicating statements of "obviously doubtful veracity must approach the level of publishing a 'knowing, calculated falsehood.' "[194] Whether the defendant acted recklessly is a substantially subjective determination.[195]

An employer who accuses an employee of misconduct is entitled to rely upon the truthfulness of the reports of its own agents whose duties included detecting such misconduct:

> It would be quite unreasonable to say that an employer should disbelieve the statements of agents upon whose truthfulness he

---

190. *Fenning v. S.G. Holding Corp.*, 47 N.J. Super. at 117; *Sokolay v. Edlin*, 65 N.J. Super. 112, 124-27 (App. Div. 1961); *Abella v. Barringer Resources, Inc.*, 260 N.J. Super. 92, 103 (Ch. Div. 1992) (finding no abuse of business/occasional privilege in the filing of an SEC form containing allegedly defamatory statement regarding officer's termination from employment and noting that plaintiffs had not presented a "prima facie case of malice").

191. *Bainhauer v. Manoukian*, 215 N.J. Super. at 42 (following four tests set forth in the Restatement (Second) of Torts). If the qualified privilege is of a type not discussed herein (*e.g.*, reports of official proceedings), different standards for determining abuse apply. See Restatement (Second) of Torts, §599 Comment c, p. 287. *See Kass v. Great Coastal Express, Inc.*, 152 N.J. 353, 356 (1998) ("A publisher abuses the privilege 'if (1) the publisher knows the statement is false or the publisher acts in reckless disregard of its truth or falsity; (2) the publication serves a purpose contrary to the interests of the qualified privilege; or (3) the statement is excessively published.'"), quoting *Williams v. Bell Telephone Laboratories, Inc.*, 132 N.J. 109 (1993).

Query whether the rationale of *Fees* will apply to employees who make defamatory statements regarding their employers or co-workers that arguably fall under the Conscientious Employee Protection Act, N.J.S.A. 34A:19-1, *et seq*, and other Whistleblower statutes discussed in Chapter 2, §§2-8 to 2-26.

192. *Williams v. Bell Tel. Lab., Inc.*, 132 N.J. 109, 121 (1993); *Erickson v. Marsh & McLennan* Co., 117 N.J. 539, 565 (1990); *Bainhauer v. Manoukian*, 215 N.J. Super. 9, 42 (1987). *Accord Rogozinski*, 152 N.J. Super. at 155-57; Restatement (Second) of Torts, §600 & Comment b, pp. 288-89. In this context—as proof of abuse of the privilege—knowledge of falsity or reckless disregard must be proved by clear and convincing evidence. *Kass v. Great Coastal Express, Inc.*, 152 N.J. 353, 358 (1998).

193. Restatement (Second) of Torts, §600 Comment b, p. 289. *See Dairy Stores, Inc. v. Sentinel Pub. Co.*, 104 N.J. 125, 149-150 (1986); *Lawrence v. Bauer Pub. & Printing Ltd.*, 89 N.J. 451, 466, *cert. denied*, 459 U.S. 999 (1982). *See Rogozinski v. Airstream By Angell*, 152 N.J. Super. at, 156-57; *Sokolay v. Edlin*, 65 N.J. Super. 112, 123-24, 126 (App. Div. 1961) (privilege is abused when defendant has "full knowledge" of the untruthfulness of his statement); *Jerolamon v. Fairleigh Dickinson Univ.*, 199 N.J. Super. 179, 185 (App. Div. 1985) (privilege is abused where defendant "prepares false and fabricated reports knowing that they are such"). *Id.*

194. *Lawrence v. Bauer Pub. & Printing Ltd.*, 89 N.J. 451, 466, *cert. denied*, 459 U.S. 999 (1982).

195. *Dairy Stores, Inc. v. Sentinel Pub. Co.*, 104 N.J. 125, 149 (1986). Where an employee-plaintiff was in charge during the period of workplace thefts, and the disappearance of the property in question was unexplained, the employer had reasonable grounds to believe that the employee stole the property and thus did not act recklessly in accusing him. *Sokolay v. Edlin*, 65 N.J. Super. 112, 127 (App. Div. 1961).

> should be entitled to rely. The fact that the defendant chose to rely upon the veracity of those persons entrusted with the duty of detecting and reporting suspect activities by company employees cannot be considered as evidence of express malice on the employer's behalf. In this regard it has been held that where a publisher relies upon the statement of a single person in whose truthfulness he has confidence, and who apparently speaks of what he knows, without attempting to verify the statement by further inquiry of other parties, affords no ground for concluding that such action was not taken in good faith.[196]

Conclusive proof as to plaintiff's wrongdoing is not required.[197]

Second, the privilege is lost if the statement was *not* made primarily for the purpose of furthering the protected interest.[198] The defendant's primary motive or purpose is dispositive.[199] The existence of spite, ill will, indignation, resentment, or vindictiveness does not vitiate the qualified privilege where the defendant acted for a proper purpose.[200] Third, the privilege is lost by "excessive publication," which means the defendant knowingly published the defamatory statement to some person not reasonably believed to be necessary for the accomplishment of the purpose that is protected by the privilege.[201] As the Restatement (Second) of Torts states:

> Often the only practicable means of communicating defamatory matter involves a probability or even a certainty that it will reach many persons whose knowledge of it is of no value in accomplishing the purpose for which the privilege is given. In this case, the publication is not excessive or an abuse of the privilege, if the importance of the interest involved, the gravity of the

---

196. *Jorgensen v. Pennsylvania R.R. Co.*, 25 N.J. 541, 567 (1958).

197. *Sokolay v. Edlin*, 65 N.J. Super. 112, 126-27 (App.Div. 1961).

198. *Bainhauer v. Manoukian*, 215 N.J. Super. 9, 43 (App.Div. 1987); *Sokolay v. Edlin*, 65 N.J. Super. 112, 127 (App.Div. 1961) (employer properly furthering its own interest and employees' interest in accusing plaintiff-employee of theft and assisting police investigation); *Murphy v. Johns-Manville Products Corp.*, 45 N.J. Super. 478, 495 (App. Div.), *certif. denied*, 25 N.J. 55 (1957), (quoting Prosser); Restatement (Second) of Torts, §603, p. 291; Prosser & Keeton on the Law of Torts, §115, p. 834. *Williams v. Bell Tel. Lab., Inc.*, 132 N.J. 109, 121 (1993).

199. *Fees v. Trow*, 105 N.J. 330, 341-42 (1987); *Sokolay v. Edlin*, 65 N.J. Super. 112, 127 (App. Div. 1961); *Murphy v. Johns-Manville Products Corp.*, 45 N.J. Super. at 495 (plaintiff's allegation that his employer discharged him because he refused to accept the employer's workers' compensation settlement and not because of his stealing was based on mere suspicion); *Garziano v. E.I. du Pont de Nemours & Co.*, 818 F.2d 380, 391 (5th Cir. 1987) (plaintiff alleged that he was discharged not for sexual harassment, but because he had filed a sick pay grievance; court held plaintiff failed to show this was the true motivation for his employer's actions); Prosser & Keeton on the Law of Torts, §115, p. 834.

> harm threatened to it and the inconvenience of any other means of communication make the publication reasonable.[202]

The nature of the information communicated also affects the extent of publication that may be warranted. While an employer might justifiably advertise publicly the fact that he has discharged his general collection agent, he would not be justified in publicly announcing the discharge of his cook or butler.[203]

Fourth, the privilege is lost if the publication contains defamatory matter that is not reasonably believed to be necessary to accomplish the purpose for which the occasion is privileged.[204] It has been said that the terms used by the defendant must not be "utterly beyond and disproportionate to the facts which the defendant has reason to believe."[205] However, the mere fact that the defendant used lan-

---

200. *Jorgensen v. Pennsylvania R.R. Co.*, 25 N.J. 541, 568 (1958); *Sokolay v. Edlin*, 65 N.J. Super. 112, 127 (App.Div. 1961); *Murphy v. Johns-Manville Products Corp.*, 45 N.J.Super. 478, 495 (App.Div.), *certif. denied*, 25 N.J. 55 (1957); *Fahr v. Hayes*, 50 N.J.L. 275, 280 (Sup.Ct. 1888) (vendor's indignation toward plaintiff-trade customer who allegedly stole defendant's merchandise did not amount to an abuse of privilege); *Rogozinski v. Airstream By Angell*, 152 N.J. Super 133, 155, 157 (Law Div. 1977), *modified on other grounds*, 164 N.J. Super. 465 (App.Div. 1979) (privilege not abused even though record was replete with evidence of ill will, vindictiveness, and personal animosity between plaintiff and defendant).

In *Fees v. Trow*, 105 N.J. 330, 341-42 (1987), the plaintiff argued that the defendant accused plaintiff of caressing the breasts of an institutionalized person to get revenge for plaintiff's remark to defendant, in front of their supervisor, that defendant consumed too many Digel pills. The Supreme Court held, as a matter of law, that there was no showing of improper motive on defendant's part:

> We are asked to infer from [the Digel] incident ... that defendant exhibited some ill will towards plaintiff one week before the [molestation] report, that she harbored these feelings for a week, and that she then relayed the information in her report with the primary purpose of harming plaintiff. There is nothing to suggest that defendant's reaction to the supposed slight was *so emotional or excessive* as to indicate that she might act in furtherance of a hostile motive. *Disagreements between co-workers over the course of a working relationship are not uncommon. Feelings of anger and irritation aroused in everyday conversation need not—and presumably most often do not—result in actions designed to visit harm on the source of that anger.*

Fees v. Trow, 105 N.J. 330, 343 (1987) (emphasis added).

201. *Williams v. Bell Tel. Lab., Inc.*, 132 N.J. 109, 121 (1993); *Bainhauer v. Manoukian*, 215 N.J. Super. 9, 43 (App.Div. 1987); Restatement (Second) of Torts, §604, p. 292; *Sokolay v. Edlin*, 65 N.J. Super. 112, 125 (App. Div. 1961) (employer did not abuse privilege by accusing plaintiff-employee of theft in front of co-workers); *Fahr v. Hayes*, 50 N.J.L. 275, 279-80 (Sup. Ct. 1888) (issue is whether the defendant purposefully sought the opportunity to make the communication in front of third persons with no legal interest in hearing it); *Garziano v. E.I. du Pont de Nemours & Co.*, 818 F.2d 380, 392-93 (5th Cir. 1987) ("The law recognizes that an employer's and employees' interests and duties coincide when the conditions of employment are implicated"; therefore, the employer properly informed all employees in the plant the essential reasons for plaintiff's discharge); Prosser & Keeton on the Law of Torts §115, p. 832.

202. Restatement (Second) of Torts, §604, comment b, p. 293.

203. *King v. Patterson*, 49 N.J.L. 417, 421 (E. & A. 1887) (*dicta*).

204. *Bainhauer v. Manoukian*, 215 N.J. Super. at 43; Restatement (Second) of Torts, §§605 & 605A, pp. 295-96; Prosser & Keeton on the Law of Torts, §115, p. 832; *Garziano v. E.I. du Pont de Nemours & Co.*, 818 F.2d 380, 391-92 (5th Cir. 1987).

205. *Fahr v. Hayes*, 50 N.J.L. 275, 279 (Sup.Ct. 1888).

guage that was angry and intemperate is not enough to establish an abuse of the qualified privilege.[206]

The plaintiff bears the burden of proving an abuse of the privilege by clear and convincing evidence.[207] If there is no evidence, or not more than a scintilla of evidence, of malice, it is the duty of the court to withdraw that issue from the jury.[208]

3-13:4 Truth

Truth is an affirmative defense and as to every particular must be strictly proved by the defendant.[209] That is, a defamatory statement is presumed to be false unless the defendant proves its truth.[210] Motive is irrelevant; "even if maliciously made, a true statement is not actionable."[211]

The modern view is that the defendant is not required to prove "the literal truth of the accusation in every detail"; rather, "it is sufficient to show that the imputation is substantially true, or, as it is often put, to justify the 'gist,' the 'sting,' or the 'substantial truth' of the defamation."[212] That is, "the truth must be as broad as the defamatory imputation or 'sting' of the statement."[213]

In view of the proposition that the plaintiff must prove that the defendant acted negligently in publishing the defamatory statement,[214] the Restatement (Second) of Torts has suggested that, by necessity, the plaintiff must also plead and prove the

---

206. *Garziano v. E.I. du Pont de Nemours & Co.*, 818 F.2d 380, 392 (5th Cir. 1987).

207. *Williams v. Bell Tel. Lab., Inc.*, 132 N.J. 109, 121 (1993); *Erickson v. Marsh & McLennan Co.*, 117 N.J. 539,566-67 (1990), *See Fees v. Trow*, 105 N.J. 330, 342 (1987); *Jorgensen v. Pennsylvania R.R. Co.*, 25 N.J. 541,565-66 (1958); *Sokolay v. Edlin*, 65 N.J. Super. 112, 125-27 (App.Div. 1961); *Rogozinski v. Airstream By Angell*, 152 N.J. Super. 133, 154, 157 (Law Div. 1977), *modified on other grounds*, 164 N.J.Super. 465 (App.Div. 1979); Prosser & Keeton on the Law of Torts, §115, p. 835.

208. *Fees v. Trow*, 105 N.J. 330, 344 (1987); *Dairy Stores, Inc. v. Sentinel Pub. Co.*, 104 N.J. 125, 157 (1986); *Jorgensen v. Pennsylvania R.R. Co.*, 25 N.J. 541, 569 (1958); *Sokolay v. Edlin*, 65 N.J. Super. 112, 130 (App.Div. 1961); *Murphy v. Johns-Manville Products Corp.*, 45 N.J. Super. 478, 495-96 (App.Div.), *certif. denied*, 25 N.J. 55 (1957).

209. *Wilson v. Savino*, 10 N.J. 11, 16-17 (1952); *Hartley v. Newark Morning Ledger Co.*, 134 N.J.L. 217, 219 (E. & A. 1946); *Neigel v. Seaboard Finance Co.*, 68 N.J. Super. 542, 552 (App.Div. 1961).

210. *Dijkstra v. Westerink*, 168 N.J. Super. 128, 134 (App.Div. 1979), *certif. denied*, 81 N.J. 329 (1979) (same). Truth is a complete defense even in those situations where the defendant believed the defamatory statement to be false or acted in reckless disregard thereof. Restatement (Second) of Torts, §600 Comment d, p. 289; *Rogozinski v. Airstream By Angell*, 152 N.J.Super. 133, 147 (Law Div. 1977), *modified on other grounds*, 164 N.J.Super. 467 (App.Div. 1978) (defamatory statement presumed to be false).

211. *Schiavone Construction Co. v. Time, Inc.*, 619 F.Supp. 684, 700 (D.N.J. 1988).

212. Prosser & Keeton on the Law of Torts, §116, p. 842. *Accord Herrmann v. Newark Morning Ledger Co.*, 48 N.J. Super. 420, 431-32. (App. Div.), *aff'd on reh.*, 49 N.J. Super. 551 (App. Div. 1958).

213. *Lawrence v. Bauer Pub. & Printing Ltd.*, 89 N.J. 451, 460, *cert. denied*, 459 U.S. 999 (1982).

214. *See Bainhauer v. Manoukian*, 215 N.J. Super. 9,31 (App. Div. 1987).

falsity of the statement.[215] Prosser, *et al.*, have rejected this conclusion with respect to private plaintiff defamation claims;[216] so have the New Jersey courts.[217]

3-14 Damages

In cases of slander other than slander *per se*, special damages must be proved before the plaintiff is permitted to recover damages.[218] Under the traditional rule, damages were presumed when the defamation involved slander *per se* or libel; however, the continued viability of that rule in New Jersey is doubtful.[219]

Special damages involve a material or pecuniary loss, such as a loss of business or other specific economic benefits.[220] Emotional distress resulting from the defamation does not constitute special damage, and this is so even if the distress causes serious physical illness.[221] Likewise, expenses incurred in refuting the

---

215. Restatement (Second) of Torts, §613 Comment j, pp. 310-11. The Second Restatement has no official position on this issue. Restatement (Second) of Torts, §613 Caveat, p. 307. *See Id.* §581A & Comment b, pp. 235-36.

216. Prosser & Keeton on the Law of Torts, §116, pp. 839-40.

217. *Rogozinski v. Airstream By Angell*, 152 N.J. Super. 133, 146-47 (Law Div. 1977), *modified on other grounds*, 164 N.J.Super. 465 (App.Div. 1979). *See DeVries v. McNeil Consumer Products Co.*, 250 N.J.Super. 159, 168 (App.Div. 1991) (referring to truth as a defense); *Lawrence v. Bauer Pub. & Printing Ltd.*, 89 N.J. 451, 460, *cert. denied*, 459 U.S. 999 (1982) (without discussion, treating truth as a defense and citing the *Rogozinski* discussion of this issue). *Accord Vassallo v. Bell*, 221 N.J.Super. 347, 376 (App.Div. 1987) (public plaintiff bears the burden of proving falsity).

Part of the argument against requiring the plaintiff to prove falsity of the statement as part of his *prima facie* case has been that the U.S. Supreme Court has not yet so held. *See Rogozinski*, 152 N.J. Super. at 147. In *Philadelphia Newspaper, Inc. v. Hepps*, 475 U.S. 767, 768-69 (1986), the Court held "that, at least where a newspaper publishes speech of public concern, a private-figure plaintiff cannot recover damages without also showing that the statements at issue are false." Given this development and the New Jersey courts' willingness to follow the lead of the Second Restatement on other issues such as privilege and negligence, the New Jersey courts may ultimately impose on at least some private plaintiffs the burden of proving falsity.

218. *See Arturi v. Tiebie*, 73 N.J. Super. 217, 222 (App. Div. 1962).

219. The traditional rule has been that harm to the plaintiff's reputation is presumed from the publication of a libel or slander *per se*. Prosser & Keeton on the Law of Torts, §112, p. 843; nn. 16, 20, 21, & 26, *supra*. In *Gertz v. Welch*, the Supreme Court held that at least in cases involving public figures, constitutional limitations preclude the recovery of presumed damages absent proof that the defendant knew the defamatory matter was false or acted in reckless disregard of its falsity. The Restatement (Second) of Torts, §621, p. 319 has taken the position that this rule should be extended to private plaintiff defamation actions, with the consequence that all plaintiffs be required to prove either actual damage to reputation or actual malice. At least two New Jersey courts have assumed that New Jersey will follow the Restatement (Second) of Torts lead. *Rogozinski v. Airstream By Angell*, 152 N.J. Super. at 146-47 (noting that the United States Supreme Court opinion in *Gertz* "apparently denies the court the right to presume damages"); *see also Vassallo v. Bell*, 221 N.J.Super. 347, 378 (App.Div. 1987) ("states may not permit recovery of presumed damages even in a case involving a private plaintiff in the absence of a showing of knowledge of falsity or reckless disregard of the truth"). *See also Sisler v. Gannett Co., Inc.*, 104 N.J. 256, 280 (1986) (in defamation cases involving a public plaintiff or a matter of public concern presumed damages may not be awarded absent a finding of *New York Times* malice). The Reporter's Note to the Restatement (Second) of Torts, §621 counts New Jersey as one of the jurisdictions following its approach. Restatement (Second) Torts, Appendix, §621 Reporter's Note, p. 186 (1981), citing *Rogozinski*.

defamatory communication do not constitute special damages.[222] Special damages are strictly limited to those damages that are reasonably foreseeable or are the normal consequence of the defamation.[223] The special damage must result from the conduct of a person other than the defamer and the defamed.[224]

Once special damages are proved (or in those situations where special damages are not required[225]), plaintiff may recover general damages (past and future), such as damage to reputation, mental suffering, physical sickness, wounded feelings, and humiliation.[226]

The defendant may offer evidence of the plaintiff's general bad reputation or bad character in order to mitigate damages.[227] However, a mere rumor that the plaintiff committed the particular act charged in the defamatory statement is not admissible unless it is first established that the rumor was so widely distributed as to affect plaintiff's general reputation.[228] Proof that the defendant was merely repeating what others had said is admissible.[229]

Moreover, where (a) there has been an abuse of a qualified privilege and (b) the harm resulting from the abuse is severable from the harm which resulted from the proper exercise of the privilege, the defendant is liable only for the excess harm resulting from the abuse.[230]

---

220. *See Arturi v. Tiebie*, 73 N.J. Super. 217, 222 (App.Div. 1962); *Bock v. Plainfield Courier-News*, 45 N.J. Super. 302, 309 (App. Div. 1957); Prosser & Keeton on the Law of Torts, §116A, p. 844; §112, p. 794 (loss of customers, loss of a particular contract, loss of employment). These damages are "special" in the sense that they must be supported by specific proof and will not be assumed to result from the wrongful conduct.

221. *See Arturi v. Tiebie*, 73 N.J. Super. 217, 222-23 (App. Div. 1962); Prosser & Keeton on the Law of Torts, §112, p. 794.

222. Prosser & Keeton on the Law of Torts, §112, p. 794.

223. *See King v. Patterson*, 49 N.J.L. 417, 432 (E. & A. 1887); Prosser & Keeton on the Law of Torts, §116A, p. 844.

224. *See Arturi v. Tiebie*, 73 N.J. Super. 217, 223 (App.Div. 1962); Restatement (Second) of Torts, §575 Comment b, p. 198.

225. *See* n. 218, *supra*.

226. *See Arturi v. Tiebie*, 73 N.J. Super. 217, 222-23 (App.Div. 1962); *Bock v. Plainfield Courier-News*, 45 N.J. Super. 302, 311 (App. Div. 1957).

227. Prosser & Keeton on the Law of Torts, §116A, p. 847; *Fodor v. Fuchs*, 79 N.J.L. 529, 531 (E. & A. 1910) (also noting that testimony of particular facts affecting plaintiff's character are not admissible). *See Schiavone Construction Co. v. Time, Inc.* 646 F. Supp. 1511, 1515 (D.N.J. 1986) *aff'd in part on other grounds*, 847 F.2d 1069 (3d Cir. 1988), wherein Judge Sarokin addressed the "libel proof plaintiff" doctrine—which he says has not been addressed by the New Jersey state courts—under which either (1) "certain plaintiffs have such poor reputations on a particular issue that no further statements on that issue could cause injury" or (2) "the unchallenged portion of a communication may so damage a plaintiff's reputation that the challenged portion may be found to cause no further meaningful injury." Judge Sarokin held that the libel proof plaintiff doctrine is a part of First Amendment defamation law.

228. Prosser & Keeton on the Law of Torts, §116A, pp. 847-48. *See also Suart v. News Publishing Co.*, 67 N.J.L. 317, 317-18 (E. & A. 1902); *Schiavone Construction Co. v. Time, Inc.*, 646 F. Supp. at 1516.

229. Prosser & Keeton on the Law of Torts, §116A, p. 848; *Hartley v. Newark Morning Ledger Co.*, 134 N.J.L. 217, 222 (E. & A. 1946).

Under appropriate circumstances, an award of punitive damages may be made. When the defamatory statement involves a matter of public concern, public and private plaintiffs alike bear the burden of proving actual malice under the *New York Times v. Sullivan* standard to recover punitive damages.[231] However, where there is a private plaintiff and no matter of public concern is involved, the common law burden of proving express malice—a wrongful personal intent to injure[232] —may suffice.[233] For a detailed discussion of punitive damages in defamation suits see Ghiardi & Kircher, *Punitive Damages Law & Practice*, §§13.01-.15.

Under New Jersey law, a defamation plaintiff can recover punitive damages even if he has not suffered any compensatory damages, so long as he has suffered nominal damages; that is, "some injury, loss, or detriment".[234] Different considerations, beyond the scope of this analysis, apply in actions governed by the First Amendment (*e.g.*, as in a public figure's action against the media).[235]

VI. FRAUD

3-15 Requisites

Legal fraud or misrepresentation requires proof of a "material representation of a presently existing or past fact, made with knowledge of its falsity and with the intention that the other party rely thereon, resulting in reliance by that party to his detriment."[236] Thus, a plaintiff must show: (a) a misrepresentation; (b) sci-

---

230. Restatement (Second) of Torts, §599 Comment b, pp. 286-87; §604 Comment c, p. 294; §605A Comment b, pp. 296-97.

231. *See Gertz v. Welch*, 418 U.S. 323, 349-50 (1974); *Vassallo v. Bell*, 221 N.J.Super. 347, 374-75 (App.Div. 1987).

232. *See Weiss v. Weiss*, 95 N.J.L. 125, 127 (E. & A. 1920); *Neigel v. Seaboard Finance Co.*, 68 N.J.Super. 542, 554 (App. Div. 1961); *Bock v. Plainfield Courier-News*, 45 N.J.Super. 302, 309, 312 (App. Div. 1957); *Schiavone Construction Co. v. Time, Inc.* 646 F. Supp. 1511, 1518 (D.N.J. 1986), *aff'd in part on other grounds*, 847 F.2d 1069 (3d Cir. 1988).

233. *See Dun & Bradstreet, Inc. v. Greenmoss Builders, Inc.*, 472 U.S. 749, 751-52 (1985) (showing of actual malice not constitutionally required for award of punitive damages in suit involving a private figure plaintiff and speech of purely private concern); *Burke v. Deiner*, 97 N.J. 465, 477 & n.2 (1984) (to recover punitive damages in public defamation action, plaintiff must prove actual malice; mere spite, hostility, hatred, or deliberate intent to harm will be insufficient where defendant did not act with actual knowledge of the falsity of the statement or in reckless disregard thereof); *Vassallo v. Bell*, 221 N.J.Super. 347, 374, 377-78 & n.7 (App.Div. 1987) (contrasting burdens for recovering punitive damages in public and private defamation suits).

234. *Schiavone Construction Co. v. Time, Inc.*, 646 F. Supp. at 1517, citing *Nappe v. Anschelewitz, Barr, Ansell & Bonello*, 97 N.J. 37 (1984).

235. *See eg.*, N.J.S.A. 2A: 43-2; *Schiavone Construction Co. v. Time, Inc.*, 646 F. Supp. 1511, 1518-20 (D.N.J. 1986), *aff'd in part on other grounds*, 847 F.2d 1069, 1081-82 (3d Cir. 1988).

enter; (c) reasonable reliance; and (d) detriment. Further, the allegations of a fraud must be pled with specificity.[237]

In equitable fraud, knowledge of the falsity of the statement is not necessary. Proof of the other elements—misrepresentation, intent that the other party rely on the representation, reasonable reliance, and detriment—remains essential. Relief is limited to equitable remedies, such as recission and reformation of an agreement, and not monetary damages only.[238]

Normal rules for proof of fraud apply in the employment context.[239]

3-15:1 Material Misrepresentation

To form the basis of an action for fraud, the misrepresentation must be material and it must relate to a present or past fact.[240] Opinions or promises with respect to future actions are normally insufficient, thus distinguishing this tort from actions in contract or quasi-contract.[241] However, a false representation of an existing intention—false state of mind—with respect to a future action has been held to constitute actionable misrepresentation.[242] To have a false state of mind, the defendant must have had no intention at the time he made the representation of

---

236. *Nappe v. Anschelewitz, Barr, Ansell & Bonello*, 97 N.J. 37, 51-52 (1984); *Jewish Center v. Whale*, 86 N.J. 619, 624 (1981); *Shebar v. Sanyo Business Systems Corp.*, 218 N.J. Super. 111, 117 (App. Div. 1987), *aff'd*, 111 N.J. 276 (1988); *Labus v. Navistar Int'l Trans. Corp.*, 740 F. Supp. 1053, 1065 (D.N.J. 1990); *SL Indust. v. American Motorists Ins. Co.*, 128 N.J. 188, 208-09 (1992). *See also Louis Schlessinger Co. v. Wilson*, 22 N.J. 576, 585-86 (1956); *Tonelli v. Khanna*, 238 N.J. Super. 121, 129 (App. Div.), *certif. denied*, 121 N.J. 657 (1990); *Foont-Freedenfeld Corp. v. Electro-Protective Corp.*, 126 N.J. Super. 254, 257 (App. Div. 1973), *aff'd*, 64 N.J. 197 (1974).

237. N.J.R. 4:5-8 ("In all allegations of misrepresentation, fraud ... particulars of the wrong, with dates and items if necessary, shall be stated insofar as practicable."); *see Fravega v. Security Savings & Loan Ass'n*, 192 N.J. Super. 213, 223 (Ch. Div. 1983). *See Pitak v. Bell Atlantic Network Servs., Inc.*, 928 F. Sppp. 1354, 1368-69 (D.N.J. 1996) (explaining elements); *McDonald's Corp. v. Miller*, 1994 WL 507822 (D.N.J. Sept. 14, 1994), *aff'd*, 60 F.3d) 815 (3d Cir. 1995) (plaintiff claimed he was fraudulently induced to stay in the McDonald's franchise program after it had already been determined he would not be awarded a franchise; claim dismissed for failure to specify who made the allegedly false statements, when the statements were made, who decided not to grant him a franchise and when that was decided, whether the statements were made with the knowledge they were false, and whether the statements could be considered factual as a matter of law).

238. *Jewish Center v. Whale*, 86 N.J. 619, 625 (1981); *Foont-Freedenfeld Corp. v. Electro-Protective* Corp., 126 N.J. Super. 254, 257 (App. Div. 1973); *Gherardi v. Trenton Board of Educ.*, 53 N.J. Super. 349, 366 (App. Div. 1958). *See generally Chrisomalis v. Chrisomalis*, 260 N.J. Super. 50-56 (App. Div. 1992) (matrimonial case; defining legal and equitable fraud).

239. *See Labus v. Navistar Int'l Trans. Corp.*, 740 F. Supp. 1053, 1066 (D.N.J. 1990) ("Defendants cite no authority that holds misrepresentation claims are reserved for incidents arising outside the employer-employee context. This court's own research has not revealed any such limitation.").

240. *Jewish Center v. Whale*, 86 N.J. 619, 624-25 (1981).

241. *See Tonelli v. Khanna*, 238 N.J.Super. 121, 129 (App.Div.), *certif. denied*, 121 N.J. 657 (1990); *Kooba v. Jacobitti*, 59 N.J. Super. 496,500-01 (App. Div. 1960); *Ocean Cape Hotel Corp. v. Masefield Corp.*, 63 N.J. Super. 369, 380 (App. Div. 1960).

fulfilling the promise.[243] And although this may be proved through circumstantial evidence, the burden is heavy:

> This lack of intention can be established by circumstantial evidence of subsequent acts and subsequent events or by evidence the representation was impossible to fulfill based upon contingencies or circumstances known to the promisor at the time the statement was made but unknown to the promisee. This burden is not met by mere proof of non-performance; failure to perform does not impose on the promisor the burden of showing his performance was due to circumstances arising after the making of the agreement.[244]

Based upon this rule, the United States District Court in *Mallon v. Prudential Property & Casualty Ins. Co.*, rejected an employee's claim of fraud based upon the employer's statements such as "this is the home office, this is where your future can really lie," and "we really need you down here."[245] Plaintiff alleged those statements were made with a false state of mind because the heavy workload he was assigned made performance impossible. Summary judgment was granted to defendant because plaintiff and defendant were both aware of the nature of the job; defendant had no reason to believe plaintiff, an experienced claims consultant, would not be able to perform; and there was evidence in the record that non-performance by defendant was due to circumstances arising after the agreement and out of its control.[246] Thus, the court concluded, there could have been no false state of mind.

In contrast, in *Shebar v. Sanyo Business Systems Corp.*, the Appellate Division found plaintiff entitled to trial on his fraud claim based on the allegation that at

---

242. *Capano v. Borough of Stone Harbor*, 530 F. Supp. 1254, 1264 (D.N.J. 1982). *Silvestre v. Bell Atlantic Corp.*, 973 F. Supp. 475, 485 (D.N.J. 1997) (plaintiff must "establish a 'false state of mind'—that the defendant had no intention to perform a future event or action at the time that the material representation was made"), *aff'd*, 156 F.3d 1225 (3d Cir. 1998). *Tarino v. Kraft Foodservice, Inc.*, 1996 WL 84680, p.*11 (D.N.J. 1996) ("Misrepresentation concerning a future event is only actionable if the defendant had a false state of mind."); *Pitak v. Bell Atlantic Network Servs., Inc.*, 928 F. Supp. 1354, 1367-68 (D.N.J. 1996) (no indication that employer did not intend to assist employees in finding other jobs, of 77 individuals whose jobs were eliminated, all but 18 were relocated).

243. *See Stochastic Decisions v. DiDomenico*, 236 N.J. Super. 388, 395-96 (App. Div. 1989), *certif. denied*, 121 N.J. 607 (1990); *Mallon v. Prudential Property & Casualty Ins. Co.*, 688 F. Supp. 997, 1008 (D.N.J. 1988); *Ocean Cape Hotel Corp. v. Masefield Corp.*, 63 N.J. Super. 369, 381 (App. Div. 1960).

244. *Mallon v. Prudential Property & Casualty Ins. Co.*, 688 F. Supp. 997, 1008-09 (D.N.J. 1988) (citation omitted). *See Stochastic Decisions v. DiDomenico*, 236 N.J. Super. 388, 395-96 (App. Div. 1989), *certif. denied*, 121 N.J. 607 (1990).

245. 688 F. Supp. at 1009. *See Tarino v. Kraft Foodservice, Inc.*, 1996 WL 84680, p.*11 (D.N.J. 1996) (suggesting that vague statements that the employer would help plaintiff develop and maintain accounts would be insufficient; complaint dismissed on other grounds).

246. *Id.*

the time Sanyo superiors convinced him to forego a competitor's job offer, they had a present intention to dismiss him. Plaintiff had been advised by an executive recruiter that Sanyo was looking for a replacement, and he in fact was terminated within a short period thereafter.[247]

A job applicant's misrepresentations with respect to his background and experience may support an action for fraud. Thus, in *Jewish Center v. Whale*, the Supreme Court found a material misrepresentation in a rabbi applicant's statement that he had served as an administrator for Israel's Ministry of Education Foreign Student Department during a period when he in fact had been a fugitive and a prisoner:

> That representation, relating as it does to defendant's skill and ability to perform the duties of a rabbi, is without question material to an evaluation of a candidate for the position of rabbi of plaintiff congregation.[248]

3-15:2 Scienter

The plaintiff alleging legal fraud must prove scienter, "meaning knowledge of the falsity of the representation, with an intent that the other party rely thereon."[249] Thus, if a totally false representation is made unknowingly, an action for fraud will not lie. If there was honest belief, *however unreasonable*, that a representation was true, there is insufficient basis for deceit.[250]

3-15:3 Reliance

The general rule is that reliance must be objectively reasonable to support a claim for fraud.[251] It is unclear, however, whether that is the rule under New Jersey law.[252] Two separate lines of cases seem to be at odds. In *Jewish Center v. Whale*, the Supreme Court rejected the defendant employee's argument that misrepresentations on his job application were not actionable because a reasonable inquiry by the employer would have revealed the truth. It stated that one who en-

---

247. *Shebar v. Sanyo Business Systems Corp.*, 218 N.J. Super. 111, 117-18 (App. Div. 1987), *aff'd*, 111 N.J. 276 (1988).

248. 86 N.J. 619, 625 (1981).

249. *Nappe v. Anschelewitz, Barr, Ansell & Bonello*, 97 N.J. 37 52-53 (1984).

250. *See Tonelli v. Khanna*, 238 N.J.Super. 121, 129 (App.Div.), *certif. denied*, 121 N.J. 657 (1990).

251. *See also Pioneer Nat'l Title Ins. Co. v. Lucas*, 155 N.J. Super. 332, 342-43 (App. Div.), *aff'd*, 78 N.J. 320 (1978) (a person led by fraud into a trap owes no duty to the one who does the trapping).

252. *See B.F. Hirsch v. Enright Refining Co., Inc.*, 751 F.2d 628, 632-33 (3d Cir. 1984).

gages in fraud may not urge that one's victim should have been more circumspect or astute.[253]

Other cases, however, hold quite clearly that reliance must be reasonable:

> Reliance by plaintiff is another necessary element of a cause of action for fraud. According to general decisional law, that reliance must have been justifiable, for example, when facts to the contrary were not obvious or did not provide a warning making it patently unreasonable that plaintiff not pursue further investigation, under the circumstances that the means for such further investigation were readily apparent and, if pursued, would reveal the falsity of the representation.[254]

Where an individual to whom a false representation is made chooses to conduct an independent investigation of the subject matter, proof of reliance becomes more difficult: "he will be deemed to have relied on his own investigation and charged with knowledge of whatever he could have discovered by a reasonable investigation."[255] One court has defined the standard in the employment context as the following:

> [P]laintiff's reliance on the representation must be justifiable, for example, where facts to the contrary were not obvious or did not provide a warning, or where plaintiff did not reasonably pursue further investigation that would have revealed the falsity of the representation.[256]

---

253. *Jewish Center v. Whale*, 86 N.J. 619, 626 n.1 (1981). *See also Bilotti v. Accurate Forming Corp.*, 39 N.J. 184, 205 (1963) ("the law is settled in this State that fraudulent misconduct is not excused by the credulity or negligence of the victim or by the fact that he might have discovered the fraud by making his own prior investigation"). *Cf. Golden v. Northwestern Mutual Life Ins. Co.*, 229 N.J. Super. 405, 415 (App. Div. 1988) (where independent investigation made and relied on there can be no action for fraud). *But see Rubenstein v. Rubenstein*, 20 N.J. 359, 367 (1956) ("the modern doctrine of fraud ... tends to disregard the question whether misrepresentations were such as would have deceived a reasonable person, and confines the question to whether the misrepresentations were intended to deceive and did so.")

254. *Shebar v. Sanyo Business Systems Corp.*, 218 N.J. Super. 111, 117 (App.Div. 1987), *aff'd*, 111 N.J. 276 (1988) (describing elements of proof of fraud as including "plaintiff's reasonable reliance"); *Labus v. Navistar Int'l Trans. Corp.*, 740 F. Supp. 1053, 1066 (D.N.J. 1990). *See International Minerals and Mining Corp. v. Citicorp North America, Inc.*, 736 F. Supp. 587, 598 (D.N.J. 1990) ("the purported reliance must have been reasonable under the circumstances or no ground for recovery will exist"); *Feldman v. U.S. Sprint Communications Co.*, 714 F.Supp. 727, 732 (D.N.J. 1989) (where employee continued to sell products in reliance on allegedly fraudulent representations as to compensation summary judgment on fraud claim denied); *Nappe v. Anschelewitz, Barr, Ansell & Bonello*, 189 N.J. Super. 347, 355 (App. Div. 1983); *aff'd in part and rev'd in part*, 97 N.J. 37 (1984).

255. *DSK Enterprises, Inc. v. United Jersey Bank*, 189 N.J. Super. 242, 251 (App.Div.), *certif. denied*, 94 N.J. 598 (1983). *See Golden v. Northwestern Mutual Life Ins. Co.*, 229 N.J.Super. 405, 415 (App.Div. 1988).

256. *Labus v. Navistar Int'l Trans. Corp.*, 740 F. Supp. 1053, 1066 (D.N.J. 1990).

3-15:4 Detriment/Damages

Proof of actual damages is no longer essential to a cause of action in fraud. In *Nappe v. Anschelewitz, Barr, Ansell & Bonello*, the Supreme Court abandoned the common law rule, which had been based upon the distinction between causes in trespass and trespass on the case:

> [F]raudulent conduct constitutes unfair dealing whether or not actual damages are shown. Even if the person relying on the falsehood were unable to establish actual damages, he should be entitled to vindicate his rights through an award of nominal damages and in appropriate cases to punish the defendant through an award of punitive damages.[257]

Abandonment of the damage requirement, however, does not eliminate the need to prove detriment; rather it permits plaintiff to recover where he can prove he was harmed but cannot prove by how much. The jury instruction approved by the Court in *Nappe v. Anschelewitz, Barr, Ansell & Bonello* was the following:

> [I]f you find that there was actionable conduct [as previously defined by the court] on the part of the defendant and you reasonably believe that he sustained damages, but they are not computable, ... but you feel that there has been sufficient evidence that he was damaged, you should in light of the questions I would submit if you so find, enter an award of nominal damages.[258]

3-15:5 Clear and Convincing Evidence

The party asserting a fraud bears the burden of proving that fraud; it is not presumed. When equitable remedies are sought, fraud must be proved by clear and convincing evidence.[259] Some cases suggest that as a general rule all fraud must

---

257. *Nappe v. Anschelewitz, Barr, Ansell & Bonello,* 97 N.J. 37, 53 (1984). Justice Schreiber's opinion relates to all intentional torts: "We hold, therefore, that compensatory damages are not an essential element of an intentional tort committed wilfully and without justification where there is some loss, detriment, or injury, and that nominal damages may be awarded in such cases in the absence of compensatory damages." The Supreme Court previously held in *Jewish Center v. Whale*, 86 N.J. 619, 626 (1981), that actual damage was not essential to proof of equitable fraud: "Actual loss in the financial sense is not required before equity may act; equity looks not to the loss suffered by the victim but rather to the unfairness of allowing the perpetrator to retain a benefit unjustly conferred." *Cf. Labus v. Navistar Int'l Trans. Corp.*, 740 F.Supp. 1053, 1065 (D.N.J. 1990) ("Plaintiff must show proof of actual detriment susceptible to a jury's or other fact finder's evaluation in compensatory damages") (citing *Nappe, supra*).

258. 97 N.J. 37, 54 (1984). *Contra Labus v. Navistar Int'l Trans. Corp.*, 740 F. Supp. 1053, 1065 (D.N.J. 1990) (plaintiff alleging fraud must prove actual detriment susceptible to a jury's or other fact finder's evaluation in compensatory damages).

be proved by clear and convincing evidence;[260] but others hold that when only legal remedies are sought, a preponderance of the evidence suffices.[261]

VII. NEGLIGENT MISREPRESENTATION

3-16 Requisites

A cause of action for negligent misrepresentation exists when (1) a party negligently provides false information; (2) plaintiff is a reasonably foreseeable recipient of the representation for its proper business purpose; (3) plaintiff justifiably relies on the representation; and (4) the representation is the proximate cause of plaintiff's injuries.[262] Where there is a duty to disclose information, or such a duty is assumed, failure to make a statement may form the basis of a misrepresentation claim.[263]

3-17 Duty to Disclose

In *Berry v. Playboy Enterprises, Inc.*,[264] the Appellate Division found that plaintiff employee stated a claim for negligent misrepresentation based upon the allegation that defendant employer had negligently failed to provide her an adequate description of health benefit coverages. It held that an employer that undertakes to explain and advise as to employee benefit options assumes a duty to

---

259. *Stochastic Decisions v. DiDomenico*, 236 N.J. Super. 388, 395-96 (App. Div. 1989), *certif. denied*, 121 N.J. 607 (1990); *Albright v. Burns*, 206 N.J. Super. 625, 636 (App. Div. 1986); *R.A. Intile Realty Co. v. Raho*, 259 N.J. Super. 438, 475 (Law Div. 1992).

260. *See Stochastic Decisions v. DiDomenico*, 236 N.J. Super. at 395-96 (plaintiff sought money damages; court stated fraud "must be proven through clear and convincing evidence"); *Albright v. Burns*, 206 N.J. Super. 625, 636 (App. Div. 1986) (same).

261. *See, e.g., Mate v. American Brands, Inc.*, 1990 WL 69177, p. *3 (D.N.J. 1990) (because plaintiff sought only monetary damages, fraud could be proved by preponderance of evidence); *Armel v. Crewick*, 71 N.J. Super. 213, 218 (App. Div. 1961) ("where fraud or misrepresentation is made the basis of an action at law, plaintiff is called upon to establish his claim by only a preponderance of the evidence"); *Schmidt v. Schmidt*, 220 N.J. Super. 46, 50 (Ch. Div. 1987) ("Fraud is never presumed but must be clearly and convincingly proved through the use of direct or circumstantial evidence by the party who asserts it . ... To demonstrate fraud in equity actions the proofs must be clear and convincing so as to 'demonstrate a high probability ... or a strong probability, or that it is much more probable than not, that there was fraud.' "). *See also Fischetto Paper Mill Supply, Inc. v. Quigley Co., Inc.*, 3 N.J. 149, 152-53, 155 (1949).

262. *See Karu v. Feldman*, 119 N.J. 135, 146-47 (1990).

263. *See, e.g., H. Rosenblum, Inc. v. Adler*, 93 N.J. 324 (1983) (inaccurate financial statement by accountant); *Berry v. Playboy Enterprises, Inc.*, 195 N.J. Super. 520 (App. Div. 1984), *certif. denied*, 99 N.J. 231 (1985) (non-disclosure of terms of health coverage plan by employer). *Cf. Karu v. Feldman*, 119 N.J. 135 (1990) (bank had no duty at time plaintiff added name to certificates of deposits to advise of possible withdrawal penalties if that name were later deleted).

264. 195 N.J. Super. 520 (App. Div. 1984), *certif. denied*, 99 N.J. 231 (1985).

perform that function with due care; that where such function is performed negligently and proximately causes harm, recovery may be had.[265] In *Wells v. Wilbur B. Driver Co.*, the court stated that such a disclosure duty on the part of any employer might arise in a number of ways, such as "any express contractual undertakings, including the employer-employee relationship or because of a course of dealing with its employees."[266] Damages for negligent misrepresentations are limited to "recovery for actual losses due to reliance on the misstatement."[267]

VIII. TORTS OF EMPLOYEES

3-18 Overview

The primary bases upon which an employer may be liable for the torts of employees are *respondeat superior* and negligent hiring and supervision. Under *respondeat superior* an employer is responsible for only those acts committed within the scope of employment. Negligent hiring, however, covers acts outside the scope of employment as well.[268]

3-18:1 *Respondeat Superior*

An employer may be held liable for the torts of its employees under the doctrine of *respondeat superior* only when that employee is acting within the scope of his employment.[269] In defining the "scope of employment," New Jersey follows the Restatement (Second) of Agency, §228 (1957):

> (1) Conduct of a servant is within the scope of employment if, but only if (a) it is of the kind he is employed to perform; (b) it occurs substantially within the authorized time and space limits; (c) it is actuated, at least in part, by a purpose to serve the master,

---

265. 195 N.J. Super. 520, 529-32 (App. Div. 1984), *certif. denied*, 99 N.J. 231 (1985); *see Wells v. Wilbur B. Driver Co.*, 121 N.J. Super. 185 (Law Div. 1972). The court in *Berry v. Playboy Enterprises, Inc.*, discussed and rejected pre-emption by the NLRA, but did not address pre-emption by the Employee Retirement Income Security Act. 195 N.J. Super. at 525-27. It is not apparent why ERISA should not have pre-empted this plaintiff's claim, and that issue should be kept in mind in all cases of this nature involving representations and/or non-disclosure with respect to an employee benefit plan.

266. 121 N.J. Super. at 203-04.

267. *Karu v. Feldman*, 119 N.J. 135, 147 (1990).

268. *See Cosgrove v. Lawrence*, 214 N.J. Super. 670, 679-80 (Law Div. 1986), *aff'd*, 215 N.J. Super. 561 (App. Div. 1987).

269. *DiCosala v. Kay*, 91 N.J. 159, 168-69 (1982); *Gilborges v. Wallace*, 78 N.J. 342, 351 (1978); *GNOC v. Aboud*, 715 F. Supp. 644, 649 (D.N.J. 1989).

> and; (d) if force is intentionally used by the servant against another, the use of force is not unexpectable by the master.
>
> (2) Conduct of a servant is not within the scope of employment if it is different in kind from that authorized, far beyond the authorized time and space limits or too little actuated by a purpose to serve the master.[270]

The principle is an elastic one, highly dependent upon the facts of the case. The Appellate Division has described the standard as merely a means of determining whether an action was authorized.[271] However, it has also quoted authority to the effect that the standard "is obviously no more than a bare formula to cover the unordered and unauthorized acts of the servant for which it is found to be expedient to charge the master with liability, as well as to exclude other acts for which it is not."[272]

3-18:2 Nature of the Conduct

To be acting within the scope of employment, the employee must normally be performing a task of the kind for which he is paid. Thus, an IRS agent driving to a fast food restaurant for lunch was not engaged in conduct of the kind he was employed to perform.[273] And, a therapist's sexual relations with a patient were not "conduct of the kind he was employed to perform within the scope of his employment."[274] But issuance of checks without approval, by employees whose job it was to issue such checks after obtaining approval, created a fact question for the jury as to the scope of employment.[275]

Criminal acts and intentional torts of employees are normally—but not always—found to be outside the scope of employment. "In practice, only rarely do intentional torts fall within the scope of employment."[276] When a consciously

---

270. *See DiCosala v. Kay*, 91 N.J. 159, 169 (1982); *Commercial Union Ins. Co. v. Burt Thomas-Aitken Construction Co.*, 49 N.J. 389, 392 n. 1 (1967).

271. *See Wright v. Globe Porcelain Co.*, 72 N.J. Super. 414, 422 (App. Div. 1962) ("the servant's act, even in advancing his master's interest, must have been authorized, either expressly or impliedly, to hold the master liable.").

272. *Gotthelf v. Property Mgt. Systems*, 189 N.J.Super. 237, 240 (App.Div.), *certif. denied*, 95 N.J. 219 (1983), quoting Prosser on the Law of Torts, §70 (4th ed. 1971). *See also Cosgrove v. Lawrence*, 214 N.J.Super. 670, 675 (App.Div. 1986).

273. *See Government Employees Ins. Co. v. U.S.*, 678 F. Supp. 454, 456 (D.N.J. 1988). The agent was neither paid for his lunch period nor entitled to reimbursement for the lunch he ate. *Id.*

274. *See Cosgrove v. Lawrence*, 215 N.J. Super. 561, 563 (App. Div. 1987).

275. *See Marley v. Palmyra Borough*, 193 N.J. Super. 271, 295 (Law Div. 1983) (interpreting Tort Claims Act, N.J.S.A. 59:3-14).

criminal or tortious action is done for the employer's purposes or is reasonably expectable by the employer, the employer will be liable.[277]

In *Roth v. First Nat'l State Bank of New Jersey*, one of defendant's tellers tipped off robbers about plaintiff's habit of obtaining cash for his check- cashing business in the early morning hours, and the robbers successfully used that information to steal from plaintiff. The Appellate Division rejected plaintiff's claim against the employer bank on the ground that the tip by the teller was outside the scope of her employment. It was found to be "outrageously criminal," not in the service of the employer's interests, unconnected with actual bank work, and effectuated away from the bank and outside of banking hours.[278] Similarly, thefts of personal property from the employer's tenants have been found outside the scope of employment.[279]

Scope of employment is intimately related to the scope of the employee's authority, and that is determined in practical, not technical, terms. For example, an employer will not be heard to say a particular task was within an employee's job scope if performed carefully, but not if performed negligently.[280] Nor does lack of knowledge of the employee's negligence in performing a job function remove it from the scope of employment.[281]

(a) Time and Location

Actions taken within the scope of employment normally occur "substantially within the authorized time and space limits" of the job.[282] A car accident during the unpaid lunch hour of an employee whose job duties did not include driving did not meet this requirement.[283] Sexual relations between a therapist and patient

---

276. *Schultz v. Roman Catholic Archdiocese of Newark*, 95 N.J. 530, 535 n.1 (1984) (*dicta*; Charitable Immunity Act bars claim for negligent hiring).

277. *See Roth v. First Nat'l State Bank of New Jersey*, 169 N.J. Super. 280, 286 (App. Div.), *certif. denied*, 81 N.J. 338 (1979); *see also Gibson v. Kennedy*, 23 N.J. 150 (1957).

278. *Roth v. First Nat'l State Bank of New Jersey*, 169 N.J. Super. at 287.

279. *See Gotthelf v. Property Mgt. Systems*, 189 N.J. Super. 237 (App. Div.), *certif. denied*, 95 N.J. 219 (1983).

280. *See Wright v. Globe Porcelain Co.*, 72 N.J. Super. 414, 418-19 (App. Div. 1962) (an employer cannot avoid responsibility for an employee's negligence by telling him to act carefully). *Cf. GNOC v. Aboud*, 715 F.Supp. 644, 650 (D.N.J. 1989) (jury issue whether casino employees were acting within the scope of employment if they offered gamblers alcohol in violation of rules).

281. *See Wollerman v. Grand Union Stores, Inc.*, 47 N.J. 426, 429 (1966) (employer is liable for employee's negligence in performing job duties whether aware of it or not).

282. See Restatement (Second) of Agency, §228 (1)(6).

283. *See Government Employees Ins. Co. v. U.S.*, 678 F. Supp. 454, 456 (D.N.J. 1988).

occurring not only in his office, but also in parks and his home, was found not within the authorized time and space limits of his job.[284]

(b) Purpose

Where the purpose of an act is merely furtherance of the employee's own purposes, the act is obviously not within the scope of employment and the employer is not liable.[285] Thus, courts have had little difficulty in finding employers not responsible for the crimes of employees committed for their own purposes and personal gain. Vicarious liability has been denied on this basis where the agents and employees of a property owner were alleged to have stolen personal property of tenants.[286] Similarly, a bank was found not liable for a teller's collusion with robbers and tip-off as to a customer's banking habits.[287] And an intoxicated police officer extorting gambling proceeds with his service revolver was acting for his own purposes and not those of his employer, even though on duty.[288]

In some cases, however, criminal acts may be intended to further the employer's business, and thus fall within the scope of employment. For example, the trainman who uses excessive force in dealing with a passenger may in some circumstances be acting within the scope of employment:

> The outrageous quality of an employee's act may well be persuasive in considering whether his motivation was purely personal, but if the employee is within the scope of employment and intends to further the employer's business, the employer is chargeable even though the employee's conduct be "imbecilic."[289]

If the conduct is activated by a purpose to serve the employer, the fact that the act is prohibited by the employer is not determinative.[290] However, the existence of a general or indirect benefit to the employer does not necessarily mean that an

---

284. *See Cosgrove v. Lawrence*, 214 N.J. Super. 670, 677 (Law Div. 1986), *aff'd*, 215 N.J. Super. 561 (App. Div. 1987).

285. *See Wright v. Globe Porcelain Co.*, 72 N.J. Super. 414, 418 (App. Div. 1962).

286. *See Gotthelf v. Property Mgt. Systems*, 189 N.J. Super. 237 (App. Div.), *certif. denied*, 95 N.J. 219 (1983).

287. *See Roth v. First Nat'l State Bank of New Jersey*, 169 N.J. Super. 280 (App. Div.), *certif. denied*, 81 N.J. 338 (1979).

288. *See Snell v. Murray*, 117 N.J. Super. 268, 273 (Law Div. 1971), *aff'd*, 121 N.J. Super. 215 (App. Div. 1972) ("If a servant or agent deviates from the business of his master or principal and, while in the pursuit of his own ends, commits a tort, the master or principal cannot be held liable for the damage inflicted.").

289. *Gibson v. Kennedy*, 23 N.J. 150, 157-58 (1957) (citation omitted) (jury question as to whether employee was acting for the employer's purposes); *cf.* Restatement (Second) of Agency §228 (1)(d) (1957) (if force is intentionally used by an employee, it is within the scope of employment only if the use of force is not unexpectable).

action was taken for the purpose of serving him. For example, the allegation that an employee's efficiency was increased by eating at a fast-food restaurant did not make the employee's drive to the restaurant an action taken for the employer's purposes.[291]

Use of the employer's machinery or other instrumentality for the action complained of creates a rebuttable presumption that the employee was acting within the scope of his employment.[292] Thus, the employee driving a vehicle owned by his employer is presumed to be acting within the scope of his employment. Moreover, where a specific trip in the employer's vehicle serves the employee's private interests and also furthers the employer's business, the employer is liable.[293]

(c) Exception

The private employer of a notary public has been found not liable for his alleged negligence under a theory of *respondeat superior* due to policy reasons related to the status of the notary as a public officer.[294]

3-18:3 Negligent Hiring/Retention

A cause of action for negligent hiring of employees was first recognized by the Supreme Court in *DiCosala v. Kay.*[295] Plaintiff in that case was a young boy on a social visit to his uncle, an employee of the Boy Scouts who occupied a cabin

---

290. *See Cosgrove v. Lawrence*, 214 N.J. Super. 670, 678 (Law Div. 1986), *aff'd*, 215 N.J. Super. 561 (App. Div. 1987); *Wright v. Globe Porcelain Co.*, 72 N.J. Super. 414, 423 (App. Div. 1962) (fact question whether loading dock employee who was prohibited from driving trucks acted within the scope of employment when he turned a truck around to complete loading it, and got into an accident while doing so); *Donio v. U.S.*, 746 F.Supp. 500, 505-06 (D.N.J. 1990) (statements by Assistant United States Attorney to newspaper within scope of employment under New Jersey standard, even if inaccuracies made them in violation of Justice Department rules); *GNOC v. Aboud*, 715 F.Supp. 644, 650 (D.N.J. 1989) (the fact that casino employees were prohibited from offering alcohol to gamblers not determinative of *respondeat superior* issue with respect to alleged violation of that rule).

291. *See Government Employees Ins. Co. v. U.S.*, 678 F. Supp. 454, 456 (D.N.J. 1988).

292. *Gilborges v. Wallace*, 78 N.J. 342, 351-52 (1978).

293. *Id.* at 351.

294. *Commercial Union Ins. Co. v. Burt Thomas-Aitken Construction Co.*, 49 N.J. 389 (1967).

295. 91 N.J. 159 (1982). Previous cases looked favorably on the cause of negligent hiring without expressly deciding the issue. *See, e.g., Bennett v. T & F Distributing Co.*, 117 N.J.Super. 439 (App.Div. 1971), *certif. denied*, 60 N.J. 350 (1972) (summary judgment properly denied as to customer's claim that the vacuum cleaner company negligently hired violent criminal as door-to-door salesman). *See also Peer v. Newark*, 71 N.J.Super. 12 (App.Div. 1961), *certif. denied*, 36 N.J. 300 (1962) (city liable for injuries caused by police officer's off-duty use of weapon, because of negligent training). *Cf. Nivins v. Sievers Hauling Corp.*, 424 F.Supp. 82 (D.N.J. 1976).

owned by the Scouts. During the course of that visit, another Scout employee, also on a social visit to the Uncle's cabin, accidentally shot the young boy with a loaded gun owned by the uncle. Plaintiff alleged the employer was liable for the negligence of these employees under theories of *respondeat superior* and negligent hiring/retention of the employees.[296]

The court rejected *respondeat superior* liability because neither employee's alleged negligent acts were within the scope of employment. However, it recognized a cause of action for negligent hiring or retention of employees pursuant to which an employer may be found indirectly accountable for the torts of employees committed outside the scope of employment, not because the employee was acting for the employer as in the case of *respondeat superior*, but because the employer was negligent in exposing the public to a dangerous or unfit employee.[297]

The tort of negligent hiring/retention has two elements of proof:

> The first involves the knowledge of the employer and foreseeability of harm to third persons. An employer will only be held responsible for the torts of its employees beyond the scope of the employment where it knew or had reason to know of the particular unfitness, incompetence or dangerous attributes of the employee and could reasonably have foreseen that such qualities created a risk of harm to other persons.
>
> * * *
>
> The second required showing is that, through the negligence of the employer in hiring the employee, the latter's incompetence, unfitness or dangerous characteristics proximately caused the injury.[298]

The foreseeability essential to creation of a legal duty in this context focuses on "whether [the employer] should have foreseen that its conduct unreasonably enhanced a hazard that would be injurious to those coming within the range of such a hazard."[299] The negligence of the employer in hiring or retaining the employ-

---

296. In its subsequent opinion in *Schultz v. Roman Catholic Archdiocese of Newark*, 95 N.J. 530 (1984), a majority of the Court held a claim for negligent hiring barred by New Jersey's Charitable Immunity Act. N.J.S.A. 2A:53A-7 to -11. Justice Handler's dissent, joined in by Justices Schreiber and Pollock, noted that the defendant Boy Scouts of America in *DiCosala v. Kay*, 91 N.J. 159, 174 (1982), was a charitable entity. 95 N.J. 530, 540-41. *See Rivera v. Alonso*, 1989 U.S.Dist. LEXIS 12378 (D.N.J. 1989) (negligent hiring claim against Roman Catholic Diocese of Paterson dismissed under New Jersey Charitable Immunity Act).

297. The Court stated: "[T]he tort of negligent hiring addresses the risk created by exposing members of the public to a potentially dangerous individual, while the doctrine of *respondeat superior* is based on the theory that the employee is the agent or is acting for the employer. Therefore the scope of employment limitation on liability which is part of the respondeat superior doctrine is not implicit in the wrong of negligent hiring." 91 N.J. at 172-73. *See also Pacifico v. Froggatt*, 249 N.J. Super. 153, 154 (Law Div. 1991).

ee—as opposed to mere negligence of the employee—must be the proximate cause of the injury.[300] There must be proof that "through the negligence of the employer in hiring or retaining the employee, the employee's unfitness or dangerous characteristics proximately caused the injury."[301] As described by the Supreme Court in *DiCosala*,

> [The] question presented is whether the employer, knowing of its employee's unfitness, incompetence or dangerous attributes when it hired or retained its employee, should have reasonably foreseen the likelihood that the employee through his employment would come into contact with members of the public, such as the plaintiff, under circumstances that would create a risk of danger to such persons because of the employee's qualities.[302]

Justice Handler's explanation of how the Boy Scout's retention of plaintiff's uncle as an employee was negligence that proximately caused the boy's injury is inexplicable except as a policy decision. Plaintiff was a *family member* on a social visit with his mother that just happened to occur on Scout property. The facts simply do not logically fit the stated rationale of the negligent hiring doctrine of preventing employers from exposing the public to a known danger.

The subsequent Appellate Division decision in *Johnson v. Usdin Louis Co., Inc.*, also involving harm to the family of an employee, followed the articulated rule of *DiCosala* and reached a less expansive result. The employee in *Johnson* had taken nitric acid from his place of employment and used it to assault his estranged wife and daughter. The wife's claim against the employer for negligent retention of her husband as an employee was rejected as a matter of law. The employer had no duty because it was not aware that the husband had dangerous

---

298. *DiCosala v. Kay*, 91 N.J. 159, 173-74 (1982) (citations omitted). .*See Lingar v. Live-In Companions, Inc.*, 300 N.J. Super. 22, 31-32 (App. Div. 1997), reversing summary judgment in favor of defendant home-care agency. Plaintiffs were a customer of the agency and a spouse who required care. They claimed the agency was negligent in sending an employee into their home who had an extensive criminal record, abandoned the invalid spouse and stole several items. While questioning whether the defendant could have obtained the employee's criminal record if it had tried to, the court nonetheless found it "arguable that '[i]f an employer wishes to give an employee the indicia of authority to enter into the living quarters of others, it has the responsibility of first making some inquiry with respect to whether it is safe to do so.'" *See Johnson v. Usdin Louis Co., Inc.*, 248 N.J.Super. 525, 528-29 (App.Div.), *certif. denied*, 126 N.J. 386 (1991).

299. *Johnson v. Usdin Louis Co., Inc.*, 248 N.J.Super. 525, 529 (App.Div. 1991).

300. *See DiCosala v. Kay*, 91 N.J. 159, 174 (1982) ("We now expressly recognize the tort of negligent hiring or retention of an incompetent, unfit, or dangerous employee and hold that one may be liable for injuries to third persons proximately caused by such negligence.").

301. *Johnson v. Usdin Louis Co., Inc.*, 248 N.J.Super. 525, 528 (App.Div. 1991).

302. *See DiCosala v. Kay*, 91 N.J. 159, 177 (1982).

characteristics. The mere fact that dangerous substances were made available in the workplace imposed no special duty on the employer:

> [I]f a legal duty was found to exist based on the facts and total circumstances in the present case, that would mean that virtually all employees would be exposed to liability. For instance, gasoline station attendants, butchers and even secretaries, work with dangerous products or implements which could be taken home from the job and used to criminally assault a family member. Public policy dictates that there should be no liability absent a showing that the employer reasonably should have foreseen an unreasonably enhanced hazard.[303]

Claims of negligent hiring of an employee that are asserted by a co-employee are barred by the exclusive remedy provision of the New Jersey Workers' Compensation Act.[304]

3-19 Punitive Damages

Punitive damages may not be recovered against an employer for the wrongful acts of its employee unless (1) the act was specifically authorized, participated in, or ratified by the master; or (2) the employee who committed the wrongful act or authorized or ratified it was so high in authority as to be fairly considered executive in character.[305] Ratification of an employee's actions may come in diverse forms. In *Cappiello v. Ragen Precision Industries, Inc.*, the Appellate Division held that a corporate employer ratified the actions of its employees by participating in a single defense with them in an action by another employee to recover sales commissions.[306] For a detailed discussion of the circumstances under which punitive damages may be imposed upon an employer for the acts of its employees, see Ghiardi and Kircher, *Punitive Damages Law & Prac.* §§24.01-.07.

---

303. *Johnson v. Usdin Louis Co., Inc.*, 248 N.J.Super. 525, 530-31 (App. Div.), *certif. denied*, 126 N.J. 386 (1991).

304. *See Cremen v. Harrah's Marina Hotel Casino*, 680 F.Supp. 150, 155-56 (D.N.J. 1988).

305. *GNOC v. Aboud*, 715 F.Supp. 644, 651 (D.N.J. 1989); *Winkler v. Hartford Accident & Indemnity Co.*, 66 N.J.Super. 22, 29 (App.Div.), *certif. denied*, 34 N.J. 581 (1961).

306. *Cappiello v. Ragen Precision Industries, Inc.*, 192 N.J.Super. 523, 531 (App.Div. 1984); *see Security Aluminum Window Mfg. Corp. v. Lehman Assocs., Inc.*, 108 N.J.Super. 137, 147 (App. Div. 1970).

Chapter 4

Law Against Discrimination

I. OVERVIEW

4-1 Introduction

The New Jersey Law Against Discrimination (LAD) was enacted in 1945.[1] Adopted pursuant to the state's police power, the LAD fulfills the provisions of the state constitution guaranteeing civil rights and promotes the general welfare and economic prosperity of the state by prohibiting unlawful discrimination in employment.[2]

Except as otherwise permitted by law, the LAD outlaws unlawful employment discrimination against any person by reason of age, ancestry, atypical hereditary cellular or blood trait (AHCBT), liability for service in the Armed Forces of the United States, color, creed, handicap, marital status, national origin, nationality, sex, genetic information, refusal to submit to genetic testing, refusal to provide genetic information, or race of that person, or of that person's spouse, partners, members, stockholders, directors, officers, managers, superintendents, agents, employees, business associates, suppliers, or customers.[3] The LAD is somewhat inconsistent in that certain types of discrimination are mentioned in one section

1. L.1945, c.169, as amended and supplemented, N.J.S.A. 10:5-1 *et seq.* The LAD was found constitutional in *Levitt & Sons, Inc. v. New Jersey Div. Against Discrimination*, 31 N.J. 514, 531-34, *app. dism'd*, 363 U.S. 418 (1960); *Jones v. Haridor Realty Corp.*, 37 N.J. 384, 390-95 (1962); *David v. Vesta Co.*, 45 N.J. 301, 310-18 (1965). The LAD does not deprive regulated persons of their federally-protected rights of freedom of speech and association. *Kiwanis Int'l v. Ridgewood Kiwanis Club*, 627 F.Supp. 1381, 1389-90 (D.N.J.), *rev'd on other grounds*, 806 F.2d 468 (3d Cir. 1986), *reh'g en banc denied*, 811 F.2d 247 (3d Cir.), *cert. dism'd*, 483 U.S. 1050 (1987); *Roberts v. Keansburg Bd. of Educ.*, 5 N.J.A.R. 208, 239-42, 261 (DCR 1983). Nor does it subject them to involuntary servitude. *David v. Vesta Co.*, 45 N.J. at 319-21.

2. N.J.S.A. 10:5-2, -3, -4; *Shaner v. Horizon Bancorp.*, 116 N.J. 433, 436, 455-56 (1989); *Andersen v. Exxon Co.*, 89 N.J. 483, 492 (1982).

3. N.J.S.A. 10:5-3, -4, -4.1, -12. Two additional categories of persons—municipal general assistance recipients and qualified Medicaid applicants—are also protected by the LAD, but not in the context of employment discrimination. N.J.S.A. 10:5-12.2, -5(ee).

of the statute but not in another. It is not clear in all instances whether those omissions are inadvertent or intentional.[4]

The LAD does not forbid all discrimination, only that which is based on these specifically-enumerated characteristics.[5] It expressly defines the classes of employment practices that are prohibited.[6] Generally, the opportunity to obtain employment without being subjected to unlawful discrimination is a civil right.[7]

The LAD is construed in combination with other New Jersey laws to maximize the protections afforded victims of discrimination.[8] It does not repeal the "Civil Rights Law" or any other New Jersey law relating to discrimination because of ancestry, liability for service in the Armed Forces, color, creed, handicap, marital status, national origin, race, or sex.[9] It does not automatically render invalid statutes that authorize otherwise unlawful discrimination, particularly subsequently enacted statutes.[10] It does not displace the New Jersey Constitution,[11] or bar, exclude, or otherwise affect any other right or action, civil or criminal, which exists independently of any right thereunder.[12] However, common law claims that dulicate claims under the LAD will be barred.[13] Provisions of the LAD will not be deemed repealed or displaced by other statutes unless the statutory incompatibility is inescapable.[14]

---

4. *See, e.g.*, *Zahorian v. Russell Fitt Real Estate Agency*, 62 N.J. 399, 410-11 (1973) (Legislature's partial omission of marital status and sex discrimination in N.J.S.A. 10:5-6 was inadvertent and is supplied by judicial construction). Certain inconsistencies are clearly unintended. For example, L.1977, c.96, §2 amended N.J.S.A. 10:5-12(g)(1)-(3) and (h)(1)-(3) to include nationality discrimination in each of the six paragraphs of N.J.S.A. 10:5-12(g) and (h). When N.J.S.A. 10:5-12 was amended 18 days later by L.1977, c.122, §2, the references to nationality discrimination were, apparently unintentionally, not included in the above-mentioned six paragraphs. When N.J.S.A. 10:5-12 was next amended, by L.1979, c.86, §2, nationality discrimination was added back to only four of the six paragraphs.

5. *Jones v. College of Medicine & Dentistry of New Jersey*, 155 N.J.Super. 232, 236 (App. Div. 1977), *certif. denied*, 77 N.J. 482 (1978). *See, e.g.*, *Floyd v. State of New Jersey*, 1991 WL 143456, p.*4 (D.N.J. 1991) (LAD protects black persons and males, but not the distinct class composed of "black males"). The Legislature "has focused upon general, rather than specific, classifications of societal groups who historically have been the objects of discrimination." *Whateley v. Leonia Bd. of Educ.*, 141 N.J.Super. 476, 479 (Ch.Div. 1976).

6. N.J.S.A. 10:5-12(a)-(e); -5(d), -4.1. *But see UAW v. Mahwah*, 119 N.J.Super. 389, 392 n.1 (App. Div. 1972) (suggesting without explanation that the specific acts of discrimination set forth in N.J.S.A. 10:5-12 are not exclusive).

7. N.J.S.A. 10:5-4, -4.1; *Shaner v. Horizon Bancorp.*, 116 N.J. 433, 436 (1989); *Andersen v. Exxon Co.*, 89 N.J. 483, 491 (1982).

8. N.J.S.A. 10:5-3; *Grigoletti v. Ortho Pharmaceutical Corp.*, 118 N.J. 89, 108 (1990); *Clowes v. Terminix Int'l, Inc.*, 109 N.J. 575, 590-91 (1988).

9. N.J.S.A. 10:5-27, -4.1. *See Jackson v. Consolidated Rail Corp.*, 223 N.J.Super. 467, 482 (App. Div. 1988) (LAD supplements other state laws concerning civil rights). When the LAD was amended in 1951 to prohibit discrimination based on liability for service in the armed forces and in 1970 to bar discrimination premised on marital status or sex, the Legislature specifically amended the non-repealer provision of N.J.S.A. 10:5-27 to reflect these new protected classes. When the Legislature amended the LAD in 1962, 1977, and 1981 to bar discrimination based on age, nationality, and AHCBT, it did not make a similar amendment.

The LAD is to be interpreted fairly and justly with due regard to the interests of all parties.[15] Where a literal reading will lead to a result not in harmony with the fundamental purpose and design of the statute, "the spirit of the law will control the letter."[16] The LAD is not to be construed to:

1. Require or authorize any act otherwise prohibited by law.[17]
2. Prevent the award of set-aside contracts by boards of education for small, women's, and minority businesses, as authorized by N.J.S.A. 18A:18A-51 *et seq.*[18]
3. Conflict with the child labor provisions of the Labor Code, N.J.S.A. 34:2-1 *et seq*,[19] or require the employment of any person under the age of 18.

Amendments to the LAD are applied only prospectively, "unless the changes are merely procedural or the Legislature specifically indicates otherwise."[20]

---

10. *See, e.g., In re Petition for Substantive Certification filed by Warren Tp.*, 247 N.J.Super. 146, 167-68 (App. Div. 1991), *rev'd*, 132 N.J. 1 (1993); *Pineman v. Paramus*, 4 N.J.A.R. 407, 412 (DCR 1981), *aff'd*, No. A-5336-80 (App. Div. Apr. 1, 1982); *Chausmer v. Commissioners of Employees' Retirement System of Newark*, 150 N.J.Super. 379 (App. Div. 1977). *But see New Jersey Dept. of Labor v. Cruz*, 45 N.J. 372 (1965) (N.J.S.A. 34:9-1, which prohibits employment of aliens on public works projects, impliedly repealed by LAD). *Cf. Boylan v. State*, 116 N.J. 236, 249-50 (1989), *cert. denied*, 494 U.S. 1061 (1990) (mandatory retirement authorization of N.J.S.A. 10:3-1 not in conflict with the mandatory retirement prohibition of LAD in view of the introductory language of N.J.S.A. 10:3-1 ("Any provision of law ... to the contrary notwithstanding")); *McKay v. Horn*, 529 F.Supp. 847 (D.N.J. 1981) (declining to decide whether N.J.S.A. 43:21-5a, which reduces unemployment compensation benefits by other periodic retirement benefits payable to recipients, violates the LAD's prohibition against age discrimination).

11. *Shaner v. Horizon Bancorp.*, 116 N.J. 433, 456 (1989); *Gray v. Serruto Builders, Inc.*, 110 N.J.Super. 297, 306-07 (Ch.Div. 1970); *Peper v. Princeton Univ. Bd. of Trustees*, 77 N.J. 55 (1978).

12. N.J.S.A. 10:5-27. *See Shaner v. Horizon Bancorp.*, 116 N.J. at 453.

13. *Shaner v. Horizon Bancorp*, 116 N.J. at 453 (LAD precludes common law wrongful discharge claim aimed at vindicating the same rights); *Catalane v. Gilian Instrument Corp.*, 271 N.J. Super. 476, 491-92 (App. Div.), *certif. denied*, 136 N.J. 298 (1994); *DeCapua v. Bell Atlantic-New Jersey*, 313 N.J. Super 110 (Law Div. 1998); *Caldwell v. KFC Corp.*, 958 F. Supp. 962, 970 (D.N.J. 1997).

14. *Hinfey v. Matawan Regional Bd. of Educ.*, 77 N.J. 514, 527-28 (1978); *Boylan v. State*, 116 N.J. at 249-50.

15. N.J.S.A. 10:5-27; *Jansen v. Food Circus Supermarkets, Inc.*, 110 N.J. 363, 374 (1988); *Andersen v. Exxon Co.*, 89 N.J. 483, 496, 500 (1982); *Dixon v. Rutgers*, 110 N.J. 432 (1988).

16. *New Jersey Builders, Owners & Managers Ass'n v. Blair*, 60 N.J. 330, 338 (1972).

17. N.J.S.A. 10:5-2.1. *See, e.g., N.J. Attorney General Formal Opinion No. 1-1989*, pp. 4-5 (Oct. 6, 1989), 125 N.J.L.J. 100, 100-01 (Jan. 11, 1990) (LAD does not legalize the illegal use of controlled dangerous substances and illegal users are *per se* not handicapped for purposes of LAD). *Cf. New Jersey Dept. of Labor v. Cruz*, 45 N.J. 372 (1965) (LAD, as well as several other statutes, impliedly repealed N.J.S.A. 34:9-1, which made it unlawful to hire aliens for public works projects).

18. N.J.S.A. 10:5-2.1.

19. N.J.S.A. 10:5-2.1.

4-2 Scope of Coverage of LAD

The LAD prohibits discrimination in contexts other than the employment relationship, including places of public accommodation,[21] transactions involving real property,[22] and a variety of other contractual relationships.[23] Discrimination in these other contexts is addressed herein only to the extent relevant to the employment relationship.

4-3 New Jersey Constitution

The Supreme Court has looked to the state constitution as a source of protection against employment discrimination in those few cases where the LAD affords no relief.[24] In *Peper v. Princeton Univ. Bd. of Trustees,* the Court held that Article 1, Paragraph 1 of the Constitution[25] bars sex discrimination in *private* employment, despite the lack of any reference therein to sex, discrimination, employment, or conduct by private persons.[26] The Court did so by applying the equal protection guarantees that are implicit in Article 1, Paragraph 1:

> It is impermissible to employ gender-based distinctions premised upon "archaic and overbroad" stereotypes regarding the

---

20. *Peper v. Princeton Univ. Bd. of Trustees,* 77 N.J. 55, 73 (1978) (amendment expanding the scope of the term "employer" (N.J.S.A. 10:5-5(e)) regulated by the LAD applied prospectively only). *Accord Sprague v. Glassboro State College,* 161 N.J.Super. 218, 224 n.1 (App. Div. 1978) (amendment to the provision specifying unlawful employer practices (N.J.S.A. 10:5-12(a)) applied prospectively only).

21. *See* N.J.S.A. 10:5-4, -4.1, -5(l), (v), -12(f)-(i), (k); N.J.A.C. 13:13-4.1 *et seq.*

22. *See* N.J.S.A. 10:5-4, -4.1, -5(n)-(p), -9.1, -12(g)-(i), (k); N.J.A.C. 13:9; N.J.A.C. 13:10-1.1 *et seq.*; N.J.A.C. 13:13-3.1 *et seq.*

23. *See* N.J.S.A. 10:5-12(l)-(n), -4.1.

24. *See, e.g., Peper v. Princeton Univ. Bd. of Trustees,* 77 N.J. 55, 76-80 (1978) (state courts have power to enforce the rights recognized by the New Jersey Constitution even in the absence of implementing statutes). A plaintiff may pursue the same claim under the LAD and the state constitution. *Gray v. Serruto Builders, Inc.,* 110 N.J.Super. 297, 307 (Ch.Div. 1970); *Lloyd v. Stone Harbor,* 179 N.J.Super. 496, 508 (Ch.Div. 1981); *Weber v. LDC/Milton Roy,* 42 FEP 1507, 1516 (D.N.J. 1986).

25. Article 1, Paragraph 1 of the Constitution provides:

> All persons are by nature free and independent, and have certain natural and unalienable rights, among which are those of enjoying and defending life and liberty, of acquiring, possessing, and protecting property, and of pursuing and obtaining safety and happiness.

26. *Peper v. Princeton Univ. Bd. of Trustees,* 77 N.J. at 77-80. *See In re Dickerson Estate,* 193 N.J.Super. 353, 370 n.9 (Ch.Div. 1983).

Article One, Paragraph Five of the State Constitution has also been found to be a source of protection against sex discrimination. *Gallagher v. Bayonne,* 102 N.J.Super. 77, 81-83 (Ch.Div.), *aff'd on other grounds,* 106 N.J.Super. 401 (App. Div. 1969), *aff'd o.b.,* 55 N.J. 159 (1969). Article One, Paragraph Five provides:

> No person shall be denied the enjoyment of any civil or military right, nor be discriminated against in the exercise of any civil or military right, nor be segregated in the militia or in the public schools, because of religious principles, race, color, ancestry or national origin.

> economic dependency of women and thus to deny a female wage earner protection for her family equal to that afforded a comparable male wage earner.
>
> * * *
>
> [T]he equal protection of the laws means that no person or class of persons shall be denied the protection of the laws enjoyed by other persons or classes of persons in their lives, liberty and property, and in the pursuit of happiness, both as respects privileges conferred and burdens imposed.[27]

The Court reiterated its *Peper* holding ten years later, stating that "[t]he right to be free from discrimination is firmly supported by the protections of Article I, paragraph 1 of the ... Constitution."[28]

The extent to which other classifications are protected by the Constitution remains unsettled. In *State of New Jersey v. Gilmore*, the Supreme Court observed that Article 1, Paragraphs 1 and 5, define the "core cognizable groups" protected: groups defined by ancestry, color, national origin, race, religion, or sex.[29] The Court left open whether other groups protected by the LAD "might in certain contexts be cognizable groups." [30]

Age

In *Shaner v. Horizon Bancorp.*, the Supreme Court suggested that "[i]t may be that like [sex] discrimination ..., age discrimination would deprive an older person of the right to acquire property that a younger person possesses, thereby constituting a violation of the equal protection guarantees of our Constitution."[31] However, eight days earlier, in *Boylan v. State*, the Court had declined to hold that firefighters and law enforcement officers who were forced by state law to retire at age 65 were deprived of their constitutional right to equal protection.[32]

---

27. *Peper v. Princeton Univ. Bd. of Trustees*, 77 N.J. at 79, *quoting Tomarchio v. Greenwich Tp.*, 75 N.J. 62, 73 (1977), and *Washington Nat'l Ins. Co. v. New Jersey Unemployment Compensation Comm'n Bd. of Review*, 1 N.J. 545, 553 (1949).

Article One, Paragraph Five of the New Jersey Constitution is also a source of equal protection guarantees. *Taxpayers Ass'n of Weymouth Tp. v. Weymouth Tp.*, 80 N.J. 6, 42 (1976), *app. dism'd and cert. denied*, 430 U.S. 977 (1977); *Gray v. Serruto Builders, Inc.*, 110 N.J.Super. 297, 307 (Ch.Div. 1970). The equal protection guarantees of the State Constitution afford protection analogous or superior to the Equal Protection Clause of the Fourteenth Amendment. *Peper v. Princeton Univ. Bd. of Trustees*, 77 N.J. at 79.

28. *Dixon v. Rutgers*, 110 N.J. 432, 452 (1988).

29. *State of New Jersey v. Gilmore*, 103 N.J. at 526-27 n.3 (1986) (criminal case involving the exercise of peremptory challenges on the basis of race). Each of these groups is a suspect or semi-suspect classification that triggers strict or intermediate scrutiny under the Equal Protection Clause of the Fourteenth Amendment. *Id. Accord Gray v. Serruto Builders, Inc.*, 110 N.J.Super. 297, 307 (Ch.Div. 1970) (race discrimination).

30. *State of New Jersey v. Gilmore*, 103 N.J. at 526-27 n.3.

Marital Status

The Supreme Court has declined to find a denial of equal protection in the recognition of certain privacy rights as to acts engaged in by married but not unmarried couples.[33]

Sexual Orientation

The Appellate Division has held that child custody may not be denied or restricted on the basis of a parent's sexual orientation, with a concurring judge stating that: "The Federal and State Constitutions are blind to the generic differences between homosexuals and heterosexuals when their legal and constitutional rights are at issue."[34]

Retaliation

In *Drinkwater v. Union Carbide Corp.*, a federal district court held that New Jersey would not recognize a cause of action under its constitution for retaliatory discharge for complaining about sexual harassment.[35]

With one significant exception, the standards of proof applicable to employment discrimination actions under the New Jersey Constitution are generally the same as those used in LAD actions.[36] Under the LAD, proof of discriminatory

---

31. *Shaner v. Horizon Bancorp.*, 116 N.J. 433, 456 (1989). *See Taxpayers Ass'n of Weymouth Tp.*, 80 N.J. at 42 (recognizing age as a protected characteristic under N.J. Const. Art. 1, ¶¶1 and 5, and noting that "age, at least where the classification burdens the young rather than the old, is not a 'suspect' criterion"); *Robinson v. Sizes Unlimited, Inc.*, 685 F.Supp. 442, 448-49 (D.N.J. 1988) (recognizing an age-based employment discrimination case under Art. 1, ¶1). *Cf. Weber v. LDC/Milton Roy*, 42 FEP 1507, 1516 (D.N.J. 1986) (denying employer's motion for summary judgment on the merits of plaintiff's age discrimination claim under ADEA, LAD, and N.J. Const. Art. 1, ¶1; no discussion of whether such a constitutional cause of action exists). Presumably age restrictions imposed by the New Jersey Constitution would not violate Article 1, Paragraph 1 or 5. Examples of such age restrictions are discussed in §4-29:1.

32. *Boylan v. State*, 116 N.J. 236, 250-51 (1989), *cert. denied*, 494 U.S. 1061 (1990) (also noting that "age is not a suspect or 'quasi-suspect' classification"). *Cf. Reiser v. Passaic County Employees Retirement System Pension Commission*, 147 N.J.Super. 168 (Law Div. 1976) (statute that denies surviving spouse benefits to a spouse who is more than 15 years younger than the decedent-employee if the employee was age 50 or older when they married does not violate New Jersey or federal equal protection guarantees); *McKay v. Horn*, 529 F.Supp. 847 (D.N.J. 1981) (declining to decide whether N.J.S.A. 43:21-5a, which reduces unemployment compensation benefits by other periodic retirement benefits payable to recipients, violates New Jersey Constitution and LAD; also holding statute did not violate federal equal protection guarantees); *Paterson Tavern & Grill Owners Ass'n v. Hawthorne*, 108 N.J.Super. 433, 439-40 (App. Div.), *rev'd on other grounds*, 57 N.J. 180 (1970) (local ordinance prohibiting employment in bars of entertainers under the age of 21 is "patently unreasonable" and invalid); *Gregory v. Ashcroft*, 501 U.S. 452, 111 S.Ct. 2395, 115 L.Ed.2d 410 (1991) (mandatory retirement of appointed state-court judges does not violate federal equal protection guarantees).

33. *State of New Jersey v. Lair*, 62 N.J. 388, 396-97 (1973).

34. *M.P. v. S.P.*, 169 N.J.Super. 425, 427 and at 440 (Halpern, P.J., concurring) (App. Div. 1979).

35. 56 FEP 495, 497-98 (D.N.J. 1991). The Third Circuit, in an earlier appeal in that case, expressed doubts about the existence of such a cause of action under the state constitution. *Drinkwater v. Union Carbide Corp.*, 904 F.2d 853, 863-64 n.21 (3d Cir. 1990). *Cf. Smith v. Ebasco Constructors, Inc.*, 1988 WL 44143 (D.N.J. 1988) (employee allegedly discharged for blowing the whistle on cost overruns and delays on a publicly-financed project does not have a property interest in continued employment protected by N.J. Const. Art. 1, ¶1).

motive is not required under the theory of disparate-impact discrimination.[37] In contrast, proof of discriminatory intent or purpose is always a prerequisite to a violation of the equal protection guarantees of the New Jersey Constitution, even under a disparate-impact analysis.[38]

4-4 Pre-emption of the LAD

In limited circumstances, federal law may pre-empt the LAD and its regulations. Pre-emption will most likely occur in the context of §514 of the Employee Retirement Income Security Act of 1974 (ERISA),[39] §301 of the Labor Management Relations Act of 1947 (LMRA),[40] §3 of the Railway Labor Act of 1926 (RLA),[41] and §14(a) of the Age Discrimination in Employment Act of 1967 (ADEA), 29 U.S.C.A. §633(a).[42] In addition, LAD claims by federal employees are pre-empted to the extent they are covered by federal statute, such as Title VII.[43]

Section 514(a) of ERISA provides that the provisions of ERISA supersede any and all state laws insofar as they relate to any employee benefit plan.[44] As interpreted by the courts, §514 pre-empts all LAD actions alleging discrimination in connection with employee benefit plans governed by ERISA in the following situations:[45]

---

36. *Peper v. Princeton Univ. Bd. of Trustees*, 77 N.J. 55, 83 (1978); *Jackson v. Consolidated Rail Corp.*, 223 N.J.Super. 467, 483 (App. Div. 1988); *Weber v. LDC/Milton Roy*, 42 FEP 1507, 1516 (D.N.J. 1986). *Cf. Christian Bros. Inst. v. Northern New Jersey Interscholastic League*, 86 N.J. 409, 418 (1981) ("a rational basis [for a classification] would be sufficient to withstand any [equal protection] challenge under Article I, paragraphs 1 and 5 of the New Jersey Constitution").

37. *See* §4-41.

38. *In re Petition for Substantive Certification filed by Warren Tp.*, 247 N.J.Super. 146, 166-67, 175 (App. Div. 1991), *rev'd*, 132 N.J. 1 (1993); *In re Petition for Substantive Certification filed by Denville Tp.*, 247 N.J.Super. 186, 195 (App. Div. 1991), *rev'd*, 132 N.J. 1 (1993).

39. 29 U.S.C.A. §1144

40. 29 U.S.C.A. §185

41. 45 U.S.C.A. §153

42. 29 U.S.C.A.§633(a); *See also Edge v. Pierce*, 540 F.Supp. 1300, 1305 (D.N.J. 1982) (claim that federal agency's interpretation and application of federal housing program deprived plaintiffs of their civil rights under LAD and New Jersey Constitution "may very well be pre-empted" by federal law); *Fisher v. Quaker Oats Co.*, 233 N.J.Super. 319 (App. Div.), *certif. denied*, 117 N.J. 628 (1989) (ADEA does not pre-empt enforcement of LAD merely because LAD affords plaintiffs a longer statute of limitations). *Cf. Hernandez v. Region Nine Housing Corp.*, 146 N.J. 645 (1996) (adverse administrative determination by the EEOC did not bar subsequent LAD civil suit based on the same facts).

43. *Pearce v. U.S.*, 1983 WL 30277, 35 FEP 1788, 1789-90 (D.N.J. 1983). *See generally* 4 *Employment Discrimination Coordinator (RIA)* ¶53,361 (1990 rev.); 3 *Employment Discrimination Coordinator (RIA)* ¶24,110 (1990 rev.); Schlei & Grossman, *Employment Discrimination Law*, Ch.33, §III.D. (1983 & 1989 supp.).

44. 29 U.S.C.A. §1144(a). There are some limited exceptions to the broad pre-emptive scope of ERISA. *See* 29 U.S.C.A. §1144(b), (d).

1. When the employment practice challenged is lawful under Title VII or the ADEA.[46]
2. When the employment practice is unlawful under Title VII or the ADEA and plaintiff has failed to file a complaint under the LAD within the time period required for filing charges with the EEOC.[47]

Section 301 of the LMRA pre-empts LAD claims that are based directly on rights created in a collective bargaining agreement or whose resolution is substantially dependent upon an analysis of the terms of the agreement.[48] If the LAD claim is properly resolved without reference to the agreement, there is no preemption.[49] However, where the claim is inextricably intertwined with rights and standards as defined in a collective bargaining agreement, the LAD claim will be preempted.[50]

---

45. *See generally* Teresia B. Jovanovic, Annotation, *Pre-emption of State Fair Employment Laws Under Provisions of §514 of [ERISA]*, 72 A.L.R.Fed. 489 (1985). *See Joyce v. RJR Nabisco Holdings Corp.*, 126 F.3d 166 (3d Cir. 1997) (plaintiff's claim that employer violated the LAD by failing to accommodate his disability not pre-empted by ERISA where its "sole relationship to an employee benefit plan is that upon termination from his job, [plaintiff] was no longer eligible for the long-term disability benefits").

46. *Shaw v. Delta Air Lines, Inc.*, 463 U.S. 85, 95-106 (1983) (New York Human Rights Law); *Nolan v. Otis Elevator Co.*, 102 N.J. 30, 37-48, *cert. denied*, 479 U.S. 820 (1986) (LAD).

47. *Nolan v. Otis Elevator Co.*, 102 N.J. at 37-48. Under both Title VII and the ADEA, a charge must be filed with the EEOC within 300 days after the alleged unlawful employment practice occurred or within 30 days after receiving notice that the DCR has terminated its review of the aggrieved person's complaint, whichever is earlier. 42 U.S.C.A. §2000e-5(e) (Title VII); 29 U.S.C.A. §626(d)(2) (ADEA). In contrast, in cases not involving ERISA-governed employee benefit plans, the shorter limitations period provided for in the ADEA does not pre-empt the longer limitations period provided by the LAD. *Fisher v. Quaker Oats Co.*, 233 N.J.Super. at 322-24. *Alston v. Atlantic Electric Co.*, 962 F. Supp. 616, 625 (D.N.J. 1997) (ERISA preempted age discrimination claims under the LAD which related to covered benefit plans where plaintiffs failed to comply with administrative filing requirements under the ADEA; in that situation, "preemption of plaintiffs' NJLAD claims in no way impairs federal law.")

48. *See Lingle v. Norge Div. of Magic Chef, Inc.*, 486 U.S. 399 (1988); *Caterpillar Inc. v. Williams*, 482 U.S. 386 (1987); *IBEW v. Hechler*, 481 U.S. 851 (1987); *Allis-Chalmers Corp. v. Lueck*, 471 U.S. 202 (1985); *United Steelworkers of America v. Rawson*, 496 U.S. 362, 110 S.Ct. 1904, 109 L.Ed.2d 362 (1990); *Maher v. New Jersey Transit Rail Operations, Inc.*, 239 N.J.Super. 213, 223-25 (App. Div. 1990), *aff'd in part, rev'd in part on other grounds*, 125 N.J. 455, 470-75, 479-85 (1991); *Carrington v. RCA Global Communications, Inc.*, 762 F.Supp. 632, 639-42 (D.N.J. 1991).

49. *Id.* The United States District Court for the District of New Jersey has denied preemption where it was based upon a non-discrimination provision in a collective bargaining agreement. *Carrington v. RCA Global Communications, Inc.*, 762 F. Supp. 632, 639-42 (D.N.J. 1991). *Accord Nieves v. Individualized Shirts*, 961 F. Supp. 782, 792-93 (D.N.J. 1997) (plaintiff's disability discrimination claim not preempted because it was not based on and did not require interpretation of the collective bargaining agreement); *Mitchell v. Village Super Market, Inc.*, 926 F. Supp. 476 (D.N.J. 1996) (plaintiff's LAD claim of discriminatory discharge from union not preempted where no breach of duty of fair representation alleged). *Cf. Kube v. New Penn Motor Express, Inc.*, 865 F. Supp. 221, 228-30 (D.N.J. 1994) (plaintiff's disability discrimination claim could be resolved without reference to the labor agreement's provisions on medical exams and modified work plans, and thus was not preempted; court suggests in dicta that LAD claims are never preempted).

The §301 preemption analysis is equally applicable to discrimination claims raised by railway and airline employees governed by the Railway Labor Act.[51] In *Maher v. New Jersey Transit Rail Operations, Inc.*, the Appellate Division held that plaintiff's discrimination claim under the LAD was pre-empted by §3(1st)(i) of the RLA because issues of reasonable accommodation of his handicap were "inextricably intertwined" with the interpretation of the collective bargaining agreement.[52] In affirming, the Supreme Court observed that the effect of plaintiff's handicap on job performance was subject to arbitration under the agreement and the propriety of plaintiff's eventual discharge for insubordination was governed by the agreement's just-cause provision.[53] The Court rejected plaintiff's argument to the contrary on the ground it would interfere with the scheme of compulsory arbitration established by Congress.

Section 14(a) of the ADEA provides:

> Nothing in [the ADEA] shall affect the jurisdiction of any agency of any State performing like functions with regard to discriminatory employment practices on account of age except that upon commencement of action under [the ADEA] such action shall supersede any State action.[54]

This provision has been read "as applying only to actions brought in state court, rather than as applying to all actions based on state law." [55] Thus it appears that an employee may be permitted to pursue age discrimination claims under both the ADEA and New Jersey law, so long as he brings the action in federal court.[56]

Federal law may also pre-empt regulations issued by the Division on Civil Rights (DCR). For example, as explained in §4-23, the DCR's pre-employment inquiries regulation bars all inquiries about an applicant's citizenship. That pro-

---

50. *Hunter v. H.L. Yoh Co., Inc.*, 1994 WL 636992 (D.N.J. 1994) (because plaintiff's claim of discriminatory layoff and failure to recall was inextricably intertwined with recall rights, bumping rights, and "qualification" standards as defined in a collective bargaining agreement, his LAD claim was preempted.).

51. *Maher v. New Jersey Transit Rail Operations, Inc.*, 125 N.J. 455, 472-73 (1991).

52. *Maher v. New Jersey Transit Rail Operations, Inc.*, 239 N.J.Super. at 225-27. *See* Jackson, *Speech Delivered at American Bar Ass'n Meeting*, Daily Labor Report (BNA) No. 46, pp. E-9 to E-10 (Mar. 8, 1991).

53. *Maher v. New Jersey Transit Rail Operations, Inc.*, 125 N.J. at 479-80, 482-83.

54. 29 U.S.C.A. §633(a).

55. *Sussman v. Vornado, Inc.*, 90 F.R.D. 680, 690 (D.N.J. 1981), *quoting Wagner v. Sperry Univac, Div. of Sperry Rand Corp.*, 458 F.Supp. 505 (E.D. Pa. 1978). *See Corn v. Adidas USA, Inc.*, No. 85-30835(HLS), p. 5 (D.N.J. Jan. 6, 1986) (Lexis) ("It is not clear to th[is] court ... that section 633(a) necessarily results in an automatic withdrawal of a complaint pending in" the DCR; thus, before a plaintiff can assert LAD claims in a federal ADEA action, he must withdraw his verified complaint from the DCR).

56. *Sussman v. Vornado, Inc.*, 90 F.R.D. at 690.

hibition is now pre-empted in part by the federal Immigration Reform and Control Act of 1986.[57]

In appropriate circumstances, a Superior Court action asserting state law claims that are pre-empted by either ERISA or the LMRA may be removed to federal court, even if the complaint purports to assert only state-law causes of action.[58] Federal pre-emption is an affirmative defense that must be pled in the answer.[59]

4-5 Persons Protected

The LAD protects individuals seeking employment or already employed.[60] It does not protect individuals employed by their parent, spouse, or child, or in the domestic service of any person.[61]

One need not receive compensation to be deemed an "employee" under the LAD,[62] but an independent contractor is not an "employee."[63] Whether an individual is an employee or an independent contractor depends upon the economic realities of the relationship and, more significantly, the employer's right to control the "means and manner" of the individual's performance.[64] The following factors are among those considered:

> (1) the kind of occupation, with reference to whether the work usually is done under the direction of a supervisor or is done by a specialist without supervision; (2) the skill required in the particular occupation; (3) whether the employer or the individual in question furnishes the equipment used and the place of work; (4) the length of time during which the individual has worked;

---

57. Pub.L. 99-603

58. *Carrington v. RCA Global Communications, Inc.*, 762 F.Supp. at 636-37; *Metropolitan Life Ins. Co. v. Taylor*, 481 U.S. 58 (1987); *Caterpillar Inc. v. Williams*, 482 U.S. 386 (1987); *Pilot Life Ins. Co. v. Dedeaux*, 481 U.S. 41 (1987); *Ingersoll-Rand Co. v. McClendon*, 498 U.S. 133, 111 S.Ct. 478, 112 L.Ed.2d 474 (1990); *Lister v. Stark*, 890 F.2d 941 (7th Cir. 1989), *cert. denied*, 498 U.S. 1011, 111 S.Ct. 579, 112 L.Ed. 2d 584 (1990); *Bakersky v. ITT*, 1990 WL 33149 (D.N.J. 1990). To the extent *Nolan v. Otis Elevator Co.*, 560 F.Supp. 119 (D.N.J. 1982), reached a contrary conclusion, it is no longer good law in view of *Metropolitan Life Ins. Co. v. Taylor* and its progeny.

59. R.4:5-4; *Cole v. Carteret Savings Bank*, 224 N.J.Super. 446, 453 (Law Div. 1988); 5 Wright & Miller, *Federal Practice & Procedure: Civil*, §1271, pp. 439, 442 (2d ed. 1990).

60. N.J.S.A. 10:5-12, -3, -4.1.

61. N.J.S.A. 10:5-5(f). A 1992 amendment to N.J.S.A. 10:5-5(f) eliminated the exemption from coverage of individuals employed by a parent, spouse or child. L. 1992, c. 146 §4.

62. *Hebard v. Basking Ridge Fire Co.*, 164 N.J.Super. 77, 83-84 (App. Div. 1978), *app. dism'd*, 81 N.J. 294 (1979).

63. *Pukowsky v. Caruso*, 312 N.J. Super 171 (App. Div. 1998); *Carney v. Dexter Shoe Co.*, 701 F.Supp. 1093, 1101-02 (D.N.J. 1988).

64. *Id.* at 1098.

> (5) the method of payment, whether by time or by the job; (6) the manner in which the work relationship is terminated; *i.e.*, by one or both parties, with or without notice and explanation; (7) whether annual leave is afforded; (8) whether the work is an integral part of the business of the employer; (9) whether the worker accumulates retirement benefits; (10) whether the employer pays social security taxes; and (11) the intention of the parties.[65]

In appropriate circumstances, an individual who was deterred from seeking employment because of known discriminatory practices may be entitled to protection of the LAD.[66]

An introductory provision of the LAD suggests that the statute affords protection only to inhabitants of New Jersey,[67] but such a reading of the LAD is supported by neither its definitional section[68] nor its proscribed conduct section,[69] and would raise significant questions as to the federal constitutionality of the statute.[70]

Although some early trial court decisions held to the contrary, it now appears settled that a New Jersey resident who is employed in a neighboring state may not pursue employment-related causes of action under New Jersey law. In *Shamley v. ITT Corp.*, plaintiff lived in New Jersey and commuted to work in New York.[71] After he was discharged, he instituted a series of lawsuits, in New York and New Jersey courts, alleging federal discrimination and various state common-law causes of action. All of the courts involved held that New York, not New

---

65. *Carney v. Dexter Shoe Co.*, 701 F. Supp. 1093, 1098 (D.N.J. 1988) (internal quotation marks omitted), *quoting EEOC v. Zippo Mfg. Co.*, 713 F.2d 32, 37 (3d Cir. 1983). *See Pukowsky v. Caruso*, 312 N.J. Super 171 (App. Div. 1998). *Cf. Carpet Remnant Warehouse, Inc. v. Dept. of Labor*, 125 N.J. 567 (1991) (extensive discussion of whether individuals are employees or independent contractors for purposes of the Unemployment Compensation Law, N.J.S.A. 43:21-1 *et seq.*); *see generally* Restatement (Second) of Agency §220(2) (1958); Chapter 1, §1-1 *supra*.

66. *Teamsters v. U.S.*, 431 U.S. 324, 365-66, 368 (1977). *Accord Wards Cove Packing Co. v. Atonio*, 490 U.S. 642, 651 n.7, 653 (1989) (Title VII); *NAACP v. Harrison*, 749 F.Supp. 1327, 1335-36 (D.N.J. 1990), *aff'd*, 940 F.2d 792 (3d Cir. 1991) (Title VII; Town of Harrison's well-established residency requirements made it futile for non-resident black persons to apply for public employment). *Cf. Fowle v. C & C Cola*, 868 F.2d 59, 67-68 (3d Cir. 1989) (employer is not obligated to consider former employee, who had been released for lack of work, for a subsequent job opening unless former employee applies for it).

67. N.J.S.A. 10:5-3.

68. N.J.S.A. 10:5-5.

69. N.J.S.A. 10:5-12. *See* N.J.S.A. 10:5-4.1, -5(d).

70. *See, e.g., DiFalco v. Subaru of America, Inc.*, 244 N.J.Super. 530 (App. Div. 1990), *appeal dismissed,* 130 N.J. 585 (1992) (New Jersey statute, N.J.S.A. 2A:14-22, that tolls the statute of limitations on claims against non-resident—but not resident —corporate defendants violates the Commerce Clause, U.S. Const. Art. 1, §8, cl.3).

71. *Shamley v. ITT Corp.*, 869 F.2d 167 (2d Cir. 1989); *Shamley v. ITT Corp.*, 1988 N.J.Super. Lexis 530 (App. Div. 1988), *certif. denied*, 117 N.J. 44 (1989).

Jersey, law applied to the state-law causes of action.[72] One court has held that discrimination claims under the LAD survive the death of plaintiff under New Jersey's survival statute and that the executor may recover compensatory and punitive damages.[73]

4-6 Persons Regulated

The LAD prohibits unlawful employment discrimination by employers, labor organizations,[74] and employment agencies.[75] In addition, any person who (1) aids,

---

72. *Shamley v. ITT Corp.*, 869 F.2d at 172, *quoting Shamley v. ITT Corp.*, 1988 N.J.Super. Lexis at p. *2. The *Shamley* decisions were followed in *Perry v. Prudential-Bache Securities, Inc.*, 738 F.Supp. 843, 853-54 & n.6 (D.N.J. 1989), *aff'd without published op.*, 904 F.2d 696 (3d Cir.), *cert. denied*, 498 U.S. 958, 113 L.Ed. 2d 158, 111 S.Ct. 1196 (1990) (New York Human Rights Law, not LAD, applied to claims of plaintiff employed in New York). *Cf. Mullen v. New Jersey Steel Corp.*, 1989 WL 20193 (E.D. Pa. 1989) (Pennsylvania resident's action under ADEA, LAD, and New Jersey common law, pertaining to the termination of his employment in New Jersey, transferred from federal court in Pennsylvania to federal court in New Jersey); *Joyce v. Hoffmann-LaRoche*, 1987 WL 12306 (E.D. Pa. 1987) (Connecticut resident's action under ADEA, LAD, and New Jersey common law, with respect to the termination of his employment in New Jersey, transferred from federal court in Pennsylvania to federal court in New Jersey); *Freeman v. Calma Co.*, 41 FEP 1287, 1289 (E.D. Pa. 1986) (Pennsylvania resident whose sales territory included Eastern Pennsylvania and southern New Jersey, who performed most of his work in Pennsylvania, and had other significant contacts with Pennsylvania must assert his cause of action for wrongful discharge in violation of the public policy against age discrimination under Pennsylvania, not New Jersey, law). The Second Circuit, in *Shamley*, also observed that "*Robinson v. Sizes Unlimited, Inc.*, 685 F.Supp. 442, 447-48 (D.N.J. 1988), which determined that [the LAD] applied in similar circumstances," has been undermined by the Appellate Division's *Shamley* decision. *Shamley*, 869 F.2d at 172 n.4. *See also McFadden v. Burton*, 645 F.Supp. 457, 460-61, 464-66 (E.D. Pa. 1986) (when viewed from Pennsylvania's choice-of-law perspective, LAD cannot be applied to a discharged individual who is employed in Pennsylvania and resides in New Jersey; but when viewed from New Jersey's choice-of-law perspective, LAD can be applied to that individual).

73. *See Hawes v. Johnson & Johnson*, 940 F. Supp. 697, 701-02 (D.N.J. 1996).

74. A "labor organization" is any organization which exists and is constituted for the purpose, in whole or in part, of (1) collective bargaining, (2) dealing with employers concerning grievances, terms, or conditions of employment, or (3) other mutual aid or protection in connection with employment. N.J.S.A. 10:5-5(c). In *Baliko v. Stecker*, 275 N.J. Super. 182, 645 A.2d 1218 (App. Div. 1994), the Appellate Division held that in appropriate circumstances, a labor union may be liable for its members' sexual harassment of the employees of another employer. However, on remand the Law Division held the LAD would be unconstitutional if extended to statements made by union members while on a picket line.

75. N.J.S.A. 10:5-12(a)-(c). An "employment agency" is any person undertaking to procure employees or opportunities for others to work. N.J.S.A. 10:5-5(b). A Division on Civil Rights regulation, without any explanation, distinguishes between an employment agency and a "recruitment source" that refers people to employers for employment. N.J.A.C. 13:13-2.2(a). *See Failla v. City of Passaic*, 146 F.3d 149 (3d Cir. 1998) (applying Restatement of Torts to determine aiding and abetting liability; "an employee aids and abets a violation of the LAD when he knowingly gives substantial assistance or encouragement to the unlawful conduct of his employer"; shared intent not required). *Tyson v. Cigna Corp.*, 918 F. Supp. 836 (D.N.J. 1996), *aff'd* 149 F.3d 1165 (3d Cir. 1998) (aiding and abetting liability limited to supervisory employees who actively participate in discrimination; non-supervisory employees are legally incapable of aiding and abetting); *Poveromo-Spring v. Exxon Corp.*, 968 F. Supp. 219 (D.N.J. 1997) (same); *Baliko v. Stecker*, 275 N.J. Super. 182 (App. Div. 1994) ("A 'labor organization' referred to in N.J.S.A. 10:5-126 can act only through its agents. If one member assists, supports, encourages, and supplements the efforts of another in conduct which violates the LAD, the local may be liable as a principle for violating N.J.S.A. 10:5-12b and individual members may be liable as aiders and abettors for violating N.J.S.A. 10:5-12e.")

abets, or otherwise assists the commission of or attempts to commit any of the acts declared unlawful by the LAD or (2) retaliates against a person who engaged in conduct protected by the LAD violates the LAD.[76]

An "employer" is any "person" not otherwise specifically exempt, including the state, any political or civil subdivisions of the state, and all public officers, agencies, boards, or bodies.[77] Supervisory employees actively involved in the conduct complained of have been found to be "employers" under the LAD.[78]

Unlike Title VII of the Civil Rights Act of 1964 and the Age Discrimination in Employment Act (ADEA), which are inapplicable to employers with fewer than 15 or 20 employees respectively,[79] the LAD applies to all employers regardless of the number of persons they employ.[80]

An employer that sells an on-going business is not liable for the purchaser's conduct unless it participated therein.[81] Two or more individuals and/or busi-

---

76. N.J.S.A. 10:5-12(e), (d). A "person" is defined as including one or more individuals, partnerships, associations, organizations, labor organizations, corporations, legal representatives, trustees, trustees in bankruptcy, receivers, and fiduciaries. N.J.S.A. 10:5-5(a).

77. N.J.S.A. 10:5-5(e). Public employers are governed by the LAD even though review of discrimination complaints by the Division on Civil Rights "implicates an interference with the inherent managerial prerogatives of" such employers. *Teaneck Bd. of Educ. v. Teaneck Teachers Ass'n*, 94 N.J. 9, 17 (1983); *cf. Hebard v. Basking Ridge Fire Co.*, 164 N.J.Super. 77, 83-84 (App. Div. 1978), *app. dism'd*, 81 N.J. 294 (1979) (volunteer fire department that refused to permit women to join was essentially an arm of the municipality and thus an "employer" under the LAD).

The LAD presently does not exempt any specified class of persons from the definition of "employer."

78. *Andersen v. Exxon Co.*, 89 N.J. 483, 502 (1982) (personnel manager, "[a]s the individual directly responsible for refusing complainant employment, ... was a direct, active participant in the discrimination"); *Braddy v. Jersey Shore Medical Center*, 44 FEP 149, 151, 1987 WL 13002 (D.N.J. June 22, 1987) (to be deemed an "employer" an employee must have "sufficient authority" over plaintiff); *Roberts v. Keansburg Bd. of Educ.*, 5 N.J.A.R. 208, 249, 259-60 (DCR 1983) (high school principal); *Wolbert v. Stylianos, Inc.*, 9 N.J.A.R. 392, 398 (DCR 1985) (owner/supervisor of a diner); *New Jersey Div. on Civil Rights v. Slumber, Inc.*, 82 N.J. 412, 413, 415 n.2 (1980) (general manager and front desk supervisor); *Castellano v. Linden Bd. of Educ.*, 158 N.J.Super. 350, 353 (App. Div. 1978), *rev'd in part on other grounds, aff'd in part*, 79 N.J. 407 (1979) (superintendent of schools and board of education president). *Cf. Peper v. Princeton Univ. Bd. of Trustees*, 151 N.J.Super. 15, 26 (App. Div. 1977), *rev'd on other grounds*, 77 N.J. 55 (1978) ("we are not satisfied that a viable cause of action was proved against any of the individual defendant[-officers] who had varying degrees, if any, of involvement with plaintiff. We are satisfied that the discrimination proceeded from an implementation of University policy for which the University itself should ... be held responsible."); *Caldwell v. KFC Corp.*, 958 F. Supp. 962, 971 (D.N.J. 1997) (supervisory employees are liable under the LAD only to the extent they affirmatively engage in discriminatory conduct while acting in the scope of employment; omissions, acquiescence, passivity or other failures to act are insufficient). *See generally Jackson v. Concord Co.*, 101 N.J.Super. 126, 130 (App. Div. 1968), *aff'd as mod. on other grounds*, 54 N.J. 113, 125 (1969) ("Operation of [a business] in corporate form does not shield the individuals owning and acting for the corporation from responsibility. * * * Otherwise a new corporate shield could be formed to evade the [DCR's] ruling."); *Jones v. Haridor Realty Corp.*, 37 N.J. 384, 395-96 (1962) (same); *Fraser v. Robin Dee Day Camp*, 44 N.J. 480, 489-90 (1965) (trade names do not shield sole proprietor from liability under LAD).

79. 42 U.S.C.A. §2000e(b) (Title VII); 29 U.S.C.A. §630(b) (ADEA).

80. N.J.S.A. 10:5-5(e), as amended by L.1966, c.254 (deleting from the definition of "employer" the exclusion of employers with fewer than six persons in their employ).

81. *Mate v. American Brands, Inc.*, 1990 WL 69177, p. *4 (D.N.J. 1990); N.J.S.A. 10:5-12(e).

nesses may be deemed to be a single entity under the LAD if they are extensively interdependent and intermingled.[82]

II. REGULATED CONDUCT

4-7 Generally

It is an unlawful employment practice:

a. For an employer, because of the race, creed, color, national origin, ancestry, age, marital status, sex or atypical hereditary cellular or blood trait of any individual, or because of the liability for service in the Armed Forces of the United States or the nationality of any individual, to refuse to hire or employ or to bar or to discharge or to require to retire, unless justified by lawful considerations other than age, from employment such individual or to discriminate against such individual in compensation or in terms, conditions or privileges of employment; ...

b. For a labor organization, because of the race, creed, color, national origin, ancestry, age, marital status or sex of any individual, or because of the liability for service in the Armed Forces of the United States or nationality of any individual to exclude or to expel from its membership such individual or to discriminate in any way against any of its members, against any applicant for, or individual included in, any apprentice or other training program or against any employer or any individual employed by an employer; ...

c. For any employer or employment agency to print or circulate or cause to be printed or circulated any statement, advertisement or publication, or to use any form of application for employment, or to make an inquiry in connection with prospective employment, which expresses, directly or indirectly, any limitation, specification or discrimination as to race, creed, color, national origin, ancestry, age, marital status or sex or liability of any applicant for employment for service in the Armed Forces of the

82. *Fraser v. Robin Dee Day Camp*, 44 N.J. 480, 489-90 (1965); *Jones v. Haridor Realty Corp.*, 37 N.J. 384, 395-96 (1962); *Hebard v. Basking Ridge Fire Co.*, 164 N.J.Super. 77, 83-84 (App. Div. 1978), *app. dism'd*, 81 N.J. 294 (1979). *Accord Brunson v. Rutherford Lodge*, 128 N.J.Super. 66, 76-77 (Law Div. 1974) (discrimination under New Jersey Constitution).

United States, or any intent to make any such limitation, specification or discrimination, unless based upon a bona fide occupational qualification.

d. For any person to take reprisals against any person because he has opposed any practices or acts forbidden under this act or because he has filed a complaint, testified or assisted in any proceeding under this act.

e. For any person, whether an employer or an employee or not, to aid, abet, incite, compel or coerce the doing of any of the acts forbidden under this act, or to attempt to do so.

The right to be free from discrimination in employment is a civil right.[83]

4-8 Age Discrimination[84]

Unlike the Federal Age Discrimination in Employment Act, which protects employees age 40 and older,[85] the LAD's prohibition of age discrimination begins at age 18.[86] The LAD does not require the employment of any person under the age of 18, and thus, does not protect minors from age discrimination.[87]

All state statutes establishing a minimum hiring age of 21 have been effectively repealed by the 1972 age-of-majority law[88] and replaced with a minimum age of 18.[89]

---

83. N.J.S.A. 10:5-12(a) - (e).

84. The LAD's prohibition of unlawful age discrimination was added in 1962. L.1962, c.37.

85. 29 U.S.C. §631(a).

86. *Bergen Commercial Bank v. Sisler*, 307 N.J. Super. 333, 341-42 (App. Div.); *aff'd* __N.J.__ (1999). *See, e.g., Sprague v. Glassboro State College*, 161 N.J.Super. 218 (App. Div. 1978) (LAD claim by 26-year-old employee); *Fischer v. Allied Signal Corp.*, 974 F.Supp. 797, 805-06 (D.N.J. 1997) (declining to hold LAD protection limited to those over 40 but noting that a plaintiff's age is relevant to determining whether the facts of a case create an inference of age discrimination); *Robinson v. Sizes Unlimited, Inc.*, 685 F.Supp. 442, 445-46 & n.8 (D.N.J. 1988) (commenting on this distinction between the LAD and ADEA in the context of a federal court exercising supplemental jurisdiction over LAD claims in a class action); *Sperling v. Hoffmann La Roche, Inc.*, 118 F.R.D. 392, 411-13 (D.N.J.), *app. dism'd in part on other grounds, aff'd in part on other grounds*, 862 F.2d 439 (3d Cir. 1988), *aff'd*, 493 U.S. 165 (1989) (same). *See also Catalane v. Gilian Instrument Corp.*, 271 N.J. Super. 476, 489-90 (App. Div. 1994) (protection of the LAD is not limited to individuals under age 70). *But see Burke v. Township of Franklin*, 261 N.J. Super. 592, 601-02 (App. Div. 1993) (while a bit unclear, apparently limiting age discrimination protection under the LAD to individuals protected under the federal ADEA, i.e., individuals 40 years of age and older).

87. N.J.S.A. 10:5-2.1. As to age 18 generally constituting the demarcation between the period of minority and the age of majority, *see* N.J. Const. Art. 2, ¶3(a); N.J.S.A. 9:17B-1 *et seq.*; N.J.S.A. 3B:1-2. *See New Jersey State Policemen's Benevolent Ass'n v. Morristown*, 65 N.J. 160, 169-71 (1974) (recognizing the necessary, though arbitrary, nature of the age-18 demarcation).

88. N.J.S.A. 9:17B-1(a).

Despite the extension of protection to employees age 18 and older, the Legislature has noted in other statutory provisions the particular difficulty persons age 40 and older face with respect to employment opportunities. Several statutes expressly state that persons applying for public employment are not to be discriminated against because they are age 40 or older,[90] and the Displaced Homemakers Act[91] states that age 40 is "an age at which discrimination based on age is likely, and at which entry or reentry to or advancement in the labor market is difficult."[92] In discussing age discrimination under the state and federal Constitutions, the Supreme Court has indicated that where a "classification burdens the young rather than the old," a more deferential standard of review may be warranted.[93] Additionally, the Court has recognized that where age-based restrictions are justifiable, the line of demarcation is by necessity somewhat arbitrary: "Any choice of a specific [age] inevitably excludes some persons who might plausibly be admitted and include others who might plausibly have been excluded."[94]

The LAD does not prohibit the refusal to hire or promote any person over age 70,[95] but employees over age 70 may not be terminated simply because of their

---

89. *New Jersey State Policemen's Benevolent Ass'n v. Morristown*, 65 N.J. at 162-71. As to professionals and other regulated occupations, *see, e.g.*, N.J.S.A. 30:6-15.1 (blind persons operating concession stands in public facilities); N.J.S.A. 30:11-1.1 (operators of private nursing homes, private hospitals, etc.); N.J.S.A. 45:5-3, -5.2 (chiropodists and podiatrists); N.J.S.A. 45:7-49, -50 (mortuary science practitioners); N.J.S.A. 45:9-6 (doctors and surgeons); N.J.S.A. 45:9-41.4, -41.5 (chiropractors); N.J.S.A. 45:12-5 (optometrists); N.J.S.A. 45:12A-3 (orthoptists); N.J.S.A. 45:14-7 (pharmacists); N.J.S.A. 45:14B-14 (psychologists); N.J.S.A. 45:14C-15 (master plumbers); N.J.S.A. 45:15B-3 (certified shorthand reporters); N.J.S.A. 45:15C-4 (certified tree experts).

Cf. Schlei & Grossman, *Employment Discrimination Law*, ch.14, §I.A., pp. 482-83 n.6 (2d ed. 1983) (discussing similar interrelation between the federal ADEA and federal statutes containing age limitations); DCR, *A Guide for Employers to the LAD*, p. 17 (June 1986) ("[A]n employer must consider all applicants under age 70 so long as they are over the minimum age of 18 years (unless other minimum age restrictions have been imposed by federal law or regulation, such as the ICC [now Dept. of Transportation] minimum age requirement for an interstate truck driver, which is 21 [, 49 C.F.R. §391.11(b)(1) (1990)]).").

90. Age caps, statutory and otherwise, are discussed in detail in Chapter 4, §4-29:1.

91. N.J.S.A. 52:27D-43.18 *et seq.*

92. N.J.S.A. 52:27D-43.19(c).

93. *Taxpayers Ass'n of Weymouth Tp. v. Weymouth Tp.*, 80 N.J. 6, 42 (1976), *app. dism'd and cert. denied*, 430 U.S. 977 (1977) (zoning ordinance restricting mobile-home park to older persons upheld). *Cf. Boylan v. State*, 116 N.J. 236, 250-51 (1989), *cert. denied*, 494 U.S. 1061 (1990) (rejecting equal protection claim of firefighters and law enforcement officers who were forced to retire at age 65).

94. *Taxpayers Ass'n of Weymouth Tp. v. Weymouth Tp.*, 80 N.J. at 40.

95. N.J.S.A. 10:5-12(a). However, note that subject to limited exceptions, the federal ADEA, as amended in 1986, prohibits age discrimination against persons over age 70. *See* 29 U.S.C.A. §§623(i) [first subsection (i)], 631, and 633a; Schlei & Grossman, *Employment Discrimination Law*, ch.14, §I.A. (2d ed. 1983 & 1989 supp.).*See Catalane v. Gilian Instrument Corp.*, 271 N.J. Super. 476, 490-91 n.1 (App. Div. 1994) (noting, but not deciding the federal pre-emption issue raised by the LAD exception permitting the refusal to hire individuals over age 70 and the ADEA's lack of a similar exception to its general prohibition of age discrimination against individuals over age 40).

"advanced age."[96] Subject to certain exceptions discussed in §4-29:1, mandatory retirement on the basis of age is prohibited by the LAD.[97] It is impermissible to deny employment to an older person because a younger person "would be able to produce more for the [employer] in the future."[98]

4-9 Ancestry Discrimination[99]

"Ancestry" discrimination is defined with reference to the LAD's purpose of prohibiting discrimination based on "racial, religious, ethnic or national ancestry shared by numerically significant segments of the population."[100] Thus, in this context, ancestry does not mean mere "genealogical succession" or "line of descent."[101] Nor does it pertain to the parent-child relationship with a particular family.[102] As a consequence, "anti-nepotism rules may be enforced ... notwithstanding the prospective employee's exclusion solely on the basis of his 'ancestry.'"[103]

In *New Jersey Dept. of Labor v. Cruz*, the Supreme Court held that the prohibition of ancestry and national origin discrimination was intended to bar discrimination between citizens and aliens.[104]

---

96. *Dumont v. Jersey Shore Medical Center*, 1 N.J.A.R. 249 (DCR 1980). *See Catalane*, 271 N.J. Super. at 490-91 (LAD exception permitting refusal to hire individual over age 70 does not sanction age discrimination against such an individual once hired).

97. N.J.S.A. 10:5-12(a), -2.1. Claims based upon alleged forced retirement must be brought solely through the procedure initiated by filing a complaint with the Attorney General. N.J.S.A. 10:5-12.1. *See Scudder v. Media Gen., Inc.*, 1995 WL 495945, p.*8-9 (D.N.J. 1995).

98. *Flanders v. William Paterson College*, 163 N.J.Super. 225, 229 (App. Div. 1976); *Accord Polcari v. Hackensack Bd. of Educ.*, 8 N.J.A.R. 537 (DCR 1984) (impermissible to select younger employee for promotion merely because he is more likely to remain with the employer for more years than an older employee); *N.J. Attorney General Formal Opinion No. 1-1984* (July 11, 1984). If the younger person is actually more productive than the older person and productivity is the selection criterion, there would be no discrimination. N.J.S.A. 10:5-2.1.

99. The LAD has prohibited unlawful discrimination on the basis of ancestry since its enactment in 1945. L.1945, c.169. The right to obtain employment without discrimination on the basis of ancestry is a civil right. N.J.S.A. 10:5-4.

100. *Whateley v. Leonia Bd. of Educ.*, 141 N.J.Super. 476, 480 (Ch.Div. 1976).

101. *Id.* at 478-80.

102. *Bluvias v. Winfield Mutual Housing Corp.*, 224 N.J.Super. 515, 526 (App. Div. 1988), *app. dism'd*, 114 N.J. 589 (1989); *Whateley v. Leonia Bd. of Educ.*, 141 N.J.Super. at 480.

103. *Bluvias v. Winfield Mutual Housing Corp.*, 224 N.J.Super. at 526; *Whateley v. Leonia Bd. of Educ.*, 141 N.J.Super. at 480.

104. *New Jersey Dept. of Labor v. Cruz*, 45 N.J. 372, 377-78 (1965).

4-10 Armed Forces Discrimination

The prohibition of discrimination on the basis of a person's liability for service in the Armed Forces of the United States was added to the LAD in 1951.[105] Liability for service in the Armed Forces means that a person, as an individual or a member of an organized unit, is subject to (1) being ordered into active service in the United States Armed Forces by reason of membership in the National Guard, naval militia, or reserve component of the Armed Forces, or (2) being inducted into such armed forces through a system of national selective service.[106] Thus, the DCR interprets this prohibition as extending to discrimination based upon an employee's National Guard or Reserve Unit duty obligations.[107]

4-11 Atypical Hereditary Cellular or Blood Trait Discrimination

The LAD's prohibition of unlawful discrimination based on atypical hereditary cellular or blood trait (AHCBT) was added in 1981.[108] Although AHCBT is a serious medical problem, the Legislature has concluded that in virtually all cases AHCBT carriers are medically asymptomatic and therefore unaffected in their ability to work.[109]

The LAD defines "atypical hereditary cellular or blood trait" as sickle cell trait, hemoglobin C trait, thalassemia trait, Tay-Sachs trait, or cystic fibrosis trait.[110] Persons afflicted with AHCBT are carriers whose chromosomes contain both an abnormal and normal gene for the particular disease.[111]

---

105. L.1951, c.64. According to the Sponsors' Statement accompanying the 1951 legislation:

> It is the historic and fundamental obligation of all able-bodied citizens of the Republic to bear arms in defense of the State and nation. No right of any employer should be permitted to interfere or discriminate against a citizen in his exercise of the right to be ready to so serve his country by training with the National Guard, naval militia or reserve, nor should the exercise of the right of any employer to employ whom he may desire be permitted to discriminate against an individual because of his liability to induction into the armed forces. Youth must be given the opportunity of employment and the exercise of inherent civil rights, without discrimination, pending call into the armed forces in time of national emergency.

Sponsors' Statement to Assembly No. 11 (Feb. 5, 1951).

106. N.J.S.A. 10:5-5(g).

107. DCR, *Employment Guide to the LAD*, p. 10 (1989).

108. L.1981, c.185. AHCBT discrimination is mentioned in the LAD only in the provision concerning discriminatory acts by employers. *See* N.J.S.A. 10:5-12(a). Nonetheless, any person, including a labor organization or employment agency, aiding or abetting an employer in such illegal conduct would also violate the LAD. N.J.S.A. 10:5-12(e).

109. Senate Labor, Industry & Professions Committee, *Statement to Senate Committee Substitute for Senate No. 448* (June 9, 1980); *Statement to Senate No. 448* (June 23, 1980); Assembly Labor Committee, *Statement to Senate Committee Substitute for Senate No. 448* (Feb. 23, 1981).

110. N.J.S.A. 10:5-5(x).

"Sickle cell trait" is the condition wherein (1) the major natural hemoglobin components present in the blood of an individual are hemoglobin A (normal) and hemoglobin S (sickle hemoglobin) as defined by standard chemical and physical analytic techniques, including electrophoresis, and (2) the proportion of hemoglobin A is greater than the proportion of hemoglobin S or one natural parent of the individual is shown to have only normal hemoglobin components (hemoglobin A, A2, F) in the normal proportions by standard chemical and physical analytic tests.[112] "Hemoglobin C trait" is the condition wherein (1) the major natural hemoglobin components present in the blood of an individual are hemoglobin A (normal) and hemoglobin C as defined by standard chemical and physical analytic techniques, including electrophoresis, and (2) the proportion of hemoglobin A is greater than the proportion of hemoglobin C or one natural parent of the individual is shown to have only normal hemoglobin components (hemoglobin A, A2, F) in normal proportions by standard chemical and physical analytic tests.[113]

"Thalassemia trait" is the presence of the thalassemia gene which in combination with another similar gene results in the chronic hereditary disease Cooley's anemia.[114] "Tay-Sachs trait" is the presence of the Tay-Sachs gene which in combination with another similar gene results in the chronic hereditary disease Tay-Sachs.[115] "Cystic fibrosis trait" is the presence of the cystic fibrosis gene

---

111. Assembly Labor Committee, *Statement to Senate Committee Substitute for Senate No. 448* (Feb. 23, 1981).

112. N.J.S.A. 10:5-5(y). Sickle cell trait clinically is asymptomatic and normally does not result in any anemia. In contrast, sickle cell anemia, as well as three other sickle cell syndromes to a lesser degree, can result in rather severe and painful disabilities. Wyngaarden & Smith, *Cecil Textbook of Medicine*, ch.143, pp. 936-42 (18th ed. 1988); 3 Schmidt, *Attorneys' Dictionary of Medicine*, p. S-108 (1989 rev. & 1990 supp.). The sickle cell syndromes are prevalent in black persons of African or Afro-American descent, though they are also found in persons of Mediterranean ancestry (southern Italians, Sicilians, and Greeks), in Saudi Arabia, and in India. *Cecil Textbook of Medicine*, p. 937. In 1981 it was reported that approximately 10 percent of black persons in New Jersey were carriers of sickle cell anemia. Assembly Labor Committee, *Statement to Senate Committee Substitute for Senate No. 448* (Feb. 23, 1981).

113. N.J.S.A. 10:5-5(z). Approximately two percent to three percent of American blacks have hemoglobin C trait. *The Merck Manual of Diagnosis & Therapy*, ch. 96, p. 1122 (15th ed. 1987); *Cecil Textbook of Medicine*, ch. 143, p. 937.

114. N.J.S.A. 10:5-5(aa). The thalassemias are hereditary anemias resulting from mutations that affect the synthesis of hemoglobin. The most common of the thalassemias is thalassemia trait, which is a mild, clinically-insignificant anemia and is believed to protect persons from malaria. In contrast, Cooley's anemia is the name given to severe beta thalassemia, which causes severe anemia, growth retardation, enlargement of both the liver and spleen, bone marrow expansion, and bone deformities which often result in a chipmunk or mongoloid facial appearance. *Cecil Textbook of Medicine*, ch. 142, pp. 930-33. *See The Merck Manual of Diagnosis & Therapy*, ch. 96, pp. 1122-24; *Tabor's Cyclopedic Medical Dictionary*, pp. 1716-17 (15th ed. 1985); 4 Schmidt, *Attorneys' Dictionary of Medicine*, p. T-58 (1990 rev.). In the United States, the occurrence of beta thalassemia is most prevalent among ethnic groups from the Mediterranean area, parts of Africa, and Asia; the incidence of alpha thalassemia is most prevalent among persons from Asia; and the rate of thalassemia trait in these groups is three percent to five percent. *Cecil Textbook on Medicine*, p. 930. In 1981 it was reported that 10 percent of Italian-Americans and Greek-Americans in New Jersey were carriers of thalassemia. Assembly Labor Committee, *Statement to Senate Committee Substitute for Senate No. 448* (Feb. 23, 1981).

which in combination with another similar gene results in the chronic hereditary disease cystic fibrosis.[116]

4-12 Color Discrimination

The LAD has barred unlawful discrimination on the basis of color since its enactment in 1945.[117]

The court in *Corin v. Glenwood Cemetery*, a pre-LAD case, distinguished between a person being "colored" and being of "African descent."[118] To establish that a person is of color, it apparently must be shown that he is darker in skin color than many residents of Southern Europe, Cuba, or Mexico, or that either of his parents was colored.[119] The LAD protects the class of colored persons, but not the distinct class of "colored males."[120]

4-13 Creed Discrimination

The LAD has prohibited unlawful creed discrimination since its adoption in 1945.[121] Although the LAD does not define the term "creed,"[122] it seems clear that the Legislature intended it to be limited to its principal meaning, that of a religious belief.[123] This is demonstrated by the fact that various provisions of the

---

115. N.J.S.A. 10:5-5(bb). Tay-Sachs disease, an autosomal recessive disorder, is most common in persons of Eastern European Jewish (Ashkenazi) descent, and to a lesser extent among children of non-Jewish consanguineous parents. *Cecil Textbook of Medicine*, ch. 33, p. 147; *The Merck Manual of Diagnosis & Therapy*, ch. 203, pp. 2140-41, 2158-59. In 1981 it was reported that 3 percent of Ashkenazic Jews were carriers of Tay-Sachs disease. Assembly Labor Committee, *Statement to Senate Committee Substitute for Senate No. 448* (Feb. 23, 1981).

116. N.J.S.A. 10:5-5(cc). Cystic fibrosis, also an autosomal recessive disorder, is most common among white persons in the United States, and to a lesser degree among children of consanguineous parents. *Cecil Textbook of Medicine*, ch.66, p.440, ch. 33, p. 147; *The Merck Manual of Diagnosis & Therapy*, ch. 203, pp. 2140-41, ch. 193, p. 2055. In 1981 it was reported that 4 percent of white persons were carriers of cystic fibrosis. Assembly Labor Committee, *Statement to Senate Committee Substitute for Senate No. 448* (Feb. 23, 1981).

117. L.1945, c.169. The right to be free from employment discrimination on the basis of color is a civil right. N.J.S.A. 10:5-4. It is also the public policy of New Jersey. N.J.S.A. 18A:54D-2(a).

118. *Corin v. Glenwood Cemetery*, 69 A. 1083 (N.J.Ch. 1908).

119. *Id.* at 1083.

120. *Floyd v. State of New Jersey*, 1991 WL 143456, p. *4 (D.N.J. 1991).

121. L.1945, c.169. The LAD has been found inapplicable to a decision appointing a nun (and not the lay plaintiff) as an elementary school principal, on the ground that the position involved ministerial functions: "The principal is in charge of the students' religious education; she supervises the teachers, plays a significant role in curriculum development, is liaison between the school and the religious community, and is the guiding force behind the school's spiritual mission." *Sabatino v. Saint Aloysius Parish*, 288 N.J. Super. 233 (App. Div. 1996). *Cf. Gallo v. Salesian Soc'y, Inc.*, 290 N.J. Super. 616 (App. Div. 1996) (LAD did apply to religious prep school's decision to terminate a lay teacher of English and History for budgetary reasons).

LAD use the term religion (or a derivative thereof) where creed would otherwise be expected to appear.[124] It has been the stated interpretation of the Division on Civil Rights (DCR) in publications.[125] The DCR's official employment poster in the New Jersey Administrative Code refers to creed and religion, apparently interchangeably.[126] However, in its regulations pertaining to pre-employment inquiries, the DCR sets forth separate examples of impermissible inquiries relating to creed and religion.[127] As to religion, the DCR states that it is impermissible to ask (1) about an applicant's religious affiliation, church, or parish, or what religious holidays the applicant observes; or (2) for the name of the applicant's pastor or religious leader.[128]

---

122. *Webster's Third New International Dictionary of the English Language*, p. 533 (unabridged ed. 1981) defines creed as:

> [A] brief authoritative doctrinal formula beginning with such words as "Credo", "Credimus", "I believe", "We believe", intended to define what is held by a Christian congregation, synod, or church to be true and essential and exclude what is held to be false belief. ... [A] formulation or system of religious faith. ...

Accord Black's Law Dictionary, p. 370 (6th ed. 1990) ("confession or articles of faith, formal declaration of religious belief, any formula or confession of religious faith, and a system of religious belief").

123. *Shuchter v. New Jersey Div. on Civil Rights*, 117 N.J.Super. 405 (App. Div. 1971) (LAD uses "creed" to mean a person's religious beliefs or principles, as opposed to moral, philosophical, social, or political values); *N.J. Attorney General Formal Opinion No. 17-1949* (Mar. 28, 1949) ("creed" means "religious principles" as opposed to political beliefs or principles); *Fioriglio v. City of Atlantic City*, 963 F. Supp. 415, 426 (D.N.J. 1997) ("creed" does not include political beliefs espoused during a campaign: "A religious belief excludes mere personal preference grounded upon a non-theological basis, such as personal choice deduced from economic or social ideology. Rather, it must consider man's nature or the scheme of his existence as it relates in a theological framework."). *See Lige v. Montclair*, 72 N.J. 5, 15 (1976); *cf. Streeter v. Brogan*, 113 N.J.Super. 486, 490 (Ch.Div. 1971) ("creed," as used in N.J.S.A. 10:1-3, does not encompass "a moral or ethical creed apart from a formal religious creed"). Note that in 1945, on the same day the Legislature adopted the LAD, it amended N.J.S.A. 30:9-17, pertaining to discrimination by city hospitals, by, *inter alia*, substituting "creed" for "religious faith." L.1945, c.173.

124. *Cf.* N.J.S.A. 10:5-3 (discrimination based on "race, creed, color," etc. is a menace to society), N.J.S.A. 10:5-4 (opportunity to obtain employment without discrimination based on "race, creed, color," etc. is a civil right), *with* N.J.S.A. 10:5-9.1 (DCR to enforce laws against discrimination based on "race, religious principles, color," etc. in public housing and real estate); N.J.S.A. 10:5-8(c) (DCR required to take steps to further goodwill among various "racial and religious and nationality groups"); N.J.S.A. 10:5-5(l) (excluding educational facilities operated by bona fide "religious or sectarian" institutions from the definition of "a place of public accommodation"); N.J.S.A. 10:5-5(n) (exempting "religious or denominational" institutions or organizations from certain restrictions pertaining to real property); N.J.S.A. 10:5-12(a) (exempting "religious" associations or organizations from certain restrictions pertaining to employment decisions); N.J.S.A. 10:5-12.2 (permitting "religiously affiliated" skilled nursing or intermediate care facilities to use "religious affiliation" as a uniform qualification for admission); N.J.S.A. 10:5-5(e) (from 1945 to 1979, the LAD excluded from the definition of "employer" non-profit "religious" associations or corporations).

New Jersey Constitution Article 1, Paragraph 5 provides that no person is to be denied the enjoyment of any civil right or discriminated against in the exercise of such right on the basis of, *inter alia*, "religious principles." *See N.J. Attorney General Formal Opinion No. 17-1949* (Mar. 28, 1949) (1947 Constitution effectively ratified LAD); *Lige v. Montclair*, 72 N.J. at 15 (same).

125. DCR, *Employment Guide to the LAD*, pp. 10, 14 (1989).

126. N.J.A.C. 13:8-2.1.

The term "creed" includes those who adhere to a particular religious faith, those who are agnostic, and those who are non-believers.[129] One court has suggested that the protections of the LAD extend to persons who are discriminated against because they are believed to be members of a particular religious faith, even if they are not.[130]

4-13:1 Reasonable Accommodation Requirement

The Division on Civil Rights (DCR) states that an employer must reasonably accommodate an employee's religious beliefs.[131] According to the DCR, the burden of reaching a reasonable accommodation is shared by both the employer and the employee.[132]

Reasonable accommodation most commonly arises in cases where an employee, because of religious beliefs, is unable to work on the Sabbath. If working on Saturday or Sunday is a job requirement and no other arrangement can be made to reasonably accommodate the employee without unduly burdening the employer or co-employees, then the employer may refuse to hire or may fire the employee.[133]

4-13:2 Religious Membership Requirements

A religious association or organization may use religious affiliation (1) as a uniform qualification in the employment of clergy, religious teachers, or other employees engaged in the religious activities of the association or organization or (2) "in following the tenets of its religion in establishing and utilizing criteria for employment of an employee."[134]

---

127. Under the categories "creed" and "organizations," the DCR states that it is discriminatory to inquire about the private organizational or political affiliations of a job applicant. N.J.A.C. 13:7-1.1(c), (m). As noted in §92, the DCR pre-employment inquiry regulations were last amended in 1970 and the agency's 1989 *Employment Guide to the LAD* deleted the prohibition of inquiries relating to private organizational and political affiliations. This deletion is consistent with the 1949 *Formal Opinion* of the state attorney general and the post-1970 court decisions, noted in n. 117, which render this aspect of the DCR's regulations of questionable validity.

128. N.J.A.C. 13:7-1.1(d), (n).

129. *N.J. Attorney General Formal Opinion No. 17-1949* (Mar. 28, 1949).

130. *Poff v. Caro*, 228 N.J.Super. 370, 377 (Law Div. 1987).

131. DCR, *Employment Guide to the LAD*, p. 10 (1989).

132. DCR, *Employment Guide to the LAD*, p. 10 (1989); DCR, *A Guide for Employers to the LAD*, p. 19 (June 1986).

133. DCR, *Employment Guide to the LAD*, p. 10 (1989); DCR, *A Guide for Employers to the LAD*, p. 19 (June 1986).

134. N.J.S.A. 10:5-12(a). *See Peper v. Princeton Univ. Bd. of Trustees*, 77 N.J. 55, 70 (1978).

4-13:3 Genetic Information

The Genetic Privacy Act, adopted in 1996, amended the LAD to make it an unlawful employment practice for an employer to discriminate on the basis of genetic information or because of the refusal of an individual to submit to a genetic test or make available the results of a genetic test.[135] "Genetic information" means the information about genes, gene products or inherited characteristics that may derive from an individual or family member."[136] A "genetic test" is "a test for determining the presence or absence of an inherited genetic characteristic in an individual, including tests for nucleic acids such as DNA, RNA and mitrochondrial DNA, chromosomes or proteins in order to identify a predisposing genetic characteristic."[137]

4-14 Handicap Discrimination

The LAD was made applicable to physically handicapped persons in 1972 and to non-physically handicapped persons in 1978.[138] It is unlawful to discriminate against persons because they are or have been at any time handicapped, unless, in spite of reasonable accommodation, the nature and extent of their handicaps reasonably preclude or impede the adequate and safe performance of their particular employments.[139] This prohibition has been extended to protect persons

---

135. N.J.S.A. 10:5-12.11.a.

136. N.J.S.A. 10:5-5.00.

137. N.J.S.A. 10:5-5.pp.

138. L.1972, c.114; L.1978, c.137. *See* N.J.S.A. 10:5-4.1 (all provisions of LAD construed as prohibiting unlawful handicap discrimination). Ten months prior to the enactment date of the 1978 amendment, the court in *Washington Tp. v. Central Bergen Community Mental Health Center*, 156 N.J.Super. 388, 420 (Law Div. 1978), commented: "[N]o explanation has been offered as to why persons suffering from a mental handicap should be excluded from the zone of statutory protection afforded others more blessed."

In 1985, the DCR adopted detailed regulations implementing the handicap provisions of the LAD. N.J.A.C. 13:13-1.1 *et seq.* These regulations are patterned after regulations promulgated under §504 of the Rehabilitation Act of 1973, 29 U.S.C.A. §794. *See* 22 N.J.R. 1436 (May 21, 1990).

139. N.J.S.A. 10:5-4.1; N.J.S.A. 10:5-2.1; *Jansen v. Food Circus Supermarkets, Inc.*, 110 N.J. 363, 373-83 (1988); *Andersen v. Exxon Co.*, 89 N.J. 483, 496-97 (1982); N.J.A.C. 13:13-1.3(2), -2.4(e)(2), -2.5, -2.8(a)(1)-(2); DCR, *Employment Guide to the LAD*, pp. 8-9 (1989); DCR, *A Guide for Employers to the LAD*, pp. 14-15 (June 1986). *See Maher v. New Jersey Transit Rail Operations, Inc.*, 125 N.J. 455, 482 (1991) (the proviso was added by the Legislature to restrict the reach of the LAD in cases of handicap discrimination). *See McNemar v. The Disney Store, Inc.*, 91 F. 3d 610 (3d Cir. 1996) (doctrine of judicial estoppel bars employee who has certified to total and permanent disability on benefits applications from alleging in handicap discrimination case that he is qualified under the LAD and ADA), *cert. denied*, 117 S. Ct. 958, 136 L.Ed.2d 845 (1997); *Erit v. Judge, Inc.*, 961 F. Supp. 774, 779 (D.N.J. 1997) (plaintiff who claimed he was disabled at the time of discharge was judicially estopped from arguing he was capable of performing his job at the time of discharge); *Morris v. Siemens Components, Inc.*, 1996 WL 294074, p.*8 (D.N.J. 1996) (employee who represents she is disabled on a benefits application is judicially estopped from contending in a handicap discrimination claim that she is qualified to perform the job).

perceived or believed to be suffering from handicaps, whether or not the medical conditions from which they suffered in fact handicapped them.[140] However, the precise contours of "perceived handicap" discrimination remain unclear. It has been suggested, for example, that an epileptic whose condition does not adversely affect job performance, but who is nonetheless discharged because of the unfounded fears of co-employees, is a victim of perceived handicapped discrimination.[141] But because epilepsy is clearly a "handicap" under the LAD, the rationale for invoking a perceived handicap theory in that circumstance is not apparent.

The protections of the LAD have also been extended to persons who suffer from medical conditions which the employer believes will handicap them in the future.[142] However, a previously handicapped person is not protected by the LAD from actions not based upon a perception of continued handicapped status.[143]

Division on Civil Rights (DCR) regulations prohibit handicap discrimination in wages, training programs, and fringe benefits,[144] and supersede any inconsistent terms of a collective bargaining agreement.[145] An employer's wage scale may not include any distinctions based on handicap, unless permitted by state or federal law.[146] Occupational training and retraining programs, such as guidance, apprenticeship, and executive training programs, may not be conducted in a manner that would discourage or discriminate against handicapped individuals.[147]

---

140. N.J.A.C. 13:13-1.3(1); *Andersen v. Exxon Co.*, 89 N.J. 483, 495-96 n.2 (1982) (dicta); *Rogers v. Campbell Foundry Co.*, 185 N.J.Super. 109, 112-13 (App. Div. 1982), *certif. denied*, 91 N.J. 529 (1982); *Gimello v. Agency Rent-A-Car Systems, Inc.*, 250 N.J.Super. 338, 356-65 (App. Div. 1991).

141. *Jansen v. Food Circus Supermarkets, Inc.*, 214 N.J.Super. 51, 57 (App. Div. 1986), *rev'd on other grounds*, 110 N.J. 363, 370, 373-74 (1988). *Accord Pilot v. New Jersey Dept. of Health*, 7 N.J.A.R. 150, 170-73 (DCR 1982), *aff'd*, No. A-5853-81 (App. Div. Sept. 28, 1983) (individual denied promotional opportunities simply because she was an epileptic). *See Andersen v. Exxon Co.*, 89 N.J. at 495-96 n.2, 497 (" '[p]rejudice in the sense of a judgment or opinion formed before the facts are known is the fountainhead of discrimination engulfing medical disabilities which prove on examination to be unrelated to job performance or to be non-existent.' "). *Cf. Behringer v. Medical Center at Princeton*, 249 N.J.Super. 597, 612-13, 623, 634-35, 639-40 n.13, 653-54 (Law Div. 1991) (patient's right to informed consent, and thus knowledge of physician's affliction with AIDS, may result in *de facto* termination of his surgical privileges if patients, because of their fears, refuse to be treated by him).

142. *Poff v. Caro*, 228 N.J.Super. 370, 374-78 (Law Div. 1987) (landlord feared that three potential tenants, homosexual men, might later acquire AIDS); *Rogers v. Campbell Foundry Co.*, 8 N.J.A.R. 75, 85-86 (DCR 1980), *aff'd*, 185 N.J.Super. 109 (App. Div.), *certif. denied*, 91 N.J. 529 (1982) (unfounded fear that healthy job applicant with hilar shadow on lungs is predisposed to contract silicosis or pneumoconiosis).

143. *Oare v. Midlantic National Bank/Merchants*, 1990 WL 4622, 54 FEP 1530, 1533 (D.N.J. Jan. 16, 1990); N.J.A.C. 13:13-1.3(2); N.J.S.A. 10:5-4.1.

144. N.J.A.C. 13:13-2.6.

145. N.J.A.C. 13:13-2.6(d). This provision may be pre-empted by federal law. *See* §4-4, discussing §301 of the Labor Management Relations Act, 1947, 29 U.S.C.A. §185.

146. N.J.A.C. 13:13-2.6(a).

147. N.J.A.C. 13:13-2.6(b).

Fringe benefits, whether provided directly by the employer or through contracts with insurance carriers, must not discriminate on the basis of handicap.[148] Fringe benefits include (1) medical, hospital, accident, and life insurance, (2) retirement benefits, profit sharing, and bonus plans, and (3) leave.[149] Thus, for example, the same medical insurance coverage must be provided to handicapped and non-handicapped employees.[150]

The DCR regulations also contain four provisions directed to labor organizations, making it unlawful for them (1) to exclude or expel an individual from membership or an apprenticeship program because of his handicap; (2) to discriminate on the basis of an individual's handicap in regard to hiring, tenure, promotion, transfer, compensation, other terms, conditions, and privileges of employment, representation, grievances, or any other matter related to membership in or employment by the union; (3) to cause or attempt to cause an employer to discriminate against an individual because of a handicap; and (4) to engage in any of the above conduct even if the conduct is authorized or required by the union's constitution or by-laws or by a collective bargaining agreement or other contract to which the union is a party.[151]

It is an unlawful employment practice for an employer or employment agency (1) to print, circulate, or cause to be printed or circulated any statement, advertisement, or publication, (2) to use any form of employment application, or (3) to make any inquiry in connection with prospective employment that expresses, directly or indirectly, any limitation, specification, or discrimination as to handicap, or any intent to make any such limitation, specification, or discrimination, unless based upon a bona fide occupational qualification (BFOQ).[152]

---

148. N.J.A.C. 13:13-2.6(c); N.J.A.C. 13:13-2.8(a)(3)(ii). *See Szabo v. New Jersey State Firemen's Ass'n*, 230 N.J.Super. 265, 283-84 & n.12 (Ch.Div. 1988) ("There is no statutory authority [in the Association] to deny membership [benefits] because of greater actuarial risk" and potential excessive claims of a handicapped firefighter; such power may violate anti-discrimination laws such as the LAD).

149. N.J.A.C. 13:13-2.6(c). To the extent this provision regulates employee benefit plans or benefits provided pursuant to collective bargaining agreements, it may be pre-empted by federal law. *See* §4-4, discussing §514 of the Employee Retirement Income Security Act of 1974, 29 U.S.C.A. §1144, and §301 of the Labor Management Relations Act of 1947, 29 U.S.C.A. §185.

150. N.J.A.C. 13:13-2.6(c). Medical insurance programs need not cover the costs of any medical condition arising out of a pre-existing illness. N.J.A.C. 13:13-2.6(c); DCR Response to Public Comments on N.J.A.C. 13:13-1.1. *et seq.*, 17 N.J.R. 1574(a), at p. 1575 (June 17, 1985).

151. N.J.A.C. 13:13-2.7(d). This provision may be pre-empted by federal law. *See* §4-4, discussing §301 of the Labor Management Relations Act of 1947, 29 U.S.C.A. §185.

152. N.J.S.A. 10:5-12(c), -4.1. Employment advertising and job referrals, pre-employment inquiries, and the BFOQ defense are discussed in §§4-22, 4-23 and 4-30.

4-14:1 Handicap Defined

A handicap under the LAD may be physical or non-physical.[153] An individual is physically handicapped if he suffers from any physical disability, infirmity, malformation, or disfigurement caused by bodily injury, birth defect, or illness (including epilepsy).[154] Physical handicap includes, but is not limited to, any degree of paralysis, amputation, lack of physical coordination, blindness[155] or visual impediment,[156] deafness[157] or hearing impediment, muteness or speech impediment, or physical reliance on a service or guide dog,[158] wheelchair, or other remedial appliance or device.[159] An individual is non-physically handicapped if he suffers from any mental, psychological, or developmental disability, which (1) results from an anatomical, psychological, physiological, or neurological condition, and which (2) either (a) prevents the normal exercise of any bodily or mental functions or (b) is demonstrable, medically or psychologically, by accepted clinical or laboratory diagnostic techniques.[160]

---

153. N.J.S.A. 10:5-5(q). With few exceptions, the LAD does not define the specific conditions that qualify as handicaps. N.J.S.A. 50:5-5(q); *Clowes v. Terminix Int'l, Inc.*, 109 N.J. 575, 593 (1988); *Gimello v. Agency Rent-A-Car Systems, Inc.*, 250 N.J.Super. 338, 361-62 (App. Div. 1991).

154. *Jansen v. Food Circus Supermarkets, Inc.*, 110 N.J. 363, 367-68 n.1 (1988); *Pilot v. New Jersey Dept. of Health*, 7 N.J.A.R. 150 (DCR 1982), *aff'd*, No. A-5853-81 (App. Div. Sept. 28, 1983).

155. N.J.S.A. 10:5-5(r).

156. In two recent cases, employees who were legally blind in one eye were subjected to adverse employment decisions to protect their remaining vision. Neither case addressed whether the employees were handicapped within the meaning of the LAD. *Maher v. New Jersey Transit Rail Operations, Inc.*, 239 N.J.Super. 213 (App. Div. 1990), *aff'd in part, rev'd in part*, 125 N.J. 455 (1991); *Greenwood v. New Jersey State Police Training Center*, 127 N.J. 500 (1992). In *Greenwood v. State Police Training Ctr.*, the Supreme Court appears to have assumed that the plaintiff—a police trainee who was legally blind in one eye, but who did not allege a violation of the LAD—would be considered handicapped under that statute. 127 N.J. 500, 511-12 (1992).

157. The LAD defines "deaf person" as an individual (1) whose hearing is so severely impaired that he is unable to hear and understand normal conversational speech through the unaided ear alone and (2) who must depend primarily on a supportive device or visual communication such as writing, lip reading, sign language, and gestures. N.J.S.A. 10:5-5(w).

A deaf person may seek the assistance of the Director of the Division of the Deaf and Hard of Hearing, within the Department of Human Services, with respect to both investigation of alleged acts of discrimination and filing of a verified complaint with the Division on Civil Rights. N.J.S.A. 34:1-69.3. The Division of the Deaf and Hard of Hearing deems a person deaf when his sense of hearing is non-functional for ordinary life purposes. N.J.S.A. 34:1-69.6. A person with a hearing loss in excess of 25 db ISO in the 500-2,000 frequency Hz range unaided in the better ear is considered deaf. *Id.*

158. A "service dog" is a dog individually trained to meet a handicapped person's requirements, such as minimal protection work, rescue work, pulling a wheelchair, or retrieving dropped items. N.J.S.A. 10:5-5(dd).

A "guide dog" is a dog that (1) either is used to assist deaf persons or is fitted with a special harness so as to be suitable as an aid to the mobility of blind persons and used by blind persons who have satisfactorily completed a specific course of training in the use of such a dog, and (2) has been trained by an organization generally recognized by agencies involved in the rehabilitation of the blind or deaf as reputable and competent to provide dogs with training of this type. N.J.S.A. 10:5-5(s).

159. N.J.S.A. 10:5-5(q). *See, e.g., Scaravelloni v. Butterfield Enterprises, Inc.*, 8 N.J.A.R. 89 (DCR 1984) (person required to use crutches to walk after hip surgery is handicapped).

The term "handicapped" is broadly construed and is not limited to "severe" or "immutable" disabilities.[161] The protections of the LAD are not restricted to "the halt, the maimed or the blind."[162] However, a condition labelled as a disability, handicap, or disease for purposes of clinical research or medical treatment is not necessarily a "handicap" for purposes of the LAD.[163]

Acquired Immunodeficiency Syndrome (AIDS) and the human immunodeficiency virus (HIV) are handicaps under the LAD.[164] Alcoholism is also a handicap under the LAD.[165]

In re Cahill held that addiction to morphine is a handicap, stating: "Addiction, habituation or dependency which results from use of one drug or another, or as in this case, a combination of drugs, renders a person handicapped."[166] The court did not state whether the employee's use of morphine was legal or illegal, although language in the opinion suggests that the usage was illegal. This is significant because *Cahill* made no reference to *Attorney General Formal Opinion No. 1-1989*, which held that the protections of the LAD do not apply to current or former drug addicts whose addiction presently involves or involved the illegal use of controlled dangerous substances (such as morphine).[167]

---

160. N.J.S.A. 10:5-5(q). In *A.B.C. v. XYZ Corp.*, 282 N.J. Super. 494 (App. Div. 1995), the plaintiff was dismissed after he was arrested for exposing himself while on a business trip. In upholding the trial court's dismissal of the complaint because of the plaintiff's failure to provide his name and address, the Appellate Division questioned, but did not rule on, the trial court's observation that a psychosexual disorder of that sort could be considered a handicap under the LAD. *See Olson v. General Electric Astrospace*, 966 F. Supp. 312, 315-16 (D.N.J. 1997) (depression and mental illness may constitute handicaps).

161. *Clowes v. Terminix Int'l, Inc.*, 109 N.J. 575, 590, 593 (1988); *Andersen v. Exxon Co.*, 89 N.J. 483, 494-96 (1982); *Gimello v. Agency Rent-A-Car Systems, Inc.*, 250 N.J.Super. 338, 359, 361 (App. Div. 1991). Unlike the ADA, the NJLAD does not require that handicaps limit a major life activity to be protected. *Failla v. City of Passaic*, 146 F.3d 149 (3d Cir. 1998) (jury verdict finding plaintiff handicapped under LAD but not disabled under ADA not inconsistent because of differences in definitions and broader scope of the state law). *Olson v. General Electric Astrospace*, 966 F.Supp. 312, 314-15 (D.N.J. 1997).

162. *Andersen v. Exxon Co.*, 89 N.J. at 495.

163. *N.J. Attorney General Formal Opinion No. 1-1989*, pp. 2-3 (Oct. 6, 1989), 125 N.J.L.J. 100 (Jan. 11, 1990).

164. N.J.S.A. 10:5-5(q), L.1991, c.493. *See Behringer v. Medical Center at Princeton*, 249 N.J.Super. 597 (Law Div. 1991); *Poff v. Caro*, 228 N.J.Super. 370, 376-77 (Law Div. 1987). *See Plainfield Bd. of Educ. v. Cooperman*, 105 N.J. 587 (1987) (upholding state regulations establishing procedures for the admission to schools of children afflicted with AIDS or ARC). AIDS was not discussed in the 1984 edition of the DCR's *A Guide for Employers to the LAD.*

165. *Clowes v. Terminix Int'l, Inc.*, 109 N.J. at 590-95; *In re Cahill*, 245 N.J.Super. 397, 400 (App. Div. 1991); *Varga v. Union County Dept. of Public Works*, 11 N.J.A.R. 546, 554-55 (Merit Sys. Bd. 1989); *Moore v. Monmouth Beach*, No. 85-5302(AET), pp. 4-5 (D.N.J. Oct. 9, 1986) (Lexis). In *Matter of Collester*, 126 N.J. 468 (1992), a judicial discipline case, the majority referred to alcoholism as "a dreadful and ruinous disease" and stated that "[w]e in no way consider this disability and its treatment as a 'vice.'" *Id.* at 475. In a separate opinion concurring in part and dissenting in part, Justice Pollock reviewed the various state and federal statutes responding "to the medical and social characterization of alcoholism as a disease and not a vice." *Id.* at 479-80.

Obesity,[168] diabetes,[169] myocardial infarction resulting from a heart attack,[170] spinal surgery (removal of a lumbar disc and fusion) that limits physical abilities,[171] and multiple sclerosis[172] have all been found to be handicaps. In contrast, a prominent hilar shadow produced by a calcification process within the lung has been held not to constitute a handicap.[173]

Where the existence of a handicap is not readily apparent, expert medical evidence is required.[174] For example, the claim of an employee who drinks too much that he is an alcoholic does not establish that he is handicapped.[175] Be-

---

166. *In re Cahill*, 245 N.J.Super. 397, 400 (App. Div. 1991) (also noting that the Supreme Court in *Clowes* declared alcohol to be a drug). *Cf. Matter of Jackson*, 294 N.J. Super. 233, 236 n.1 (App. Div. 1996), *certif. denied*, 149 N.J. 141 (1997) (in a case involving "reasonable accommodation" of a drug-addicted employee, the court specifically notes that the underlying question whether drug addiction is protected is not before it:

> Our affirmance does not, therefore, signal agreement with the *dicta* in *Cahill*, which, in reliance upon an alcoholism case, *Clowes v. Terminix Int'l*, 109 N.J. 575, 590-95, 538 A.2d 794 (1988), stated that addiction, habituation or dependency resulting from use of any drug renders a person handicapped under the LAD. *Cahill, supra*, 245 N.J. Super. at 400, 500 A.2d 977. We note particularly the concurring opinion in *A.B.C. v. XYZ Corp.*, 282 N.J. Super. 494, 508, 660 A.2d 1199 (App. Div. 1995) (Petrella, P.J.A.D., concurring) in which it was questioned whether the statutory definition of "handicap" should be interpreted to "[afford] a remedy under the LAD where the discrimination claim is based upon conduct by an individual claimant which would otherwise constitute a crime, whether or not there is a prosecution and conviction." See N.J.S.A. 2C:35-10.

167. *N.J. Attorney General Formal Opinion No. 1-1989* (Oct. 6, 1989), 125 N.J.L.J. 100 (Jan. 11, 1990). *See A.B.C. v. XYZ Corp.*, 282 N.J.Super. 494, 508 (App. Div. 1995) (Petrella, P.J.A.D., concurring) (questioning whether LAD should apply where underlying conduct is a crime); *In the matter of Jackson*, 294 N.J. Super. 233, 236 n.1 (App. Div. 1996) (same). *Baldino v. Baldino*, 241 N.J.Super. 414 (Ch.Div. 1990) (a child will not be deemed unemancipated for purposes of a parent's child support obligations where the child voluntarily became addicted to illegal drugs because such addiction does not constitute a legally-cognizable handicap; adopting reasoning of *Formal Opinion No. 1-1989*); *Hennessey v. Coastal Eagle Point Oil*, 129 N.J. 81 (1992) (upholding random urine testing by private-sector employer to detect illicit use of drugs); *In re Carberry*, 114 N.J. 574, 578 (1989) (non-LAD case; illegal use of drugs by state troopers is "incompatible with the integrity of the State Police and with the ability ... to perform their duties."); *In re Terner*, 120 N.J. 706, 718 (1990) (drug addiction is neither a defense to nor a mitigating factor in attorney discipline cases; expressly observing: "Nor can we ignore the different legal consequences attendant on the abuse of cocaine as distinguished from alcohol. Attorneys who use cocaine or other controlled dangerous substances necessarily violate the law. We would be remiss in condoning such activity"); *Jevic v. Coca-Cola Bottling Co. of N.Y.*, 5 IER 765, 771 (D.N.J. 1990) (private employer's pre-employment drug testing policy does not violate civil or constitutional law: "We should not seek to shield [illegal drug] use by creating amorphous legal rights but should rather sanction [reasonable] policies" that "rid all work places of [the] influence [of drugs]."); *Int'l Federation of Professional & Technical Engineers v. Burlington County Bridge Comm'n.*, 240 N.J.Super. 9, 12, 26 (App. Div.), *certif. denied*, 122 N.J. 183 (1990) (upholding constitutionality of non-random drug testing of public employees; declining to rule upon claim that such testing violated N.J.S.A. 10:5-4.1).

168. *Gimello v. Agency Rent-A-Car Systems, Inc.*, 250 N.J.Super. 338, 354-65 (App. Div. 1991). *But see* Mariani, "Appellate Division Weighs In With Faulty Finding of Handicap," 15 *N.J. Labor & Employment Law Quarterly*, p. 9 (Winter 1991-92).

169. *N.J. Attorney General Formal Opinion No. 14-1974* (Oct. 7, 1974).

170. *Panettieri v. C.V. Hill Refrigeration*, 159 N.J.Super. 472, 481, 489 (App. Div. 1978).

171. *Andersen v. Exxon Co.*, 89 N.J. 483, 489-90, 494 (1982) (plaintiff could not lift objects in excess of 100 pounds and was required not to excessively twist his trunk).

172. *Levinson v. Prentice-Hall, Inc.*, 868 F.2d 558 (3d Cir. 1989).

cause many symptoms of alcoholism, standing alone, may be attributable to some other illness or condition, and given the complexity of the procedures required to make a diagnosis of alcoholism, expert medical testimony is needed.[176]

4-14:2 Reasonable Accommodation Requirement

DCR regulations require employers to provide reasonable accommodations for the handicapped.[177] DCR states that this requirement is implicit in the LAD provision that an individual may not be denied employment opportunities because of a handicap unless the nature and extent of the handicap *reasonably* precludes job performance, and that it is consistent with the principle that, absent a business necessity, job requirements that have a disparate impact on a protected class of individuals are prohibited.[178] In evaluating the reasonable accommodation requirement, due regard must be given to the interests of both the employee and employer.[179]

In particular, an employer must make a reasonable accommodation to the limitations of a handicapped applicant or employee unless the employer can demonstrate that the accommodation would impose an undue hardship on the operation of the business.[180] An employer is required to consider the possibility of reasonable accommodation prior to making an adverse employment decision based on

---

173. *Rogers v. Campbell Foundry Co.*, 185 N.J.Super. 109, 111 (App. Div. 1982), *aff'g*, 8 N.J.A.R. 75 (DCR 1980), *certif. denied*, 91 N.J. 529 (1982).

174. *Clowes v. Terminix Int'l, Inc.*, 109 N.J. 575, 597-98 (1988); *Rogers v. Campbell Foundry Co.*, 185 N.J.Super. at 111; *Gimello v. Agency Rent-A-Car Systems, Inc.*, 250 N.J.Super. at 353-55, 356-57, 361, 365. A plaintiff's treating physician may testify as to the existence of a disability; formal expert testimony is not required. *See Gaul v. AT&T, Inc.*, 955 F. Supp. 346, 349 (D.N.J. 1997), *aff'd* 134 F.3d 576 (3d Cir. 1998).

175. *Clowes v. Terminix Int'l, Inc.*, 109 N.J. at 598; *but see Gimello v. Agency Rent-A-Car Systems, Inc.*, 250 N.J.Super. at 346, 353-55, 356-57, 361, 365 (employee's obesity constituted a handicap even though his medical expert was unable to opine whether the obesity was the result of heredity, metabolism, or mere overeating).

176. *Clowes v. Terminix Int'l, Inc.*, 109 N.J. at 593, 597-99.

177. N.J.A.C. 13:13-2.5; *N.J. Attorney General Formal Opinion No. 1-1989*, pp.8-9 (Oct. 6, 1989), 125 N.J.L.J. 100, 102 (Jan. 11, 1990). *See, e.g., In re Cahill*, 245 N.J.Super. 397, 401 (App. Div. 1991); *cf. Maher v. New Jersey Transit Rail Operations, Inc.*, 239 N.J.Super. 213, 218-19, 226-27 (App. Div. 1990), *aff'd in part, rev'd in part on other grounds*, 125 N.J. 455 (1991) (illustration of attempt to reasonably accommodate an employee's handicap in the context of a collective bargaining agreement). Because the DCR's regulations were "patterned after" those promulgated under the federal Rehabilitation Act of 1973, it is appropriate to look to cases interpreting federal law for guidance. *Ensslin v. Township of N. Bergen*, 275 N.J. Super. 352, 364 (App. Div. 1994), *certif. denied*, 142 N.J. 446 (1995).

178. DCR Response to Public Comments on N.J.A.C. 13:13-1.1 *et seq.*, 17 N.J.R. 1574(a), at p.1575 (June 17, 1985); N.J.S.A. 10:5-4.1; N.J.A.C. 13:13-2.5(b)(3)(iv).

179. *Formal Opinion No. 1-1989*, p.9, 125 N.J.L.J. at 102; N.J.S.A. 10:5-27.

180. N.J.A.C. 13:13-2.5(b); *Formal Opinion No. 1-1989*, p.8, 125 N.J.L.J. at 102; DCR, *Employment Guide to the LAD*, p.9 (1989).

a finding that an individual's handicap precludes job performance.[181] Depending upon the circumstances, reasonable accommodation may include (1) making facilities readily accessible and usable to handicapped individuals; (2) job restructuring, including part-time or modified work schedules; (3) acquisition or modification of equipment or devices; and (4) job reassignments.[182] Whether an employer has made a reasonable accommodation is determined on a case-by-case basis.[183]

The following factors, among others, will be considered in determining whether an otherwise reasonable accommodation need not be made because of the undue hardship it would impose on the operation of the employer's business:

1. The overall size of the business in terms of employees, number and type of facilities, and budget.[184]
2. The nature of the operations, including the composition and structure of the workforce.[185]
3. The nature and cost of the accommodation needed.[186]
4. The extent to which accommodation would require waiver of an essential requirement of the job as opposed to a tangential or non-business necessity requirement.[187]

By necessity, the determination of undue hardship must be made on a case-by-case basis.[188]

The Appellate Division has held that where feasible, an employer should accommodate a chemically-dependent employee by affording an opportunity for

---

181. N.J.A.C. 13:13-2.5(b)(2).

182. N.J.A.C. 13:13-2.5(b)(1). *Accord* N.J.A.C. 19:53-1.8(a) (Casino Control Commission regulation). *See, e.g., Jansen v. Food Circus Supermarkets, Inc.*, 214 N.J.Super. 51, 55, 62 (App. Div. 1986), *rev'd on other grounds*, 110 N.J. 363 (1988) (reasonable accommodation of handicapped epileptic achieved by offering him employment other than as a meat cutter); *Panettieri v. C.V. Hill Refrigeration*, 159 N.J.Super. 472, 480 (App. Div. 1978) (alleged limitation on heart attack victim's ability to move heavy objects could be alleviated by use of motorized hoists and other mechanical aids or with the assistance of a co-worker); DCR, *Employment Guide to the LAD*, p.5 (1989) (failure to provide a hearing-impaired office worker with a telephone amplifying device might violate LAD).

183. N.J.A.C. 13:13-2.5(b). Ensuring that an employee be guarded against stress and criticism is not a reasonable accommodation. *Gaul v. AT&T, Inc.*, 955 F. Supp. 346, 353 (D.N.J. 1997), *aff'd* 134 F.3d 576 (3d Cir. 1998). Permitting a municipal court clerk to work at home was not a reasonable accommodation. *Melick v. Township of Oxford*, 294 N.J. Super. 386, 396-97 (App. Div. 1996).

184. N.J.A.C. 13:13-2.5(b)(3)(i); DCR, *Employment Guide to the LAD*, p.5 (1989). *Accord* N.J.A.C. 19:53-1.8(b)(1) (Casino Control Commission regulation).

185. N.J.A.C. 13:13-2.5(b)(3)(ii). *Accord* N.J.A.C. 19:53-1.8(b)(2) (Casino Control Commission regulation).

186. N.J.A.C. 13:13-2.5(b)(3)(iii); DCR, *Employment Guide to the LAD*, p. 5 (1989). *Accord* N.J.A.C. 19:53-1.8(b)(3) (Casino Control Commission regulation).

187. N.J.A.C. 13:13-2.5(b)(3)(iv).

188. *See* N.J.A.C. 13:13-2.5(b)(3)(iii)-(iv), -2.5(b).

rehabilitation; however, multiple chances to rehabilitate apparently are not required.[189] An employer who reinstated a drug abuser after he completed an inpatient drug rehabilitation program, but then fired him after he failed his first routine random drug test was found to have reasonably accommodated the employee's handicap and not to have violated the LAD.[190] A police department did not violate the LAD in terminating an officer who was rendered paraplegic in a ski accident. An essential job duty for all officers, including those assigned to desk duty, was the ability to respond to emergencies such as the control of prisoners. It would not be reasonable to require the department to restructure the job to accommodate the plaintiff.[191]

4-14:3 Performance of Handicapped Individuals

The LAD does not prohibit handicap discrimination when the handicap reasonably precludes or impedes job performance.[192] Employers are not required to tolerate criminal or egregious conduct of employees, even if the conduct in question was caused by a disability.[193] The LAD is not violated where it can reasonably be determined that an applicant or employee, because of the nature and extent of a handicap and in spite of reasonable accommodation, is unable to adequately perform the essential functions of the job.[194] That determination must

---

189. *In re Cahill*, 245 N.J.Super. 397, 401 (App. Div. 1991) (public employee addicted to morphine and alcohol). *But see N.J. Attorney General Formal Opinion No. 1-1989*, p. 9 (Oct. 6, 1989), 125 N.J.L.J. 100, 102 (Jan. 11, 1990) (reasonable accommodation duty does *not* extend to illegal drug users).

190. *In re Cahill*, 245 N.J.Super. at 401, *See In the Matter of Jackson*, 294 N.J.Super. 233 (App. Div. 1996) (same). *Accord Varga v. Union County Dept. of Public Works*, 11 N.J.A.R. 546, 551, 557 (Merit Sys. Bd. 1989) (upholding termination of drawbridge operator who was intoxicated while on duty and who had previously utilized an employee-assistance program for his drinking problem, including a detoxification program and a rehabilitation program).

191. *Ensslin v. Township of N. Bergen*, 275 N.J. Super. 352 (App. Div. 1994), *certif. denied*, 142 N.J. 446 (1995).

192. N.J.S.A. 10:5-4.1; *Jansen v. Food Circus Supermarkets, Inc.*, 110 N.J. 363, 373-83 (1988); *Clowes v. Terminix Int'l, Inc.*, 109 N.J. 575, 594 (1988); *Andersen v. Exxon Co.*, 89 N.J. 483, 497 (1988); *Maher v. New Jersey Transit Rail Operations, Inc.*, 125 N.J. 455, 481, 482 (1991) (also noting that the Legislature, in N.J.S.A. 10:5-4.1, "recognized a job-performance-related difference between" handicap discrimination and discrimination based on other characteristics such as race). *See* N.J.S.A. 10:5-2.1. The protection afforded an employer by N.J.S.A. 10:5-4.1 (the subject of this section) is "no greater" than that afforded by N.J.S.A. 10:5-2.1. *Andersen*, 89 N.J. at 497. An employee who cannot perform the essential job functions even with a reasonable accommodation is not "an otherwise qualified handicapped" person and therefore is not entitled to protection under the LAD. *Ensslin v. Township of N. Bergen*, 275 N.J. Super. 352, 369 (App. Div. 1994).

193. *Barbera v. DiMartino*, 305 N.J.Super. 617, 640 (App. Div. 1997) (plaintiff's assault of a supervisor, caused by a psychotic episode, was nonetheless a legitimate nondiscriminatory reason for terminating and not rehiring him. "We are in line with the federal authority that laws protecting the handicapped from employment discrimination are not intended to protect against crime or egregious conduct which, if committed by any other employee, would have warranted the adverse employment decision.")

194. *Jansen v. Food Circus Supermarkets, Inc.*, 110 N.J. at 375, expressly approving N.J.A.C. 13:13-2.8(a), -2.4(e)(2); *Andersen v. Exxon Co.*, 89 N.J. at 496-97; N.J.S.A. 10:5-4.1; N.J.S.A. 10:5-2.1.

be based upon an objective standard supported by individualized factual evidence, rather than general assumptions that a particular handicap would interfere with the individual's ability to perform the duties of the particular job.[195]

Adequate performance must be viewed in terms of whether the handicapped individual, with reasonable accommodation, is performing at the level considered acceptable when evaluating other employees.[196] Each employee or applicant should be assessed to determine whether he has the physical and non-physical abilities to adequately perform the job.[197] Then the employer, based upon the medical report(s) and relevant records (such as an employee's work and medical histories), must make an independent, objectively-reasonable determination of the individual's qualification for the position.[198]

But "because of the limits imposed by a handicap, the [LAD] must be applied sensibly with due consideration to the interests of the employer, employee, and the public,"[199] and "there should be no second-guessing the employer."[200] If an employer reasonably arrives at the conclusion that a handicap would preclude or impede performance, it will not be liable for handicap discrimination even if the trier of facts disagrees with the conclusion.[201]

4-14:4 Safety Hazards Created by Handicapped Employees

The LAD does not prohibit discrimination against handicapped employees where the employer can demonstrate that even with reasonable accommodation, the handicap would make employment in a particular job hazardous to the safety or health of the handicapped employee or others.[202] An employer's determination to that effect must be based upon an objective standard supported by indi-

---

195. N.J.A.C. 13:13-2.8(a)(1); *see Clowes v. Terminix Int'l, Inc.*, 109 N.J. at 592-93 (degree of impairment varies among persons with the same handicap); *Andersen v. Exxon Co.*, 89 N.J. at 497-98, 500.

196. DCR Response to Public Comments on N.J.A.C. 13:13-1.1 *et seq.*, 17 N.J.R. 1574(a), at p.1575 (June 17, 1985); N.J.S.A. 10:5-2.1.

197. *Andersen v. Exxon Co.*, 89 N.J. at 497-98, 500, 502; *Panettieri v. C.V. Hill Refrigeration*, 159 N.J.Super. 472, 478-81, 486-89 (App. Div. 1978).

198. *Andersen v. Exxon Co.*, 89 N.J. at 497-98, 500, 502; *Jansen v. Food Circus Supermarkets, Inc.*, 110 N.J. at 379-80; *Panettieri v. C.V. Hill Refrigeration*, 159 N.J.Super. at 487-90.

199. *Jansen v. Food Circus Supermarkets, Inc.*, 110 N.J. at 374; *Andersen v. Exxon Co.*, 89 N.J. at 496, 500; *Panettieri v. C.V. Hill Refrigeration*, 159 N.J.Super. at 492; *Behringer v. Medical Center at Princeton*, 249 N.J.Super. at 645-47, 649, 657-58 (Law Div. 1991); N.J.S.A. 10:5-27.

200. *Clowes v. Terminix Int'l, Inc.*, 109 N.J. at 595, *quoting Andersen v. Exxon Co.*, 89 N.J. at 496; *Panettieri v. C.V. Hill Refrigeration*, 159 N.J.Super. at 487; *Pilot v. New Jersey Dept. of Health*, No. A-5853-81, slip op. at p. 6 (App. Div. Sept. 28, 1983), *aff'g*, 7 N.J.A.R. 150 (DCR 1982); *In re Cahill*, 245 N.J.Super. 397, 399, 401 (App. Div. 1991) (ALJ's decision to give drug abuser one more chance reversed by Merit System Board, which was affirmed by Appellate Division).

201. *Panettieri v. C.V. Hill Refrigeration*, 159 N.J.Super. at 487; *Andersen v. Exxon Co.*, 89 N.J. at 496-97.

vidualized factual or scientifically-validated evidence, and not general assumptions.[203] Thus, an expert medical evaluation is normally required, followed by the employer's independent, objectively-reasonable determination that it is probable that the individual poses a hazard to himself or others in the workplace.[204]

A hazard exists when the risk of serious harm or death is materially enhanced.[205] Factors to be weighed in making that determination include:

1. The likelihood of the risk actualizing (the "probability").

---

202. *Jansen v. Food Circus Supermarkets, Inc.*, 110 N.J. at 375, expressly approving N.J.A.C. 13:13-2.8(a)(2), -2.4(e)(2); N.J.S.A. 10:5-4.1; N.J.S.A. 10:5-2.1; *Maher v. New Jersey Transit Rail Operations, Inc.*, 125 N.J. 455, 481 (1991); *In re Cahill*, 245 N.J.Super. 397, 400-01 (App. Div. 1991); *Panettieri v. C.V. Hill Refrigeration*, 159 N.J.Super. at 491-93 (Legislature did not intend to require employers to let handicapped employees further injure themselves or aggravate their handicaps and then obligate the employers to pay workers' compensation); *Rogers v. Campbell Foundry Co.*, 185 N.J.Super. 109, 111 (App. Div. 1982), *aff'g*, 8 N.J.A.R. 75, 85-86 (DCR 1980), *certif. denied*, 91 N.J. 529 (1982) (employer failed to establish that complainant's lung condition would predispose him to contracting silicosis or pneumoconiosis); *Behringer v. Medical Center at Princeton*, 249 N.J.Super. 597, 646-47 (Law Div. 1991). *See Greenwood v. State Police Training Ctr.*, 127 N.J. 500, 511-12 (1992) (dicta).

203. *Jansen v. Food Circus Supermarkets, Inc.*, 110 N.J. at 368, 374, 375, 377-79, (the mere fact that an epileptic may suffer a seizure on the job is not by itself sufficient basis for an adverse action). *Accord Behringer v. Medical Center at Princeton*, 249 N.J.Super. at 613, 646-47; *Panettieri v. C.V. Hill Refrigeration*, 159 N.J.Super. at 492-93 (even if it were true that all heart attack victims are at greater risk of repeat attacks, "each heart attack victim must be individually evaluated to determine whether he has the stamina, the dexterity, and the strength to do the job without a material risk of recurrence"); *Rogers v. Campbell Foundry Co.*, 8 N.J.A.R. 75, 82-84 (DCR 1980), *aff'd*, 185 N.J.Super. 109, 111 (App. Div.), *certif. denied*, 91 N.J. 529 (1982). *But see In re Cahill*, 245 N.J.Super. at 400 (stating it was "obvious" that a chemically-dependent firefighter is unable to safely perform his job).

In appropriate circumstances, an employer may take immediate action to isolate an employee until it ascertains the nature and extent of risk presented by the employee's presence in the workplace. The employer's investigation should be completed as promptly as practicable under the circumstances and limitations on the employee should be the least restrictive necessary. *See, e.g.*, *Behringer v. Medical Center at Princeton*, 249 N.J.Super. at 606, 610-15, 645, 658; *Jansen v. Food Circus Supermarkets, Inc.*, 110 N.J. at 369-70.

204. *Jansen v. Food Circus Supermarkets, Inc.*, 110 N.J. at 376-79; *Barbera v. Di Martino*, 305 N.J.Super. 617, 632 n.5 (App. Div. 1997); *Rogers v. Campbell Foundry Co.*, 185 N.J.Super. at 111; *Behringer v. Medical Center at Princeton*, 249 N.J.Super. at 610-15, 646-47, 658. *But see In re Cahill*, 245 N.J.Super. at 400-01 (no medical reports needed where it is "obvious" that the handicap precludes safe performance; chemically-dependent firefighter); *Varga v. Union County Dept. of Public Works*, 11 N.J.A.R. at 555-56 (despite the absence of medical evidence or direct proof that the employee, while intoxicated, failed to perform any of the specific functions of a drawbridge operator, it was evident that such employee presented a materially-enhanced risk of serious injury). An inadequate medical report will not justify an adverse employment action. *Jansen v. Food Circus Supermarkets, Inc.*, 110 N.J. at 379-80, 383 ("reasonable degree of certainty" required). *See Greenwood v. State Police Training Ctr.*, 127 N.J. 500, 511 (1992) (dicta; "[a]n employer may not base a decision to discharge an employee for safety reasons on subjective evaluations or conclusory medical reports. Rather, the employer must produce factual or scientifically-validated evidence indicating that employment of the disabled employee will probably cause substantial injury to that employee or others") (citations omitted).

205. *Jansen v. Food Circus Supermarkets, Inc.*, 110 N.J. at 375; *Barbera v. Di Martino*, 305 N.J.Super. 617, 632 n.5 (App. Div. 1997); *Panettieri v. C.V. Hill Refrigeration*, 159 N.J.Super. at 492-93. The *Jansen* Court variously referred to a "materially enhanced risk of serious harm" as a "serious threat of injury," a "reasonable degree of certainty" that injury will "probably" result, and a "reasonable probability of substantial harm." 110 N.J. at 374-75, 383. *Accord Behringer v. Medical Center at Princeton*, 249 N.J.Super. 597, 606, 646-47, 651-58 (Law Div. 1991).

2. The extent of the harm if the risk is actualized (the "gravity").
3. The number of persons who would be affected if the risk takes effect in harm (the "scope").
4. The ease or difficulty of minimizing the risk (the "burden").[206]

Applying these rules to employees with AIDS, it is the position of the DCR that an employer may take adverse action only if it is demonstrated that exposure to a person with AIDS would jeopardize the health and safety of co-employees or others.[207] Thus, it has been found permissible for a hospital to bar a physician with HIV seropositivity or AIDS from performing medical procedures that pose any risk of HIV/AIDS transmission to patients and to require that patients be advised of a physician's HIV/AIDS status before any surgery is performed.[208] In contrast, restrictions on an epileptic lab technician, such as prohibiting her from working where infectious disease assays were handled, was found unreasonable in the absence of objective medical evidence of a safety risk or an adequate trial period, with safeguards, to ascertain whether she could function safely.[209]

Differential treatment of a handicapped individual may not be based upon (1) the preferences or unreasonable fears of co-employees, clients, customers, or the employer;[210] (2) an anticipated or actual increase in the cost of insurance under a group or employee insurance plan;[211] or (3) an unsubstantiated assumption that

---

206. *Behringer v. Medical Center at Princeton*, 249 N.J.Super. at 651-58. *See generally United States v. Carroll Towing Co.*, 159 F.2d 169, 173 (2d Cir. 1947); Restatement, (Second) of Torts §293 (1965).

207. DCR, *Employment Guide to the LAD*, p. 10 (1989).

208. *Behringer v. Medical Center at Princeton*, 249 N.J.Super. at 606, 615, 657-58. Although the probability of a surgeon transmitting the AIDS virus is extremely low (.0025 percent), the gravity of the harm to patients is immense, ranging from HIV-testing for a year or more, changes in sexual practices and child-bearing, anxiety as to whether the virus in fact was transmitted, and, if transmitted, death. *Id.* at 606, 625, 627-28 & n.8, 631, 651-53, 657-58.

209. *Pilot v. New Jersey Dept. of Health*, 7 N.J.A.R. 150, 171, 173-74 (DCR 1982), *aff'd*, No. A-5853-81, slip op. at p. 8 (App. Div. Sept. 28, 1983).

210. *Jansen v. Food Circus Supermarkets, Inc.*, 110 N.J. at 370, 373, 374. For example, it is impermissible for an employer to refuse to hire a qualified epileptic because of a fear that other employees will be frightened by a seizure and quit. *Id.* at 370, 373-74. *Cf. Behringer v. Medical Center at Princeton*, 249 N.J.Super. at 612-13, 623, 634-35, 639-40 n.13, 653-54 (patients' right to informed consent, and thus knowledge of physician's affliction with AIDS, may result in *de facto* termination of his physician's surgical privileges if patients, because of their fears, refuse to be treated by him).

211. N.J.A.C. 13:13-2.8(a)(3)(ii); N.J.A.C. 13:13-2.6(c). *See Panettieri v. C.V. Hill Refrigeration*, 159 N.J.Super. at 492 ("fear that reemployment of any heart [attack] victim, whatever the disabling extent of his cardiac condition, will increase the risk of recurrence and hence a work-connected death or disability with a concomitant insurance premium increase, is not a legitimate basis for his rejection"); *Szabo v. New Jersey State Firemen's Ass'n*, 230 N.J.Super. 265, 283-84 & n.12 (Ch.Div. 1988) (denial of membership benefits because of greater actuarial risk and potential excessive claims of handicapped firefighter may violate anti-discrimination laws, including the LAD).

the individual will have a high rate of absenteeism in the future.[212] However, a handicapped individual may be discharged for unexplained absenteeism.[213]

4-14:5 Testing

Division on Civil Rights (DCR) regulations prohibit the use of employment tests or other selection criteria that in fact or effect screen out handicapped persons, unless (1) the test score or criterion is shown to be job related for the position and (2) alternative job-related tests or criteria that screen out fewer handicapped individuals are not available.[214] Employment tests must accurately reflect, with the benefit of reasonable accommodation, the handicapped individual's job skills, aptitude, or competency, and not the individual's impaired sensory, manual, or speaking skills, except where those skills are the factors the test is designed to measure and are necessary to perform the job.[215] The DCR states that an AIDS test is not a proper condition of employment, except where an infected person could not perform essential job functions without jeopardizing the health and safety of others.[216]

DCR regulations do permit an employer to condition an offer of employment on the results of a medical examination performed after the offer but before work begins as long as (1) all offerees are subject to the examination and (2) the exam results are used to disqualify offerees only when a discovered disability, even with reasonable accommodation, would preclude safe or adequate performance of the job.[217] To ensure that the examining physician considers abilities on an individual basis, the examination should evaluate the degree to which the

---

212. N.J.A.C. 13:13-2.8(a)(3)(iii). The DCR advises:

> A major element of successful job performance is the employee's actual availability to perform the job. If a handicapped employee is absent for whatever reasons in excess of the organization's *normally allowable absentee rate* and if such absences interfere with the employee's ability to do his job or interfere with the normal functions of the business, then the employer may take appropriate action against such individual [, including termination].

DCR, *A Guide for Employers to the LAD*, p. 15 (June 1986).

213. *Yekel v. General Biscuit Brands, Inc.*, 1991 WL 43024, p. *3 (D.N.J. 1991).

214. N.J.A.C. 13:13-2.3(a). Pre-employment testing is discussed generally in §4-23. The DCR's guidance documents pertaining to handicap testing do not reflect the more recent developments in disparate-impact analysis, which are discussed in §4-41.

215. N.J.A.C. 13:13-2.3(b).

216. DCR, *Employment Guide to the LAD*, p. 10 (1989).

217. N.J.A.C. 13:13-2.4(e)(1)-(2); DCR, *Employment Guide to the LAD*, p. 9 (1989). *See Andersen v. Exxon Co.*, 89 N.J. 483, 489 (1982) (applicant with orthopedic handicap required to undergo pre-employment medical evaluation); *Rogers v. Campbell Foundry Co.*, 185 N.J.Super. 109, 111 (App. Div. 1982), *aff'g*, 8 N.J.A.R. 75 (DCR 1980), *certif. denied*, 91 N.J. 529 (1982) (pre-employment medical exam revealed hilar shadow on lungs).

offeree has compensated for the handicap and the rehabilitation he has received or is receiving.[218]

Employers may make pre-offer demands for medical evidence of ability to perform the job where they have become aware through lawful means that an applicant has a handicap of a type that raises legitimate concerns regarding his ability to perform the job.[219] In deciding whether to require an applicant to submit medical evidence, and in evaluating the evidence submitted, the employer must act reasonably.[220]

To ensure that pre-employment medical examinations are fair and physicians' judgments are informed, the examining physician should be provided with an accurate, current job description.[221] The standard by which the DCR determines whether an employer has engaged in handicap discrimination "does not involve [the] correctness of a company doctor's decision, but rather the thoroughness of the procedures that led to the conclusion and the reasonableness of the conclusion itself."[222] An employer is not liable for every mistaken judgment of an examining physician if the doctor is carefully informed of the job requirements and the employer independently reviews and acts upon a reasonable medical report.[223] However, blind reliance on an uninformed or inadequate medical report is no defense.[224]

4-15 Marital Status Discrimination[225]

The LAD's prohibition of unlawful discrimination on the basis of marital status bars employment decisions based on the fact that a person is either married

---

218. N.J.A.C. 13:13-2.4(c); DCR Response to Public Comments on N.J.A.C. 13:13-1.1 *et seq.*, 17 N.J.R. 1574(a), at p. 1575 (June 17, 1985).

219. DCR Response to Public Comments on N.J.A.C. 13:13-1.1 *et seq.*, 17 N.J.R. 1574(a), at p. 1575 (June 17, 1985). *See, e.g.*, DCR, *A Guide for Employers to the LAD*, p.14 (June 1986) (an employer may require an epileptic who sometimes has seizures to submit a medical certification of job fitness).

220. DCR Response to Public Comments on N.J.A.C. 13:13-1.1 *et seq.*, 17 N.J.R. 1574(a), at p. 1575 (June 17, 1985).

221. *Andersen v. Exxon Co.*, 89 N.J. 483, 502, 498 (1982); *Panettieri v. C.V. Hill Refrigeration*, 159 N.J.Super. 472, 479, 488 (App. Div. 1978); DCR Response to Public Comments on N.J.A.C. 13:13-1.1 *et seq.*, 17 N.J.R. 1574(a), at p. 1575 (June 17, 1985); DCR, *Employment Guide to the LAD*, p. 14 (1989).

222. DCR, *Employment Guide to the LAD*, p. 9 (1989); DCR, *A Guide for Employers to the LAD*, p. 15 (June 1986).

223. *Andersen v. Exxon Co.*, 89 N.J. at 502; *Panettieri v. C.V. Hill Refrigeration*, 159 N.J.Super. at 487-89 (App. Div. 1978).

224. *Jansen v. Food Circus Supermarkets, Inc.*, 110 N.J. at 379.

225. The LAD's prohibition of marital status discrimination was added in 1970. L.1970, c.80.

or single.[226] It does not bar employers from maintaining and enforcing anti-nepotism rules.[227]

A rule that requires the discharge of married employees who engage in sexual activity out of wedlock (*i.e.*, adultery) but not unmarried employees engaged in sexual activity (*i.e.*, fornication) violates the LAD.[228] One court has suggested, without explanation, that discrimination against homosexuals because of a fear they may contract AIDS constitutes marital status discrimination.[229]

A provision of state law requiring a widow or widower to remain unmarried to retain eligibility for a pension does not violate the LAD, because the LAD expressly provides that it does not interfere with the operation of bona fide retirement, pension, employee benefit, or insurance plans.[230]

4-16 National Origin Discrimination

The LAD has prohibited unlawful national origin discrimination since its enactment in 1945.[231] In *New Jersey Dept. of Labor v. Cruz*, the Supreme Court held that the prohibition of ancestry and national origin discrimination was intended to bar discrimination between citizens and aliens.[232]

4-17 Nationality Discrimination

The prohibition against unlawful discrimination on the basis of nationality was added to the LAD in 1977.[233] The evident purpose of that legislation was to curb pressure placed on American businesses by the Arab boycott of Jewish business-

226. *Thomson v. Sanborn's Motor Express, Inc.*, 154 N.J.Super. 555, 560 (App. Div. 1977). *Cf. Kurman v. Fairmount Realty Corp.*, 8 N.J.A.R. 110 (DCR 1985) (landlord violated LAD by refusing to rent apartment to two persons of the opposite sex who were not married to each other); *N.J. Attorney General Formal Opinion No. 7-1983* (July 5, 1983) (lending institution may not inquire as to the marital status of a prospective borrower to ascertain creditworthiness, but may, at the appropriate stage of the application process, make such an inquiry when necessary to obtain an enforceable security lien).

227. *Thomson v. Sanborn's Motor Express, Inc.*, 154 N.J.Super. at 561-64; *Slohoda v. United Parcel Service, Inc.*, 193 N.J.Super. 586, 592-93 (App. Div. 1984).

228. *Slohoda v. United Parcel Service, Inc.*, 193 N.J.Super. at 589-92; *Slohoda v. United Parcel Service, Inc.*, 207 N.J.Super. 145, 148-56 (App. Div. 1986), *certif. denied*, 104 N.J. 400 (1986).

229. *Poff v. Caro*, 228 N.J.Super. 370, 378 (Law Div. 1987).

230. *Chausmer v. Commissioners of Employees' Retirement System of Newark*, 150 N.J.Super. 379, 382 (App. Div. 1977). Another statutory provision requires that every group health insurance policy offer coverage for maternity care without regard to the marital status of the participants. *See* Chapter 11, §11-11, *infra*.

231. L.1945, c.169.

232. *New Jersey Dept. of Labor v. Cruz*, 45 N.J. 372, 377-78 (1965).

233. L.1977, c.96. Nationality is mentioned in some provisions of the LAD, but not others. Compare N.J.S.A. 10:5-12(a)-(b) with N.J.S.A. 10:5-12(c).

es and individuals.[234] At the same time that nationality was added as a protected classification, the LAD was amended to provide that it does not prohibit legitimate distinctions between citizens and aliens that are required by federal law or are otherwise necessary to promote the national interest.[235] Thus, an employer may restrict employment to United States citizens in those circumstances.[236]

4-18 Race Discrimination

The LAD has prohibited unlawful race discrimination since its enactment in 1945.[237] One court has suggested that the protections of the LAD extend to persons who are discriminated against because they are believed to be members of a certain race when in fact they are not.[238]

In a case of race discrimination, plaintiff's color is not relevant. For example, in *Kearny Generating System v. Roper*, the employer did not hire complainant, a black man, but instead employed a Caucasian, a black, and two Hispanic persons.[239] In ruling in favor of complainant, the DCR deemed one of the Hispanic men to be a "white" person. On appeal, the court observed that the color of the Hispanic man had no bearing on the issues and was one of many reasons why the DCR's decision was manifestly wrong.[240]

---

234. Upon signing the legislation, Governor Byrne stated: "This bill establishes a principle. ... In the political climate of today, it's Israel. Next year it could be Ireland, Poland or Italy." Press Release to Assembly No. 2234 (May 19, 1977).

235. N.J.S.A. 10:5-3. The reference to "federal law" was explained by Governor Byrne in the press release that accompanied his signing the 1977 legislation:

> The Governor had hoped that federal legislation against discriminatory boycotts would have been passed by this time "and we recognized in this bill the appropriateness of having the federal government deal with this legislation," he said.

Gov. Byrne, *Press Release to Assembly No. 2334*, ¶5 (May 19, 1977).

Even before the 1977 amendment, the Supreme Court had held that alienage discrimination was barred by the 1945 adoption of the LAD, which prohibited discrimination on the basis of ancestry or national origin. *New Jersey Dept. of Labor v. Cruz*, 45 N.J. 372, 377-78 (1965).

236. N.J.S.A. 10:5-12(a).

237. L.1945, c.169.

238. *Poff v. Caro*, 228 N.J.Super. 370, 377 (Law Div. 1987). *See Clowes v. Terminix Int'l, Inc.*, 7 N.J.A.R. 206, 231 (DCR 1984), *rev'd on other grounds*, No. A-3886-84 (App. Div. May 8, 1986), *aff'd*, 109 N.J. 575 (1988) (quoting Congressional reports that state that Title VII prohibits perceived race discrimination); *Rogers v. Campbell Foundry Co.*, 8 N.J.A.R. 75, 85 (DCR 1980), *aff'd*, 185 N.J.Super. 109 (App. Div.), *certif. denied*, 91 N.J. 529 (1982) (same).

239. *Kearny Generating System v. Roper*, 184 N.J.Super. 253 (App. Div.), *certif. denied*, 91 N.J. 254 (1982).

240. *Kearny Generating System v. Roper*, 184 N.J.Super. at 260-63.

4-19 Sex Discrimination[241]

The LAD and New Jersey's Equal Pay Act (EPA) further "a distinctive public policy directed to improving the status of women in the work force, particularly with respect to their compensation."[242] "Traditional ideas" about what females should look like and "stereotyped conceptions" about their abilities are improper criteria for evaluating women in the workplace.[243]

An employer may violate the LAD by paying women lower wages than it pays to men performing similar work.[244] It is unlawful to assign a heavier work load or additional duties (*e.g.*, laundry, washing, serving, and assisting the cook) to female employees performing the same job functions as male employees.[245] Likewise, it is impermissible to limit promotional opportunities to men when both male and female employees are qualified therefor.[246]

4-19:1 Sex-Plus Discrimination

"Sex-plus" discrimination is discrimination based upon sex plus another characteristic;[247] for example, a refusal to hire women with small children, or the imposition of grooming requirements upon women but not upon men. Under "sex plus" analysis, discrimination will be found when an appearance/grooming requirement is based on sex, plus some other characteristic which: (1) is of an im-

---

241. The prohibition against unlawful sex discrimination was added to the LAD in 1970. L.1970, c.80. *See Sillery v. Fagan*, 120 N.J.Super. 416, 426-31 (Dist.Ct. 1972) (reviews the evolution of women's rights in New Jersey and takes judicial notice of the "Women's Liberation Movement"). One court, without explanation, suggested that discrimination against homosexuals because of a fear that they might acquire AIDS would constitute sex discrimination. *Poff v. Caro*, 228 N.J.Super. 370, 378 (Law Div. 1987).

242. *Grigoletti v. Ortho Pharmaceutical Corp.*, 118 N.J. 89, 108 (1990).

243. *Drinkwater v. Union Carbide Corp.*, 904 F.2d 853, 862-63 (3d Cir. 1990); *Nat'l Organization for Women v. Little League Baseball, Inc.*, 127 N.J.Super. 522, 533 (App. Div.), *summarily aff'd without op.*, 67 N.J. 320 (1974); *Gallagher v. Bayonne*, 102 N.J.Super. 77, 82 (Ch.Div. 1968), *aff'd on other grounds*, 106 N.J.Super. 401 (App. Div.), *aff'd on opinion below*, 55 N.J. 159 (1969); *Paterson Tavern & Grill Owners Ass'n v. Hawthorne*, 57 N.J. 180, 183-84, 186 (1970).

244. *Grigoletti v. Ortho Pharmaceutical Corp.*, 118 N.J. 89; *Decker v. Elizabeth Bd. of Ed.*, 153 N.J.Super. 470 (App. Div. 1977), *certif. denied*, 75 N.J. 612 (1978); *Terry v. Mercer County Freeholders Bd.*, 173 N.J.Super. 249 (App. Div. 1980), *aff'd on other grounds*, 86 N.J. 141 (1981). *Cf. Elmwood Park Educ. Ass'n v. Elmwood Park Bd. of Educ.*, 3 N.J.A.R. 249 (Comm'r Ed. 1980) (payment of lower wages to coaches performing comparable duties solely because of the sex of the student participants violates the Education Code).

245. *Countiss v. Trenton State College*, 77 N.J. 590, 592-95 (1978); *Terry v. Mercer County Freeholders Bd.*, 173 N.J.Super. at 252. *See Terry v. Mercer County Freeholders Bd.*, 86 N.J. 141, 144 (1981).

246. *Terry v. Mercer County Freeholders Bd.*, 173 N.J.Super. at 252. *Cf. Slohoda v. United Parcel Service, Inc.*, 193 N.J.Super. 586, 590 (App. Div. 1984) (LAD would be violated if females, but not males, were discharged because of an illicit sexual affair).

247. Schlei & Grossman, *Employment Discrimination Law*, ch.12, §VI (2d ed. 1983 & 1989).

mutable nature; or (2) involves a fundamental right of an employee; or (3) significantly affects the employment opportunities of one sex.[248]

In *Twomey v. Englewood Hospital Ass'n*, a female nurse was suspended for failing to wear her nurse's cap.[249] Male nurses were not required to wear them. The ALJ, applying the sex-plus test, held that the hospital did not violate the LAD because the cap requirement did not involve an immutable characteristic or fundamental right and did not significantly affect complainant's employment opportunities.[250] The ALJ found no evidence that the requirement was either designed to demean or stereotype female nurses or used as a pretext for imposing deliberate disparate treatment on females.[251]

The Director of the Division on Civil Rights reversed, finding that the sex-plus approach was plainly inconsistent with the language of the statute.[252] Instead, the Director adopted the following test, under which it found the cap requirement illegal:

> So long as [personal appearance standards] find some justification in commonly accepted social norms and are reasonably related to the employer's business needs, such regulations are not necessarily violations of [the LAD] even though the standards prescribed differ somewhat for men and women. However, the situation is different where ... two sets of employees performing the same function are subjected on the basis of sex to two entirely separate dress codes.[253]

The Appellate Division, in an unpublished, *per curiam* opinion, summarily reversed, simply stating that:

> Our examination and consideration of this matter convinces us that the findings of fact and conclusions of law ... rendered ... by

---

248. *See Twomey v. Englewood Hospital Ass'n*, 5 N.J.A.R. 188, 193, 195 (DCR 1981), *rev'd*, No. A-3523-80 (App. Div. June 14, 1982), *certif. denied*, 91 N.J. 568 (1982); *Rivera v. Trump Plaza Hotel & Casino*, 305 N.J.Super. 596, 602-604 (App. Div. 1997) (hair length policy did not violate LAD; male plaintiffs failed to establish defendant was the unusual employer that disciminates against the majority).

249. *Twomey v. Englewood Hospital Ass'n*, 5 N.J.A.R. 188 (DCR 1981), *rev'd*, No. A-3523-80 (App. Div. June 12, 1982), *certif. denied*, 91 N.J. 568 (1982).

250. *Id.* at 194.

251. *Id.* at 193. The hospital's stated reasons for the policy were tradition, personal pride, and ease of identification. *Id.*

252. N.J.S,A. 10:5-4. That section provides:

> *All persons* shall have the opportunity to obtain employment ... without discrimination because of ... sex, subject only to *conditions* and *limitations applicable alike* to *all persons*.

Twomey v. Englewood Hospital Ass'n, 5 N.J.A.R. at 195-96, *quoting* N.J.S.A. 10:5-4.

253. *Id.* at 196.

> [the ALJ] are persuasive, compelling and represent proper interpretation of [N.J.S.A. 10:5-4 and N.J.S.A. 10:5-12(a)].[254]

4-19:2 Pregnancy Discrimination

Discrimination against women because of pregnancy violates the LAD.[255] A woman:

> is entitled to work as long as she is able to perform her job. When she is no longer able to work, she should receive the same consideration given to those taking disability leave. When she returns from disability leave she is entitled to the same seniority, benefits, etc., as well as a comparable position if similarly disabled employees are entitled to such.[256]

Thus, the DCR has opined that it is permissible for an employer, pursuant to a general disability policy, to ask a pregnant employee to obtain a physician's certification as to the expected date of delivery and estimated period of confinement.[257] DCR states that it is *not* permissible for an employer to set a specific date for the commencement of pregnancy leave.[258] However, employers should limit the period of leave to that granted for other disabilities.[259] When the employee has recovered from her pregnancy, she must be permitted to return to work to the same extent as persons with other disabilities or illnesses are al-

---

254. *Twomey v. Englewood Hospital Ass'n*, No. A-3523-80, slip op. at p. 1 (App. Div. June 14, 1982) (Judges Michels, McElroy, & Coleman), *rev'g*, 5 N.J.A.R. 188 (DCR 1981), *certif. denied*, 91 N.J. 568 (1982). *See also Manco v. Irvington*, 126 N.J.Super. 148 (App. Div. 1973), *aff'd on opinion below*, 64 N.J. 142 (1974) (non-LAD case; sustaining fire department directive concerning style and length of hair); *Gimello v. Agency Rent-A-Car Systems, Inc.*, 250 N.J.Super. 338 (App. Div. 1991) (employee fired for being a "fat slob" victim of handicap discrimination under LAD).

255. *Castellano v. Linden Bd. of Educ.*, 79 N.J. 407 (1979); *Gilchrist v. Haddonfield Bd. of Educ.*, 155 N.J.Super. 358, 367-69 (App. Div. 1978); *Farley v. Ocean Tp. Bd. of Educ.*, 174 N.J.Super. 449, 451-52 (App. Div.), *certif. denied*, 85 N.J. 140 (1980); DCR, *Employment Guide to the LAD*, p. 10 (1989). The DCR does not consider pregnancy by itself to be a disability. DCR, *A Guide for Employers to the LAD*, p. 13 (June 1986); *cf. Castellano v. Linden Bd. of Educ.*, 158 N.J.Super. 350, 358-62 (App. Div. 1978), *rev'd in part on other grounds, aff'd in part*, 79 N.J. 407 (1979) (discussion of pregnancy as a disability or illness for purposes of various laws).

256. DCR, *Employment Guide to the LAD*, p. 10 (1989); DCR, *Your Employment Rights*, p. 9 (Nov. 1986); DCR, *A Guide for Employers to the LAD*, pp. 13-14 (June 1986).

257. DCR, *A Guide for Employers to the LAD*, p. 13 (June 1986).

258. DCR, *A Guide for Employers to the LAD*, p. 13 (June 1986). In *Castellano v. Linden Bd. of Educ.*, the Appellate Division stated that it was not deciding whether an employer can require a pregnant employee to commence maternity leave at a particular stage of the pregnancy. 158 N.J.Super. at 357 n.3. Nonetheless, the court quoted at length from an Iowa case that struck down a regulation requiring maternity leave to commence by the end of the fifth month. 158 N.J.Super. at 356-57.

259. DCR, *A Guide for Employers to the LAD*, p. 14 (June 1986).

lowed.[260] Conversely, men must be afforded the same disability benefits, such as leave, as are given to pregnant women.[261]

A provision of a collective bargaining agreement that requires a pregnant teacher to commence a mandatory leave of absence after the seventh month of pregnancy, and to remain on leave until the next school year following resolution of the pregnancy, and does not treat other disabilities similarly, violates the LAD.[262] Likewise, a policy that only pregnant teachers will not be rehired for the following academic year violates the LAD.[263] In contrast, a school board's policy not to rehire "any nontenured teacher, male or female, who gives the Board advance [notice] of an anticipated absence [for any reason] of substantial duration in the coming school year," does not violate the LAD.[264]

A sick-leave provision of a collective bargaining agreement that is interpreted to cover all disabilities or illnesses except pregnancies violates the LAD.[265] However, a provision of the Education Code that limits the award of long-term contracts to members of the professional staff at state colleges who have achieved five years of probationary employment within six consecutive years does not discriminate against women; in fact, it substantially benefits women for maternity-leave purposes.[266]

Note should be made of the federal Pregnancy Discrimination Act of 1978 (PDA), which added subsection (k) to §701 of the Civil Rights Act of 1964:

> The terms "because of sex" or "on the basis of sex" include, but are not limited to, because of or on the basis of pregnancy, childbirth, or related medical conditions; and women affected by pregnancy, childbirth, or related medical conditions shall be treated the same for all employment-related purposes, including receipt of benefits under fringe benefit programs, as other persons not so affected but similar in their ability or inability to

---

260. *Castellano v. Linden Bd. of Educ.*, 158 N.J.Super. at 357.

261. DCR, *A Guide for Employers to the LAD*, p. 14 (June 1986). *See* Assembly Labor Committee, *Statement to Senate No. 748*, reprinted following N.J.S.A. 34:2-21.15 (explaining why N.J.S.A. 43:21-29 was amended in 1980 to eliminate the presumption of disability given to pregnant women seeking temporary disability benefits for the four-weeks before and after birth).

262. *Castellano v. Linden Bd. of Educ.*, 158 N.J.Super. 350, 354-58 (App. Div. 1978), *rev'd in part on other grounds, aff'd in part*, 79 N.J. 407 (1979).

263. *Gilchrist v. Haddonfield Bd. of Educ.*, 155 N.J.Super. 358, 368 (App. Div. 1978).

264. *Gilchrist v. Haddonfield Bd. of Educ.*, 155 N.J.Super. at 368. *Gilchrist* was discussed favorably in *Castellano v. Linden Bd. of Educ.*, 79 N.J. 407, 412 (1979).

265. *Castellano v. Linden Bd. of Educ.*, 79 N.J. at 409, 412-13; *Farley v. Ocean Tp. Bd. of Educ.*, 174 N.J.Super. 449, 452-53 (App. Div.), *certif denied*, 85 N.J. 140 (1980).

266. *Jaeger v. State of New Jersey*, 176 N.J.Super. 222 (App. Div. 1980), *certif. denied*, 85 N.J. 504 (1981) (apparently decided under the New Jersey Constitution and the LAD); N.J.S.A. 18A:60-14.

> work ... This subsection shall not require an employer to pay for health insurance benefits for abortion, except where the life of the mother would be endangered if the fetus were carried to term, or except where medical complications have arisen from an abortion: *Provided*, That nothing herein shall preclude an employer from providing abortion benefits or otherwise affect bargaining agreements in regard to abortion.[267]

In *Formal Opinion No. 2-1979*, the State Attorney General held that this subsection of Title VII invalidated the provisions of New Jersey's temporary disability benefits law that allowed women to collect disability benefits for normal pregnancy under state and private plans for a maximum of only eight weeks, while all other disability claimants were eligible for up to 26 weeks.[268]

4-20 Sexual Orientation Discrimination

A 1992 amendment to the LAD prohibits discrimination on the basis of sexual or affectional orientation.[269] However, it specifically provides that:

> With respect only to affectional or sexual orientation, nothing contained herein shall be construed to require the imposition of affirmative action, plans or quotas as specific relief from an unlawful employment practice or unlawful discrimination.[270]

A 1990 state-court rule prohibits lawyers from engaging, in a professional capacity, in conduct involving discrimination based on sexual orientation.[271] A 1991 executive order provides that all Executive Branch departments and agencies must prohibit sexual orientation discrimination in any matter relating to state employment.[272] And, several provisions of the Criminal Code provide that criminal

267. 42 U.S.C.A. §2000e(k).

268. *N.J. Attorney General Formal Opinion No. 2-1979* (Feb. 9, 1979). *See* Chapter 10, §255.

269. N.J.S.A. 10:5-12, as amended by L.1991, c.519. "Affectional or sexual orientation," is defined as "male or female heterosexuality, homosexuality or bisexuality by inclination, practice, identity or expression, having a history thereof or being perceived, presumed or identified by others as having such orientation." N.J.S.A. 10:5-5(ff), as amended by L.1991, c.519, §3. *See Presbytery of N.J. of The Orthodox Presbyterian Church v. Florio*, 902 F. Supp. 492 (D.N.J. 1995) (rejecting challenge to aiding and abetting provisions of LAD as facially unconstitutional when applied to sexual orientation discrimination; abstaining under *Railroad Comm'n of Texas v. Pullman Co.*, 312 U.S. 496 (1941), from deciding whether those provisions are unconstitutional as applied to minister), *aff'd* 99 F.3d 101 (3d Cir. 1977).

270. N.J.S.A. 10:5-27, as amended by L.1991, c.519, §9.

271. N.J. Rule of Professional Conduct 8.4(g).

272. Executive Order No. 39, ¶1 (Aug. 16, 1991).

conduct purposely motivated on the basis of an individual's sexual orientation is subject to harsher penalties.[273]

One court strained to stretch the reach of the LAD to cover sexual orientation discrimination before it was so amended. In *Poff v. Caro*, a landlord refused to rent an apartment to three homosexual men because he feared that they might later acquire AIDS and expose his family to the disease.[274] After ruling that AIDS is a handicap covered by the LAD and that discrimination against persons perceived to be handicapped is barred by the LAD, the court held that discrimination against persons who are neither handicapped nor perceived to be presently handicapped is unlawful when based on a belief that they might subsequently become handicapped.[275] The court then suggested, without explanation, that discrimination against homosexuals because of a fear that they might acquire AIDS would constitute sex or marital status discrimination.[276] Finally, the court closed its opinion by stating:

> To refuse to extend [the] protection [of the LAD] to homosexuals because they may be more susceptible to a dread disease would mark a return to a past of judging individuals on the basis of ignorance and prejudice. A home is a basic human need. Homosexuals also need homes. They should not be denied that basic need by a democratic and caring society.[277]

4-21 Apprenticeship Programs

The LAD expressly prohibits discrimination by labor organizations in apprentice or training programs, because of age, ancestry, eligibility for service in the Armed Forces, color, creed, handicap, marital status, national origin, nationality, race, or sex.[278] Although there is no similar express prohibition of employer dis-

---

273. N.J.S.A. 2C:12-1(e); N.J.S.A. 2C:33-4(d); N.J.S.A. 2C:44-3.

274. *Poff v. Caro*, 228 N.J.Super. 370 (Law Div. 1987).

275. *Id.* at 376-78.

276. *Id.* at 378.

277. *Id.* at 381. *See also Behringer v. Medical Center at Princeton*, 249 N.J.Super. 597, 635 (Law Div. 1991) (" 'the majority of people infected with HIV in the United States are members of groups that are traditionally disfavored. Even before the AIDS epidemic, gays and intravenous ... drug users were subject to persistent prejudice and discrimination.' "); *One Eleven Wines & Liquors v. New Jersey Div. of Alcoholic Beverage Control*, 50 N.J. 329, 339 (1967) (ABC improperly disciplined licensees for permitting "apparent homosexuals" to congregate in bars; noting: "Though in our culture homosexuals are indeed unfortunates, their status does not make them criminals or outlaws. ...[S]o long as their public behavior conforms with currently acceptable standards of decency and morality, they may, at least in the present context, be viewed as having the equal right to congregate" within bars).

278. N.J.S.A. 10:5-12(b), -4.1.

crimination in apprenticeship programs, such conduct would violate the general proscriptions of the LAD.[279] Thus, the Division on Civil Rights (DCR) regulations pertaining to apprenticeship programs are expressly applicable to both labor organizations and employers.[280] They prohibit discrimination in both the recruitment and selection of apprentices and in the terms and conditions of employment applicable after selection.[281]

BFOQs

Reasonable minimum age requirements for apprenticeship programs are permitted.[282] Labor organizations may maintain single-sex programs where sex is a bona fide occupational qualification (BFOQ) reasonably necessary to normal operation of the particular program.[283]

The extent to which maximum age requirements may be maintained is unclear. The 1984 edition of the Division on Civil Rights' (DCR) booklet, *A Guide for Employers to the LAD*, condoned the use of a maximum age limit for entry into apprenticeship programs approved by the U.S. Bureau of Apprenticeship and Training.[284] The next edition of the *Guide*, issued in June 1986, deleted reference to this issue.[285] On its face, the LAD makes no provision for a maximum age requirement, except for the general allowance of refusals to hire applicants over age 70.[286] The DCR's 1984 interpretation is consistent with the longstanding federal approach to this issue:

> Age limitations for entry into bona fide apprenticeship programs were not intended to be affected by the [ADEA]. Entry into most apprenticeship programs has traditionally been limited to youths under specified ages. This is in recognition of the fact that ap-

---

279. *See* N.J.S.A. 10:5-12(a), -4.1.

280. N.J.A.C. 13:5-1.1 *et seq.* These regulations were last amended in 1970 and thus fail to reflect subsequent amendments prohibiting discrimination on the basis of atypical hereditary cellular or blood trait (employers only), handicap, and nationality. *See* N.J.S.A. 10:5-12(a)-(b), -4.1. The DCR's general handicap regulations prohibit the conduct of apprentice and training programs in a manner that discourages or otherwise discriminates against handicapped individuals. N.J.A.C. 13:13-2.6(b).

281. N.J.A.C. 13:5-1.2(a).

282. N.J.S.A. 10:5-2.1.

283. N.J.S.A. 10:5-12(b); N.J.A.C. 13:5-1.2(a)(3). Although the DCR apprenticeship regulations refer to the single sex BFOQ defense only in connection with labor organizations, *see* N.J.A.C. 13:5-1.2(a)(3), there is no apparent reason for not extending it to employers. N.J.S.A. 10:5-2.1 expressly provides that nothing in the LAD is to be construed to prohibit the establishment or maintenance of BFOQs, and N.J.S.A. 10:5-12(a) explicitly states that an employer may refuse to employ an individual on the basis of sex where sex is a BFOQ.

284. DCR, *A Guide for Employers to the LAD*, p. 15 (1984). *See* 29 C.F.R. §1625.13 (1990); 29 C.F.R. §521.1 *et seq.* (1990).

285. DCR, *A Guide for Employers to the LAD*, pp. 16-17 (June 1986).

286. *See* N.J.S.A. 10:5-12(a)-(b); N.J.S.A. 10:5-2.1 (expressly permitting a reasonable *minimum* age for apprenticeship programs).

> prenticeship is an extension of the educational process to prepare young men and women for skilled employment. Accordingly, the prohibitions contained in the [ADEA] will not be applied to bona fide apprenticeship programs which meet the standards specified in [29 C.F.R.] §§521.2 and 521.3. ...[287]

Procedures

The sponsor of an apprenticeship program must make full information public at least one month before the final deadline for applications.[288] Disclosure must be made to, among others, the public media, schools, employment service offices, and organizations having contact with persons qualified for the program, including organizations in contact with members of racial and ethnic minority groups.[289]

Each applicant who satisfies the minimum qualifications for the program must be given at least two weeks' advance written notice of the time to appear for any selection procedures.[290] Applicants must be selected for enrollment in the order of their scores under the selection procedures.[291]

Each time a new apprenticeship program begins, the application and selection process must be repeated anew.[292] All documents pertaining to an apprenticeship program, such as applications, test papers, and announcements, must be retained by the sponsor for at least two years after the final date for filling applications and made available to DCR upon request.[293]

A program sponsor that delegates the selection process to the Apprenticeship Information Center of the New Jersey State Employment Service is presumed to

---

287. 29 C.F.R. §1625.13 (1990). *See Quinn v. N.Y. State Elec. & Gas Corp.*, 569 F.Supp. 655, 661-64 (N.D.N.Y. 1983) (EEOC's apprenticeship regulation contravenes the ADEA and thus is invalid); *EEOC Letter on ADEA/Apprenticeship Programs* (1987), reprinted in 1 *EEOC Compliance Manual (BNA)*, pp.N:1301-02 (Aug. 1987) (rejecting *Quinn* and readopting regulation).

288. N.J.A.C. 13:5-1.3(a). Information that must be disclosed includes where and when applications may be filed and minimum qualifications required, such as age, education, work experience, and physical condition. *Id.* The regulations contain boilerplate language that must be included in all announcements, notices, and forms used in connection with apprenticeship programs. *See* N.J.A.C. 13:5-1.8(a). Readers are cautioned that the regulations, last amended in 1970, fail to reflect the fact that the LAD has been subsequently amended to outlaw discrimination on the basis of impermissible characteristics other than those listed in the regulations; *e.g.*, handicap. The boilerplate language should be modified accordingly.

289. N.J.A.C. 13:5-1.4(a).

290. N.J.A.C. 13:5-1.5.

291. N.J.A.C. 13:5-1.6, -1.10.

292. N.J.A.C. 13:5-1.7(a). Unsuccessful applicants from a prior program must be permitted to apply for a new program and given equal treatment and consideration if they possess the minimum qualifications announced for the new program. N.J.A.C. 13:5-1.7(b).

293. N.J.A.C. 13:5-1.9.

be in compliance with the LAD.[294] An apprenticeship program will also be presumed in compliance with the LAD if:

1. The sponsor complies with the provisions of N.J.A.C. 13:5-1.2 to -1.9 (DCR apprenticeship regulations).[295]
2. The selection procedures are designed, administered, scored, and interpreted by or under the supervision of impartial professionals qualified to perform such services.[296]
3. The qualifications required of applicants and the tests used in the selection procedures have been demonstrated to have reasonably high correlations to the work that apprentices and journeypersons actually perform.[297]
4. The program conforms to all apprenticeship program guidelines established by the Director of the DCR.[298]

4-22 Employment Advertising and Referrals

The LAD bars the use of advertisements that directly or indirectly discriminate or express any limitations based upon the impermissible characteristics set forth therein.[299] Division on Civil Rights (DCR) regulations on advertising are applicable to employers, labor organizations, employment agencies, newspapers, and other media (collectively referred to as "advertisers").[300]

An advertiser violates the LAD by circulating an advertisement relating to employment, employment opportunities, job openings, union membership, apprenticeship programs, or any of the terms and conditions thereof that "expresses, overtly or subtly, directly or indirectly, any limitation, specification, preference or discrimination" based on age, ancestry, color, creed, marital status, national origin, race, or sex, unless based on a bona fide occupational qualification (BFOQ) for the particular job advertised.[301] An advertisement that discourages handicapped persons from applying for a job for which they are qualified or for

294. N.J.A.C. 13:5-1.11.

295. N.J.A.C. 13:5-1.12(a).

296. N.J.A.C. 13:5-1.12(a)(1)-(2).

297. N.J.A.C. 13:5-1.12(a)(3)-(4).

298. N.J.A.C. 13:5-1.12(a)(5). No such guidelines have been established by the Director.

299. N.J.S.A. 10:5-12(a)-(b).

300. N.J.A.C. 13:11-1.1 *et seq.*; N.J.A.C. 13:13-2.1. The Supreme Court has found the regulations valid. *Passaic Daily News v. Blair*, 63 N.J. 474 (1973). Only the general employment advertising rules were before the Court. The rules pertaining to handicap discrimination were not enacted until 1985.

membership in a labor organization also violates the LAD.[302] However, an advertiser may include a statement of particular physical or mental abilities reasonably necessary for performance.[303]

The use of words such as Black, Negro, colored, white, restricted, interracial, segregated, Christian, Jewish, men, women, girl, boy, gal, guy, married, single, able-bodied persons, or any other words or expressions that "tend to influence, persuade or dissuade, encourage or discourage, attract or repel" any person because of the aforementioned impermissible characteristics violates the LAD.[304] However, the Director, in an order issued against any employer, labor organization, or employment agency, may require advertisements pertaining to employment opportunities to include the words "equal opportunity" or any substantially similar term.[305]

It is unlawful to run advertisements under specific column headings that are impermissible characteristics[306] (*e.g.*, "Help Wanted-Men") even where the otherwise impermissible characteristic is a BFOQ.[307]

When sex is not a BFOQ, the advertisement should use a gender neutral job title when practicable.[308] If use of a neutral job title is not practicable, the non-neutral title must be accompanied by either the description "M/W" or the job title that is the sex counterpart of the non-neutral job title,[309] such as "waiter/waitress" or "draftsman M/W." [310]

The DCR, upon request, will render an oral or written opinion concerning whether an otherwise impermissible characteristic is a BFOQ for a particular job

---

301. N.J.A.C. 13:11-1.1(a), -1.4(a). Because the regulations have not been amended since 1972, they do not reflect the subsequent extension of coverage to discrimination based upon atypical hereditary cellular or blood trait (employers only), nationality (employers and labor organizations only), and handicap. *See, e.g.*, N.J.S.A. 10:5-12(a)-(c), -4.1. However, handicap discrimination in employment advertising is now covered by N.J.A.C. 13:13-2.1, which is discussed throughout this section. Also note that the regulations, without explanation, do not address unlawful discrimination on the basis of eligibility for service in the Armed Forces, which has been prohibited by the LAD since 1951. L.1951, c.64, amending, *inter alia*, N.J.S.A. 10:5-12(a)-(c).

302. N.J.A.C. 13:13-2.1(a)-(b).

303. N.J.A.C. 13:13-2.1(a).

304. N.J.A.C. 13:11-1(b); N.J.A.C. 13:13-2.1(a).

305. N.J.A.C. 13:11-1.2. *Cf.* N.J.A.C. 13:6-1.16(b), which permits contractors on public works contracts to use advertisements that state the contractor is an "equal opportunity employer."

306. N.J.A.C. 13:11-1.3; DCR, *Employment Guide to the LAD*, p. 11 (1989); DCR, *A Guide for Employers to the LAD*, p. 20 (June 1986).

307. *Passaic Daily News v. Blair*, 63 N.J. 474, 491 (1973); *cf.* N.J.A.C. 13:11-1.3 (no BFOQ exception stated) with N.J.A.C. 13:11-1.1(a), -1.4(a) (BFOQ exception stated). A column heading of "Men and Women" is permissible. N.J.A.C. 13:11-1.4.

308. N.J.A.C. 13:11-1.4(b); DCR, *A Guide for Employers to the LAD*, p. 21 (June 1986).

309. N.J.A.C. 13:11-1.4(c); DCR, *A Guide for Employers to the LAD*, p. 21 (June 1986). DCR guidance documents provide an extensive list of examples of prohibited terms and permissible substitutes. N.J.A.C. 13:13-2.1(a); N.J.A.C. 13:11-1.4(d); DCR, *A Guide for Employers to the LAD*, pp. 21-23 (June 1986).

for which an advertisement is to be published.[311] The DCR's opinion is binding if it is rendered before publication and the request fully and accurately discloses the relevant facts about the particular job.[312]

The DCR has also adopted regulations directed specifically to job referrals of handicapped persons, making it unlawful (1) for an employer to knowingly use any employment agency or recruitment source that does not refer handicapped individuals or that discriminates against such individuals; (2) for an employment agency or labor organization to fail or refuse to refer individuals for employment because of their handicaps; (3) for an employment agency or labor organization to comply with an employer's request for referrals if the request indicates, directly or indirectly, that the employer will discriminate against handicapped individ-

---

310. The DCR has provided a list of terms it deems sex-neutral:

Accountant	Counselor	Operator
Administrator	Couple	Orderly
Advisor	Custodian	Pharmacist
Aide	Demonstrator	Photographer
Analyst	Dentist	Porter
Artist	Designer	Presser
Assistant	Director	Printer
Attendant	Dishwasher	Programmer
Auditor	Dispatcher	Receptionist
Bartender	Doctor	Representative
Beautician	Driver	Secretary
Bookkeeper	Electrician	Stenographer
Cabinet Maker	Engineer	Stylist
Caretaker	Estimator	Superintendant
Carpenter	Executive	Supervisor
Cashier	Guard	Technician
Caterer	Helper	Teller
Clerical	Inspector	Trainee
Clerk	Instructor	Typist
Closer	Interviewer	Welder
Consultant	Machinist	Worker
Cook	Manager	Writer
Coordinator	Mechanic	

311. N.J.A.C. 13:11-1.6(a); DCR, *Employment Guide to the LAD*, pp. 11-12 (1989); N.J.S.A. 52:14B-8.

312. N.J.A.C. 13:11-1.6(c); N.J.S.A. 52:14B-8. If the person placing the advertisement informs the media company (1) that the DCR has opined that the restriction set forth in the advertisement constitutes a BFOQ and (2) of the identification number assigned by the DCR to that opinion, the media company will not violate the LAD by publishing the specific advertisement in good faith and in reasonable reliance upon the aforesaid representations. N.J.A.C. 13:11-1.6(e). If a media company has reasonable doubts about the legitimacy of the advertisement or the advertiser's representations, the prudent course for the media company is to wait for clearance from the DCR before publishing the ad. *See Passaic Daily News v. Blair*, 63 N.J. 474, 478-79, 491-93 (1973).

uals; and (4) for an employment agency or labor organization to classify handicapped individuals in any manner which would, in fact or effect, deprive them of employment opportunities or otherwise affect employee status.[313]

4-23 Pre-employment Inquiries and Tests

The LAD expressly prohibits employers and employment agencies from making pre-employment inquiries[314] which directly or indirectly express any limitation, specification, or discrimination as to age, ancestry, eligibility for service in the Armed Forces, color, creed, handicap, marital status, national origin, race, and sex, or any intent to make such limitation, specification, or discrimination, unless based upon a bona fide occupational qualification (BFOQ).[315]

Pre-employment inquiries should be job-related and designed to elicit an applicant's qualifications.[316] According to the DCR, inquiries about prior work experience and education should be made only if necessary to determine whether the applicant can perform the job.[317] Regulations specifically addressed to handicaps prohibit inquiries that elicit information tending to divulge the existence of a handicap or health condition not reasonably related to the applicant's fitness to perform the duties of the job.[318] Inquiries about a handicap or health problem that would impede satisfactory job performance are permissible, but only if the applicant (1) is provided with an accurate description of the job duties involved and (2) is asked to provide information regarding reasonable accommodations that could be made if the inquiry reveals that the applicant is handicapped.[319]

Further, an employer may invite applicants to indicate whether and to what extent they are handicapped if the inquiry is made in connection with a required or

---

313. N.J.A.C. 13:13-2.2.

314. Both written and oral pre-employment inquiries are covered. N.J.A.C. 13:7 Foreword.

315. N.J.S.A. 10:5-12(c), -4.1. Atypical heredity cellular or blood trait (AHCBT) and nationality are omitted from the section of the LAD relating to pre-employment inquiries, but are included in the section prohibiting discrimination in hiring. *Cf.* N.J.S.A. 10:5-12(c) with N.J.S.A. 10:5-12(a).

316. DCR, *Employment Guide to the LAD*, p. 12 (1989); DCR, *A Guide for Employers to the LAD*, p. 9 (June 1986); DCR, *Your Employment Rights*, p. 10 (Nov. 1986).

317. DCR, *Employment Guide to the LAD*, p. 12 (1989); DCR, *A Guide for Employers to the LAD*, p. 9 (June 1986). The DCR's June 1986 *A Guide for Employers to the LAD*, at pp. 11 and 31, states that (1) employers may not ask whether an applicant is a high school graduate, unless that requirement is job related and a business necessity, because of the potential disparate impact such inquiry may have on minorities, but that (2) it is permissible to ask an applicant to disclose the highest grade completed and/or to detail his or her educational background.

318. N.J.A.C. 13:13-2.4(a).

319. N.J.A.C. 13:13-2.4(a); DCR, *Employment Guide to the LAD*, p. 17 (1989). Inquiries regarding an individual's handicap should be made only when the applicant's response is likely to be used for a non-discriminatory purpose.

voluntary affirmative action program to correct past discrimination or in compliance with instructions or requirements of a local, state, or federal agency.[320] Information obtained about such an individual's handicap must be maintained on separate forms, kept confidential and in good faith solely for the purpose of complying with the law, and not be used for unlawful discriminatory purposes.[321]

The DCR's regulations contain a list of prohibited and acceptable pre-employment questions.[322] The DCR's *Employment Guide to the LAD*, issued in 1989, contains another table of sample inquiries, many of which overlap those in the regulations.[323] In the chart that follows, the sample inquiries are taken from the DCR regulations verbatim. Significant additions made by the *Employment Guide* are noted in italics and/or footnotes. Significant deletions made by the *Employment Guide* are shown by brackets.[324]

(a) Name

It is Discriminatory to Inquire About:[325]

1. The fact of a change of name or the original *name* of an applicant whose name has been *legally* changed.
2. Maiden name of a married woman

320. N.J.A.C. 13:13-2.4(b). *See, e.g.*, §503 of the Rehabilitation Act of 1973, 29 U.S.C.A. §793(a) ("Any contract in excess of $2,500 entered into by any Federal ... agency ... shall contain a provision requiring that, in employing persons to carry out such contract, the party contracting with the United States shall take affirmative action to employ ... qualified [handicapped] individuals").

Such an inquiry must clearly state, in writing, that (1) the requested information is intended for use only in connection with the aforesaid program or agency instructions or requirements; (2) the information will be kept confidential; (3) the applicant is not required to disclose the information; and (4) refusal to provide the information will not subject the applicant to any adverse treatment. N.J.A.C. 13:13-2.4(b).

321. N.J.A.C. 13:13-2.4(c). The regulations also permit officially-recognized agencies to keep records needed to provide services to individuals requiring employment assistance or rehabilitation. N.J.A.C. 13:13-2.4(d).

322. N.J.A.C. 13:7-1.1. These regulations were last amended in 1970 and fail to reflect subsequent amendments to the LAD outlawing certain unlawful employment practices based upon AHCBT (employers only), handicap, and nationality (employers only). *See* N.J.S.A. 10:5-12(A), (C), -4.1.

323. DCR, *Employment Guide to the LAD*, pp. 14-17 (1989).

324. The DCR regulations, but not the *Employment Guide*, have the force and effect of law. However, the sample permissible inquiries listed in the regulations that conflict with subsequent amendments to the LAD and/or with federal law (*e.g.*, Immigration Reform & Control Act of 1986, Pub.L. 99-603) should not be used. *See New Jersey Builders, Owners & Managers Ass'n v. Blair*, 60 N.J. 330, 334 (1972); 37 Lefelt, *New Jersey Practice: Administrative Law & Practice*, §73 (1988).

325. The *Employment Guide* describes these inquiries as ones which "should be avoided." DCR, *Employment Guide to the LAD*, p. 14 (1989).

It is Permissible to Inquire About:

[Maiden name of a married woman applicant.]

1. Whether or not the applicant ever worked under another name or was the applicant educated under another name. (Allowable only when the data is needed to verify the applicant's qualifications)

(b) Birthplace and Residence

It is Discriminatory to Inquire About:

1. Birthplace of applicant.
2. Birthplace of applicant's parents.

[3. Requirement that applicant submit birth certificate, naturalization or baptismal record.]

3. Own home, rent, board or live with parents.[326]

4. Citizenship.

5. Address of applicant's spouse and children who are dependents.

It is Permissible to Inquire About:

[1. Applicant's place of residence and address of applicant's wife and children who are dependents.][327]

1. Are you either a U.S. citizen or an alien authorized to work in the U.S.?

2. Requiring applicant to produce documents INS has set forth to satisfy IRCA of 1986 (I-9).[328]

---

326. Inquiries about home ownership, and other inquiries that address credit-worthiness or garnishment records are considered impermissible by the DCR unless required by business necessity, because significantly more minorities and women are poor and would be disproportionately impacted. DCR, *Employment Guide to the LAD*, p. 13 (1989); DCR, *A Guide for Employers to the LAD*, pp. 12-13 (June 1986); DCR, *Your Employment Rights*, p. 10 (Nov. 1986). *Cf. Wilson v. Sixty-Six Melmore Gardens*, 106 N.J.Super. 182, 185 (App. Div. 1969) (court stated that it did "not necessarily concur in all the subordinate findings and inferences" of the DCR hearing examiner that the landlord's use of a credit check "was a device designed to avoid rentals to Negroes"); *N.J. Attorney General Formal Opinion No. 7-1983* (July 5, 1983) (lending institution may not inquire as to the marital status of a prospective borrower to ascertain credit-worthiness, but may, at the appropriate stage of the application process, make such an inquiry when necessary to obtain an enforceable security lien).

327. The DCR notes that identification inquiries, such as name, address, and telephone number, are permissible. DCR, *Employment Guide to the LAD*, p. 12 (1989); DCR, *Your Employment Rights*, p. 10 (Nov. 1986); DCR, *A Guide for Employers to the LAD*, p. 9 (June 1986).

3. Length of applicant's residence in New Jersey and/or city where the employer is located.

[(c) Creed][329]

It is Discriminatory to Inquire About:

[1. Private organizational affiliations of applicant.]

[2. Political affiliations of applicant.]

(d) *Creed*/Religion

It is Discriminatory to Inquire About:

1. Applicant's religious affiliations.[330]
2. Church, parish, or religious holidays observed by applicant.

It is Permissible to Inquire About:

1. Unions or professional organizations, as long as that information is not used to violate the National Labor Relations Act or other federal statutes.

(e) Race or Color

It is Discriminatory to Inquire About:

1. Applicant's race.

2. Color of applicant's skin, eyes, hair, [and so forth] *distinguishing physical characteristics, scars, markings.*

---

328. According to the DCR:

> Under the Immigration Reform and Control Act of 1986, [Pub.L. 99-603,] an employer must verify the legal status of all employees or job applicants hired or applying after Nov. 6, 1986. Therefore, the [LAD] does not prohibit an inquiry that is necessary to comply with this law. An example of this would be asking applicants to verify that they are either U.S. citizens or legal aliens. However, it might be a violation of the [LAD] to ask for information pertaining to national origin or citizenship status, if such information is not necessary to comply with federal law.

DCR, *Employment Guide to the LAD*, p. 13 (1989).

329. The DCR's 1970 regulations addressed "creed" as including more than religious beliefs. As noted in §82, that definition is inconsistent with a 1949 Formal Opinion of the state attorney general and post-1970 court decisions.

330. *See, e.g., Clover Hill Swimming Club v. Goldsboro*, 47 N.J. 24, 27, 30 (1966).

It is Permissible to Inquire About:

[General distinguishing physical characteristics, such as scars, or markings.]

(f) Photographs

It is Discriminatory to Inquire About:

1. Photographs with application.
2. Photographs after interview but before hiring.

(g) Age

It is Discriminatory to Inquire About:

1. Date of birth or age of an applicant except when such information is needed for or to:
   i. Maintain apprenticeship requirements based upon a reasonable minimum age;
   ii. Satisfy the provisions of either State or federal minimum age statutes;
   iii. Avoid interference with the operation of the terms and conditions and administration of any bona fide retirement, pension, employee benefit or insurance plan or program;
   iv. Verify that applicant is above the minimum legal adult age. … but without asking for a birth certificate;
   [v. Age specifications or limitations in a newspaper employment advertisement which might bar workers under or over a certain age.]

2. Age specifications, limitations, or implications in a newspaper advertisement that might bar workers under or over a certain age.

3. Driver's license number (contains driver's age).

It is Permissible to Inquire About:

1. Applicant may be asked if s/he is over the minimum legal working age.

[(h) Citizenship]

It is Discriminatory to Inquire About:

[Any and all inquiries into whether applicant is now or intends to become a citizen of the U.S., or any other inquiry related to the aspect of citizenship. (*See Dept. of Labor and Industry v. Cruz*, N.J., 1965.[331])]

(i) National Origin and Ancestry

It is Discriminatory to Inquire About:

1. Applicant's lineage, ancestry, national origin, descent, parentage, or nationality.
2. Nationality of applicant's parents or spouse.

(j) Language

It is Discriminatory to Inquire About:

1. Applicant's mother tongue.
2. Language commonly used by applicant *at* [or in applicant's] *home.*
3. How the applicant acquired *the* ability to read, write, or speak a foreign language.

It is Permissible to Inquire About:

1. Language*s* applicant speaks [and/or writes] fluently *(only if job related).*

(k) Relatives

It is Discriminatory to Inquire About:

1. Name and/or address of any relative of applicant [other than spouse and children who are his dependents].
2. Name of applicant's spouse and dependent children.
3. Names of persons with whom applicant resides.

It is Permissible to Inquire About:

[1. Names of applicant's spouse and dependent children.]

---

331. *New Jersey Dept. of Labor v. Cruz*, 45 N.J. 372 (1965).

[2. Names of relatives already employed by their company.]
[3. Names of persons with whom applicant resides.]
4. Name and address of person to be notified in case of accident or emergency.
[5. Whether the applicant has ever worked for the same employer under a different name.]

(l) Military Experience

It is Discriminatory to Inquire About:

1. Applicant's military experience in other than U.S. armed forces.
2. National Guard or Reserve units of applicant.
3. Draft classification or other eligibility for military service.
4. Applicant's whereabouts in [1914-1918,] 1941-45, [or] 1950-53 *or 1964-73.*

It is Permissible to Inquire About:

1. Military experience of applicant in the armed forces [of the United States and dates and conditions of discharge][332] *only when used for employment history.*
[2. Applicant's service in a particular branch of the armed forces.]
3. Whether applicant has received any notice to report for duty in the armed forces.

[(m) Organizations]

It is Discriminatory to Inquire About:

[All clubs, social fraternities, societies, lodges, or organizations to which the applicant belongs, other than professional, trade, or service organizations.]

---

332. The 1970 regulations permit an employer to ask an applicant the dates and conditions of a military discharge. N.J.A.C. 13:7-1.1(l). The DCR's June 1986 *A Guide for Employers to the LAD*, at p. 31, states that an employer may not inquire as to the dates, conditions, and type of military discharge. The DCR's 1989 *Employment Guide to the LAD*, at p. 16, is silent on this issue.

It is Permissible to Inquire About:

[1. Applicant's membership in any union or professional or trade organization.]

[2. Names of any service organizations of which applicant is a member.]

(n) References

It is Discriminatory to Inquire About:

The name of applicant's pastor or religious leader.

It is Permissible to Inquire About:

1. Names of persons willing to provide professional and/or character reference for applicant.

[2. Names of persons who suggested applicant apply for a position with the employer.]

2. *Name and address of person to be notified in case of accident or emergency.*

(o) Sex and Marital Status[333]

It is Discriminatory to Inquire About:

1. *Sex or marital status or any questions that would be used to detemine same.*
2. *Number of dependents, number of children.*
3. *Spouse's occupation.*[334]

---

333. The DCR's *Your Employment Rights*, p. 10 (Nov. 1986), adds that it is impermissible to ask a female about child-care arrangements she has made, because it "assumes that women with minor children are bad employment risks because of their absentee potential." DCR, *A Guide for Employers to the LAD*, pp. 10-11 (June 1986). The use of "code words" directed to minority employees (such as "all of you" and "that one in there" may imply a discriminatory intent and constitute harassment). *Aman v. Cort Furniture Rental Corp.*, 85 F.3d 1074, 1082-83 (3d Cir. 1996). *See Kelly v. Bally's Grand, Inc.*, 285 N.J. Super. 422, 434 (App. Div. 1995) ("evidence of age based statements of bias aimed at plaintiff by her supervisor, together with the evidence of poorer evaluations and written reprimands" sufficient to establish *prima facie* case of harassment on the basis of age or age discrimination). *Cf. Lawrence v. National Westminster Bank*, 1996 WL 506043, p.*5 (D.N.J. 1995), *aff'd in part and rev'd in part*, 98 F. 3d 61 (3d Cir. 1996) ("Statements from plaintiff's superiors that he is not "as he used to be" or that "he had to have a higher energy level" do not give rise to an inference that plaintiff was terminated because he was disabled.")

334. The DCR states that this question is impermissible because it is based on "the stereotyped assumption that if a husband is offered a job advancement in another area, the wife will automatically quit her job to relocate with him. Many employers are also reluctant to hire a woman if she is the second 'breadwinner' in the family." DCR, *A Guide for Employers to the LAD*, pp. 10-11 (June 1986).

(p) Arrest and Conviction Record[335]

It is Discriminatory to Inquire About:

1. *The number and kinds of arrest of an applicant.*

It is Permissible to Inquire About:

1. *Convictions that bear a relationship to the job, and have not been expunged or sealed by a court.*

(q) Height and Weight

It is Discriminatory to Inquire About:

1. *Any inquiry into height or weight of applicant, unless justified by business necessity.*

(r) Disabilities

It is Discriminatory to Inquire About:

1. *Any general inquiry as to whether applicant has any physical or mental disability.*

It is Permissible to Inquire About:

1. *Does applicant have any disabilities that would prevent him or her from satisfactorily performing the job. Must be accompanied by job descriptions and mention of reasonable accommodation.*[336]

The DCR recommends that all employment applications include an affirmation of the employer's policy of equal employment opportunity.[337] The agency has published a sample pre-employment application, but states that it is not intended to serve as a model application.[338]

---

335. According to the DCR, an arrest is not an indication of guilt or ability to perform a job, and screening out applicants on the basis of their arrest records may have a disparate impact on minorities. DCR, *Employment Guide to the LAD*, p. 13 (1989); DCR, *A Guide for Employers to the LAD*, p. 12 (June 1986). It recommends that if a permissible inquiry concerning convictions is to be made, applicants should be advised that a conviction is not an absolute bar to all employment. DCR, *A Guide for Employers to the LAD*, p. 12 (June 1986).

336. The DCR's June 1986 *A Guide for Employers to the LAD*, at p. 31, provided the following example:

> [Q]uestions concerning hearing impairments are acceptable on applications for a telephone operator position.

337. DCR, *A Guide for Employers to the LAD*, pp. 25-26 (June 1986).

In evaluating the legality of pre-employment tests, the DCR follows the approach set forth in *Griggs v. Duke Power Co.*, 401 U.S. 424 (1971), *Albemarle Paper Co. v. Moody*, 422 U.S. 405 (1975), and the Uniform Guidelines on Employee Selection Procedures (UGESP), 29 C.F.R. 1607.1 *et seq.* (1990).[339]

4-24 Posting Requirements

Division on Civil Rights (DCR) regulations require all employers, labor organizations, and employment agencies to display the official employment poster issued by the DCR in locations easily visible to all employees and applicants for employment.[340] A copy of the current edition of the DCR employment poster may be obtained by contacting the DCR's Trenton, New Jersey office. The sample poster reprinted in the New Jersey Administrative Code is long out-of-date and should not be used.[341]

4-25 Harassment

Harassment of an employee on the basis of a characteristic protected by the LAD is prohibited.[342] All employees have the right to a workplace environment that is free of discriminatory intimidation, harassment, and hostility, such as sexual harassment, gender-based harassment, and racial name-calling.[343]

In appropriate circumstances, harassment may constitute a petty disorderly persons or disorderly persons offense under the Criminal Code.[344] If the harassment is purposely motivated by color, ethnicity, race, religion, or sexual orientation, the offender may be guilty of a crime of the fourth degree.[345] In addition,

---

338. DCR, *A Guide for Employers to the LAD*, pp. 34-35 (June 1986). Applications may be submitted to the DCR for review and approval. *Id.* at pp. 9-10.

339. DCR, *A Guide for Employers to the LAD*, pp. 11-12 (June 1986). The UGESP are supplemented by EEOC explanatory text and interpretive questions and answers, neither of which are published in the Code of Federal Regulations. These supplementary materials, along with the UGESP, are reprinted in 8 *Fair Employment Practices Manual (BNA)*, pp. 403:349-458 (Mar. 1990).

340. N.J.A.C. 13:8-1.2. The LAD provides for the posting of notices as may be required by regulation. N.J.S.A. 10:5-12(j).

341. *See* N.J.A.C. 13:8-2.1. At times, the DCR has also published its official poster in Spanish. *See, e.g.*, 8B *Fair Employment Practices Manual (BNA)*, p. 455:2752 (Feb. 1980).

342. *Erickson v. Marsh & McLennan Co.*, 117 N.J. 539, 555-59 (1990); *Drinkwater v. Union Carbide Corp.*, 904 F.2d 853, 859-63 (3d Cir. 1990); *Muench v. Township of Haddon*, 255 N.J. Super. 288 (App. Div. 1992); *Giudice v. Drew Chemical Corp.*, 210 N.J.Super. 32, 38 (App. Div.), *certif. denied in part, certif. granted in part and remanded on other grounds*, 104 N.J. 465 (1986); *Jackson v. Consolidated Rail Corp.*, 223 N.J.Super. 467, 474-75 (App. Div. 1988).

sexual harassment that constitutes a sexual assault, criminal sexual contact, or lewdness may subject the actor to criminal punishment.[346]

4-25:1 Sexual Harassment

Sexual harassment consists of unwelcomed sexual advances, requests for sexual favors, and/or verbal or physical conduct of a sexual nature that results in an alteration of the terms and conditions of employment.[347] "Hostile environment" sexual harassment involves harassing conduct that has the purpose or effect of unreasonably interfering with an individual's work performance or creating an intimidating, hostile, or offensive working environment.[348] "Quid pro quo" sexual harassment involves situations where (1) submission to harassing sexual conduct is, explicitly or implicitly, made a term or condition of an individual's employment or (2) submission to or rejection of such conduct by an individual is used as a basis for employment decisions affecting that individual.[349]

Under both approaches, the harassing conduct must be unwelcomed and coercive, as opposed to consensual.[350] The LAD prohibits both heterosexual and homosexual sexual harassment.[351] One trial court has held that same sex

---

343. LAD decisions involving racial harassment include *Taylor v. Metzger*, 152 N.J. 490 (1998); *White v. PSE&G Co.*, 8 N.J.A.R. 335, 355-56, 364-65 (DCR 1984), *aff'd*, No. A-1496-84 (App. Div. 1986), and *Jackson v. Consolidated Rail Corp.*, 223 N.J.Super. at 474-75. Harassment based on an individual's handicap is briefly mentioned in *Maher v. New Jersey Transit Rail Operations, Inc.*, 125 N.J. 455, 461, 479-80 (1991). *See Levinson v. Prentice-Hall, Inc.*, 868 F.2d 558 (3d Cir. 1989) (plaintiff ridiculed because of his handicap).

In *Muench v. Township of Haddon*, 255 N.J. Super. 288 (App. Div. 1992), the Appellate Division held that gender-based harassment need not be sexual in nature to violate the LAD. "[W]hether the offending conduct is in the form of sexual advances or intimidation and hostility toward a woman solely because she is a woman, the result is the same. ... Interpreting the LAD as prohibiting pervasive and hostile nonsexual harassment best serves the Act's underlying goal of eradicating discrimination in the workplace." *Id.* at 298.

344. N.J.S.A. 2C:33-4(a)-(c) (harassment); N.J.S.A. 2C:12-1(a) (simple assault).

345. N.J.S.A. 2C:33-4(d); N.J.S.A. 2C:12-1(e).

346. N.J.S.A. 2C:14-1 to -4. *See generally* 33 Miller, *New Jersey Practice: Criminal Law*, ch.10 (2d ed. 1990); Cannel, *N.J. Criminal Code Annotated*, Comments to N.J.S.A. 2C:14-1 *et seq.* (1992 ed.).

347. *Lehmann v. Toys 'R' Us, Inc.*, 132 N.J. 587 (1993). *Erickson v. Marsh & McLennan Co.*, 117 N.J. 539, 555-56 (1990); *Reynolds v. Atlantic City Convention Center Authority*, 1990 WL 267417, 53 FEP 1852, 1867 (D.N.J. 1990), *aff'd without published op.*, 925 F.2d 419 (3d Cir. 1991); DCR, *Employment Guide to the LAD*, p. 18 (1989); DCR, *Sexual Harassment*, p. 3 (1989); *Cf. Burlington Indus., Inc. v. Ellerth*, 118 S. Ct. 2257 (1998); *Faragher v. Boca Raton*, 118 S. Ct. 2275 (1998).

348. *Lehmann v. Toys 'R' Us, Inc.*, 132 N.J. 587 (1993); *Woods-Pirozzi v. Nabisco Foods*, 290 N.J. Super. 252 (App. Div. 1996); *Lynch v. New Deal Delivery Service, Inc.*, 974 F. Supp. 441 (D.N.J. 1997). *See also Burlington Indus., Inc., v. Ellerth*, 118 S. Ct. 2257 (1998); *Faragher v. Boca Raton*, 118 S. Ct. 2275 (1998); *Harris v. Forklift Systems, Inc.*, 510 U.S. 17 (1993). *Cf. Erickson v. Marsh & McLennan Co.*, 117 N.J. at 555-56; *Reynolds v. Atlantic City Convention Center Authority*, 53 FEP at 1864; *Maher v. New Jersey Transit Rail Operations, Inc.*, 125 N.J. 455, 480-81 (1991) (complainant was "required to labor under conditions that were unreasonably different from those of other employees"; handicap discrimination).

349. *Erickson v. Marsh & McLennan Co.*, 117 N.J. at 555-56; *Wolbert v. Stylianos, Inc.*, 9 N.J.A.R. 392, 395-400 (DCR 1985); *Reynolds v. Atlantic City Convention Center Authority*, 53 FEP at 1864.

heterosexual harassment based on gender stereotyping (i.e., heterosexual male harassing another heterosexual male because he does not fit the stereotyped definition of masculine) is actionable.[352]

Hostile Environment Harassment

To establish a hostile environment claim under the LAD, plaintiff must demonstrate that the conduct in question was unwelcome, that it occurred because of his or her sex and that a reasonable person of the same sex would consider it sufficiently severe or pervasive to alter the conditions of employment and create an intimidating, hostile, or offensive working environment.

> For the purposes of establishing and examining a cause of action, the test can be broken down into four prongs: the complained-of conduct (1) would not have occurred but for the employee's gender; and it was (2) severe or pervasive enough to make a (3) reasonable woman believe that (4) the conditions of employment are altered and the working environment is hostile or abusive. However, the second, third, and fourth prongs, while separable to some extent, are interdependent. One cannot inquire whether the alleged conduct was "severe or pervasive" without knowing how severe or pervasive it must be. The answer to that question lies in the other prongs: the conduct must be severe or pervasive enough to make a reasonable woman believe that the conditions of employment are altered and her working environment is hostile.[353]

With respect to the first requirement, the *Lehmann* Court made clear that not all harassment violates the LAD; "if a supervisor is equally crude and vulgar to all employees, regardless of their sex, no basis exists for a sex harassment claim. Although the supervisor may not be a nice person, he is not abusing a plaintiff

---

350. *Erickson v. Marsh & McLennan Co.*, 117 N.J. at 556-57; *Reynolds v. Atlantic City Convention Center Authority*, 53 FEP at 1864. *See Meritor Savings Bank v. Vinson*, 477 U.S. 57, 68-69 (1986) (under Title VII, the conduct must be "unwelcomed"; the focus is not on the "voluntariness" of the plaintiff's participation). Although the Supreme Court does not mention the unwelcomeness requirement in *Lehmann*, its subsequent opinion in *In re Brenner*, 147 N.J. 314, 318 (1997), a judicial discipline case, confirms that under the LAD, like Title VII, proof of unwelcomeness is part of plaintiff's case. *See Meritor Savings Bank v. Vinson*, *supra*, at 65.

351. *Lehmann v. Toys 'R' Us, Inc.*, 132 N.J. 587, 604 (1993); *Caldwell v. KFC Corp.*, 958 F. Supp. 962, 970 (D.N.J. 1997).

352. *Zalewski v. Overlook Hospital*, 300 N.J. Super. 202 (Law Div. 1996); *See Oncale v. Sundowner Offshore Services, Inc.*, 118 S. Ct. 998 (1998). Note that under *Lehmann*, 132 N.J. at 605-06, the male plaintiff in a sexual harassment case may in some circumstances face an increased burden of proving that his employer "is the rare employer who discriminates against the historically-privileged group." *Id* at 606. *See Erickson, supra,* 117 N.J. at 551.

353. *Lehmann v. Toys 'R' Us, Inc.*, 132 N.J. 587 (1993).

because of her sex."[354] The second prong, requiring that the conduct complained of be severe or pervasive, is in accord with the U.S. Supreme Court opinion in *Meritor Savings Bank v. Vinson*.[355] Other decisions had required that the conduct be both severe and persistent.[356] The *Lehmann* Court found the dual requirement unacceptable because it "would bar actions based on a single, extremely severe incident, or, perhaps, even those based on multiple but randomly-occurring incidents of harassment." Although recognizing that it would be a "rare and extreme" case in which a single incident would be severe enough to alter the terms and conditions of employment to the point that a reasonable woman would consider it abusive, the *Lehman* Court stated that was possible.[357] In *Taylor v. Metzger*, the Court found that a single but extreme racial epithet uttered publicly by the head of the office to a subordinate was sufficient to create a jury question as to whether it was severe.[358]

Creation of working conditions that a reasonable woman would condider abusive or hostile is all the "harm" a plaintiff must demonstrate to state a claim for sexual harassment under the LAD. The line of federal cases requiring proof that the hostile environment severely affected the psychological well-being of plaintiff was specifically rejected by the *Lehmann* Court.[359]

---

354. *Id.* That obscenity is in the air generally but is not directed at particular persons, is directed by men at both men and women, and is practiced by women, including plaintiff, are significant factors in negating the existence of an actionable hostile environment. *Reynolds v. Atlantic City Convention Center Authority*, 1990 Wl 267417, 53 FEP 1852, 1866 (D.N.J. 1990), *aff'd without published op.*, 925 F.2d 419 (3d Cir. 1991).

355. 477 U.S. 57, 67 (1986).

356. *See Drinkwater v. Union Carbide Corp.*, 904 F.2d at 863; *Reynolds v. Atlantic City Convention Center Authority*, 63 FED at 1865 (the harassment must be "'sufficiently severe and persistent to affect seriously the psychological well being' [or work performance] of the employee, a finding to be based on 'the totality of the circumstances.'"). In *Meritor Savings Bank v. Vinson*, 477 U.S. at 67 (under Title VII, "[f]or sexual harassment to be actionable, it must be sufficiently severe or pervasive 'to alter the conditions of [the victim's] employment and create an abusive working environment.'"); *Porta v. Rollins Environmental Services (N.J.), Inc.*, 654 F. Supp. at 1282 (same).

357. "Although it will be a rare and extreme case in which a single incident will be so severe that it would, from the perspective of a reasonable woman, make the working environment hostile, such a case is certainly possible. The LAD was designed to prevent the harm of hostile working environments. No purpose is served by allowing that harm to go unremedied merely because it was brought about by a single, severe incident of harassment rather than by multiple incidents of harassment." *Lehmann v. Toys "R" Us, Inc.*, 132 N.J. 587, 606-07 (1993).

358. *Taylor v. Metzger*, 152 N.J. 490 (1998). *See Woods-Pirozzi v. Nabisco Foods*, 290 N.J. Super. 252, 270-71 (App. Div. 1996) (jury issue created on "severe or pervasive" requirement where plaintiff alleged that incidents occurred "every so often" within a year; that "you're a woman and a pain in my ass" was said frequently; that plaintiff was called a "loser" about "once or twice a week"; and that references to "PMS" were made once or twice a month); *Lynch v. New Deal Delivery Service Inc.*, 974 F. Supp. 441, 451 (D.N.J. 1997) (female co-workers' hiring of a male stripper for plaintiff's birthday; male supervisor's invitations to dinner and to work out; male supervisor's requests for the key to the corporate apartment where plaintiff stayed; and other sexual conduct involving other employees did not meet "severe or pervasive" standard).

In adopting the objective standard of a reasonable person of plaintiff's sex (designated the "reasonable woman" standard for ease of reference) the Court expressed a dual objective: (1) that recovery should be limited to cases of real harassment and not the idiosyncratic reactions of hypersensitive employees; and (2) that the incorporation of community standards should not be used to perpetuate discrimination through conclusions such as "a reasonable woman would expect sexual harassment on entering a historically male-dominated workplace." The Court found a gender-specific standard necessary due to perceived differences in the ways men and women view sexual conduct in the workplace, i.e. men being flattered and women being intimidated.[360]

Quid Pro Quo Harassment

To prove quid-pro-quo harassment, an employee generally must establish the following *prima facie* case:

1. The employee is a member of a protected class.
2. The employee was subjected to unwelcomed sexual harassment to which members of the opposite sex were not.
3. The harassment complained of was based on sex.
4. The employee's reaction to the harassment complained of affected tangible aspects of her compensation, terms, conditions, or privileges of employment. Acceptance or rejection of the harassment by the employee must be an expressed or implied condition to the receipt of a job benefit or the cause of a tangible job detriment. The employee must establish that she was deprived of a job benefit that she was otherwise qualified to receive because of the employer's use of a prohibited criterion in making the employment decision.[361]

Once the *prima facie* case is made, the burden of production shifts to defendant to rebut the presumption of discrimination with a legitimate, non-discriminatory reason for the adverse action.[362] If the articulation burden is satisfied, plaintiff bears the burden of demonstrating that the articulated reason is pretex-

---

359. 132 N.J. at 607-09. The United States Supreme Court decision in *Harris v. Forklift Systems, Inc.*, 510 U.S. 17 (1993), is in accord.

360. 132 N.J. at 614-15.

361. The usefulness of the *quid pro quo*/hostile environment distinction has been questioned. *See Burlington Indus., Inc. v. Ellerth,* 118 S.Ct. 2257 (1998). *See generally, Henson v. Dundee*, 682 F.2d 897, 909-11 & n.22 (11th Cir. 1982) (Title VII); *Spencer v. General Elec. Co.*, 894. F2d 651, 658 (4th Cir 1990) (Title VII).

362. *Spencer v. General Elec. Co.*, 894 F.2d at 659; *Craig v. Y&Y Snacks, Inc.*, 721 F.2d 77, 79-80 (3d Cir. 1983) (Title VII).

tual and that the employment decision was based on intentional sex discrimination.[363] In deciding whether conduct constitutes sexual harassment, the totality of the circumstances must be examined.[364] Among others, the following factors are considered:

> [T]he nature of the alleged harassment, the background and experience of the plaintiff, her coworkers, and supervisors, the totality of the physical environment of the plaintiff's work area, the lexicon of obscenity that pervaded the environment of the workplace both before and after the plaintiff's introduction into its environs, coupled with the reasonable expectation of the plaintiff upon voluntarily entering that environment.[365]

By necessity, claims of sexual harassment must be resolved on a case-by-case basis.[366]

Third-Party Harassment

In certain circumstances, persons who have not been directly subjected to the harassing conduct may have an actionable claim. Under "third party" sexual harassment, if employment opportunities or benefits are bestowed because of an individual's submission to quid-pro-quo harassment, then other persons who were qualified for but denied those opportunities or benefits have been subjected to unlawful sex discrimination.[367] However, as the Supreme Court made clear in *Erickson v. Marsh & McLennan Co.*, the third-party sexual harassment theory does not reach adverse employment decisions resulting solely from a consensual, non-coercive romantic relationship between a supervisor and another employee.[368] There must be additional evidence of sexual hostility, such as facts dem-

---

363. *Spencer v. General Elec. Co.*, 894 F.2d at 659; *Craig v. Y&Y Snacks, Inc.*, 721 F.2d at 79-80.

364. *Reynolds v. Atlantic City Convention Center Authority*, 1990 WL 267417, 53 FEP 1852, 1865 (D.N.J. 1990), *aff'd without published op.*, 925 F.2d 419 (3d Cir. 1991); 29 C.F.R. §1604.11(b) (1990).

365. *Reynolds v. Atlantic City Convention Center Authority*, 53 FEP at 1866 (internal quotation marks and emphasis omitted). *See* 29 C.F.R. §1604.11(b) (1990).

366. *Id.* at 1866; 29 C.F.R. §1604.11(b) (1990).

367. *Erickson v. Marsh & McLennan Co.*, 117 N.J. at 557; DCR, *Employment Guide to the LAD*, p. 18 (1989); DCR, *Sexual Harassment*, p. 4 (1989); DCR, *Your Employment Rights*, p. 11 (Nov. 1986); 29 C.F.R. §1604.11(g) (1990).

368. *Woods-Pirozzi v. Nabisco Foods,* 290 N.J. Super. 252, 268-69 (App. Div. 1996) (extent of employer's control over third-party harasser is a factor to consider). *See Erickson v. Marsh & McLennan Co.*, 117 N.J. at 557-59, 561. *See Drinkwater v. Union Carbide Corp.*, 904 F.2d at 860-62 (extensive discussion of *Erickson*). *See generally* EEOC, *Policy Guide on Employer Liability for Sexual Favoritism Under Title VII* (Jan. 12, 1990), reprinted in 8 *Fair Employment Practices Manual (BNA)*, pp. 405:6817-21 (Apr. 1990), and in 1 *EEOC Compliance Manual (BNA)*, pp. N:5051-58 (Feb. 1990). In *Erickson*, plaintiff claimed that he was accused of sexual harassment and then discharged so that his supervisor's paramour could be promoted. The Court found no violation of the LAD in view of the facts that the romantic relationship was voluntary and both men and women would be denied the promotion because of the favoritism exhibited toward the paramour.

onstrating that "the environment was so charged with sexual innuendo as to create an atmosphere that discriminated against" plaintiff on the basis of sex, that the romantic couple flaunted the nature of their relationship, or that romantic relationships were prevalent in the workplace.[369]

Employer Liability

Employers may be liable for sexual harassment committed by supervisors, by non-supervisory employees, and in some circumstances by third parties (*e.g.*, customers or outside contractors), if the employers knew or should have known about the conduct, had control over the harasser, and failed to take prompt and appropriate corrective action.[370] In *Lehmann v. Toys 'R' Us, Inc.*, the Supreme Court established a three-tiered standard for determining when employers may be liable for hostile environment sexual harassment by supervisors. First, with respect to equitable remedies—such as hiring or reinstating the victim, disciplining or terminating the harasser, providing back or front pay and taking remedial actions in the workplace—the employer is strictly liable.

However, with respect to compensatory damages, the employer will be liable for a hostile environment created by a supervisory employee only under agency principles, as set forth in the Restatement (Second) of Agency. That means that the employer will be responsible for actions taken by the supervisor within the scope of employment. It also means that the employer will be liable for actions taken by the supervisor outside the scope of his employment, if:

(a) the employer intended the conduct;

(b) the employer was negligent or reckless;

---

369. *Drinkwater v. Union Carbide Corp.*, 904 F.2d at 861-63 ("it is the environment, not the relationship, that is actionable"). The Supreme Court made clear in *Lehmann v. Toys 'R' Us, Inc.*, 132 N.J. 587 (1993), that the conduct alleged to create a hostile work environment need not have been directed to the plaintiff:

> [T]he plaintiff may use evidence that other women in the workplace were sexually harassed. The plaintiff's work environment is affected not only by conduct directed at herself but also by the treatment of others. A woman's perception that her work environment is hostile to women will obviously be reinforced if she witnesses the harassment of other female workers. Therefore, we hold that the plaintiff need not personally have been the target of each or any instance of offensive or harassing conduct.

370. *See Woods-Pirozzi v. Nabisco Foods*, 290 N.J. Super. 252, 268-269 (App. Div. 1996) (extent of employer's control over third-party harasser is a factor to consider); *Erickson v. Marsh & McLennan Co.*, 117 N.J. at 559-60; *Reynolds v. Atlantic City Convention Center Authority*, 53 FEP at 1865; *Vasto v. Vornado, Inc.*, 8 N.J.A.R. 481, 496-97, 504 (DCR 1983); *White v. PSE&G Co.*, 8 N.J.A.R. 335, 355-56, 364-65 (DCR 1984), *aff'd*, No. A-1496-84 (App. Div. July 16, 1986) (racial harassment by non-supervisory employee); DCR, *Sexual Harassment*, p. 4 (1989); DCR, *Employment Guide to the LAD*, p. 18 (1989); DCR, *A Guide for Employers to the LAD*, pp. 17-19 (June 1986); 29 C.F.R. §1604.11(d)-(e) (1990). The EEOC's guidelines add that the constructive or actual knowledge of supervisors is imputed to the employer and that in determining an employer's liability for the conduct of third parties the EEOC considers the extent of the employer's control over, and any other legal responsibility that the employer may have with respect to, the conduct of such third parties. 29 C.F.R. §1604.11(d)-(e) (1990).

(c) the conduct violated a nondelegable duty of the employer; or

(d) the supervisor purported to act or speak on behalf of the employer and there was reliance upon apparent authority, or he was aided in accomplishing the tort by the existence of the agency relationship.[371]

In discussing these criteria, the Court noted that an employer's failure to establish, publicize and enforce an anti-harassment policy might constitute negligence: "the absence of effective preventative mechanisms will present strong evidence of an employer's negligence." Other courts have held that "an effective grievance procedure—one that is known to the victim and that timely stops the harassment—shields the employer from NJLAD liability for a hostile environment.[372] By definition, there is no negligence if the procedure is effective. A policy known to potential victims also eradicates apparent authority the harasser might otherwise possess."[373]

Finally, an employer will be liable for punitive damages for hostile environment harassment by a supervisory employee only in the event of actual participation by upper management or willful indifference.[374]

The Appellate Division has also held that a labor union may be liable for its members' harassment of another entity's employees on a construction site, because the LAD imposes liability on labor organizations and on individuals who "aid or abet" illegal discrimination.[375]

The Division on Civil Rights (DCR) instructs employers to conspicuously post an anti-sexual harassment policy that reflects top management's disapproval of such conduct.[376] Supervisory training programs should include discussions of techniques to prevent, stop, and/or correct sexual harassment.[377] An internal

---

371. *See Woods-Pirozzi v. Nabisco Foods*, 290 N.J. Super. 252, 271-72 (App. Div. 1996) (harassing employee was not acting within the scope of employment where the employer had a well-publicized policy against harassment; employer not negligent where harassment procedure utilized, albeit not perfectly; employee's supervisory position may have aided in harassment).

372. *Bouton v. BMW of N. Am., Inc.*, 29 F.3d 103, 106-11 (3d Cir. 1994). *See Burlington Indus., Inc. v. Ellerth*, 118 S. Ct. 2257 (1998); *Faragher v. Boca Raton*, 118 S. Ct. 2275 (1998).

373. *Bouton v. BMW of N. Am., Inc.*, 29 F.3d 103, 106-11 (3d Cir. 1994), The nature and degree of discipline required or appropriate when harassment is found to have ocurred remains unclear. In *Matter of Judge Edward Seaman*, 133 N.J. 67 (1993), a judicial disciplinary matter, the Court interpreted its own standards as requiring only a two-month suspension of a high level employee who was found by clear and convincing evidence to have engaged in a pattern of abusive conduct of his judicial law clerk, including two corroborated incidents of inappropriate touching.

374. *See Woods-Pirozzi v. Nabisco Foods*, 290 N.J. Super. 252, 273 (App. Div. 1996) (dismissing punitive damages claim).

375. N.J.S.A. 10:5-12(b) and N.J.S.A. 10:5-12(e). *Baliko v. Stecker*, 275 N.J. Super. (App. Div. 1994) (on remand, the Law Division held that the LAD would be unconstitutional if extended to statements made by union members on a picket line).

grievance procedure, containing confidentiality safeguards, should be established and published.[378]

The DCR recommends that a victim of sexual harassment:

1. Immediately document what occurred, including all remarks and actions; dates, times, and locations of the incidents; and the victim's feelings and responses during and after the incidents.
2. Discuss the problem with someone.
3. Give written notification of the incident to the appropriate supervisor, personnel officer, or EEO/AA official, and state that corrective action is demanded. If this person is the harasser or seems sympathetic to the harasser, complain to someone else in authority in the company.
4. Not quit his or her job because the employer is obligated to take corrective action.
5. File a verified complaint with the DCR if immediate corrective action is not taken.[379]

All claims of sexual harassment should be immediately investigated by the employer, in the same manner as other employee complaints.[380] If the investigation confirms the allegations made, immediate corrective action should be taken, including counselling and, if appropriate, suspending, demoting, or discharging the offender.[381]

---

376. DCR, *Employment Guide to the LAD*, p. 19 (1989); DCR, *A Guide for Employers to the LAD*, p. 18 (June 1986); DCR, *Sexual Harassment*, p. 5 (1989). The EEOC recommends that employers take all steps necessary to prevent harassment, including affirmatively raising the issue, expressing strong disapproval, developing appropriate sanctions, and installing and advising employees of a complaint procedure. 29 C.F.R. §1604.11(f) (1990).

377. DCR, *Employment Guide to the LAD*, p. 19 (1989); DCR, *A Guide for Employers to the LAD*, p. 18 (June 1986).

378. *Id.*

379. DCR, *Your Employment Rights*, p. 11 (Nov. 1986); DCR, *Sexual Harassment*, pp. 5-6 (1989).

380. *Erickson v. Marsh & McLennan Co.*, 117 N.J. at 560; DCR, *A Guide for Employers to the LAD*, p. 18 (June 1986); DCR, *Sexual Harassment*, p. 5 (1989). If the investigation does not confirm the allegations, it is unlawful for the employer to take adverse action against the complainant if s/he had complained in good faith. *See* §4-26. When the employer asserts as a defense in litigation that it conducted an appropriate investigation followed by remedial action, if necessary, the investigation may be discoverable. *See Payton v. New Jersey Turnpike Auth.*, 148 N.J. 524 (1997); *Harding v. Dana Transp., Inc.*, 914 F. Supp. 1084 (D.N.J. 1996).

381. *Erickson v. Marsh & McLennan Co.*, 117 N.J. at 560; *Vasto v. Vornado, Inc.*, 8 N.J.A.R. at 496, 504; DCR, *A Guide for Employers to the LAD*, pp. 18-19 (June 1986); DCR, *Sexual Harassment*, p. 5 (1989). *See* 29 C.F.R. §1604.11(d)-(f) (1990).

4-26 Retaliation

It is an unlawful employment practice to take reprisals against any person because he (1) has opposed any practices or acts outlawed by the LAD *or* (2) has or intends to file a complaint, testify, or assist in any proceeding under the LAD.[382] Thus, employers who have denied promotions to, or filed suit against, employees who pressed claims of discrimination have been guilty of unlawful retaliation.[383]

The determination of what constitutes statutorily-protected opposition to unlawful practices must be made on a case-by-case basis.

> [The] courts have ... to balance the purpose of the Act to protect persons engaging reasonably in activities opposing sexual discrimination, against [the Legislature's] equally manifest desire not to tie the hands of employers in the objective selection and control of personnel... The standard can be little more definitive than the rule of reason applied by a judge or other tribunal to given facts. The requirements of the job and the tolerable limits of conduct in a particular setting must be explored.[384]

An employee who in good faith complains about a prohibited practice is protected, even if the employer, the court, or the DCR ultimately determines that the alleged violation did not occur.[385] But, where allegations of employer misconduct are "raised as a 'smokescreen in challenge to the supervisor's legitimate criticism,' rather than voiced in good faith opposition to perceived employer misconduct," recovery for retaliatory discharge will be denied.[386]

---

382. N.J.S.A. 10:5-12(d); N.J.A.C. 13:4-15.2(a); DCR, *Employment Guide to the LAD*, p. 8 (1989); *Weiss v. Parker Hannifan Corp.*, 747 F.Supp. 1118, 1128-30 (D.N.J. 1990); *White v. PSE&G Co.*, 8 N.J.A.R. 335, 383-84 (DCR 1984), *aff'd*, No. A-1496-84 (App. Div. July 16, 1986). Filing of a complaint is not requisite. *Vasto v. Vornado, Inc.*, 8 N.J.A.R. 481, 496, 506 (DCR 1983); *Weiss v. Parker Hannifan Corp.*, 747 F.Supp. at 1124, 1130.

383. *See Jamison v. Rockaway Tp. Bd. of Educ.*, 242 N.J.Super. 436 (App. Div. 1990) (denial of promotion because employee successfully pursued discrimination claim unlawful); *Buzogany v. Roller Bearing Co.*, 47 FEP 1485, 1988 WL 363820 (D.N.J. July, 26, 1988) (filing defamation suit against employee in retaliation for his pursuit of age discrimination suit unlawful).

384. *Porta v. Rollins Environmental Services (N.J.), Inc.*, 654 F.Supp. 1275, 1284 (D.N.J. 1987), *aff'd without published op.*, 845 F.2d 1014 (3d Cir. 1988) (internal quotation marks omitted). *See* N.J.S.A. 10:5-27.

385. *Drinkwater v. Union Carbide Corp.*, 904 F.2d 853, 865-66 (3d Cir. 1990) (an employer is not free to retaliate against a plaintiff simply because she failed to properly build her sexual harassment claim).

386. *Porta v. Rollins Environmental Services (N.J.), Inc.*, 654 F.Supp. at 1284. An employee who objected to his removal from a position, but did not allege that the removal was discriminatory, was not engaged in protected conduct at that time. *DeJoy v. Comcast Cable Communications, Inc.*, 968 F. Supp. 963 (D.N.J. 1997). *See Reyes v. McDonald Pontiac GMC Truck, Inc.*, 997 F.Supp. 614, 619 (D.N.J. 1996) (where plaintiff never complained that outbursts and name calling were sexual in nature or that they constituted sexual harassment, she was not engaged in protected activity).

A co-employee defending against a charge of sexual harassment is not engaged in protected activity.[387] However, in *Craig v. Suburban Cablevision, Inc.*, 140 N.J. 623 (1995), the Supreme Court held that co-employees who alleged that they were retaliated against because the employer *perceived* them as supporting a complaining employee had standing to sue, despite the fact that they neither sought to exercise rights under the LAD themselves nor said or did anything to aid or abet the complaining employee in her cause. And the Appellate Division has held that a letter from an employee's wife to the Governor, complaining about alleged reverse discrimination, constituted a "protected activity" that satisfied the first prong of the test.[388]

Retaliation against an employee because he is conducting a pre-suit investigation before filing a discrimination action may violate the LAD.[389] However, wrongful conduct by an employee during such an investigation, such as unauthorized removal of files, would normally warrant disciplinary action, and might defeat the employee's retaliation claim.[390]

4-27 Aiding, Abetting, and Attempting Discrimination

It violates the LAD to aid, abet, incite, compel, or coerce the doing of any act prohibited thereby or to attempt to do so.[391] The Third Circuit has held that a "shared intent" to violate the LAD is not requisite to aiding and abetting liability, only knowing assistance or encouragement of a substantial nature. [392] A high

387. *Erickson v. Marsh & McLennan Co.*, 117 N.J. 539, 559-60 (1990) (not retaliation to fire an employee who hired an attorney to defend against sexual-harassment charges); *Drinkwater v. Union Carbide Corp.*, 904 F.2d at 864-65 (explaining *Erickson*).

388. *Wachstein v. Slocum*, 265 N.J.Super. 6, 19 (App. Div.), *certif. denied*, 134 N.J. 563 (1993).

389. *Velantzas v. Colgate-Palmolive Co.*, 109 N.J. 189, 192-93 & n.1 (1988). *Cf.* 42 U.S.C.A. §2000e-3(a) with N.J.S.A. 10:5-12(d). In *Velantzas*, the Supreme Court held that the "retaliatory discharge of an at-will employee for pressing an employment discrimination claim constitutes a discharge that violates clearly mandated public policy interests." The Court permitted plaintiff to proceed with a *Pierce* public-policy cause of action based on her allegations that she was fired because she asked to examine her personnel file to establish a sex discrimination case. The Court observed that such a retaliatory firing violates the public policy expressed in the anti-retaliation provision of Title VII of the Civil Rights Act of 1964, a provision essentially identical to the LAD's anti-retaliation provision.

390. *Cf. NLRB v. Brookshire Grocery Co.*, 919 F.2d 359, 361-66 (5th Cir. 1990) (employee engaged in protected activity forfeits such protection by surreptitiously taking confidential personnel evaluations of co-employees from supervisor's office; to take a contrary position "would elevate pilferage to the status of a protected activity"); *Gimello v. Agency Rent-A-Car Systems, Inc.*, 250 N.J.Super. 338, 350, 353 (App. Div. 1991) (in a LAD handicap discrimination case, court noted that discharged employee took several documents that the employer alleged belonged to it).

391. N.J.S.A. 10:5-12(e). *Cf.* N.J.S.A. 10:5-12(n), which adds the terms "induce" and "conspire" to the list of misconduct by persons assisting the violation of N.J.S.A. 10:5-12(l) or (m). As discussed in §4-22, the DCR has specific regulations addressing the potential aiding and abetting liability of media companies for publishing employment advertisements that violate the LAD.

school principal who created and encouraged a sexually-abusive tone and atmosphere among faculty members that continued to be felt even after he was transferred to another school was held guilty of inciting male teachers to participate in the unlawful conduct.[393]

An employer may file a complaint with the Division on Civil Rights (DCR) requesting assistance by conciliation or other remedial action when one or more of the employer's employees refuse or threaten to refuse to cooperate with the provisions of the LAD.[394]

4-28 Constructive Discharge

A constructive discharge occurs when an employer knowingly permits conditions of employment so intolerable that a reasonable person subject to them would resign.[395] "The issue in a constructive discharge case is whether the employer has done indirectly what it may not do directly by knowingly permitting conditions in employment 'so intolerable that a reasonable person subject to them would resign.' "[396] If the analysis utilized by the Supreme Court in the sex-

---

392. In *Failla v. City of Passaic*, 146 F.3d 149 (3d Cir. 1998), the Third Circuit applied the Restatement of Torts standard for determining aiding and abetting liability. It held that:

> The Restatment requires that an aider and abettor knowingly give assistance or encouragement. It does not incorporate the shared intent requirement rejected in *Passaic Daily News* [*v. Blair*, 308 A.2d 649, 656 (N.J. 1973)]....Accordingly, we predict that the New Jersey Supreme Court would find that an employee aids and abets a violation of the LAD when he knowingly gives substantial assistance or encouragement to the unlawful conduct of his employer.

The Third Circuit specifically rejected the analysis in *Tyson v. Cigna Corp.*, 918 F. Supp. 836, 840, 841 (D.N.J. 1996), *aff'd*, 149 F.3d 1165 (3d Cir. 1998), where the District Court held that non-supervisory employees may not be personally liable under the LAD, and that supervisory employees may be liable only if they actively participate in the discrimination and share the requisite intent:

> Thus, in order to aid or abet another to commit an unlawful act, it is necessary that the defendant wilfully and knowingly associate himself in some way with the unlawful act, and that he wilfully and knowingly seek by some act to make the unlawful act succeed. "The aider and abettor must share the same intent as the one who actually committed the offense. There must be a community of purpose between the actual perpetrator and the aider and abettor."
>
> * * *
>
> In addition, we hold that it is necessary that a supervisor affirmatively engage in discriminatory conduct in order to find individual liability. Mere inaction, passivity, or acquiescence do not in our view rise to the level of aiding and abetting. They do not have the elements of willfulness, intent or commonality of goals—of active purpose—that "aid or abet" requires.

393. *Roberts v. Keansburg Bd. of Educ.*, 5 N.J.A.R. 208, 250, 261 (DCR 1983). *See Frank v. Ivy Club*, 120 N.J. 73, 95 (1990), *cert. denied*, 498 U.S. 1073 (1991) (complaint filed with DCR alleging that a private, nonsectarian university violated the LAD by aiding and abetting public-accommodation gender discrimination committed by eating clubs that were integrally connected to the university).

394. N.J.S.A. 10:5-13.

395. *Muench v. Township of Haddon*, 255 N.J. Super. 288, 302 (App. Div. 1992).

396. *Hyman v. Atlantic City Medical Center*, 1998 WL 135249, p.*11 (D.N.J. 1998).

ual harassment context were to be applied to constructive discharge claims, the issue would be whether a reasonable member of the same protected class as the plaintiff would have felt compelled to resign.[397]

A continuous pattern of harassment over a period of years may constitute constructive discharge.[398] However, a plaintiff's own subjective beliefs are not enough.[399]

4-29 Bona Fide Employee Benefit Plans

The LAD does not interfere with operation of the terms or conditions and administration of any bona fide retirement, pension, employee benefit, or insurance plan or program, including any state or locally administered public retirement system, provided the provisions of those plans or programs are not used to establish a mandatory retirement age.[400] In view of the potential pre-emption of the LAD with respect to employee benefit plans governed by the Employee Retirement Income Security Act of 1974 (ERISA), New Jersey courts will likely interpret the LAD's employee benefit plan provision in harmony with the parallel provision of the federal Age Discrimination in Employment Act of 1967 (ADEA), such that employee benefit plan practices that are lawful under the ADEA will also be lawful under the LAD.[401]

In a 1984 guidance document, the Division on Civil Rights (DCR) stated:

> Generally, any pension plan or retirement program is exempt from the [LAD], if:

---

397. *Lehmann v. Toys 'R' Us, Inc.*, 132 N.J. 587 (1993). *But see Woods-Pirozzi v. Nabisco Foods*, 290 N.J. Super. 252, 276-77 (App. Div. 1996) (constructive discharge claim in sexual harassment case dismissed as a matter of law where one alleged harasser had been discharged and the other was no longer supervising plaintiff; the employer "did not knowingly permit discriminatory conditions so intolerable that a reasonable person subject to them would resign"); *Hyman v. Atlantic City Medical Center*, 1998 WL 135249, p.*9 (D.N.J. 1998) (referring to a "reasonable person in plaintiff's shoes").

398. *Aman v. Cort Furniture Rental Corp.*, 85 F.3d 1074, 1084 (3d Cir. 1996).

399. *Hyman v. Atlantic City Medical Center*, 1998 WL 135249, p*10 (D.N.J. 1998). In *Kass v. Brown Boveri Corp.*, 199 N.J. Super. 42 (App. Div. 1985), defendant attempted to reclassify plaintiff to a lesser job status, allegedly in contravention of his employment contract. The Appellate Division observed that plaintiff "was unjustifiably placed in the position of submitting to ... discharge, accepting a demotion or resorting to a resignation so he might obtain employment in the future without the stigma of discharge." *Id.* at 50. *Cf. Harvard v. Bushberg Bros.*, 137 N.J. Super. 537, 542 (App. Div. 1975), *certif. gr.*, 71 N.J. 493 (1976), *app. dism'd by stipulation*, as stated in *Castellano v. Linden Bd. of Educ.*, 79 N.J. 407, 417 (1979) (employee denied promotion should have continued in her present position until suitable alternative employment found; LAD case).

400. N.J.S.A. 10:5-2.1. *See Nolan v. Otis Elevator Co.*, 102 N.J. 30, 48-50, *cert. denied*, 479 U.S. 820 (1986) (brief discussion of the ADEA's bona fide employee benefit plan exception, 29 U.S.C.A. §623(f)(2), and voluntary early retirement programs).

401. *See, e.g., Nolan v. Otis Elevator Co.*, 197 N.J.Super. 468, 472, 474-75 (App. Div. 1984), *rev'd on other grounds*, 102 N.J. 30, *cert. denied*, 479 U.S. 820 (1986).

1. It is bona fide (actuarially justified and not an attempt to frustrate the purpose of the law).
2. Well defined and administered fairly within the definitions.[402]

The employee benefit plan exception has been found to insulate from attack municipal pension plans which, in accordance with state law, require widows and widowers to remain unmarried in order to remain eligible for a pension.[403]

4-29:1 Mandatory Retirement

As a general rule the LAD prohibits mandatory retirement, unless "justified by lawful considerations other than age."[404] This prohibition may not be circumvented by inclusion of an age for mandatory retirement in a bona fide retirement, pension, employee benefit, or insurance plan or program.[405] There are, however, certain narrowly-defined exceptions.[406] An employee who has attained age 70 and is serving under tenure at a public or private institution of higher education may, at the option of the institution, be required to retire.[407] Justices of the New Jersey Supreme Court,[408] judges of the Superior Court,[409] and judges of the Tax Court[410] are subject to mandatory retirement at age 70.[411] Members of the State Police, except for the Superintendent, are subject to mandatory retirement at age

---

402. DCR, *A Guide for Employers to the LAD*, p. 16 (1984). The DCR states that because pension plans and mandatory retirement involve highly technical and sophisticated areas of the law, employers with specific concerns should contact the DCR for advice. In *Rutgers Council of AAUP Chpts. v. Rutgers, the State University,* 298 N.J. Super. 442, 450-51 (App. Div. 1997), *certif. denied*, 153 N.J. 48 (1998), the Appellate Division held that the denial of health benefits to unmarried domestic partners of university employees did not violate the LAD because the State Health Benefit Plan was *bona fide* and the LAD unambiguously exempts such benefit and insurance programs.

403. *Chausmer v. Commissioners of Employees' Retirement System of Newark*, 150 N.J.Super. 379, 382 (App. Div. 1977).

404. N.J.S.A. 10:5-12(a), -2.1; *Swarts v. Sherwin-Williams Co.*, 244 N.J.Super. 170, 176 (App. Div. 1990).

405. N.J.S.A. 10:5-2.1. As to whether this provision of the LAD may be pre-empted by §514 of the Employee Retirement Income Security Act of 1974 (ERISA), 29 U.S.C. §1144, or §301 of the Labor Management Relations Act of 1947, 29 U.S.C. §185, *see* §4-4.

406. N.J.S.A. 10:5-12(a); DCR, *Employment Guide to the LAD*, p. 11 (1989). These exceptions are premised, in part, on the belief that mandatory retirement "opens opportunities" for other persons. *Boylan v. State*, 116 N.J. 236, 251 (1989), *cert. denied*, 494 U.S. 1061 (1990).

407. N.J.S.A. 10:5-2.2; DCR, *A Guide for Employers to the LAD*, p. 16 (June 1986); DCR, *Your Employment Rights*, p. 8 (Nov. 1986). *See generally Univ. of Medicine & Dentistry of New Jersey v. AAUP,* 223 N.J.Super. 323 (App. Div. 1988), *aff'd on opinion below,* 115 N.J. 29 (1989) (setting forth history, purpose, and scope of this exception).

408. N.J. Const. Art. 6, §6, ¶3; N.J.S.A. 43:6A-7; N.J.S.A. 10:3-1.

409. N.J. Const. Art. 6, §6, ¶3; N.J.S.A. 43:6A-7; N.J.S.A. 10:3-1.

410. N.J.S.A. 2A:3A-15, -19; N.J.S.A. 43:6A-7; N.J.S.A. 10:3-1.

411. In *Gregory v. Ashcroft*, 501 U.S. 452, 111 S.Ct. 2395, 115 L.Ed.2d 410 (1991), the Court held that the ADEA's prohibition against mandatory retirement is not applicable to appointed state-court judges.

55.[412] Members of a police or fire department employed in the service of the State, a county, or a municipality may be subject to mandatory retirement at age 65 or 70.[413]

No other public employees in the service of the state, a county, or a municipality may be required to retire upon attainment of a particular age, unless the employer can show either (1) that the retirement age bears a manifest relationship to the employment in question, or (2) that the employee is unable to adequately perform his duties.[414] If the employer is able to meet either of these subjective standards[415] for permitting mandatory retirement, a contract of tenure or similar arrangement providing for tenure will not bar the employer from requiring the employee to retire.[416]

A private employee, but apparently not a public employee,[417] may be required to retire upon the attainment of a particular age if the employee (1) has been employed in a bona fide executive or high policy-making position for the two years immediately preceding[418] and (2) is entitled to an immediate, non-forfeitable annual retirement benefit of at least $27,000 from a pension, profit-sharing, savings, or deferred retirement plan, or any combination of those plans, of the employer.[419]

Relief for unlawful mandatory retirement under the LAD[420] is limited to administrative proceedings before the DCR.[421] Moreover, the Director of the DCR,

---

412. N.J.S.A. 53:5A-8(a), (c); N.J.S.A. 10:3-1. In *Boylan v. State*, 116 N.J. 236, the Supreme Court held that the mandatory retirement of firefighters and law enforcement officers violates neither the ADEA nor the LAD. *Accord N.J. Attorney General Informal Opinion No. 12-1987* (Feb. 11, 1987).

413. N.J.S.A. 43:15A-99; N.J.S.A. 43:16A-5(1); N.J.S.A. 43:16-1; N.J.S.A. 43:16-1.1; N.J.S.A. 10:3-1; DCR, *A Guide for Employers to the LAD*, p. 16 (June 1986); DCR, *Your Employment Rights*, p. 8 (Nov. 1986). *See* commentary in preceding footnote.

414. N.J.S.A. 10:3-1. This provision states that it supersedes any other State law to the contrary. For example, N.J.S.A. 40A:9-154.6, which permits the mandatory retirement of municipal superintendents of public works at age 70, is no longer enforceable unless one of the two exceptions set forth in the text above is satisfied.

415. Governor's Reconsideration & Recommendation Statement to Assembly No. 1042, L.1985, c.73 (N.J.S.A. 10:3-1 sets forth a subjective standard to govern when a public employer may require an employee to retire because of age), reprinted following N.J.S.A. 10:3-1.

416. N.J.S.A. 10:3-1.

417. N.J.S.A. 10:3-1 provides that, notwithstanding any other law (*e.g.*, the LAD), mandatory retirement of *public* employees is impermissible except for those employees specifically enumerated in N.J.S.A. 10:3-1. N.J.S.A. 10:5-2.2, the provision permitting mandatory retirement of tenured employees of higher education institutions, expressly states it is applicable to public employees regardless of N.J.S.A. 10:3-1. In contrast, N.J.S.A. 10:5-12(a), the provision of the LAD setting forth this executive exception, contains no similar language suspending the bar of N.J.S.A. 10:3-1.

418. A "bona fide executive" is a top-level employee who exercises substantial executive authority over a significant number of employees and a large volume of business. N.J.S.A. 10:5-12(a). A "high policymaking position" is a position in which the individual plays a significant role in developing and recommending implementation of policy. N.J.S.A. 10:5-12(a). These definitions were designed to conform with regulations under the ADEA. Governor's Reconsideration & Recommendation Statement to Assembly No. 1042, L.1985, c.73, reprinted following N.J.S.A. 10:3-1.

in granting relief to the aggrieved party, is limited to ordering reinstatement with back pay and interest.[422]

4-29:2 Voluntary Retirement Incentives

As discussed in the preceding section, the LAD prohibits mandatory retirement except in limited circumstances. It does not, however, prohibit employers from offering, and employees from accepting, financial incentives to retire early.[423] For example, in *Swarts v. Sherwin-Williams Co.*, the court held that the LAD was not violated by an employer's offer of 21 weeks' severance pay, in addition to early retirement benefits to which the employee was already entitled, as an inducement to retire.[424]

On occasion, the Legislature has enacted special legislation designed to induce state and/or local employees to accept voluntary early retirement by creating narrowly-defined windows of opportunity within which enhanced retirement benefits are available.[425] These early retirement programs have been justified as means of rewarding dedicated employees, reducing the need for involuntary layoffs, saving employers the higher costs associated with senior employees, and infusing "new blood" into school districts.[426]

---

419. N.J.S.A. 10:5-12(a); N.J.S.A. 10:3-1. A public employee's remedy would be under N.J.S.A. 10:3-1, not N.J.S.A. 10:5-12(a), -12.1.

Compliance with this provision of the LAD will not necessarily insulate an employer from liability for age discrimination, because the ADEA affords greater protection to employees. In particular, under the ADEA, the retirement allowance threshold is $44,000, not $27,000, and the bona fide executive/high policymaker exemption is limited to employees age 65 and over. 29 U.S.C.A. §631(c)(1).

420. N.J.S.A. 10:5-12(a))

421. N.J.S.A. 10:5-12.1.

422. N.J.S.A. 10:5-12.1. A public employee who is mandatorily retired in contravention of N.J.S.A. 10:3-1 is entitled to reinstatement, back pay, and interest. N.J.S.A. 10:3-1.

423. *Swarts v. Sherwin-Williams Co.*, 244 N.J.Super. 170, 174-79 (App. Div. 1990). *See Nolan v. Otis Elevator Co.*, 102 N.J. 30, 48-50, *cert. denied*, 479 U.S. 820 (1986) (brief discussion of voluntary early retirement programs under the ADEA).

424. *Swarts v. Sherwin-Williams Co.*, 244 N.J.Super. at 174-79. Note that in 1990 Congress amended §4 of the ADEA, 29 U.S.C.A. §623, to expressly permit voluntary early retirement incentive plans.

425. *See, e.g.*, L.1991, c.137 (certain state employees); L.1991, c.206 (certain state police officers); L.1991, c.229 (certain non-state public employees); L.1991, c.230 (certain other public employees); L.1991, c.231 (certain school board employees).

426. Schwaneberg, "Early Retirement Plan Enacted for Localities," *The Star-Ledger* of Newark, p. 9 (July 27, 1991), quoting co-sponsors of L.1991, c.229; L.1991, c.230; and L.1991, c.231; 18 *Pension Reporter (BNA)*, pp. 1517-18 (Aug. 19, 1991).

4-30 Bona Fide Occupational Qualifications

The LAD provides generally that it does not prohibit the establishment and maintenance of bona fide occupational qualifications (BFOQs).[427] It provides specifically that employers are not prohibited from refusing to hire any individual on the basis of sex, and labor organizations are not prohibited from excluding individuals from apprenticeship programs on the basis of sex, where sex is a BFOQ reasonably necessary to the normal operation of the particular business or enterprise.[428]

Nor are employers or employment agencies prohibited from circulating advertisements, using employment applications, or making inquiries in connection with prospective employment that express limitations, specifications, or discrimination as to age, ancestry, eligibility for service in the Armed Forces, color, creed, handicap, marital status, national origin, race, or sex, if based upon a BFOQ.[429]

DCR regulations provide that the employer, labor organization, or employment agency bears the burden of establishing that an otherwise impermissible characteristic is a BFOQ.[430] A BFOQ will not be found to exist where it is based on, *inter alia*:

1. A characteristic generally attributable to a protected class, rather than the individual capacities of the members of that class.[431]
2. Assumptions as to the comparative general employment characteristics of persons of a particular protected class, such as their turnover rate.[432]

---

427. N.J.S.A. 10:5-2.1. This provision was added in 1962 when the LAD was amended, among other things, to prohibit age discrimination. L.1962, c.37.

428. As to employers, *see* N.J.S.A. 10:5-12(a). This provision was added in 1970 at the same time the LAD was amended to prohibit discrimination based on sex or marital status. L.1970, c.80. *See* N.J.A.C. 13:11-1.5; *Passaic Daily News v. Blair*, 63 N.J. 474 (1973) (upholding validity of DCR regulations). As to labor organizations, *see* N.J.S.A. 10:5-12(b); N.J.A.C. 13:5-1.2(a)(3).

429. N.J.S.A. 10:5-12(c), -4.1. *See* N.J.A.C. 13:7 Foreword; N.J.A.C. 13:11-1.1(a), -1.5. Employment advertising and pre-employment inquiries are discussed in §§4-1 and 4-23.

430. N.J.A.C. 13:11-1.5(c). *See Spragg v. Shore Care*, 293 N.J. Super. 33, 51-52 (App. Div. 1996) ("It must be understood that the burden is on the employer to establish the facts bringing it within the BFOQ exception. The employer must show that there is a factual basis for its conclusion that the essence of its business operation would be undermined by failing to employ members of one sex exclusively. ...The test is one of business necessity, not business convenience.").

431. N.J.A.C. 13:11-1.5(b); *Passaic Daily News v. Blair*, 63 N.J. at 478, 492.

432. N.J.A.C. 13:11-1.5(d)(1); *Passaic Daily News v. Blair*, 63 N.J. at 492. *See, e.g., Hayman v. Funk*, 8 N.J.A.R. 27, 31, 33 (DCR 1984) (higher turnover rate of black employees).

3. Stereotyped characteristics of the protected classes, such as their mechanical ability or aggressiveness.[433]
4. Customer, client, co-worker, or employer preference.[434]
5. Historical usage, tradition, or custom.[435]
6. The necessity of providing separate facilities of a personal nature, such as rest or dressing rooms.[436]

Sex is a BFOQ where an employee of a particular sex is necessary for authenticity or genuineness (such as for an actor or actress, a fashion model, or a male vocalist), or where the job necessarily involves intimate personal contact with persons of the opposite sex (*e.g.* masseuse, masseur or dressing room attendant).[437] Thus, it has been found permissible for a juvenile detention center to limit employment as "girl supervisors" to females and as "boy supervisors" to males, because it would be "inappropriate to have men strip-searching girl inmates and women strip-searching boy inmates."[438] However, it is not permissible for volunteer fire companies to limit their membership to men.[439]

In view of the Supreme Court's observation that the DCR's BFOQ regulations are substantially similar to the guidelines adopted by the EEOC and utilized by

---

433. N.J.A.C. 13:11-1.5(d)(2); *Passaic Daily News v. Blair*, 63 N.J. at 492. *See, e.g.*, *Hayman v. Funk*, 8 N.J.A.R. 27 (respondents believed, based on experience with three prior employees, that black employees as a group are "undependable" and "unreliable"); *Goodman v. London Metals Exchange, Inc.*, 86 N.J. 19, 27, 32 (1981) (employer believed that women were reluctant to be away from home for four or five days at a time).

434. N.J.A.C. 13:11-1.5(d)(3). *See, e.g.*, *EEOC v. Sedita*, 755 F.Supp. at 811 (under Title VII, defendant must prove that clients would stop patronizing a women's health club if males were hired as employees). The Appellate Division has held that where the BFOQ is based on customer preferences, the employer has the additional burden to prove that there are no reasonable alternatives to the sex-based policy. "Thus, to satisfy its burden based on client privacy rights, an employer has to show that its clients would not consent to service by members of the opposite sex, and that clients would stop patronizing the business if members of the opposite sex were allowed to perform the service." *Spragg v. Shore Care*, 293 N.J. Super. 33, 52 (App. Div. 1996).

435. N.J.A.C. 13:11-1.5(d)(3). *But see Twomey v. Englewood Hospital Ass'n*, 5 N.J.A.R. 188 (DCR 1981), *rev'd*, No. A-3523-80 (App. Div. June 14, 1982), *certif. denied*, 91 N.J. 568 (1982). *Twomey* is discussed at length in §4-19:1.

436. N.J.A.C. 13:11-1.5(d)(4).

437. N.J.A.C. 13:11-1.5(e); *Passaic Daily News v. Blair*, 63 N.J. at 478; DCR, *Employment Guide to the LAD*, pp. 11-12 (1989); DCR, *A Guide for Employers to the LAD*, pp. 20-21 (June 1986). *See, e.g.*, *Paterson Tavern & Grill Owners Ass'n v. Hawthorne*, 108 N.J.Super. 433, 441 (App. Div.), *rev'd on other grounds*, 57 N.J. 180 (1970) (positing that the refusal to employ women in an all-male Turkish bath establishment would be permissible); *EEOC v. Sedita*, 755 F.Supp. 808 (N.D. Ill. 1991) (women's fitness center failed to prove that its policy of not hiring males was a BFOQ under Title VII); *Nat'l Organization for Women v. Little League Baseball, Inc.*, 127 N.J.Super. 522, 532 (App. Div.), *summarily aff'd without op.*, 67 N.J. 320 (1974) (the LAD's sex BFOQ pertaining to public accommodations is facially limited to situations involving the changing of clothes and the performance of bodily functions). *Cf. UAW v. Johnson Controls, Inc.*, 499 U.S. 187, 111 S.Ct. 1196, 113 L.Ed.2d 158, 178 n.4 (1991) (Blackman, J., for the Court), with 113 L.Ed.2d at 187 n.8 (White, J., concurring in part). *See Spragg v. Shore Care*, 293 N.J. Super. 33, 52-53 (App. Div. 1996) (trial judge properly permitted jury to decide legitimacy of asserted BFOQ defense to assigning male home health care aids to male patients only; job duties included toileting, changing clothes and cleaning intimate body parts, all performed in the clients' homes).

the federal courts under Title VII,[440] the United States Supreme Court's opinion in *UAW v. Johnson Controls, Inc.*, striking down a policy that barred all fertile women from jobs involving lead exposure, is instructive.[441] Because the policy in *Johnson Controls* was not facially neutral, the Court applied a BFOQ analysis, and not the more lenient business-necessity standard applicable to facially-neutral policies challenged as having a disparate impact on a protected class.[442] The Court then parsed the language of §703(e)(1) of Title VII,[443] which is in relevant aspects identical to the BFOQ language of the New Jersey statute.[444]

> First, the job qualification must not be so peripheral to the central mission of the employer's business that no discrimination could be reasonably *necessary* to the normal operation of the particular business.
>
> * * *
>
> Second, the employer must show either that all or substantially all persons excluded would be unable to perform safely and efficiently the duties of the job involved, or that it is impossible or highly impractical to deal with them on an individual basis.[445]

The DCR will provide advance guidance as to whether a particular pre-employment inquiry or employment advertisement falls within the BFOQ exception.[446] The DCR's opinion may also be obtained as to whether an otherwise impermissible characteristic is a BFOQ for a particular job for which an advertisement is to be published.[447] The DCR's opinion, whether oral or written, is binding on the agency as long as it is rendered before publication and the request fully and accurately disclosed the relevant facts pertaining to the particular job.[448]

---

438. *Terry v. Mercer County Freeholders Bd.*, 173 N.J.Super. 249, 252, 255 (App. Div. 1980), *aff'd on other grounds*, 86 N.J. 141 (1981). *See Csizmadia v. Fauver*, 746 F.Supp 483 (D.N.J. 1988) (civil rights suit against N.J. Dept. of Corrections challenging the method of assignment of male and female correction officers and involving the competing concerns of the officers' employment rights, the prisoners' privacy and religious rights, and the state's interest in maintaining security; LAD claims dismissed on Eleventh Amendment grounds).

439. *Hebard v. Basking Ridge Fire Co.*, 164 N.J.Super. 77 (App. Div. 1978), *app. dism'd*, 81 N.J. 294 (1979). Some statutes create BFOQs. For example, N.J.S.A. 30:8-10, which permits a sheriff to hire up to three county jail matrons, specifies that the matrons must be female.

440. *Passaic Daily News v. Blair*, 63 N.J. at 492.

441. *UAW v. Johnson Controls, Inc.*, 499 U.S. 187, 111 S.Ct. 1196, 113 L.Ed.2d 158 (1991).

442. *Id.* at 170-74. The BFOQ defense is an affirmative defense as to which defendant bears the burden of persuasion.

443. 42 U.S.C.A. §2000e-2(e)(1).

444. N.J.S.A. 10:5-12(a).

III. STANDARDS OF PROOF

4-31 Overview

In *Peper v. Princeton Univ. Bd. of Trustees*, the New Jersey Supreme Court recognized two separate methods of proof of discrimination under the New Jersey Constitution, the LAD, and other state laws:

> "Disparate treatment" ... is the most easily understood type of discrimination. The employer simply treats some people less favorably than others because of their race, color, [*etc.*]. Proof of discriminatory motive is critical, although it can in some situations be inferred from the mere fact of differences in treatment. Undoubtedly disparate treatment was the most obvious evil Congress had in mind when it enacted Title VII.
>
> Claims of disparate treatment may be distinguished from claims that stress "disparate impact." The latter involve employment practices that are facially neutral in their treatment of different groups but that in fact fall more harshly on one group than another and cannot be justified by business necessity. Proof of discriminatory motive ... is not required under a disparate impact theory.[449]

---

445. *UAW v. Johnson Controls, Inc.*, 113 L.Ed.2d at 184 (White, J., concurring in part) (internal quotation marks omitted). *Accord N.J. Attorney General Formal Opinion No. 5-1983* (Apr. 21, 1983) (discussing ADEA's BFOQ in the context of New Jersey's mandatory retirement statutes); *EEOC v. State of New Jersey*, 620 F.Supp. 977, 981-82 (D.N.J. 1985) (opinion on denial of preliminary injunction), *supplemented*, 631 F.Supp. 1506, 1513-14 (D.N.J. 1986) (opinion on the merits), *aff'd without published op.*, 815 F.2d 694 (3d Cir. 1987) (mandatory retirement of N.J. State Police at age 55 is a BFOQ under ADEA); *N.J. Attorney General Formal Opinion No. 1-1984* (July 11, 1984) (New Jersey's maximum hiring age for firefighters and law enforcement officers violative of ADEA unless justified as a BFOQ; insufficient evidence to support BFOQ); *Dumont v. Jersey Shore Medical Center*, 1 N.J.A.R. 249, 258 (DCR 1980) (failure of proof that security guard's "advanced age" was a BFOQ warranting his termination). *But see Sgambati v. Fairview*, 3 N.J.A.R. 412, 413-14 (DCR 1981) (Attorney General argues that statutory maximum hiring ages applicable to paid firefighters and law enforcement officers not violative of LAD); *Pineman v. Paramus*, 4 N.J.A.R. 407, 412, 414 (DCR 1981), *aff'd*, No. A-5336-80 (App. Div. Apr. 1, 1982) (DCR holds that aforesaid maximum hiring ages not violative of LAD). *See The Passaic Daily News v. Blair*, 63 N.J. 474, 492 (1973).

446. N.J.A.C. 13:7 Foreword; N.J.S.A. 52:14B-8. Pre-employment inquiries are discussed in §4-23.

447. N.J.A.C. 13:11-1.6(a); *Passaic Daily News v. Blair*, 63 N.J. at 478; DCR, *Employment Guide to the LAD*, pp. 11-12 (1989); DCR, *A Guide for Employers to the LAD*, pp. 20-21 (June 1986); N.J.S.A. 52:14B-8. Employment advertising is discussed in §4-22.

448. N.J.A.C. 13:11-1.6(c); *Passaic Daily News v. Blair*, 63 N.J. at 479. The requesting party should obtain from the DCR the identification (or clearance) number the agency has assigned to the request. *See* N.J.A.C. 13:11-1.6(d)-(e); DCR, *Employment Guide to the LAD*, p. 12 (1989).

In meeting their burdens of production and persuasion, the parties may not rest upon the mere allegations of the pleadings or conclusory and unsupported assertions and denials contained in affidavits or trial testimony.[450]

4-32 Disparate Treatment—*McDonnell Douglas* Test

New Jersey courts have traditionally "looked to federal law as a key source of interpretive authority" for the substantive and procedural standards that govern claims under the LAD.[451] As explained in *Grigoletti v. Ortho Pharmaceutical Corp.*,[452] the Supreme Court has adopted for use under the LAD the analysis outlined by the United States Supreme Court in *McDonnell Douglas Corp. v. Green*:[453]

> [T]he *McDonnell Douglas* approach established the elements of a *prima facie* case of unlawful discrimination. The plaintiff must demonstrate by a preponderance of the evidence that he or she (1) belongs to a protected class, (2) applied and was qualified for a position for which the employer was seeking applicants, (3) was rejected despite adequate qualifications, and (4)

---

449. *Peper v. Princeton Univ. Bd. of Trustees*, 77 N.J. 55, 81-82 (1978), *quoting Teamsters v. United States*, 431 U.S. 324, 335-36 n.15 (1977) (citations omitted). The disproportionate impact of a facially-neutral policy may be circumstantial evidence of the intent to discriminate needed to prove a case under the disparate treatment theory. *Massarsky v. General Motors Corp.*, 706 F.2d 111, 118 & n.14 (3d Cir.), *cert. denied*, 464 U.S. 937 (1983). Disparate treatment may sometimes be shown through statistical proofs, although their usefulness will depend upon the totality of the surrounding facts and circumstances. *Maietta v. United Parcel Service, Inc.*, 749 F.Supp. 1344, 1372 (D.N.J. 1990), *aff'd without published op.*, 932 F.2d 960 (3d Cir. 1991).

450. *Retter v. Georgia Gulf Corp.*, 755 F.Supp. 637, 640-44 (D.N.J. 1991), *aff'd*, 975 F.2d 1551 (3d Cir. 1992); *Maietta v. United Parcel Service, Inc.*, 749 F.Supp. at 1357 & n.20, 1371-72; *Reynolds v. Atlantic City Convention Center Authority*, 1990 WL 267417, 53 FEP 1852 (D.N.J. 1990), *aff'd without published op.*, 925 F.2d 419 (3d Cir. 1991); *Baxter v. AT&T Communications*, 712 F.Supp. 1166 (D.N.J. 1989).

451. *Grigoletti v. Ortho Pharmaceutical Corp.*, 118 N.J. 89, 97 (1990) (listing prior decisions of the Court applying the analysis of federal anti-discrimination statutes). The use of federal standards under the LAD provides a "reasonable degree of symmetry and uniformity" among the various overlapping statutory schemes. *Id.* at 107, 108. Nonetheless, in appropriate circumstances, New Jersey courts "are free to apply our own concept of that which is right and proper." *Castellano v. Linden Bd. of Educ.*, 158 N.J. Super. 350, 360 (App. Div. 1978), *aff'd in part, rev'd in part on other grounds*, 79 N.J. 407 (1979) (declining to follow a U.S. Supreme Court Title VII decision pertaining to pregnancy disability benefits). *See also Burke v. Township of Franklin*, 261 N.J. Super. 592, 601-02 (App. Div. 1993) (looking to the ADEA for guidance in interpreting the LAD and reading into the LAD the federal statutory provision limiting age discrimination protection to individuals 40 years of age and older); *Waldron v. SL Indus., Inc.*, 849 F. Supp. 996 (D.N.J. 1994), *rev'd on other grounds*, 56 F.3d 491 (3d Cir. 1995) ("Age discrimination claims under the LAD and the ADEA are governed by the same standards and burden of proof structures applicable under Title VII of the Civil Rights Act of 1964.").

452. *Grigoletti v. Ortho Pharmaceutical Corp.*, 118 N.J. at 97-98, *quoting Andersen v. Exxon Co.*, 89 N.J. 483, 492 (1982), and *Erickson v. Marsh & McLennan Co.*, 117 N.J. 539, 550 (1990) (footnotes appearing in the indented quote in the text above have been suppied).

453. 411 U.S. 792 (1973).

after rejection the position remained open and the employer continued to seek applicants for persons of plaintiff's qualifications.[454] Establishment of the *prima facie* case gives rise to a presumption that the employer unlawfully discriminated against the applicant. The burden of going forward then shifts to the employer to rebut the presumption of undue discrimination by articulating some legitimate, nondiscriminatory reason for the employee's rejection.[455] The plaintiff then has the opportunity to prove by a preponderance of the evidence that the legitimate nondiscriminatory reason articulated by the defendant was not the true reason for the employment decision but was merely a pretext for discrimination.[456] In such cases the ultimate burden of persuading the trier of fact that the defendant intentionally discriminated against the plaintiff remains at all times with the plaintiff; only the burden of going forward shifts.[457]

However, the Court has never embraced the *McDonnell Douglas* test literally, invariably, or inflexibly. We have recognized [, as has the Supreme Court,] that the *McDonnell Douglas* criteria "provide only a general framework for analyzing unlawful discrimination claims and must be modified where appropriate."

---

454. Where an employer has no need to solicit additional applicants, a rejected candidate will be unable to invoke the *McDonnell Douglas* test because the fourth prong by definition cannot be satisfied. *Lloyd v. Stone Harbor*, 179 N.J. Super. 496, 520-21 (Ch. Div. 1981); *Oare v. Midlantic National Bank/Merchants*, 54 FEP at 1532-33.

455. Defendant is not required to prove that the proffered reason or reasons were the exclusive basis for the adverse action. *Retter v. Georgia Gulf Corp.*, 755 F. Supp. 637, 639, 643 (D.N.J. 1991).

456. Plaintiff "may succeed in this either directly by persuading the court that a discriminatory reason more likely motivated the employer or indirectly by showing that the employer's proffered explanation is unworthy of credence." *Slohoda v. United Parcel Service, Inc.*, 207 N.J. Super. 145, 155 (App. Div.) *cert. denied*, 104 N.J. 400 (1986), *quoting Texas Dept. of Community Affairs v. Burdine*, 450 U.S. 248, 256 (1981). *Accord Turner v. Schering-Plough Corp.*, 901 F.2d 335, 342 (3d Cir. 1990) (evidence of "inconsistencies and implausibilities" in defendant's proffered explanation of the adverse employment action); *Mate v. American Brands, Inc.*, 1990 WL 69277, p. *5 (D.N.J. 1990) (same). *See, e.g.*, *Gimello v. Agency Rent-A-Car Systems, Inc.*, 250 N.J. Super. 338, 345-50, 352-54 (App. Div. 1991). *See Johnson v. Penske Truck Leasing Co.*, 949 F. Supp. 1153, 1172 (D.N.J. 1996) (to establish pretext, employee "must point to some evidence from which a factfinder could reasonably disbelieve [the employer's] articulated legitimate, non-discriminatory reason or infer that discrimination was more likely than not a motivating or determinative cause of employment action"); *Ditzel v. University of Medicine & Dentistry of New Jersey*, 962 F. Supp. 595, 604 (D.N.J. 1997) (plaintiff cannot merely show that the employer's decision was wrong; courts are not permitted to second-guess performance standards or make personnel decisions).

457. If plaintiff establishes that defendant's asserted reasons for the adverse employment action were pretextual, he still must establish that defendant engaged in intentional discrimination. *Retter v. Georgia Gulf Corp.*, 755 F. Supp. at 643; *Erickson v. Marsh & McLennan Co.*, 117 N.J. at 561 (an "employee can be fired for a false cause or no cause at all. That firing may be unfair but it is not illegal.").

The *McDonnell Douglas* shifting-burden formula need not be employed when plaintiff has direct evidence of discrimination.[458]

Plaintiff's continuing burden of persuasion was re-emphasized in *St. Mary's Honor Ctr. v. Hicks*[459] where the Supreme Court held that defendant need not persuade the court it was actually motivated by the articulated reasons. The employer's burden after plaintiff proves a *prima facie* case is only to produce evidence of a nondiscriminatory reason. Once the employer does that, the plaintiff must persuade the jury not just that the reason articulated by defendant was not the "real reason" for the challenged action, but that the "real reason" was intentional discrimination. The trier of fact is free to infer intentional discrimination if it disbelieves the employer's proffered reasons and also finds that plaintiff has presented a *prima facie* case. However: "It is not enough, in other words, to disbelieve the employer; the fact finder must believe the plaintiff's explanation of intentional discrimination."[460]

New Jersey courts have applied the *Hicks* analysis to claims under the LAD.[461]

4-32:1 The *Prima Facie* Case

The elements of plaintiff's *prima facie* case will vary depending upon the circumstances, and the courts are divided as to precisely what the fourth prong of the *prima facie* case requires. The first three prongs are well-settled: plaintiff must prove that (1) he is a member of the protected class, (2) he was qualified for the job he sought or was performing the job at a level that met the employer's legitimate expectations, and (3) adverse action was taken against him.

Some decisions describe the fourth prong as requiring plaintiff to prove only that the employer sought someone to perform the same work after he was removed from the position.[462] Others describe the fourth prong as requiring proof that the employer sought replacements with the same or lesser qualifications than

---

458. *Baxter v. AT&T Communications*, 712 F. Supp. 1166, 1172 (D.N.J. 1989); *Oare v. Midlantic National Bank/Merchants*, 54 FEP at 1532; *Glover v. Canada Dry Bottling Co.*, 1990 WL 43739, p. *3 (D.N.J. 1990). *See* §4-33.

459. 509 U.S. 502 (1993).

460. *St. Mary's Honor Center v. Hicks*, 509 U.S. 502 (1993).

461. *Maiorino v. Schering-Plough Corp.*, 302 N.J. Super. 323 (App. Div.), *certif. denied*, 152 N.J. 189 (1997); *Murray v. Newark Housing Authority*, 311 N.J. Super. 163, 174 (Law Div. 1998). *See McKenna v. Pacific Rail Serv.*, 32 F.3d 820 (3d Cir. 1994) (predicting New Jersey Supreme Court would adopt the *Hicks* rule under the LAD, and that the court would not limit that rule to prospective application); *Waldron v. SL Indus.*, 56 F.3d 491 (3d Cir. 1995) (applying *Hicks* to LAD claim); *Tarino v. Kraft Foodservice, Inc.*, 1996 WL 84670, p. *6 (D.N.J. 1996); *McKenzie v. Merck & Co.*, 1993 WL 493306 at *5-6 (D.N.J. Nov. 24, 1993) (applying *Hicks* to LAD claim); *Stewart v. Personnel Pool of Am., Inc.*, 1993 WL 525575, at *3 (D.N.J. Dec. 16, 1993), *aff'd*, 30 F.3d 1488 (3d Cir. 1994) (same).

the plaintiff.[463] Still others require proof that the position was filled by someone outside the protected class who had qualifications similar to plaintiff's.[464] However, a mere showing that there was a change in personnel in plaintiff's department is insufficient to satisfy the fourth element of the *prima facie* case; it must be demonstrated that the employer sought a replacement for plaintiff.[465]

When plaintiff's job has been eliminated as part of a reduction in force (RIF), he need not establish that the employer sought a replacement, but only that "he was laid off from a job for which he was qualified while other workers not in the protected class were retained."[466] Some opinions have held that because the LAD does not prohibit "essential belt tightening having no discriminatory motive,"[467] plaintiff's burden of persuasion is heightened in the case of a RIF:

---

462. *Maher v. New Jersey Transit Rail Operations, Inc.*, 125 N.J. 455, 480-81 (1991); *Clowes v. Terminix Int'l, Inc.*, 109 N.J. 575, 597 (1988); *Jansen v. Food Circus Supermarkets, Inc.*, 110 N.J. 363, 382 (1988); *Erickson v. Marsh & McLennan Co.*, 117 N.J. 539, 550-51, 553-54 (1990); *Gimello v. Agency Rent-A-Car Systems, Inc.*, 250 N.J. Super. 338, 355-56 (App. Div. 1991).

463. In both *Clowes* and *Erickson*, the Court indicated that it was quoting the four-part test set forth in *Loeb v. Textron, Inc.*, 600 F.2d 1003 (1st Cir. 1979). In *Loeb*, the fourth part was actually stated as follows: the "employer sought a replacement with qualifications similar to [plaintiff's], thus demonstrating a continued need for the same services and skills." 600 F.2d at 1013. *Accord Maietta v. United Parcel Service, Inc.*, 749 F. Supp. at 1371 (also noting that *Loeb* held the evidence that the replacement was not a member of the protected class may be probative of discrimination). *See Catalane v. Gilian Instrument Corp.*, 271 N.J. Super. 476, 496-97 (App. Div.), *cert. denied*, 136 N.J. 298 (1994) (to establish *prima facie* case of age-biased discharge plaintiff was required to prove "that: 1) he was a member of the protected class; 2) he was performing the job at the level that met the employer's legitimate expectations; 3) he was discharged; and 4) the employer sought another to perform the same work after the complainant had been removed from the position").

464. *See, e.g.*, *Keller v. Orix Credit Alliance, Inc.*, 130 F.3d 1101, 1108 (3d Cir. 1997); *Waldron v. SL Industries*, 56 F.3d 491, 494 (3d Cir. 1995); *Greenberg v. Camden Vocational Schools*, 310 N.J. Super. 189, 198-99, 201 (App. Div. 1998).

465. *Id.* at 554-55 (fact that defendant had three account executives prior to plaintiff's discharge and four at the time of trial insufficient to meet plaintiff's *prima facie* burden). *Cf. Baxter v. AT&T Communications*, 712 F. Supp. at 1173 (mere change in supervisors does not establish that plaintiff was intentionally given inadequate training because of his race).

466. *Baker v. The National State Bank*, 312 N.J. Super. 268 (App. Div.), *certif. granted*, 156 N.J. 425 (1998); *Murray v. Newark Housing Authority*, 311 N.J. Super. 163, 172 (Law Div. 1998) ("To establish disparate treatment as a result of age in a reduction in force case such as this in which plaintiff's job was eliminated, plaintiff must establish initially that: (1) statutory protections against age discrimination apply to him; (2) he was laid off from a job for which he was qualified; and (3) other, younger workers were treated more favorably.") (footnote omitted). *Turner v. Schering-Plough Corp.*, 901 F.2d at 342. *Accord Massarsky v. General Motors Corp.*, 706 F.2d 111, 118 & n.13 (3d Cir.), *cert. denied*, 464 U.S. 937 (1983); *Baxter v. AT&T Communications*, 712 F. Supp. at 1172; *Reilly v. Prudential Prop. & Cas. Ins. Co.*, 653 F. Supp. 725, 730-32 (D.N.J. 1987); *Johnson v. Trenton State College*, 1985 WL 6095, 40 FEP 1505, 1507 (D.N.J. Sept. 11, 1985); *Gorham v. AT&T Co.*, 762 F. Supp. 1138, 1143 (D.N.J. 1991). *See Geldreich v. American Cyanamid Co.*, 299 N.J. Super. 478, 489-90 (App. Div. 1997) (employee terminated in RIF made *prima facie* case by showing that job duties were reassigned to substantially younger employees; it was not incumbent upon plaintiff to prove that the persons who succeeded to his job functions were of equal or lesser qualifications); *Jackson v. Georgia-Pacific Corp.*, 296 N.J. Super. 1, 17 (App. Div. 1996) (jury correctly instructed that plaintiff was required to prove adequate job performance as part of his *prima facie* case), *certif. denied*, 149 N.J. 141 (1997); *Leahey v. Singer Sewing Co.*, 302 N.J. Super. 68, 76 (Law Div. 1996) (to demonstrate a *prima facie* case in reduction-in-force cases, "the plaintiff must show that he [she] was qualified, he [she] was laid off, and other unprotected workers were retained.").

> [C]laimant must [be able] to demonstrate specific evidence that could support an inference that the employer did not act for non-discriminatory reasons.
>
> ***
>
> [E]vidence...demonstrat[ing] only that [claimant] performed competently in his previous jobs [is insufficient because] ... the essence of a RIF is that competent employees who in more prosperous times would continue and flourish with a company may nevertheless have to be fired.[468]

However, that line of authority was rejected by the Appellate Division in *Baker v. The National State Bank.*[469] Moreover, an employer is not obligated by the LAD to preserve the employment of a member of the protected class by bumping another employee.[470]

In a failure-to-promote case, the *McDonnell Douglas prima facie* case requires proof that similarly-situated persons outside the protected class—individuals with equivalent qualifications working in the same job category—were promoted while plaintiff was not.[471] Qualifications would include educational level, job experience, and quality of work performed.[472] In age discrimination cases the al-

---

467. *McBride v. Princeton Univ.*, 1991 WL 66758, p. *5 (D.N.J. April 24, 1991) (internal quotation marks omitted), *aff'd*, 950 F.2d 723 (3d Cir. 1991). In *O'Shea v. The News Tribune*, 95 N.J.A.R. 2d (CRT) 21 (1995), the Administrative Law Judge set the following standard for establishing a *prima facie* case of alleged discriminatory failure to recall. The complainant must demonstrate:

(1) he is a member of a protected class,

(2) he was qualified for the position from which he was terminated and had recall rights in that position,

(3) that despite his qualifications he was not recalled, and

(4) other employees with a lesser right to recall were recalled.

Id. at 22 (*citing Lanyon v. University of Delaware*, 544 F. Supp. 1262 (D. Del. 1982), *aff'd*, 709 F.3d 1493 (3d Cir. 1983)). *See EEOC v. MCI Int'l, Inc.*, 829 F. Supp. 1438 (D.N.J. 1993).

468. *Id.* at pp. *6-7, quoting *Healy v. New York Life Ins. Co.*, 860 F.2d 1209, 1219-20 (3d Cir. 1988), *cert. denied*, 490 U.S. 1098 (1989).

469. 312 N.J. Super. 268 (App. Div. 1998). *See also Geldreich v. American Cyanamid Co.*, 299 N.J. Super. 478, 489-91 (App. Div. 1997). *Cf. Murray v. Newark Housing Authority, supra,* n. 456.

470. *McBride v. Princeton Univ.*, 1991 WL 66758 at p. *5 (D.N.J.), *aff'd*, 950 F.2d 723 (3d Cir. 1991).

471. In *Peper v. Princeton Univ. Bd. of Trustees*, 77 N.J. 55, 84-85 (1978), a failure to promote case, the Court described plaintiffs' *prima facie* burden as including proof "that he or she is a member of a protected class and qualified for the position sought, but was denied the position while others of similar or lesser qualification achieved it"). Same "job category" means plaintiff and the person(s) preferred were in the same "promotional stream" and had similar responsibilities. *Id.* at 85; *Dixon v. Rutgers*, 110 N.J. 432, 444-45 (1988). *See Esposito v. Township of Edison*, 306 N.J. 280, 289 (App. Div. 1997), *certif. denied*, 156 N.J. 384 (1998).

472. *Peper v. Princeton Univ. Bd. of Trustees*, 77 N.J. at 85. *See Andersen v. Exxon Co.*, 89 N.J. 483, 491, 499 (1982) (experience, education, intelligence, skills, stamina, physical strength, dexterity).

legedly favored employee must be "sufficiently younger" to warrant an inference of discrimination.[473]

In a reverse discrimination case, the rebuttable presumption of discrimination established by a *prima facie* case does not apply. Instead, the first prong of the employee's proofs is modified to require the employee to show that he has been victimized by an unusual employer who discriminates against the majority.[474] This is an appropriate burden to place on a plaintiff in such an unusual discrimination case.[475] It may be satisfied by offering evidence that the employer viewed the plaintiff's majority status in a negative light.[476] The Appellate Division has held that when a majority-group plaintiff alleges discrimination because he associated with a member of the protected group, that is the "functional equivalent of being a member of the protected group."[477]

As the level of job increases, the issues of proof become more difficult because matters of personality and subjective judgments of immediate supervisors become more critical in the decision making process.[478] The mere fact that an employee who had previously received favorable performance evaluations commences to receive unfavorable ones from a new supervisor with a different management philosophy is not indicative of discrimination.[479] Similarly, positive performance evaluations while employed in a lower-level position are insufficient proof that an employee has the requisite qualifications for a higher-level position.[480] Plaintiff must make a "persuasive showing ... that the decision not to promote him was based upon something other than a bona fide evaluation of his qualifications" for the job.[481] When the relative qualifications or skills of sev-

---

473. *Turner v. Schering-Plough Corp.*, 901 F.2d 335, 342 (3d Cir.), *cert. denied*, 464 U.S. 937 (1983) ("considerably younger").

474. *Erickson v. Marsh & McLennan Co., Inc.*, 117 N.J. 539, 551 (1990) (reverse sex discrimination case); *Bergen Commercial Bank v. Sisler*, 307 N.J. Super. 333, 344 (App. Div.), *certif. granted*, 153 N.J. 216 (1998) (reverse age discrimination).

475. Adverse action against a member of the majority carries none of the inherent implications of motivation that form the basis of the *McDonnell Douglas* method of proof.

476. *Bergen Commercial Bank v. Sisler*, 307 N.J. Super. 333, 347 (App. Div.), *aff'd*, __N.J.__ (1999).

477. *O'Lone v. N.J. Dept. of Corrections*, 313 N.J. Super. 249 (App. Div. 1998) (white employee who refused to stop dating African American).

478. *Peper v. Princeton Univ. Bd. of Trustees*, 77 N.J. at 80-81; *Turner v. Schering-Plough Corp.*, 901 F.2d at 342-46; *Fowle v. C & C Cola*, 868 F.2d 59, 61 (3d Cir. 1989) (when executive positions are involved, "particularly abstract considerations" are implicated).

479. *Turner v. Schering-Plough Corp.*, 901 F.2d at 343-44.

480. *Fowle v. C & C Cola*, 868 F.2d at 67; *Gorham v. AT&T Co.*, 762 F. Supp. 1138, 1139-44 (D.N.J. 1991).

481. *Peper v. Princeton Univ. Bd. of Trustees*, 77 N.J. at 86.

eral applicants are in issue, it is error to exclude or not consider evidence of the applicants' qualifications.[482]

Qualified/Performing at an Acceptable Level

Courts have held that to satisfy the second prong, the employee may show either that he was performing his job at a level that met his employer's reasonable expectations or that his qualifications were similar to those of other similarly situated employees.[483] At this stage, in the *prima facie* case, plaintiff must show only that he was objectively qualified and not that his performance met the employer's subjective requirements.[484] Subjective qualification, including elements such as leadership and management effectiveness, is considered in determining whether the employer's legitimate, nondiscriminatory reason for the employment action was a pretext.[485]

4-32:2 The Employer's Burden of Production

Among others, the following reasons have been held to constitute legitimate, nondiscriminatory justifications:

1. The employee was contentious and adversely reacted to management's criticism of his performance.[486]
2. The employee and a supervisor had a genuine "personality conflict."[487]

---

482. *Kearny Generating System v. Roper*, 184 N.J. Super. 253, 262-63 (App. Div.), *certif. denied*, 91 N.J. 254 (1982); *Jamison v. Rockaway Tp. Bd. of Educ.*, 242 N.J. Super. 436, 444-51 (App. Div. 1990); *Jones v. College of Medicine & Dentistry of New Jersey*, 155 N.J. Super. 232, 236-40 (App. Div. 1977), *certif. denied*, 77 N.J. 482 (1978); *Dungee v. Northeast Foods, Inc.*, 940 F. Supp. 682, 689 (D.N.J. 1996) (plaintiff's subjective belief that she was more qualified for the job does not create an issue of fact for the jury). *But see Flanders v. William Paterson College*, 163 N.J. Super. 225, 230-31 (App. Div. 1976).

483. *Greenberg v. Camden County Vocational and Technical Schools*, 310 N.J. Super. 189, 202-03 (App. Div. 1998); *Bennun v. Rutgers, The State University*, 941 F.2d 154, 176 (3d Cir. 1991), *cert. denied*, 502 U.S. 1066, 112 S. Ct. 956, 117 L.Ed. 2d 124 (1992).

484. *Baker v. The National State Bank*, 312 N.J.Super. 268, 284-85 (App. Div.), *certif. granted*, 156 N.J. 425 (1998); *Matczak v. Frankford Candy and Chocolate Co.*, 136 F.3d 933, 939 (3d Cir. 1997).

485. *Baker v. The National State Bank*, 312 N.J. Super. 268 (App. Div.), *certif. granted*, 156 N.J. 425 (1998). *See, e.g.*, *Gorham v. AT&T Co.*, 762 F. Supp. 1138, 1143-44 (D.N.J. 1991); *Oare v. Midlantic National Bank/Merchants*, 1990 WL 4622, 54 FEP 1530, 1532-33 (D.N.J. Jan. 16, 1990). With respect to subjective qualifications, such as leadership and managerial skills, *see Fowle v. C & C Cola*, 868 F.2d 59, 64-65 (3d Cir. 1989); *Gorham v. AT&T Co.*, 762 F. Supp. at 1144.

486. *Erickson v. Marsh & McLennan Co.*, 117 N.J. 539, 560-61 (1990); *Gorham v. AT&T Co.*, 762 F. Supp. 1138, 1144 (D.N.J. 1991); *Bellissimo v. Westinghouse Elec. Co.*, 764 F.2d 175, 182 (3d Cir. 1985), *cert. denied*, 475 U.S. 1035 (1986) (Title VII not violated by discharging "an adequate but strident, touchy, and difficult" in-house attorney whose presence in the workforce created an "unfortunate and destructive conflict of personalities").

3. The employee was discharged because he could not interface with co-employees and supervisors.[488]
4. The employee was not rehired because her attitude toward her work, the public, and other employees was very poor.[489]
5. The employee, though competent, was believed not to be able to deal with the public or project the desired image and was too eccentric (e.g., she carried her lunch in a child's lunch box decorated with cartoon characters).[490]
6. The employee promoted had a better attendance record, had more supervisory experience, and was a better communicator.[491]
7. The employee was discharged because of his unsatisfactory performance.[492]
8. The faculty member was denied tenure because he failed to earn his doctorate and did not have the requisite other qualifications that would compensate for such failure.[493]
9. The manager was demoted because of his performance deficiencies in areas such as leadership and interpersonal skills.[494]
10. The employee had an absenteeism problem.[495]
11. The employee was discharged because clients complained about his performance.[496]

---

487. *Velantzas v. Colgate-Palmolive Co.*, 109 N.J. 189, 194 n.2 (1988), *citing Wheeler v. Snyder Buick, Inc.*, 794 F.2d 1228, 1233 (7th Cir. 1986) (also noting that an employer does not violate Title VII if it discharges an employee because of a good-faith, albeit mistaken, belief that a legitimate cause for discharge exists); *Johnson v. Trenton State College*, 1985 WL 6095, 40 FEP 1505, 1509 (D.N.J. Sept. 11, 1985).

488. *Retter v. Georgia Gulf Corp.*,755 F. Supp. 637, 640 (D.N.J. 1991); *Gorham v. AT&T Co.*, 762 F. Supp. at 1144.

489. *Lloyd v. Stone Harbor*, 179 N.J. Super. 496, 520 (Ch. Div. 1981) (N.J. Constitution).

490. *Kiss v. New Jersey Dept. of Community Affairs*, 171 N.J. Super. 193, 200-01 (App. Div. 1979).

491. *Weiss v. Parker Hannifan Corp.*, 747 F. Supp. 1118, 1127 (D.N.J. 1990).

492. *Clowes v. Terminix Int'l, Inc.*, 109 N.J. 575, 600 (1988); *Retter v. Georgia Gulf Corp.*, 755 F. Supp. at 642; *Mullen v. New Jersey Steel Corp.*, 733 F. Supp. 1534, 1549-52 (D.N.J. 1990); *Gorham v. AT&T Co.*, 762 F. Supp. at 1144; *Yekel v. General Biscuit Brands, Inc.*, 1991 WL 43024, p. *3 (D.N.J. 1991).

493. *Sprague v. Glassboro State College*, 161 N.J. Super. 218, 220-25 (App. Div. 1978); *Countiss v. Trenton State College*, 77 N.J. 590, 596-97 (1978) (also noting that it was permissible for college to adopt more rigorous tenure requirements and apply them to previously-hired tenure-track teachers). When a decision to hire, promote or grant tenure to one person rather than another is reasonably attributable to an honest even though partially subjective evaluation of their qualifications, no inference of discrimination can be drawn. *Chow v. Rutgers, The State Univ.*, 283 N.J. Super. 524, 540 (App. Div. 1995), *certif. denied*, 145 N.J. 374 (1996).

494. *Turner v. Schering-Plough Corp.*, 901 F.2d 335, 342-44 (3d Cir. 1990). *See Casseus v. Elizabeth Gen. Medical Ctr.*, 287 N.J. Super. 396, 405-06 (App. Div. 1996) ("it should require no citation to state that an employee's poor performance in discharging his duties is a legitimate nondiscriminatory reason to fire or demote the employee").

12. The employee was terminated because, despite ample training opportunities, he was not performing at the level his employer expected of similarly-situated employees.[497]
13. The sales manager failed to collect accurate information from his accounts, inaccurately and sloppily completed required documentation, and otherwise did not follow proper office procedures.[498]
14. The worker ignored departmental policies and failed to complete assignments properly.[499]
15. The worker was terminated for falsifying company records.[500]
16. The employee was discharged for insubordination and violation of workplace safety rules.[501]
17. The applicant, although qualified, was not hired because another candidate had more maintenance and hands-on experience.[502]
18. The applicant, although qualified, was not selected because another applicant had "personal attributes which enhanced the applicant's value to the prospective employer."[503]
19. The applicant failed to achieve a satisfactory score on a written, nondiscriminatory employment test.[504]
20. The applicant was not hired because he appeared to be weak in direct sales and not aggressive enough.[505]

---

495. *Jones v. College of Medicine & Dentistry of New Jersey*, 155 N.J. Super. 232, 236, 239 (App. Div. 1977), *certif. denied*, 77 N.J. 482 (1978); *Yekel v. General Biscuit Brands, Inc.*, 1991 WL 43024, p. *3 (D.N.J. 1991). *Cf. Galante v. Sandoz, Inc.*, 196 N.J. Super. 568, 570 (App. Div. 1984), *app. dism'd*, 103 N.J. 492 (1986) (employee may be discharged for violating an "absenteeism policy that treated work-injury absences like all other absences, whether for illness, ..., non-work injury or other, less necessitous, circumstances").

496. *Retter v. Georgia Gulf Corp.*, 755 F. Supp. 637, 639-40 (D.N.J. 1991).

497. *Baxter v. AT&T Communications*, 712 F. Supp. 1166, 1173-74 (D.N.J. 1989).

498. *Retter v. Georgia Gulf Corp.*, 755 F. Supp. at 640-42.

499. *Oare v. Midlantic National Bank/Merchants*, 1990 WL 4622, 54 FEP 1530, 1533 (D.N.J. Jan. 16, 1990).

500. *Maietta v. United Parcel Service, Inc.*, 749 F. Supp. 1344, 1349, 1371-72 (D.N.J. 1990), *aff'd without published op.*, 932 F.2d 960 (3d Cir. 1991); *Oare v. Midlantic National Bank/Merchants*, 54 FEP at 1533; *Glover v. Canada Dry Bottling Co.*, 1990 WL 43739, p. *3 (D.N.J. 1990) (observing that the employer had a good-faith belief that plaintiff engaged in wrongdoing).

501. *Weiss v. Parker Hannifan Corp.*, 747 F. Supp. 1118, 1130, 1131 (D.N.J. 1990); *Mullen v. New Jersey Steel Corp.*, 733 F. Supp. 1534, 1549-52 (D.N.J. 1990).

502. *Kearny Generating System v. Roper*, 184 N.J. Super. 253, 259, 261, 263 (App. Div.), *certif. denied*, 91 N.J. 254 (1982).

503. *Kearny Generating System v. Roper*, 184 N.J. Super. at 261. *Accord Jones v. College of Medicine & Dentistry of New Jersey*, 155 N.J. Super. 232, 239 (App. Div. 1977), *certif. denied*, 77 N.J. 482 (1978).

504. *Patrolmen's Benevolent Ass'n v. East Brunswick*, 180 N.J. Super. 68, 72 (App. Div. 1981).

505. *Mate v. American Brands, Inc.*, 1990 WL 69177, p. *5 (D.N.J. 1990).

21. The employer was reducing its workforce.[506]
22. The administrator was laid off during a cutback instead of other employees because she did not have tenure and clerical staff was reduced by attrition.[507]
23. The employee was laid off in accordance with the company's seniority system that contained an exception only for students enrolled in the employer's fully-accredited college.[508]
24. The non-tenured teacher, who was going to be on an extended leave of absence, was not rehired in order to avoid a detrimental interruption in the continuity of classroom instruction.[509]
25. The public employee was denied certain benefits given to older employees in order to remedy previous age discrimination.[510]
26. The lower-rated employee was selected pursuant to a non-discriminatory application of the Civil Service Act's "rule of three."[511]
27. The applicant was not hired because of the employer's anti-nepotism rule.[512]

---

506. *Velantzas v. Colgate-Palmolive Co.*, 109 N.J. 189, 194 n.2 (1988), *citing Pendleton v. New York State Dept. of Correctional Services*, 615 F. Supp. 522, 526 (S.D.N.Y. 1985), *aff'd without published op.*, 788 F.2d 6 (2d Cir.), *cert. denied*, 479 U.S. 835 (1986); *Pittman v. LaFontaine*, 756 F. Supp 834, 837 n.2, 839 (D.N.J. 1991) (restating holding in *Pittman v. Immunomedics, Inc.*, No. A-0905-89 (N.J. App. Div. Oct. 5, 1990)); *Turner v. Schering-Plough Corp.*, 901 F.2d 335, 344-45 (3d Cir. 1990); *Reilly v. Prudential Prop. & Cas. Ins. Co.*, 653 F. Supp. 725, 727-28, 730-31 (D.N.J. 1987); *Johnson v. Trenton State College*, 1985 WL 6095, 40 FEP 1505, 1507-10 (D.N.J. Sept. 11, 1985); *McBride v. Princeton Univ.*, 1991 WL 66758, p. *6 (D.N.J. Apr. 24, 1991), *aff'd*, 950 F.2d 723 (3d Cir. 1991); *Kapossy v. McGraw-Hill, Inc.*, 921 F. Supp. 234, 244 (D.N.J. 1996). *But see Murray v. Newark Housing Authority*, 311 N.J. Super. 163, 176-77 (Law Div. 1998) (employer did not meet its burden of production where it showed that some but not all employees in plaintiff's classification had to be laid off for economic reasons, but its explanation for plaintiff's selection—random picks—was found inadequate as a matter of law by the court).

507. *Johnson v. Trenton State College*, 40 FEP at 1508.

508. *Massarsky v. General Motors Corp.*, 706 F.2d 111, 118-20 (3d Cir.), *cert. denied*, 464 U.S. 937 (1983).

509. *Gilchrist v. Haddonfield Bd. of Educ.*, 155 N.J. Super. 358, 368 (App. Div. 1978). *Cf. Castellano v. Linden Bd. of Educ.*, 79 N.J. 407, 412 (1979) (approving of *Gilchrist*, but observing that such a policy "cannot be adhered to blindly at the expense of the civil rights of teachers").

510. *Simon v. Police & Firemen's Retirement System Bd. of Trustees*, 233 N.J. Super. 186, 196-97 (App. Div.), *certif. denied*, 117 N.J. 652 (1989).

511. *Kiss v. New Jersey Dept. of Community Affairs*, 171 N.J. Super. 193, 200-02 (App. Div. 1979).

512. *Bluvias v. Winfield Mutual Housing Corp.*, 224 N.J. Super. 515, 526 (App. Div. 1988), *app. dism'd*, 114 N.J. 589 (1989); *Whateley v. Leonia Bd. of Educ.*, 141 N.J. Super. 476, 480 (Ch. Div. 1976); *Thomson v. Sanborn's Motor Express, Inc.*, 154 N.J. Super. 555, 558-64 (App. Div. 1977); *Slohoda v. United Parcel Service, Inc.*, 193 N.J. Super. 586, 592-93 (App. Div. 1984).

28. The applicant was not hired because the employer gives first preference to relatives, friends, and long-standing customers, even if less qualified.[513]
29. The employer did not interview applicants who previously earned in excess of 30 to 50 cents or more an hour above the company's wage scale.[514]
30. A mentally handicapped employee assaulted his supervisor during a psychotic episode.[515]

4-32:3 Plaintiff's Proof of Pretext/Intentional Discrimination

Once the defendant meets its burden of production, plaintiff must meet his ultimate burden of proving that the employer's stated reasons were a pretext and that the real reason for the employer's action was intentional discrimination.[516] Plaintiff can create an issue of fact sufficient to send the question of intentional discrimination to the jury by showing either (1) that defendant's articulated legitimate reasons are untrue; or (2) that intentional discrimination was more likely than not a determinative factor in the decision.[517]

Under the first prong, plaintiff must present evidence that rebuts the employer's stated reasons for the job action, thus allowing the jury to conclude that discrimination was the real reason. However, it is not enough just to show that the employer was wrong or mistaken: "Rather, the ... plaintiff must demonstrate such weaknesses, implausibilities, inconsistencies, incoherencies, or contradictions in the employer's proffered legitimate reasons for its actions that a reasonable factfinder could rationally find them unworthy of credence."[518] The employee must show "not merely that the employer's proffered reasons were wrong, but that it was so plainly wrong that it could not have been the employer's real reason."[519]

---

513. *Hayman v. Funk*, 8 N.J.A.R. 27, 39-40 (DCR 1984).

514. *Hunter v. Wando Optical Corp.*, 2 N.J.A.R. 42 (DCR 1980).

515. *Barbera v. DiMartino*, 305 N.J. Super. 617, 619 (App. Div. 1997).

516. The Appellate Division has held that once the employer meets its burden of articulating a legitimate nondiscriminatory reason, the presumption and burden-shifting of the *prima facie* case become irrelevant and the jury need only be instructed on the ultimate issue of whether there was intentional discrimination. *Baker v. The National State Bank*, 312 N.J. Super. 268 (App. Div.), *certif. granted*, 156 N.J. 425 (1998).

517. *Keller v. Orix Credit Alliance, Inc.*, 130 F.3d 1101, 1108 (3d Cir. 1997); *Fuentes v. Perskie*, 32 F.3d 759, 764 (3d Cir. 1994); *Ferraro v. Bell Atlantic Co., Inc.*, 2 F. Supp. 2d 577, 586 (D.N.J. 1998).

518. *Keller v. Orix Credit Alliance, Inc.*, 130 F.3d 1101, 1108-09 (3d Cir. 1997), quoting *Fuentes v. Perskie*, 32 F.3d 759, 765 (3d Cir. 1994).

519. *Keller v. Orix Credit Alliance, Inc.*, 130 F.3d 1101, 1109 (3d Cir. 1997).

Alternatively, under the second prong, plaintiff may present other evidence which if believed would allow a jury to conclude that discrimination played a role in the decision making process and that it had a determinative influence on the outcome of that process.[520] "In other words, under this prong, [plaintiff] must point to evidence that proves discrimination in the same way that critical facts are generally proved—based solely on the natural probative force of the evidence."[521] Evidence that the employer is not providing the whole story, prefers employees not in the protected class or behaves inconsistently or contradictorily may be sufficient. [522]

4-33 Dual Motives/*Price Waterhouse* Test

It is unsettled who bears the ultimate burden of persuasion where two or more factors, one of which violates the LAD, played a role in an adverse employment decision. A sharply-divided United States Supreme Court held, in *Price Waterhouse v. Hopkins*, that once a plaintiff in a case under Title VII of the Rights Act of 1964 demonstrates through direct evidence that an impermissible criterion played a motivating or substantial part in an adverse action, the burden of persuasion, not merely the burden of production, shifts to defendant to prove "by a preponderance of the evidence that it would have made the same decision even if it had not taken the [impermissible characteristic] into account."[523] The Civil

---

520. *Maiorino v. Schering-Plough Corp.*, 302 N.J. Super. 323, 344 (App. Div.), *certif. denied*, 152 N.J. 189 (1997); *Greenberg v. Camden Vocational Schools*, 310 N.J. Super. 189, 198-200 (App. Div. 1998) (an employee successfully meets this burden by persuading the court that a discriminatory reason more likely motivated the employer or indirectly by showing that the employer's proffered explanation is unworthy of credence; the standard is whether evidence of inconsistencies and implausibilities in the employer's proffered reasons for discharge reasonably could support an inference that the employer did not act for non-discriminatory reasons).

521. *Keller v. Orix Credit Alliance, Inc.*, 130 F.3d 1101, 1111 (3d Cir. 1997).

522. *Greenberg v. Camden County Vocational and Technical Schools*, 310 N.J. Super. 189, 204 (App. Div. 1998).

523. *Price Waterhouse v. Hopkins*, 490 U.S. 228, 258 (1989) (plurality opinion). The EEOC's interpretation of *Price Waterhouse* is set forth in EEOC, *Policy Guide on Recent Developments in Disparate Treatment Theory* (Mar. 7, 1991), reprinted in 8 *Fair Employment Practices Manual (BNA)*, pp. 405:6915-25 (Mar. 1991), and in 1 *EEOC Compliance Manual (BNA)*, pp. N:2119-34 (Apr. 1991). The evidence presented by plaintiff to support application of the mixed motives analysis must directly reflect a discriminatory or retaliatory animus on the part of a person involved in the decisionmaking process. *Dungee v. Northeast Foods, Inc.*, 940 F. Supp. 682, 691 (D.N.J. 1996). Circumstantial evidence may satisfy this burden if it is tied directly to the alleged discriminatory animus; reliance on presumptions created by a prima facie case is not permitted. *Id. See Jackson v. Georgia-Pacific Corp.*, 296 N.J. Super. 1, 19 (App. Div. 1996) ("Unless there is evidence which can be fairly said to directly reflect unlawful bias, the case should be treated as a pretext case."), *certif. denied*, 149 N.J. 141 (1997); *Fischer v. Allied Signal Corp.*, 974 F. Supp. 797, 804 (D.N.J. 1997) (mixed motive analysis not applicable absent direct evidence that decisionmakers placed substantial negative reliance on an illegitimate criterion in reaching their decision; general age-biased comments about plaintiffs' department, but not specifically directed to plaintiffs did not suffice).

Rights Act of 1991[524] (1991 CRA) partially overruled *Price Waterhouse* by providing that proof that the same action would have been taken in the absence of the impermissible motivating factor serves only to limit the nature of remedy available and not to avoid liability.[525]

Although the issue is unsettled under the LAD, the New Jersey Supreme Court has made passing, favorable reference to *Price Waterhouse.* In *Grigoletti v. Ortho Pharmaceutical Corp.*, one of the issues presented concerned standards of proof in equal pay cases.[526] In reaching the conclusion that in appropriate circumstances the burden of persuasion shifts to defendant once plaintiff establishes a *prima facie* case of unequal pay for equal work, the Court surveyed its earlier burden-shifting cases and the *Price Waterhouse* decision.[527]

The *Price Waterhouse* approach is essentially identical to the test the United States Supreme Court adopted in the *Mt. Healthy* and *Transportation Management* cases.[528] The New Jersey Supreme Court has applied the same test in several different state-law contexts,[529] although it has expressly noted that the LAD has not been one of them.[530] One Appellate Division decision applied the dual-motive analysis of *Mt. Healthy* in a retaliatory discharge case.[531]

---

524. S.1745.

525. 42 U.S.C. §2000e-2(m). The court in that instance

> (i) may grant declaratory relief, injunctive relief (except as provided in clause (ii)), and attorney's fees and costs demonstrated to be directly attributable only to the pursuit of a claim under section 703(m); and
>
> (ii) shall not award damages or issue an order requiring any admission, reinstatement, hiring, promotion, or payment described in subparagraph (A).

42 U.S.C. §2000e-5(g)(2)(B).

526. *Grigoletti v. Ortho Pharmaceutical Corp.*, 118 N.J. 89 (1990). *See Dungee v. Northeast Foods, Inc.*, 940 F. Supp. 682, 690-91 (D.N.J. 1996) ("Because age and sex discrimination claims under NJLAD are analyzed using Title VII and ADEA standards, the *Price Waterhouse* burden-shifting scheme would be equally applicable"); *Kapossy v. McGraw-Hill, Inc.*, 921 F. Supp. 234, 240 (D.N.J. 1996) (suggesting in dicta that the Price Waterhouse burden-shifting scheme would apply under the LAD); *Jackson v. Georgia-Pacific Corp.*, 296 N.J. Super. 1, 18-19 (App. Div. 1996) (same), *certif. denied*, 149 N.J. 141 (1997).

527. *Id.* at 108.

528. *Price Waterhouse v. Hopkins*, 490 U.S. at 248-50. In *Mt. Healthy City School Dist. Bd. of Educ. v. Doyle*, 429 U.S. 274 (1977), the issue was whether a public school teacher had been discharged for exercising his First Amendment rights of free speech. In *NLRB v. Transportation Management Corp.*, 462 U.S. 393 (1983), the question presented was whether an employee was terminated for engaging in protected union activity.

529. *See, e.g., In re Bridgewater Tp.*, 95 N.J. 235, 240-45 (1984) (adverse employment action against a public-sector worker for engaging in union activities; noting: this test "is the best yet established for determining causation in dual motive cases"); *Comite Organizador de Trabajadores Agricolas v. Molinelli*, 114 N.J. 87, 99-100 (1989) (adverse action against private-sector employees; New Jersey Const. Art. I, ¶19).

530. *In re Bridgewater Tp.*, 95 N.J. at 243 n.3.

531. *Jamison v. Rockaway Tp. Bd. of Educ.*, 242 N.J.Super. 436 (App. Div. 1990).

4-34 Retaliation Claims

Claims of retaliation for engaging in protected activity have generally been subject to a modified version of the *McDonnell Douglas* analysis. Plaintiff's *prima facie* case requires proof that (1) he was engaged in protected activity, *known* by the alleged retaliator, (2) he was subjected to an adverse employment decision as a result, and (3) there was a causal connection between the protected activity and the retaliation.[532] Plaintiff must have had a reasonable belief that the employer's conduct violated the LAD at the time he engaged in the protected activity.[533] The requisite "causal connection"

> may be demonstrated by evidence of circumstances that justify an inference of retaliatory motive, such as protected conduct closely followed by the adverse action. The timing of the termination in relation to the notice of the employee's complaint, however, does not create an inference without more evidence of a causal connection.[534]

A causal connection may also be demonstrated by evidence that plaintiff was treated differently from others after having engaged in the protected conduct.[535]

If plaintiff establishes a *prima facie* case, the burden of production then shifts to defendant to articulate some legitimate, non-retaliatory reason for the adverse action.[536] If defendant meets this articulation burden, then plaintiff must demon-

---

532. *Erickson v. Marsh & McLennan Co.*, 117 N.J. 539, 560 (1990); *Velantzas v. Colgate-Palmolive Co.*, 109 N.J. 189, 193 n.1 (1988) (non-LAD case), *citing Wrighten v. Metropolitan Hospitals, Inc.*, 726 F.2d 1346, 1354 (9th Cir. 1984) (Title VII); *Woods-Pirozzi v. Nabisco Foods*, 290 N.J. Super. 252, 274-75, 675 A.2d 527 (App. Div. 1996); *Jamison v. Rockaway Tp. Bd. of Educ.* 242 N.J.Super. 436, 445, 447 (App. Div. 1990); *Drinkwater v. Union Carbide Corp.*, 904 F.2d 853, 865 (3d Cir. 1990); *Reyes v. McDonald Pontiac GMC Truck, Inc.*, 997 F. Supp. 614, 619 (D.N.J. 1998); *Ferraro v. Bell Atlantic Co.*, 2 F. Supp. 2d 577, 587 (D.N.J. 1998); *Weiss v. Parker Hannifan Corp.*, 747 F.Supp. 1118, 1128-31 (D.N.J. 1990); *Delli Santi v. CNA Ins. Cos.*, 88 F.3d 192 (3d Cir. 1996). In *Wachstein v. Slocum*, 265 N.J. Super. 6 (App. Div.), *certif. denied*, 134 N.J. 563 (1993), the Appellate Division found that a letter from the employee's wife to the Governor, protesting alleged reverse discrimination, constituted a "protected activity" which satisfied the first prong of that test. *Id.* at 19.

533. *Drinkwater v. Union Carbide Corp.*, 904 F.2d at 865-66. Reasonableness is determined on the basis of the law at the time plaintiff formed the belief. *Id.*

534. *McBride v. Princeton Univ.*, 1991 WL 66758 at p. *4 (D.N.J.), *aff'd*, 950 F.2d 723 (3d Cir. 1991) (internal quotation marks and citations omitted). *See Quiroga v. Hasbro, Inc.*, 934 F.2d 497, 501 (3d Cir. 1991) ("While we held [in *Avdel v. Jalil*, 873 F.2d 701 (3d Cir. 1989)] that the 'timing of the discharge in relation to Jalil's EEOC complaint may suggest discriminatory motives,' *Jalil*, 873 F.2d at 709, we stopped short of creating an inference based upon timing alone"), *cert. denied*, 502 U.S. 940 (1991). *Delli Santi*, 88 F.3d 192 ("timing alone will not suffice to prove retaliatory motive").

535. *McBride v. Princeton Univ.* at p. *5.

536. *Velantzas v. Colgate Palmolive Co.*, 109 N.J. at 193 n.1, *quoting Wrighten v. Metropolitan Hospitals, Inc.*, 726 F.2d at 1354; *Jamison v. Rockaway Tp. Bd. of Educ.*, 242 N.J.Super. at 445, 447. *Delli Santi v. CNA Ins. Cos.*, 88 F.3d 192, 199 (3rd Cir. 1996); *Reyes v. McDonald Pontiac GMC Truck, Inc.*, 997 F. Supp. 614, 619 (D.N.J. 1998).

strate by a preponderance of the evidence that a discriminatory intent motivated defendant's action.[537] Plaintiff may do this indirectly, by proving that defendant's proffered explanation is a pretext for the retaliation, or directly, by demonstrating that a discriminatory reason more likely motivated defendant's action.[538]

One Appellate Division decision suggests that *McDonnell Douglas* is insufficient in cases alleging retaliatory failure to hire or promote. It combined the *McDonnell Douglas* and dual-motive analyses and held that once plaintiff satisfies the third step of the modified *McDonnell Douglas* test by proving that the employer's articulated reason for failure to promote is a pretext or that a discriminatory reason more likely motivated the employer, a presumption is created that the adverse action was the product of unlawful retaliatory intent.[539] The employer then bears the burden of persuading, by a preponderance of the evidence, that the adverse action would have been taken regardless of the retaliatory motive.[540] Defendant may meet this burden by proving that other job applicants or employees had better qualifications than plaintiff.[541]

4-35 Handicap Discrimination

Defendant's burden of proof in a handicap discrimination case depends upon whether it seeks to (1) advance a non-discriminatory reason for the adverse action or (2) establish the reasonableness of the otherwise discriminatory act.[542] If

---

537. *Jamison v. Rockaway Tp. Bd. of Educ.*, 242 N.J.Super. at 445; *Weiss v. Parker Hannifan Corp.*, 747 F.Supp. at 1130, 1131; *McBride v. Princeton Univ.*, 1991 WL 66758 at p. *6 (D.N.J. Apr. 24, 1991), *aff'd*, 950 F.2d 723 (3d Cir. 1991); *Delli Santi v. CNA Ins. Cos.*, 88 F.3d 192, 199 (3rd Cir. 1996); *Reyes v. McDonald Pontiac GMC Truck, Inc.*, 997 F. Supp. 614, 619 (D.N.J. 1998).

538. *Jamison v. Rockaway Tp. Bd. of Educ.*, 242 N.J.Super. at 445, 447, *citing Wrighten v. Metropolitan Hospitals, Inc.*, 726 F.2d at 1354; *McBride v. Princeton Univ.*, 1991 WL 66758 at p. *6; *Reyes v. McDonald Pontiac GMC Truck, Inc.*, 997 F. Supp. 614, 619 (D.N.J. 1998).

539. *Jamison v. Rockaway Tp. Bd. of Educ.*, 242 N.J.Super. at 445-47, *citing Wrighten v. Metropolitan Hospitals, Inc.*, 726 F.2d at 1354.

540. *Jamison v. Rockaway Tp. Bd. of Educ.*, 242 N.J.Super. at 446-47, 451, *citing Wrighten v. Metropolitan Hospitals, Inc.*, 726 F.2d at 1354. *But see Delli Santi*, 88 F.3d 192 (quoting from and applying *Jamison* but also noting that under *Jalil v. Avdel Corp.*, 873 F.2d 701, 706 (3d Cir. 1988), *cert. denied*, 493 U.S. 1023 (1990), the "ultimate burden of persuasion always remains with the employee who seeks to prove a retaliation claim). *Cf. Morris v. Siemens Components, Inc.*, 1996 WL 294074, p.*5 (D.N.J. 1996) ("A defendant is entitled to summary judgment on a plaintiff's claim for retaliatory discharge if it can demonstrate that: (1) the plaintiff is unable to establish a prima facie case of retaliatory discharge; or (2) if plaintiff can establish a prima facie case, the plaintiff cannot produce sufficient evidence of pretext to rebut the defendant's asserted legitimate reason for discharge.") (alleged retaliation for filing workers' compensation claim).

541. *Jamison v. Rockaway Tp. Bd. of Educ.*, 242 N.J.Super. at 446-47, 451, *citing Ruggles v. California Polytechnic State Univ.*, 797 F.2d 782, 786-87 (9th Cir. 1986), *citing Mt. Healthy City School Dist. Bd. of Educ. v. Doyle*, 429 U.S. 274 (1977).

defendant takes the former approach, the traditional *McDonnell Douglas* standard of proof applies, with plaintiff retaining the ultimate burden of persuasion.[543] An employer who takes the second approach, however, effectively admits that plaintiff's handicap played a role in the adverse decision, but claims that it played a legitimate role.[544] In such cases, the burden of persuasion shifts to defendant to establish by objective evidence that it reasonably arrived at the conclusion that plaintiff, because of the nature and extent of his handicap and in spite of reasonable accommodation, is either unable at present to adequately perform the essential functions of the job or creates a materially enhanced risk of serious harm to himself or others in the workplace.[545]

Regardless of which approach is used, plaintiff must establish that he was handicapped (or perceived to be handicapped) at the time of the adverse employment action.[546] Plaintiff must prove that his employer was aware of his handicap at the time of the complained-of action.[547] Plaintiff also bears the initial burden of proving that he was qualified for the position in terms of both general qualifications—*e.g.*, experience, education, intelligence, and skills—and physical/non-physical qualifications, such as stamina, physical strength, and dexterity.[548] Only

---

542. *Jansen v. Food Circus Supermarkets, Inc.*, 110 N.J. 363, 382 (1988); *Maher v. New Jersey Transit Rail Operations, Inc.*, 125 N.J. 455, 481 (1991); *Clowes v. Terminix Int'l, Inc.*, 109 N.J. 575, 595-600 (1988); *Panettieri v. C.V. Hill Refrigeration*, 159 N.J.Super. 473, 485-87 (App. Div. 1978).

543. *Jansen v. Food Circus Supermarkets, Inc.*, 110 N.J. at 382-83; *Clowes v. Terminix Int'l, Inc.*, 109 N.J. at 595-97; *Panettieri v. C.V. Hill Refrigeration*, 159 N.J.Super. at 485-86; *Yekel v. General Biscuit Brands, Inc.*, 1991 WL 43024, pp. *2-3 (D.N.J. 1991).

544. *Jansen v. Food Circus Supermarkets, Inc.*, 110 N.J. at 381, 383; *Andersen v. Exxon Co.*, 89 N.J. 483, 493, 498-500 (1982); *Panettieri v. C.V. Hill Refrigeration*, 159 N.J.Super. at 484-86; *Behringer v. Medical Center at Princeton*, 249 N.J.Super. 597, 646 (Law Div. 1991). *Ensslin v. Township of N. Bergen*, 275 N.J. Super. 352, 363, 646 A.2d 452 (App. Div. 1994), *certif. denied*, 142 N.J. 446 (1995) ("Where, as here, an employer maintains that it has reasonably concluded that the employee's handicap precluded performance of the job, and has terminated the employee for that reason, the burden of proof is on the employer.").

545. *Jansen v. Food Circus Supermarkets, Inc.*, 110 N.J. at 374-75, 376, 381, 383; *Andersen v. Exxon Co.*, 89 N.J. at 498-500; *Panettieri v. C.V. Hill Refrigeration*, 159 N.J.Super. at 484-87; N.J.A.C. 13:13-2.8(a)(1)-(3); N.J.A.C. 13:13-2.4(e)(2); N.J.S.A. 10:5-4.1; N.J.S.A. 10:5-2.1. An employee who needs reasonable accommodation must so advise his employer. "[B]efore an employer must make an accommodation for the physical or mental limitation of an employee, the employer must have knowledge that such a limitation exists. *Lawrence v. National Westminster Bank*, 1995 WL 506043, p.*6 (D.N.J. 1995), *aff'd*, 98 F.3d 61 (3d Cir. 1996).

546. *Clowes v. Terminix Int'l, Inc.*, 109 N.J. at 597-98; *Jansen v. Food Circus Supermarkets, Inc.*, 110 N.J. at 373, 377, 381-83; *Andersen v. Exxon Co.*, 89 N.J. at 493, 499-500.

547. *Illingworth v. Nestle U.S.A., Inc.*, 926 F.Supp. 482 (D.N.J. 1996).

548. *Andersen v. Exxon Co.*, 89 N.J. at 499; *Panettieri v. C.V. Hill Refrigeration*, 159 N.J.Super. at 491; *Yekel v. General Biscuit Brands, Inc.*, 1991 WL at pp. *2-3. An employee who represents that she is disabled on a benefits application is judicially estopped from contending in her handicap discrimination suit that she was able to perform the job. An employee cannot be simultaneously unable to work and qualified to perform the duties of her position. *Morris v. Siemens Components, Inc.*, 1996 WL 294074, p.*8-9 (D.N.J. 1996).

when those requirements have been met will the burden of production or pursuasion (depending on which defense is asserted) shift to the defendant.[549]

4-36 Equal Pay

In *Grigoletti v. Ortho Pharmaceutical Corp.*, the Supreme Court outlined two methods of proving discrimination in pay.[550] The first, based on the federal Equal Pay Act, requires proof that employees of different sexes are given different rates of pay for "substantially equal" work.[551] This equal-work comparison focuses on whether the jobs held by the men and women "have a common core of tasks, that is, whether a significant portion of the two jobs is identical."[552] It involves a comparison of the job requirements, skills, efforts, responsibilities, and working conditions involved, rather than an analysis of the skills or other qualifications of the people holding the jobs.[553]

If plaintiff establishes a *prima facie* case of unequal pay for substantially equal work, then the burden of persuasion shifts to defendant to establish by a preponderance of the evidence one of the following four affirmative defenses: "that the wage disparity is the result of (i) a seniority system, (ii) a merit system, (iii) a system which measures earnings by quantity or quality of production, or (iv) a differential based on any factor other than sex."[554]

An employee may also prove a claim of wage discrimination under the Title VII standard established in *McDonnell Douglas*.[555] In such a case, plaintiff need

---

549. *Andersen v. Exxon Co.*, 89 N.J. 499.

550. *Grigoletti v. Ortho Pharmaceutical Corp.*, 118 N.J. 89 (1990).

551. *Id.* at 109-11, 114; *McBride v. Princeton Univ.*, 1991 WL 66758, pp. *8-9 (D.N.J.), *aff'd* 950 F.2d 723 (3d Cir. 1991). Such a showing creates a "virtually inescapable" inference of unlawful discrimination that must be rebutted by the employer, *Grigoletti v. Ortho Pharmaceutical Corp.*, 118 N.J. at 108-09.

552. *Grigoletti v. Ortho Pharmaceutical Corp.*, 118 N.J. at 102, 111, 113 (internal quotation marks omitted). *See Dubrowsky v. Stern, Lavinthal, Norgaard & Daly*, 922 F. Supp. 985 (D.N.J. 1996) (comparing tasks performed by associates at law firm, including factors such as hours billed, responsibility, time pressure and difficulty, and denying firm's motion for summary judgment on female associate's equal pay claim).

553. *Id.* at 102, 111, 113-14; *McBride v. Princeton Univ.*, 1991 WL 66758 at p.*8. (D.N.J.), *aff'd*, 950 F. 2d 723 (3d Cir. 1991). Job requirements would include education and prior work experience. *Grigoletti v. Ortho Pharmaceutical Corp.*, 118 N.J. at 102. Although job titles are considered in determining whether jobs are equal, it is job content that is controlling. *Id.* at 114.

554. *Grigoletti v. Ortho Pharmaceutical Corp.*, 118 N.J. at 102, 103, 109-11, 114; *McBride v. Princeton Univ.*, 1991 WL 66758 at p. *8. *Bitsko v. Main Pharmacy, Inc.*, 289 N.J. Super. 267, 272, 673 A.2d 825 (App. Div. 1996) (in applying the standard established in *Grigoletti v. Ortho Pharmaceutical Corp.*, 118 N.J. 89 (1990), the Appellate Division found that the EPA defense of "any factor other than sex" has substantially the same meaning as the "legitimate non-discriminatory reason" factor in the *McDonnell Douglas* formula). *See Dubrowsky v. Stern, Lavinthal, Norgaard & Daly*, 922 F. Supp. 985, 993 (D.N.J. 1996) (denying law firm's motion for summary judgment on "market forces" defense; "It is not legitimate under the EPA to pay an equally qualified woman less than a man because of her inferior bargaining power in the market as a woman.").

not prove that the jobs in question were "substantially equal," only that they were "similar."[556] However, satisfaction of that less exacting burden of a *prima facie* case shifts only the burden of coming forward, and not the burden of proof.[557] Defendant is then required only to articulate a legitimate, nondiscriminatory reason for the wage disparity, and plaintiff retains the ultimate burden of persuading that she was intentionally discriminated against because of her sex.[558]

4-37 Sexual Harassment

The standards of proof applicable to cases of sexual harassment are discussed in §4-37.

4-38 Reverse Discrimination

The burden of proof when a person not in a protected class alleges a violation of the LAD is more demanding. In particular, the first prong of plaintiff's *prima facie* case requires proof that the employer is the "unusual employer who discriminates against the majority."[559] In *Erickson v. Marsh & McLennan Co.*, the Supreme Court held that plaintiff's proof that he was discharged so a supervisor's female paramour could be promoted and that another male employee was replaced with a female was insufficient as a matter of law to establish that his employer was the requisite "unusual employer."[560]

---

555. *Grigoletti v. Ortho Pharmaceutical Corp.*, 118 N.J. at 101, 110; *McBride v. Princeton Univ.*, 1991 WL 66758 at p. *9. The *McDonnell Douglas* approach is discussed in §4-32 *et seq.* The DCR apparently followed a similar approach in a case involving unequal pay based on race discrimination. *See White v. PSE&G Co.*, 8 N.J.A.R. 335, 361-67, 382-87 (DCR 1984), *aff'd*, No. A-1496-84 (App. Div. July 16, 1986).

556. *Grigoletti v. Ortho Pharmaceutical Corp.*, 118 N.J. at 101, 110; *McBride v. Princeton Univ.*, 1991 WL 66758 at p. *9 (a mere showing of "rough similarity" is insufficient), *aff'd*, 950 F.2d 723 (3d Cir. 1991).

557. *Grigoletti v. Ortho Pharmaceutical Corp.*, 118 N.J. at 101, 103, 109-10; *McBride v. Princeton Univ.*, 1991 WL 66758 at p. *9. Defendant is not limited to the four affirmative defenses in overcoming the *prima facie* case. *Grigoletti*, 118 N.J. at 103.

558. *Grigoletti v. Ortho Pharmaceutical Corp.*, 118 N.J. at 109-10; *McBride v. Princeton Univ.*, 1991 WL 66758 at pp. *9-10.

559. *Erickson v. Marsh & McLennan Co.*, 117 N.J. 539, 551-52 (1990); *Grigoletti v. Ortho Pharmaceutical Corp.*, 118 N.J. 89, 107-08 (1990); *Wachstein v. Slocum*, 265 N.J. Super. 6, 13-14 (App. Div.), *certif. denied*, 134 N.J. 563 (1993); *Harel v. Rutgers, The State University*, 5 F. Supp. 2d 246, 264 (D.N.J. 1998). *See Flanders v. William Paterson College*, 163 N.J.Super. 225, 233-35 (App. Div. 1976); *Talman v. Burlington County College Bd. of Trustees*, 169 N.J.Super. 535, 542, 537 (App. Div.), *certif. denied*, 81 N.J. 407 (1979), *ovr'ld on other grounds*, *Goodman v. London Metals Exchange, Inc.*, 86 N.J. 19, 41 n.5 (1981), and *Terry v. Mercer County Freeholders Bd.*, 173 N.J.Super. 249, 254 (App. Div. 1980), *modified*, 86 N.J. 141, 147-54 (1981). *See also Patrolmen's Benevolent Ass'n v. East Brunswick*, 180 N.J.Super. 68, 72-74 (App. Div. 1981).

4-39 Causation

In all cases of disparate treatment, the ultimate issue is proximate causation.[561]

4-40 After-Acquired Evidence

The New Jersey Supreme Court has not yet addressed the question whether after-acquired evidence of employee misconduct should affect either liability or the extent of damages recoverable in an NJLAD action.[562] The United States District Court for the District of New Jersey has predicted that New Jersey will follow the federal rule and hold that after-acquired evidence of employee misconduct does not preclude liability, but that it may limit plaintiff's recovery.[563] In *Miller v. Beneficial Management Corp.*,[564] the court held that the defendant could "negate relief, not liability," with after-acquired evidence that plaintiff lied on her resume and removed confidential documents from the employer's offices,

---

560. *Erickson v. Marsh & McLennan Co.*, 117 N.J. at 552-53; *Lehmann v. Toys 'R' Us, Inc.* 132 N.J. 587, 605-06 (1993) (where a man alleges that facially-neutral conduct was directed at him because of his sex he must show that the employer is the rare employer who discriminated against the historically privileged majority group) (*dicta*). In *Wachstein v. Slocum*, 265 N.J. Super. 6, 18 (App. Div.), *certif. denied*, 134 N.J. 563 (1993), the Appellate Division found no evidence of discrimination in Public Defender's statements about combatting discrimination and pursuing affirmative action by replacing white male supervisors with blacks and women. Similarly, in *Harel v. Rutgers, The State University*, 5 F. Supp. 2d 246 (D.N.J. 1998), a Title VII case, the court found insufficient an alleged policy to encourage the advancement of women where the actual numbers of male and female faculty members granted tenure did not reflect a general disposition to discriminate against men. *But see DeCapua v. Bell Atlantic-New Jersey, Inc.*, 313 N.J. Super. 110 (Law Div. 1998) (where white male plaintiff alleged a hostile work environment based upon reverse discrimination, he was not required to prove systemic discrimination by his employer against the majority).

561. *See Goodman v. London Metals Exchange, Inc.*, 86 N.J. 19, 29 (1981) (there must be a "causal relationship" between the discriminatory conduct and the adverse employment action); *Countiss v. Trenton State College*, 77 N.J. 590, 599 (1978) (discrimination must be a "substantial factor" in the adverse action); *Levinson v. Prentice-Hall, Inc.*, 868 F.2d 558, 560 (3d Cir. 1989) (a "substantive or determinative factor"); *Slohoda v. United Parcel Service, Inc.*, 207 N.J.Super. 145, 155 (App. Div.), *certif. denied*, 104 N.J. 400 (1986) (discriminatory intent must be "a determinative factor" in the adverse action); *Baxter v. AT&T Communications*, 712 F.2d 1166, 1172 (D.N.J. 1989) (same); *Jackson v. Consolidated Rail Corp.*, 223 N.J.Super. 467, 473, 477 (App. Div. 1988) (the impermissible criterion was "a determinant factor ... more likely than not motivat[ing]" the adverse action); *Turner v. Schering-Plough Corp.*, 901 F.2d 335, 342 (3d Cir. 1990) (age need not be the sole factor though it must have made a difference in the decision); *Harvard v. Bushberg Bros.*, 137 N.J.Super. 537, 540 (App. Div. 1975), *certif. gr.*, 71 N.J. 493 (1976), *app. dism'd by stipulation, as stated in Castellano v. Linden Bd. of Educ.*, 79 N.J. 407, 417 (1979) (discrimination played at least a part and was a causal factor); *Flanders v. William Paterson College*, 163 N.J.Super. 225, 231 (App. Div. 1976) (discrimination was the deciding factor); *Floyd v. State of New Jersey*, 1991 WL 143456, p. *3 (D.N.J. 1991) ("but for" test). *See generally Scafidi v. Seiler*, 119 N.J. 93, 101-09 (1990), and *Battenfeld v. Gregory*, 247 N.J.Super. 538, 548-50 (App. Div. 1991), comparing the "substantial factor" and "but for" tests as applied in medical malpractice cases.

562. *Nicosia v. Wakefern Food Corp.*, 136 N.J. 401 (1994) (declining to address the issue).

563. See *McKennon v. Nashville Banner Publishing Co.*, 513 U.S. 353 (1995).

564. 855 F. Supp. 691 (D.N.J. 1994).

because back pay under both Title VII and the LAD was equitable in nature. To negate relief, the employer would have to establish that plaintiff "engaged in the misconduct [and defendant] would have terminated [plaintiff] if it had known of this misconduct at the time it had occurred," not just that it could have. The court held that because compensatory and punitive damages under the LAD are legal (not equitable) remedies, they are not barred by such proof.[565]

4-41 Disparate Impact

Claims of "disparate impact"

> involve employment practices that are facially neutral in their treatment of different groups but that in fact fall more harshly on one group than another and cannot be justified by business necessity. Proof of discriminatory motive ... is not required under a disparate impact theory.[566]

The method of proof of disparate impact claims under the LAD remains unsettled. The Supreme Court has not addressed in detail the elements of proof required under this approach; however, the Appellate Division has applied the federal standard as established by the Civil Rights Act of 1991.[567]

To make a *prima facie* case of disparate impact discrimination under Title VII of the Civil Rights Act of 1964 (Title VII), as amended by the Civil Rights Act of 1991 (1991 CRA), plaintiff must first demonstrate "that a respondent uses a particular employment practice that causes a disparate impact on the basis of race, color, religion, sex, or national origin."[568] Plaintiff must demonstrate that each particular practice complained of has a disparate impact, unless he can demonstrate to the court that the elements of respondent's decision-making process are not capable of separation for analysis. In that event only, the decision-making process may be analyzed as one employment practice.[569]

To be actionable, a disparity must be significant.[570] Any statistical analyses used must be based upon a proper comparison "between the racial composition of [the at-issue jobs] and the racial composition of the qualified ... population in

---

565. *Id.* at 716-17.

566. *Peper v. Princeton Univ. Bd. of Trustees*, 77 N.J. 55, 81-82 (1978), *quoting Teamsters v. United States*, 431 U.S. 324, 335-36 n.15 (1977) (citations omitted). *Accord Massarsky v. General Motors Corp.*, 706 F.2d 111, 117, 120 (3d Cir.), *cert. denied*, 464 U.S. 937 (1983) (ADEA and LAD); *Reilly v. Prudential Prop. & Cas. Ins. Co.*, 653 F.Supp. 725, 729 (D.N.J. 1987) (LAD, ADEA, and Title VII).

567. *Esposito v. Township of Edison*, 306 N.J. Super. 280, 289-90 (App. Div. 1997).

568. 42 U.S.C. 2000e-2(k)(1)(A)(i).

the relevant labor market" who would seek such jobs.[571] This approach to statistical evidence has been endorsed by New Jersey courts.[572]

Once plaintiff establishes a *prima facie* case under the federal law, defendant must "demonstrate that the challenged practice is job related for the position in question and consistent with business necessity."[573] Alternatively, defendant may demonstrate that the practice in question does not cause the disparate impact, in which case proof of job relatedness and business necessity is not required.[574] It is specifically stated in the designated legislative history of the 1991 CRA that

> The terms "business necessity" and "job related" are intended to reflect the concepts enunciated by the Supreme Court in *Griggs v. Duke Power Co.*, 401 U.S. 424 (1971), and in the other Supreme Court decisions prior to *Wards Cove Packing Co. v. Atonio*.[575]

---

569. 42 U.S.C. 2000e-2(k)(1)(B)(i). This portion of the 1991 CRA is an apparent acceptance of the requirement in *Wards Cove Packing Co. v. Atonio*, 490 U.S. 642 (1989), that plaintiffs identify the specific employment practice that is alleged to be responsible for the observed statistical disparity. *Id.* at 656-57, 653 & n.8. As stated by the DCR in *Hunter v. Wando Optical Corp.*, 2 N.J.A.R. 42, 50 (DCR 1980):

> In any case ... concerning statistical proofs in the selection process, one needs to locate, as precisely as possible, the point in the selection process at which the alleged discrimination occurred. Without such specificity, the development of a sharply focused statistical proof on which one can rely with confidence is impossible.

Existing standards for determining whether a "disparate impact" exists appear to have been left intact by the 1991 CRA. *See, e.g.* BNA, Daily Labor Report, Special Supplement No. 218, pp. 1-2 (Nov. 12, 1991).

570. *Wards Cove Packing Co. v. Atonio*, 490 U.S. at 645-46, 656-58. *Accord Massarsky v. General Motors Corp.*, 706 F.2d at 117, 120; *Reilly v. Prudential Prop. & Cas. Ins. Co.*, 653 F.Supp. at 729, 732. The policy must have an adverse effect on "a disproportionate number of members of the protected group." *Id.* at 120. "An adverse effect on a single employee, or even a few employees, is not sufficient to establish disparate impact." *Id.* at 121. *Accord Meacham v. Bell Telephone Laboratories, Inc.*, 1990 WL 299805, p. *13 n.7 (D.N.J. 1990) (LAD and Title VII). Statistical proof, not pure conjecture, is required to establish an actionable case of disparate impact. *Massarsky*, 725 F.2d at 121.

571. *Wards Cove Packing Co. v. Atonio*, 490 U.S. at 650, 653-54 (internal quotation marks omitted). Where labor market statistics are difficult to ascertain, certain other statistics, such as the racial composition of the pool of qualified applicants for the at-issue jobs, may be utilized. *Id.* at 651. *See Richmond v. J.A. Croson Co.*, 488 U.S. 469, 501-02 (1989); *Hunter v. Wando Optical Corp.*, 2 N.J.A.R. at 48-50, 53, 57.

572. The *Wards Cove* approach to statistical analysis was followed in *State of New Jersey v. Kennedy*, 247 N.J.Super. 21, 33 (App. Div. 1991) (case involving allegations that state police discriminatorily enforce traffic laws against minorities). In *Lige v. Montclair*, 72 N.J. 5 (1976), the Supreme Court *in dicta* questioned the use of general population statistics as a comparison base for the racial mix of an employer's workforce:

> A population comparison ignores the fact that all segments of the population may not be equally qualified for the positions in question, ... and different groups within the population may have different levels of desire for the particular job. ...

Id. at 12 n.3 (internal quotation marks omitted). *See also NAACP v. Harrison*, 749 F.Supp. 1327, 1337-41 (D.N.J. 1990), *aff'd*, 940 F.2d 792 (3d Cir. 1991) (Title VII challenge to Town of Harrison's residency requirement for municipal employment).

573. 42 U.S.C. §2000e-2 (k)(1)(A)(i).

574. 42 U.S.C. §2000e-2 (k)(1)(B)(ii).

575. *Interpretive Memorandum*, Vol. 137 Congressional Record S 15276 (daily ed. Oct. 25, 1991).

In *Griggs*, these terms were described variously as requiring "that any given requirement ... have a manifest relationship to the employment in question;"[576] and that a practice bear a demonstrable relationship to successful performance of the jobs for which it was used.[577]

The 1991 CRA also permits plaintiffs to establish a case of disparate impact by demonstrating the availability of a less discriminatory practice which the respondent refuses to adopt.[578] Two Appellate Division decisions differ from that approach to the alternate means factor. They hold that if plaintiff establishes a *prima facie* case of disparate impact, and defendant shows that its policy furthers "a legitimate, bona fide [business] interest,"[579] plaintiff is then required to establish that feasible "alternative means are available which serve that interest with less discriminatory effect."[580]

The 1991 CRA shifts the burden of persuasion to the defendant. It states that proof of disparate impact proves an unlawful employment practice when, *inter alia*, "*respondent fails to demonstrate* that the challenged practice is job related for the position in question and consistent with business necessity."[581] The Supreme Court had held in *Wards Cove* that only the burden of production—not the burden of persuasion—shifts, and federal court decisions before that were divided on the issue.[582]

---

576. 401 U.S. at 432.

577. 401 U.S. at 431. *Accord Massarsky v. General Motors Corp.*, 706 F.2d at 118, 120 ("manifest relationship" between the policy and the employment); *Reilly v. Prudential Prop. & Cas. Ins. Co.*, 653 F.Supp. at 732; *NAACP v. Harrison*, 940 F.2d 792, 798, 801-05 (3d Cir. 1991). *See Esposito v. Township of Edison*, 306 N.J. Super. 280, 290 (App. Div. 1997) (written examinations and credits for college used as components of promotional policies for police officers were job-related and consistent with business necessity).

578. The "alternative employment" concept is determined as of the day prior to the decision in *Wards Cove*. 42 U.S.C. §2000e-2(k)(1)(C). There the Court held that any alternative practices put forward as proof that incumbent practices were not employed for non-discriminatory reasons

> must be equally effective as [defendants'] chosen hiring procedures in achieving [defendants'] legitimate employment goals. Moreover, [f]actors such as the cost or other burdens of proposed alternative selection devices are relevant in determining whether they would be equally as effective as the challenged practice in serving the employer's legitimate business goals.

490 U.S. at 660-61 (internal quotation works omitted). *Accord Massarsky v. General Motors Corp.*, 706 F.2d at 120; *Reilly v. Prudential Prop. & Cas. Ins. Co.*, 653 F.Supp. at 732.

579. *In re Petition for Substantive Certification filed by Warren Tp.*, 247 N.J.Super. 146, 177, 169-70 (App. Div. 1991), *rev'd*, 132 N.J. 1 (1993) (internal quotation marks omitted); *In re Petition for Substantive Certification filed by Denville Tp.*, 247 N.J.Super. 186, 196 (App. Div. 1991), *rev'd*, 132 N.J. 1 (1993).

580. *In re Petition for Substantive Certification filed by Warren Tp.*, 247 N.J.Super. at 170, 169, 176-77; *In re Petition for Substantive Certification filed by Denville Tp.*, 247 N.J.Super. at 196. *Contra* DCR, *A Guide for Employers to the LAD*, p.12 (June 1986) ("The burden of proving that a test is job related...[and] that no other less discriminatory selection method is feasible" is on defendant).

581. 42 U.S.C. §2000e-2 (k)(1)(A). "Demonstrates" is defined in the 1991 CRA as meeting the burdens of proof and persuasion. 42 U.S.C. §2000e(m).

The Appellate Division seemed to endorse a non-shifting burden in *Jones v. College of Medicine & Dentistry of New Jersey*, where it stated that "discrimination cases are no different from others in resting the burden of proof by a preponderence of the evidence upon the complaining party."[583] The New Jersey Supreme Court has not squarely addressed this issue, but language in *Lige v. Montclair* is in harmony with a non-shifting burden approach.[584] In *Lige*, the Division on Civil Rights (DCR) determined that the *Wonderlic* test used by a municipal employer had a "disproportionately negative effect on blacks" in view of the facts, among others, that 67 percent of the white applicants and only 16 percent of the black candidates passed the exam and the test had not been professionally validated to show job-relatedness.[585] The DCR held that once plaintiff made a *prima facie* showing of disparate impact, the "burden of going forward" shifted to defendant to "offer significant evidence establishing the job relatedness of the written ... tests."[586]

On appeal to the Supreme Court, the disparate-impact analysis was not at issue, but the Court nonetheless questioned whether the employer should bear the burden of proving test validations: "lack of job relatedness does not necessarily support a finding that the test was racially discriminatory."[587]

In *Countiss v. Trenton State College*, the Court applied the disparate-impact approach to an employment policy permitting coaches of male teams to teach three hours a week less than coaches of female teams. Noting that all coaches were the same sex as the athletes they coached, the court found "disparate treatment which

---

582. *Wards Cove Packing Co. v. Atonio*, 490 U.S. at 658-60. The Third Circuit had opined that plaintiffs retain the burden of persuasion in both disparate treatment and disparate-impact cases under Title VII, the ADEA, and the LAD: "[I]t is illogicial to impose a heavier burden on a defendant in a case where a neutral policy results in disparate impact than in one where the charge is unlawful animus." *NAACP v. Medical Center, Inc.*, 657 F.2d 1322, 1335 (3d Cir. 1981) (*en banc*) (Title VII of the Civil Rights Act).

583. *Jones v. College of Medicine & Dentistry of New Jersey*, 155 N.J.Super. 232, 238, 236-37 (App. Div. 1977), *certif. denied*, 77 N.J. 482 (1978). *See Patrolmen's Benevolent Ass'n v. East Brunswick*, 180 N.J.Super. 68, 72 (App. Div. 1981) (plaintiff "failed to meet her burden of proving by a preponderance of the credible evidence that the testing procedure employed by [defendant] on the written part of the examination was discriminatory."); *Thomson v. Sanborn's Motor Express, Inc.*, 154 N.J.Super. 555, 562-63 (App. Div. 1977) (if plaintiff establishes a *prima facie* case of disparate impact, defendant must "go forward with proof justifying the business reasons for its policy"). *Contra Giammario v. Trenton Bd. of Ed.*, 203 N.J.Super. 356, 363 (App. Div.), *certif. denied*, 102 N.J. 336 (1985), *cert. denied*, 475 U.S. 1141 (1986) (discussed *infra* at n. 577).

584. *Lige v. Montclair*, 72 N.J. 5 (1976). At least one federal trial court had applied *Wards Cove* to an LAD claim. *Meacham v. Bell Telephone Laboratories, Inc.*, 1990 WL 299805, pp. *2, 6 n.4, 8 n.7, 13 nn.4 &7 (D.N.J. 1990) (LAD and Title VII).

585. *Lige v. Montclair*, 72 N.J. 5, 7-8, 11 (1976). The *Wonderlic* test consists of 50 questions testing vocabulary comprehension, computation of mathematical problems, deductive reasoning, and general knowledge. *Id.* at 8.

586. *Id.* at 11-12. The DCR adopted the disparate impact analysis of *Griggs v. Duke Power Co.*, 401 U.S. 424 (1971). *Lige v. Montclair*, 72 N.J. at 11-12 n.3.

was not shown to be justified by educational ('business') considerations," and a disparate impact that justified a finding of discrimination in the absence of invidious intent.[588] And in *Shaner v. Horizon Bancorp.*, the Court noted that "a presumption of invidious motive or intent [is created] if the claimant can show that an employment practice ... has a significant discriminatory impact."[589]

The Appellate Division has applied the disparate-impact analysis in several other cases. In *Castellano v. Linden Bd. of Educ.*, collective bargaining agreement provisions applicable to pregnancy but not other disabilities and requiring mandatory leaves of absence were found to have a disparate impact on women.[590] The employer's "business necessity" defense that there was a need for "continuity of instruction" during the school year, while "unquestionably a valid consideration," was held to be an insufficient justification because no other extended absences due to disability were subject to the policy.[591] In contrast, a school board policy of not rehiring "any nontenured teacher, male or female, who gives the Board advance [notice] of an anticipated absence [for any reason] of substantial duration in the coming school year" does not violate the LAD.[592]

In *Giammario v. Trenton Bd. of Ed.*, the court held that monetary considerations in collective bargaining may justify an adverse impact on older employees:

---

587. *Lige v. Montclair,* 72 N.J. at 12 n.3. In *Giammario v. Trenton Bd. of Ed.*, 203 N.J.Super. 356, 363 (App. Div.), *certif. denied,* 102 N.J. 336 (1985), *cert. denied,* 475 U.S. 1141 (1986), the court, without citation to any authority, held that the burden of persuasion shifts to defendant to show that the employment practice was legally justified. Relying on §4(f)(1) of the federal ADEA, the court stated that an employer can defend a disparate-impact case by showing that the differentiation was based on "reasonable factors other than age" (RFOA). If *Giammario* based the burden-of-persuasion shift on §4(f)(1) of the ADEA, it was mistaken. The RFOA defense (as well as the good-cause defense of §4(f)(3) of the ADEA) is not an affirmative defense that shifts the burden of persuasion to defendants. *Marshall v. Westinghouse Elec. Corp.*, 576 F.2d 588, 591 (5th Cir. 1978), *reh'g denied*, 582 F.2d 966 (5th Cir. 1978); *EEOC v. Westinghouse Electric Corp.*, 725 F.2d 211, 222 (3d Cir. 1983), *cert. denied*, 469 U.S. 820 (1984), *overruled on other grounds, EEOC v. Westinghouse Electric Corp.*, 930 F.2d 329 (3d Cir. 1991). *Contra Criswell v. Western Airlines, Inc.*, 709 F.2d 544, 552-53 (9th Cir. 1983), *aff'd on other grounds*, 472 U.S. 400, 408 n.10 (1985). In *In re Vey,* 124 N.J. 534, 543 (1991), a case involving the denial of a civil service appointment because of alleged mental unfitness, the Court held that although "this is not an employment-discrimination case, we believe that the [employing] agency 'should reasonably bear the burden of establishing the job-validity of its * * * psychological tests.' "

588. *Countiss v. Trenton State College*, 77 N.J. 590, 595 (1978). *Cf. Elmwood Park Educ. Ass'n v. Elmwood Park Bd. of Educ.*, 3 N.J.A.R. 249 (Comm'r Ed. 1980) (payment of lower wages to coaches performing comparable work solely on the basis of the sex of the student participants violated the Education Code).

589. *Shaner v. Horizon Bancorp.*, 116 N.J. 433, 437 (1989).

590. *Castellano v. Linden Bd. of Educ.*, 158 N.J.Super. 350 (App. Div. 1978), *rev'd in part on other grounds*, 79 N.J. 407 (1979).

591. *Id.* at 355-56. The court added that rights guaranteed by the LAD may not be bargained away at the collective bargaining table. *Id.* at 358.

592. *Gilchrist v. Haddonfield Bd. of Educ.*, 155 N.J.Super. 358, 368 (App. Div. 1978). *Gilchrist* was discussed favorably in *Castellano v. Linden Bd. of Educ.*, 79 N.J. 407, 412 (1979).

> Although monetary considerations cannot normally justify policies which [have a disparate impact], the rule must be different with respect to labor negotiations—an exercise in which fiscal effect is a primary factor. [I]t is inevitable in the negotiation process that some employees will fare better than others. If facially neutral negotiating compromises which turn out to have an unintended disparate impact on people of differing age are discrimination under ADEA or LAD, labor negotiations become chaotic. Compromises will often lie in the area of retroactivity which by definition will relate to seniority, a quality with a high correlation to age. Making new benefits prospective only is a rational and usual compromise often employed in negotiations.
>
> * * *
>
> [A] facially neutral provision in a labor contract which impacts adversely on an older age group in an incidental manner does not violate the ADEA or the LAD.[593]

The *Giammario* court noted that some commentators argue that the disparate-impact analysis should not be applied in age discrimination cases.[594] While many courts have applied the disparate-impact theory in age cases, they have tempered its application by requiring a stronger showing at the *prima-facie* case stage or by making a more searching review of the record.[595] The reason for this heightened standard was explained in *Kephart v. Institute of Gas Technology*:

> [S]tatistics, while of some aid in showing discriminatory intent, are not significant in age discrimination cases unless the disparities in treatment are quite large. The reason such evidence is of little value in assessing discriminatory intent was explained in *Laugesen v. Anaconda Co.*: "[I]t is apparent that in the usual case, absent any discriminatory intent, discharged employees will more often than not be replaced by those younger than they,

---

593. *Giammario v. Trenton Bd. of Ed.*, 203 N.J. Super. at 363-64. *Cf. Donnelly v. Exxon Research & Engineering Co.*, 12 FEP 417 (D.N.J. 1974), *aff'd without published op.*, 521 F.2d 1398 (3d Cir. 1975) (policy of terminating any employee whose efficiency was not evaluated at least 75 percent of his current salary does not violate ADEA); *Geller v. Markham*, 635 F.2d 1027 (2d Cir. 1980), *cert. denied*, 451 U.S. 945 (1981) (policy of hiring teachers with five or less years of experience violated ADEA); *Markham v. Geller*, 451 U.S. 945 (1981) (Rehnquist, J., dissenting from denial of *certiorari*).

594. *Giammario v. Trenton Bd. of Ed.*, 203 N.J.Super. at 362. *See Esposito v. Township of Edison*, 306 N.J. Super. 280 (App. Div. 1997) (utilizing both disparate impact and disparate treatment analysis in age discrimination case).

595. *See, e.g.*, *Massarsky v. General Motors Corp.*, 706 F.2d 111, 120 (3d Cir.), *cert. denied*, 464 U.S. 937 (1983) (ADEA and LAD).

> for older employees are constantly moving out of the labor market, while younger ones move in."[596]

The applicability of the disparate-impact approach to age discrimination cases under the LAD is further hampered by the fact that the LAD protects all employees age 18 and older, whereas the federal ADEA is limited to age 40 and over.[597] Thus, under the LAD, nearly all employees are in the protected age class.

If a facially-neutral policy that has a disparate impact is sanctioned by the New Jersey Constitution, it probably does not violate the LAD.[598]

IV. ENFORCEMENT

4-42 The Division on Civil Rights

The Division on Civil Rights (DCR) within the Department of Law and Public Safety is charged with enforcement of the LAD.[599] It consists of the Attorney General and the Commission on Civil Rights.[600]

The Attorney General has broad powers under the LAD, including, but not limited to the following:

1. Exercise all powers of the DCR not vested in the Commission, and administer the work of the DCR.[601]
2. Appoint the DCR Director, who acts in the place of and has the powers of the Attorney General, along with other employees as are deemed necessary to carry out the work of the DCR.[602]

---

596. *Kephart v. Institute of Gas Technology*, 630 F.2d 1217, 1224, 1219 (7th Cir. 1980), *cert. denied*, 450 U.S. 959 (1981) (citations omitted), *quoting Laugesen v. Anaconda Co.*, 510 F.2d 307, 313-14 n.4 (6th Cir. 1975) (also noting that Congress did not intend the ADEA to prevent an employer from achieving a reasonable age balance in its employment structure).

597. *See, e.g., Massarsky v. General Motors Corp.*, 706 F.2d at 121.

598. *Cf. Ballou v. New Jersey Dept. of Civil Service*, 148 N.J.Super. 112, 119, 124-26 (App. Div. 1977), *aff'd*, 75 N.J. 365 (1978) (provision of Civil Service Act that gives employment preference to veterans and has disparate impact on females is sanctioned by New Jersey's Constitution and does not violate the Equal Protection Clause of the Fourteenth Amendment). *Accord Personnel Administrator of Massachusetts v. Feeney*, 442 U.S. 256 (1979).

599. N.J.S.A. 10:5-6, -5.1, -5(h).

600. N.J.S.A. 10:5-7, -5(i)-(j); *David v. Vesta Co.*, 45 N.J. 301, 321 (1965). The Commission on Civil Rights is empowered to: (1) consult with and advise the Attorney General with respect to the work of the DCR; (2) survey and study the operations of the DCR; and (3) report to the governor and Legislature with respect to the DCR, as it deems in the public interest. N.J.S.A. 10:5-10.

601. N.J.S.A. 10:5-8; *David v. Vesta Co.*, 45 N.J. 301, 321 (1965).

602. N.J.S.A. 10:5-8(e); *David v. Vesta Co.*, 45 N.J. at 321.

3. Enact suitable rules and regulations, including rules of practice, to carry out the provisions of the LAD.[603]
4. Conduct investigations, receive complaints, and conduct hearings thereon other than complaints received and hearings held pursuant to the provisions of the LAD.[604]
5. In connection with any investigation or hearing held pursuant to the LAD, among other things, subpoena witnesses, require the production of documents, conduct such discovery procedures as deemed necessary, and administer oaths.[605]
6. Regulate the powers and practices of county and municipal offices of civil rights.[606]

The expressed powers of the DCR are liberally construed, and are augmented by such incidental powers as are reasonably necessary or appropriate to fully effectuate its legislative mandate.[607] Subject to the limitations of the LAD, the Ad-

---

603. N.J.S.A. 10:5-8(g), (i), -18; *General Motors Corp. v. Blair*, 129 N.J.Super. 412, 418 (App. Div. 1974). Agency rules that have been duly promulgated under properly delegated powers have the force and effect of law. *State of New Jersey v. Atlantic City Elec. Co.*, 23 N.J. 259, 270 (1957); 37 Lefelt, *New Jersey Practice: Administrative Law & Practice*, §71 (1988). Courts will give "considerable weight" to the DCR's construction of the LAD, as reflected in the DCR's published rules. *Passaic Daily News v. Blair*, 63 N.J. 474, 484 (1973). A rule that is not properly adopted in accordance with the Administrative Procedure Act, N.J.S.A. 52:14B-1 *et seq.*, will not have the force of law. *See* 37 Lefelt, *New Jersey Practice: Administrative Law & Practice*, §§74-76, 90 (1988); *In re Boyan*, 246 N.J.Super. 300, 319-30 (App. Div. 1991) (Petrella, J., concurring), *rev'd*, 127 N.J. 266 (1992). A rule that conflicts with the enabling statute will be invalidated by a reviewing court. *New Jersey Builders, Owners & Managers Ass'n v. Blair*, 60 N.J. 330, 334 (1972); *see generally* 37 Lefelt, *New Jersey Practice: Administrative Law & Practice*, §73 (1988). There is a rebuttable presumption that rules enacted pursuant to the LAD are valid. *United Building & Construction Trades Council v. Mayor & Council of Camden*, 88 N.J. 317, 325 (1982), *rev'd on other grounds*, 465 U.S. 208 (1984). Rules that have been adopted subsequent to the events in controversy, while not binding authority as to the dispute in question, are nonetheless entitled to some deference. *See, e.g.*, *Jansen v. Food Circus Supermarkets, Inc.*, 110 N.J. 363, 375 (1988).

The DCR has issued various booklets explaining the scope of the LAD. Although the guidelines contained therein do not have the force of law, they nonetheless constitute administrative interpretations of the LAD by the enforcing agency and thus are entitled to "great weight." *Peper v. Princeton Univ. Bd. of Trustees*, 77 N.J. 55, 69-70 (1978) (Attorney General's interpretation of the LAD entitled to "great weight"). *Accord Lige v. Montclair*, 72 N.J. 5, 18 (1976) (Court looked to the DCR's *Employer Guide to the [LAD]* (1965) for guidance).

The consistent position taken by the DCR over a period of years in administrative proceedings is entitled to great weight. *Clowes v. Terminix Int'l, Inc.*, 109 N.J. 575, 590-91 (1988). "The meaning ascribed to legislation by the administrative agency responsible for its implementation, including the agency's contemporaneous construction, long usage, and practical interpretation, is persuasive evidence of the Legislature's understanding of its enactment." *Cedar Cove, Inc. v. Stanzione*, 122 N.J. 202, 212 (1991).

604. N.J.S.A. 10:5-8(h).

605. N.J.S.A. 10:5-8(i).

606. N.J.S.A. 10:5-14.2, -14.3.

607. *United Building & Construction Trades Council v. Mayor & Council of Camden*, 88 N.J. at 325; 37 Lefelt, *New Jersey Practice: Administrative Law & Practice*, §7 (1988); N.J.S.A. 10:5-3, -27; N.J.A.C. 13:13-1.2(a); N.J.A.C. 13:4-1.2(a)-(b).

ministrative Procedure Act[608] and due process, the DCR has broad discretion to follow such procedures as it deems most appropriate in implementing the LAD.[609]

4-43 DCR Declaratory Rulings and Advisory Opinions

Upon the request of any interested person, the DCR may make a declaratory ruling on the applicability of the LAD or its regulations to any person or state of facts.[610] Opportunity for a hearing must be provided.[611] A declaratory ruling by the DCR binds the agency and all parties to the proceedings on the state of facts alleged,[612] and is a final order subject to direct appeal to the Superior Court, Appellate Division.[613] The DCR's right to issue declaratory rulings does not affect its right or practice to render advisory opinions.[614]

4-44 Director's Investigations

The Director may conduct investigations to determine the extent of compliance with the LAD, regardless of whether a complaint has been filed.[615] All investigatory, subpoena, and discovery powers otherwise available to the Director may be used in these investigations.[616] In an investigation of an employer, the Director may require submission of all information reasonably necessary to effectuate the LAD.[617]

---

608. N.J.S.A. 52:14B-1 *et seq.*

609. *Frank v. Ivy Club*, 228 N.J.Super. 40, 54, 62 (App. Div. 1988), *rev'd on other grounds*, 120 N.J. 73 (1990), *cert. denied*, 498 U.S. 1073 (1991); *Hinfey v. Matawan Regional Bd. of Educ.*, 77 N.J. 514, 530-31 (1978). *Accord Shaner v. Horizon Bancorp.*, 116 N.J. 433, 438 (1989) (DCR "has far-ranging and comprehensive jurisdiction ... and broad and flexible power to combat discrimination").

610. N.J.S.A. 52:14B-8. Requests may even be made by a complainant or respondent during a DCR enforcement proceeding. *General Motors Corp. v. Blair*, 129 N.J.Super. 412, 425-26, 417 (App. Div. 1974). For a fuller discussion of declaratory rulings, *see* 37 Lefelt, *New Jersey Practice: Administrative Law & Practice*, §83 (1988).

611. N.J.S.A. 52:14B-8.

612. *Id.*

613. *Id.*

614. *Id.*

615. N.J.A.C. 13:4-2.1(a), (e). Any person entitled to file a complaint may request an investigation. *See, e.g.*, *New Jersey Div. on Civil Rights v. Slumber, Inc.*, 82 N.J. 412, 413-14 (1980); *New Jersey Builders, Owners & Managers Ass'n v. Blair*, 60 N.J. 330, 335 (1972).

616. N.J.A.C. 13:4-2.1(b), -2.2.

617. N.J.A.C. 13:4-2.1(d). This includes the age, ancestry, color, etc., of employees, employment records, and procedures for advertising, hiring, testing, seniority, promotion and discharge.

4-45 Enforcement Proceedings

With one exception, a person claiming to be aggrieved by an unlawful employment practice may pursue relief in either the Division on Civil Rights (DCR) or the Superior Court.[618] The procedures employed in DCR proceedings have been found to satisfy administrative due-process requirements under New Jersey and federal law.[619]

4-46 Arbitration Agreements

Agreements to arbitrate employment disputes may include discrimination claims. If an employee has entered into a contract providing for such arbitration, his LAD claim must be submitted to arbitration and may not be pursued before the DCR or in a civil action.[620] However, any such agreement to waive statutory remedies under the LAD must be clearly and unmistakeably established; contractual language alleged to constitute a waiver will not be read expansively.[621] While language providing for arbitration of "any dispute" has been found effective, the "better course would be the use of language reflecting that the employee, in fact, knows that other options such as federal and state administrative remedies and judicial remedies exist; that the employee also knows that by signing the contract, those remedies are forever precluded; and that, regardless of the

---

618. N.J.S.A. 10:5-13. Claims of mandatory retirement in violation of the LAD may be heard only by the DCR. N.J.S.A. 10:5-12.1.

If an adequate basis for federal subject matter jurisdiction exists, such as complete diversity of citizenship or supplemental jurisdiction, the aggrieved party may institute suit in federal court instead of state court.

619. *Frank v. Ivy Club*, 120 N.J. 73, 79, 98 (1990), *cert. denied*, 498 U.S. 1073 (1991); *Pittman v. LaFontaine*, 756 F.Supp. 834, 845-46 (D.N.J. 1991) (also noting: "The fact that [a plaintiff] failed to avail [her]self of the full procedures provided by state law does not constitute a sign of their inadequacy," quoting *Kremer v. Chemical Construction Corp.*, 456 U.S. 461, 485 (1982)); *Hermann v. Fairleigh Dickinson Univ.*, 183 N.J.Super. 500, 503-04 (App. Div.), *certif. denied*, 91 N.J. 573 (1982) (plaintiff failed to request a hearing or seek judicial review); *Ferrara v. Tappan Co.*, 722 F.Supp. 1204, 1205-06 (D.N.J. 1989) (due process not violated by offering plaintiff choice of remedial options); *Giammario v. Trenton Bd. of Ed.*, 203 N.J.Super. 356, 364-65 (App. Div.), *certif. denied*, 102 N.J. 336 (1985), *cert. denied*, 475 U.S. 1141 (1986); *Sprague v. Glassboro State College*, 161 N.J.Super. 218, 225-29 (App. Div. 1978). *Cf. O'Hara v. Camden County Vocational School Bd. of Educ.*, 590 F.Supp. 696, 703 (D.N.J. 1984), *aff'd as modified on other grounds*, 760 F.2d 259 (table), 36 EPD 35135 (3d Cir. 1985) (OAL's procedures meet the requirements of federal due process: "The important due process criterion is the *opportunity* to present one's evidence, and it is irrelevant that the party declined to take advantage of [the] opportunity" to present evidence to the ALJ; Title VII case).

One court has held that DCR proceedings that terminate in findings of no probable cause do not afford complainants adequate due process. *Wood v. Garden State Paper Co.*, 577 F.Supp. 632, 634-37 (D.N.J. 1983). That decision has not been followed in any reported decisions and has been expressly rejected by several courts. *Giammario v. Trenton Bd. of Ed.*, 203 N.J.Super. at 365; *Ferrara v. Tappan Co.*, 722 F.Supp. at 1205; *Pittman v. LaFontaine*, 756 F.Supp. at 846; *see O'Hara v. Camden County Vocational School Bd. of Educ.*, 590 F.Supp. at 703.

nature of the employee's complaint, he or she knows that it can only be resolved by arbitration."[622] A defendant invoking arbitration as a bar to an LAD proceeding must raise it as an affirmative defense in the answer or else risk waiving it.[623]

4-46:1 Collective Bargaining Grievance Procedures

Grievance procedures provided for by collective bargaining agreements need not be exhausted before filing a verified complaint with the DCR.[624] The mere

---

620. *Alamo Rent A Car, Inc. v. Galarza*, 306 N.J. Super. 384, 388-89 (App. Div. 1997); *Young v. Prudential Ins. Co. of America, Inc.*, 297 N.J. Super. 605, 621 (App. Div.), *certif. denied*, 149 N.J. 408 (1997); *Nicholson v. CPC Int'l Inc.*, 46 FEP 1019, 1023 (D.N.J. 1988), *aff'd on other grounds*, 877 F.2d 221, 231 (3d Cir. 1989), *overruled*, *Gilmer v. Interstate/Johnson Lane Corp.*, 500 U.S. 20, 111 S.Ct. 1647, 114 L.Ed.2d 26 (1991) (referring all state-law claims, including LAD claim, to arbitration); *Steck v. Smith Barney, Harris Upham & Co.*, 661 F.Supp. 543, 547-48 (D.N.J. 1987) (same); *Moore v. Merrill Lynch, Pierce, Fenner & Smith, Inc.*, 1991 WL 149881, pp. *8-10 (D.N.J. 1991) (post-*Gilmer* decision). *Cf. Burke v. Merrill Lynch & Co.*, 52 FEP 244 (D.N.J. 1989), *order aff'd and app. dism'd without published op.*, 897 F.2d 520 (3d Cir. 1990) (staying LAD claims and deferring decision as to whether such claims must be arbitrated), with *Fregara v. Jet Aviation Business Jets*, 764 F.Supp. 940 (D.N.J. 1991) (same judge holding that employee claiming a *Woolley* implied contract based upon an employee handbook required to utilize the final and binding grievance procedure set forth in handbook).

If an employee is asserting claims under the ADEA, a similar result would obtain if the arbitration agreement is not part of a collective bargaining agreement. *See Gilmer v. Interstate/Johnson Lane Corp.*, 500 U.S. 20, 111 S.Ct. 1647, 114 L.Ed.2d 26; *Moore v. Merrill Lynch, Pierce, Fenner & Smith, Inc.*, 1991 WL 149881, pp. *8-10. In *Alexander v. Gardner-Denver Co.*, 415 U.S. 36 (1974), the Court held that Title VII claims need not be submitted to arbitration pursuant to a collective bargaining agreement. Many courts have extended the *Gardner-Denver* holding to cases not involving collective bargaining agreements. *See, e.g.*, *Alford v. Dean Witter Reynolds, Inc.*, 905 F.2d 104 (5th Cir. 1990), *vacated*, 500 U.S. 930 (1991). The Court's analysis in *Gilmer* clearly suggests that *Gardner-Denver* is limited to arbitration provisions contained in collective bargaining agreements. Indeed, one week after *Gilmer* was issued, the Court vacated the *Alford* decision and remanded to the Fifth Circuit for further consideration in light of *Gilmer*. *Dean Witter Reynolds, Inc. v. Alford*, 500 U.S. 930, 111 S.Ct. 2050, 114 L.Ed.2d 456 (1991).

Also noteworthy is the fact that one week after *Gilmer* was decided the Court denied *certiorari* in a California case where a court had held, as a matter of federal law, that claims under the California Fair Employment and Housing Act must be arbitrated pursuant to an arbitration clause in a private employment contract. *Cook v. Barratt American, Inc.*, 268 Cal.Rptr. 629 (App. 4th Dist. 1990), *cert. denied*, 500 U.S. 932, 111 S.Ct. 2052, 114 L.Ed.2d 458 (1991).

Because public employers in New Jersey cannot agree to binding arbitration of the prerogatives of management—such as decisions pertaining to the hiring, transfer, promotion, and dismissal of employees—claims that such decisions were based on unlawful discrimination are not subject to binding arbitration and may be litigated before the DCR or in Superior Court. *Teaneck Bd. of Educ. v. Teaneck Teachers Ass'n*, 94 N.J. 9 (1983); *Jersey City Educ. Ass'n v. Jersey City Bd. of Educ.*, 218 N.J.Super. 177, 194 (App. Div. 1987). *Young v. Prudential Ins. Co.*, 297 N.J. Super. 605 (App. Div. 1997) requiring arbitration of LAD claim, but not CEPA claim, pursuant to arbitration agreement in the National Association of Securities Dealers (NASD) U-4 form); *Great Western Mortgage Corp. v. Peacock*, 110 F.3d 222 (3d Cir. 1997) (requiring arbitration of sexual harassment claim under the LAD, pursuant to a signed arbitration agreement; employment contract exception to the Federal Arbitration Act is limited to individuals employed directly in the channels of commerce; making agreement to arbitrate a condition of employment does not make it involuntary), *certif. denied*, 118 S. Ct. 299, 139 L.Ed.2d 230.

621. *Alamo Rent A Car, Inc. v. Galarza*, 306 N.J. Super. 384, 391 (App. Div. 1997) (arbitration of LAD claim not required where employment agreement provided for arbitration of alleged violations of agreement; fact that the agreement guaranteed freedom from discrimination and harassment didn't turn employee's LAD claim into a contract claim).

existence of a general contractual grievance procedure does not bar filing of an administrative charge of discrimination or a civil suit.[625] Nonetheless, utilization of grievance procedures is encouraged because they "often provide an expedited resolution of discrimination claims and clear the air of much misunderstanding."[626] The LAD does not affect the contractual right of employees who are disciplined for violating the LAD from challenging that discipline in grievance and arbitration proceedings under their collectively negotiated agreement.[627]

4-46:2 Impact of Prior Determinations

Because employment discrimination claimants frequently pursue their disputes in more than one forum (*e.g.*, arbitration and then court, the Division on Civil Rights and then court) issues regularly arise as to the evidentiary and preclusive effects of the first tribunal's determination.

Arbitration

The Supreme Court has held that an employee who fails to raise a discrimination claim in arbitration conducted by his union is not barred by the entire-controversy doctrine from filing that claim with the DCR.[628] An adverse

---

622. *Id.* at 394.

623. *Moore v. Merrill Lynch, Pierce, Fenner & Smith, Inc.*, 1991 WL 149881, pp. *10-11; R.4:5-4. *See* Pressler, *Current N.J. Court Rules*, Comments to R.4:5-4 (1999 ed.).

624. *Thornton v. Potamkin Chevrolet*, 94 N.J. 1, 5-8 (1983); *Teaneck Bd. of Educ. v. Teaneck Teachers Ass'n*, 94 N.J. 9, 20-21 (1983); *Dixon v. Rutgers*, 110 N.J. 432, 460 (1988); *Roberts v. Keansburg Bd. of Educ.*, 5 N.J.A.R. 208, 220, 237 (DCR 1983); *Vasto v. Vornado, Inc.*, 8 N.J.A.R. 481, 506 (DCR 1983). *See Nieves v. Individualized Shirts*, 961 F. Supp. 782, 791-92 (D.N.J. 1997) (United States Supreme Court decision in *Gilmer v. Interstate/Johnson Lane Corp.*, 500 U.S. 20 (1991) does not extend to arbitration provisions in collective bargaining agreements; plaintiff's failure to exhaust that remedy did not bar assertion of her purely statutory claims in court). *See Gallo v. Salesian Soc'y, Inc.*, 290 N.J. Super. 616 (App. Div. 1996) (plaintiff not required to grieve her LAD claim).

625. *Gallo v. Salesian Society, Inc.*, 290 N.J. Super. 616, 656 (App. Div. 1996). *See also Alamo Rent A Car, Inc. v. Galarza*, 306 N.J. Super. 384, 390 (App. Div. 1997).

626. *Teaneck Bd. of Educ. v. Teaneck Teachers Ass'n*, 94 N.J. at 18. *See, e.g., Dixon v. Rutgers*, 110 N.J. at 436-37.

627. *New Jersey Turnpike Auth. v. New Jersey Turnpike Supervisors Ass'n*, 143 N.J. 185 (1996) (court rejects the Turnpike Authority's contention that the LAD preempted an alleged sexual harasser's right to arbitration over his discipline, holding that the employer's right to adopt and implement policies against sexual harassment 'is distinct from the employees' ability to seek review of disciplinary actions based on allegations of sexual harassment.'). *See also Nieves v. Individualized Shirts*, 961 F. Supp. 782, 792-93 (D.N.J. 1997) (plaintiff's disability claim not preempted because it was not based on and did not require interpretation of the collective bargaining agreement); *Hunter v. H.L. Yoh Co., Inc.*, 1994 WL 636992 (D.N.J. Oct. 6, 1994) (plaintiff's race discrimination claim dismissed as pre-empted by §301 of the Labor Management Relations Act, 29 U.S.C. §185; since plaintiff's claim depended upon whether he was "qualified" to be rehired after being laid off in a cutback, and such recall rights were dependent upon the collective bargaining agreement, the court held that plaintiff's LAD claims were "inextricably intertwined with considerations of the terms of the labor contract").

628. *Thornton v. Potamkin Chevrolet*, 94 N.J. 1 (1983).

determination in union arbitration similarly fails to bar a subsequent filing with the DCR:

> [I]n either public or private employment, although of evidential value, neither failure to present nor unsuccessful prior submission of [a discrimination] claim to an available [collective-bargaining] arbitration process will foreclose an employee's statutory right to present the claim to the [DCR].[629]

Nonetheless, the arbitrator's decision is admissible into evidence and should be afforded such weight as the following factors warrant: "what evidence was considered; what procedures were employed to test credibility; whether the hearing was informal and casual; whether the award was brief and cursory or detailed; whether a well-reasoned formal award was intrinsically persuasive."[630]

Unemployment Compensation

In *Hahn v. Arbat Systems Ltd., Inc.*, the Appellate Division held that a final determination in an unemployment compensation proceeding that there was no evidence that plaintiff was discriminated against was not entitled to preclusive effect in a subsequent civil action for employment discrimination.[631] However, unemployment compensation records may be entered into evidence in a subsequent discrimination proceeding.[632]

Although the Unemployment Compensation Law expressly prohibits the evidentiary use of certain documents in subsequent proceedings,[633] the Law Division held in an unpublished 1990 opinion that recorded tapes and transcripts of hearings held before the Appeals Tribunal and Board of Review were discoverable and admissible in a civil action for wrongful discharge instituted by an employee who had pursued a claim for compensation benefits in the Division.[634] The Division subsequently issued an Administrative Instruction providing that requests for copies of

---

629. *Teaneck Bd. of Educ. v. Teaneck Teachers Ass'n*, 94 N.J. 9, 20-21 (1983). The decisions in *Thornton* and *Teaneck* should be read in light of the discussion in §4-46.

630. *Thornton v. Potamkin Chevrolet*, 94 N.J. at 8.

631. *Hahn v. Arbat Systems Ltd., Inc.*, 200 N.J.Super. 266, 268-69 (App. Div. 1985). *Cf. Gimello v. Agency Rent-A-Car Systems, Inc.*, 250 N.J.Super. 338, 351 (App. Div. 1991) (State Division of Unemployment notice of determination admitted into evidence in DCR proceeding); *DeMarco v. Thatcher Furnace Co.*, 102 N.J.Super. 258, 278 (Ch.Div. 1968) (final determination in unemployment compensation proceeding that plaintiff was not discharged for work-related misconduct not binding in subsequent civil action for wrongful discharge because employer bore the burden of persuasion in first proceeding and plaintiff bears that burden in the second).

632. In *Clowes v. Terminix Int'l, Inc.*, 109 N.J. 575, 583-84 (1988), an ALJ admitted records from an unemployment compensation proceeding in a handicap discrimination case. The records indicated that (1) plaintiff had stated that he was discharged for lack of work due to the off-season and because he was one of the last hired and (2) the employer had stated that plaintiff was discharged because he was too ill to continue working.

633. N.J.S.A. 43:21-11(g).

hearing tapes and other claims-related information will be honored "only when such requests are made [in writing] by a party to the hearing and the tape is for use in a [pending] civil action between the [same] parties which involves issues similar to those involved in the unemployment proceeding."[635]

EEOC and DCR Determinations

EEOC probable cause determinations which are shown to be trustworthy may be admissible in actions under the LAD and federal anti-discrimination laws.[636] An adverse administrative determination by the EEOC does not bar a subsequent LAD suit in state court..[637] Judicially-unreviewed DCR probable cause determinations are admissible in subsequent Title VII and ADEA lawsuits,[638] as well as in proceedings before the Commissioner of Education.[639] However, findings of probable cause made by the DCR are generally not admissible in subsequent proceedings before the DCR in the same case.[640]

Judicially-unreviewed state administrative agency findings of no discrimination are entitled to preclusive effect under 42 U.S.C.A. §1983,[641] "substantial

---

634. *Boardwalk Regency Corp. v. New Jersey Div. of Unemployment & Temporary Disability Ins.*, No. ATL-L-003119-89 P.W. (Law Div. May 7, 1990). The court concluded that the claimant and the employer, as participants in the administrative proceedings, were not members of the general public to whom the statutory bar was addressed. *Boardwalk Regency*, slip op. at pp. 3-4. A similar argument was adopted in *EEOC v. Associated Dry Goods Corp.*, 449 U.S. 590, 598-603 (1981) (complainants and respondents in EEOC administrative proceedings are not members of the "public" to whom prelitigation disclosure of information in EEOC's files is barred by Title VII). *See Rogozinski v. Airstream By Angell*, 152 N.J.Super. 133, 153 (Law Div. 1977), *modified on other grounds*, 164 N.J.Super. 465 (App. Div. 1979) (N.J.S.A. 43:21-11(g) is designed to protect the confidentiality interests of the employee and employer).

635. Dept. of Labor, Div. of Unemployment & Disability Ins., *Administrative Instruction No. IMT-189.*

636. *Stewart v. Personnel Pool of Am., Inc.*, 1993 WL 525575, at *6 (D.N.J., Dec. 16, 1993), *aff'd*, 30 F.3d 1488 (3d Cir. 1994) (admissibility of EEOC determination "is a decision to be made by the trial court in the exercise of its discretion"; where the administrative determination is shown to be untrustworthy it should not be considered). *Mullen v. New Jersey Steel Corp.*, 733 F.Supp. 1534, 1540-42 & n.7, 1551 (D.N.J. 1990) (preliminary determinations of EEOC and portions of its files admissible in evidence in ADEA/LAD action); *Abrams v. Lightolier, Inc.*, 702 F.Supp. 509, 511-12 (D.N.J. 1988) (EEOC preliminary determinations admissible); *Campbell Soup Co. v. Liberty Mut. Ins. Co.*, 239 N.J.Super. 403, 406 (App. Div.), *certif. denied*, 122 N.J. 163 (1990) (same); *Tuma v. American Can Co.*, 373 F.Supp. 218, 229 (D.N.J. 1974) (EEOC determination admissible in subsequent Title VII action); *Tuma v. American Can Co.*, 367 F.Supp. 1178, 1189 (D.N.J. 1973) (same).

637. *Hernandez v. Region Nine Housing Corp.*, 146 N.J. 645 (1996).

638. *Astoria Federal Savings & Loan Ass'n v. Solimino*, 501 U.S. 104, 111 S.Ct. 2166, 115 L.Ed.2d 96 (1991).

639. *Perry v. Glen Rock Bd. of Educ.*, 1 N.J.A.R. 300, 303 (Comm'r Ed. 1981).

640. *See* §4-49:9. *Muench v. Township of Haddon*, 255 N.J. Super. 288, 305-06 (App. Div. 1992).

641. *Univ. of Tennessee v. Elliott*, 478 U.S. 788, 795-99 (1986). *See Mancuso v. No. Arlington*, 203 N.J.Super. 427 (Law Div. 1985), (§1983 action of plaintiff who unsuccessfully challenged his discharge from public employment in an administrative proceeding before the Civil Service Commission barred by the doctrines of issue preclusion and claim preclusion; plaintiff's appropriate course of action would have been to file a timely appeal with the Appellate Division); *See Farley v. No. Bergen Tp. Bd. of Educ.*, 705 F.Supp. 223, 225, 228-29 (D.N.J. 1989) (in §1983 action, defendant precluded from relitigating factual issues resolved by an ALJ, after a hearing, and affirmed by the Commissioner of Education).

weight" under Title VII,[642] and deference under the ADEA.[643] In contrast, a state court judgment affirming a state agency's findings of no discrimination is preclusive under all of these three statutes.[644]

A final determination of an LAD claim by the DCR bars any further action on the same grievance in state trial court, and vice versa. The pendency of an appeal from an administrative determination does not diminish its preclusive effect.[645]

A final determination by the Division on Civil Rights also bars an action in federal court for the same LAD claim.[646]

4-46:3 Waiver of LAD Rights

A person protected by the LAD may waive his rights if the waiver is knowing and voluntary.[647] In evaluating whether a waiver is enforceable, New Jersey ap-

---

642. *Univ. of Tennessee v. Elliott*, 478 U.S. at 795-99. *See Delaine v. Western Temporary Services*, 32 FEP 593, 1983 WL 143570 (D.N.J. 1983).

In *O'Hara v. Camden County Vocational School Bd. of Educ.*, 590 F.Supp. 696, 701-04 (D.N.J. 1984), *modified on other grounds*, 760 F.2d 259 (table), 36 EPD 35135 (3d Cir. 1985), the court held that the findings of an ALJ, affirmed by both the Commissioner of Education and the State Board of Education, that plaintiff's outlandish conduct warranted her dismissal were entitled to preclusive effect in her Title VII sex discrimination case. It is unclear whether *O'Hara* survives the subsequent decision in *Elliott*, because *Elliott* was based on language in Title VII that requires the EEOC to give "substantial weight" to findings made by state fair employment practices agencies, such as the DCR. *O'Hara* did not involve such an agency.

643. *Astoria Federal Savings & Loan Ass'n v. Solimino*, 501 U.S. 104, 111 S.Ct. 2166, 115 L.Ed.2d 96; 29 C.F.R. §§1601.75(a), 1601.80 (1990) (in cases processed by DCR pursuant to the worksharing agreement, EEOC accepts the findings and resolutions of DCR without case-by-case review); DCR/EEOC Worksharing Agreement, pp. 1, 3 (1990-91).

644. *Univ. of Tennessee v. Elliott*, 478 U.S. at 792 & n.3, *citing Kremer v. Chemical Construction Corp.*, 456 U.S. 461 (1982); *Pittman v. LaFontaine*, 756 F.Supp. 834, 840-47 (D.N.J. 1991) (DCR finding of no probable cause that was affirmed by the Appellate Division). In *Wood v. Garden State Paper Co.*, 577 F.Supp. 632 (D.N.J. 1983), the court refused to give preclusive effect to a DCR finding of no probable cause that was affirmed by the Appellate Division, on the ground that DCR procedures failed to satisfy due process. The *Wood* court's analysis of the DCR's procedures is inaccurate and has been rejected in subsequent reported decisions. *Cf. Ivy Club v. Edwards*, 943 F.2d 270, (3d Cir. 1991), *cert. denied*, 503 U.S. 914 (1992) (DCR's determination of federal constitutional issue that was not reviewed during subsequent state court appeal from DCR's finding of discrimination not preclusive in subsequent §1983 action).

645. *O'Hara v. Camden County Vocational School Bd. of Educ.*, 590 F.Supp. at 702 (final administrative determination of State Board of Education entitled to preclusive effect in Title VII case even though appeal pending in Appellate Division). *Cf. Gregory Marketing Corp. v. Wakefern Food Corp.*, 207 N.J.Super. 607, 621-24 (Law Div. 1985), *overruled in part, Watkins v. Resorts Int'l Hotel & Casino, Inc.*, 124 N.J. 398 (1991) (State-court antitrust action barred by *res judicata* and collateral estoppel in view of federal court judgment in earlier action that is on appeal). *See Hernandez v. Region Nine Housing Corp.*, 146 N.J. 645 (1996) (adverse administrative determination by the EEOC does not bar subsequent LAD suit in state court).

646. *Tummala v. Merck & Co., Inc.*, 1995 WL 669220, p.*11-12 (D.N.J. 1995), *aff'd*, 111 F.3d 127 (3d Cir. 1997); *Harter v. GAF*, 150 F.R.D. 502, 514-15 (D.N.J. 1993).

647. *Swarts v. Sherwin-Williams Co.*, 244 N.J.Super. 170, 176-79 (App. Div. 1990); *Mullen v. New Jersey Steel Corp.*, 733 F.Supp. 1534, 1543-48 (D.N.J. 1990). *See Keelan v. Bell Communications Research*, 289 N.J. Super. 531 (App. Div. 1996) (applying *Swarts* standard to a CEPA claim; analyzing factors; holding requirements of the federal Older Workers' Benefit Protection Act, 29 U.S.C. § 626, inapplicable to waiver of state law claim, but useful as guidance as to voluntariness).

plies the "totality of the circumstances" standard, which includes, among others, the following factors:

1. Plaintiff's education, business experience, and awareness of his legal rights.
2. Whether defendant encouraged or discouraged plaintiff to consult with an attorney and whether plaintiff actually consulted with or was represented by counsel.
3. The amount of time plaintiff had possession of or access to the agreement before signing it, including time to consult an attorney.
4. The role plaintiff had in deciding the terms of the agreement.
5. The clarity and specificity of the agreement.
6. Whether the consideration given in exchange for the waiver exceeded the employee benefits plaintiff was already entitled to by contract or law.[648]

A waiver of rights under the LAD must be plainly expressed in clear and unmistakable terms.[649] The district court has held that an employee ratified an invalid release by accepting the benefits of a severance agreement and failing to complain about discrimination until after all periodic severance payments had been paid in full.[650]

4-46:4 Jurisdiction of the DCR

The DCR has "far-ranging and comprehensive jurisdiction in the field of civil rights,"[651] to prevent and eliminate discrimination prohibited by the LAD.[652]

---

648. *Swarts v. Sherwin-Williams Co.*, 244 N.J.Super. at 177, adopting the standard set forth by the Third Circuit in *Coventry v. U.S. Steel Corp.*, 856 F.2d 514 (3d Cir. 1988); *Mullen v. New Jersey Steel Corp.*, 733 F.Supp. at 1543. *See also Cirillo v. Arco Chemical Co.*, 862 F.2d 448 (3d Cir. 1988); *Valenti v. Int'l Mill Services, Inc.*, 1987 WL 54444, 45 FEP 1054 (3d Cir. 1987), *opinion vacated*, Jan. 22, 1988; *Sullivan v. Boron Oil Co.*, 831 F.2d 288 (table case), 8 EBC 2590 (3d Cir. 1987). In 1990, Congress enacted new subsection (f) to Section 7 of the ADEA, 29 U.S.C.A. §626(f), which establishes stringent standards for the enforceability of waivers of ADEA rights.

649. *Dixon v. Rutgers*, 110 N.J. 432, 460-61 (1988) (finding no waiver of access to discovery materials). *Cf. Ahrensfield v. New Jersey State Bd. of Educ.*, 124 N.J.L. 231, 234 (Sup.Ct. 1940), *aff'd*, 126 N.J.L. 543 (E. & A. 1941) (in an action under N.J.S.A. 10:1-1, N.J.S.A. 18A:6-6, and N.J. Const. Art. 1, ¶1, the court observed that plaintiff's "resignations were free from fraud, coercion and duress and ... were altogether voluntary").

650. *Mullen v. New Jersey Steel Corp.*, 733 F.Supp. at 1548, 1541; *O'Shea v. Commercial Credit Corp.*, 930 F.2d 358, 362-63 (4th Cir), *cert. denied*, 502 U.S. 859, 112 S.Ct. 177, 116 L.Ed.2d 139 (1991) (ADEA).

651. *Shaner v. Horizon Bancorp.*, 116 N.J. 433, 438 (1989) (internal quotations marks omitted).

652. N.J.S.A. 10:5-6; N.J.S.A. 10:5-13; N.J.S.A. 10:5-12; N.J.S.A. 10:5-4.1.

Acts of employment discrimination committed by governmental agencies are subject to the enforcement powers of the DCR,[653] but governmental actions in the exercise of basic regulatory responsibilities are not.[654] Thus, for example, the DCR does not have jurisdiction to review charges of discrimination in connection with (1) a duly-enacted zoning ordinance;[655] (2) insurance rates approved by the Commissioner of Insurance;[656] or (3) the rules and regulations of the Department of Personnel.[657]

Jurisdictional issues are resolved by the DCR before proceeding to the merits of the verified complaint.[658] If necessary, the Director may seek legal guidance from the Attorney General regarding the DCR's jurisdiction over a controversy.[659]

Prosecution of a civil action under the LAD in the courts effectively divests the DCR of jurisdiction. When two administrative agencies have concurrent jurisdiction over an employment discrimination dispute, the agency with the "predominate interest" should initially hear the matter.[660] In recognition of administrative comity and to avoid conflicts between the two agencies, the Director, in reaching a final decision, will apply the doctrines of claim preclusion, issue preclusion, entire controversy, and the like.[661] If the complaint is filed only with the agency with the non-predominate interest, it should be transferred to the other agency.[662]

---

653. *Teaneck Bd. of Educ. v. Teaneck Teachers Ass'n*, 94 N.J. 9, 17 (1983); *N.J. Attorney General Formal Opinion No. 2-1975* (Jan. 31, 1975); N.J.S.A. 10:5-5(e).

654. *UAW v. Mahwah*, 119 N.J.Super. 389, 392 (App. Div. 1972); *N.J. Attorney General Formal Opinion No. 5-1976* (Feb. 9, 1976).

655. *UAW v. Mahwah*, 119 N.J.Super. at 392.

656. *N.J. Attorney General Formal Opinion No. 2-1975* (Jan. 31, 1975).

657. *N.J. Attorney General Formal Opinion No. 5-1976* (Feb. 9, 1976).

658. *See, e.g., Frank v. Ivy Club*, 120 N.J. 73, 79-83, 92-96 (1990), *cert. denied*, 498 U.S. 1073 (1991) (issue raised by the DCR). The DCR may schedule a factfinding conference to discover facts relevant to the jurisdictional issue, *Id.* at 80-92, and if there is no disputed fact, resolve the question without a contested case hearing. *Id.* at 80-81, 93, 98-102, 110. If the issues of the DCR's jurisdiction and the occurrence of discrimination are very closely intermixed, it is permissible to conduct a joint hearing on both issues and then resolve the jurisdictional dispute. *Clover Hill Swimming Club v. Goldsboro*, 47 N.J. 25, 37 (1966). In certain circumstances, respondent may also challenge the jurisdiction of the DCR by instituting an action in lieu of prerogative writ in the Superior Court.

659. *See, e.g., Hinfey v. Matawan Regional Bd. of Educ.*, 77 N.J. 514, 519, 534 (1978); *Chai v. New Jersey Div. on Civil Rights*, 160 N.J.Super. 176, 177 (App. Div. 1977), *certif. denied*, 77 N.J. 511 (1978); *UAW v. Mahwah*, 119 N.J.Super. 389, 391 (App. Div. 1972); *N.J. Attorney General Formal Opinion No. 5-1976* (Feb. 9, 1976); *N.J. Attorney General Formal Opinion No. 2-1975* (Jan. 31, 1975).

660. *Balsley v. No. Hunterdon Regional Sch. Dist. Bd. of Educ.*, 117 N.J. 434, 439-47 (1990) (sex discrimination claim by high school student); *Hinfey v. Matawan Regional Bd. of Educ.*, 77 N.J. at 531-34 (sex, age, and marital status discrimination in public school employment and curricula); N.J.A.C. 1:1-17.5 *et seq.*

4-46:5 DCR/EEOC Worksharing Agreement

Because of their similarity of functions and volume of workloads, the DCR and the U.S. Equal Employment Opportunity Commission (EEOC) annually enter into a Worksharing Agreement designed to further the goals of the laws they enforce.[663] The Agreement reduces duplication of effort by dividing primary responsibility for charge resolution between the two agencies.[664] The DCR and EEOC state that they defer to final determinations made by each other, but in practice, that is not always the case.

Pursuant to the Worksharing Agreement, each agency assists claimants in completing the forms required for filing charges with both.[665] Each has designated the other as its agent for receiving complaints.[666]

Subject to certain exceptions, discrimination charges within the concurrent jurisdiction of the DCR and the EEOC are processed as set forth below:[667]

1. The DCR has primary responsibility for resolution of the following charges:
   a. All charges initially received by the DCR.
   b. All charges that allege more than one basis of discrimination, at least one of which is not covered by the laws administered by the EEOC but is covered by the LAD.
   c. All charges where the EEOC is required to dismiss the charge because of federal court decisions or internal EEOC policy, but the DCR can process it.
   d. All disability discrimination charges against Respondents over which EEOC lacks jurisdiction.
   e. A charge where the DCR is a party to a conciliation agreement or consent decree that is relevant to the disposition of the charge.

---

661. *Hackensack v. Winner*, 82 N.J. 1, 31-38 (1980) (employment dispute within the concurrent jurisdiction of PERC and the Civil Service Commission); *Balsley v. No. Hunterdon Regional Sch. Dist. Bd. of Educ.*, 117 N.J. at 440, 446; *Hinfey v. Matawan Regional Bd. of Educ.*, 77 N.J. at 532; N.J.A.C. 1:1-17.6(c). *But see Perry v. Glen Rock Bd. of Educ.*, 1 N.J.A.R. 300, 302-03, 308 (Comm'r Ed. 1981) (Commissioner declined to give any preclusive effect to DCR's finding of no probable cause and then determined, *de novo*, that the employer did not violate the LAD).

662. *Balsley v. No. Hunterdon Regional Sch. Dist. Bd. of Educ.*, 117 N.J. at 439, 445, 447; *Hinfey v. Matawan Regional Bd. of Educ.*, 77 N.J. at 520, 530. An agency decision to retain or transfer a complaint is subject to the abuse-of-discretion standard of review. *Jamison v. Rockaway Tp. Bd. of Educ.*, 171 N.J.Super. 549, 551-53 (App. Div. 1979).

663. DCR/EEOC Worksharing Agreement, pp. i-ii (1999).

664. Worksharing Agreement, p. iii-iv..

665. Worksharing Agreement, pp.ii.

666. Worksharing Agreement, p. ii.

667. Worksharing Agreement, pp. iii-iv and addendum.

f. Charges alleging retaliation for filing a charge or cooperating with the DCR.

2. The EEOC has primary responsibility for resolving the following charges:

a. All charges initially received by the EEOC.

b. All Title VII, ADA, ADEA and concurrent Title VII/ADA charges received by the DCR more than 180 days after the date of the violation.[668]

c. All charges against designated divisions of the New Jersey Department of Law and Public Safety (*e.g.*, Office of the Attorney General, DCR, Division of Motor Vehicles).

d. All charges filed by the EEOC Commissioners.

e. A charge where the EEOC is a party to a conciliation agreement or consent decree that is relevant to the disposition of the charge.

f. Charges alleging retaliation for filing a charge or cooperating with the EEOC.

g. Concurrent Title VII/EPA charges.

h. All charges against the DCR or its parent organization where the parent organization exercises direct or indirect control over the charge decision-making process.

i. Charges also covered by the Immigration Reform and Control Act.

j. Complaints referred to the EEOC by the Department of Justice, Office of Federal Contract Compliance Programs, or federal fund-granting agencies under 29 CRR §1640, 1641 and 1691.

4-47 Commencing Proceedings Before the DCR

To commence proceedings in the DCR, the aggrieved person,[669] or his attorney,[670] files with the DCR[671] a written verified complaint,[672] on a printed form approved by the DCR,[673] stating the names and addresses of the aggrieved person (complainant) and the person alleged to have violated the LAD (respondent);

668. Worksharing Agreement p. iii.

669. Subject to certain exceptions discussed later in this section, only actual victims of discrimination have standing to pursue a claim under the LAD. N.J.S.A. 10:5-13; *Patrolmen's Benevolent Ass'n v. East Brunswick*, 180 N.J.Super. 68, 72-73 (App. Div. 1981); *Bluvias v. Winfield Mutual Housing Corp.*, 224 N.J.Super. 515, 526 n.6 (App. Div. 1988), *app. dism'd*, 114 N.J. 589 (1989); *Watkins v. Resorts Int'l Hotel & Casino, Inc.*, 124 N.J. 398 (1991).

the particulars of the alleged violation, including a brief statement of the pertinent facts, the impermissible characteristic (*e.g.*, age) allegedly relied upon by the respondent, the section of the LAD allegedly violated, and the county in which the alleged discrimination occurred; and such other information as may be required by the DCR.[674] The complaint must be verified[675] and include an entire-controversy certification.[676]

A complainant with claims for relief under other state or federal statutes (*e.g.*, 42 U.S.C.A. §1981 or Title VII) or constitutions (*e.g.*, deprivation of equal protection), should assert them in the verified complaint and may not pursue them in an independent civil action.[677] Although the DCR lacks jurisdiction to resolve these claims (unless they involve issues that are relevant and necessary to resolution of the LAD claim), the Appellate Division will resolve them upon appeal from an adverse decision of the DCR.[678] However, federal statutory claims which may be pursued only in federal court should not be barred by a failure to raise them in a verified complaint or appeal therefrom.[679]

Under appropriate circumstances, verified complaints may also be filed by:

---

670. If necessary, the DCR will assist complainant in completing a verified complaint. N.J.A.C. 13:4-3.2(a). *See, e.g., Pittman v. LaFontaine*, 756 F.Supp. 834, 837-38 (D.N.J. 1991). Representation of parties by lawyers or non-lawyers in DCR and OAL proceedings is governed by N.J.A.C. 13:4-2.3(b)(4) and N.J.A.C. 1:1-5.1 *et seq. See generally* 37 Lefelt, *New Jersey Practice: Administrative Law & Practice*, §§125-32 (1988); Carter, *Handbook of Civil Practice in the Courts of New Jersey*, §14.7.3. (1988 & 1990 supp.).

671. The verified complaint may be filed at one of the DCR's regional offices or with any official or investigator of the DCR. N.J.A.C. 13:4-3.1. As explained in the preceding section, the EEOC is authorized to accept verified complaints on behalf of the DCR. All subsequent pleadings should be filed with a regional office only. N.J.A.C. 13:4-3.3(b).

Verified complaints may also be filed with authorized municipal offices of civil rights. *See* N.J.S.A. 10:5-18, -14.2. Although the LAD is silent on the issue, verified complaints may also be filed with authorized county offices of civil rights. *See* N.J.S.A. 10:5-18, -14.2, -14.3.

672. While the case is pending in the DCR, complainant may not file an amended verified complaint without approval of the Director. N.J.A.C. 13:4-6.3(a). *See, e.g., Frank v. Ivy Club*, 228 N.J.Super. 40, 48 (App. Div. 1988), *rev'd on other grounds*, 120 N.J. 73 (1990), *cert. denied*, 498 U.S. 1073 (1991); *Lige v. Montclair*, 72 N.J. 5, 6-7 (1976); *Levitt & Sons, Inc. v. New Jersey Div. Against Discrimination*, 56 N.J.Super. 542, 545, 553-55 (App. Div. 1959), *aff'd on other grounds*, 31 N.J. 514, 519-20, *app. dism'd*, 363 U.S. 418 (1960) (amendments adding new parties must be filed within limitations period).

673. *See* N.J.A.C. 13:4-3.4(a).

674. N.J.S.A. 10:5-13; N.J.A.C. 13:4-3.4, -3.5, -4.1; N.J.A.C. 1:1-3.1, -6.1; *Dixon v. Rutgers*, 110 N.J. 432, 455 (1988) (allegations of discrimination should be set forth with sufficient particularity and complaint should incorporate any and all available relevant information). *See* R.1:4-7 and R.1:4-8.

675. N.J.A.C. 13:4-3.5(a)(7). *See* R.1:4-7 and R. 1:4-8.

676. N.J.A.C. 13:4-3.5(a)(6). *Cf.* R.4:30A (entire-controversy doctrine); R.4:5-1 (notice of other actions). Complainant has a continuing obligation to notify the DCR if he files a related complaint with another agency or court. N.J.A.C. 13:4-3.5(a)(6).

677. *Christian Bros. Inst. v. Northern New Jersey Interscholastic League*, 86 N.J. 409, 413-16 (1981).

678. *Id.* at 415-16. *Cf. Simon v. Police & Firemen's Retirement System Bd. of Trustees*, 233 N.J.Super. 186, 196-97 (App. Div. 1989), *aff'g*, 12 N.J.A.R. 476, 491 (PFRS 1988), *certif. denied*, 117 N.J. 652 (1989) (resolving LAD and constitutional claims on appeal from the PFRS Bd. of Trustees).

- — groups or associations dedicated to the elimination of discrimination by employers and unions[680]
- — the Comissioners of Education and Labor, the Attorney General and the Director of the DCR[681]
- — the Director of the Division of the Deaf and Hard of Hearing.[682]
- — the Public Advocate[683]
- — an employer.[684]

Upon receipt of a verified complaint, the DCR notifies complainant in writing of (1) his rights under the LAD, including the right to file a complaint in the Superior Court to be heard before a jury; (2) the jurisdictional limitations of the DCR; and (3) without interpretation, any other provisions of the LAD that may apply to the verified complaint.[685] Once a proceeding has been commenced and while it is pending in the DCR, no civil action with respect to the same grievance may be instituted in the Superior Court.[686]

The DCR serves a copy of the verified complaint upon each respondent named therein by registered or certified mail, return receipt requested, or by any other means authorized by R.4:4-4 (service of process).[687]

---

679. *See, e.g.*, 29 U.S.C.A. §§1140, 1132(e)(1) (federal courts have exclusive jurisdiction of ERISA discrimination claims). *See Watkins v. Resorts Int'l Hotel & Casino, Inc.*, 124 N.J. 398, 413-14 (1991).

680. N.J.S.A. 10:5-17; N.J.A.C. 13:4-4.1(b). *See, e.g.*, *Hinfey v. Matawan Regional Bd. of Educ.*, 77 N.J. 515, 517 (1978) (employment and education discrimination action commenced by representatives of NOW); *Nat'l Organization for Women v. Little League Baseball, Inc.*, 127 N.J.Super. 522 (App. Div.), *summarily aff'd without op.*, 67 N.J. 320 (1974) (public accommodation case).

681. Such complaints are normally filed where a victim fails to complain or the discrimination is pervasive or far-reaching. N.J.S.A. 10:5-13; *Jackson v. Concord Co.*, 54 N.J. 113, 124 (1969); N.J.A.C. 13:4-4.2(a); N.J.A.C. 1:1-3.1. *See, e.g.*, *Lige v. Montclair*, 72 N.J. 5, 6-7 (1976) (Director); *New Jersey Div. on Civil Rights v. Slumber, Inc.*, 82 N.J. 412, 414 (1980) (Director).

682. N.J.S.A. 34:1-69.3.

683. N.J.S.A. 52:27E-28 to -32; N.J.S.A. 10:5-17; N.J.A.C. 13:4-6.5(a), -6.2(a); N.J.A.C. 1:1-16.1 *et seq. See Maher v. New Jersey Transit Rail Operations, Inc.*, 125 N.J. 455, 459, 479 (1991) (Public Advocate participated in appellate proceedings as an amicus curiae); *Edmond v. New Jersey Dept. of the Public Advocate*, 137 N.J. Super. 82, 83 (App. Div. 1975), *certif. denied*, 69 N.J. 445 (1976) (Public Advocate did not abuse discretion in refusing to institute action to compel DCR to reopen proceedings on complaint filed with DCR by appellant).

684. N.J.S.A. 10:5-13.

685. N.J.S.A. 10:5-13.

686. N.J.S.A. 10:5-27; *Christian Bros. Inst. v. Northern New Jersey Interscholastic League*, 86 N.J. 409, 415 (1981); *Fuchilla v. Layman*, 109 N.J. 319, 336, *cert. denied*, 488 U.S. 826 (1988); *Gray v. Serruto Builders, Inc.*, 110 N.J.Super. 297, 300 (Ch.Div. 1970); *Hermann v. Fairleigh Dickinson Univ.*, 183 N.J.Super. 500, 503-04 (App. Div.), *certif. denied*, 91 N.J. 573 (1982); *Ferrara v. Tappan Co.*, 722 F.Supp. 1204, 1205-06 (D.N.J. 1989) (plaintiff allowed only one bite at the apple); *Corn v. Adidas USA, Inc.*, No. 85-30835(HLS), p.5 (D.N.J. Jan. 6, 1986) (Lexis) (before a plaintiff can assert LAD claims in a federal ADEA action, he must withdraw his verified complaint from the LAD).

Respondent must file a verified answer with the DCR within 20 days after service of the verified complaint.[688] Affirmative defenses in the answer are deemed denied by complainant.[689]

The DCR attempts to resolve all cases within 180 days after filing of the verified complaint.[690] If a case is still pending at that time, complainant may file a written request to present the action personally or by counsel to the Office of Administrative Law (OAL).[691] Transfer must be granted unless the Director (1) has found that no probable cause exists to credit the allegations of the verified complaint or (2) has otherwise dismissed the verified complaint.[692]

4-47:1 DCR Investigation

Subject to the specific procedural mandates of the LAD and the Administrative Procedure Act, the Director has broad discretion in case handling.[693] The DCR will generally start an investigation upon receipt of a verified complaint,[694] but where the allegations are patently outside the LAD, a finding of no probable cause and an order of dismissal will be issued before any investigation is undertaken.[695]

---

687. N.J.S.A. 10:5-15; N.J.A.C. 13:4-3.6. Although there is no set time within which the DCR must give respondent notice, service normally is made within 60 days after the verified complaint is filed.

688. N.J.S.A. 10:5-16; N.J.A.C. 13:4-5.1(b). *See* R.1:4-7 and R.1:4-8. The answer must contain in short and plain terms respondent's defenses to each claim asserted and must specifically admit or deny each allegation or paragraph of the verified complaint N.J.A.C. 13:4-5.1(b)-(c).

689. N.J.A.C. 13:4-5.1(d).

690. DCR, *Complaint Processing Under the LAD* (March 1982), reprinted in 8B *Fair Employment Practices Manual (BNA)*, p.455:2741 (Apr. 1984), and 3 *Employment Practices Guide (CCH)*, ¶25,780 (1984). *See* N.J.S.A. 10:5-13. The LAD does not require that a finding of probable cause be made within the 180-day period. *Hardwick v. Newark Morning Ledger Co.*, No. A-1084-83, slip op. at p.4 (App. Div. Sept. 27, 1984), *aff'g*, 8 N.J.A.R. 249 (DCR 1983), *certif. denied*, 99 N.J. 215 (1984).

691. N.J.S.A. 10:5-13; N.J.A.C. 13:4-12.1(c). *See, e.g., Frank v. Ivy Club*, 120 N.J. 73, 92 (1990), *cert. denied*, 498 U.S. 1073 (1991); *Roberts v. Keansburg Bd. of Educ.*, 5 N.J.A.R. 208, 209 (DCR 1983); *Clowes v. Terminix Int'l, Inc.*, 109 N.J. 575, 584 (1988). The intent of this provision is to permit complainant to accelerate the resolution of the case. Assembly Judiciary, Law, Public Safety & Defense Committee, *Statement to Senate No. 3101 With Assembly Committee Amendments* (Dec. 17, 1979). By making such a request, complainant waives the right to have the DCR's attorney prosecute the case in the OAL. N.J.A.C. 13:4-12.1(f).

692. N.J.S.A. 10:5-13; N.J.A.C. 13:4-12.1(d). The DCR must act upon the request within 30 days. N.J.A.C. 1:1-4.1(a). If the verified complaint has been dismissed, the final determination of the Director may exclude any other action, civil or criminal, based on the same grievance of the complainant.

693. *Frank v. Ivy Club*, 228 N.J.Super. 40, 54, 62 (App. Div. 1988), *rev'd on other grounds*, 120 N.J. 73 (1990), *cert. denied*, 498 U.S. 1073 (1991).

694. N.J.S.A. 10:5-14; N.J.A.C. 13:4-6.1(a); *Pittman v. LaFontaine*, 756 F.Supp. 834, 845 (D.N.J. 1991); *Howard Savings Inst. v. Francis*, 133 N.J.Super. 54, 57 (App. Div. 1975).

695. N.J.A.C. 13:4-6.1(d), -6.4(a).

4-47:2 Discovery

The Director may conduct discovery as necessary, including, but not limited to, interrogatories and oral depositions.[696] DCR discovery requests must be rationally related to legitimate purposes under the LAD and must not be unreasonable, oppressive, or unduly onerous.[697] When directed to a party, they need not be supported by a subpoena.[698] The DCR is not prohibited from reviewing respondent's answers to interrogatories and the results of its investigation with complainant before deciding whether to issue a finding of probable cause.[699]

When DCR discovery requests seek disclosure of trade secrets or other confidential or privileged information, protective orders may be entered.[700] When protected information is produced, the agency must employ adequate safeguards against disclosure.[701]

Before a determination of probable cause is made, the parties normally have no right to take discovery,[702] and the DCR's own requests at that time may not require respondent to search for or collate voluminous quantities of information.[703] The Director, upon motion by a party or the DCR itself, may order that the testimony of a witness, whether or not residing in New Jersey, be taken by deposition if it is shown that (1) the witness' testimony is material and (2) the witness is unable or cannot be compelled to attend the hearing.[704]

---

696. N.J.S.A. 10:5-8(i), (d); N.J.A.C. 13:4-6.1(a); *Howard Savings Inst. v. Francis*, 133 N.J.Super. 54, 57, 58 (App. Div. 1975).

697. *General Motors Corp. v. Blair*, 129 N.J.Super. 412, 425 (App. Div. 1974); *Howard Savings Inst. v. Francis*, 133 N.J.Super. at 61-62. In a disparate-treatment case, records of other comparable employees whom plaintiff alleges received favorable treatment may be discovered in appropriate circumstances. *Dixon v. Rutgers*, 110 N.J. 432, 443, 458 (1988).

A reasonable period of time to comply with discovery requests must be provided. *General Motors Corp. v. Blair*, 129 N.J.Super. at 425-26.

698. *General Motors Corp. v. Blair*, 129 N.J.Super. at 419-20.

699. *Hardwick v. Newark Morning Ledger Co.*, No. A-1084-83, slip op. at p. 7 (App. Div. Sept. 27, 1984), *aff'g*, 8 N.J.A.R. 249, 269-70 (DCR 1983), *certif. denied*, 99 N.J. 215 (1984); *Hayman v. Funk*, 8 N.J.A.R. 27, 48-49 (DCR 1984).

700. *See* N.J.A.C. 13:4-8.3(a), -6.4(a); N.J.A.C. 1:1-10.1(c), -10.2(c); R.4:10-3; *Dixon v. Rutgers*, 110 N.J. 432, 438 (1988); *In re Solid Waste Utility Customer Lists*, 106 N.J. at 522-24.

701. *See Dixon v. Rutgers*, 110 N.J. at 438.

702. *Howard Savings Inst. v. Francis*, 133 N.J.Super. at 58-61 (abuse-of-discretion standard of review). *But see Frank v. Ivy Club*, 120 N.J. 73, (1990), *cert. denied*, 498 U.S. 1073 (1991).

703. *Howard Savings Inst. v. Francis*, 133 N.J.Super. 54, 61.

704. N.J.A.C. 13:4-8.4(a). Depositions are conducted in accordance with the rules governing depositions in the Superior Court. N.J.A.C. 13:4-8.4(a). *See* R.4:14 and R.4:15. If the case is not going to be processed expeditiously, the parties should be permitted to take depositions for the preservation of relevant evidence. *Decker v. Elizabeth Bd. of Ed.*, 153 N.J.Super. 470, 474 (App. Div. 1977), *certif. denied*, 75 N.J. 612 (1978); *Hardwick v. Newark Morning Ledger Co.*, No. A-1084-83, slip op. at pp. 3-4 (App. Div. Sept. 27, 1984), *aff'g*, 8 N.J.A.R. 249 (DCR 1983), *certif. denied*, 99 N.J. 215 (1984).

When the DCR serves interrogatories, it advises of the consequences of failure to answer or move to strike.[705] They include entry of an order requiring answers within 10 days and advising that any further default will result in a waiver of procedural rights before the DCR and an admission that the interrogatories, if answered, would have established facts in accordance with the claim of complainant.[706]

If the order is not complied with, the relief specified will be imposed and default entered,[707] and if a petition to vacate is not made and granted, the case is transferred to the OAL for hearing on a default basis.[708] The proofs at that hearing consist of the order of entry of default and supporting affidavit, respondent's implied answers to the interrogatories, and any other evidence proffered by complainant.[709] The ALJ decides whether the facts presented constitute a violation of the LAD and, if so, the amount of damages or other recommended relief.[710] A final order adopting, rejecting, or modifying the ALJ's decision is entered by the Director.[711]

The DCR may also move in Superior Court to compel responses to its discovery request.[712] When the discovery involved is a deposition or request to produce documents, the DCR may file a motion for an order to show cause, supported by an affidavit stating the circumstances.[713] If the DCR discovery request was by way of subpoena, the remedies set forth in the following section obtain. When the discovery involved is interrogatories or requests for admissions, the DCR

---

705. N.J.A.C. 13:4-8.3(a); *General Motors Corp. v. Blair*, 129 N.J.Super. at 422. A motion to strike must be supported by affidavit and/or brief and will be ruled upon by the Director on the papers. N.J.A.C. 13:4-8.3(b).

706. N.J.A.C. 13:4-8.3(a); *General Motors Corp. v. Blair*, 129 N.J.Super. at 417, 422-23.

707. N.J.A.C. 13:4-8.3(c); *General Motors Corp. v. Blair*, 129 N.J.Super. at 417. The order must be supported by an affidavit of a DCR representative in the form specified in N.J.A.C. 13:4-8.3(d). *Id.* at 417.

708. N.J.A.C. 13:4-8.3(e); *General Motors Corp. v. Blair*, 129 N.J.Super. at 417, 422. A petition to vacate default must be supported by (1) an affidavit establishing good cause for reopening the case and (2) full and complete answers to all of the interrogatories. N.J.A.C. 13:4-8.3(g); *General Motors Corp. v. Blair*, 129 N.J.Super. at 422.

709. N.J.A.C. 13:4-8.3(i), -8.3(c)(1); *General Motors Corp. v. Blair*, 129 N.J.Super. at 417, 423. No evidence proffered by respondent may be admitted. N.J.A.C. 13:4-8.3(i); *General Motors Corp. v. Blair*, 129 N.J.Super. at 417, 423.

710. N.J.A.C. 13:4-8.3(i); *General Motors Corp. v. Blair*, 129 N.J.Super. at 417.

711. N.J.A.C. 13:4-8.3(j)-(k); N.J.S.A. 10:5-17; *General Motors Corp. v. Blair*, 129 N.J.Super. at 417-18.

712. N.J.S.A. 10:5-14.1, -19; N.J.A.C. 13:4-9.3(a); R.1:9-6(b)-(c); R.4:67-6(b)(2).

713. R.1:9-6(b)-(c); R.4:67-6(b)(2). *See, e.g., Vornado, Inc. v. Potter* 159 N.J.Super. 32 (App. Div.), *certif. denied*, 77 N.J. 489 (1978). For a fuller discussion of this topic, *see* Pressler, *Current N.J. Court Rules*, Comments to R.1:9-6 and R.1:10 (1999 ed.); 1 Del Deo & Klock, *New Jersey Practice: Court Rules Annotated*, Comment & Annotations to R.1:9-6 and R.1:10 (4th ed. 1988); 4 Walzer, *New Jersey Practice: Civil Practice Forms*, §53.36 (1991).

may commence a summary action for an order to show cause in Superior Court.[714]

One who fails to comply with a Superior Court order for discovery may be held in contempt of court.[715] A purposeful or knowing refusal to comply with a court order, or a willful refusal to comply with the Director's discovery order may subject the violator to indictment for a fourth-degree crime.[716]

4-47:3 Subpoena Power

The Director may administer oaths and subpoena witnesses to appear and give testimony under oath in connection with any investigation or hearing conducted pursuant to the LAD.[717] A subpoenaed witness may be required to produce for examination any evidence relating to the subject matter of the investigation or hearing.[718] A corporate respondent represented by counsel may be compelled to produce employees or documents by a notice in lieu of subpoena served upon counsel.[719]

Motions to quash or modify a subpoena may be filed with the Director.[720] Failure to comply with a subpoena is punishable in a contempt proceeding in Superior Court.[721]

The privilege against self-incrimination does not excuse a witness subpoenaed by the Attorney General, the Director, or an ALJ from testifying or producing evidence.[722] This is because the LAD expressly provides "transactional immunity"

---

714. R.4:67-6; R.4:67-1; R.4:67-2; N.J.S.A. 10:5-14.1, -19.

715. N.J.S.A. 2A:10-1; R.1:10; N.J.S.A. 2C:1-5(c); N.J.S.A. 2C:29-9(a).

716. N.J.S.A. 2C:29-9(a) (court orders); N.J.S.A. 10:5-26; N.J.S.A. 13:4-9.3(a) (director's orders).

717. N.J.S.A. 10:5-8(i), (d); N.J.A.C. 13:4-6.1(a), -8.1(b), -9.1; *Pittman v. LaFontaine*, 756 F.Supp. 834, 845 (D.N.J. 1991). The Director's statutory power to issue subpoenas was upheld in *Vornado, Inc. v. Potter* 159 N.J.Super. 32, 36 (App. Div.), *certif. denied*, 77 N.J. 489 (1978).

718. N.J.S.A. 10:5-8(i); N.J.A.C. 13:4-6.1(a), -8.1(b), -9.1.

719. N.J.A.C. 13:4-9.1(e). *See* R.1:9-1 and -2 (notice in lieu of subpoena). Note that contempt sanctions are not available for non-compliance with the demand of a notice in lieu of subpoena. *See* Pressler, *Current N.J. Court Rules*, Comments to R.1:9-1 (1999 ed). Subpoenas requiring only the production of evidence may be answered without a personal appearance by mailing copies of the documents to the DCR. N.J.A.C. 13:4-9.2(b). Counsel using such subpoenas should comply with the implicit ethical considerations set forth in R.4:14-7(c).

720. *In re Vornado, Inc.*, 159 N.J.Super. at 36; N.J.A.C. 13:4-6.2.

721. N.J.S.A. 10:5-8(i); N.J.A.C. 13:4-9.3. *See, e.g.*, *In re Vornado, Inc.*, 159 N.J.Super. at 32. If the subpoena was issued by the Director upon the application of a party, that party may seek to enforce the subpoena in Superior Court in the name of the DCR. N.J.A.C. 13:4-9.3(b); *cf.* R.4:67-6(a)(2).

For a discussion of subpoena enforcement proceedings, *see* Pressler, *N.J. Current Court Rules*, Comments to R.1:9-6 and R.1:10 (1999 ed.); 1 Del Deo & Klock, *New Jersey Practice: Court Rules Annotated*, Comments & Annotations to R.1:9-6 and R.1:10 (4th ed. 1988); 4 Walzer, *New Jersey Practice: Civil Practice Forms*, §53.36 (1991).

to a witness invoking the self-incrimination privilege, which immunity protects the witness from later prosecutions relating to the subject matter of the testimony given or evidence produced.[723] Inasmuch as the privilege against self-incrimination applies only to natural persons, the immunity extended by the LAD protects only individuals.[724] Regardless of the immunity granted by the LAD, the witness may be prosecuted or subjected to penalty or forfeiture for any perjury or contempt in answering, failing to answer, or producing or failing to produce evidence in accordance with the subpoena.[725] Any testimony given or evidence produced by the witness is admissible against the witness in the perjury or contempt proceeding.[726]

4-47:4 Fact-Finding Conference

The DCR's investigation typically includes one or more fact-finding conferences (FFCs).[727] The FFC normally does not constitute a hearing on or adjudication of the merits, but rather, a "culling-out process" leading to an initial determination of whether probable cause exists to believe that unlawful discrimination has occurred.[728]

---

722. N.J.S.A. 10:5-11. As to the definition of incrimination under New Jersey law, *see* Biunno, *Current N.J. Rules of Evidence*, Comments to Evid. R. 24 (1991 ed.); 2B Del Deo & Klock, *New Jersey Practice: Court Rules Annotated*, Comments & Annotations to Evid. R. 24 (1987).

723. N.J.S.A. 10:5-11. The immunity language of N.J.S.A. 10:5-11 is nearly identical to the transactional immunity language of §1 of the Model State Witness Immunity Act (1952) (reprinted in 9C *Uniform Laws Annotated*, p. 206 (1957)) and Rule 732 of the Uniform Rules of Criminal Procedure (1974 & 1987 editions) (reprinted in 10 *Uniform Laws Annotated*, pp. 340-54 (Master Ed. 1974 & Special Pamphlet 1989)). When New Jersey adopted the Model State Witness Immunity Act in 1968, N.J.S.A. 2A:81-17.3, the Legislature substituted "use immunity" for "transactional immunity." *Cf.* N.J.S.A. 11A:2-17 (affording use immunity in Civil Service proceedings). The immunity granted under the LAD is broader than (1) the immunity normally granted to public employees who testify before a court, grand jury, or the State Commission of Investigation, N.J.S.A. 2A:81-17.2a *et seq.*, and (2) the absence of immunity provided to certain municipal employees, N.J.S.A. 40:69A-167.

724. N.J.S.A. 10:5-11; *New Jersey Builders, Owners & Managers Ass'n v. Blair*, 60 N.J. 330, 340-41 (1972); Biunno, *Current N.J. Rules of Evidence*, Comments to N.J.R.E. 503 (1999 ed.); *McCormick on Evidence*, §128 (3d ed. 1984).

725. N.J.S.A. 10:5-11. *See* Biunno, *Current N.J. Rules of Evidence*, Comments to N.J.R.E. 503 (1999 ed.); 32 Arnold, *New Jersey Practice: Criminal Practice & Procedure*, §905 (2d ed. 1980). As to the criminal offense of perjury, *see* N.J.S.A. 2C:28-1. Although N.J.S.A. 10:5-11 does not refer to a witness' liability for false swearing under N.J.S.A. 2C:28-2, case law under N.J.S.A. 2A:81-17.2a2 (the public employee use immunity statute) has imposed such liability, finding that the immunity statute used the term "perjury" in the generic sense of "false testimony." *State of New Jersey v. Mullen*, 67 N.J. 134, 136-38 (1975).

726. N.J.S.A. 10:5-11. *See* Biunno, *Current N.J. Rules of Evidence*, Comments to N.J.R.E. 502 (1999 ed.); 32 Arnold, *New Jersey Practice: Criminal Practice & Procedure*, §905 (2d ed. 1980).

727. The FFC is used to obtain evidence, identify issues, learn the parties' positions, and explore the possibility of settlement. N.J.A.C. 13:4-2.3(a)(1), -6.1(a); *Frank v. Ivy Club*, 120 N.J. 73, 80-81, 98-99 (1990), *cert. denied*, 498 U.S. 1073 (1991); *Pittman v. LaFontaine*, 756 F.Supp. 834, 845 (D.N.J. 1991). The DCR may engage an administrative law judge (ALJ) to pursue settlement. N.J.A.C. 1:1-4.2.

The DCR gives written notice of the FFC, including the individuals requested to attend on behalf of each party and any documents a party is requested to provide.[729] Upon prior notice to the DCR, the parties may bring additional witnesses.[730] A party may be accompanied at the FFC by counsel or another representative and, if necessary, a translator.[731]

The FFC is typically conducted by a DCR Investigator[732] who controls which witnesses will be heard and in which order.[733] Witnesses may be sequestered, but counsel and one representative of each party are entitled to remain.[734] Because the FFC is not considered a hearing on the merits, all questioning is normally done by the fact finder.[735] However, the fact finder may permit the parties or counsel to ask questions,[736] introduce and examine documents, present unsworn testimony, and make oral and written legal arguments.[737] The DCR may ask the parties to provide affidavits from witnesses who appeared at the FFC.[738] Statements made by the parties at the FFC or during the DCR's investigation may be used against them during the hearing on the merits.[739]

---

728. N.J.A.C. 13:4-2.3(a)(1); N.J.A.C. 13:4-2.3(b)(6); *Frank v. Ivy Club*, 228 N.J.Super. at 56-58. If the FFC reveals no genuine issue of material fact, the fact finder may recommend to the Director that the matter be determined without first conducting a plenary contested-case hearing. *See Frank v. Ivy Club*, 120 N.J. at 80-81, 93, 98-102, 110.

729. N.J.A.C. 13:4-2.3(a)(2). Requests for adjournments of FFCs are granted only if good cause is shown and normally must be made at least 10 days in advance of the scheduled date. N.J.A.C. 13:4-2.3(d)(1). If a party or witness refuses or fails to attend a scheduled FFC, the DCR may either proceed without the missing party or subpoena him to appear at a rescheduled FFC. N.J.A.C. 13:4-2.3(d)(2), (e). *See, e.g., Gimello v. Agency Rent-A-Car Systems, Inc.*, 250 N.J.Super. 338, 352 (App. Div. 1991). If a party fails to provide the documents requested, the DCR may also issue a subpoena for these documents. N.J.A.C. 13:4-2.3(e).

730. N.J.A.C. 13:4-2.3(b)(2); *Pittman v. LaFontaine*, 756 F.Supp. 834, 845 (D.N.J. 1991); *Hayman v. Funk*, 8 N.J.A.R. 27, 47 (DCR 1984).

731. N.J.A.C. 13:4-2.3(b)(4); *Pittman v. LaFontaine*, 756 F.Supp. at 845.

732. N.J.A.C. 13:4-2.3(b)(1), -6.1(a). *See, e.g., Pittman v. LaFontaine*, 756 F.Supp. at 838. A party is not entitled to demand that the Director or Office of Administrative Law (OAL) conduct the FFC. *Frank v. Ivy Club*, 228 N.J.Super. 40, 55 (App. Div. 1988), *rev'd on other grounds*, 120 N.J. 73, 97 (1990), *cert. denied*, 498 U.S. 1073 (1991). In an appropriate case, a higher-level DCR employee may be assigned to conduct the FFC. *See, e.g., Frank v. Ivy Club*, 120 N.J. 73, 81 (1990), *cert. denied*, 498 U.S. 1073 (1991) (Chief of the DCR's Bureau of Enforcement assigned).

733. N.J.A.C. 13:4-2.3(b)(2). In contrast to hearings on the merits of a discrimination claim, testimony given at an FFC need not be under oath. *See Frank v. Ivy Club*, 120 N.J. at 81, 98, *rev'g*, 228 N.J.Super. at 61-62; N.J.S.A. 10:5-16.

734. N.J.A.C. 13:4-2.3(b)(2). *Cf.* Fed. R. Evid. 615; 37 Lefelt, *New Jersey Practice: Administrative Law & Practice*, §221 (1988); Pressler, *Current N.J. Court Rules*, Comments to R.1:8-6 (1999 ed.).

735. N.J.A.C. 13:4-2.3(b)(6).

736. N.J.A.C. 13:4-2.3(b)(6). *See, e.g., Frank v. Ivy Club*, 120 N.J. at 81, 98 (parties directly cross-examined each other); *Pittman v. LaFontaine*, 756 F.Supp. at 838, 845 (parties permitted to question each other through the DCR investigator).

737. *See, e.g., Frank v. Ivy Club*, 120 N.J. at 81, 98-99.

738. N.J.A.C. 13:4-2.3(b)(3).

If the case is not settled at the FFC, the Investigator may continue to collect documents and interview witnesses as needed.[740]

4-47:5 Probable Cause Determination

Upon conclusion of the investigation, the Investigator prepares and submits Findings of the Investigation to his supervisor for approval, and if approved, to the Director for review.[741] If the Director determines there is no probable cause for crediting the allegations of the verified complaint, a final order of dismissal is entered.[742] That is an appealable order, and bars any other action, civil or criminal, based on the same grievance of complainant.[743]

If the Director concludes there is "a reasonable ground of suspicion supported by facts and circumstances strong enough in themselves to warrant [in] a cautious man . . . the belief that the law is being violated,"[744] a finding of probable cause is entered, and the DCR endeavors to resolve the matter by conference, conciliation, and persuasion.[745] The quantum of evidence required to establish probable cause is less than that needed to prevail on the merits.[746]

---

739. *See, e.g.*, *Hayman v. Funk*, 8 N.J.A.R. 27, 35-36 (DCR 1984); *Vasto v. Vornado, Inc.*, 8 N.J.A.R. 481, 488, 489 (DCR 1983) (DCR field representative called to testify as to statements made by respondent's representatives at conferences); *Dixon v. Rutgers*, 110 N.J. 432, 440 (1988) (DCR field investigator submitted affidavit recounting discussions with defendant's employees); *Lige v. Montclair*, 72 N.J. 5, 7-8 (1976); *Zahorian v. Russell Fitt Real Estate Agency*, 62 N.J. 399, 403-04 (1973). However, offers of settlements and proposed stipulations are not admissible during the hearing. N.J.A.C. 1:1-15.10; N.J.A.C. 13:4-2.3(c)(2). *Cf.* N.J.R.E. 408, 410; Fed. R. Evid. 408.

740. DCR, *Employment Guide to the LAD*, p. 19 (1989); DCR, *Sexual Harassment*, p. 7 (1989). *See, e.g.*, *Pittman v. LaFontaine*, 756 F.Supp. 834, 838, 845-46 (D.N.J. 1991).

741. *See* N.J.S.A. 10:5-14. *See, e.g.*, *Hermann v. Fairleigh Dickinson Univ.*, 183 N.J.Super. 500, 502-03 (App. Div.), *certif. denied*, 91 N.J. 573 (1982); *Sprague v. Glassboro State College*, 161 N.J.Super. 218, 220, 223, 224 (App. Div. 1978).

742. N.J.S.A. 10:5-14, -13; N.J.A.C. 13:4-6.1(b), (d); N.J.A.C. 13:4-15.3. A finding of no probable cause means the DCR has determined that the alleged unlawful employment practice did not occur or cannot be proved. DCR, *Employment Guide to the LAD*, p. 19 (1989); DCR, *Sexual Harassment*, p. 8 (1989); DCR, *Your Employment Rights*, p. 13 (Nov. 1986).

743. N.J.S.A. 10:5-27; *Pittman v. LaFontaine*, 756 F.Supp. 834, 842-44 (D.N.J. 1991); *Hermann v. Fairleigh Dickinson Univ.*, 183 N.J.Super. at 503-05; *Giammario v. Trenton Bd. of Ed.*, 203 N.J.Super. 356, 364-65 (App. Div.), *certif. denied*, 102 N.J. 336 (1985), *cert. denied*, 475 U.S. 1141 (1986); *Ferrara v. Tappan Co.*, 722 F.Supp. 1204, 1205-06 (D.N.J. 1989).

744. *Frank v. Ivy Club*, 228 N.J.Super. 40, 56 (App. Div. 1988), *rev'd on other grounds*, 120 N.J. 73 (1990), *cert. denied*, 498 U.S. 1073 (1991), *quoting Sprague v. Glassboro State College*, 161 N.J.Super. 218, 225 (App. Div. 1978). *Accord* DCR, *Employment Guide to the LAD*, p. 19 (1989) (a belief that discrimination may exist); DCR, *Your Employment Rights*, p. 3 (Nov. 1986) (same); DCR, *Sexual Harassment*, p. 7 (1989) (a finding that there is sufficient evidence to suspect that discrimination occurred).

745. N.J.S.A. 10:5-14; N.J.A.C. 13:4-6.1(b)-(c); N.J.A.C. 13:4-11.1(a).

746. *Frank v. Ivy Club*, 228 N.J.Super. at 56, 63; *Sprague v. Glassboro State College*, 161 N.J.Super. at 224-25.

Complainant and respondent are given copies of the Director's probable cause determination order and the Findings of the Investigation.[747] Following the determination, the DCR's records of factual statements made at the Fact Finding Conference are discoverable,[748] but records of settlement discussions during the FFC are not.[749] The Appellate Division has held that a probable cause determination was properly excluded from evidence under New Jersey Rule of Evidence 403.[750]

4-48 Conciliation

When a finding of probable cause issues, the DCR immediately begins conciliation efforts,[751] which must conclude within 45 days.[752] The conciliation conference is attended only by representatives of respondent and the DCR.[753] A respondent's failure to attend may be deemed an unsuccessful attempt at conciliation.[754] Conversations between respondent (and respondent's representatives) and DCR personnel during conciliation conferences are confidential and may not be disclosed by the DCR personnel.[755] However, complainant will be advised of any settlement offers made by respondent.[756]

Conciliation agreements or consent orders that are intended to be complete and final dispositions, subject only to fulfillment of their terms, must be enforced first before the DCR.[757]

---

747. N.J.A.C. 13:4-6.1(c)-(d), -6.4(b); N.J.S.A. 10:5-14.

748. N.J.A.C. 13:4-2.3(c)(1). As to the discovery of the DCR's files generally, *see* §4-49:5.

749. N.J.A.C. 13:4-2.3(c)(2).

750. *Muench v. Township of Haddon*, 255 N.J. Super 288, 305-06 (App. Div. 1992) ("It is conclusory material compiled by an investigator for the Division solely for the purpose of determining whether there was any basis for continuing the administrative process. Further, the jury might well have placed undue significance on the investigator's 'conclusion,' when in fact the investigator makes no findings, but simply determines that the matter should proceed further. Moreover, we presume all of the evidence presented to the investigator will be presented to the jury for its ultimate and independent resolution based on its judgment of the evidence presented during trial.").

751. N.J.S.A. 10:5-14; N.J.A.C. 13:4-6.1(b), -11.1(a); *David v. Vesta Co.*, 45 N.J. 301, 322 (1965); *Howard Savings Inst. v. Francis*, 133 N.J.Super. 54, 58 (App. Div. 1975). *See, e.g.*, *New Jersey Div. on Civil Rights v. Slumber, Inc.*, 166 N.J.Super. 95, 102-04 (App. Div.), *app. dism'd in part without op.*, 81 N.J. 334 (1979), *conditionally modified in part on other grounds, aff'd in part on other grounds*, 82 N.J. 412 (1980).

Respondent is given at least five days' advance notice of the conciliation conference and the fact that a public hearing will be held if conciliation is unsuccessful. N.J.A.C. 13:4-11.1(b)-(c).

752. N.J.S.A. 10:5-14.

753. DCR, *Employment Guide to the LAD*, p. 20 (1989); DCR, *Sexual Harassment*, p. 8 (1989); DCR, *Your Employment Rights*, p. 13 (Nov. 1986).

754. N.J.A.C. 13:4-11.1(e).

755. N.J.S.A. 10:5-14; N.J.A.C. 13:4-11.1(d); N.J.S.A. 10:5-16.

756. DCR, *Employment Guide to the LAD*, p. 20 (1989); DCR, *Sexual Harassment*, p. 8 (1989).

4-49 Hearing

Upon failure of conciliation or in advance of conciliation if the Director believes warranted,[758] a public hearing is scheduled.[759] If the DCR unreasonably delays scheduling a hearing and respondent is thereby prejudiced, the verified complaint may be dismissed.[760]

The Director may hear the case himself or transfer it to the OAL for a hearing and initial decision by an Administrative Law Judge (ALJ).[761] If the case is transferred,[762] the Administrative Procedure Act (APA)[763] and the Uniform Administrative Procedure Rules (UAPRs)[764] govern the hearing and issuance of the initial decision and final order.[765] In such cases, the DCR's attorney will prosecute the case in the OAL and on appeal, if necessary.[766]

---

757. *Christian Bros. Inst. v. Northern New Jersey Interscholastic League*, 86 N.J. 409, 415-19 (1981); N.J.S.A. 10:5-17.

758. One such circumstance is where the Director believes conciliation would be fruitless. N.J.A.C. 13:4-12.1(a); Pesin, *Summary, Analysis & Comment on "Anti-Discrimination" Legislation of New Jersey*, 68 N.J.L.J. 225, 227 (July 5, 1945); N.J.A.C. 1:1-8.1(c).

759. N.J.S.A. 10:5-15, N.J.A.C. 13:4-12.1(a)-(b); N.J.A.C. 1:1-8.1(a), (c); N.J.A.C. 1:1-14.1; *David v. Vesta Co.*, 45 N.J. 301, 322, 326 (1965); *Howard Savings Inst. v. Francis*, 133 N.J.Super. 54, 58 (App. Div. 1975).

760. *See, e.g.*, *Hughes v. Cypress Garden Apartments, Inc.*, 118 N.J.Super. 374 (App. Div. 1972) (eleven-month delay in scheduling hearing following failed conciliation conference seriously prejudiced respondent because the passage of time rendered memories hazy and murky, thereby warranting dismissal of the verified complaint); *Decker v. Elizabeth Bd. of Ed.*, 153 N.J.Super. 470, 474-75 (App. Div. 1977), *certif. denied*, 75 N.J. 612 (1978) (44-month delay in scheduling hearing following filing of verified complaint was not excusable because of DCR's heavy backlog of cases; nonetheless, because respondent was not prejudiced by delay, complaint not dismissed and complainant still entitled to recover prejudgment interest); *Andersen v. Exxon Co.*, 7 N.J.A.R. 289, 303-04 (DCR 1980), *aff'd*, No. A-2940-79 (App. Div. Feb. 25, 1981), *aff'd as modified on other grounds*, 89 N.J. 483 (1982) (prejudgment interest awarded despite delays before DCR); *Gimello v. Agency Rent-A-Car Systems, Inc.*, 250 N.J.Super. 338, 369-70 (App. Div. 1991) (DCR's five-year, nine-month delay in processing case did not warrant denying complainant relief in the absence of unfair prejudice to respondent). *Cf. General Motors Corp. v. Blair*, 129 N.J.Super. 412, 425 (App. Div. 1984) (DCR claimed that all employment discrimination claims require expeditious processing).

761. N.J.S.A. 52:14F-8(b); N.J.A.C. 13:4-1.1; N.J.A.C. 1:1-8.1(a); *Frank v. Ivy Club*, 228 N.J.Super. 40, 55 (App. Div. 1988), *rev'd on other grounds*, 120 N.J. 73 (1990), *cert. denied*, 498 U.S. 1073 (1991).

762. If a case is pending in the DCR more than 180 days after the verified complaint is filed, complainant is entitled, with two exceptions, to have the matter transferred to the OAL for hearing and to prosecute the case personally or through counsel. By filing such a request, complainant waives the right to have the DCR's attorney prosecute the case; however, the DCR's attorney may still attend preliminary proceedings, such as prehearing conferences, to determine whether the DCR should intervene. N.J.A.C. 13:4-12.1(f). *Cf.* N.J.A.C. 1:1-16.5, -16.6. Upon its application to the OAL, the DCR must be permitted to intervene. N.J.S.A. 10:5-13; N.J.A.C. 13:4-12.1(f), -6.5(c), -6.2(a); N.J.A.C. 1:1-16.3(c). Even if the DCR does not intervene, copies of pleadings, briefs, or legal memoranda filed with the OAL must be mailed to the DCR's attorney. N.J.S.A. 10:5-13; N.J.A.C. 13:4-12.1(f).

763. The APA is codified as N.J.S.A. 52:14B-1 *et seq. See also* the OAL law, N.J.S.A. 52:14F-1 *et seq.*

764. The UAPRs appear in N.J.A.C. 1:1-1.1 *et seq.*

4-49:1 Hearing by Director

If the Director decides not to transfer a case to the OAL, he must conduct the hearing and issue his decision personally and directly.[767] In that event, the APA and the UAPRs apply only with respect to procedures for conducting hearings and issuing final orders.[768]

4-49:2 Interim Relief

If the Director determines that a complainant may be irreparably harmed before hearing or disposition, the DCR may seek appropriate temporary injunctive relief in Superior Court.[769] Complainant may similarly apply for temporary injunctive relief in cases before the OAL and not involving the DCR.[770]

The standards for granting temporary injunctive relief are set forth in *Poff v. Caro*:

> Preliminary injunctive relief should not issue except when necessary to prevent irreparable harm. Such relief should be withheld when the right underlying the claim is unsettled; nor should preliminary injunctive relief be granted when all material facts are controverted.
>
> To prevail on such an application, the movant must make a preliminary showing of a reasonable probability of ultimate success on the merits. This requirement is tempered by the principle that mere doubt as to the validity of the claim is not an adequate basis for refusing to maintain the status quo. The Court must also weigh the relative hardship to the parties resulting from the grant or denial of preliminary injunctive relief. The Court must

---

765. N.J.A.C 13:4-1.1, -12.4; N.J.A.C. 1:1-1.1. *See* Lefelt, *New Jersey Practice: Administrative Law and Practice*, §110 (1988). Note that the UAPRS supersede any inconsistent DCR regulations pertaining to procedural aspects of the hearing and decisionmaking process, except for DCR regulations that incorporate requirements of the LAD. N.J.A.C. 1:1-1.1(b). Similarly, UAPRs are superseded to the extent inconsistent with the provisions of the LAD. N.J.A.C. 1:1-1.1(a).

766. N.J.S.A. 10:5-16; *Jackson v. Concord Co.*, 54 N.J. 113, 117 n.2 (1969).

767. *Frank v. Ivy Club*, 228 N.J.Super. 40, 55 (App. Div. 1988), *rev'd on other grounds*, 120 N.J. 73 (1990), *cert. denied*, 498 U.S. 1073 (1991); N.J.S.A. 52:14F-8(b).

768. N.J.A.C. 13:4-1.1, -12.4; N.J.A.C. 1:1-1.1; N.J.S.A. 52:14F-8(b). *See* 37 Lefelt, *New Jersey Practice: Administrative Law & Practice*, §110 (1988).

769. N.J.S.A. 10:5-14.1; N.J.A.C. 13:4-12.3; R.4:67-2(a). *See* R.4:52. N.J.S.A. 10:5-14.1 officially filled a statutory void that was noted and judicially remedied nine months earlier in *Pfaus v. Feder*, 88 N.J.Super. 468 (Ch.Div. 1965). *See Pfaus v. Palermo*, 97 N.J.Super. 4, 8 (App. Div. 1967).

770. N.J.A.C. 13:4-12.3; R.4:52.

> always consider and apply principles of justice, equity and morality.[771]

Because the LAD specifically authorizes the DCR to seek injunctive relief, the court must not "adopt a grudging or narrow approach" when reviewing such an application.[772] Nonetheless, because injunctive relief is a "drastic remedy," the court must "exercise ... exacting judicial discretion" when reviewing the Director's application.[773] Any injunctive relief ordered should be limited to the extent "reasonably necessary to preserve the *status quo*" and should be protective of the interests of all the parties.[774]

A party may apply directly to the Director for interim emergency relief where irreparable harm will result in the absence of an expedited decision in a contested case.[775] The Director may hear the application or refer it to the OAL.[776]

4-49:3 Transfer to the Office of Administrative Law

The parties normally learn that a dispute has been transferred to the Office of Administrative Law (OAL) when it sends them a notice of filing.[777] The notice also advises the parties to commence discovery, of the controlling hearing procedures, and of their right to be represented by counsel or other qualified non-lawyers.[778]

---

771. *Poff v. Caro*, 228 N.J.Super. 370, 375 (Law Div. 1987) (citations omitted). The standards for granting preliminary injunctive relief in discrimination cases filed in federal court are discussed in *EEOC v. State of New Jersey*, 620 F.Supp. 977, 980, 983-98 (D.N.J. 1985) (opinion on application for immediate injunctive relief), *supplemented*, 631 F.Supp. 1506 (D.N.J. 1986) (opinion on merits), *aff'd without published op.*, 815 F.2d 694 (3d Cir. 1987).

772. *Poff v. Caro*, 228 N.J.Super. at 375-76, *quoting Pfaus v. Palermo*, 97 N.J.Super. at 8.

773. *Pfaus v. Feder*, 88 N.J.Super. at 476.

774. *Pfaus v. Palermo*, 97 N.J.Super. at 9; N.J.S.A. 10:5-27.

775. N.J.A.C. 1:1-12.6. *See* N.J.A.C. 13:4-6.4(a); N.J.A.C. 13:4-15.1. *See generally* 37 Lefelt, *New Jersey Practice: Administrative Law & Practice*, §196 (1988). *See, e.g., Jamison v. Rockaway Tp. Bd. of Educ.*, 242 N.J.Super. 436, 443 (App. Div. 1990) (Director's denial of emergent relief reversed on interlocutory appeal); *cf. Balsley v. No. Hunterdon Regional Sch. Dist. Bd. of Educ.*, 117 N.J. 434, 437 (1990) (in an education discrimination case within the concurrent jurisdiction of the DCR and Commissioner of Education, Commissioner adopted ALJ's recommended restraining order permitting female student to try out for high school football team).

776. N.J.A.C. 1:1-12.6(c). If the matter is referred to the OAL, an ALJ will issue an initial decision, which is subject to review by the Director. N.J.A.C. 1:1-12.6(i)-(j).

777. N.J.A.C. 1:1-9.5(a). The procedures discussed in this Section and the following sections with respect to proceedings in the OAL apply with equal force to cases retained by the Director, except that an initial decision is not issued.

The discussion that follows addresses only the highlights of practice before the OAL. For a more complete discussion, see 37 Lefelt, *New Jersey Practice: Administrative Law & Practice*, chs. 4-7 (1988). *See also* Davis, *Administrative Law Treatise* (2d ed. 1978-84 & 1989 supp.) (six volumes).

778. N.J.A.C. 1:1-9.5(a), -10.4(a)-(b). *See* N.J.A.C. 1:1-5.1 *et seq.*

4-49:4 Discovery

Prior to a hearing, the parties generally may engage in the full range of paper discovery available in civil actions.[779] Depositions and physical and mental examinations are allowed only on motion for good cause shown.[780]

The Supreme Court, in *Dixon v. Rutgers*, set forth the general standards governing discovery in DCR proceedings and in Superior Court actions:

> [W]e believe that "a plaintiff claiming discriminatory treatment ought not to be entitled to a general inquisition into the [defendant's] files merely on the strength of having filed a complaint." A plaintiff must do more than merely allege that a [defendant] has violated the LAD.
>
> * * *
>
> [T]he [DCR or trial] court has a responsibility to satisfy itself that the charge is valid and that the material requested is "relevant" to the charge, and more generally to assess any contentions by the employer that the demand for information is too indefinite or has been made for an illegitimate purpose.[781]

Sanctions, including reasonable counsel fees, may be imposed for discovery abuses.[782] Protective orders should be entered as to confidential materials, ensur-

---

779. *See* N.J.A.C. 1:1-10.1 *et seq*.; N.J.A.C. 1:1-1.3(a). *See, e.g., Dixon v. Rutgers*, 110 N.J. 432 (1988); *Clowes v. Terminix Int'l, Inc.* 7 N.J.A.R. 206, 207 (DCR 1984), *rev'd on other grounds*, No. A-3886-84 (App. Div. May 8, 1986), *aff'd*, 109 N.J. 575 (1988) (order compelling discovery).

780. N.J.A.C. 1:1-10.2(c). *See, e.g., Flanders v. William Paterson College*, 163 N.J.Super. 225, 230-31 (App. Div. 1976) (hearing examiner did not abuse discretion in denying respondent permission to question DCR's investigator about the identity of individuals with whom he spoke during his investigation and the substance of such conversations). In deciding such a motion, the ALJ weighs, *inter alia*, the specific need for these forms of discovery, the extent to which the information sought cannot be obtained in other ways, any undue hardship to a party, and matters of expense, privilege, trade secret, or oppressiveness. N.J.A.C. 1:1-10.2(c). *Cf.* N.J.A.C. 13:4-8.4(a) (in deciding whether to permit a deposition, DCR Director considers the materiality of deponent's testimony and whether the witness is unable or cannot be compelled to attend the hearing). An order granting such discovery must specify a reasonable time limit on the length of the deposition or examination. N.J.A.C. 1:1-10.2(c).

If a delay in hearing deprives a party of the testimony of a material witness, then the ALJ should permit the deposition of that witness. *Decker v. Elizabeth Bd. of Ed.*, 153 N.J.Super. 470, 474 (App. Div. 1977), *certif. denied*, 75 N.J. 612 (1978); N.J.A.C. 13:4-8.4(a). In deciding whether to draw an adverse inference from a party's failure to produce a witness at an evidentiary hearing the DCR considers whether the party attempted to secure the witness' testimony by deposition. *Gimello v. Agency Rent-A-Car Systems, Inc.*, 250 N.J.Super. 338, 352 (App. Div. 1991).

781. *Dixon v. Rutgers*, 110 N.J. at 454-55 (citations omitted). Discovery is "relevant" if it has "any tendency in reason to prove any material fact." *Id.* at 442. In making the relevancy determination, the tribunal should consider whether the information sought is available from other sources and its importance to the issues presented. *Id.* at 456. While discovery "need not be circumscribed by the narrow allegations of the complaint, [it] should nevertheless be reasonably limited to the end that a fair adjudication may obtain." *General Motors Corp. v. Blair*, 129 N.J.Super. 412, 425 (App. Div. 1974).

ing that discovery of them "is not unnecessarily broad and that access to them is limited."[783]

Adverse discovery rulings may be appealed interlocutorily to the Director of the DCR.[784] An adverse ruling of the Director may be appealed to the Appellate Division by means of a motion for leave to appeal.[785]

4-49:5 Discovery of the DCR's Files

A party may obtain discovery of specified materials in the DCR's file,[786] upon written request and notice, after (1) a finding of probable cause has been made, (2) the case has been transferred to the Office of Administrative Law (OAL) at complainant's request, (3) a final DCR determination has issued, or (4) the case has been closed by the DCR.[787] Requests for discovery should be made promptly, because the DCR destroys its files one year after closing the case or final court action, whichever is later. If the purpose of the request is to oppress any party or delay resolution of the case, the Director may refuse or limit discovery of the DCR's file.[788]

The DCR will produce three classes of documents:

1. Statements made by any person during the course of the DCR's investigation, other than (a) DCR work product, (b) intra-agency communications, and (c) attorney-client communications.
2. Factual written reports of the Investigator.

---

782. N.J.A.C. 1:1-10.5; N.J.A.C. 1:1-14.4; *In re Uniform Administrative Procedure Rules*, 90 N.J. 85, 106 (1982). *See, e.g., Clowes v. Terminix Int'l, Inc.*, 7 N.J.A.R. 206, 207-08, 220 (DCR 1984), *rev'd on other grounds*, No. A-3886-84 (App. Div. May 8, 1986), *aff'd*, 109 N.J. 575 (1988).

783. *Dixon v. Rutgers*, 110 N.J. at 435. For example, confidential, non-discoverable material can be redacted; access to the confidential materials that are produced can be limited to the parties, their counsel, and their experts; relevant portions of deposition transcripts can be sealed; and use of the confidential information may be limited to the specific litigation. *Id.* at 456-57.

784. N.J.A.C. 1:1-14.10; *Dixon v. Rutgers*, 110 N.J. at 440.

785. *See Dixon v. Rutgers*, 110 N.J. at 440; *Howard Savings Inst. v. Francis*, 133 N.J.Super. 54, 57 (App. Div. 1975).

786. N.J.A.C. 13:4-8.2(a), -2.3(c)(1); *Hayman v. Funk*, 8 N.J.A.R. 27, 49 (DCR 1984). The parties may also have common-law and statutory rights of access to the DCR's files. *See* New Jersey Right to Know Law, N.J.S.A. 47:1A-1 *et seq.*; 34 Pane, *New Jersey Practice: Local Government Law*, §§281-84 (1987 & current supp.); 37 Lefelt, *New Jersey Practice: Administrative Law & Practice*, §88, p. 105 & n.3, §§149-50 (1988 & current supp.).

787. N.J.A.C. 13:4-8.2(a). *See, e.g., New Jersey Div. on Civil Rights v. Slumber, Inc.*, 166 N.J.Super. 95, 100-01 & n.3 (App. Div.), *app. dism'd in part without op.*, 81 N.J. 334 (1979), *conditionally modified in part on other grounds, aff'd in part on other grounds*, 82 N.J. 412, 416-17 (1980).

788. N.J.A.C. 13:4-8.2(b). If the case is pending before the OAL, objections to discovery are to be made to the ALJ, with notice to the Director. *Id.*

3. Factual written data, factual written reports, or documentary information.[789]

The DCR is barred by statute from producing or otherwise disclosing the content of any record containing conversations between DCR representatives and respondents at conciliation conferences.[790] The DCR is barred by regulation from producing any records reflecting settlement discussions during fact-finding conferences.[791]

The reports that typically appear in the DCR's file and that normally will be produced by the agency include: Complainant Interview Form; Humiliation Interview Questions; Investigator's Case Progress Reports; discovery produced by the parties; Pre-Fact Finding Interview Report; Fact Finding Conference Report; Post Conference Report; Listing of Documents To Support Investigator's Findings; Final Case Disposition Report; and various form correspondence between the DCR and either the parties or the EEOC.

4-49:6 Subpoenas

The ALJ or the Clerk of the OAL may issue subpoenas to compel the attendance of a person to testify and/or produce evidence at a hearing or deposition.[792] Refusal to obey a subpoena may result in (1) an inference that the testimony or evidence not provided is unfavorable or (2) the imposition of sanctions, ranging from costs incurred by the other party to dismissal of the cause or award of the requested relief.[793] The party that requested issuance of the subpoena may seek enforcement by filing a motion for an order to show cause in Superior Court.[794]

---

789. N.J.A.C. 13:4-8.2(a)(1)(3). *See, e.g., New Jersey Div. on Civil Rights v. Slumber, Inc.*, 166 N.J.Super. at 100-01 & n.3.

790. N.J.S.A. 10:5-14, -16; N.J.A.C. 13:4-11.1.

791. N.J.A.C. 13:4-2.3(c)(2).

792. N.J.S.A. 10:5-8(i); N.J.A.C. 1:1-11.1(a), -14.6(n), -15.12(c); N.J.A.C. 13:4-9.1(f); *David v. Vesta Co.*, 45 N.J. 301, 322 (1965). *See, e.g., Clover Hill Swimming Club v. Goldsboro*, 47 N.J. 24, 28, 37 (1966). The procedures for serving and moving to quash subpoenas are set forth in the UAPRs. *See* N.J.A.C. 1:1-11.1 *et seq.*

793. N.J.A.C. 1:1-11.4, -14.4.

794. N.J.A.C. 1:1-11.5. Because the subpoena power of the OAL is derived from the power invested in the DCR by the LAD, the earlier discussion in §4-47:3 pertaining to enforcement of DCR subpoenas is applicable here. *See Wright v. Plaza Ford*, 164 N.J.Super. 203, 212-13 (App. Div. 1978); *Hayes v. Gulli*, 175 N.J.Super. 294 (Ch.Div. 1980).

4-49:7 Informal Disposition

Informal disposition of the case may be made by stipulation, agreed settlement, or consent order.[795] The full terms of the settlement must be disclosed, either in a written consent order or stipulation or orally on the record.[796] If the ALJ finds that the settlement is voluntary, consistent with the LAD, and fully dispositive of the case, an initial decision approving and incorporating the full settlement terms will be issued.[797] If the DCR consents to the settlement terms, the ALJ's decision is deemed the final decision of the Director.[798]

4-49:8 Summary Disposition

A party may move for summary decision by filing a motion supported by a brief and, if necessary, affidavits.[799] To withstand the motion, the adverse party must file an affidavit setting forth specific facts demonstrating a genuine issue as to material facts which can be resolved only in an evidentiary proceeding.[800] The DCR must grant the non-moving party a plenary contested-case hearing only if "*material* disputed adjudicative facts" exist.[801]

The motion must be decided within 45 days of the submission (return) date.[802] As is the case with all motions in the OAL, a motion for summary decision is decided on the papers unless the ALJ directs oral argument.[803]

4-49:9 Presentation of Evidence

In a hearing before the ALJ, complainant's case is presented by the DCR's attorney.[804] Respondent must appear in person or by representative and submit tes-

795. N.J.S.A. 52:14B-9(d); N.J.A.C. 1:1-14.7(a). The UAPRs make available to the parties settlement conferences and mediation as means to encourage consensual resolution of disputes. *See* N.J.A.C. 1:1-9.1(c); N.J.A.C. 1:1-20.1 *et seq.*

796. N.J.A.C. 1:1-19.1(a).

797. N.J.A.C. 1:1-19.1(b).

798. N.J.A.C. 1:1-19.1(b)(2).

799. N.J.A.C. 1:1-12.5(a)-(b). *See, e.g., Frank v. Ivy Club*, 120 N.J. 73, 92, 95 (1990), *cert. denied*, 498 U.S. 1073 (1991) (affirming summary disposition in favor of complainant); *Pineman v. Paramus*, 4 N.J.A.R. 407 (DCR 1981), *aff'd*, No. A-5336-80 (App. Div. Apr. 1, 1982). *See generally* 37 Lefelt, *New Jersey Practice: Administrative Law & Practice*, §194 (1988).

800. N.J.A.C. 1:1-12.5(b); *Frank v. Ivy Club*, 120 N.J. at 95, 98-99.

801. *Frank v. Ivy Club*, 120 N.J. at 98; *Frank v. Ivy Club*, 228 N.J.Super. 40, 54 (App. Div. 1988), *rev'd on other grounds*, 120 N.J. 73 (1990), *cert. denied*, 498 U.S. 1073 (1991) (defining "adjudicative facts").

802. N.J.A.C. 1:1-12.5(c), -12.2(b).

803. N.J.A.C. 1:1-12.2(e).

804. N.J.S.A. 10:5-16; *David v. Vesta Co.*, 45 N.J. 301, 322 (1965); *Howard Savings Inst. v. Francis*, 133 N.J.Super. 54, 58 (App. Div. 1975).

timony,[805] and may be represented by counsel.[806] At the ALJ's discretion, complainant may intervene, present testimony, and be represented by counsel.[807] All parties to the proceeding may present oral and documentary evidence and argument on all issues involved, submit rebuttal evidence, and conduct such cross-examination as may be required, in the discretion of the ALJ, for a full and true disclosure of the facts.[808] Witnesses may be sequestered.[809] If necessary, the ALJ, with the parties or counsel present, may take a view of the workplace to resolve a dispute in issue.[810]

Testimony at a hearing must be under oath and recorded verbatim.[811] Any party may require that a hearing transcript be prepared at his expense.[812] Unless special circumstances warrant, the hearing is open to the public.[813]

The hearing is a *de novo* proceeding and, as such, neither party may use the DCR finding of probable cause as evidence of the merits of the verified com-

---

805. N.J.S.A. 10:5-16; N.J.S.A. 52:14B-9(c).

806. N.J.S.A. 10:5-16; *Howard Savings Inst. v. Francis*, 133 N.J.Super. at 58. As to the practice of law by non-lawyer representatives in DCR and OAL proceedings, *see* N.J.A.C. 1:1-5.1 *et seq.* and N.J.A.C. 13:4-2.3(b)(4). *See generally* 37 Lefelt, *New Jersey Practice: Administrative Law & Practice*, §§125-32 (1988).

807. N.J.S.A. 10:5-16; N.J.S.A. 52:14B-9(c); N.J.A.C. 1:1-16.1 *et seq.*; N.J.A.C. 13:4-6.5(c); *David v. Vesta Co.*, 45 N.J. at 322; *Howard Savings Inst. v. Francis*, 133 N.J.Super. at 58. The procedures to be followed by a person seeking to intervene are set forth in N.J.A.C. 1:1-16.1 *et seq.* N.J.A.C. 13:4-6.5(c).

808. N.J.S.A. 52:14B-10(a), -9(c); N.J.A.C. 1:1-14.7(b)-(g); *David v. Vesta Co.*, 45 N.J. at 322. *Cf. Jamison v. Rockaway Tp. Bd. of Educ.*, 242 N.J.Super. 436, 444-51 (App. Div. 1990) (ALJ erred in excluding respondent's evidence concerning the comparative qualifications of complainant and other employee considered for promotion), *Kearny Generating System v. Roper*, 184 N.J.Super. 253, 262-63 (App. Div.), *certif. denied*, 91 N.J. 254 (1982) (hearing examiner erred in ruling evidence of relative qualifications of applicants not relevant), and *Jones v. College of Medicine & Dentistry of New Jersey*, 155 N.J.Super. 232, 236-40 (App. Div. 1977), *certif. denied*, 77 N.J. 482 (1978) (selection decisions involve comparisons of relative qualifications), with *Flanders v. William Paterson College*, 163 N.J.Super. 225, 230-31 (App. Div. 1976) (hearing examiner did not abuse discretion in barring respondent's evidence regarding comparative qualifications of complainant and the employee who was retained).

Closing arguments may be presented, N.J.A.C. 1:1-14.7(e), but unless permitted or requested by the ALJ, post-hearing briefs may not be submitted. N.J.A.C. 1:1-14.7(f).

809. 37 Lefelt, *New Jersey Practice: Administrative Law & Practice*, §221 (1988). *Cf.* N.J.A.C. 13:4-2.3(b)(2) (sequestration at DCR fact-finding conferences); Fed. R. Evid. 615; Pressler, *Current N.J. Court Rules*, Comments to R.1:8-6 (1999 ed.).

810. *See, e.g., Panettieri v. C.V. Hill Refrigeration*, 159 N.J.Super. 472, 480 (App. Div. 1978). *See* N.J.S.A. 2A:77-1 *et seq.*

811. N.J.S.A. 10:5-16; N.J.A.C. 1:1-14.1(a); *David v. Vesta Co.*, 45 N.J. 301, 322, 326 (1965); *Howard Savings Inst. v. Francis*, 133 N.J.Super. 54, 58 (App. Div. 1975).

812. N.J.S.A. 10:5-24; N.J.S.A. 52:14B-9(e); N.J.A.C. 1:1-14.11.

813. N.J.A.C. 1:1-14.1. Similarly, the transcript or sound recording of the hearing is considered a public record open to inspection and copying. *See* N.J.A.C. 1:1-14.11(g)-(h).

plaint.[814] However, a finding of probable cause may be used to confirm and corroborate the credibility of witnesses.[815]

4-49:10 Rules of Evidence

The hearing need not be in accordance with the formal rules of evidence;[816] generally, all relevant evidence is admissible.[817] The ALJ may exclude evidence if its probative value is substantially outweighed by the risk that its admission will either (1) unduly consume time or (2) create substantial danger of undue prejudice or confusion.[818] Rules of privilege recognized by law are applicable.[819] Hearsay evidence is admissible and is accorded whatever weight the ALJ deems appropriate in view of the nature, character, and scope of the evidence, the circumstances of its creation and production, and its reliability.[820] Evidence concerning attempted conciliation, settlement discussions, and failed mediation efforts is inadmissible.[821] The ALJ may take notice of (1) judicially-noticeable facts and (2) generally recognized technical or scientific facts within the specialized knowledge of the DCR or the ALJ.[822]

---

814. *Hardwick v. Newark Morning Ledger Co.*, 8 N.J.A.R. 249, 269 n.1 (DCR 1983), *aff'd*, No. A-1084-83 (App. Div. Sept. 27, 1984), *certif. denied*, 99 N.J. 215 (1984); *Hayman v. Funk*, 8 N.J.A.R. 27, 35-36, 50 (DCR 1984).

815. *Hayman v. Funk*, 8 N.J.A.R. at 35-36.

816. N.J.S.A. 52:14B-10(a),(d); N.J.S.A. 10:5-16; N.J.A.C. 1:1-15.1(c). *See* N.J.A.C. 1:1-15.1 *et seq.* (OAL evidence rules); 37 Lefelt, *New Jersey Practice: Administrative Law & Practice*, §§202-24 (1988); Biunno, *Current N.J. Rules of Evidence*, Comments to N.J.R.E. 101 (1999 ed.).

817. N.J.S.A. 52:14B-10(a); N.J.A.C. 1:1-15.1(c). *Cf. Dixon v. Rutgers*, 110 N.J. 432, 442 (1988) (defining relevancy in the context of discovery in an employment discrimination proceeding); Evid. R. 7.

818. N.J.S.A. 52:14B-10(a); N.J.A.C. 1:1-15.1(c); *Cf.* Evid. R. 4.

819. N.J.S.A. 52:14B-10(a); N.J.A.C. 1:1-15.4. *See Dixon v. Rutgers*, 110 N.J. at 446-59. The privilege against self-incrimination would not be available to a subpoenaed witness in view of the LAD's grant of transactional immunity. N.J.S.A. 10:5-11. *See* §4-47:3.

820. N.J.A.C. 1:1-15.5(a), -15.12. *See, e.g., Hardwick v. Newark Morning Ledger Co.*, 8 N.J.A.R. 249, 262, 279 (DCR 1983), *aff'd*, No. A-1084-83 (App. Div. Sept. 27, 1984), *certif. denied*, 99 N.J. 215 (1984); *Gimello v. Agency Rent-A-Car Systems, Inc.*, 250 N.J.Super. 338, 354 (App. Div. 1991) (unreliable hearsay rejected by ALJ); *Lige v. Montclair*, 72 N.J. 5, 8 n.2 (1976). *See* Biunno, *Current N.J. Rules of Evidence*, Comments to N.J.R.E. 101 (1998 ed.). If hearsay evidence has been admitted, there must be some legally competent evidence to support each ultimate finding of fact to ensure reliability and avoid the fact or appearance of arbitrariness. N.J.A.C. 1:1-15.5 (residuum rule); *Clowes v. Terminix Int'l, Inc.*, 109 N.J. 575, 599 (1988) (residuum rule violated); *Goodman v. London Metals Exchange, Inc.*, 86 N.J. 19, 29 (1981) ("there must be a residuum of legal and competent evidence in the record to support" the DCR's decision); Biunno, *Current N.J. Rules of Evidence*, Comments to N.J.R.E. 101 (1998 ed.).

821. N.J.S.A. 10:5-16, -14; N.J.A.C. 13:4-11.1(d), -2.3(c)(2); N.J.A.C. 1:1-15.10, -20.1(a)(3)(i)-(iii). *See* N.J.R.E. 408, 410; Fed. R. Evid. 408.

822. N.J.S.A. 52:14B-10(b); N.J.A.C. 1:1-15.2(a)-(b). *See* N.J.R.E. 201-202 (judicial notice).

4-49:11 Amending the Pleadings

Amendments to pleadings may be permitted when (1) they are in the interest of efficiency and avoiding hyper-technical pleading requirements and (2) they will not create undue prejudice.[823] Amendments to conform to the evidence presented at hearing may also be allowed.[824]

4-50 Initial Decision of the ALJ

After a hearing, the ALJ sets forth recommended findings of fact and conclusions of law, based exclusively upon the evidence, stipulations, and matters officially noticed.[825] If appropriate, adverse inferences may be drawn from the failure of a party to produce a witness.[826] The experience, technical competence, and specialized knowledge of the DCR or the ALJ may be utilized in the evaluation of evidence, provided it is disclosed on the record.[827] The ALJ's recommended report and decision (commonly referred to as the "initial decision"), must be based upon sufficient, competent, and credible evidence, in final form and fully dispositive of all issues in the case, and filed with the DCR Director within 45 days after the the hearing closes.[828] Motions for reconsideration are not permitted;[829] however, motions to reopen the record are permitted.[830]

---

823. N.J.S.A. 10:5-16. N.J.A.C. 1:1-6.2(a); N.J.A.C. 13:4-6.3(b)-(c). *See, e.g., White v. PSE&G Co.*, 8 N.J.A.R. 335, 337 (DCR 1984), *aff'd*, No. A-1496-84 (App. Div. July 16, 1986). *Cf. Balsley v. No. Hunterdon Regional Sch. Dist. Bd. of Educ.*, 117 N.J. 434, 437 (1990) (in an education discrimination dispute filed with the Commissioner of Education, over which the DCR would have had concurrent jurisdiction, ALJ permitted complainant, subsequent to settlement of the merits, to amend complaint to include claim for counsel fees under LAD).

824. N.J.A.C. 13:4-6.3(c); N.J.A.C. 1:1-6.2(a). *See, e.g., Roberts v. Keansburg Bd. of Educ.*, 5 N.J.A.R. 208, 250 (DCR 1983); *New Jersey Div. on Civil Rights v. Slumber, Inc.*, 82 N.J. 412, 415-16 (1980). *See* R.4:9-2 (amending pleadings to conform to evidence).

825. N.J.S.A. 52:14B-9(f); N.J.S.A. 10:5-17; N.J.S.A. 52:14B-10(c); N.J.A.C. 1:1-15.1(a), -18.1(a), 60-18.3(c); *Clowes v. Terminix Int'l, Inc.*, 109 N.J. 575, 586 (1988); *David v. Vesta Co.*, 45 N.J. 301, 326 (1965). *See Noble Oil Co. v. New Jersey Dept. of Environmental Protection*, 123 N.J. 474, 476-77 (1991) ("Administrative agencies must 'articulate the standards and principles that govern their discretionary decisions in as much detail as possible.' ").

826. *See, e.g., Zahorian v. Russell Fitt Real Estate Agency*, 62 N.J. 399, 404 (1973); *Andersen v. Exxon Co.*, 7 N.J.A.R. 289, 302 (DCR 1980), *aff'd*, No. A-2940-79 (App. Div. Feb. 25, 1981), *aff'd as modified on other grounds*, 89 N.J. 483 (1982); *Gimello v. Agency Rent-A-Car Systems, Inc.*, 250 N.J.Super. 338, 352 (App. Div. 1991). *See* N.J.A.C. 1:1-11.4 (party who fails to comply with hearing subpoena may suffer inference that evidence or testimony not produced is unfavorable). *See generally N.J. Model Jury Charges*, §1.16 (3d ed. 1990).

827. N.J.S.A. 52:14B-10(b).

828. N.J.S.A. 52:14B-10(c); N.J.A.C. 1:1-18.1(b), (d); *Clowes v. Terminix Int'l, Inc.*, 109 N.J. at 585-86. The 45-day limit may be extended, for good cause shown, upon certification by the directors of the OAL and DCR. N.J.S.A. 52:14B-10(c); N.J.A.C. 1:1-18.8.

The parties of record must be served with the recommended report and decision, along with an indication of the date of receipt thereof by the Director of the DCR. N.J.S.A. 52:14B-10(c); N.J.A.C. 1:1-18.3(b).

4-50:1 Filing Exceptions to the Initial Decision

All parties may file exceptions, objections, and replies to the ALJ's recommended report and decision, and present argument to the Director of the DCR, either orally or in writing, as directed by the DCR.[831] Exceptions must be filed and served within 13 days after the ALJ's decision is mailed to the parties, and any reply must be filed and served within five days after receipt of the exceptions.[832] The reply may include cross-exceptions or submissions in support of the ALJ's decision.[833]

4-51 Final Decision of the Director

The Director may adopt, reject, or modify the recommended report and decision of the ALJ.[834] He may also remand the case to the ALJ for further action on specific issues or arguments not previously raised or incompletely considered.[835] If the Director fails to act on the recommended report and decision within 45 days after receipt, the ALJ's decision is deemed adopted as the final decision of the Director.[836] In all events, it is the Director's, not the ALJ's, ultimate responsibility to decide adjudicated matters brought before the DCR.[837]

---

829. N.J.A.C. 1:1-18.5(a). *Cf. Pineman v. Paramus*, 4 N.J.A.R. 407, 409 (DCR 1981), *aff'd*, No. A-5336-80 (App. Div. Apr. 1, 1982) (motion for reconsideration of interlocutory order); *Hayman v. Funk*, 8 N.J.A.R. 27, 45 (DCR 1984) (motion to vacate and for new hearing).

830. N.J.A.C. 1:1-18.5(b)-(c). If the motion is made prior to the filing of the ALJ's decision, it is addressed to the ALJ and may be granted only in extraordinary circumstances. N.J.A.C. 1:1-18.5(c). Once the ALJ's decision has been filed, such motion must be addressed to the Director of the DCR. N.J.A.C. 1:1-18.5(b).

831. N.J.S.A. 52:14B-10(c); N.J.A.C. 1:1-18.4. *See, e.g., Frank v. Ivy Club*, 120 N.J. 73, 93 (1990), *cert. denied*, 498 U.S. 1073 (1991); *Clowes v. Terminix Int'l, Inc.*, 109 N.J. 575, 585 (1988).

832. N.J.A.C. 1:1-18.4. These limits may be extended, for good cause shown, upon certification by the directors of the OAL and DCR. N.J.S.A. 52:14B-10(c); N.J.A.C. 1:1-18.8. *See, e.g., Hardwick v. Newark Morning Ledger Co.*, 8 N.J.A.R. 249, 268 (DCR 1983), *aff'd*, No. A-1084-83 (App. Div. Sept. 27, 1984), *certif. denied*, 99 N.J. 215 (1984) (extension granted in view of counsel's vacation schedule).

833. N.J.A.C. 1:1-18.4(d).

834. N.J.S.A. 10:5-17; N.J.S.A. 52:14B-10(c); N.J.S.A. 52:14F-7(a); N.J.A.C. 1:1-18.3(c)(12), -18.6(a); *Clowes v. Terminix Int'l, Inc.* 109 N.J. 575, 587 (1988). The findings and conclusions of the ALJ are not binding on the Director. N.J.A.C. 1:1-18.1(c); *Clowes*, 109 N.J. at 586.

835. N.J.A.C. 1:1-18.7(a).

836. N.J.S.A. 52:14B-10(c); N.J.S.A. 10:5-17; N.J.A.C. 1:1-18.3(c)(12), -18.6(c); *Clowes v. Terminix Int'l, Inc.*, 109 N.J. at 586-87. The 45-day limit may be extended, for good cause shown, upon certification by the directors of the OAL and DCR. N.J.S.A. 52:14B-10(c); N.J.A.C. 1:1-18.8. *See, e.g., Clowes v. Terminix Int'l, Inc.*, 7 N.J.A.R. 206, 222 (DCR 1984), *rev'd on other grounds*, No. A-3886-84 (App. Div. May 8, 1986), *aff'd*, 109 N.J. 575 (1988).

837. *Clowes v. Terminix Int'l, Inc.*, 109 N.J. at 586; *Clover Hill Swimming Club v. Goldsboro*, 47 N.J. 25, 37 (1966); *Hardwick v. Newark Morning Ledger Co.*, 8 N.J.A.R. at 275; N.J.A.C. 1:1-18.1(c).

The Director's final decision or order must be in writing or stated in the record.[838] The final decision must include findings of fact and conclusions of law, although the Director may incorporate by reference any or all of the recommended findings and conclusions of the ALJ.[839] The final decision must be based exclusively upon evidence of record and matters officially noticed.[840] The Director is not required to "personally read the entire record or transcript but rather is only required to consider and appraise a personal understanding of the evidence contained in the record."[841] If the Director rejects or modifies the ALJ decision, his final decision must clearly state in sufficient detail the nature of the rejection or modification, the reasons for it, the specific evidence of record and interpretation of law upon which it is based, and the precise change in result or disposition caused by it.[842] Rejection or modification of an ALJ's findings of fact must be based upon substantial evidence in the record.[843]

The final decision of the Director is effective (1) on the date of delivery or the date of mailing of the decision to the parties, whichever occurs first, or (2) on any date after the aforesaid date as may be provided by the order.[844] Upon motion by the Director, a party, or the DCR's attorney, the Director may reopen the proceeding for good cause shown.[845] Upon motion by a party, the Director may grant a stay of the decision pending appeal.[846] If the motion is denied, it may be renewed in the Appellate Division of Superior Court.[847]

The final determination of the Director precludes any other action, civil or criminal, based on the same grievances of complainant.[848]

---

838. N.J.S.A. 52:14B-10(d); *Hardwick v. Newark Morning Ledger Co.*, 8 N.J.A.R. at 274-75.

839. N.J.S.A. 10:5-17; N.J.S.A. 52:14B-10(d); *Frank v. Ivy Club*, 228 N.J.Super. 40, 46-47 (App. Div. 1988), *rev'd on other grounds*, 120 N.J. 73, 80 (1990), *cert. denied*, 498 U.S. 1073 (1991); *David v. Vesta Co.*, 45 N.J. 301, 326 (1965).

840. N.J.S.A. 10:5-17; N.J.S.A. 52:14B-10(d), -9(f); *B.C. v. Cumberland Regional School Dist.*, 220 N.J.Super. 214, 231 (App. Div. 1987); *Hardwick v. Newark Morning Ledger Co.*, 8 N.J.A.R. at 275.

841. *B.C. v. Cumberland Regional School Dist.*, 220 N.J.Super. at 230 (agency head may rely upon a summary of the record prepared by the ALJ or a subordinate).

842. N.J.A.C. 1:1-18.6(b); *Hardwick v. Newark Morning Ledger Co.*, 8 N.J.A.R. at 274-75. *See, e.g., Rogers v. Campbell Foundry Co.*, 8 N.J.A.R. 75 (DCR 1980), *aff'd*, 185 N.J.Super. 109 (App. Div.), *certif. denied*, 91 N.J. 529 (1982). *Cf. Hardwick*, 8 N.J.A.R. at 273-80 (rejecting ALJ's credibility findings), with *Hayman v. Funk*, 8 N.J.A.R. 27, 45-47 (DCR 1984) (accepting ALJ's credibility findings).

843. N.J.S.A. 1:1-18.6(b); *Hardwick v. Newark Morning Ledger Co.*, 8 N.J.A.R. at 275.

844. N.J.S.A. 52:14B-10(e). The date of delivery or mailing is to be stamped on the face of the decision. N.J.S.A. 52:14B-10(e).

845. N.J.A.C. 13:4-14.1; N.J.A.C. 1:1-18.5(b). *See, e.g., Farley v. Ocean Tp. Bd. of Educ.*, 174 N.J.Super. 449, 453 (App. Div.), *certif. denied*, 85 N.J. 140 (1980) (Director may reopen, rehear, and modify prior orders; abuse-of-discretion standard of review on appeal); *Panettieri v. C.V. Hill Refrigeration*, 159 N.J.Super. 472, 493-95 (App. Div. 1978).

846. R.2:9-7. *See, e.g., Frank v. Ivy Club*, 228 N.J.Super. at 51.

847. R.2:9-7.

4-52 Summary Enforcement Proceedings in the Superior Court

The LAD provides two methods of summary enforcement designed "to enable the Director to secure full compliance with the [LAD] and the complete effectuation of the particular terms ... of his orders."[849]

After the filing of a verified complaint, the Director may proceed against any person in a summary manner in Superior Court to (1) compel compliance with any of the provisions of the LAD or (2) prevent violations or attempts to violate the LAD or attempts to interfere with or impede the enforcement of any provision of the LAD.[850] The effectiveness of a summary proceeding has been dimin-

---

848. N.J.S.A. 10:5-27; *Christian Bros. Inst. v. Northern New Jersey Interscholastic League*, 86 N.J. 409, 415 (1981); *Hermann v. Fairleigh Dickinson Univ.*, 183 N.J.Super. 500, 503-05 (App. Div.), *certif. denied*, 91 N.J. 573 (1982); *Giammario v. Trenton Bd. of Ed.*, 203 N.J.Super. 356, 364-65 (App. Div.), *certif. denied*, 102 N.J. 336 (1985), *cert. denied*, 475 U.S. 1141 (1986) (DCR finding of no probable cause barred subsequent civil action alleging same discriminatory conduct under a continuing violation theory); *Gray v. Serruto Builders, Inc.*, 110 N.J.Super. 297, 300 (Ch.Div. 1970); *Pittman v. LaFontaine*, 756 F.Supp. 834, 842-43 (D.N.J. 1991); *Butler v. Sherman, Silverstein & Kohl, P.C.*, 755 F.Supp. 1259, 1266 (D.N.J. 1990); *Ferrara v. Tappan Co.*, 722 F.Supp. 1204, 1205-06 (D.N.J. 1989) (plaintiff allowed only one bite at the apple).

When the DCR administratively closes its case-file upon the withdrawal or abandonment of the verified complaint by complainant without having rendered a substantive decision on the merits (such substantive decisions include, *e.g.*, a finding of no probable cause or a finding, after a hearing, of no discrimination), there has been no "final determination" within the meaning of N.J.S.A. 10:5-27. *Weber v. LDC/Milton Roy*, 42 FEP 1507, 1515-16 (D.N.J. 1986); *Leese v. Doe*, 182 N.J.Super. 318 (Law Div. 1981); *Corn v. Adidas USA, Inc.*, No. 85-30835(HLS), p. 5 (D.N.J. Jan. 6, 1986) (Lexis); Poff, *Letters to Editor*, 116 N.J.L.J. 292 (Aug. 29, 1985), 117 N.J.L.J. 118 (Jan. 30, 1986) (DCR Director believes LAD should be amended to provide that claimant withdrawing claim from DCR may not commence suit in court). *See, e.g., Jansen v. Food Circus Supermarkets, Inc.*, 110 N.J. 363, 372 (1988) (complainant withdrew verified complaint filed with DCR and then filed civil action). However, if the DCR closes its file upon the entry of a conciliation agreement or consent order that settles the dispute, there has been a "final determination" for purposes of the LAD.

The court in *Weber v. LDC/Milton Roy* also held that there is no "final determination" when the DCR closes its file upon receipt of the EEOC's final determination letter in cases where the EEOC, pursuant to the DCR/EEOC Worksharing Agreement (*see* §4-46:5), conducts the investigations and makes the discrimination determinations. The second holding in *Weber* vitiates the salutory purposes of the Worksharing Agreement by requiring the DCR to duplicate the efforts of the EEOC to have its dispositions treated as final determinations. *See EEOC v. Commercial Office Products Co.*, 486 U.S. 107, 122 (1988); DCR/EEOC Worksharing Agreement, pp. 1, 3 (1990-91). The holding also interferes with the comity and deference that the EEOC and DCR accord to each other. *See, e.g.*, 29 C.F.R. §§1601.75(a), 1601.80 (1990) (in cases processed by the DCR pursuant to the Worksharing Agreement, the EEOC accepts the findings and resolutions of the DCR without case-by-case review by the EEOC); *Mullen v. New Jersey Steel Corp.*, 733 F.Supp. 1534, 1540-42 (D.N.J. 1990) (detailed illustration of DCR closing its files upon finding of no probable cause by EEOC; jurisdictional issue not addressed in *Mullen*); DCR/EEOC Worksharing Agreement, pp. 1, 3 (1990-91). Finally, the second *Weber* holding is inconsistent with the text of the LAD inasmuch as the DCR's determination to take no further action on a verified complaint upon receipt of the EEOC's determination effectively dismisses the complaint, thereby precluding complainant from either seeking to have the matter transferred to the Office of Administrative Law or reinstituting the grievance in the Superior Court. *See* N.J.S.A. 10:5-13; N.J.S.A. 10:5-27. Complainant's statutorily-mandated course of action is to file an appeal with the Appellate Division. For similar reasons, the decision in *Smith v. Hartford Fire Ins. Co.*, 1985 WL 2828 (E.D.Pa. 1985), holding that the DCR's dismissal of a verified complaint as time-barred under N.J.S.A. 10:5-18 (*see* §4-56) is not a "final determination," is wrongly decided.

849. *General Motors Corp. v. Blair*, 129 N.J.Super. 412, 419 (App. Div. 1974).

ished by the 1990 amendments to the LAD which permit a party charged with unlawful employment discrimination to demand a jury trial.[851] Thus, if there is a genuine issue as to a material fact, defendant is entitled to have the summary proceedings converted into a plenary action.[852]

The Director may also institute a summary civil action to enforce an order he has issued.[853] If civil penalties are not in issue, the enforcement proceeding is commenced by complaint for an order to show cause, pursuant to R.4:67.[854] If civil penalties are in issue, the enforcement action is commenced by complaint, pursuant to R.4:70 and N.J.S.A. 2A:58-1 *et seq.* (Penalty Enforcement Law).[855]

Although the LAD expressly states that summary enforcement actions are to be commenced by the Director, a 1990 court rule amendment now permits enforcement proceedings to be instituted by a complainant in whose favor a written order affording specific relief has been entered by the Director.[856]

In these summary enforcement proceedings, the trial court generally lacks jurisdiction to rule on the validity of the agency order;[857] exclusive jurisdiction to review DCR decisions is in the Appellate Division.[858]

---

850. N.J.S.A. 10:5-14.1; *Jackson v. Concord Co.*, 54 N.J. 113, 124 (1969). The procedures to be followed in such summary actions are set forth in R.4:67. For a fuller discussion of summary actions, *see* Pressler, *Current N.J. Court Rules*, Comments to R.4:67 (1999 ed.); 2A Del Deo, *New Jersey Practice: Court Rules Annotated*, Comments & Annotations to R.4:67 (3d ed. 1973 & 1990 supp.); 37 Lefelt, *New Jersey Practice: Administrative Law & Practice*, §332 (1988); 4A Walzer, *New Jersey Practice: Civil Practice Forms*, ch. 83 (1991).

851. L.1990, c.12, §2, amending N.J.S.A. 10:5-13.

852. R.4:67-4(b); R.4:67-5.

853. N.J.S.A. 10:5-19; *David v. Vesta Co.*, 45 N.J. 301, 323, 327-28 (1965).

854. *See* R.4:67, particularly R.4:67-6; N.J.S.A. 10:5-19.

855. *See* R.4:70, particularly R.4:70-1(b); R.4:67-1(a); N.J.S.A. 10:5-19. For a fuller discussion of penalty enforcement proceedings, *see* Pressler, *Current N.J. Court Rules*, Comments to R.4:70 (1999 ed.); 2A Del Deo, *New Jersey Practice: Court Rules Annotated*, Comments & Annotations to R. 4:70 (3d ed. 1973 & 1990 supp.); 37 Lefelt, *New Jersey Practice: Administrative Law & Practice*, §332 (1988 & current supp.).

856. R.4:67-6(a)(2); *cf.* N.J.A.C. 13:4-9.3(b) (subpoena enforcement proceeding instituted by party). Upon timely application, the DCR has a right to intervene. R.4:67-6(b)(3). *Cf.* N.J.S.A. 10:5-13 (intervention by DCR generally).

857. R.4:67-6(c)(3). There are exceptions to this rule. For example, in summary proceedings to enforce an agency subpoena or discovery order, the trial court has authority to review the validity of the subpoena or order. R.4:67-6(c)(2); R.1:9-6. And where the proposed administrative action has not been preceded by the creation in the agency of a record which is amenable to appellate review, the validity of the agency's order may be challenged by defendant in a summary enforcement action. *See State Farm Mutual Auto. Ins. Co. v. New Jersey Dept. of Public Advocate*, 227 N.J.Super. 99, 131-34 (App. Div. 1988), *aff'd*, 118 N.J. 336 (1990); *Philadelphia Newspapers, Inc. v. New Jersey Dept. of Law & Public Safety*, 232 N.J.Super. 458, 466 (App. Div. 1989). Absent unusual circumstances, the latter exception would not be applicable to DCR proceedings.

858. R.2:2-3(a)(2); R.2:2-4.

4-53 Commencing Proceedings in the Superior Court

In lieu of proceeding in the DCR, an aggrieved person may institute a civil action in the Superior Court.[859] Prosecution of such action bars the filing of a verified complaint with the DCR during the pendency of the action.[860] A final determination by the court precludes plaintiff from filing a verified complaint with the DCR with respect to the same grievance.[861] An employee who files a verified complaint with the DCR, but voluntarily withdraws it before a final determination is made, is not precluded from filing a civil suit in Superior Court on the same claim.[862] A civil action may not be filed in the case of unlawful mandatory retirement; relief for such conduct may be sought only administratively, in a proceeding before the DCR.[863]

The complaint should state the allegations of discrimination with sufficient particularity and incorporate any and all available relevant information.[864] A motion to amend pleadings to add new claims of discrimination normally should be granted, even if tardily made, as long as defendant had notice of the precise claims being added from the beginning of the litigation.[865] Any party may demand a trial by jury of claims arising under the LAD.[866] The principles govern-

---

859. N.J.S.A. 10:5-13. Although the LAD speaks in terms of instituting a suit in the "Superior Court," LAD claims may also be heard in federal district court as long as there is subject matter jurisdiction (*e.g.*, diversity or supplemental). *Butler v. Sherman, Silverstein & Kohl, P.C.*, 755 F.Supp. 1259, 1266 n.9 (D.N.J. 1990). *See generally* 17 Wright, Miller & Cooper, *Federal Practice & Procedure: Jurisdiction*, §4211 (2d ed. 1988). However, a LAD claim against the state of New Jersey cannot be pursued in federal court, unless the state waives its Eleventh Amendment immunity. *Csizmadia v. Fauver*, 746 F.Supp. 483, 488 (D.N.J. 1990) (N.J. Dept. of Corrections); *Johnson v. New Jersey Transit Rail Operations, Inc.*, 1988 WL 24148 (D.N.J. 1988) (stating legal principle), *overruled, Fitchik v. New Jersey Transit Rail Operations, Inc.*, 873 F.2d 655 (3d Cir.) (*en banc*), *cert. denied*, 493 U.S. 850 (1989) (holding N.J. Transit is not an alter ego of state of New Jersey). *See generally* 13 Wright, Miller & Cooper, *Federal Practice & Procedure: Jurisdiction*, §3524 (2d ed. 1984).

As noted in §4-4, a plaintiff wishing to sue under both the LAD and the ADEA must institute suit in federal, not state, court.

860. N.J.S.A. 10:5-13; *Balsley v. No. Hunterdon Regional Sch. Dist. Bd. of Educ.*, 117 N.J. 434, 442 (1990) (prosecution of a civil action "divests" the DCR of jurisdiction); *Fuchilla v. Layman*, 109 N.J. 319, 336, *cert. denied*, 488 U.S. 826 (1988). The pendency of a Superior Court action likewise bars the filing of a verified complaint with an authorized municipal office of civil rights. N.J.S.A. 10:5-13, -14.2, -14.3. Although the LAD is silent on the issue, the pendency of the Superior Court action should also bar the filing of a verified complaint with an authorized county office of civil rights. *See* N.J.S.A. 10:5-13, -14.2, -14.3.

861. *Pittman v. LaFontaine*, 756 F.Supp. 834, 842 (D.N.J. 1991); *Butler v. Sherman, Silverstein & Kohl, P.C.*, 755 F.Supp. at 1266; *Ferrara v. Tappan Co.*, 722 F.Supp. 1204, 1205-06 (D.N.J. 1989) (a plaintiff is permitted only one bite at the apple); N.J.S.A. 10:5-27. *See Hackensack v. Winner*, 82 N.J. 1, 31-38 (1980) (administrative agencies obligated to apply doctrines of claim preclusion, issue preclusion, and entire controversy).

862. *Aldrich v. Manpower Temporary Servs.*, 277 N.J. Super. 500 (App. Div.), *certif. denied*, 139 N.J. 442 (1994) (also noting that where administrative hearings have commenced and "estoppel principles" might rise, the Administrative Law Judge might recommend against permitting withdrawal). *Id.* at 506.

863. *See* §4-29:1.

864. *Dixon v. Rutgers*, 110 N.J. 432, 455 (1988).

ing discovery in employment discrimination cases pending in the Superior Court are essentially the same as those applicable in DCR proceedings, which are discussed in §4-49:4.[867]

When an action is pending in the Superior Court, a party filing a pleading, brief, or legal memorandum with the court is obligated to mail a copy to the DCR.[868] Upon application to the Superior Court, the DCR must be permitted to intervene in the proceedings.[869]

A respondent challenging the jurisdiction of the DCR or the constitutionality of the LAD on persuasive grounds may file an action in lieu of prerogative writ in the Superior Court, Law Division.[870] Constitutional challenges to the LAD and the DCR's exercise of jurisdiction thereunder may also be cognizable in federal district court.[871] A party seeking to ascertain whether certain conduct is in conformance with the requirements of the LAD or the LAD's constitutionality may institute an action for a declaratory judgment in the trial division of Superior Court.[872]

---

865. *Grigoletti v. Ortho Pharmaceutical Corp.*, 226 N.J.Super. 518, 532 (App. Div. 1988), *aff'd in part on opinion below, rev'd and modified on other grounds*, 118 N.J. 89, 114 (1990). *See* R.4:9-1.

866. N.J.S.A. 10:5-13. *See* R.1:8-1(b); R.4:35-1. A jury trial may be had regardless of whether the action is pending in the Chancery Division or the Law Division. *See O'Neill v. Vreeland*, 6 N.J. 158, 167-68 (1951).

867. *Dixon v. Rutgers*, 110 N.J. at 441-59.

868. N.J.S.A. 10:5-13.

869. N.J.S.A. 10:5-13; R.4:33-3. Note that the LAD mandates that the DCR's intervention motion be granted. In contrast, the applicable court rule, R.4:33-2, gives the trial court discretion to deny such motions. It has yet to be judicially determined whether, to the extent inconsistent, R.4:33-2 supersedes N.J.S.A. 10:5-13. *See* N.J. Const. Art. 6, §2, ¶3; *Winberry v. Salisbury*, 5 N.J. 240, *cert. denied*, 340 U.S. 877 (1950); *cf.* R.1:13-9 (appearance by amicus curiae); R.4:67-6(b)(3) (mandatory intervention by agency in summary enforcement action).

870. *Levitt & Sons, Inc. v. New Jersey Div. Against Discrimination*, 31 N.J. 514, 523, 536 (1960), *app. dism'd*, 363 U.S. 418 (1960); R.4:69-1 *et seq.* Proceedings in the DCR may be stayed pending resolution of the civil action. R.4:69-3. *See, e.g., Levitt*, 31 N.J. at 520.

Where respondent's challenge to the constitutionality of the LAD or the jurisdiction of the DCR is not based on substantial grounds or involves the resolution of material facts within the scope of the DCR's expertise, an action in lieu of prerogative writ will not lie. *Princeton First Aid & Rescue Squad, Inc. v. New Jersey Div. on Civil Rights*, 124 N.J.Super. 150 (App. Div.), *certif. denied*, 63 N.J. 555 (1973); *Ward v. Keenan*, 3 N.J. 298, 308-09 (1949); *Levitt*, 31 N.J. at 523; Pressler, *Current N.J. Court Rules*, Comment to R.4:69-5 (1999 ed.). In such case, the challenge must be raised by way of motion or answer filed in the DCR, with any adverse ruling thereon being subject to review by the Appellate Division. *Princeton First Aid*, 124 N.J.Super. at 152-53. *See, e.g., Twomey v. Englewood Hospital Ass'n*, 5 N.J.A.R. 188, 189 (DCR 1981), *rev'd on other grounds*, No. A-3523-80 (App. Div. June 14, 1982), *certif. denied*, 91 N.J. 568 (1982).

871. *Tiger Inn v. Edwards*, 636 F.Supp. 787, 789 (D.N.J. 1986). The federal court, however, may abstain from deciding the constitutional issue and stay the proceedings pending clarification by the DCR and State courts of the meaning of unsettled provisions of the LAD. 636 F.Supp. at 790-92; *Ivy Club v. Edwards*, 943 F.2d 270 (3d Cir. 1991), *cert. denied*, 503 U.S. 914 (1992).

4-54 Remedies

The Legislature has determined that persons subjected to unlawful discrimination may suffer diverse and substantial personal hardships which give rise to remedies under the LAD, including compensatory and punitive damages.[873] The unlawful discrimination must be the proximate cause of the damages suffered by the aggrieved party.[874]

4-54:1 In DCR Proceedings

The Director's "power to fashion remedies is as broad and flexible as needed to comport with the preeminent social significance of the LAD's purposes and objects."[875] Nonetheless, the Director's "orders must be reasonably related to the findings upon which they rest and must avoid undue breadth."[876]

When the Director has determined that an unlawful employment practice has occurred, he will order respondent to cease and desist and to take such affirmative action as he deems necessary to effectuate the purposes of the LAD.[877] Affirmative action that may be ordered includes, *inter alia*, hiring, reinstatement, or upgrading of employees, with or without back pay; restoration to membership in

---

872. N.J.S.A. 2A:16-50 *et seq.*; R.4:42-3. *See, e.g., Passaic Daily News v. Blair*, 63 N.J. 474 (1973); *Help-U-Sell of Teaneck v. Teaneck*, 207 N.J.Super. 600 (Law Div. 1985); *Ebler v. Newark*, 54 N.J. 487 (1969); *David v. Vesta Co.*, 45 N.J. 301, 309 (1965).

873. N.J.S.A. 10:5-3. Examples listed in the statute include economic loss; time loss; physical and emotional stress; search and relocation difficulties; anxiety caused by lack of information, uncertainty, and resultant planning difficulty; career, education, family, and social disruption; adjustment problems; and severe emotional trauma, illness, homelessness, or other irreparable harm resulting from the strain of employment controversies. *Id.*

874. *Reynolds v. Atlantic City Convention Center Authority*, 1990 WL 267417, 53 FEP 1852, 1872 (D.N.J. 1990), *aff'd without published op.*, 925 F.2d 419 (3d Cir. 1991); *Countiss v. Trenton State College*, 77 N.J. 590, 597, 599 (1978).

875. *Shaner v. Horizon Bancorp.*, 116 N.J. 433, 438 (1989) (internal quotation marks and alterations omitted), *citing, inter alia, Castellano v. Linden Bd. of Educ.*, 79 N.J. 407, 417 (1979) (Handler, J., concurring and dissenting). *Accord Nat'l Organization for Women v. Little League Baseball, Inc.*, 127 N.J.Super. 522, 538 (App. Div.), *summarily aff'd without op.*, 67 N.J. 320 (1974).

876. *Castellano v. Linden Bd. of Educ.*, 79 N.J. at 415 (Schreiber, J., concurring and dissenting) (internal quotation marks omitted).

877. N.J.S.A. 10:5-17. *See Dixon v. Rutgers*, 110 N.J. 432, 459 (1988) (LAD is designed not only to give redress to the individual complainant but also to enjoin further discriminatory practices as to all persons). *See, e.g., Frank v. Ivy Club*, 120 N.J. 73, 96, 111 (1990), *cert. denied*, 498 U.S. 1073 (1991) (cease and desist order directing eating clubs to admit women as members); *Andersen v. Exxon Co.*, 89 N.J. 483, 502 (1982) (DCR authorized to issue cease and desist order against company and supervisor who effectuated company's discriminatory conduct); *Roberts v. Keansburg Bd. of Educ.*, 5 N.J.A.R. 208, 269 (DCR 1983) (requiring employer's affirmative action officer to explain to employees the school's sexual harassment complaint procedure, that retaliation for making such a complaint will not occur, and their right to file a complaint with the DCR).

a labor organization; or extension of full and equal accommodations, advantages, facilities, and privileges to all persons.[878] Such an order may require that the victim of discrimination, if qualified, be appointed, reinstated, or promoted—either immediately or to the first open position—and granted retroactive seniority and benefits.[879]

In a case involving discriminatory denial of seniority and promotions, the New Jersey Supreme Court utilized the "rightful place" theory. *Terry v. Mercer County Bd. of Chosen Freeholders*.[880] The affected employees were granted retroactive seniority and immediate pay increases to the level they would have had if not wrongfully denied promotions. However, they were required to wait for actual promotion until positions became available; no incumbent employees were "bumped." In *Granziel v. City of Plainfield*,[881] , in contrast, the Appellate Division ordered the reinstatement of an employee discriminatorily discharged because of a handicap, despite the fact that an innocent co-employee would have to be bumped.

The Supreme Court has left open the issue whether the DCR may order an educational institution to grant tenure to a victim of discrimination.[882] The Court did suggest that at a minimum there would have to be a "substantial causal relation" between the discriminatory conduct and the complainant's failure to meet

---

878. N.J.S.A. 10:5-17. *See, e.g.*, *Terry v. Mercer County Freeholders Bd.*, 86 N.J. 141, 147-58 (1981). *Cf. Simon v. Police & Firemen's Retirement System Bd. of Trustees*, 233 N.J.Super. 186 (App. Div.), *certif. denied*, 117 N.J. 652 (1989) (upholding State Division of Pension's interim regulation permitting employees who were denied the opportunity to transfer from one public retirement system to another because of unlawful age discrimination to transfer cost-free in order to remediate the previous inequity). A DCR order directing an employer and its employees to provide services to all persons without discrimination does not violate the Thirteenth Amendment of the U.S. Constitution (prohibition against involuntary servitude). *Sellers v. Philip's Barber Shop*, 46 N.J. 340, 348-49 (1966).

879. *Terry v. Mercer County Freeholders Bd.*, 86 N.J. at 146-59 (adopting the "rightful place" remedial theory; also declaring that such relief is not inconsistent with the "rule of three" applicable to civil service appointments); *Flanders v. William Paterson College*, 163 N.J.Super. 225, 233-35 (App. Div. 1976) (one plaintiff entitled to retroactive promotion to full professorship; other plaintiff entitled to reinstatement with tenure); *Pilot v. New Jersey Dept. of Health*, 7 N.J.A.R. 150, 175, 180 (DCR 1982), *aff'd*, No. A-5853-81 (App. Div. Sept. 28, 1983) (complainant entitled to immediate promotion, with retroactive seniority; if necessary, a provisional appointee is to be displaced or a new position created); *Polcari v. Hackensack Bd. of Educ.*, 8 N.J.A.R. 537, 556-58 (DCR 1984) (complainant retroactively awarded salary grade of the position he was denied); *White v. PSE&G Co.*, 8 N.J.A.R. 335, 384-85 (DCR 1984), *aff'd*, No. A-1496-84 (App. Div. July 16, 1986) (same); *Dumont v. Jersey Shore Medical Center*, 1 N.J.A.R. 249, 259 (DCR 1980) (reinstatement). Innocent employees who have been favored by an employer's discriminatory actions normally will not be removed from their positions to redress the unlawful discrimination. *Polcari v. Hackensack Bd. of Educ.*, 8 N.J.A.R. at 556; *White v. PSE&G Co.*, 8 N.J.A.R. at 384; *Terry v. Mercer County Freeholders Bd.*, 86 N.J. at 155 n.3, 156-57.

880. 86 N.J. 141 (1981)

881. 279 N.J. Super. 104 (App. Div. 1995), *certif. granted and remanded*, 142 N.J. 513 (1995).

882. *Countiss v. Trenton State College*, 77 N.J. 590, 595-99 (1978).

the tenure requirements.[883] In a case decided two years earlier, the Appellate Division upheld the DCR's award of tenure to a faculty member.[884]

The courts have differed over whether the DCR may order a college to direct "all appropriate individuals and/or committees to consider for faculty promotions any and all qualified women *before giving consideration to any and all men who have substantially similar qualifications*."[885] One court approved this provision as long as it is not used "to prefer women above men or to subordinate the promotion of qualified men to women in a manner of reverse discrimination."[886]

Another court rejected the provision, believing that it compelled discrimination by requiring preferential treatment of females.[887]

A respondent may be ordered to:

1. Evaluate complainant's qualifications under the criteria in effect at the time of the discrimination instead of under more stringent qualifications adopted thereafter.[888]
2. Establish objective job qualifications that relate solely and directly to the ability of employees to safely and adequately perform their duties.[889]
3. Engage in affirmative recruitment, hiring, and promotion of qualified members of the protected group discriminated against.[890]
4. Give written notice of reasons for subsequent promotion denials to members of the protected group.[891]
5. Establish pay-equity policies.[892]

---

883. *Id.* at 597, 599.

884. *Flanders v. William Paterson College*, 163 N.J.Super. at 230-31.

885. *Id.* at 233, 234-35 (emphasis added); *Talman v. Burlington County College Bd. of Trustees*, 169 N.J.Super. 535, 542, 537 (App. Div.), *certif. denied*, 81 N.J. 407 (1979), *ovr'ld on other grounds*, *Goodman v. London Metals Exchange, Inc.*, 86 N.J. 19, 41 n.5 (1981).

886. *Flanders v. William Paterson College*, 163 N.J.Super. at 235.

887. *Talman v. Burlington County College Bd. of Trustees*, 169 N.J.Super. at 542. The court in *Talman* was obviously aware of the *Flanders* decision, having cited it for another point. *Talman*, 169 N.J.Super. at 538. The Appellate Division, in *Terry*, attempted to harmonize *Talman* and *Flanders*. *Terry v. Mercer County Freeholders Bd.*, 173 N.J.Super. 249, 254 (App. Div. 1980), *modified*, 86 N.J. 141, 147-54 (1981).

888. *Pineman v. Paramus*, 4 N.J.A.R. 407, 418 (DCR 1981), *aff'd*, No. A-5336-80 (App. Div. Apr. 1, 1982).

889. *Hebard v. Basking Ridge Fire Co.*, 164 N.J.Super. 77, 85-86 (App. Div. 1978), *app. dism'd*, 81 N.J. 294 (1979). New qualifications may not be ordered applied retroactively to the employer's entire current workforce.

890. *Flanders v. William Paterson College*, 163 N.J.Super. at 233-35. *Cf. Terry v. Mercer County Freeholders Bd.*, 86 N.J. 141, 153 (1981) (retroactive relief limited to the actual victims of discrimination as opposed to the members of the protected class as a whole).

891. *Flanders v. William Paterson College*, 163 N.J.Super. at 233-35.

6. Expunge references to an employee's termination and filing of a discrimination complaint from her work record and advise all prospective employers only of complainant's period of employment, the job she performed, and the fact she was a good employee.[893]
7. Give written notice of the DCR's remedial order, as well as written instructions prohibiting discrimination, to its agents and employees.[894]
8. Include in employment advertisements the term "equal opportunity" or any substantially similar term.[895]
9. Post on the premises, in a specifically prescribed fashion, notices of its complaint policies and include such notice in all advertising.[896]
10. Post a copy of the DCR's remedial order[897] and the DCR's official anti-discrimination poster.[898]
11. Report to the Director the manner of its compliance with the order.[899]
12. Maintain and allow inspection of records and report statistics to the DCR to ensure that appropriate corrective action has been taken.[900]

A respondent who unlawfully refused to enter a contract may be ordered to sign the contract.[901] Discriminatory provisions in a contract may be excised and

---

892. *Id.*

893. *Hardwick v. Newark Morning Ledger Co.*, 8 N.J.A.R. 249, 273, 280 (DCR 1983), *aff'd*, No. A-1084-83 (App. Div. Sept. 27, 1984), *certif. denied*, 99 N.J. 215 (1984); *Twomey v. Englewood Hospital Ass'n*, 5 N.J.A.R. 188, 198 (DCR 1981), *rev'd on other grounds*, No. A-3523-80 (App. Div. June 14, 1982), *certif. denied*, 91 N.J. 568 (1982) (suspension).

894. *Jackson v. Concord Co.*, 54 N.J. 113, 121, 125 (1969); *Sellers v. Philip's Barber Shop*, 46 N.J. 340, 344 (1966).

895. N.J.A.C. 13:11-1.2.

896. *New Jersey Div. on Civil Rights v. Slumber, Inc.*, 166 N.J.Super. 95, 103 (App. Div.), *app. dism'd in part without op.*, 81 N.J. 334 (1979), *conditionally modified in part on other grounds, aff'd in part on other grounds*, 82 N.J. 412 (1980); *Jackson v. Concord Co.*, 54 N.J. at 121, 125.

897. *Zahorian v. Russell Fitt Real Estate Agency*, 62 N.J. 399, 407, 409-10 (1973); *Jackson v. Concord Co.*, 54 N.J. at 121, 125; *Sellers v. Philip's Barber Shop*, 46 N.J. at 344.

898. *Jackson v. Concord Co.*, 54 N.J. at 121, 125; N.J.S.A. 10:5-12(j).

899. N.J.S.A. 10:5-17. *See, e.g., New Jersey Div. on Civil Rights v. Slumber, Inc.*, 166 N.J.Super. at 103; *Pilot v. New Jersey Dept. of Health*, 7 N.J.A.R. 150, 176, 180 (DCR 1982), *aff'd*, No. A-5853-81 (App. Div. Sept. 28, 1983).

900. DCR, *A Guide for Employers to the LAD*, pp. 27-28 (June 1986). *See, e.g., Zahorian v. Russell Fitt Real Estate Agency*, 62 N.J. at 406-07, 409-10 (respondent required for two years to report monthly a listing of apartment vacancies and the names, addresses, sex, ages, etc. of all prospective tenants); *Jackson v. Concord Co.*, 54 N.J. 121, 125 (respondent directed to maintain certain records for review by DCR).

the contract, as reformed, may be enforced.[902] A respondent may be directed to delete discriminatory provisions from its personnel manual.[903]

Back Pay

Back pay is designed to make complainants whole to the fullest extent possible by restoring them to the status they would have occupied but for the unlawful discrimination.[904] For example, if a female employee is paid less than her male counterpart and is required to perform additional duties, she is entitled to recover back pay for both the wage differential between their salaries and the extra duties she performed.[905]

In selecting the appropriate remedy, the Director may use reasonably certain bases, such as market prices or values, or contract or advertised terms and conditions, to determine particulars or performance.[906] For example, in a civil action alleging wage discrimination based on sex and marital status, the higher salary paid to a married male who replaced plaintiff is evidential of her damages.[907] Where employees are paid on a straight-commission basis, the back-pay award of an applicant unlawfully denied employment can be based on the averaged salary of the persons holding the position applied for.[908]

In appropriate circumstances, the salary of the highest paid person in the relevant job classification may be used instead of the salary of the person who re-

---

901. *Jones v. Haridor Realty Corp.*, 37 N.J. 384, 389 (1962); *David v. Vesta Co.*, 45 N.J. 301, 319-20 (1965).

902. *Kiwanis Int'l v. Ridgewood Kiwanis Club*, 627 F.Supp. 1381, 1394-95 (D.N.J.), *rev'd on other grounds*, 806 F.2d 468 (3d Cir. 1986), *reh'g en banc denied*, 811 F.2d 247 (3d Cir.), *cert. dism'd*, 483 U.S. 1050 (1987).

903. *Twomey v. Englewood Hospital Ass'n*, 5 N.J.A.R. 188, 197-98 (DCR 1981), *rev'd on other grounds*, No. A-3523-80 (App. Div. June 14, 1982), *certif. denied*, 91 N.J. 568 (1982).

904. *Clowes v. Terminix Int'l, Inc.*, 7 N.J.A.R. 206, 233 (DCR 1984), *rev'd on other grounds*, No. A-3886-84 (App. Div. May 8, 1986), *aff'd*, 109 N.J. 575 (1988); *Goodman v. London Metals Exchange, Inc.*, 86 N.J. 19, 34-35 (1981); *Weiss v Parker Hannifan Corp.*, 747 F.Supp. 1118, 1132 (D.N.J. 1990) (civil action). *See, e.g., Panettieri v. C.V. Hill Refrigeration*, 159 N.J.Super. 472, 478 (App. Div. 1978) (Director included mandatory overtime in back-pay award); *Rogers v. Campbell Foundry Co.*, 8 N.J.A.R. 75, 87 (DCR 1980), *aff'd*, 185 N.J.Super. 109 (App. Div.), *certif. denied*, 91 N.J. 529 (1982) (overtime).

905. *Terry v. Mercer County Freeholders Bd.*, 173 N.J.Super. 249, 252-53 (App. Div. 1980), *aff'd on other grounds*, 86 N.J. 141, 146 (1981).

906. N.J.S.A. 10:5-17. *See, e.g., Zahorian v. Russell Fitt Real Estate Agency*, 62 N.J. 399, 406, 410 (1973) (economic, out-of-pocket loss calculated under the "loss of the bargain" approach to damages); *Gimello v. Agency Rent-A-Car Systems, Inc.*, 250 N.J.Super. 338, 368-69 (App. Div. 1991) (upholding DCR's use of IRS's methodology for valuing employee benefits); *Pilot v. New Jersey Dept. of Health*, 7 N.J.A.R. 150, 176, 180 (DCR 1982) *aff'd*, No. A-5853-81 (App. Div. Sept. 28, 1983) (back pay calculated in accordance with the State Compensation Plan).

907. *Healey v. Dover Tp.*, 208 N.J.Super. 679, 683-84 (App. Div. 1986), *ovr'ld on other grounds, Fuchilla v. Layman*, 109 N.J. 319, *cert. denied*, 488 U.S. 826 (1988).

908. *See, e.g., Goodman v. London Metals Exchange, Inc.*, 86 N.J. at 28; *Rogers v. Campbell Foundry Co.*, 8 N.J.A.R. at 87.

placed the wrongfully discharged employee.[909] Back pay would include pay raises;[910] lost fringe benefits, such as employer-paid contributions to a retirement program;[911] and unreimbursed medical expenses due to the loss of health insurance coverage.[912]

Where the award of back pay would be too speculative or cannot be supported with reasonable certainty, back pay will be denied.[913] However, because back pay is an equitable remedy, "mathematical certainty and exactitude is not required, especially as long as the award is based on a reasonable method of calculation."[914]

In calculating a back-pay award, the DCR does not deduct unemployment compensation payments received by complainant because such payments must be repaid to the state.[915] However, earnings and benefits from new employment will be deducted.[916] Entitlement to additional back pay ceases once the employee has obtained a comparable position.[917] In cases involving welfare recipients, the DCR notifies the county welfare board of the award of back pay.[918]

---

909. *Gimello v. Agency Rent-A-Car Systems, Inc.*, 250 N.J.Super. 338, 367-68 (App. Div. 1991).

910. *Dumont v. Jersey Shore Medical Center*, 1 N.J.A.R. 249, 260 (DCR 1980) (employee who regularly received annual 5 percent merit increases entitled to such increases in calculating back pay during period following his wrongful discharge and his salary upon reinstatement); *White v. PSE&G Co.*, 8 N.J.A.R. 335, 385 (DCR 1984), *aff'd*, No. A-1496-84 (App. Div. July 16, 1986).

911. *Flanders v. William Paterson College*, 163 N.J.Super. 225, 230 (App. Div. 1976).

912. *Weiss v. Parker Hannifan Corp.*, 747 F.Supp. 1118, 1126, 1132-33 (D.N.J. 1990). It has not been resolved under the LAD whether a wrongfully-discharged employee is required to mitigate damages by exercising either the right to continue health benefits pursuant to the Consolidated Omnibus Budget Reconciliation Act of 1985 (COBRA), 29 U.S.C.A. §1161 *et seq.*, or the right to convert to an individual insurance policy.

913. *Andersen v. Exxon Co.*, 7 N.J.A.R. 289, 299, 301, 306-07 (DCR 1980), *aff'd*, No. A-2940-79 (App. Div. Feb. 25, 1981), *aff'd as modified on other grounds*, 89 N.J. 483 (1982) (back pay denied in part to seasonal employee whose chance of being selected for full-time employment was less than 50 percent).

914. *Weiss v. Parker Hannifan Corp.*, 747 F.Supp. at 1132. *See Shaner v. Horizon Bancorp.*, 116 N.J. 433, 443-45 & n.1 (1989).

915. *Vasto v. Vornado, Inc.*, 8 N.J.A.R. 481, 503 (DCR 1983), *citing Newark v. Copeland*, 171 N.J.Super. 571, 575 (App. Div. 1980); *Hardwick v. Newark Morning Ledger Co.*, 8 N.J.A.R. 249, 272 (DCR 1983), *aff'd*, No. A-1084-83 (App. Div. Sept. 27, 1984), *certif. denied*, 99 N.J. 215 (1984) (same); *Dumont v. Jersey Shore Medical Center*, 1 N.J.A.R. at 259 (invoking collateral source rule). *See* N.J.S.A. 2A:15-97 (1987 legislation limiting scope of collateral source rule in personal injury civil actions).

916. *Goodman v. London Metals Exchange, Inc.*, 86 N.J. 19, 34, 42 (1981); *Gimello v. Agency Rent-A-Car Systems, Inc.*, 250 N.J.Super. 338, 366-69 (App. Div. 1991) (value of company car deducted); *Weiss v. Parker Hannifan Corp.*, 747 F.Supp. at 1132-33. In appropriate cases, earnings from part-time employment will also be deducted. *Andersen v. Exxon Co.*, 7 N.J.A.R. at 306-07; *Weiss v. Parker Hannifan Corp.*, 747 F.Supp. at 1126, 1132-33; *Hayman v. Funk*, 8 N.J.A.R. 27, 42-43 (DCR 1984).

917. *Weiss v. Parker Hannifan Corp.*, 747 F.Supp. at 1132; *Rogers v. Campbell Foundry Co.*, 8 N.J.A.R. 75, 76, 87 (DCR 1980), *aff'd*, 185 N.J.Super. 109 (App. Div.), *certif. denied*, 91 N.J. 529 (1982) (back-pay period terminated upon new employment and not revived by a subsequent 10-month period of unemployment).

918. *Hardwick v. Newark Morning Ledger Co.*, 8 N.J.A.R. at 272-73.

Mitigation

A victim of discrimination has a duty to mitigate damages.[919] Mitigation is an affirmative defense and, as such, defendant bears the burden of persuasion on this issue.[920] Defendant must establish that comparable employment opportunities were available.[921] In measuring comparability, the following factors, among others, are considered: the particular requirements, responsibilities, and skills of the job plaintiff was denied, job location, and rate of compensation.[922] With the passage of a reasonable period of time, the circumstances peculiar to the claimant may dictate that she lower expectations and accept employment with less pay, involving different work, or at a more distant location.[923] If qualifying opportunities existed, "unreasonable refusals to accept proffered employment or failure to exercise reasonable diligence in seeking other suitable positions trigger mitigation principles."[924]

---

919. *Goodman v. London Metals Exchange, Inc.*, 86 N.J. at 34-42; *Clowes v. Terminix Int'l, Inc.*, 7 N.J.A.R. 206, 234 (DCR 1984), *rev'd on other grounds*, No. A-3886-84 (App. Div. May 8, 1986), *aff'd*, 109 N.J. 575 (1988). *Abrams v. Lightolier*, 841 F. Supp. 584, 595-96 (D.N.J. 1994), *aff'd*, 50 F.3d 1204 (3d Cir. 1995) (failure to mitigate under LAD causes a reduction in back pay; it is not a waiver of back pay).

920. *Goodman v. London Metals Exchange, Inc.*, 86 N.J. at 40-41. To the extent that *Talman v. Burlington County College Bd. of Trustees*, 169 N.J.Super. 535, 538-39 (App. Div.), *certif. denied*, 81 N.J. 407 (1979), and *Dumont v. Jersey Shore Medical Center*, 1 N.J.A.R. 249, 250, 258-59 (DCR 1980), placed the burden of persuasion on both the employer and the employee, they have been overruled by *Goodman*. *Goodman v. London Metals Exchange, Inc.*, 86 N.J. at 41 n.5; *Hardwick v. Newark Morning Ledger Co.*, 8 N.J.A.R. at 271.

921. *Goodman v. London Metals Exchange, Inc.*, 86 N.J. at 41; *Meacham v. Bell Telephone Laboratories, Inc.*, 1990 WL 299805, p. *13 (D.N.J. 1990).

922. *Goodman v. London Metals Exchange, Inc.*, 86 N.J. at 36-37 (detailed discussion). Where the victim of discrimination was a job applicant, the nature, location, and compensation of the applicant's prior employment may also be considered. *Id.* at 42.

923. *Goodman v. London Metals Exchange, Inc.*, 86 N.J. at 38-40. *See, e.g., Gimello v. Agency Rent-A-Car Systems, Inc.*, 250 N.J.Super. 338, 351-52, 366-67 (App. Div. 1991) (employee who reasonably accepted lower-paying job in order to mitigate damages is still entitled to differential back pay during the period of re-employment until his new earnings become equivalent to what he would have earned in the former job).

924. *Goodman v. London Metals Exchange, Inc.*, 86 N.J. at 35; *Meacham v. Bell Telephone Laboratories, Inc.*, 1990 WL299805 at p. *13. *Cf. Reynolds v. Atlantic City Convention Center Authority*, 1990 WL 267417, 53 FEP 1852, 1872 (D.N.J. 1990), *aff'd without published op.*, 925 F.2d 419 (3d Cir. 1991) (union-hall worker who claimed sex discrimination by employer and failed to go back to the union hall for equivalent opportunities failed to prove that her damages were proximately caused by the alleged wrongful act). Mitigation requires that the claimant do more than make three or four informal inquiries about job opportunities. *Talman v. Burlington County College Bd. of Trustees*, 169 N.J.Super. at 541. *Cf. Hardwick v. Newark Morning Ledger Co.*, 8 N.J.A.R. at 254, 264, 271 (mitigation found where complainant went to more than five different employers and respondent did not present any evidence that jobs were available for which complainant did not apply). Once the claimant stops seeking full-time employment, entitlement to further lost wages and benefits ceases. *Gilchrist v. Haddonfield Bd. of Educ.*, 155 N.J.Super. 358, 364 (App. Div. 1978); *Hardwick*, 8 N.J.A.R. at 254, 261, 264-65. The fact that a co-employee, who had better qualifications and left the employer on friendly terms, immediately found a new job is not necessarily indicative of a lack of diligence on complainant's part. *Vasto v. Vornado, Inc.*, 8 N.J.A.R. 481, 498 (DCR 1983). This is because a wrongfully-terminated employee is less likely to receive a favorable recommendation from the former employer and may have to tell prospective employers the reasons for leaving the last job. *Id.* at 498; *Hardwick v. Newark Morning Ledger Co.*, 8 N.J.A.R. at 264; *Gimello v. Agency Rent-A-Car Systems, Inc.*, 250 N.J.Super. at 351.

An employee denied a promotion normally is required to continue in his present position until suitable alternative employment is located.[925] In such case, the employee is entitled to recover only the difference between her current salary and the salary she would have earned had she been promoted.[926]

Compensatory Damages

Minor or incidental awards of compensatory damages may be made for medical expenses and pain, suffering, and humiliation.[927] Interest may be awarded in order to make the complainant whole.[928] *Per quod* claims are not permitted under the LAD.[929]

The DCR may not award punitive damages or more than incidental compensatory damages.[930] In *Shaner v. Horizon Bancorp.*, the Court noted that the broad remedial powers of the DCR, set forth in N.J.S.A. 10:5-17, include the power to award legal relief such as compensatory damages for out-of-pocket expenses and incidental damages for pain, suffering, and humiliation.[931] The Court then noted

---

925. *Harvard v. Bushberg Bros.*, 137 N.J.Super. 537, 542 (App. Div. 1975), *certif. gr.*, 71 N.J. 493 (1976), *app. dism'd by stipulation, as stated in Castellano v. Linden Bd. of Educ.*, 79 N.J. 407, 417 (1979).

926. *Id.* at 542.

927. *Zahorian v. Russell Fitt Real Estate Agency*, 62 N.J. 399, 410-16 (1973) (Director authorized to make "minor" or "incidental" awards of compensatory damages, as opposed to "substantial" awards; $750 award for pain and suffering upheld). *See, e.g., Frank v. Ivy Club*, 120 N.J. 73, 96, 111 (1990), *cert. denied*, 498 U.S. 1073 (1991) ($5,000 award for humiliation); *Andersen v. Exxon Co.*, 89 N.J. 483, 502-03 (1982) ("a moderate token award" of $500); *Gimello v. Agency Rent-A-Car Systems, Inc.*, 250 N.J.Super. 338, 366 (App. Div. 1991) ($10,000 for pain, suffering, and humiliation, and $2,876 for "incidental compensatory damages"); *Rogers v. Campbell Foundry Co.*, 185 N.J.Super. 109, 113 (App. Div. 1982), *aff'g*, 8 N.J.A.R. 75 (DCR 1980), *certif. denied*, 91 N.J. 529 (1982) ($750 for pain and suffering); *Roberts v. Keansburg Bd. of Educ.*, 5 N.J.A.R. 208, 253, 266 (DCR 1983) ($4,000 awarded to 3 complainants for pain, suffering, and humiliation); *Vasto v. Vornado, Inc.*, 8 N.J.A.R. at 499-500, 507-08 (award of $750 for humiliation, pain, and suffering and $12 for cost of prescription); *Wolbert v. Stylianos, Inc.*, 9 N.J.A.R. 392, 399 (DCR 1985) (award of $7,500 for pain, humiliation, and suffering and $22 for cost of doctor visit).

In contrast to the limited nature of compensatory relief available in DCR proceedings, full compensatory damages are available in civil actions under the LAD. *See, e.g., Jackson v. Consolidated Rail Corp.*, 223 N.J.Super. 467, 476-81 (App. Div. 1988). Nonetheless, the quantum of compensatory damages awarded must not be "so disproportionate to the injuries described by the plaintiff as to constitute a manifest injustice and shock the conscience." *Id.* at 478 (internal quotation marks omitted) ($600,000 award vacated in view of limited injuries sustained).

In a civil action under the LAD, a court held that (1) nominal damages for emotional distress are presumed ($500 in that case) unless actual damages are proved; (2) such distress must be "the natural, proximate, reasonable and foreseeable result" of the discrimination; and (3) aggravating circumstances, such as public and rude humiliation, may warrant a larger damage award. *Gray v. Serruto Builders, Inc.*, 110 N.J.Super. 297, 312-19 (Ch.Div. 1970). In a subsequent case, *Castellano v. Linden Bd. of Educ.*, 79 N.J. 407, 410-12 (1979), the Court vacated the Director's award of $600 in humiliation damages, holding that there was not a "substantial basis" for the award in view of the "nebulous" evidence presented. One court has suggested that *Castellano* stands "for the proposition that in cases against public bodies the evidence of emotional distress must be substantial to sustain a monetary award, not that nominal awards against discriminatory private employers and others are improper." *Andersen v. Exxon Co.*, No. A-2940-79, slip op. at p. 12 (Feb. 25, 1981), *aff'd as modified on other grounds*, 89 N.J. 483 (1982). On appeal, the Supreme Court, in *Andersen*, explained that "*Castellano* is distinguishable ... because the discriminatory actions in *Castellano* were taken in compliance with contractual provisions ... negotiated in good faith." 89 N.J. at 503.

that a judicial action permits "more extensive individual relief in terms of monetary damages than might otherwise obtain in an administrative proceeding"—*e.g.*, compensatory damages and punitive damages.[932]

Eight months after *Shaner* was decided, the Legislature amended the LAD to overturn the holding in *Shaner* that jury trials were not available in LAD civil actions.[933] The new legislation also made clear that compensatory and punitive damages are available under the LAD by amending (1) N.J.S.A. 10:5-3 (legislative findings) to provide that common-law remedies, including compensatory and punitive damages, are to be available to all persons protected by the LAD and (2) the paragraph of N.J.S.A. 10:5-13 pertaining to suits in the Superior Court to provide that all common-law remedies, which are *in addition to* those remedies provided by the LAD, are available to a successful plaintiff.[934] The Legislature did *not* amend N.J.S.A. 10:5-17, the provision laying out the DCR's remedial powers. This pattern of amendments suggests that the Legislature intended to retain the dichotomy of remedies set forth in *Shaner*, thereby precluding the DCR from awarding punitive damag-

---

928. *Decker v. Elizabeth Bd. of Ed.*, 153 N.J.Super. 470, 472, 475 (App. Div. 1977), *certif. denied*, 75 N.J. 612 (1978); *Rogers v. Campbell Foundry Co.*, 8 N.J.A.R. 75, 87 (DCR 1980) *aff'd*, 185 N.J.Super. 109 (App. Div.), *certif. denied*, 91 N.J. 529 (1982); *Milazzo v. Exxon Corp.*, 243 N.J.Super. 573 (Law Div. 1990) (civil action); *Weiss v. Parker Hannifan Corp.*, 747 F.Supp. 1118, 1133-34 (D.N.J. 1990) (civil action). Interest is calculated in accordance with R.4:42-11. *Hardwick v. Newark Morning Ledger Co.*, 8 N.J.A.R. 249, 264-65, 281 (DCR 1983), *aff'd*, No. A-1084-83 (App. Div. Sept. 27, 1984), *certif. denied*, 99 N.J. 215 (1984) (pre- and post-judgment interest); *Vasto v. Vornado, Inc.*, 8 N.J.A.R. 481, 499 (DCR 1983); *Clowes v. Terminix Int'l, Inc.*, 7 N.J.A.R. 206, 233-34 (DCR 1984), *rev'd on other grounds*, No. A-3886-84 (App. Div. May 8, 1986), *aff'd*, 109 N.J. 575 (1988); *Milazzo v. Exxon Corp.*, 243 N.J.Super. at 576-77; *Weiss v. Parker Hannifan Corp.*, 747 F.Supp. at 1134 n.3.

929. *Catalane v. Gilian Instrument Corp.*, 271 N.J. Super. 476, 500 (App. Div.), *cert. denied*, 136 N.J. 298 (1994).

930. The standards applicable to the award of punitive damages are discussed in §4-54:5. In *Maczik v. Gilford Park Yacht Club*, 271 N.J. Super. 439, 446-49 (App. Div. 1994), a public accommodation case, the Appellate Division reiterated that the DCR's power to award compensatory damages is limited to incidental awards, upheld an award of $10,000, but described "that amount as approaching, if not at, the limit of an 'incidental' award." *Id.* at 448, n.3. The court further held that the DCR lacks power to make any awards of punitive damages. *Id.* at 449-54.

931. *Shaner v. Horizon Bancorp.*, 116 N.J. 433, 439-40 (1989). *Accord Zahorian v. Russell Fitt Real Estate Agency*, 62 N.J. 399, 410-16 (1973).

932. *Shaner v. Horizon Bancorp.*, 116 N.J. at 441, *citing Erickson v. Marsh & McLennan Co.*, 227 N.J.Super. 78, 84-85 (App. Div. 1988). *See, e.g.*, *Jackson v. Consolidated Rail Corp.*, 223 N.J.Super. 467, 476-81 (App. Div. 1988). At the time *Shaner* was decided, *Erickson* was pending on appeal in the Supreme Court. The Court thereafter, on other grounds, affirmed in part and reversed in part the Appellate Division's decision. *Erickson v. Marsh & McLennan Co.*, 117 N.J. 539 (1990).

933. L.1990, c.12, §2.

934. L.1990, c.12, §§1-2. It appears that the Legislature added the language regarding punitive damages in part because the Supreme Court had never directly ruled on the issue, which had been recently contested in several civil actions. *See, e.g.*, *Jackson v. Consolidated Rail Corp.*, 223 N.J.Super. at 482 (punitives available); *Levinson v. Prentice-Hall, Inc.*, 868 F.2d 558, 560, 562-63 (3d Cir. 1989) (same); *O'Shea v. RCA Global Communications*, 1984 WL 49044, 117 LRRM 2880, 2884-85 (D.N.J. July 24, 1984) (punitives not available).

es or more than incidental compensatory damages.[935] The failure of the Legislature to expressly state that the DCR may award punitive damages may be in recognition of the possible unconstitutionality of such a legislative grant of power to an administrative tribunal.[936]

Relief on Behalf of Absent Parties

In any case where the Director, the Attorney General, or an appropriate organization is the complainant before the DCR on behalf of unnamed individuals or a class of individuals, any of the remedies or relief allowed by the LAD may be awarded to the unnamed individual victims of the unlawful discrimination.[937] However, procedural due process requires that the DCR give respondents timely notice of the Director's intention to seek relief on behalf of unnamed individuals and their names.[938] The unnamed individuals for whom the Director may seek relief must be persons who suffered discrimination within 180 days prior to the filing of the verified complaint.[939] Respondents must be given a fair opportunity to meet the evidence pertaining to the "unnamed" persons by cross-examination and presentation of rebuttal proofs.[940] Any person who violates the LAD is liable for a penalty of not more than $2,000 for the first offense and not more than $5,000 for each subsequent offense.[941] The amount of the penalty to be imposed is determined by the Director based upon the circumstances and is to be included in the Director's order.[942] Penalties collected by the Director are payable into the State Treasury for the general purposes of the State.[943]

Miscellaneous

---

935. *See Maczik v. Gilford Park Yacht Club*, 271 N.J. Super. 439, 449-54 (App. Div. 1994) (public accommodation case holding that DCR lacks power to award punitive damages). As noted elsewhere in this section, the DCR has explicit power to award treble damages in specified situations (N.J.S.A. 10:5-17) and penalties (N.J.S.A. 10:5-14.1a).

936. *See Wright v. Plaza Ford*, 164 N.J.Super. 203, 210-18 (App. Div. 1978) (workers' compensation statute, in contrast to LAD, by empowering administrative officers to adjudicate and punish for contempt, violated constitutional doctrine of separation of powers); *David v. Vesta Co.*, 45 N.J. 301, 323, 328 (1965) (penal sanctions for willful violations of DCR orders can be imposed only by judicial process).

937. N.J.S.A. 10:5-17. *See Shaner v. Horizon Bancorp.*, 116 N.J. 433, 445, 453 (1989). *See, e.g., New Jersey Div. on Civil Rights v. Slumber, Inc.*, 82 N.J. 412, 416-17 (1980).

938. *New Jersey Div. on Civil Rights v. Slumber, Inc.*, 82 N.J. at 416-17.

939. *Id.* at 414 & n.1; N.J.S.A. 10:5-18.

940. *New Jersey Div. on Civil Rights v. Slumber, Inc.*, 82 N.J. at 417.

941. N.J.S.A. 10:5-14.1a. *See, e.g., Jamison v. Rockaway Tp. Bd. of Educ.*, 242 N.J.Super. 436, 444 n.1 (Director awarded $5,000 penalty to victim of racial retaliation; award vacated on other grounds). *See* N.J.S.A. 10:5-19; N.J.S.A. 2A:58-1 *et seq.* (Penalty Enforcement Law).

942. N.J.S.A. 10:5-14.1a. *See Poff v. Caro*, 228 N.J.Super. 370, 380 (Law Div. 1987) (suggesting that where respondent's wrongful conduct was not motivated by ill will but rather by understandable, though unfounded, fear of AIDS, and respondent was willing to eliminate the discrimination prior to the DCR hearing, penalties would not be warranted).

943. N.J.S.A. 10:5-14.1a.

There is one significant exception to the broad remedies permitted under the LAD. An employee who has been mandatorily retired in contravention of the LAD may seek relief only in an administrative proceeding before the DCR and the employee's remedy is limited to reinstatement with back pay and interest.[944]

Once liability is established, the Director may request the parties to attempt to reach a voluntary resolution of the damages issues.[945] In the exercise of discretion, the Director may order that only the corporate respondent, and not the individual respondent who effectuated the corporate policy, pay the damages awarded.[946] The respondent and its employees may be ordered not to engage in any retaliatory conduct against the complainant or any other participant in the DCR proceedings.[947]

4-54:2 In Superior Court Proceedings

In actions tried in the Superior Court, all remedies available in common-law tort actions, including compensatory and punitive damages, are available to a prevailing plaintiff.[948]

These are in addition to the remedies otherwise provided by the LAD or another statute.[949] The court may grant remedies similar to those the Director is authorized to award pursuant to N.J.S.A. 10:5-17.[950]

4-54:3 Front Pay

Front pay may be awarded by the Court in lieu of reinstatement when disharmony and acrimony would result from plaintiff's return to the workplace.[951] Front pay is limited to the reasonable period required for plaintiff to reestablish his rightful place in the job market.[952]

---

944. N.J.S.A. 10:5-12.1. *Cf.* N.J.S.A. 10:3-1 (a public employee involuntarily retired in contravention of N.J.S.A. 10:3-1 is entitled to reinstatement with back pay and interest).

945. *Clowes v. Terminix Int'l, Inc.*, 7 N.J.A.R. at 234; *Andersen v. Exxon Co.*, 7 N.J.A.R. 289, 308 (DCR 1980), *aff'd*, No. A-2940-79 (App. Div. Feb. 25, 1981), *aff'd as modified on other grounds*, 89 N.J. 483, 503 (1982).

946. *Andersen v. Exxon Co.*, 89 N.J. at 502 n.8. *Cf. Peper v. Princeton Univ. Bd. of Trustees*, 151 N.J.Super. 15, 26 (App. Div. 1977), *rev'd on other grounds*, 77 N.J. 55 (1978) (only university, not the individual defendant-officers who had varying, if any, involvement with plaintiff, liable to plaintiff).

947. *See, e.g.*, *Jackson v. Concord Co.*, 54 N.J. 113, 120-21, 125 (1969); *Roberts v. Keansburg Bd. of Educ.*, 5 N.J.A.R. 208, 269 (DCR 1983); *Jamison v. Rockaway Tp. Bd. of Educ.*, 242 N.J.Super. 436, 440 (App. Div. 1990).

948. N.J.S.A. 10:5-13; N.J.S.A. 10:5-3.

949. N.J.S.A. 10:5-13.

950. *Shaner v. Horizon Bancorp.*, 116 N.J. 433, 440-41 (1989); N.J.S.A. 10:5-13.

951. *Levinson v. Prentice Hall, Inc.*, 868 F.2d at 563; *Weiss v. Parker Hannifan Corp.*, 747 F. Supp. at 1135.

4-54:4 Emotional Distress Damages

Damages for pain and suffering may be recovered under the LAD.[953] Expert testimony is not required.[954] The Third Circuit has held that objective corroboration is not required either.[955] Nonetheless, plaintiff must demonstrate that there is "a substantial basis for compensation."[956]

The amounts of jury awards for pain and suffering have varied widely and frequently have been reduced by the Court.[957]

4-54:5 Punitive Damages

Prerequisites

Not every violation of the LAD warrants an award of punitive damages.[958] Punitive damages are to be awarded only in "exceptional" cases where the defendant's conduct is "especially egregious."[959] This is consistent with the general rule that "something more than the commission of a tort is always required for punitive damages."[960] As with other intentional torts,[961] proof of intentional dis-

---

952. *Weiss v. Parker Hannifan Corp.*, 747 F. Supp. at 1135.

953. N.J.S.A. 10:5-3.

954. *Rendine v. Pantzer*, 141 N.J. 292, 312 (1995). *See Delli Santi v. CNA Ins. Cos.*, 88 F.3d 192, 205 (3d Cir. 1996); *McKenna v. Pacific Rail Service*, 32 F.3d 820, 834 (3d Cir. 1994).

955. *Delli Santi v. CNA Ins. Cos.*, 88 F.3d 192, 205 (3d Cir. 1996).

956. *See McKenna v. Pacific Rail Service*, 32 F.3d 820, 834 (3d Cir. 1994) (if plaintiff establishes "objectively identifiable, medically verified" symptoms from which a jury could infer causation expert testimony is not requisite to an award of emotional distress damages). *Hyman v. Atlantic City Medical Center*, 1998 WL 135249, p.*14 (D.N.J. 1998) (allegations that plaintiff felt hurt and upset at not having been given a going away party, "a card, a goodbye, nothing, cold, you know, to do that to a good employee" insufficient as a matter of law).

957. *See and compare*: *Rendine v. Pantzer*, 141 N.J. 292 (1995) (awards of approximately $105,000 and $125, 000 upheld); *Delli Santi v. CNA Ins. Cos.*, 88 F.3d 192 (affirming district court's conditional grant of a new trial on damages unless plaintiff accepted a remittitur of emotional distress damages from $300,000 to $5,000; collecting cases); *Abrams v. Lightolier, Inc.*, 841 F. Supp. 584, 592-94 (D.N.J. 1994), *aff'd*, 50 F.3d 1204 (3d Cir. 1995) (reducing award of emotional distress damages from $100,000 to $2,500 due to paucity of proof; discussing standards); *Spragg v. Shore Care*, 293 N.J. Super. 33, 63 (App. Div. 1996) (vacating award of $42,500 emotional distress damages as excessive); *Murray v. Newark Housing Authority*, 311 N.J. Super. 163, 180 (Law Div. 1998) (awarding $4,000 to plaintiff who said that for two years he felt depressed and ashamed and could picture himself only looking for a job, that at times he felt ill, suffered headaches, stomach pains and vomiting, and that his relations with his wife had deteriorated).

958. *Catalane v. Gilian Instrument Corp.*, 271 N.J. Super. 476, 500-01 (App. Div. 1994), *cert. denied*, 136 N.J. 298 (1994).

959. *Rendine v. Pantzer*, 141 N.J. 292, 313-14 (1995); *Catalane v. Gilian Instrument Corp.*, 271 N.J. Super. 476, 500-01 (App. Div.), *certif. denied*, 136 N.J. 298 (1994) (holding that "punitive damages are only to be awarded in exceptional cases even where the LAD has been violated"); *Maczik v. Gilford Park Yacht Club*, 271 N.J. Super. 439, 446 (App. Div. 1994) ("Punitive damages, on the other hand, are distinct from compensatory damages, require a greater threshold basis, and are assessed only when the wrongdoer's conduct is especially egregious.") (public accommodation case); *Delli Santi v. CNA Ins. Cos.*, 88 F.3d 192 (3d Cir. 1996) (affirming district court's refusal to submit punitive damages to the jury; collecting cases).

crimination alone is not enough.[962] In order to justify an award of punitive damages, there must be "actual malice."[963] "There must be an intentional wrongdoing in the sense of an 'evil-minded act' or an act accompanied by a wanton and willful disregard for the rights of another .... The key to the right to punitive damages is the wrongfulness of the intentional act."[964] The burden has also been described as requiring "wantonly reckless or malicious conduct reflecting intentional wrongdoing in the sense of an evil-minded act or a disregard of the rights of another." Punitive damages have been upheld in the following circumstances:

- employees were targeted for layoff during a reduction in force, then trumped-up reasons for their selection were created, then they were replaced.[965]

Proofs of punitive damages have been found insufficient in the following circumstances:

---

960. *DiGiovanni v. Pessel*, 55 N.J. 188, 190 (1970); *Catalane v. Gilian Instrument Corp.*, 271 N.J. Super. 476, 500 (App. Div.), *certif. denied*, 136 N.J. 298 (1994); *Jackson v. Consolidated Rail Corp.*, 223 N.J. Super. 467, 483 (App. Div. 1988); *Levinson v. Prentice-Hall, Inc.*, 868 F.2d 558 (3d Cir. 1989).

961. *See Weir v. McEwan*, 94 N.J.L. 92, 94 (N.J. Sup. Ct. 1920); *Neigel v. Seaboard Finance Co.*, 68 N.J. Super. 542, 554 (App. Div. 1961); *Intermilo, Inc. v. L.P. Enters, Inc.*, 19 F.3d 890, 893-94 (3d Cir. 1994) (conduct "more outrageous than that comprising the [intentional] tort at issue must be proven" to support a claim for punitive damages, despite finding of liability for tortious interference with prospective economic advantage and the intentional nature of that tort).

962. *Catalane v. Gilian Instrument Corp.*, 271 N.J. Super. 476, 500 (App. Div.), *certif. denied*, 136 N.J. 298 (1994); *Jackson v. Consolidated Rail Corp.*, 223 N.J. Super. 467, 483 (App. Div. 1988); *Murray v. Newark Housing Authority*, 311 N.J. Super. 163, 181 (Law Div. 1998) (there must be additional evidence of outrageous conduct to distinguish the punitive damages case from the ordinary, though still reprehensible, case of age discrimination). *See Levinson v. Prentice-Hall, Inc.*, 868 F.2d 558 (3d Cir. 1989) (circumstances present which support punitive damages do not suggest that in every LAD employment discrimination case in which there is a basis for compensatory damages it follows that punitive damages are also available). *Weiss v. Parker Hannifan Corp.*, 747 F. Supp. 1118, 1135-36 (D.N.J. 1990) (punitive damages should only be awarded in exceptional LAD cases, and proof must go beyond the intent requirement for proving a disparate treatment claim). Federal civil rights law is similar: punitive damages are available for violation of 42 U.S.C. §1981, that prohibits racial discrimination in employment, even where compensatory damages are due, only "under certain circumstances." *Johnson v. Railway Express Agency*, 421 U.S. 454, 460 (1975). Federal civil rights law generally requires egregious conduct or a showing of willfulness or malice on the part of the defendant before punitive damages are appropriate. *Beauford v. Sister of Mercy-Province of Detroit*, Inc., 816 F.2d 1104, 1109 (6th Cir.), *cert. denied*, 484 U.S. 913 (1987). Even where evidence is sufficient to support a finding of intentional discrimination, it is improper to submit the question of punitive damages to the jury unless the record additionally supports a finding of evil intent or callous, reckless, or egregious disregard of plaintiffs' rights. *Beauford*, 816 F.2d at 1109. *See also Stephens v. South Atlantic Canners, Inc.*, 848 F.2d 484, 489-90 (4th Cir.), *cert. denied*, 488 U.S. 996 (1988) ("Although any form of discrimination constitutes reprehensible and abhorrent conduct, not every lawsuit under section 1981 calls for submission of this extraordinary remedy to a jury.")

963. *Rendine v. Pantzer*, 141 N.J. 292, 314 (1995); *Herman v. Sunshine Chemical Specialties, Inc.*, 133 N.J. 329, 337 (1993).

964. *Nappe v. Anschelewitz, Barr, Ansell & Bonello*, 97 N.J. 37, 49-50 (1984), quoted with approval in *Rendine v. Pantzer*, 141 N.J. 292, 314 (1995).

• employer assigned only men to provide home care to male patients; at worst the employer picked the wrong way to correct a perceived problem with patients' rights.[966]

• in a sexual harassment case where only one supervisor was alleged to have harassed, and where employer's handling of internal complaint may have been negligent but not "especially egregious."[967]

The Punitive Damages Act

Although claims under the LAD are exempt from the cap on punitive damages established by the Punitive Damages Act, the rest of that law applies. [968] It mandates an exacting review of the proofs before punitive damages may be submitted to the jury. [969] It also requires proof by clear and convincing evidence that "the harm suffered was the result of the defendant's acts or omissions and such acts or omissions were actuated by actual malice or accompanied by a wanton and willful disregard of persons who foreseeably might be harmed."[970]

The statute also obligates the trial judge to examine any award before its entry to ascertain whether it is reasonable in amount and justified by the circumstances of the case.[971] If not, the judge may reduce or eliminate the award.[972]

Employer Liability

---

965. *Baker v. The National State Bank*, 312 N.J. 268 (App. Div.), *certif. granted*, 156 N.J. 425 (1998);. Punitive damages were awarded in the following cases: *Milazzo v. Exxon Corp.*, 243 N.J.Super. 573, 574 (Law Div. 1990) ($100,000); *Levinson v. Prentice-Hall, Inc.*, 868 F.2d 558 (3d Cir. 1989) ($2,300,000 award vacated and remanded for redetermination); *Jackson v. Consolidated Rail Corp.*, 223 N.J.Super. 467 (App. Div. 1988) ($1,000,000 awarded, case remanded)

966. *Spragg v. Shore Care*, 293 N.J. Super. 33, 59-61 (App. Div. 1996).

967. *Woods-Pirozzi v. Nabisco Foods*, 290 N.J. Super. 252, 273 (App. Div. 1996) *See Gray v. Serruto Builders, Inc.*, 110 N.J. Super. 297, 319 (Ch. Div. 1970), and *Weiss v. Parker Hannifan Corp.*, 747 F. Supp. 1118, 1135-36 (D.N.J. 1990), where punitive damages were denied for lack of "exceptional" circumstances.

968. N.J.S.A. 2A:15-5.9 to 5.17.

969. *Cf. Silverman v. King*, 247 N.J. Super. 534, 537 (App. Div. 1991) (trial court has duty, even in intentional tort cases, to examine the evidence to determine whether it presents a factual basis for a reasonable jury to conclude that a basis for punitive damages is present); *Delli Santi v. CNA Ins. Cos.*, 88 F.3d 192 (3d Cir. 1996) (affirming district court's refusal to submit punitive damages to the jury; collecting cases); *Woods-Pirozzi v. Nabisco Foods*, 290 N.J. Super. 252, 273 (App. Div. 1996) (dismissing punitive damages claim in sexual harassment case where plaintiff did not allege that anyone other than her immediate supervisor engaged in harassing conduct, and where employer's handling of internal complaint may have been negligent, but was not "especially egregious" or "willfully indifferent").

970. N.J.S.A. 2A:15-5.12(a).

971. N.J.S.A. 2A:15-5.14(a).

972. *Id.*

An employer may not be liable for punitive damages absent (1) actual participation by upper management; or (2) willful indifference.[973] It remains unsettled precisely how "upper management" will be defined. [974]

Public Entity Liability

Public employers have been held liable for punitive damages under the LAD.[975]

4-54:6 Counsel Fees

In any employment action or proceeding under the LAD, the prevailing party may be awarded a reasonable counsel fee.[976] Fees may be assessed against a public body that will have to pay them from tax dollars.[977] However, fees may not be assessed against a losing plaintiff unless it is determined that the case was

---

973. *Lehman v. Toys 'R' Us, Inc.*, 132 N.J. 587, 625 (1993); *Rendine v. Pantzer*, 141 N.J. 292, 313-14 (1995) (applying Lehmann). *See Maczik v. Gilford Park Yacht Club*, 271 N.J. Super. 439, 446 (App;. Div. 1994); *Coleman v. Kaye*, 89 F.3d 1491 (3d Cir. 1996), *cert. denied*, ___ U.S.___, 117 S. Ct. 754, 136 L.Ed.2d 691 (1997) (punitive damages awarded when conduct is especially egregious; therefore employer liable only in the event of participation by upper management or willful indifference); *Kapossy v. McGraw Hill, Inc.*, 921 F. Supp. 234, 244-45 (D.N.J. 1996) ("punitive damages are available under the NJLAD upon a showing of the employer's participation in or willful indifference to the wrongful conduct on the part of upper management, and that the offending conduct was 'especially egregious.'... An NJLAD claim will only rarely support an award of punitive damages.").

974. In *Baker v. The National State Bank*, 312 N.J. Super. 268 (App. Div.), *certif. granted*, 156 N.J. 425 (1998), the Appellate Division found that a Senior V.P. of Branch Operations was clearly upper management where he had responsibility for an entire system of 50 branches in seven counties; six regional vice presidents and three vice presidents reported to him; he was appointed by and reported to the president and CEO of the Bank; and he participated in senior management meetings. *See Maioramo v. Schering-Plough Corp*; 302 N.J. Super. 323 (App. Div.), *certif. denied*, 152 N.J. 189 (1997) (reversing jury duty award because jury not instructed that upper management involvement was required).

975. *Gares v. Willingboro Township*, 90 F.3d 720 (3d Cir. 1996); *Murray v. Newark Housing Authority*, 311 N.J. Super. 163, 181 n.16 (Law Div. 1998).

976. N.J.S.A. 10:5-27.1. *See, e.g., Roberts v. Keansburg Bd. Of Educ.*, 5 N.J.A.R. 208, 253-55, 266-68 (DCR 1983) ($19,120 awarded); *Vasto v. Vornado, Inc.*, 8 N.J.A.R. 481, 500-02, 508 (DCR 1983) ($5,551 awarded); *Pilot v. New Jersey Dept. of Health*, 7 N.J.A.R. 150, 177, 180 (DCR 1982), *aff'd*, No. A-5853-81 (App. Div. Sept. 28, 1983) ($6,795 awarded); *White v. PSE&G Co.*, 8 N.J.A.R. 335, 388 (DCR 1984) *aff'd*, No. A-1496-84 (App. Div. July 16, 1986) ($18,371 awarded); counsel fees may be awarded with respect to appellate proceedings. *Levinson v. Prentice-Hall, Inc.*, 1989 WL 65622 (D.N.J. 1989) (extensive discussion of how to determine whether a party has "prevailed" on appeal). It has been suggested that special circumstances may warrant denying a prevailing party a fee award. *See Davidson v. Roselle Park Soccer*, 304 N.J. Super. 352, 360 (Ch. Div. 1997) (while plaintiff's lack of good faith effort to settle would not in itself warrant denial of fees, it was "a persuasive factor"); *H.I.P. v. K. Hovnanian at Mahwah VI, Inc.*, 291 N.J. Super. 144, 157 (Law Div. 1996); *Jackson v. Georgia-Pacific Corp.*, 296 N.J. Super. 1, 23-25 (App. Div. 1996), *certif. denied*, 149 N.J. 141 (1997).

977. *Robb v. Ridgewood Bd. of Educ.*, 269 N.J. Super. 394, 403 (Ch. Div. 1993); *Murray v. Newark Housing Authority*, 311 N.J. Super. 163, 180-81 (Law Div. 1998); *Failla v. City of Passaic*, 146 F.3d 149 (3d Cir. 1998) ("The mere fact that the City is a public entity does not relieve it of its obligation to pay attorneys' fees when it is found liable for unlawful discrimination).

brought in bad faith.[978] "Bad faith" is a subjective standard and requires more than a finding that a complaint was frivolous or meritless.[979]

A "prevailing party" has been described as one who has achieved a substantial portion of the relief it sought; one who has succeeded on any significant portion of the relief it sought.[980]

It is not clear whether a party who settles a discrimination complaint is a "prevailing party" within the meaning of N.J.S.A. 10:5-27.1.[981] The Supreme Court left the issue undecided in *Balsley v. No. Hunterdon Regional Sch. Dist. Bd. of Educ.*, although it observed that it is the DCR's position that counsel fees should not be available in administrative proceedings when settlements occur before hearing.[982] It is also unresolved whether a *pro se* plaintiff is entitled to counsel fees under the LAD.[983]

Calculation of Fees

The amount of counsel fees is within the sound discretion of the tribunal.[984] The proper starting point is calculating the "lodestar" amount, which is the num-

---

978. N.J.S.A. 10:5-27.1. This restriction on the recovery of counsel fees is limited to "respondents." Under the LAD, a respondent is a party charged in a verified complaint filed with the DCR with violating the LAD. N.J.S.A. 10:5-15. As such, the "bad faith" limitation is facially limited to proceedings commenced in the DCR. It is significant to note that the counsel fee provision was added to the LAD by L.1979, c.404, the same legislation that amended N.J.S.A. 10:5-13 to expressly permit aggrieved persons the option of proceeding before the DCR or in court. This would suggest that the counsel fee provision is applicable in the same manner regardless of where the proceeding is pending. *See, e.g., Brown v. Fairleigh Dickinson Univ.*, 560 F.Supp. 391, 406 (D.N.J. 1983) (denying defendant counsel fees because plaintiff's LAD civil action was not brought in bad faith).

Apart from the LAD, parties to a civil action in state court may seek counsel fees under the frivolous litigation statute, N.J.S.A. 2A:15-59.1, and/or R. 1:4-8. In federal court actions, counsel fees may be recoverable under Federal Rule of Civil Procedure 11 and/or 28 U.S.C.A. §1927. *See Quiroga v. Hasbro, Inc.*, 934 F.2d 497 (3d Cir. 1991) (LAD and Title VII); *see also Chambers v. NASCO, Inc.*, 501 U.S. 32, 111 S.Ct. 2123, 115 L.Ed.2d 27 (1991).

979. *Brown v. Fairleigh Dickinson Univ.*, 560 F. Supp. at 406-07, 403-04. This standard is significantly higher than the standard applicable in Title VII and other federal civil rights actions, where bad faith is not required. *Id.*

980. *See Davidson v. Roselle Park Soccer*, 304 N.J. 352, 356 (Ch. Div. 1997) ("In order to be considered a prevailing party a plaintiff must demonstrate: (1) success on a significant issue which benefits the party bringing suit; (2) a factual causal nexus between plaintiff's litigation and the relief obtained; and (3) that the relief obtained had a basis in law;" where relief was given voluntarily and case was dismissed as moot, plaintiff did not prevail); *H.I.P. v. K. Hovnanian at Mahwah VI, Inc.*, 291 N.J. Super. 144, 154 (Law Div. 1996) ("[A] prevailing party is one who achieves a substantial portion of the relief it sought."). "[A] prevailing party is one who achieves a substantial portion of the relief it sought." *H.I.P. v. K. Hovnanian at Mahwah VI, Inc.*, 291 N.J. Super. 144 (Law Div. 1996). *See Robb v. Ridgewood Bd. of Educ.*, 269 N.J. Super. 394, 400 (Ch. Div. 1993) ("To be a prevailing party, a plaintiff must have 'succeeded on any significant claim affording it some of the relief sought.'"). *See generally Silva v. Autos of Amboy, Inc.*, 267 N.J. Super. 546, 555-560 (App. Div. 1993) (consumer fraud case discussing fees in civil rights actions). *See Abrams v. Lightolier*, 50 F.3d 1204, 1223-26 (3d Cir. 1995) (discussing what expenses, other than the cost of attorney time, may be recovered as part of a reasonable attorney's fee). Where plaintiff's reemployment was not sought in complaint or ordered in litigation, that reemployment did not make him a prevailing party. *Robb v. Ridgewood Bd. of Educ.*, 269 N.J. Super. 394, 400 (Ch. Div. 1993) ("To be a prevailing party, a plaintiff must have 'succeeded on any significant claim affording it some of the relief sought.'").

ber of hours reasonably necessary to successfully prosecute the claim times a reasonable hourly rate.[985] "Trial courts should not accept passively the submissions of counsel to support the lodestar amount."[986] The lodestar calculation requires the court to carefully and critically evaluate the hours and the hourly rate put forth by counsel.[987] The party requesting the fee bears the burden of proving that it is reasonable.[988]

Hourly rates must be "fair, realistic and accurate."[989] To take into account delay in payment, the hourly rate at which compensation is to be awarded should

---

981. In *Balsley v. No. Hunterdon Regional Sch. Dist. Bd. of Educ.*, 117 N.J. 434, 448 (1990), the Court noted that in *Singer v. State of New Jersey*, 95 N.J. 487, 494, *cert. denied*, 469 U.S. 832 (1984), it adopted the following test for determining whether a litigant is a "prevailing party" under the Civil Rights Attorney's Fees Awards Act of 1976, 42 U.S.C.A. §1988: was the action "causally related to securing the relief obtained" and were the party's efforts "a necessary and important factor in obtaining the relief"? (internal quotation marks omitted). In *Texas State Teachers Ass'n v. Garland Independent School Dist.*, 489 U.S. 782, 791-93 (1989), the Court adopted the following test for determining whether a plaintiff is a prevailing party under §1988: did plaintiff succeed on "any significant issue in litigation which achieve[d] some of the benefit the parties sought in bringing suit'" such that there is a "material alteration of the legal relationship of the parties"? Neither *Singer* nor *Garland* involved a settlement. The *Singer/Garland*-type analysis was held applicable to settlements in *Girandola v. Allentown*, 208 N.J. Super. 437 (App. Div. 1986) (Environmental Rights Act, N.J.S.A. 2A:35A-10(a)), and has been applied in LAD cases not involving settlements. *See, e.g., Levinson v. Prentice-Hall, Inc.*, 1989 WL 65622 (D.N.J. 1989). *See H.I.P. v. K. Hovnanian at Mahwah VI, Inc.*, 291 N.J. Super. 144, 676 A.2d 1166 (Law Div. 1996) (fees awarded under LAD and other statutes in connection with consent order).

982. *Balsley v. No. Hunterdon Regional Sch. Dist. Bd. of Educ.*, 117 N.J. at 448-49. The Appellate Division, in *Balsley*, had ruled that plaintiff was a "prevailing party" entitled to counsel fees because her case was settled by consent order. *Balsley v. No. Hunterdon Regional High Sch. Bd. of Educ.*, 225 N.J. Super. 221, 229-30 (App. Div. 1988), *rev'd on other grounds*, 117 N.J. 434 (1990). *See Poff v. Caro*, 228 N.J. Super. 370, 380 (Law Div. 1987). *Cf. Brewster v. Keystone Ins. Co.*, 238 N.J. Super. 580, 585-86 & n.4 (App. Div. 1990) (under R. 4:42-9(a)(6), an insured who obtains a pretrial settlement in an amount greater than that which he was offered prior to institution of suit is a "successful claimant" entitled to counsel fees).

983. *Cf. Schlichtman v. New Jersey Highway Auth.*, 243 N.J. Super. 464, 475 (Law Div. 1990) (*pro se* plaintiff not entitled to counsel fees in breach of contract and negligence action); *Kay v. Ehrler*, 499 U.S. 432, 111 S.Ct. 1435, 113 L.Ed.2d 486 (1991) (*pro se* attorney not entitled to counsel fees under 42 U.S.C.A. §1988; also noting that the federal circuits are in agreement that a non-lawyer, *pro se* plaintiff is not entitled to counsel fees).

984. *Roberts v. Keansburg Bd. of Educ.*, 5 N.J.A.R. 208, 254 (DCR 1983) ("[A]n award of counsel fees under LAD is not mandatory."); *Jackson v. Georgia-Pacific Corp.*, 296 N.J. Super. 1, 25 (App. Div. 1996) (same), *certif. denied*, 149 N.J. 141 (1997).

985. *Id.; Blakey v. Continental Airlines, Inc.*, 2 F. Supp. 2d 598, 602 (1998); *Levinson v. Prentice-Hall, Inc.*, 1989 WL 656622 (D.N.J. 1989). "Trial courts should not accept passively the submissions of counsel to support the lodestar amount." *Rendine v. Pantzer*, 141 N.J. 292, 337. Hourly rates must be "fair, realistic and accurate," but "[t]o take into account delay in payment, the hourly rate at which compensation is to be awarded should be based on current rates rather than those in effect when the services were performed." *Id.* Contemporaneously kept time sheets will normally be required. *Szczepanski v. Newcomb Medical Ctr., Inc.*, 141 N.J. 346 (1995).

986. *Rendine v. Pantzer*, 141 N.J. 292, 335 (1995). That determination "requires the trial court to evaluate carefully and critically the aggregate hours and specific hourly rates advanced by counsel for the prevailing party to support the fee application." *Id. See Blakey v. Continental Airlines, Inc.*, 2 F. Supp. 2d 598, 602 (D.N.J. 1998).

be based on current rates rather than those in effect when the services were performed.[990]

Compensable time is that which is reasonably necessary. Unproductive or duplicative time should not be included.[991] Hours that would not be billed to one's client should not be "billed" to one's adversary under statutory authority.[992] The lodestar may be reduced to account for a partial loss or limited success.[993] However, a proportional reduction in the lodestar "based simply or solely on a mathematical approach comparing the total number of issues in the case with those actually prevailed upon cannot serve as the basis for determining a reasonable fee for the prevailing party."[994] The method to be used rests in the equitable discretion of the court.[995]

The records supporting a fee application must be "sufficiently detailed" to permit the tribunal to make an independent assessment of whether the hours claimed are justified.[996] Contemporaneously kept time sheets normally will be re-

---

987. *Rendine v. Pantzer*, 141 N.J. 292, 334-35 (1995); *Blakey v. Continental Airlines, Inc.*, 2 F. Supp. 2d 598, 602 (1998).

988. *Blakey v. Continental Airlines, Inc.*, 2 F. Supp. 2d 598, 602 (1998).

989. *Rendine v. Pantzer*, 141 N.J. 292, 337 (1995).

990. *Rendine v. Pantzer*, 141 N.J. 292, 337 (1995). *See Baker v. The National State Bank*, 312 N.J. Super. 268 (App. Div.), *certif. granted*, 156 N.J. 425 (1998) (awarding fees at the $250 per hour rate set forth in plaintiffs' retention agreement instead of the $300 per hour rate that counsel stated was her current standard). *See also Blakey v. Continental Airlines, Inc.*, 2 F. Supp. 2d 598, 602-04 (D.N.J. 1998) (awarding fees at the rate of $300 per hour for experienced and skilled partner and $100 to $150 per hour for associates; noting that rates set by plaintiffs' counsel for use in contingency and fee-shifting cases may be suspect as a guide if they are not rates actually billed and paid under non-contingent fee arrangements).

991. *Id.; Hensley v. Eckerhart*, 461 U.S. 424, 434-37 (1983) (§1988). *Hurley v. Atlantic City Police Dept.*, 1996 WL 549298 (D.N.J. 1996) (awarding plaintiff counsel fees after deducting time spent on unsuccessful claims; also detailing the nature and extent of costs recoverable); *Robb v. Ridgewood Bd. of Educ.*, 269 N.J. Super. 394, 410 (Ch. Div. 1993) (reducing fees by 80% to account for unsuccessful efforts). Fees for time spent preparing a fee petition have been awarded, but at a lower rate. *Id. at 410-13. Cf. Abrams v. Lightolier, Inc.*, 50 F.3d 1204, 1222 (3d Cir. 1995) (noting that in determining a reasonable fee, the court must consider deducting time spent on unsuccessful claims, but affirming magistrate's decision not to reduce fees on that basis here.)

992. *Blakey v. Continental Airlines, Inc.*, 2 F. Supp. 2d 598, 604-05 (D.N.J. 1998) (deducting fees requested for, *inter alia*, time spent contacting the media : "It takes a lot of *chutzpah* to not only participate in such media contact during the litigation, but to bill for it.").

993. "[L]imited success may limit the fees awarded." *Blakey v. Continental Airlines, Inc.*, 2 F. Supp. 2d 598, 604 (D.N.J. 1998).

994. *Robb v. Ridgewood Bd. of Educ.*, 269 N.J. Super. 394, 402 (Ch. Div. 1993). If the court believes the lodestar is excessive in relation to the degree of plaintiff's success, it may "attempt to identify specific hours that should be eliminated, or it may simply reduce the award to account for the limited success." *Id.* at 405.

995. *See Rendine v. Pantzer*, 141 N.J. 292, 336 (1995); *Robb v. Ridgewood Bd. of Educ.*, 269 N.J. Super. 394, 402 (Ch. Div. 1993); *H.I.P. v. K. Hovnanian at Mahwah VI, Inc.*, 291 N.J. Super. 144(Law Div. 1996) (reducing fee for excessive hours and limited success; "Research may have been time consuming here because of the novelty to these attorneys of the precise issues in the case. But the fee shifting statutes do not contemplate the losing party has to pay for the learning experience of attorneys for the prevailing party.").

996. *Levinson v. Prentice-Hall, Inc.*, 1989 WL 65622, p. *5 (D.N.J. 1989). *See generally* R. 4:42-9(b)-(d).

quired.[997] The subject matter of the time expenditures must be identified in a manner that allows the tribunal to determine their reasonableness with a "high degree of certainty."[998] Vague entries and terse summaries will not suffice to support a fee award.[999]

While the amount of the compensatory damages award may be taken into account in awarding attorney's fees, there is no rule that the fees must be less than the damages.[1000]

The fact that a prevailing litigant was represented by or received financial assistance from a public interest organization or law firm has been found inadequate grounds for denying an award or not using prevailing market rates.[1001]

Enhancement

A trial court, after having carefully established the amount of the lodestar fee, may consider whether to increase that fee to reflect the risk of nonpayment in cases in which the attorney's compensation entirely or substantially is contingent on a successful outcome.[1002]

---

997. *Id.* Reconstruction of time is not an automatic bar to recovery, but it is strongly disfavored except in exceptional circumstances. *Szczepanski v. Newcomb Medical Center,* 141 N.J. 346, 367 (1995); *H.I.P. v. Hovnanian at Mahwah VI, Inc.*, 291 N.J. Super. 144 (Law Div. 1996) (disallowing fees not supported by actual time records).

998. *Blakey v. Continental Airlines, Inc.*, 2 F. Supp. 2d 598, 604 (D.N.J. 1998) (court may deduct for hours that are inadequately documented). *Levinson v. Prentice-Hall, Inc.*, 1989 WL 65622, p. *5. (internal quotation marks omitted).

999. *Id.* at p. *6.

1000. *Szczepanski v. Newcomb Medical Ctr., Inc.*, 141 N.J. 346 (1995). *See Abrams v. Lightolier, Inc.*, 50 F.3d 1204, 1222 (3d Cir. 1995) (affirming fees of $546,379.59 in case where damages were $473,953). However, "[t]he trial court's responsibility to review carefully the lodestar fee request is heightened in cases in which the fee requested is disproportionate to the damages recovered. In such cases the trial court should evaluate not only the damages prospectively recoverable and actually recovered, but also the interest to be vindicated in the context of the statutory objectives, as well as any circumstances incidental to the litigation that directly or indirectly affected the extent of counsel's efforts." *Id.*

The existence of a contingent fee arrangement is considered a factor reducing the risk of nonpayment. *Id.* However, it does not serve as a cap on the amount of a "reasonable fee." *Szczepanski v. Newcomb Medical Center, Inc.*, 141 N.J. 346 (1995). The "reasonable counsel fee payable to the prevailing party under fee-shifting statutes is determined independently of the provisions of the fee agreement between that party and his or her counsel. The statutory-fee award may be comparable to or substantially different from the amount payable under a negotiated fee agreement. *Id.*

1001. *Roberts v. Keansburg Bd. of Educ.*, 5 N.J.A.R. at 254, 267-68. *Accord Blum v. Stenson*, 465 U.S. 886, 892-95 (1984) (Civil Rights Attorney's Fees Awards Act of 1976); *Spoto v. McCarroll*, 250 N.J. Super. 66 (App. Div. 1991) (under R. 4:42-9(a), there is no reason to distinguish between publicly-funded legal-service organizations and private law firms in awarding counsel fees). *See Balsley v. No. Hunterdon Regional Sch. Dist. Bd. of Educ.*, 12 N.J.A.R. 232, 235, 251 (St.Bd.Ed.), *rev'd on other grounds*, 225 N.J. Super. 221 (App. Div. 1988), *rev'd*, 117 N.J. 434 (1990) (ALJ awarded counsel fee to student represented by ACLU in an education discrimination case; fee award vacated on other grounds). Additionally, in "actions involving public-interest law firms, defense counsel may not insist on the waiver or settlement of statutory fees as a condition of or before the settlement of the merits claim." *Coleman v. Fiore Bros., Inc.*, 113 N.J. 594, 611 (1989) (consumer fraud class action).

"[C]ontingency enhancements in fee-shifting cases ordinarily should range between five and fifty-percent of the lodestar fee, with the enhancement in typical contingency cases ranging between twenty and thirty-five percent of the lodestar. Such enhancements should never exceed one-hundred percent of the lodestar, and an enhancement of that size will be appropriate only in the rare and exceptional case in which the risk of non-payment has not been mitigated at all, i.e., where the 'legal' risk constitutes 'an economic disincentive independent of that created by the basic contingency in payment ... [and] the result achieved ... is significant and of broad public interest.[1003]

1002. *See Rendine v. Panter,* 141 N.J. 292 (1995)*; Roberts v. Keansburg Bd. of Educ.*, 5 N.J.A.R. at 255; *Singer v. State of New Jersey*, 95 N.J. 487, 499 (1984). *Roberts* and *Singer* cited the following 12 factors:

1. The time and labor required.
2. The novelty and difficulty of the question presented.
3. The skill required to perform the legal services properly.
4. The preclusion of other employment by counsel due to the acceptance of the case.
5. The customary fee for similar work in the geographic area.
6. Whether the fee is fixed or contingent.
7. The time limitations imposed by the client or the circumstances.
8. The amount involved and the results obtained.
9. The experience, reputation, and ability of the attorneys retained.
10. The undesirability of the case.
11. The nature and length of the professional relationship with the client.
12. Awards in similar cases.

Roberts v. Keansburg Bd. of Educ., 5 N.J.A.R at 254-55; *Singer v. State of New Jersey*, 95 N.J. at 498 n.4. These twelve factors are derived from *Johnson v. Georgia Highway Express, Inc.*, 488 F.2d 714, 717-19 (5th Cir. 1974), and are discussed in detail in Schlei & Grossman, *Employment Discrimination Law*, ch.39, pp. 1486-1509 (2d ed. 1983). It is noteworthy that these 12 factors are nearly identical to the factors, enumerated in New Jersey Rule of Professional Conduct 1.5(a) and incorporated by reference in R.4:42-9(b), used by the courts in determining reasonable counsel fees under various New Jersey counsel fee provisions. *Rendine v. Pantzer*, 141 N.J. 292. "[C]ontingency enhancements in fee-shifting cases ordinarily should range between five and fifty-percent of the lodestar fee, with the enhancement in typical contingency cases ranging between twenty and thirty-five percent of the lodestar. Such enhancements should never exceed one-hundred percent of the lodestar, and an enhancement of that size will be appropriate only in the rare and exceptional case in which the risk of nonpayment has not been mitigated at all, *i.e.*, where the 'legal' risk constitutes 'an economic disincentive independent of that created by the basic contingency in payment * * * [and] the result achieved * * * is significant and of broad public interest.'" *Id. See H.I.P. v. K. Hovnanian at Mahwah VI, Inc.*, 291 N.J. Super. 144 (Law Div. 1995) (allowing 5 percent enhancement for contingency risk after reducing the lodestar claimed due to both excessive hours and limited success); *Gallo v. Salesian Society, Inc.*, 290 N.J. Super. 616 (App. Div. 1996) (affirming trial court's reduction of the lodestar and denial of enhancement).

1003. *Rendine v. Pantzer*, 141 N.J. 292 (1995). *See Baker v. The National State Bank*, 312 N.J. Super. 268 (1998) (upholding 50% enhancement where plaintiffs' counsel was extremely successful, noting it was at the high end under *Rendine*), *certif. granted*, 156 N.J. 425 (1998); *See H.I.P. v. K. Hovnanian at Mahwah VI, Inc.*, 291 N.J. Super. 144 (Law Div. 1995) (allowing 5 percent enhancement for contingency risk after reducing the lodestar claimed due to both excessive hours and limited success); *Gallo v. Salesian Society, Inc.*, 240 N.J. Super. 616 (App. Div. 1996) (affirming trial court's reduction of the lodestar and denial of enhancement).

4-54:7 Criminal Offenses

Any person who willfully (1) resists, prevents, impedes, or interferes with the DCR's performance of its duties under the LAD or (2) violates an order of the Attorney General or Director is guilty of a crime of the fourth degree and subject to imprisonment for up to one year and/or a fine of not more than $500.[1004] Failure to comply with such an order pending judicial review, which presumably must be timely invoked, does not constitute a willful violation of the order.[1005]

4-55 Affirmative Action

Upon a finding of an unlawful employment practice, a respondent in a DCR proceeding or a defendant in a civil action may be ordered "to take such affirmative action, including, but not limited to, hiring, reinstatement or upgrading of employees, with or without back pay, or restoration to membership, in any respondent labor organization, or extending full and equal accommodations, advantages, facilities, and privileges to all persons, as ... will effectuate the purpose of [the LAD], and including a requirement for report of the manner of compliance."[1006] The LAD contains no other provision pertaining to affirmative action.[1007]

The regulations issued by the DCR, however, set forth certain affirmative action requirements that are applicable even in the absence of a finding of a violation of the LAD. A labor organization or employer that sponsors an apprenticeship program is obligated to publicly disseminate full information about the program to, among others, schools, employment service offices, and organizations having contacts with persons qualified for the program, including those which have contact with persons belonging to racial and ethnic minority groups.[1008] Employers must take affirmative steps to reasonably accommodate the needs of handicapped individuals.[1009]

1004. N.J.S.A. 10:5-26; N.J.S.A. 2C:1-5(b); N.J.S.A. 2C:43-1(b); *David v. Vesta Co.*, 45 N.J. 301, 323, 327 (1965). In *Passaic Daily News v. Blair*, 63 N.J. 474, 488 (1973), the Court noted that a willful violation of the LAD or a DCR rule does not give rise to criminal sanctions.

1005. N.J.S.A. 10:5-26.

1006. N.J.S.A. 10:5-17.

1007. The LAD does provide that it is not to be construed as to prevent the award of set-aside contracts by boards of education for small, women's, and minority businesses, as permitted by N.J.S.A. 18A:18A-51 *et seq*. N.J.S.A. 10:5-2.1. *See* §4-1. The public works employment discrimination law, N.J.S.A. 10:2-1 *et seq*., and the Public School Contracts Law, N.J.S.A. 18A:18A-1 *et seq*., contain similar provisions.

1008. N.J.A.C. 13:5-1.4(a)(2).

1009. N.J.A.C. 13:13-2.5.

Unless an employer is a federal or state contractor, it generally is not required to implement an affirmative action program or take affirmative steps to employ minorities, women, or the handicapped.[1010] Anti-discrimination laws do not require an employer to give preferential treatment to members of a protected class.[1011]

It is now settled that hiring quotas are not permissible under the LAD or any other State anti-discrimination law. In *Lige v. Montclair*, the Supreme Court struck down a one-for-one hiring and promotion quota for police and fire officers that was ordered by the DCR.[1012] The Court held that racial quotas contravened the prohibition of the state constitution that "No person shall be ... discriminated against ... because of race."[1013]

The legality of hiring goals is not as clear. In *United Building & Construction Trades Council v. Mayor & Council of Camden*, the Supreme Court held that the concerns raised in *Lige* are not present when goals are involved.[1014] *United Building* involved a City of Camden ordinance requiring all public works contractors to make every effort to employ not less than 25 percent minority workers in each trade utilized during a construction project. In upholding the ordinance against a State and federal equal protection challenge, the Court noted that the Camden goal requirements

> do not require the contractor to hire non-qualified employees or to disregard meaningful differences in employee qualifications. The regulations require only that the contractor make a good faith effort to attain the minority hiring goals.[1015]

1010. DCR, *Employment Guide to the LAD*, p. 6 (1989); DCR, *A Guide for Employers to the LAD*, p. 22 (June 1986). *Cf. Kearny Generating System v. Roper*, 184 N.J.Super. 253, 256, 262 (App. Div.), *certif. denied*, 91 N.J. 254 (1982) (employer had an affirmative action program designed to increase the percentage of its minority employees to match the percentage of minorities in the county); *Jones v. College of Medicine & Dentistry of New Jersey*, 155 N.J.Super. 232, 238 (App. Div.), *certif. denied*, 77 N.J. 482 (1977).

1011. *Kearny Generating System*, 184 N.J.Super. at 261; *Texas Dept. of Community Affairs v. Burdine*, 450 U.S. 248, 259 (1981) (Title VII).

1012. *Lige v. Montclair*, 72 N.J. 5 (1976).

1013. *Id.* at 15; N.J. Const. Art. 1, ¶5. *Accord Hebard v. Basking Ridge Fire Co.*, 164 N.J.Super. 77, 85-86 (App. Div. 1978), *app. dism'd*, 81 N.J. 294 (1979) (DCR may not direct that new job qualifications be applied retroactively to all current employees). *See, e.g., Terry v. Mercer County Freeholders Bd.*, 86 N.J. 141, 152-58 (1981) (victim of discrimination entitled to next available promotional opportunity); *Flanders v. William Paterson College*, 163 N.J.Super. 225, 231-35 (App. Div. 1976) (plaintiff entitled to immediate promotion); *Pilot v. New Jersey Dept. of Health*, 7 N.J.A.R. 150, 175, 180 (DCR 1982), *aff'd*, No. A-5853-81 (App. Div. Sept. 28, 1983) (same). *See Taxman v. Board of Educ. of Piscataway*, 91 F.3d 1547 (3d Cir. 1996) (school district violated Title VII when it selected white employee for layoff over equally qualified black employee based upon race and for the purpose of "diversity;" nonremedial affirmative action invalid under statute), *cert. granted*, 117 S. Ct. 2506, *cert. dismissed*, 118 S. Ct. 595 (1997).

1014. *United Building & Construction Trades Council v. Mayor & Council of Camden*, 88 N.J. 317, 335 (1982), *rev'd on other grounds*, 465 U.S. 208 (1984).

1015. *Id.* at 335.

In reaching this result, the Court rejected the contention that Camden was required to demonstrate with specificity the existence of past discrimination in the local construction industry to justify the goals.[1016]

That analysis, however, was rejected by the United States Supreme Court, in *Richmond v. Croson Co.*.[1017] The Court there invalidated a municipal set-aside program because (1) the municipality could not identify with specificity past racial discrimination in the municipality's construction industry, (2) the set-aside was not narrowly tailored to remedy the effects of the perceived discrimination, and (3) the municipality failed to consider alternative, race-neutral means to achieve the same result.[1018] It thus appears that for hiring goals to withstand an equal protection challenge, the strict standards of *Richmond* must be adhered to.

Note should be made of Public Transportation Act of 1979,[1019] which requires New Jersey Transit Corporation to establish an affirmative action program under which equal employment opportunity is to be provided to rehabilitated offenders[1020] and members of minority groups qualified in all employment categories, including the handicapped.[1021] The County Transportation Authorities Act,[1022] requires county transportation authorities to establish affirmative action programs guaranteeing equal employment opportunity to members of minority groups.[1023] Additional affirmative action statutes of note include:

1016. *United Building & Construction Trades Council v. Mayor & Council of Camden*, 88 N.J. at 333-37. *United Building* was followed in *Jersey City Educ. Ass'n v. Jersey City Bd. of Educ.*, 218 N.J.Super. 177 (App. Div. 1987). In that case, the public employer replaced its one-for-one quota system with an ad hoc promotion list created by the Interim Superintendent of Schools that placed Hispanic candidates first, Black candidates second, and all other candidates third. The court upheld the legality of the list without extended discussion.

In *Patrolmen's Benevolent Ass'n v. East Brunswick*, 180 N.J.Super. 68 (App. Div. 1981), the employer, in an attempt to recruit more qualified women, lowered the passing test score of a police officers' physical agility test from 70 to 50 and created for the first time two separate lists of qualified candidates—one for males and one for females. The court upheld these revised procedures in view of the facts that the lowering of the passing score did not result in unqualified candidates being appointed and the lists did not result in a quota system. *See also In re Dickerson Estate*, 193 N.J.Super. 353, 370-72 (Ch.Div. 1983) (preferences).

1017. 488 U.S. 469, 489-509 (1989). *Cf. United Building & Construction Trades Council v. Mayor & Council of Camden*, 88 N.J. at 333-37. *See Adarand Constructors, Inc. v. Pena*, 515 U.S. 200, 115 S. Ct. 2097, 132 L.Ed.2d 158 (1995) (all racial classifications by federal, state, or local government subject to strict scrutiny).

1018. *Richmond v. J.A. Croson Co.*, 488 U.S. 469, 498-506 (1989). *See Wygant v. Jackson Bd. of Ed.*, 476 U.S. 267 (1986); *Sheet Metal Workers v. EEOC*, 478 U.S. 421 (1986); *NAACP v. Harrison*, 940 F.2d 792, 805-08 (3d Cir. 1991).

1019. N.J.S.A. 27:25-1 *et seq.*

1020. The determination whether a convicted offender is rehabilitated apparently is made in accordance with N.J.S.A. 2A:168A-1 *et seq.* (rehabilitated convicted offenders). *Cf.* N.J.S.A. 5:12-90(h), -91(d) (rehabilitation criteria of the Casino Control Act).

1021. N.J.S.A. 27:25-12(a). The Casino Control Act contains a nearly identical provision, N.J.S.A. 5:12-135(c).

1022. N.J.S.A. 40:35B-1 *et seq.*

1023. N.J.S.A. 40:35B-39(b).

1. N.J.S.A. 18A:7A-35(h)—provision of the state takeover of failed local school districts law requiring the state district superintendent to ensure that the district is in compliance with all applicable affirmative action laws and regulations.
2. N.J.S.A. 18A:54D-1 *et seq.*—the Technical Training for Minorities and Women Act, designed to encourage a higher rate of minority and female participation in apprenticeship and other training programs.
3. N.J.S.A. 34:15B-11 *et seq.*—the Jobs Training Act, designed to provide job training and employment opportunities for the unemployed, underemployed, economically disadvantaged, displaced, etc.
4. N.J.S.A. 52:18A-89.1 *et seq.*—the Investment in United States Corporations Doing Business in Northern Ireland Law, designed to encourage such corporations to engage in affirmative action practices in Northern Ireland.

4-56 Statutes of Limitation

The LAD provides that a verified complaint must be filed with the DCR within 180 days after the alleged act of unlawful employment discrimination in order to be timely.[1024] A verified complaint is deemed filed on the date it is received in any of the DCR's regional offices or by any official or Investigator of the DCR.[1025] In appropriate circumstances, such as where a preliminary complaint is filed within the 180-day period but the verified complaint is not filed until a few days after the period, the verified complaint may be held to relate back to the date of filing of the preliminary complaint, if respondent has not been prejudiced thereby.[1026]

The LAD is silent with respect to the statute of limitations applicable to civil actions commenced thereunder.[1027] In *Montells v. Haynes*, [1028] the Supreme

1024. N.J.S.A. 10:5-18; N.J.S.A. 10:5-13; N.J.A.C. 13:4-3.1. *See, e.g., Alaya v. Ramapo College*, 1 N.J.A.R. 342 (DCR 1980). The 180-day period set forth in N.J.S.A. 10:5-18 pertains only to administrative, not civil, actions. *Fuchilla v. Layman*, 109 N.J. 319, 336, *cert. denied*, 488 U.S. 826 (1988); *Nolan v. Otis Elevator Co.*, 197 N.J.Super. 468, 473 (App. Div. 1984), *rev'd on other grounds*, 102 N.J. 30, *cert. denied*, 479 U.S. 820 (1986). This limitation also applies to verified complaints filed with authorized municipal offices of civil rights. N.J.S.A. 10:5-18, -14.2, and should apply to verified complaints filed with authorized county municipal offices of civil rights. *See* N.J.S.A. 10:5-18, -14.2, -14.3.

1025. N.J.A.C. 13:4-3.3(a).

1026. *Decker v. Elizabeth Bd. of Ed.*, 153 N.J.Super. 470, 473-74 (App. Div. 1977), *certif. denied*, 75 N.J. 612 (1978).

Court held that a two-year limitations period governs all civil suits under the LAD, because the injuries suffered as a consequence of employment discrimination more closely resemble injuries to the person, and because the shorter period comports with the LAD's purposes of efficiency and avoidance of stale claims. However, because the decisions before it were divided as to whether a two-year or six-year limitations period applied,[1029] the Court made its rule prospective, applicable to acts or omissions occurring after the date of the opinion.

As discussed in §4-4, when a LAD action alleges discrimination in connection with an employee benefit plan governed by ERISA, if the employment practice challenged is unlawful under Title VII or the ADEA and plaintiff has failed to file a complaint under the LAD within the time period for filing charges with the EEOC (generally 300 days), plaintiff's LAD action is effectively pre-empted by ERISA. In circumstances such as these, plaintiff must comply with the limitations period of Title VII or the ADEA.[1030]

1027. *Fuchilla v. Layman*, 109 N.J. at 336; *Lautenslager v. Supermarkets General Corp.*, 252 N.J.Super. 660, 661 (Law Div. 1991)

1028. 133 N.J. 282 (1993)

1029. *See* Editorial, *The [LAD]: Time for Clarification*, 115 N.J.L.J. 408 (Apr. 11, 1985); Poff, *Letter to Editor*, 116 N.J.L.J. 292 (Aug. 29, 1985) (Director of DCR joins in *New Jersey Law Journal* Editorial Board's Recommendation that the Legislature resolve the confusion concerning the applicable limitations period); *Skadegaard v. Farrell*, 578 F.Supp. 1209, 1213 (D.N.J. 1984) (limitations period under LAD "not entirely settled"); Jacobs, *It's Time to Clarify LAD Statute of Limitations*, 124 N.J.L.J. 969 (Oct. 19, 1989); Duffy, *Appellate Division Should Follow Its Own Lead*, 128 N.J.L.J. 551 (June 20, 1991).

The decisions under the LAD were as follows:

1.*180 days*: *Erdmann v. Union County Regional High Sch. Bd. of Educ.*, 541 F.Supp. 388, 391, 394, 396-97 (D.N.J. 1982), *modified on other grounds*, 34 FEP 1379 (D.N.J. 1984) (LAD and N.J.S.A. 18A:6-6). This holding is facially inconsistent with the subsequent decision in *Fuchilla*, 109 N.J. at 336, where the Court stated that the 180-day period of N.J.S.A. 10:5-18 "pertains only to administrative actions" before the DCR.

2.*Two years*: *White v. Johnson & Johnson Products, Inc.*, 712 F.Supp. 33, 36-38 (D.N.J. 1989); *Pachilio v. Union Carbide*, 1990 WL 4630, pp.*1-2 (D.N.J. 1990); *Moore v. Monmouth Beach*, No. 85-5302(AET) (D.N.J. Oct. 9, 1986) (Lexis).

3.*Six years*: *Leese v. Doe*, 182 N.J.Super. 318 (Law Div. 1981); *Nolan v. Otis Elevator Co.*, 197 N.J.Super. 468, 473-74 (App. Div. 1984), *rev'd on other grounds*, 102 N.J. 30, *cert. denied.*, 479 U.S. 820 (1986) (summarily holding that N.J.S.A. 2A:14-1, not N.J.S.A. 2A:14-2, applies; no discussion of the issue); *Fisher v. Quaker Oats Co.*, 233 N.J.Super. 319, 320 (App. Div.), *certif. denied.*, 117 N.J. 628 (1989) (merely restates *Nolan* holding); *Lautenslager v. Supermarkets General Corp.*, 252 N.J.Super. 660 (Law Div., 1991); *Mucci v. Moonachie Board of Education*, 37 FEP 65, 68 (D.N.J.), *modified on other grounds*, 37 FEP 1284 (D.N.J. 1985) (noting that the limitations period issue is unsettled); *Meacham v. Bell Telephone Laboratories, Inc.*, 1990 WL 299805, pp.*4-5 (D.N.J. 1990); *Carrington v. RCA Global Communications, Inc.*, 762 F.Supp. 632, 642-45 (D.N.J. 1991). *Cf. Elmwood Park Educ. Ass'n v. Elmwood Park Bd. of Educ.*, 3 N.J.A.R. 249, 272 (Comm'r Ed. 1980) (comparable worth case under N.J.S.A. 18A:6-6; Commissioner of Education chose the six-year period of N.J.S.A. 2A:14-1 over the 180-day period of N.J.S.A. 10:5-18). One panel of the Appellate Division questioned, but did not resolve, whether *Leese* "was correctly decided". *Healey v. Dover Tp.*, 208 N.J.Super. 679, 682 (App. Div. 1986), *ovr'ld on other grounds*, *Fuchilla v. Layman*, 109 N.J. 319, *cert. den*ied, 488 U.S. 826 (1988). The judge who decided *Mucci* thereafter rejected the six-year limitations period in *Pachilio* in view of intervening case law developments (discussed *infra*).

1030. *See* Pressler, *Current N.J. Court Rules*, Comment to R.4:5-4, (1999 ed.).

It has been suggested that the discovery rule should be extended to claims asserted under the LAD.[1031] When the Legislature amended N.J.S.A. 10:5-18 in 1979, it was proposed that the following italicized language be added as well:

> Any complaint filed in the [DCR] ... must be so filed within 180 days after the alleged act of discrimination *became known or should have become known to the complainant.*[1032]

The intent of the italicized words was to expand the time for filing a complaint until complainant discovered the alleged wrongful act.[1033] The italicized language was deleted prior to passage of the 1979 amendments to the LAD.

In cases involving discrimination in wages, each pay period in which discriminatory wages are paid constitutes a new or "continuing" violation of the LAD, thus recommencing the limitations period as to these new violations.[1034] However, an action for wage discrimination will be dismissed as time barred if the wage disparity is the result of a time-barred discriminatory act, such as hiring plaintiff at a lower rank or denying plaintiff a promotional opportunity, thereby placing plaintiff at a lower position on a facially-neutral salary scale or seniority system.[1035]

Application of the continuing violation theory is inappropriate where "an employee invokes it seeking to resurrect and litigate grievances long past by merely appending them to a current complaint."[1036] However, if the continuing violation

---

1031. *See Healey v. Dover Tp.*, 208 N.J.Super. 679, 684 (App. Div. 1986), *overruled on other grounds, Fuchilla v. Layman*, 109 N.J. 319, *cert. denied*, 488 U.S. 826 (1988) (LAD), and *Lloyd v. Stone Harbor*, 179 N.J.Super. 496, 515 n.1 (Ch.Div. 1981) (N.J. Const. Art. 1, ¶¶1 & 5), finding, on facts presented, that the discovery rule would not have saved plaintiffs' claims from the bar of the Tort Claims Act's statute of limitations.

1032. Senate No. 3101, §4 (Second Copy Reprint).

1033. Senate Law, Public Safety & Defense Committee, *Statement to Senate No. 3101* (Aug. 6, 1979); *Sponsors' Statement to Senate No. 3101* (Feb. 20, 1979).

1034. *Decker v. Elizabeth Bd. of Ed.*, 153 N.J.Super. 470, 473-74 (App. Div. 1977), *certif. denied*, 75 N.J. 612 (1978); *Terry v. Mercer County Freeholders Bd.*, 173 N.J.Super. 249, 253 (App. Div. 1980), *aff'd on other grounds*, 86 N.J. 141 (1981); *White v. PSE&G Co.*, 8 N.J.A.R. 335, 385 (DCR 1984), *aff'd*, No. A-1496-84 (App. Div. July 16, 1986). *Accord Bazemore v. Friday*, 478 U.S. 385, 395-96 (1986) (Brennan, J., concurring opinion joined by all other Members of the Court), and 478 U.S. at 387 n.1 (per curiam opinion of the Court) (Title VII).

1035. *Alaya v. Ramapo College*, 1 N.J.A.R. 342 (DCR 1980); *Perry v. Glen Rock Bd. of Educ.*, 1 N.J.A.R. 300, 301-04 (Comm'r Ed. 1981). *Accord Bazemore*, 478 U.S. at 396 n.6 (Brennan, J., concurring opinion joined by all other Members of the Court). *See McBride v. Princeton Univ.*, 1991 WL 66758, p.*9 (D.N.J. 1991), *aff'd* 950 F.2d 723 (3d Cir. 1991). *But see White*, 8 N.J.A.R. at 361-67, 374-76, 382-87 (unclear analysis).

1036. *Erdmann v. Union County Regional High Sch. Bd. of Educ.*, 541 F.Supp. 388, 392, 394 (D.N.J. 1982), *mod. on other grounds*, 34 FEP 1379 (D.N.J. 1984) (LAD, Title VII, and N.J.S.A. 18A:6-6); *Porta v. Rollins Environmental Services (N.J.), Inc.*, 654 F.Supp. 1275, 1281 (D.N.J. 1987), *aff'd without published op.*, 845 F.2d 1014 (3d Cir. 1988) ("plaintiff must do more than show the occurrence of 'isolated or sporadic acts of intentional discrimination'"). *See Jurinko v. Wiegard Co.*, 477 F.2d 1038, 1042, 1047 (3d Cir.), *vacated on other grounds*, 414 U.S. 970 (1973) (under Title VII, where plaintiffs allege three discrete acts of discrimination, only the last of which is within the limitations period, recovery is limited to the last act).

is the result of the consistent application of a discriminatory employment practice, policy, or procedure and plaintiff has brought a timely complaint of a current violation based on defendant's use of that practice, policy, or procedure, the otherwise time-barred acts of discrimination may be litigated.[1037] For example, paying women less than men performing the same work and requiring female employees to perform additional duties not required of their male counterparts are continuing violations.[1038]

In such case, a back-pay award is not limited to the period covered by the statute of limitations, but rather, relief may be granted as far back as the effective date of the *unlawful* conduct.[1039] When application of the continuing violation doctrine is inappropriate, the untimely acts of alleged discrimination only "constitute relevant background evidence in a proceeding in which the status of a current practice is at issue, but separately considered, [they are] merely ... unfortunate event[s] in history which [have] no present legal consequences."[1040]

New Jersey's Tort Claims Act is not applicable to claims filed under the LAD.[1041] Because the statute of limitations is an affirmative defense, a defendant must plead it in the answer.[1042]

1037. *Erdmann v. Union County Regional High Sch. Bd. of Educ.*, 541 F.Supp. at 392-94 (no continuing violation where plaintiff failed to show that the pattern of alleged discriminatory conduct was the result of a policy or practice used by defendants in making employment decision with respect to the protected class generally); *Pilot v. New Jersey Dept. of Health*, No. A-5853-81, slip op. at p.2 (App. Div. Sept. 28, 1983), *aff'g*, 7 N.J.A.R. 150, 168-69, 176-77 (DCR 1982) ("a continuous and systematic policy of limit[ing] [complainant's] opportunity over the span of [her] employment" because of her perceived handicap); *Alaya v. Ramapo College*, 1 N.J.A.R. at 347; *White v. PSE&G Co.*, 8 N.J.A.R. at 361-67, 374-76, 382-87; *Levitt & Sons, Inc. v. New Jersey Div. Against Discrimination*, 56 N.J.Super. 542, 553-55 (App. Div. 1959), *aff'd on other grounds*, 31 N.J. 514, 519-20, *app. dism'd*, 363 U.S. 418 (1960) (complainants' claims barred by limitations period where it was not shown that they were discriminated against during the period). *Cf. Lorance v. AT&T Technologies, Inc.*, 490 U.S. 900 (1989) (under Title VII, it is the allegedly discriminatory adoption of a seniority system that is nondiscriminatory in form and application and not the actual application of the system that triggers the running of the limitations period).

1038. *Terry v. Mercer County Freeholders Bd.*, 173 N.J.Super. at 252-53; *White v. PSE&G Co.*, 8 N.J.A.R. at 361-67, 374-76, 382-87 (race discrimination).

1039. *Terry v. Mercer County Freeholders Bd.*, 173 N.J.Super. at 253 (the limitations period "is not a restriction on damages"); *Pilot v. New Jersey Dept. of Health*, 7 N.J.A.R. 150, 176-77 (DCR 1982), *aff'd*, No. A-5853-81 (App. Div. Sept. 28, 1983); *White v. PSE&G Co.*, 8 N.J.A.R. at 386. *Cf. Elmwood Park Educ. Ass'n v. Elmwood Park Bd. of Educ.*, 3 N.J.A.R. 249, 272 (Comm'r Ed. 1980) (back-pay award in a comparable worth case under Education Code limited to the period of the statute of limitations).

1040. *Erdmann v. Union County Regional High Sch. Bd. of Educ.*, 541 F.Supp. at 394, *quoting United Air Lines, Inc. v. Evans*, 431 U.S. 553, 558 (1977). *Accord Hedgpeth v. New Jersey Dept. of Law & Public Safety*, 1997 WL 17057, 44 FEP 1390, 1393-94 (D.N.J. 1987) (same); *McBride v. Princeton Univ.*, 1991 WL 66758, p.*9 (D.N.J. Apr. 24, 1991), *aff'd*, 950 F.2d. 723 (3d Cir. 1991).

1041. *Fuchilla v. Layman*, 109 N.J. 319, 321, 335-38, *cert. denied*, 488 U.S. 826 (1988); N.J.S.A. 59:8-1 *et seq*. The court in *Lloyd v. Stone Harbor*, 179 N.J.Super. 496, 507, 511-12 (Ch.Div. 1981), held that the Tort Claims Act does apply to employment discrimination claims under N.J. Const. Art. 1, ¶¶1 and 5. The reasoning in *Fuchilla* suggests that the Tort Claims Act would not be applicable to such constitutional claims.

1042. R.4:5-4.

Chapter 5

Employee Privacy

I. INTRODUCTION

5-1 Generally

Employees may assert a right to privacy in the workplace under common law and public policy. In *Hennessey v. Coastal Eagle Point Oil Co.,*[1] the Supreme Court held that constitutional and common-law privacy rights express a public policy of privacy in New Jersey. Thus, in appropriate circumstances, an employee may maintain a *Pierce*[2] action for violation of public policy based on employment actions that infringe on protected privacy rights.[3] The extent of the public policy of privacy in the workplace is not clearly defined, but rather is determined by balancing the employee's individual right to privacy with the competing public interest.[4] Other factors relevant to the inquiry are the extent of the intrusion and its effect on employee dignity; the existence of advance notice to employees of the possibility of the intrusion, how it will be done and how the results will be used; limitation of the intrusion to the extent actually required to satisfy the employer's legitimate purposes; and nondisclosure of private information obtained except for the necessary and legitimate purposes of the intrusion.[5]

---

1. 129 N.J. 81 (1992). *See* Chapter 2, §§2-2 to 2-7.
2. *Pierce v. Ortho Pharmaceutical Corp.*, 84 N.J. 58 (1980).
3. 129 N.J. 81, 99. As the *Hennessey* court made clear, "more is needed than simply the breach of public policy affecting a single person's rights to constitute the breach of a 'clear mandate' of public policy that Pierce requires." A clear mandate of public policy must be one that on balance is beneficial to the public. *Id.* at 100.
4. In *Hennessey*, a drug-testing case, the court balanced the employee's privacy right against the public interest in public safety. Factors it considered included (1) a showing of drug-use among employees; (2) potential dangers in the job assignment at issue; and (3) inability of the employer to detect drug use through other means.
5. 129 N.J. 81, 106-07.

New Jersey common law also recognizes a tort of unreasonable intrusion on seclusion. "'One who intentionally intrudes, physically or otherwise, upon the solitude or seclusion of another or his private affairs or concerns, is subject to liability to the other for invasion of his privacy, if the intrusion would be highly offensive to a reasonable person.'"[6]

II. OFFICE SEARCHES

5-2 Generally

The New Jersey Supreme Court has not directly considered the extent to which private employers may search the offices and belongings of employees. Although earlier lower court decisions found constitutional search and seizure protections inapplicable to private, non-governmental conduct,[7] the Court's opinion in *Hennessey v. Coastal Eagle Point Oil*[8] suggests that while such protections do not apply directly, they nonetheless constrain employer conduct as expressions of public policy which in appropriate circumstances will support a *Pierce* claim. Thus, public employee cases provide useful guidance. In *O'Connor v. Ortega*,[9] the United States Supreme Court held that "a warrant or probable cause standard does not apply when a government employer searches an employee's office, desk, or file cabinet to retrieve government property or to investigate work-related misconduct."[10] Such a search is justified "where there are reasonable grounds for suspecting that a search will turn up evidence that the employee is guilty of work-related misconduct."[11]

---

6. *Hennessey v. Coastal Eagle Point Oil Co.*, 129 N.J. 81, 95-96 (1992) (quoting RESTATEMENT (SECOND) OF TORTS § 652B (1977)). *See Bisbee v. John C. Conover Agency*, 186 N.J. Super. 335, 340 (App. Div. 1982) ("The thrust of this aspect of the tort is, in other words, that a person's private, personal affairs should not be pried into...The converse of this principle is, however, of course, that there is no wrong where defendant did not actually delve into plaintiff's concerns, or where plaintiff's activities are already public or known").

7. *See State v. Robinson*, 86 N.J. Super. 308 (Law Div. 1965) (search of employee's locker by a private detective hired by a private employer did not implicate the Fourth Amendment and therefore the exclusionary rule was inapplicable). *See also State v. Pohle*, 166 N.J. Super. 504 (App. Div.), *certif. denied*, 81 N.J. 328 (1979) (evidence acquired by an inspection search of an air freight shipment by an airline employee should not have been suppressed because there was no state action).

8. 129 N.J. 81 (1992).

9. 480 U.S. 709 (1987). *Contra State v. Ferrari*, 136 N.J. Super. 61 (Law Div. 1975) (government employer's search of employee's office and desk violated the Fourth Amendment; no New Jersey constitutional claim presented).

10. 480 U.S. at 721. *See Gossmeyer v. McDonald*, 128 F.3d 481, 490 (7th Cir. 1997) (citing *O'Connor v. Ortega*, 480 U.S. 709, 719-26 (1987)).

11. 480 U.S. 709, 766. *See Wassen v. Sonoma County Junior College District*, 4 F. Supp. 2d 893, 905 (N.D. Ca. 1997) (citing *Ortega*, 480 U.S. at 726).

The "workplace" that is subject to search under *Ortega* includes "those areas and items that are related to work and are generally within the employer's control" such as hallways, cafeterias, offices, desks, and file cabinets.[12] That is so "even if the employee has placed personal items in them, such as a photograph placed in a desk or a letter placed on an employee bulletin board."[13] Moreover, employees' expectations of privacy in the workplace may be reduced by virtue of actual office practices, procedures or by legitimate regulation.[14] Thus, employers who give employees advance notice that offices and desks are subject to search are more likely to have their actions upheld.[15] When an employee does have a reasonable expectation of privacy in the area searched, the employee's interest will be balanced against the public interest and the need for supervision, control and the efficient operation of the workplace.[16]

III. E-MAIL AND INTERNET USE

5-3 Generally

The New Jersey Supreme Court has not yet addressed the extent to which employers may monitor employee e-mail and internet use. Under *Hennessey*, advance notice to employees that e-mail and internet use must be strictly limited to business purposes, and that all communications are considered the property of the employer and therefore subject to review would be a significant factor in determining the employee's legitimate expectations and the validity of the employer's actions.

---

12. 480 U.S. at 715-16.

13. 480 U.S. at 716. However,

> Not everything that passes through the confines of the business address can be considered part of the workplace context, however. An employee may bring closed luggage to the office prior to leaving on a trip, or a handbag or briefcase each workday. While whatever expectation of privacy the employee has in existence and the outward appearance of the luggage is affected by its presence in the workplace, the employee's expectation of privacy in the *contents* of the luggage is not affected in the same way. The appropriate standard for a workplace search does not necessarily apply to a piece of closed personal luggage, a handbag, or a briefcase that happens to be within the employer's business address.

Id.

14. *Ortega*, 480 U.S. at 717. ("The employee's expectation of privacy must be assessed in the context of the employment relation. An office is seldom a private enclave free from entry by supervisors, other employees, and business and personal invitees... .Given the great variety of work environments in the public sector, the question whether an employee has a reasonable expectation of privacy must be addressed on a case-by-case basis.").

15. *See Hennessey v. Coastal Eagle Point Oil Co.*, 129 N.J. 81, 106-07 (1992).

16. *See Wasson v. Sonoma County Junior College District*, 4 F. Supp. 2d 893, 905 (N.D. Ca. 1997).

Decisions from other jurisdictions have upheld employer actions based upon the discovery of inappropriate context in monitored e-mail. In *Smyth v. Pillsbury Co.*,[17] the United States District Court for the Eastern District of Pennsylvania upheld the discharge of an employee for transmitting "inappropriate and unprofessional comments" over the employer's internal e-mail system, despite the employee's claim that he had been assured that e-mail communications would remain confidential and privileged and that they could not be intercepted and used as grounds for termination or reprimand.[18] The employee failed to show a violation of a clear mandate of public policy under Pennsylvania law inasmuch as "the company's interest in preventing inappropriate and unprofessional comments or even illegal activity over its e-mail system outweighs any privacy interest the employee may have in those comments."[19]

E-mail sent by a public carrier may be protected by the Omnibus Crime Control and Safe Streets Act of 1968, as amended by the Electronic Communications Privacy Act of 1986 (ECPA),[20] and the New Jersey Wire Tapping and Electronic Control Act.[21] The Acts prohibit third-parties from gaining access to or disclosure of e-mail without authorization such as consent from the user.[22] However, two exceptions may apply to most situations in which an employer would monitor e-mail. The first applies to inspections done in the normal course of business which are necessary for business purposes or to protect the employer's rights or property.[23] The second exception applies to monitoring that is consented to by one of the parties to the communication.[24] Thus, if an employee's consent to interception were obtained, the Acts would not apply.

---

17. *See Hennessey v. Coastal Eagle Point Oil Co.*, 129 N.J. 81, 106-07 (1992).

18. *Smyth v. Pillsbury Co.*, 914 F. Supp. 97, 98 (E.D. Pa. 1996).

19. *See id.* at 101. The court found that there was no reasonable expectation of privacy in e-mail communications voluntarily made by an employee to his supervisor; that once the employee utilized an e-mail used by the entire company, any reasonable expectation of privacy was lost. *See also Cyber Promotions, Inc. v. America Online, Inc.*, 948 F. Supp. 436 (E.D. Pa. 1996) (in the absence of state action, a private entity may restrict unsolicited e-mail from reaching its subscribers).

20. 18 U.S.C. § 2510, *et seq.*

21. N.J.S.A. 2A:156A-1, *et seq.* The New Jersey Act, enacted in 1969, largely follows the federal statute. *State v. Minter*, 116 N.J. 269 (1989); *Pascale v. Carolina Freight Carriers Corp.*, 898 F.Supp. 276, 281 (D.N.J. 1995). New Jersey courts look to constructions of the federal act when interpreting the state law. *Id.*; *State v. Lane*, 279 N.J. Super. 209 (App. Div. 1995).

22. 18 U.S.C. § 2511.

23. 18 U.S.C. § 2510(5)(a) excepts from the Act's definition of a covered interception device "any telephone or telegraph instrument, equipment or facility, or any component thereof, (i) furnished to the subscriber or user by a provider of wire or electronic communication service in the ordinary course of its business and being used by the subscriber or user in the ordinary course of its business or furnished by such subscriber or user for connection to the facilities of such service and used in the ordinary course of its business; or (ii) being used by a provider of wire or electronic communication service in the ordinary course of its business, or by an investigative or law enforcement officer in the ordinary course of his duties."

The Acts do not apply to e-mail sent through an employer's internal e-mail system.[25]

IV. CONSENSUAL RELATIONSHIPS

5-4 Generally

{Reserved}

V. POLYGRAPH TESTS

5-5 Generally

With only limited exceptions, it is a disorderly persons offense for any employer in New Jersey to influence, request or require an employee or prospective employee to take or submit to a lie detector test as a condition of employment or continued employment.[26] The employer need not terminate the employee or directly threaten the employee for a violation to occur; the psychological pressure of a request is enough,[27] even if the employee signs a waiver stating that he is voluntarily submitting.[28] It is not a violation if (1) the employer is authorized to manufacture, distribute or dispense controlled dangerous substances pursuant to the provisions of the "New Jersey Controlled Dangerous Substances Act;"[29] and (2) the employee or prospective employee is or will be directly involved in the manufacture, distribution, or dispensing of, or will have access to, legally distributed controlled dangerous substances.[30] When a test is permissible, it must be

---

24. 18 U.S.C. § 2511(2)(d) ("It shall not be unlawful under this chapter for a person not acting under color of law to intercept a wire or oral communication where such person is a party to the communication or where one of the parties to the communication has given prior consent to such interception unless such communication is intercepted for the purpose of committing any criminal or tortious act in violation of the Constitution or laws of the United States or of any State or for the purpose of committing any other injurious act."); N.J.S.A. 2A:156A-4d.

25. 18 U.S.C. § 2510, 2511(1); N.J.S.A. 2A:156A-2a., 156A-3.

26. N.J.S.A. 2C:40A-1. Cf. 29 U.S.C. § § 2001 to 2009. *See generally Engel v. Township of Woodbridge*, 124 N.J. Super. 307 (App. Div. 1973) (police officer could not be dismissed for failure to submit to lie detector test).

27. *State v. Community Distributors*, 123 N.J. Super. 589 (Law Div. 1973), *aff'd*, 64 N.J. 479 (1974) (although employer asked, but did not require, employees to take lie detector test, given psychological pressure to appease employer, employer's actions were deemed a "condition of employment" thus violating the predecessor to N.J.S.A. 2C:40A-1).

28. *State v. Berkey Photo, Inc.*, 150 N.J. Super. 56 (App. Div. 1977) (lie detector tests violated predecessor statute despite the facts that employees signed waivers stating they took the tests voluntarily and tests were given at the suggestion of police to uncover theft; they were still a condition of employment or continued employment).

29. N.J.S.A. 24:21-1, *et seq.*

30. N.J.S.A. 2C:40A-1.

limited to a period of no greater than 5 years preceding the test. Questioning must be limited to the work of the employee or prospective employee and the individual's improper handling, use or illegal sale of legally distributed controlled dangerous substances, as well as standard baseline questions necessary and for the sole purpose of establishing a normal test pattern.[31] Any employee or prospective employee who is required to take a lie detector test as a precondition of employment or continued employment has the right to be represented by legal counsel.[32] A copy of the report containing the results of the lie detector test shall be in writing and shall be provided, upon request, to the individual who has taken the test.[33] Information obtained from the test may not be released to anyone else.[34] The individual taking the test must be informed that he has a right to present the employer with the results of an independently administered second lie detector test before any employment decision about him is made.[35]

VI. BACKGROUND CHECKS

5-6 Generally

Pursuant to regulations issued by the Superintendent of the State Police, with approval of the Attorney General, employers may obtain certain criminal conviction records from the State Bureau of Investigation[36] "for purposes of determining a person's qualifications for employment, volunteer work or other performance of services."[37] Any person or entity may obtain from the State Bureau of Investigation (1) all records of convictions in New Jersey State courts; (2) all records of pending arrests and charges for violations of New Jersey laws, regardless of their age, unless the records have been expunged pursuant to law.[38]

Requests for criminal history record information for purposes of employment must be made on prescribed forms[39] signed by the subject of the request.[40] In addition, the employer making the request must sign a certification that: (1) it is authorized to re-

31. *Id.*
32. *Id.*
33. *Id.*
34. *Id.*
35. *Id.*
36. N.J.S.A. 53:1-20.6; N.J.A.C. 13:59-1.1, *et seq.*
37. N.J.A.C. 13:59-1.2(a)(2).
38. N.J.A.C. 13:59-1.2(a).
39. N.J.A.C. 13:59-1.4.
40. N.J.A.C. 13:59-1.2(b).

ceive criminal history information in conformity with the regulation;[41] (2) the records will be used by the employer solely for the purpose of determining the subject's qualifications for employment, volunteer work or other performance of services;[42] (3) the records will not be disseminated to persons for unauthorized purposes;[43] (4) it will otherwise comply with the requirements of N.J.A.C. 13:59-1.6(a);[44] (5) it will give the subject of the inquiry adequate notice to complete or challenge the accuracy of the records provided by the SBI;[45] (6) if asked by the subject of the inquiry, it will give him a reasonable period in which to correct or complete records provided by the SBI;[46] (7) it will not presume guilt for any pending arrests or charges indicated on records received from the SBI;[47] and (8) it will otherwise comply with the requirements of N.J.A.C. 13:59-1.6(b).[48] All records produced by the SBI must include a warning reiterating the above-stated limitations on its use and dissemination and rights of the subjects of the information.[49]

---

41. N.J.A.C. 13:59-1.2(b)(1).

42. N.J.A.C. 13:59-1.2(b)(2).

43. N.J.A.C. 13:59-1.2(b)(3).

44. N.J.A.C. 13-1.6(a) provides: "Access to criminal history record information for non-criminal justice purposes, including licensing and employment, is restricted to authorized requesters as defined by this chapter. Such requesters shall limit their use of criminal history record information solely to the authorized purpose for which it was obtained and Criminal History Record Information furnished by the SBI [State Bureau of Information] shall not be disseminated by authorized requesters to persons not authorized to receive the records for authorized purposes."

45. N.J.A.C. 13:59-1.2(c)(1).

46. N.J.A.C. 13-59-1.2(c)(2).

47. N.J.A.C. 13-59-1.2(c)(3).

48. N.J.A.C. 13:59-1.6(b) provides: "If Criminal History Record Information may be used to disqualify a person from holding any position, employment or license or performing any services, whether compensated or uncompensated, the person acting on behalf of the authorized requester making such determination shall provide the applicant with adequate notice to complete or challenge the accuracy of any information obtained in the Criminal History Record. The applicant shall be afforded a reasonable period of time to correct or complete the record. A person shall not be presumed guilty of any pending charges or arrests for which there are no final dispositions indicated on the record.

49. N.J.A.C. 13:59-1.6 (c). All such records must include the following statement:

> Use of this record is governed by Federal and State regulations. Unless fingerprints accompanied your inquiry, the State Bureau of Identification cannot guarantee this record relates to the person who is the subject of your request. Use of this record shall be limited solely to the authorized purpose for which it was given and it shall not be disseminated to any unauthorized persons. This record shall be destroyed immediately after it has served its intended and authorized purposes. Any person violating Federal or State regulations governing access to Criminal History Record Information may be subject to criminal and/or civil penalties.
>
> If this record may disqualify an applicant for any purpose, the person making the determination shall provide the applicant with an opportunity to complete and challenge the accuracy of the information contained in the Criminal History Record. The applicant shall be afforded a reasonable period of time to correct and complete this record. A person is not presumed guilty of any charges or arrests for which there are no final dispositions indicated on the record. This record is certified as a true copy of the Criminal History Record Information on file for the assigned State identification number.

In appropriate circumstances, failure of an employer to conduct a criminal check of a prospective employee may be evidence of negligent hiring.[50]

---

50. *See Lingar v. Live-In Companions, Inc.*, 300 N.J. Super. 22, 30-33 (App. Div. 1997) (dicta; under statute and regulations in effect at the time of employee's hiring, records of criminal convictions were not accessible; question whether employer failed to exercise due care in hiring employee by not adequately investigating his background was for the jury based upon the totality of the circumstances; failure to conduct a criminal background check was not in itself determinative).

Chapter 6

The Family Leave Act

I. OVERVIEW

6-1 Generally

The New Jersey Family Leave Act[1] ("FLA") was designed to promote stability and security in the state's evolving family structures:

> The Legislature finds and declares that the number of families in the State in which both parents or a single parent is employed outside of the home has increased dramatically and continues to increase and that due to lack of employment policies to accommodate working parents, many individuals are forced to choose between job security and parenting or providing care for ill family members. The Legislature further finds that it is necessary to promote the economic security of families by guaranteeing jobs to wage earners who choose to take a period of leave upon the birth or placement for adoption of a child or serious health condition of a family member.[2]

Although there is now a federal Family and Medical Leave Act and family leave policies in many other states.[3] New Jersey's FLA has been described as "one of the most far-reaching."[4] It requires public and private employers to provide covered employees up to 12 weeks leave of absence upon the birth or adop-

---

1. N.J.S.A. 34:11B-1 *et seq.* DCR regulations interpreting the FLA are codified at N.J.A.C. 13:14-1.1 *et seq.* Regulations interpreting the Act with respect to employees of state and local governments have been adopted by the Merit System Board and are codified at N.J.A.C. 4A:6-1.21 *et seq.*

2. N.J.S.A. 34:11B-2. "The Act was adopted in 1989 and represents the culmination of a comprehensive legislative effort to maintain the integrity of the family unit and promote flexibility and productivity in the work place. The purpose of the legislation is to adjust public and private policy to accommodate the changing needs of the modern family." *D'Alia v. Allied-Signal Corp.*, 260 N.J. Super. 1, 6 (App. Div. 1992).

3. 42 *Pension & Profit Sharing Report*, No. 4 (April 26, 1991); Goldstein, "Job-Security v. Caretaking," *New Jersey Lawyer,* July-Aug. 1990, at 30.

tion of a child or the serious health condition of a child, parent or spouse. In most cases, it guarantees reinstatement to the same or similar position when leave ends. By its terms, the FLA also requires the continuation of certain employee medical benefits during leave, but that provision has been found pre-empted by federal law with respect to plans subject to the Employee Retirement Income Security Act ("ERISA").[5] However, the Federal Family and Medical Leave Act, which provides largely paralell benefits, requires that coverage under group health plans must be maintained "for the duration of such leave and at the level and under the conditions coverage would have been provided if the employee had continued in employment continuously for the duration of the leave."[6]

Both "child" and "parent" are defined broadly under the Act. Child includes biological, adopted, foster and stepchildren as well as legal wards, all of whom must be either under 18 years of age or incapable of self care because of a physical or mental impairment.[7] A parent is defined as anyone who has a parental relationship with a child as defined by law, including adoptive, foster and stepparents, parents-in-law, and those having custody, guardianship or visitation rights.[8] A "serious health condition" includes any injury, illness, impairment or mental or physical condition requiring either in-patient care or continuing medical supervision or treatment by a health care provider.[9]

Because family leave provided under the Act is dependent upon the employee's need to care for another, rather than upon his own disability, it is separate and distinct from maternity and other forms of disability leave.[10] As a consequence, family leave based upon birth or adoption of a child is available to both men and women. In fact, under the Division of Civil Rights' regulations, more than one employee in a family may be entitled to family leave at the same time, even if they are employed by the same employer.[11] Moreover, the Act specifical-

---

4. Mayer and Beach, "Family Leave Act : Mrs. Cleaver Goes to Work", 125 *N.J.L.J.* 879 (April 5, 1990); "Family Leave Law Takes Effect Amid Division," *The Star Ledger* of Newark, May 7, 1990, p.1; "N.J. a Leader, Leave Act Confounds Attorneys," *National Law Journal*, April 2, 1990, pp.3, 32.

5. See §6-7.

6. 29 U.S.C.A. 2614(c).

7. N.J.S.A. 34: 11B-3(a).

8. N.J.S.A. 34:11B-3(h).

9. N.J.S.A. 34:11B-3(l); N.J.A.C. 13:14-1.2.

10. N.J.S.A. 34:11B-13; N.J.A.C. 13:14-1.6. Family leave was designed to fill the gap left by the Temporary Disability Benefits Law and expand job protections to men and women who want to take time off to care for a baby after the physical disability associated with pregnancy has ended. *D'Alia v. Allied-Signal Corp.*, 260 N.J. Super. 1, 7-8 (App. Div. 1992).

11. N.J.A.C. 13:14-1.12.

ly provides that any rights granted thereunder are in addition to and shall not adversely affect rights provided under the Temporary Disability Benefits Law.[12]

Limitations on the employee rights created by the FLA include notice and verification requirements, restrictions upon moonlighting and non-consecutive leave, and the right to deny leave to certain highly paid employees where substantial and grievous economic injury to business operations would otherwise result.[13]

---

12. N.J.S.A. 34:11B-13. The Temporary Disability Benefits Law is discussed in Chapter 10.

13. N.J.S.A. 34:11B-4(h)(i); N.J.A.C. 13:14-1.9. In an April 1991 poll of 177 executives in attendance at a labor and employment conference, 130 responded to questions about their experience with FLA in its first year. Seventy percent said they had received requests for family leave, and of those, 35 percent said they had received five or more requests for leave. Daily Labor Report, No. 86, p.A-4 (May 3, 1991).

II. COVERAGE

6-2 Employers Subject to FLA

The FLA was phased into effect over a four-year period. On May 4, 1990, it became applicable to employers who employed 100 or more individuals for 20 or more workweeks during the then-current or preceding calendar year. On May 4, 1991, coverage was extended to employers of 75 or more such employees, and on May 4, 1993 coverage will be expanded again to include employers of 50 or more such employees.[14] All public and private employers that employ the requisite number of employees are subject to the Act, including sole proprietorships and joint ventures.[15]

An individual is "employed" within the scope of the FLA if he is working for compensation, including working under an ongoing contractual relationship in which the employer has retained substantial control over employment opportunities or the terms and conditions of employment.[16] The statute itself is silent as to whether employees working outside of New Jersey must be included in determining applicability of the FLA, but regulations promulgated by the DCR require the inclusion of all employees "who have worked each working day for 20 or more workweeks during the current or immediately preceding calendar year," regardless of whether they work out-of-state or within the state, and regardless of whether they themselves are eligible for family leave.[17] The DCR's regulations also provide that under certain circumstances, to be determined on a case-by-case basis, employees of the employer's divisions, subsidiaries and other related entities, must also be included. The four factors listed in the regulation as pertinent to this determination are those traditionally applied in labor law "single employer analyses," *i.e.*:

i. The interrelationship of the employer's operation;

ii. The degree of centralized control of labor relations;

---

14. N.J.S.A. 34:11B-3(f); N.J.A.C. 13:14-1.2. In *Essex Crane Corp. v. Dir., Civ. Rights*, 294 N.J. Super. 101 (App. Div. 1996), the court held that the FLA applies to employers with 50 or more employees regardless of the state in which the employees work. Thus, although the employer had less than 12 employees in New Jersey, the employer was still subject to the FLA where it employed a total of 164 persons, albeit in six states. The United States District Court for the District of New Jersey adopted the *Essex Crane Corp.* analysis in *Callari v. Rehau, Inc.*, F. Supp. (D.N.J. 1998).

15. N.J.S.A. 34:11B-3(f).

16. N.J.S.A. 34:11B-3(d).

17. N.J.A.C. 13:14-1.2-1.3. The Appellate Division and the United States District Court have found this regulation to be valid. See n.14, *supra*.

iii. The existence of common management; and/or

iv. The degree of common ownership or financial control.[18]

6-3 Employees Eligible

An employee is covered under the FLA if he has been employed within the state by the same covered employer for at least 12 months, and for at least 1000 base hours,[19] during the 12-month period immediately preceding the leave.[20] Thus, many part-time as well as full-time employees are covered.[21] The FLA is silent as to what constitutes employment within the state. The DCR's regulations provide that an individual will be considered to be employed within the state if either (1) he works in New Jersey; or (2) he "routinely performs some work in New Jersey and [his] base of operations or the place from which such work is directed and controlled is in New Jersey."[22]

18. N.J.A.C. 13:14-1.3. The four factors in the FLA regulation are the same factors used in the test developed for jurisdictional purposes by the National Labor Relations Board. Courts have looked to that test for guidance in a variety of other contexts in determining whether a corporation may be liable for the employment practices of another corporation as a "single employer." One would expect the single employer cases to provide guidance in application of the FLA regulations, *e.g., See Chaiffetz v. Robertson Research Holding Ltd.*, 798 F.2d 731, 735 (5th Cir. 1986) (Title VII); *Mas Marques v. Digital Equipment Corp.*, 637 F.2d 24, 27 (1st Cir. 1980) (Title VII); *Saulsberry v. Atlantic Richfield Co.*, 673 F. Supp. 811, 815 (N.D. Miss. 1987) (Title VII); *Beckwith v. International Mill Services* 617 F. Supp. 187, 189 (E.D. Pa. 1985) (ADEA); *Nation v. Winn-Dixie Stores, Inc.*, 567 F.Supp. 997, 1010-11 (N.D. Ga. 1983) (Title VII). *See also American Bell, Inc. v. Federation of Tel. Workers*, 736 F.2d 879, 888-89 (3d Cir. 1984) (liability for breach of collective bargaining agreement). In *American Bell, Inc. v. Federation of Tel. Workers*, the Third Circuit observed that complete dominance of one corporation by another is a prerequisite to piercing the corporate veil: "[T]here is no policy of federal labor law" that binds a parent by the subsidiary's actions in labor matters "simply because it controls the subsidiary's stock and participates in the subsidiary's management." 736 F.2d at 886. "The court may only pierce the veil in 'specific, unusual circumstances,' lest it render the theory of limited liability useless." 736 F.2d at 886.

19. "Base hours" are the "employee's regular hours of work excluding overtime, for which an employee receives compensation." N.J.A.C. 13:14-1.2. The Appellate Division has held that hours for which an employee receives Workers Compensation benefits must be included as base hours. *Kenney v. Meadowview Nursing Center*, 308 N.J. Super. 565, 572 (App. Div. 1998).

20. N.J.S.A. 34:11B-3(e); N.J.A.C. 13:14-1.2.

21. If the part-time employee works less than five days a week, the number of days of leave to which the employee is entitled is adjusted accordingly. *See* N.J.A.C. 4A:6-1.21(c)(2)(iv); N.J.A.C. 13:14-1.2. Thus, a part-time employee who normally works four days per week is entitled to up to 48 days of leave. N.J.A.C. 13:14-1.2. This is of particular import when leave is taken non-consecutively, and it is necessary to calculate the leave period in terms of days rather than weeks.

22. N.J.A.C. 13:14-1.2.

III. TAKING LEAVE

6-4 Advance Notice of Leave Required

An employee seeking leave must provide advance notice to his employer.[23] Where the necessity for leave is foreseeable because of the expected birth or adoption of a child, the employee must provide advance notice of the *expected event* in a "reasonable" and "practicable" manner.[24] The DCR's regulations require notice in these circumstances no later than 30 days prior to commencement of the leave, except where emergent circumstances warrant shorter notice.[25]

An employee who takes leave in connection with the serious health condition of a family member must provide his employer notice at least 15 days prior to commencement of the leave, except where emergent circumstances warrant a shorter period of time.[26]

The Appellate Division has found the notice requirement satisfied even where the employee does not mention the Family Leave Act, so long as the information given is sufficient to alert the employer of the employee's plan to take time off for a purpose covered by the act. *D'Alia v. Allied-Signal Corp.*,[27] ("an employer must grant an employee all of the rights accorded by the statute once the employee apprises it of his or her desire to take a family leave because of (1) the birth or adoption of a child, or (2) the serious health condition of a family member").

Noting the employer's obligations to post notices and use other appropriate means to advise employees of their rights under the Family Leave Act, the court found that it "is incumbent upon the employer to apprise the employee of his or her rights and to effectuate them once the employee requests a leave of absence for any of the reasons provided by the Act." *Id.* at 10. Thus the court held that the employee in that case provided sufficient notice when she submitted disability forms and advised of her intent to take time off for the birth and care of her child. *See also Senape v. Middlesex County, Adult Jail Facility*[28], (employee's written and oral requests for leave to take care of a family member with a serious health condition were sufficient to raise a claim under the Act).

---

23. N.J.S.A. 34:11B-4.
24. N.J.S.A. 34:11B-4(f).
25. N.J.A.C. 13:14-1.5(c)(1).
26. N.J.A.C. 13:14-1.5(d)(1).
27. 260 N.J. Super. 1 (App. Div. 1992).
28. 95 N.J.A.R.2d (CSV) 297, 299 (1995).

6-5 Circumstances Warranting Leave

Eligible employees are entitled to a leave of absence for up to 12 weeks in order "to provide care made necessary by reason of " either: (1) the birth or placement for adoption of a child; or (2) the serious health condition of a child, parent or spouse.[29] All terms are defined broadly. A "child" within the scope of the FLA is a biological, adopted, or foster child, step-child, or legal ward, who is either less than 18 years of age or incapable of self-care because of a physical or mental impairment.[30] A "parent" is one who is the "biological parent, adoptive parent, foster parent, step-parent, parent-in-law or legal guardian, having a 'parent-child relationship' with a child as defined by law, or having sole or joint legal or physical custody, care, guardianship or visitation with a child."[31]

A "serious health condition" includes any injury, illness, impairment, or physical or mental condition requiring either (a) in-patient care in a hospital, hospice, or residential medical care facility; or (2) continuing medical treatment or continuing medical supervision by a health care provider.[32] And, perhaps most controversial, "care" is defined as including, but not limited to:

> physical care, emotional support, visitation, assistance in treatment, transportation, assistance with essential daily living matters and personal attendant services.[33]

An employer may require that a request for leave be supported by the certification of a duly licensed health care provider or other health care provider determined by the Director of the DCR to be capable of providing adequate

---

29. N.J.S.A. 34:11B-3(i),-4.

30. N.J.S.A. 34:11B-3(a); see N.J.A.C. 13:14-1.2.

31. N.J.S.A. 34:11B-3(h). The regulations combine the statutory definitions of parent and child, providing that:

> "Child," for the purpose of determining whether an employee is eligible for family leave because of such employee's parental status, means a child as defined in the Act to whom such employee is a biological parent, adoptive parent, foster parent, step-parent, or legal guardian, or has a "parent-child relationship" with a child as defined by law, or has sole or joint legal or physical custody, care, guardianship or visitation with a child.

N.J.A.C. 13:14-1.2.

32. N.J.S.A. 34:11B-3(l). The DCR regulations contain an identical definition of serious health condition. N.J.A.C. 13:14-1.2. In response to concerns that this definition might be construed to include common childhood illnesses such as the flu, DCR stated: "The extent to which a serious health condition will include childhood and other illnesses will be decided on a case-by-case basis, in accordance with the definition provided by the Legislature." 23 N.J.R. 2864 (Sept. 16, 1991).

33. N.J.A.C. 13:14-1.2. The DCR's response to a comment on its regulation when proposed suggests an employee would be considered "caring" for a child within the scope of the FLA by visiting her in a hospital and thereby providing emotional support, even though the child was receiving all physical and medical care from the hospital staff. 23 N.J.R. 2864 (Sept. 16, 1991).

certification.[34] Where the certification is for the serious health condition of a family member of the employee, it should include (a) the date on which the health condition commenced; (b) the probable duration of the condition; and (c) the medical facts within the provider's knowledge regarding the condition.[35] Where the certification is for the birth or placement of a child, it need only state the date of birth or placement for adoption.[36]

If the employer has reason to doubt a certification as to the health of a family member, it may, at its own expense, require the employee to obtain a second opinion from a health care provider designated or approved by the employer, but not employed by it on a regular basis.[37] If the second opinion is in conflict with the initial certification, the employer may require the employee to obtain a third opinion from a health care provider chosen or approved by both the employer and employee.[38] The conclusions of this third health care provider are binding upon both parties.[39]

The DCR's regulations also permit an employer to require the employee to sign a form of certification attesting that he is taking family leave for the birth or adoption of a child, or to care for a family member because of that family member's serious health condition, whichever is applicable.[40] An employer may not, however, require the employee to sign or otherwise submit a form of certification attesting to any additional facts, including the fact of eligibility for leave.[41]

An employee who refuses to provide such a certification may be denied leave,[42] and an employee who provides a false certification may be subjected to reasonable disciplinary measures.[43] The form of certification utilized by an employer must contain a warning of the consequences of providing false information or refusing to sign.[44]

---

34. N.J.S.A. 34:11B-4(e)(1); N.J.A.C. 13:14-1.10(b).

35. N.J.S.A. 34:11-B-4(e)(1); N.J.A.C. 13:14-1.10(b)(1). The provisions of the statute and the regulation are the same. *See Senape v. Middlesex County, Adult Jail Facility*, 95 N.J.A.R.2d (CSV) 297, 299 (1995) (doctor's notes which contained neither the date on which the serious health condition commenced nor its probable duration were inadequate).

36. N.J.S.A. 34:11-B-4(e)(2); N.J.A.C. 13:14-1.10(b)(2). The provisions of the statute and the regulation are the same.

37. N.J.S.A. 34:11B-4(e)(2); N.J.A.C. 13:14-1.10(b)(3).

38. N.J.S.A. 34:11B-4(e)(2); N.J.A.C. 13:14-1.10(b)(3). The employer must also bear the cost of obtaining the third opinion. *Id.*

39. N.J.A.C. 13:14-1.10(b)(3).

40. *Id.*

41. N.J.A.C. 13:14-1.10(a).

42. *Id.*

43. N.J.A.C. 13:14-1.10(a)(1).

44. *Id.*

6-6 Duration and Timing of Leave

An eligible employee is entitled to 12 weeks of leave in any 24-month period.[45] Leave based upon the birth or adoption of a child may begin at any time within one year of the date of birth or placement.[46] Under certain circumstances, leave based upon either the birth or placement of a child or the serious health condition of a family member may be taken intermittently or pursuant to a reduced leave schedule.

6-6:1 Intermittent Leave

Intermittent leave is leave taken in intervals lasting at least one week but less than 12 weeks.[47] If the leave is for the birth or adoption of a child who does not suffer from a serious health condition, leave may not be taken on an intermittent basis unless both employer and employee agree.[48] Where leave is based upon the serious health condition of a family member, however, it may be taken intermittently at the option of the employee if (1) the intermittent leave is medically necessary; (2) the leave is taken within a 12-month period for each episode of a serious health condition, (3) the employee gives the employer prior notice of the leave in a manner that is "reasonable" and "practicable"; and (4) the employee makes a reasonable effort to schedule the intermittent leave so as not to disrupt unduly the employer's operations.[49] According to the regulations, an intermittent leave disrupts unduly the employer's operations if it:

> would cause the employer measurable harm, economic or otherwise, significantly greater than any measurable harm which would befall the employer if the same employee was granted a consecutive leave.[50]

The burden of proving such a disruption is on the employer.[51]

If intermittent leave is taken with respect to more than one serious health condition episode, it must be taken within a consecutive 24-month period, or until the employee's 12 weeks of leave are used, whichever is sooner.[52]

---

45. N.J.S.A. 34:11B-4.
46. N.J.S.A. 34:11B-4(c).
47. N.J.S.A. 34:11B-4(a); *see also*, N.J.A.C. 13:14-1.2.
48. N.J.S.A. 34:11B-4(b).
49. N.J.S.A. 34:11B-4(a).
50. N.J.A.C. 13:14-1.2.
51. *Id.*
52. N.J.A.C. 13:14-1.5(d)(2).

6-6:2 Reduced Leave Schedule

Employees who take leave for the birth or adoption of a healthy child may, with the agreement of their employer, take a "reduced leave schedule." [53] Employees who take leave for any other reason are entitled to take a reduced leave schedule at their own option, whether their employer agrees or not.[54]

A reduced leave schedule is one which permits an employee to work less than his usual number of hours per workweek, but not less than his usual number of hours per workday, unless the employer and employee agree otherwise.[55] The fact that leave is taken upon a reduced leave schedule does not lessen the amount of leave to which the employee is entitled.[56] However, a reduced leave schedule may not exceed 24 consecutive weeks,[57] and only one reduced leave may be taken during any 24-month period.[58] Thus, if less than the full leave period is taken on a reduced schedule, any remaining leave may be taken only on a consecutive or an intermittent basis.[59]

As with intermittent leaves, an employee taking leave on a reduced basis must make reasonable efforts to schedule the leave so as not to disrupt unduly the employer's operations.[60] The employee must also provide prior notice to the employer of "the care, medical treatment, or continuing supervision by a health care provider necessary due to a serious health condition of a family member, in a manner which is reasonable and practicable."[61]

6-6:3 Payment During Leave

Leave required to be provided under the FLA need not be paid; it may be paid, unpaid, or partially paid.[62] If an employer provides paid family leave for less than 12 weeks, the additional weeks required to comply with the FLA may be unpaid.[63]

---

53. N.J.S.A. 34:11B-5.
54. *Id.*
55. N.J.S.A. 34:11B-3(k).
56. N.J.S.A. 34:11B-5(b).
57. N.J.S.A. 34:11B-5(a); N.J.A.C. 13:14-1.5(d)(3).
58. N.J.A.C. 13:14-1.5(d)(3).
59. *Id.*
60. N.J.S.A. 34:11B-5(b); N.J.A.C. 13:14-1.2.
61. N.J.S.A. 34:11B-5(b).
62. N.J.S.A. 34:11B-4(d).
63. *Id.*

Informal guidelines issued by the DCR after the FLA's enactment allowed employers to require employees to exhaust accrued paid leave during family leave, provided only that there was no applicable employment contract or collective bargaining agreement to the contrary.

The DCR's final regulations, in contrast, provide that only employers with an established practice are permitted to require exhaustion. Thus, an employer with a past practice requiring employees to use vacation days and personal days before taking unpaid leave may require employees to do the same with respect to family leave, thus preventing employees from extending their absence from the workplace by taking 12 weeks' family leave followed by several weeks of vacation.[64] But employers with a different past policy, or even no past policy, are prohibited by the regulations from requiring such exhaustion. The regulations leave it to the employee to decide in each instance whether or not to use vacation or other accrued paid leave as part of his family leave.[65]

6-7 Continuation of Benefits During Leave

Section 8 of the FLA provides that during the period of family leave, the employer "shall maintain coverage under any group health insurance policy, group subscriber contract or health care plan at the level and under the conditions" coverage would have been provided had the employee not taken leave.[66] It also requires that all other employment benefits be provided in accordance with the employer's policy on benefits to employees on temporary leave.[67] If benefits are normally dependent upon the type of leave taken, the statute requires that they be

---

64. N.J.A.C. 13:14-1.7.

65. The regulation provides in part:

> In situations where an employer does not have an established policy in this regard, the employee shall be entitled to utilize any accrued paid leave as part of the family leave. If such an employee determines not to utilize accrued paid leave, the employer shall not require such employee to utilize any accrued paid leave as part of the leave. Where an employer maintains leaves of absence which provide different policies and/or practices regarding the use of accrued paid leave, the employer shall treat family leave in the same manner as that other leave of absence which most closely resembles family leave.

N.J.A.C. 13:14-1.7.

66. N.J.S.A. 34:11B-8. As discussed *infra*, this requirement has been found pre-empted with respect to plans subject to the Employee Retirement Income Security Act. 29 U.S.C. §§1001, *et seq*.

DCR's regulations define a "health insurance policy" as including "all health benefits provided by an employer to an employee. Health benefits includes the opportunity provided by an employer to participate in a group health plan." N.J.A.C. 13:14-1.2.

67. N.J.S.A. 34:11B-8.

provided in the same manner as that governing the leave most closely resembling family leave.[68]

In *New Jersey Business & Industry Association v. State of New Jersey*,[69] the Law Division found §8(a) of the FLA—requiring continuation of health benefits during leave—pre-empted by the Employee Retirement Income Security Act of 1974[70] (hereinafter "ERISA"), insofar as it applies to plans subject to the federal law. The court stressed, however, that §8(a) would remain in effect with respect to plans not subject to ERISA, such as plans maintained by government employers.[71] That ruling is in accord with ERISA's broad pre-emption provisions and United States Supreme Court interpretations of same.

ERISA regulates both employee pension benefit plans and employee welfare benefit plans, the latter being defined as any plan, program or fund designed to provide "medical, surgical, or hospital care or benefits, or benefits in the event of sickness, accident, disability, death or unemployment, or vacation benefits, apprenticeship or other training programs, or day care centers, scholarship funds, or prepaid legal services. ..."[72] Under §514(a) of ERISA, state laws which "relate to" an employee benefit plan covered by the federal law are expressly pre-empted.[73] A state law is deemed to relate to an employee-benefit plan "if it has a connection with or reference to such a plan."[74]

---

68. *Id.*; *see also* N.J.A.C. 13:14-1.7.

69. 249 N.J.Super. 513 (Law Div. 1991).

70. 29 U.S.C. §§1001 *et seq.*

71. 249 N.J.Super. at 520-21.

72. 29 U.S.C. §1002(1).

73. 29 U.S.C. §1144(a). Plans maintained "solely for the purpose of complying with applicable workmen's compensation or unemployment compensation or disability insurance laws" are not pre-empted under the Act. 29 U.S.C. §1003(b)(3). Nor are state laws regulating insurance pre-empted. 29 U.S.C. §1144(b)(2)(A). However, neither an employee benefit plan covered by the Act nor a trust established under such a plan may be considered an insurance company for purposes of a state law purporting to regulate insurance companies or insurance contracts. 29 U.S.C. §1144(b)(2)(B).

74. *Shaw v. Delta Air Lines, Inc.*,463 U.S. 85, 96-97 (1983). *See, e.g.*, *Alessi v. Raybestos-Manhattan, Inc.*, 451 U.S. 504 (1981) (N.J. statute prohibiting integration of workers' compensation and pension benefits pre-empted); *Metropolitan Life Ins. Co. v. Taylor*, 481 U.S. 58 (1987) (common law contract claims pre-empted); *Metropolitan Life Ins. Co. v. Commonwealth of Massachusetts*, 471 U.S. 724 (1985) (Massachusetts statute requiring insurance policies to provide specified minimum benefits not pre-empted); *Fort Halifax Packing Co. v. Coyne*, 482 U.S. 1 (1987) (Maine statute requiring one-time severance payment upon plant closing not pre-empted).

6-8 Employment During Leave

Employees are prohibited from engaging in full-time employment during family leave, unless the employment began before the leave commenced.[75] The FLA does not address part-time employment during leave.

The DCR's regulations provide that employees may commence part-time employment while they are on leave, so long as it does not exceed half the regularly scheduled hours worked for the employer from whom the employee is on leave.[76] They further provide that an employee may continue part-time employment during leave at the same number of hours for which he was scheduled before leave commenced.[77] Employers are barred by the regulations from prohibiting part-time employment during family leave.[78]

6-9 Reinstatement

Upon an employee's return from leave, the employer must restore him to his former position or to one which is comparable in terms of pay, seniority, employment benefits and other terms and conditions of employment.[79] However, the employee is not entitled to reinstatement if during the leave period he would have lost his position due to a reduction in force or the legitimate operation of a bona fide system of layoff and recall, including one established under a collective bargaining agreement.[80] All rights under such a layoff and recall system are retained by the employee to the same extent they would have been had he not taken leave.[81]

---

75. N.J.S.A. 34:11B-4(g). DCR's regulations would also prohibit full-time employment that began prior to the leave if it is barred by law. N.J.A.C. 13:14-1.8.

76. N.J.A.C. 13:14-1.8.

77. *Id.*

78. *Id.*

79. N.J.S.A. 34:11B-7; N.J.A.C. 13:14-1.11(a). *See generally D'Alia v. Allied-Signal Corp.*, 260 N.J. Super. 1, 11 (App. Div. 1992) (job functions and number of subordinate employees may be among the factors considered in determining whether a position is equivalent)

80. N.J.S.A. 34:11B-7; N.J.A.C. 13:14-1.11(b). *Marzano v. Computer Science Corp., Inc.*, 91 F.3d 497, 511-12 (3d Cir. 1996) (court determined that there was a genuine issue of fact regarding whether or not the employer actually experienced a reduction in force which thereby precluded the court from applying the reduction in force exception to bar plaintiff's claim); *Leahey v. Singer Sewing Co.*, 302 N.J. Super. 68, 79-81 (Law Div. 1996) (setting forth factors to consider in determining whether an employer experienced a reduction in force which would enable it to rely upon the reduction in force exception in defense of a FLA claim).

81. N.J.S.A. 34:11B-7; N.J.A.C. 13:14-1.11(b).

6-10 Grounds for Denial or Revocation of Leave

As discussed in §6-5 request for leave may be denied if the employee refuses to sign a certification of the reason for the leave, or provides false certification of same.

Leave may also be denied to certain high level salaried employees on the basis of the employer's needs and without employee fault. Three statutory prerequisites must be met. First, the employee must be a salaried employee who is among the highest paid five percent of the employer's employees or one of the seven highest paid employees of the employer, whichever is larger.[82] Second, the denial must be "necessary to prevent substantial and grievous economic injury to the employer's operations."[83] And third, the employer must notify the employee of its intent to deny the leave at the time it determines the denial is necessary.[84] It appears that an employer may utilize this subsection to revoke leave after an employee has already left the work place; the statute provides that an employee who receives notice of his employer's intent to invoke this exception after his leave has commenced must return to work within 10 days.[85]

The DCR's regulations with respect to this section are particularly significant. They define "substantial and grievous economic injury" as:

> economic harm that will befall an employer which is of such a magnitude that it would substantially and adversely affect the employer's operations, considerably beyond the costs which are associated with replacing an employee who has requested family leave.[86]

That definition is substantially broader than one which was in DCR's earlier proposed regulations, and which limited the exception to injuries that would imperil the continued business operations of the employer.[87]

---

82. N.J.S.A. 34:11B-4(h)(1); N.J.A.C. 13:14-1.9. Under DCR's regulations, employees would be ranked according to their "base salary," defined as gross salary excluding overtime and bonuses and including amounts withheld for taxes, FICA and employee health and pension plan contributions. N.J.A.C. 13:14-1.9; 13:14-1.2.

The regulations also require that both New Jersey and out-of-state employees be included in the salary ranking. N.J.A.C. 13:14-1.9(a)(1).

83. N.J.S.A. 34:11B-4(h)(2). The regulations place the burden of proving this on the employer, rewriting the second prong of the test to be: "2. The employer can demonstrate that the granting of the leave would cause a substantial and grievous economic injury to the employer's operations." N.J.A.C. 13:14-1.9(a)(2).

84. N.J.S.A. 34:11B-4(h)(3); N.J.A.C. 13:14-1.9(a)(3).

85. N.J.S.A. 34:11B-4(i).

86. N.J.A.C. 13:14-1.2.

87. 22 N.J.R. 2131 (July 16, 1990).

IV. POSTING

6-11 Posting

Employers must post a conspicuous notice apprising employees of their rights and obligations under the Act and use "other appropriate means to keep its employees so informed." [88] A DCR form notice is reproduced on the next page. The FLA does not specifically set forth what other steps should be taken to keep employees informed. It has been suggested that employers should include a discussion of the FLA's provisions in any policy handbook or newsletter regarding the employer's discrimination policy.[89]

88. N.J.S.A. 34:11B-6.

89. Goldstein, "Job-Security v. Caretaking," *New Jersey Lawyer*, July-Aug. 1990, at 33.

6-11:1 Sample Notice

NOTICE

Family Leave Act

Pursuant to the Family Leave Act (N.J.S.A. 34:11B-l, et seq.), most employees who have worked at least 1,000 hours during the last 12 months are eligible to receive an unpaid leave of absence for a period not to exceed 12 weeks in a 24-month period.

Leave may be taken only for the birth or adoption of a child, or the serious health condition of a family member (i.e., child, parent or spouse).

Any leave granted to an eligible employee under this Act due to the serious health condition of a family member may be taken consecutively or intermittently, depending upon the legitimate needs of the employee. Any leave granted due to the birth or adoption of a child must be taken consecutively unless otherwise agreed to by the employer and must begin within one year of the adoption or birth.

The Act does not require an employer to grant more than 12 weeks of leave in any consecutive 24-month period.

Eligible employees must provide prior notice to the employer if requesting a leave of absence. under this Act. The employer has the right to request that an employee provide a certification issued by a health care provider in order to ensure that the employee meets the eligibility requirements.

The employer may deny a request for leave made by an otherwise eligible employee, if the employee is among the highest paid five percent or is one of the seven highest paid employees of the company, whichever is greater, and the employer can demonstrate that the leave will cause substantial and grievous economic injury to its operations.

Violations should be reported to the nearest office

- 31 Clinton Street
  P.O. Box 46001
  Newark, New Jersey 07102
  (201) 648-2700
- 1548 Atlantic Avenue
  Atlantic City, New Jersey 08401
  (609) 441-3100
- 383 West State St. CN 090
  Trenton, New Jersey 08625
  (609) 292-4605
- Camden State Office Building
  101 Haddon Avenue
  Camden, New Jersey 08103
  (609) 757-2850
- 370 Broadway
  Paterson, New Jersey 07501
  (201) 977-4500

CIVIL RIGHTS

V. ENFORCEMENT

6-12 Enforcement

Section 9 of the FLA makes it unlawful for an employer to withhold benefits or otherwise interfere with the exercise of employee rights provided thereunder. It also prohibits employers from discharging or otherwise discriminating against an individual for opposing an unlawful practice under the Act, or for instituting, testifying or giving information in connection with charges or proceedings relating to a right provided by the Act.[90]

A penalty of up to $2,000 for the first offense and up to $5,000 for each subsequent offense may be recovered in a summary civil action by the Attorney General.[91]

A private cause of action may also be maintained; the aggrieved party may either file an administrative complaint with the DCR or institute a civil action in Superior Court.[92] All remedies provided for in N.J.S.A. 10:5-17 are available under FLA, including compensatory damages and reinstatement with back pay.[93]

Punitive damages are also available, but they are capped at $10,000 per person, except in class actions or complaints by the Director of the DCR, where they may not exceed the lesser of $500,000 or one percent of the defendant's net worth.[94] The prevailing party may also recover its reasonable attorneys' fees as part of the assessment of costs, except that an employer may not be awarded attorneys fees unless the action was brought in bad faith.[95]

---

90. N.J.S.A. 34:11B-9.

91. N.J.S.A. 34:11B-10; N.J.S.A. 2A:58-1 *et seq.*

92. N.J.S.A. 34:11B-11. Complaints filed with the Division on Civil Rights are to be processed in the same manner as those filed under the Law Against Discrimination, N.J.S.A. 10:5-1, et seq., N.J.A.C. 34:14-1.16.

93. N.J.S.A. 34:11B-11.

94. *Id.* Among the relevant factors which must be considered by the Director of the DCR or the court in assessing punitive damages are (1) the compensatory damages awarded, (2) the amount of the civil penalty imposed, (3) the frequency of violation, (4) the number of persons affected by the violation, (5) the employer's resources and (6) the extent to which the violation was intentional. N.J.S.A. 34:11B-11. For a complete discussion of the remedies available under N.J.S.A. 10:5-17, see Chapter 4, §4-54.

95. N.J.S.A. 34A:11B-12.

6-13 TABLE 1: COMPARISON OF NEW JERSEY FAMILY LEAVE ACT AND FEDERAL FAMILY AND MEDICAL LEAVE ACT*

NEW JERSEY FAMILY LEAVE ACT (Citations are to Sections of the Main Volume of This Book)	**FAMILY AND MEDICAL LEAVE ACT** (Citations are to 29 U.S.C.)
§6-2 Employers Subject to FLA As of May 4, 1993, all employers of 50 or more "employees" (individuals working 20 or more workweeks during the current or preceding year). Pursuant to Division on Civil Rights regulations, employees outside of New Jersey are included in this calculation.	**§2611(4)(A)** All employers who: (1) Are engaged in commerce; and (2) Employed 50 or more employees during each of 20 or more workweeks during the current or preceding year. **Included**: 1. Those who act for the employer 2. Successors of the employer 3. Public agencies

*The FMLA expressly saves state leave laws which provide greater family or medical leave rights than does the FMLA from pre-emption. 29 U.S.C. § 2651(b). As a result, employees are entitled to leave if the conditions under *either* the FMLA or FLA are met, subject to the requirements of whichever statute applies. If the leave qualifies under both FMLA and FLA, the leave used counts concurrently against the employee's entitlement under each law. *See* 29 C.F.R. § 825.701. *Cf.* N.J.A.C. § 4A:6-1.22 (chart created by state personnel office for its use regarding state employees, comparing FMLA and FLA for relative favorability to employees).

NEW JERSEY FAMILY LEAVE ACT (Citations are to Sections of the Main Volume of This Book)	FAMILY AND MEDICAL LEAVE ACT (Citations are to 29 U.S.C.)
§6-3 Employees Eligible Employed by a covered employer within the state for at least 12 months and for at least 1,000 base hours during the 12 month period immediately preceding leave.	**§2611(1)** Employed by the employer from whom leave is sought (1) for at least 12 months and (2) for at least 1,250 hours during the previous 12 - month period. **Excluded:** Employees at worksites with fewer than 50 employees if the total number of employees of that employer within 75 miles is less than 50.

*The FMLA expressly saves state leave laws which provide greater family or medical leave rights than does the FMLA from pre-emption. 29 U.S.C. § 2651(b). As a result, employees are entitled to leave if the conditions under *either* the FMLA or FLA are met, subject to the requirements of whichever statute applies. If the leave qualifies under both FMLA and FLA, the leave used counts concurrently against the employee's entitlement under each law. *See* 29 C.F.R. § 825.701. *Cf.* N.J.A.C. § 4A:6-1.22 (chart created by state personnel office for its use regarding state employees, comparing FMLA and FLA for relative favorability to employees).

NEW JERSEY FAMILY LEAVE ACT (Citations are to Sections of the Main Volume of This Book)	FAMILY AND MEDICAL LEAVE ACT (Citations are to 29 U.S.C.)
§6-4 Advance Notice of Leave Required Expected birth or adoption • "reasonable" and "practicable" notice (interpreted in DCR regulations as requiring 30 days except in emergencies) Serious health condition • 15 days Emergencies • "reasonable" and "practicable"	**§2612(e)** Expected birth or adoption • not less than 30 days, but if date of birth or placement requires leave to begin earlier, "practicable" notice Serious health condition that is foreseeable based upon planned medical treatment • not less than 30 days, but if date of treatment requires leave to begin earlier, "practicable" notice • employee required to make reasonable effort to schedule treatment so as not to disrupt unduly the employer's operations, subject to approval of the health care provider

*The FMLA expressly saves state leave laws which provide greater family or medical leave rights than does the FMLA from pre-emption. 29 U.S.C. § 2651(b). As a result, employees are entitled to leave if the conditions under *either* the FMLA or FLA are met, subject to the requirements of whichever statute applies. If the leave qualifies under both FMLA and FLA, the leave used counts concurrently against the employee's entitlement under each law. *See* 29 C.F.R. § 825.701. *Cf.* N.J.A.C. § 4A:6-1.22 (chart created by state personnel office for its use regarding state employees, comparing FMLA and FLA for relative favorability to employees).

NEW JERSEY FAMILY LEAVE ACT **(Citations are to Sections of the Main Volume of This Book)**	**FAMILY AND MEDICAL LEAVE ACT** **(Citations are to 29 U.S.C.)**
§6-5 Circumstances Warranting Leave **Employee Certification** Employees may be required to certify as to the reason for leave. **Health Care Certification** Employers may require certification from a duly licensed health care provider. If for a serious health condition, it should include: 1. date the condition began 2. probable duration 3. medical facts regarding the condition If for birth or adoption, only the expected date of birth or placement need be included. **Second Opinion** Employer may require second opinion at its own expense...If that conflicts with the original certification, a third and binding opinion may be obtained at employer cost.	**§2613** **Health Care Certification** Employers may require certification from the health care provider. It is sufficient if it includes the following: 1. date the condition began 2. probable duration 3. medical facts regarding the condition 4. when leave is sought for caregiving, a statement that the employee is needed to give care and the amount of time for which he is needed. 5. when leave is for the employee's health condition, a statement that the employee is unable to perform the functions of his position. 6. when leave is sought on an intermittent or reduced basis, a statement that the intermittent or reduced schedule is necessary and its expected duration. **Second Opinion** Employer may require second opinion at its own expense...If that conflicts with the original certification, a third and binding opinion may be obtained at employer cost.

NEW JERSEY FAMILY LEAVE ACT (Citations are to Sections of the Main Volume of This Book)	**FAMILY AND MEDICAL LEAVE ACT (Citations are to 29 U.S.C.)**
§6-5 Circumstances Warranting Leave Birth or adoption of child. Serious health condition of a child, parent or spouse. [Note that under the state law, parent-in-law is included in the definition of parent.]	**§2612(1)** Birth of a son or daughter and to care for that son or daughter. Placement of son or daughter with the employee for adoption or foster care. Serious health condition of a spouse, son, daughter or parent for which employee will render care. Serious health condition of employee which renders him unable to perform functions of his position.
§6-6 Duration and Timing of Leave 12 weeks in any 24 month period. Leave for birth or adoption may *begin* at any time within one year of birth or placement.	**§2612** 12 weeks during any 12-month period. Entitlement to leave for birth or adoption expires after 12 months; *i.e.*, it must be *concluded* in 12 months. 29 C.F.R. §825.201.

*The FMLA expressly saves state leave laws which provide greater family or medical leave rights than does the FMLA from pre-emption. 29 U.S.C. § 2651(b). As a result, employees are entitled to leave if the conditions under *either* the FMLA or FLA are met, subject to the requirements of whichever statute applies. If the leave qualifies under both FMLA and FLA, the leave used counts concurrently against the employee's entitlement under each law. *See* 29 C.F.R. § 825.701. *Cf.* N.J.A.C. § 4A:6-1.22 (chart created by state personnel office for its use regarding state employees, comparing FMLA and FLA for relative favorability to employees).

NEW JERSEY FAMILY LEAVE ACT (Citations are to Sections of the Main Volume of This Book)	FAMILY AND MEDICAL LEAVE ACT (Citations are to 29 U.S.C.)
§6-6:1 Intermittent Leave	**§2612(b)**
Intermittent leave is taken in intervals of at least one week but less than 12 weeks. Absent agrement between employer and employee, available only for serious medical conditions and only if: • medically necessary • taken within a 12-month period for each health condition • employee gives "reasonable" and "practicable" notice • employee makes reasonable effort not to disrupt unduly the employer's operations	Intermittent leave is leave taken by the hour, day or week as the employee's needs dictate. 29 C.F.R. §825.203(b). • Not available for healthy births or adoptions unless the employer agrees • Available for serious medical conditions where medically necessary • Should not result in a reduction of the total amount of leave available • Where medical need for intermittent leave is foreseeable, employee may be required to transfer temporarily into an alternative position

*The FMLA expressly saves state leave laws which provide greater family or medical leave rights than does the FMLA from pre-emption. 29 U.S.C. § 2651(b). As a result, employees are entitled to leave if the conditions under *either* the FMLA or FLA are met, subject to the requirements of whichever statute applies. If the leave qualifies under both FMLA and FLA, the leave used counts concurrently against the employee's entitlement under each law. *See* 29 C.F.R. § 825.701. *Cf.* N.J.A.C. § 4A:6-1.22 (chart created by state personnel office for its use regarding state employees, comparing FMLA and FLA for relative favorability to employees).

<table>
<tr><th>NEW JERSEY
FAMILY LEAVE ACT
(Citations are to Sections of the Main Volume of This Book)</th><th>FAMILY AND MEDICAL
LEAVE ACT
(Citations are to 29 U.S.C.)</th></tr>
<tr><td>§6-6:2 Reduced Leave Schedule

Reduced schedule leave permits the employee to work fewer hours per week, but not fewer hours per workday (unless employer and employee agree otherwise).
• Not available for healthy births or adoptions unless the employer agrees
• Reduced leave schedule may not exceed 24 consecutive weeks
• Only one reduced leave may be taken during any 24-month period.</td><td>§2611(9); §2612(b)

Reduced leave under FMLA includes any leave schedule that reduces the usual number of hours per workweek, or hours per workday of an employee. 29 C.F.R. §825.203(c).
• Not available for healthy births or adoptions unless the employer agrees
• Available for serious medical conditions where medically necessary
• Should not result in a reduction of the total amount of leave available
• Where medical need for reduced leave is foreseeable, employee may be required to transfer temporarily into an alternative position</td></tr>
<tr><td>§6-6:3 Payment During Leave

Leave may be paid or unpaid.</td><td>§2612(c)

Leave may be paid or unpaid.</td></tr>
<tr><td>§6-7 Continuation of Benefits During Leave

Section 8 of the FLA requires the continuation of benefits during leave. It was found pre-empted by ERISA with respect to benefit plans subject to that statute.</td><td>§2614(c)

Coverage under group health plans must be maintained. However, if the employee fails to return from leave the cost of benefits must be repaid, unless the failure is due to circumstances beyond his control, such as continued illness.</td></tr>
</table>

NEW JERSEY FAMILY LEAVE ACT (Citations are to Sections of the Main Volume of This Book)	FAMILY AND MEDICAL LEAVE ACT (Citations are to 29 U.S.C.)
§6-8 Employment During Leave Full-time employment is prohibited. • DCR regulations state that certain part-time employment is permitted.	

*The FMLA expressly saves state leave laws which provide greater family or medical leave rights than does the FMLA from pre-emption. 29 U.S.C. § 2651(b). As a result, employees are entitled to leave if the conditions under *either* the FMLA or FLA are met, subject to the requirements of whichever statute applies. If the leave qualifies under both FMLA and FLA, the leave used counts concurrently against the employee's entitlement under each law. *See* 29 C.F.R. § 825.701. *Cf.* N.J.A.C. § 4A:6-1.22 (chart created by state personnel office for its use regarding state employees, comparing FMLA and FLA for relative favorability to employees).

NEW JERSEY FAMILY LEAVE ACT (Citations are to Sections of the Main Volume of This Book)	FAMILY AND MEDICAL LEAVE ACT (Citations are to 29 U.S.C.)
§6-9 Reinstatement	**§2614(a); §2614(b)**
Upon return from family leave the employee normally must be reinstated to his former position or a position that is "comparable" in terms of pay, seniority, benefits, and other terms and conditions of employment. Reinstatement is not required where a reduction in force has occurred.	Upon return from family leave the employee normally must be reinstated to his former position or an "equivalent" position with equivalent employment benefits, pay, and other terms and conditions of employment. Restoration may be denied to certain highly paid employees if: • necessary to prevent substantial and grievous economic injury to the employer's operations • the employer notifies the employee of its intent to deny restoration at the time it determines that such injury would occur; and • in any case in which the leave has commenced, the employee elects not to return to employment after receiving such notice Reinstatement is not required where the employee would have been laid off during the leave. 29 C.F.R. §825.216(a).

*The FMLA expressly saves state leave laws which provide greater family or medical leave rights than does the FMLA from pre-emption. 29 U.S.C. § 2651(b). As a result, employees are entitled to leave if the conditions under *either* the FMLA or FLA are met, subject to the requirements of whichever statute applies. If the leave qualifies under both FMLA and FLA, the leave used counts concurrently against the employee's entitlement under each law. *See* 29 C.F.R. § 825.701. *Cf.* N.J.A.C. § 4A:6-1.22 (chart created by state personnel office for its use regarding state employees, comparing FMLA and FLA for relative favorability to employees).

NEW JERSEY FAMILY LEAVE ACT (Citations are to Sections of the Main Volume of This Book)	**FAMILY AND MEDICAL LEAVE ACT** (Citations are to 29 U.S.C.)
6-10 Grounds for Denial or Revocation of Leave Leave may be denied if: • Employee refuses to certify reason for leave • Employee falsely certifies reason for leave • Employee is high level and essential -among highest paid 5% or one of 7 highest paid -denial of leave is necessary to prevent substantial and grievous economic injury to the employer's operations -employer must notify employee of its intent when the decision to deny leave is made	The FMLA does not restrict key employees' ability to take leave.

*The FMLA expressly saves state leave laws which provide greater family or medical leave rights than does the FMLA from pre-emption. 29 U.S.C. § 2651(b). As a result, employees are entitled to leave if the conditions under *either* the FMLA or FLA are met, subject to the requirements of whichever statute applies. If the leave qualifies under both FMLA and FLA, the leave used counts concurrently against the employee's entitlement under each law. *See* 29 C.F.R. § 825.701. *Cf.* N.J.A.C. § 4A:6-1.22 (chart created by state personnel office for its use regarding state employees, comparing FMLA and FLA for relative favorability to employees).

NEW JERSEY FAMILY LEAVE ACT (Citations are to Sections of the Main Volume of This Book)	FAMILY AND MEDICAL LEAVE ACT (Citations are to 29 U.S.C.)
6-12 Enforcement	**§2617**
Penalties Up to $2,000 for the first offense and up to $5,000 for each subsequent offense. Damages in private actions: All equitable remedies and compensatory damages available under the LAD in proceeding in the DCR. Punitive damages Up to $10,000 per person. In class actions or complaints by the Director of the Division on Civil Rights, up to the lesser of $500,000 or 1 percent of the defendant's net worth.	Damages equal to wages, salary, employment benefits, or other compensation denied or lost; or If no such losses have been sustained, any actual losses (such as the cost of providing care up to a sum equal to the employee's pay for 12 weeks) -plus- Interest -plus- Liquidated damages unless the employer proves it acted in good faith with a reasonable belief it was not violating the law -plus- Appropriate equitable relief.

*The FMLA expressly saves state leave laws which provide greater family or medical leave rights than does the FMLA from pre-emption. 29 U.S.C. § 2651(b). As a result, employees are entitled to leave if the conditions under *either* the FMLA or FLA are met, subject to the requirements of whichever statute applies. If the leave qualifies under both FMLA and FLA, the leave used counts concurrently against the employee's entitlement under each law. *See* 29 C.F.R. § 825.701. *Cf.* N.J.A.C. § 4A:6-1.22 (chart created by state personnel office for its use regarding state employees, comparing FMLA and FLA for relative favorability to employees).

Chapter 7

Health and Safety

I. THE RIGHT TO KNOW ACT

7-1 Introduction

The New Jersey Worker and Community Right to Know Act[1] establishes a system for disclosure and dissemination of information regarding hazardous substances in the workplace and environment.[2] The obligations imposed upon employers under the Act can be categorized generally as environmental requirements and workplace requirements.

Environmental requirements relate to substances identified by the Department of Environmental Protection and Energy (DEPE) as "environmental hazards." Covered employers have two basic responsibilities as to these substances. First, they must disclose relevant information concerning the use and/or storage of

---

1. L.1983, c.315, codified at N.J.S.A. 34:5A-1 to -31. *See Welch v. Schneider Nat'l Bulk Carriers*, 676 F. Supp. 571, 573 (D.N.J. 1987) ("The New Jersey Legislature enacted the Right to Know Act in response to the growing threat to the public health, safety, and welfare posed by the 'proliferation of hazardous substances in the environment.'").

Workplace safety is additionally addressed by the Worker Health and Safety Act, N.J.S.A. 34:6A-1 *et seq.* which guarantees workers a safe and healthful work environment. That "has long been a right protected by common law." *LePore v. National Tool & Mfg. Co.*, 224 N.J. Super. 463, 469 (App. Div 1988), *aff'd*, 115 N.J. 226 (1989). The stated purpose of that statute is the following:

> Every employer shall furnish a place of employment which shall be reasonably safe and healthful for employees. Every employer shall install, maintain and use such employee protective devices and safeguards including methods of sanitation and hygiene and where a substantial risk of physical injury is inherent in the nature of a specific work operation shall also with respect to such work operation establish and enforce such work methods, as are reasonably necessary to protect the life, health and safety of employees, with due regard to the nature of the work performed.

N.J.S.A. 34:6A-3.

2. The Act was intended to impose comprehensive requirements upon employers within the state regarding the public disclosure of information as to hazardous substances. N.J.S.A. 34:5A-27. As a result, it prohibits any county or municipality from enacting any law or ordinance regarding the disclosure of information to the extent that such disclosure is already covered by the Act. *Id.* It also expressly preempts such laws and ordinances enacted after May 11, 1983. *Id.*

each substance located at their facility by responding to environmental surveys developed by the DEPE.[3] Second, employers must ensure that containers at the facility in which the substances are stored or mixed are properly labeled.[4]

Workplace requirements relate to substances deemed by the Department of Health (DOH) to be hazardous to the health or safety of employees. Covered employers must meet reporting and labeling requirements for these substances that are similar to those imposed with respect to environmental hazards.[5] In addition, covered employers must train employees in the proper use and safe handling of any such substances to which they may be exposed.[6] Employers also must maintain a central file of information about each substance and make that file available for inspection by interested employees.[7]

As the Act was initially passed, each employer was required to meet both workplace and environmental standards. The Third Circuit has held, however, that the Occupational Safety and Health Act,[8] preempts the workplace requirements of the Act with respect to private employers.[9]

7-2 Covered Employers/OSHA Pre-emption

As initially enacted, each provision of the Right to Know Act covered all persons and corporations operating businesses included within certain enumerated Standard Industrial Classifications, as well as all state and local governments and their agencies, departments, authorities and instrumentalities.[10] At that time, the Occupational Safety and Health Administration's (OSHA's) Hazard Communication Standard imposed requirements upon manufacturing sector employers similar to those contained in the New Jersey Act.[11] Section 18 of the Occupational Safety and Health Act (OSH Act) provides that state laws pertaining to issues addressed by an OSHA standard are expressly pre-empted unless the Secretary of Labor has approved the state's plan.[12]

---

3. N.J.S.A. 34:5A-7(b); N.J.A.C. 7:1G-5.1. Employers must update the workplace survey every five years, and must notify the department and other appropriate entities which receive the survey of any additional workplace hazardous substance present during a non-reporting year by the July 15th following the change. N.J.S.A. 34:5A-10(b).

4. N.J.S.A. 34:5A-14.

5. N.J.S.A. 34:5A-7(a).

6. N.J.S.A. 34:5A-13.

7. N.J.S.A. 34:5A-12.

8. Pub. L. No. 91-596, 84 Stat. 1590 (1970), *codified at* 29 U.S.C. §§651-678 (1982) (OSH Act).

9. *See* §7-2, *infra.*

In *N.J. State Chamber of Commerce v. Hughey*,[13] the United States Court of Appeals for the Third Circuit interpreted section 18 as expressly pre-empting state laws "only to the extent that a federal standard regulating the same issue is already in effect."[14] As a result, the court concluded that the reporting and labeling requirements of the Right to Know Act were expressly pre-empted to the extent they related to workplace hazards within the manufacturing sector covered by OSHA's Hazard Communication Standard.[15] Reporting and labeling requirements relating to environmental hazards and designed to safeguard the public health and safety, however, were beyond the scope of the OSHA Act and the

---

10. N.J.S.A. 34:5A-3(h). Standard Industrial Classifications (SIC) are prepared by the federal Office of Management and Budget and are published in the Standard Industrial Classifications Manual. Businesses within the following categories were initially covered by the Right to Know Act.

> Major Group Number 07 (Agricultural Services), only Industry Number 0782—Lawn and Garden Services; Major Group Numbers 20 through 39 inclusive (Manufacturing Industries); Major Group Number 45 (Transportation by Air), only Industry Number 4511—Air Transportation, Certified Carriers, and Group Number 458—Air Transportation Services; Major Group Number 46 (Pipelines, except Natural Gas); Major Group Number 47 (Transportation Services), only Group Numbers 471—Freight Forwarding, 474—Rental of Railroad Cars, and 478—Miscellaneous Services Incidental to Transportation; Major Group Number 48 (Communication), only Group Numbers 481—Telephone Communication, and 482—Telegraph Communication; Major Group Number 49 (Electric, Gas and Sanitary Services); Major Group Number 50 (Wholesale Trade—Durable Goods), only Industry Numbers 5085—Industrial Supplies, 5087—Service Establishment Equipment and Supplies, and 5093—Scrap and Waste Materials; Major Group Number 51 (Wholesale Trade, Nondurable Goods), only Group Numbers 512—Drugs, Drug Proprietaries and Druggist's Sundries, 516—Chemicals and Allied Products, 517—Petroleum and Petroleum Products, 518—Beer, Wine and Distilled Alcoholic Beverages, and 519—Miscellaneous Nondurable Goods; Major Group Number 55 (Automobile Dealers and Gasoline Service Stations), only Group Numbers 551—Motor Vehicle Dealers (New and Used), 552—Motor Vehicle Dealers (Used Only), and 554—Gasoline Service Stations; Major Group Number 72 (Personal Services), only Industry Numbers 7216—Dry Cleaning Plants, Except Rug Cleaning, 7217—Carpet and Upholstery Cleaning, and 7218—Industrial Launderers; Major Group Number 73 (Business Services), only Industry Number 7397 Commercial Testing Laboratories; Major Group Number 75 (Automotive Repair, Services, and Garages), only Group Number 753 - Automotive Repair Shops; Major Group Number 76 (Miscellaneous Repair Services), only Industry Number 7692—Welding Repair; Major Group Number 80 (Health Services), only Group Number 806—Hospitals; and Major Group Number 82 (Educational Services), only Group Numbers 821—Elementary and Secondary Schools and 822—Colleges and Universities, and Industry Number 8249—Vocational Schools.

N.J.S.A. 34:5A-3(h). To this list, the DOH has added the following: "Major Group Number 87 (Engineering, Accounting, Research, Management and Related Services), only Industrial Number 8734—Testing Laboratories." N.J.A.C. 8:59-11.3.

11. 48 Fed. Reg. 53, 3340 (1983). As noted by the Third Circuit, the Hazard Communication Standard at that time regulated employers who were engaged in a business within Standard Industrial Codes 20-39, where chemicals are used or produced for use or distribution. Those codes correspond to the manufacturing sector of the economy. *N.J. State Chamber of Commerce v. Hughey*, 774 F.2d 587, 590 n.2 (3rd Cir. 1985).

12. 29 U.S.C. §667 (1985); *N.J. State Chamber of Commerce v. Hughey*, 774 F.2d at 592. New Jersey never sought such approval.

13. 774 F.2d 587 (3rd Cir. 1985) (*Hughey I*).

14. *Id.* at 593. The court stated: "It would thwart the overriding congressional intent to promote worker safety if federal statutes preempted state laws governing issues that are not federally regulated." *Id.*

Standard, and thus were not expressly pre-empted.[16] With regard to implied preemption,[17] the Court held that environmental reporting requirements were not impliedly pre-empted by the OSHA Act, but found the record inadequate to determine whether environmental labeling requirements were pre-empted.[18] In a subsequent appeal after remand, the court upheld a district court finding that the Act's labeling requirements with respect to environmental hazards were not impliedly pre-empted by the OSH Act.[19]

After the Third Circuit decided *Hughey I*, OSHA's hazard communication standard was amended to cover private employers outside of the manufacturing sector.[20] Although there is no case law directly addressing the issue, it is clear that under the court's holding in *Hughey I*, the Act's workplace requirements as to these employers would be similarly preempted.[21] Recognizing this, the Department of Environmental Protection and Energy (DEPE) and the Department of Health (DOH) adopted regulations that implemented the provisions of the Act in such a way as to avoid claims of preemption.[22]

Thus, both public and private employers[23] must now comply with environmental reporting and labeling requirements. In general, only public employers must make information relevant to workplace hazards available for employee inspection at the facility. Similarly, only public employers must provide training to their

---

15. *Id.* at 595. In a later opinion, *New Jersey Chamber of Commerce v. Hughey*, 868 F.2d 621, 628 (3rd Cir.), *cert. denied*, 492 U.S. 920, 109 S.Ct. 3246 (1989), (Hughey II), the court clarified its holding regarding the Act's labeling requirements. It stated: "Hughey I thus held that section 18(a) of the OSH Act expressly preempted section 14 of the New Jersey Act only to the extent that section 14(a) required the labeling of workplace hazards that were not also environmental hazards." *Id.* at 629.

16. *Hughey I*, at 595-96. In so holding, the court noted that by their terms, the OSHA standards governed only *occupational* safety and health issues. *Id.* at 593.

17. The Third Circuit relied on the rule set forth in *Fidelity Federal Savings and Loan Ass'n v. de la Cuesta*, 458 U.S. 141 (1982), and *Silkwood v. Kerr McGee Corp.*, 464 U.S. 238 (1984), in resolving the issue of implied preemption:

> [A]n intent to preempt state law will be implied if: (1) it is impossible to comply with both the state and federal law, or (2) "the state law stands as an obstacle to the accomplishment of the full purposes and objectives of Congress."

Hughey I, 774 F. Supp. at 592.

18. *Id.* at 595. The court also held that portions of the Act requiring disclosure of trade secret information were not preempted by the OSHA standard and did not constitute a taking of property without due process. *Hughey I*, 774 F.2d at 587.

19. *Hughey II*, 868 F.2d at 631.

20. 29 C.F.R. 1910, 1200(b) (1989).

21. In *Hughey II*, the court acknowledged that in light of the amendment of the OSHA standard, it could be argued that "*Hughey I's* express preemption holding should also be extended to the nonmanufacturing sector." *Hughey II*, 868 F.2d at 628 n.6. Because the parties had not raised the issue, however, the court refused to address it. *Id.*

22. N.J.A.C. 8:59-11.2; *see also* N.J.A.C. 7:1G-1.1 *et seq.*

23. N.J.A.C. 7:1G-1.2.

employees under the Act. It should be noted, however, that the New Jersey Supreme Court has stated that even the preempted portion of the Act "remains as an exposition of the state public policy on these issues."[24]

7-3 Reporting Requirements

A. The Environmental Survey

In accordance with section 4 of the Act, the DEPE has developed a list of environmental hazardous substances and a corresponding "Environmental Survey" that requires covered employers to provide information about each identified hazardous substance at their facilities.[25] The environmental hazardous substance list is based upon a list of substances developed by the DEPE in conjunction with the Industry Survey Project but may also include other substances where there is documented scientific evidence that the substances pose a threat to public health and safety.[26]

The Environmental Survey consists of the Community Right to Know Survey and the Release and Pollution Prevention Report, and requires employers to provide information about environmental hazardous substances in the workplace,

---

24. *Millison v. E.I. du Pont de Nemours & Co.*, 101 N.J. 161, 180 n.3 (1985).

25. N.J.S.A. 34:5A-4; N.J.A.C. 7:1G-1.2. The following are not included within the term "hazardous substance" as it is used in the Act:

1) Fuel in a motor vehicle;

2) Articles containing a hazardous substance in its solid form which does not present any chronic or acute health hazard to employees exposed to it;

3) Listed hazardous substances which constitute less than one percent of a mixture unless there is a total of 500 pounds or more of the substance present at the facility;

4) Special health hazard substances which are below the threshold percentage set by the DOH;

5) Hazardous substances present in the same form and concentration found in consumer products, provided that employee exposure in handling is not significantly greater than general consumer exposure during the principal use of the toxic substance;

6) Tobacco or tobacco products;

7) Wood or wood products;

8) Food, drugs, cosmetics or alcoholic beverages in a retail establishment packaged for sale to consumers;

9) Food, drugs or cosmetics intended for personal consumption by employees while in the workplace;

10) Materials gathered as evidence by a law enforcement agency and maintained in an evidence locker room;

11) Hazardous substances which are an integral part of a facility structure or furnishings; or

12) Products which are the personal property and for the personal use of an employee.

N.J.S.A. 34:5A-3(m); N.J.A.C. 8:59-1.3.

26. N.J.S.A. 34:5A-4(a). The environmental hazardous substance list shall also include any substance on the list established by the United States Environmental Protection Agency for reporting pursuant to 42 U.S.C. §11023. N.J.S.A. 34:5A-4(a).

such as the Chemical Abstract Service (CAS) number and chemical name of the relevant substances, the uses to which the substances are put, and the quantity of each substance produced, stored, used or shipped to or from the facility, the methods of storage and/or disposal of the substances, and the total amount of each discharged into the environment.[27]

Under Section seven of the Act, the employer must forward copies of the completed Environmental Survey to the DEPE and the county health department of the county in which the facility is located on the date on which Toxic Chemical Release Forms are due to be transmitted to the United States Environmental Protection Agency pursuant to 42 U.S.C. §11023.[28] Pertinent sections of the survey must also be supplied to local police and fire departments within that time.[29]

---

27. N.J.A.C. 7:1G-1.2. The regulation provides that the information required by the Environmental Survey, comprised of the Community Right to Know Survey and the Release and Pollution Prevention Report, includes but is not limited to the following:

1. The chemical name and Chemical Abstracts Service number of the environmental hazardous substance;
2. A description of the use of the environmental hazardous substance at the facility;
3. The quantity of the environmental hazardous substance produced at the facility;
4. The quantity of the environmental hazardous substance brought into the facility;
5. The quantity of the environmental hazardous substance consumed at the facility;
6. The quantity of the environmental hazardous substance shipped out of the facility as, or in, products;
7. The maximum inventory of the environmental hazardous substance stored at the facility, the methods of storage, and the frequency and methods of transfer;
8. The total stack or point-source emissions of the environmental hazardous substance;
9. The total estimated fugitive or non-point-source emissions of the environmental hazardous substance;
10. The total discharge of the environmental hazardous substance into the surface or groundwater, the treatment methods, and the raw wastewater volume and loadings;
11. The total discharge of the environmental hazardous substance into publicly owned treatment works;
12. The quantity and methods of disposal, of any wastes containing an environmental hazardous substance, the methods of on-site storage of these wastes, the location or locations of the final disposal site for these wastes, and the identity of the hauler of the wastes;
13. The total quantity of environmental hazardous substances generated at the facility, including hazardous substances generated as nonproduct output;
14. The quantity of environmental hazardous substances recycled on-site and off-site; and
15. Information pertaining to pollution prevention activities at the facility.

N.J.S.A. 34:5A-3(k).

CAS numbers are assigned to chemicals by the Chemical Abstract Service as a means of identification. N.J.S.A. 34:5A-3(a). The environmental survey is distributed to employers by the DEPE. N.J.S.A. 34:5A-3(k). The DEPE must also make available Spanish translations of the survey and all other materials prepared by it to advise the public of the availability of information under the Act. N.J.S.A. 34:5A-4.

28. N.J.S.A. 34:5A-7(b).

29. *Id.*

The DEPE may also require the employer to submit additional information clarifying statements made on the environmental survey, within 30 days of notification, or by such other date the DEPE specifies.[30] The employer must in any event provide bi-annual updates of information on the Environmental Survey.[31] Significant changes during the nonreporting year must be reported to the DEPE.[32] Moreover, the DEPE may, in its discretion, require a particular employer to update its Environmental Survey on an annual basis.[33]

If the employer believes that disclosure of the information requested on the environmental survey would reveal a trade secret, it may file a trade secret claim with the DEPE within the 90 day period.[34] Merely filing a trade secret claim, however, does not relieve the employer of the responsibility of providing the relevant information to the department. Rather, two versions of the survey—one containing the alleged trade secret information and one with that information omitted—must be submitted.[35] Pending a determination as to the validity of the trade secret claim, the employer may omit the disputed information on the copies of the survey on file at the facility and submitted to the local police, fire and county health departments.[36]

7-4 Labeling Requirements

All containers of hazardous substances must bear a label reflecting the Chemical Abstract Service number and chemical name (or trade secret registry number) of the substance.[37] When a container contains a mixture, the label must

---

30. N.J.S.A. 34:5A-9; N.J.A.C. 7:1G-5.2. If applicable, the DEPE must transmit the clarifying information to county health and local police and fire departments as it deems necessary. N.J.S.A. 34:5A-9(b); N.J.A.C. 7:1G-5.2.

31. N.J.S.A. 34:5A-9(c).

32. *Id.*

33. *Id.*

34. N.J.S.A. 34:5A-15(b). The procedure to be followed in filing a trade secret claim is discussed more fully in §7-7.

35. *Id.*

36. *Id.*

37. N.J.S.A. 34:5A-14. A container is broadly defined as any "receptacle used to hold a liquid, solid or gaseous substance, including, but not limited to, bottles, pipelines, bags, barrels, boxes, cans, cylinders, drums, cartons, vessels, vats, and stationary or mobile storage tanks." N.J.S.A. 34:5A-3(d). It does not include "process containers." *Id.* Process containers are containers other than pipelines, with a capacity of 10 gallons or less, and which are intended only for the immediate use of an employee transferring substances from labeled containers. N.J.S.A. 34:5A-3(q). Containers such as vials and beakers which are routinely reused, and containers on which labels would be obscured because of spillage, heat or other factors are also exempted as "process containers." *Id.*

Common names identified by the DOH may be substituted for chemical names. N.J.S.A. 34:5A-14(d); N.J.A.C. 8:59-5.7(a).

include relevant information[38] for each hazardous substance and each of the five most prominent substances in the mixture.[39] Substances constituting less than 1% of any mixture need not be included on the label unless a total of 500 or more pounds of the substance is present at the facility.[40]

If more than one percent of a container's contents are unknown, it must bear a label reading either "contents unknown" or "contents partially unknown."[41] If the contents are later identified, the label must be updated accordingly.[42] When an employer receives information allowing it to identify the CAS number or chemical name of the components of a material found at its facility, it must update the labels of the affected containers within five working days.[43]

Labels may also include an appropriate hazard warning as well as the name and address of the manufacturer, importer or other potentially responsible entity.[44] The contents of an unlabeled or inappropriately labeled container may not be used by an employer.[45] All containers must be labeled either before they are opened or within five working days after their arrival, whichever is sooner.[46] Where incoming containers are already labeled by the manufacturer or other entity, the employer may not remove or deface the labels unless the container is immediately labeled in accordance with the Act.[47] If the employer feels that compliance with these labeling requirements would reveal a trade secret, it may file a trade secret claim with the DOH.[48]

7-4:1 Pipelines

The employer must label pipelines at the valves located where the substances enter the facility's pipeline, and at all other normally operated valves, vents, out-

---

38. N.J.S.A. 34:5A-14(b).

39. *Id.*; N.J.A.C. 8:59-5.1(c). This is known as "universal labeling." N.J.A.C. 8:59-5.1(c).

40. N.J.S.A. 34:5A-14(b).

41. N.J.A.C. 8:59-5.1(b). Where the manufacturer of the substance is also unknown or is no longer in business, the employer may either label the container pursuant to the Act or pursuant to the Federal Resource Conservation and Recovery Act. N.J.A.C. 8:59-5.1(f).

42. N.J.A.C. 8:59-5.1(e).

43. N.J.A.C. 8:59-5.1(g).

44. N.J.A.C. 8:59-5.1(j).

45. N.J.A.C. 8:59-5.1(d).

46. N.J.A.C. 8:59-5.1(d). Containers packed within larger properly labeled containers need not be labeled until they are removed. N.J.A.C. 8:59-1(n).

47. N.J.A.C. 8:59-5.1(k). If labeling requirements present a security risk for a public employer operating a jail or prison it may request a waiver of the requirements. N.J.A.C. 8:59-5.1(l). Under the waiver employees will be permitted to get the relevant information in an alternative manner. *Id.*

48. N.J.S.A. 34:5A-15.

lets, sample connections, and drains designed to permit release of the substance from the pipeline.[49] Release points used to discharge waste materials from the facility must also be labeled.[50]

7-4:2 Reaction Vessels

Reaction vessels are containers other than process containers[51] in which the mixture or reaction of substances occurs.[52] Reaction vessels must be labeled so as to identify the substances which are added and removed from them.[53] If necessary, the label may be posted on an adjoining wall or pole located near the vessel.[54]

7-4:3 Containers Holding Two Ounces or Less

Containers that hold two ounces or less may be labeled with a code that permits emergency responders (or employees in the case of public employers) to determine the identity of the substance by use of a readily available fact sheet providing the CAS or trade secret number of the substance.[55]

7-4:4 Containers Located at Storage or Transfer Facilities

Where containers are delivered to storage or transfer facilities in stacks or on skids that make it impossible to label each container without breaking down the stacks, and the containers remain that way until they leave the facility, only the containers that face outward and that are within reach of the employees must be

---

49. N.J.S.A. 34:5A-14; N.J.A.C. 8:59-5.2(a). Where a number of valves are in close proximity to each other on a single pipeline leading to one process container, only one valve in the group must be labeled. N.J.A.C. 8:59-5.2(a). The term "normally operated" refers to those release points used at least once every 24 hours or those used monthly in connection with repairs or maintenance. *Id.*

50. N.J.A.C. 8:59-5.2(b). With respect to such discharge points, the employer may substitute a label meeting the requirement of the Resource Conservation and Recovery Act, regardless of whether it is otherwise covered by that Act. *Id.*

51. A process container is defined as "a container, excluding a pipeline, the content of which is changed frequently; a container of 10 gallons or less in capacity, into which substances are transferred from labeled containers, and which is intended only for the immediate use of the employee who performs the transfer; or a container on which a label would be obscured by heat, spillage or other factors; or a test tube, beaker, vial, or other container which is routinely used and reused." N.J.A.C. 8:59-1.3.

52. N.J.A.C. 8:59-5.1(h).

53. *Id.*

54. *Id.* Batch sheets or operating manuals reflecting the required information may be posted in place of labels. *Id.*

55. N.J.A.C. 8:59-5.1(i). As to public employees such fact sheets must be in close proximity to the work location and available without the aid of management. *Id.*

labeled.[56] Where the containers remain unopened, labeling consistent with the requirements of the United States Department of Transportation satisfies the requirements of the Act.[57] Unlabeled containers, however, must be labeled immediately upon their removal from the skid.[58]

7-4:5 Containers at Research and Development Laboratories

Containers in areas identified as research and development laboratories[59] may be labeled pursuant to a code or number system, provided that the system permits emergency responders (or employees in the case of public employers) to readily cross-reference hazardous substance fact sheets or other material so as to obtain the CAS number, chemical or common name, or trade secret registry number of the substance involved.[60]

7-5 The Right to Know Survey (Public Employers)

As required by §4 of the Act, the DOH has developed two lists of hazardous substances. The "workplace hazardous substance list" identifies substances hazardous to the health or safety of workers.[61] The "special health hazard substance list" identifies hazardous substances that pose a special threat to health and safety, and as to which employers may not assert a trade secret claim.[62] A corresponding "workplace survey" requires public employers to report the presence in their workplace of any substances listed in the workplace hazardous substance list and the special health hazard substance list.[63] The Right to Know Hazardous Substance List is a compilation of the workplace and environmental hazardous

---

56. N.J.A.C. 8:59-5.1(m). If the skids are shrink wrapped, labels must appear on all four sides of the wrapping. *Id.*

57. N.J.A.C. 8:59-5.1(d).

58. N.J.A.C. 8:59-5.1(m).

59. A research and development laboratory is defined as a "specially designated area used primarily for research, development, and testing activity, and not primarily involved in the production of goods for commercial sale, in which hazardous substances or environmental hazardous substances are used by or under the direct supervision of a technically qualified person." N.J.S.A. 34:5A-3(r).

60. N.J.S.A. 34:5A-14(a) and (b); N.J.A.C. 8:59-5.3. Public employers must make the information available to employees near the job location and without the assistance or permission of management. N.J.A.C. 8:59-5.3.

61. N.J.S.A. 34:5A-5; N.J.A.C. 8:59-1.3. The list includes environmental hazardous substances, components of mixtures regulated by OSHA and other substances determined by the DOH to pose a threat to the safety or health of employees. N.J.S.A. 34:5A-5; N.J.A.C. 8:59-9.1.

62. N.J.S.A. 34:5A-5(b); N.J.A.C. 8:59-10.1.

63. N.J.A.C. 8:59-1.3.

substance lists.[64] Similarly, the Right to Know Survey is a compilation of the workplace and environmental surveys.[65]

The DOH distributes the Right to Know Survey to covered public employers[66] who must return completed surveys to the department within 90 days.[67] Copies of the completed surveys must also be sent to the county health department,[68] the Local Emergency Planning Committee, and the local police, fire, and health departments.[69]

A public employer's responsibilities in completing the Right to Know Survey parallel those of private employers described above. Hazardous substances present at the facility must be reported in alphabetical order by common name and CAS number.[70] If the employer does not know the CAS number and chemical name of a substance or the components of a mixture, it must make a good faith attempt to obtain that information from the manufacturer or supplier of the product.[71] If it is unable to do so, it must identify the trade name of the material and provide the department with the name and address of the manufacturer or supplier.[72] Available material safety data sheets for the product must also be provided.[73]

---

64. *Id.*

65. *Id.*

66. N.J.A.C. 8:59-2.1(a). Covered employers include state and local governments as well as all agencies, departments, bureaus, authorities or instrumentalities thereof. N.J.A.C. 8:59-1.3. Public employers who indicate that there are no hazardous substances present at their facilities are exempt from the Act, except that they must continue to annually update information as to that facility and are subject to the Act's penalty provisions. N.J.S.A. 34:5A-8(b); N.J.A.C. 8:59-1.4(a). If such an exempted public employer later indicates that a hazardous substance is present at the facility, it will immediately be subject to the Act. N.J.S.A. 34:5A-8(b); N.J.A.C. 8:59-1.4(b).

67. N.J.S.A. 34:5A-7(a); N.J.A.C. 8:59-2.1(d).

68. If there is no county health department for the county where the facility is located, copies of the survey should be filed with the county clerk or designated lead agency for the county. N.J.A.C. 8:59-2.1(d).

69. N.J.S.A. 34:5A-7(a); N.J.A.C. 8:59-2.1(d).

70. N.J.A.C. 8:59-2.2(a). A substance on the Special Health Hazard Substance List that is contained in a mixture must be reported if it is either a carcinogen, mutagen or teratogen and constitutes one-tenth of one percent or more of a mixture. N.J.A.C. 8:59-2.2(a); N.J.A.C. 8:59-10.1(b). All other hazardous substances must be reported if they constitute one percent or more of a mixture or are present in a container at the facility in an aggregate of 500 pounds or more. N.J.A.C. 8:59-2.2(a); N.J.A.C. 8:59-10.1(b).

Substances stored at a public employer's facility by subcontractors must also be reported on the survey. N.J.A.C. 8:59-2.2(h).

71. N.J.A.C. 8:59-2.2(e). Written documentation of such efforts must be maintained. *Id.*

72. N.J.S.A. 34:5A-7(a); N.J.A.C. 8:59-2.2(f). Thereafter, the DOH will obtain the CAS numbers and chemical names of the substances or component parts and provide them to the employer along with the appropriate hazardous substance fact sheets and instructions regarding disclosure of the information to employees. N.J.S.A. 34:5A-7(a).

73. N.J.A.C. 8:59-2.2(f).

Like private employers, the public employer must certify that its responses to the Right to Know Survey are true and accurate.[74] If the employer believes that compliance with the reporting requirements would disclose a trade secret, it may file a trade secret claim within 90 days of receipt of the survey.[75]

Public employers must update the Right to Know Survey annually.[76] Moreover, county health departments, county clerks, lead agencies and local police and fire departments receiving copies of the completed surveys may request that the employer provide additional information concerning the survey.[77] In providing the additional information, the employer may require the receiving entity to sign an agreement protecting its confidentiality.[78]

For each hazardous substance identified on the completed Right to Know Survey, the public employer will receive a hazardous substance fact sheet from the DOH setting forth information concerning the substance.[79] Except where a trade secret claim has been made, the fact sheet will identify the substance by its chemical, trade and common names, and CAS number.[80] The information contained on the fact sheet includes, but is not limited to the following:

1. The chemical name, the Chemical Abstracts Service number, the trade name, and common names of the hazardous substance;
2. A reference to all relevant information on the hazardous substance from the most recent edition of the National Institute for Occupational Safety and Health's Registry of Toxic Effects of Chemical Substances;
3. The hazardous substance's solubility in water, vapor pressure at standard conditions of temperature and pressure, and flash point;
4. The hazard posed by the hazardous substance, including its toxicity, carcinogenicity, mutagenicity, teratogenicity, flammabili-

---

74. N.J.A.C. 8:59-2.2(g).

75. N.J.S.A. 34:5A-15.

76. N.J.A.C. 8:59-2.1(c).

77. N.J.A.C. 8:59-2.3(a). Employers must comply with such requests within 30 days. *Id.*

78. N.J.A.C. 8:59-2.3(b).

79. N.J.S.A. 34:5A-8(a); N.J.A.C. 8:59-4.3(a). Fact sheets need not be prepared for substances in generic categories. N.J.A.C. 8:59-4.1(a).

If the employer asserts a trade secret claim as to a particular substance, it may prepare its own fact sheet subject to the department's approval. N.J.A.C. 8:59-4.1(b); N.J.A.C. 8:59-4.4(a). Except in such situations, the DOH will also make Spanish translations of the fact sheet available for distribution. N.J.A.C. 8:59-4.1(d), (e); N.J.A.C. 8:59-4.3(d).

80. N.J.S.A. 34:5A-8; N.J.A.C. 8:59-4.2(a). Where a trade secret claim is made, the substance will be identified by a trade secret registry number. N.J.A.C. 8:59-4.4.

ty, explosiveness, corrosivity and reactivity, including specific information on its reactivity with water;

5. A description, in nontechnical language, of the acute and chronic health effects of exposure to the hazardous substance, including the medical conditions that might be aggravated by exposure, and any permissible exposure limits established by the federal Occupational Safety and Health Administration;
6. The potential routes and symptoms of exposure to the hazardous substance;
7. The proper precautions, practices, necessary personal protective equipment, recommended engineering controls, and any other necessary and appropriate measures for the safe handling of the hazardous substance, including specific information on how to extinguish or control a fire that involves the hazardous substance; and
8. The appropriate emergency and first aid procedures for spills, fires, potential explosions, and accidental or unplanned emissions involving the hazardous substance.[81]

Under the administrative regulations promulgated by the DOH, public employers must also obtain material safety data sheets from manufacturers, suppliers and subcontractors for all products present at the facility and purchased for the facility, and maintain records as to which hazardous substances are present in which mixtures.[82]

7-6 Employee Training (Public Employers)

Public employers must also maintain training programs by which employees are educated and provided instruction as to the hazardous substances to which they may be exposed, including those used or stored at the facility by subcontractors.[83] The training must be provided every two years and all relevant information must be provided both orally and in writing.[84] In addition, prospective employees should be notified of the availability of Right to Know Surveys and

81. N.J.A.C. 8:59-4.2(a). In short, all information relevant to the substance should be found on the fact sheet including a reference to information contained in the most recent edition of the Registry of Toxic Effects of Chemical Substance published by the National Institute for Occupational Safety and Health. N.J.A.C. 8:59-4.2(a). Moreover, the information set forth on the fact sheet must be updated by the DOH when significant new information becomes known. N.J.A.C. 8:59-4.2(b).

82. N.J.A.C. 8:59-2.2(b),(i).

hazardous substance fact sheets prior to their entering an employment agreement.[85] New employees beginning work after training has been completed must be provided with training within the first month of their employment.[86]

In addition to providing information as to the proper handling of the hazardous substances involved, the training program must advise employees of their rights under the Act and of the various obligations imposed upon the employer.[87] Notices providing this information must also be conspicuously posted on bulletin boards at the facility.[88]

7-7 Trade Secrets—Filing of Trade Secret Claims

If an employer believes that compliance with the Act will reveal a trade secret, it may file a trade secret claim with either the DOH or the DEPE, depending upon which agency is responsible for enforcement of the relevant provision of the Act.[89] The DOH and DEPE have jointly adopted rules regarding the filing of such claims and the implementation of the trade secret provisions of the Act.[90]

---

83. N.J.S.A. 34:5A-13(a); N.J.A.C. 8:59-6.2; N.J.A.C. 8:59-6.5. Except with respect to volunteers, training must be provided during paid employer time. N.J.A.C. 8:59-6.1(a).

Information and training given as to substances used or stored by subcontractors should be provided either during the normally required training session or upon the request of an employee or his representative, whichever is sooner. N.J.A.C. 8:59-6.5(a). If the information is not provided during the training session, it should be given to all exposed and potentially exposed employees in writing along with the relevant hazardous substance fact sheets or material safety data sheets if requested. N.J.A.C. 8:59-6.5(b).

If the employee's native language is Spanish and he cannot read or speak English over a 6th grade level, he must be provided training and materials in Spanish. N.J.A.C. 8:59-6.2(d).

If an unidentified substance is later identified, the employer must provide training within three months of receipt of the applicable hazardous substance fact sheets. N.J.A.C. 8:59-6.2(c).

84. N.J.S.A. 34:5A-13(a); N.J.A.C. 8:59-6.1(a)(1); N.J.A.C. 8:59-6.2(a).

85. N.J.S.A. 34:5A-13(a); N.J.A.C. 8:59-6.2(e).

86. N.J.S.A. 34:5A-13(a); N.J.A.C. 8:59-6.2(b).

87. N.J.S.A. 34:5A-13; N.J.A.C. 8:59-6.2; N.J.A.C. 8:59-6.3. The administrative regulations provide detailed information as to what areas should be covered in the training program. *Id.* Public employers should also note that less burdensome rules apply where the only hazardous exposure results from the periodic replacement of copier toner or gasoline. N.J.A.C. 8:59-6.3(f).

88. N.J.A.C. 8:59-6.3(d). The administrative regulations also require the distribution of sample fact sheets, material safety data sheets, and the Right to Know brochure developed by the DOH to advise employees of their rights. N.J.A.C. 8:59-6.3(b), (c).

89. N.J.S.A. 34:5A-15. It should be noted, however, that certain information may not be claimed to represent a trade secret. N.J.A.C. 7:1G-6.5; N.J.A.C. 8:59-3.5. For example, information which the employer must disclose pursuant to another act may not be claimed to be a trade secret. N.J.A.C. 7:1G-6.5(a)(2); N.J.A.C. 8:59-3.5(a). In addition, the name, CAS number and United States Department of Transportation number of any substance appearing on the Special Health Hazard Substance List may not be alleged to be a trade secret. N.J.A.C. 7:1G-6.5(a)(1); N.J.A.C. 8:59-3.5(a)(1).

90. N.J.A.C. 7:1G-6.1; N.J.A.C. 8:59-3.1. Private employers claiming confidentiality for trade secrets for container labeling and public employers claiming confidentiality for labeling or for reporting on Right to Know surveys shall comply with the regulations at N.J.A.C. 8:59-3.6. N.J.A.C. 7:1G-6.6 (l).

An employer seeking to assert a trade secret claim as to information requested on the environmental survey must file a claim with the DEPE within 90 days of its receipt of the survey.[91] To do so the employer must file two versions of the relevant survey with the department.[92] The first version must contain all of the information requested, including that claimed to be a trade secret.[93] The top of each page of this version should be marked "confidential" in bold type.[94] Moreover, all information claimed to be a trade secret should be highlighted or otherwise identified.[95] The second version of the survey must be identical to the first except that the alleged trade secret information must be omitted.[96] Since this version will be made available to the public, the employer must also mark it "TSC" or "trade secret claimed" so as to provide warning that information is omitted under a claim of confidentiality.[97]

Similarly, a public employer wishing to assert a trade secret claim as to information requested on the workplace survey or as to the Act's labeling requirements, or a private employer wishing to assert a trade secret claim as to the Act's labeling requirements, must do so within 90 days of its receipt of the workplace survey.[98] Unlike claims concerning the environmental surveys, however, an employer wishing to assert a trade secret claim as to the workplace survey must complete the trade secret section of the workplace survey.[99]

Along with each asserted trade secret claim both public and private employers must submit a statement setting forth (1) the time period for which the trade secret designation is requested; (2) whether the disputed information is known outside the employer's industry; (3) whether it is patented; (4) the extent to which analytical techniques could be used by others to obtain the information; (5) the alleged harm which would result from disclosure of the information; and (6) a summary of all prior trade secret determinations regarding the claim.[100] If the

---

91. N.J.S.A. 34:5A-15(b).

92. N.J.S.A. 34:5A-15(b); N.J.A.C. 7:1G-6.6(b).

93. *Id.*

94. *Id.* In addition, all documents containing information should be delivered to the appropriate department via personal delivery, certified mail or some other means providing verification of delivery in envelopes clearly marked "CONFIDENTIAL." N.J.A.C. 7:1G-6.4(f), (g); N.J.A.C. 8:59-3.4(f), (g).

95. N.J.A.C. 7:1G-6.6(b)(1).

96. N.J.S.A. 34:5A-15(b); N.J.A.C. 7:1G-6.6(b)(2).

97. N.J.A.C. 7:1G-6.6(b)(2).

98. N.J.A.C. 8:59-3.6(a).

99. *Id.* Trade secret claims regarding the labeling of a container holding a substance for which a trade secret claim was not made on the workplace survey must be filed with the DOH before employees open the container or within five working days of its arrival at the facility, whichever is sooner. N.J.A.C. 8:59-3.6(a)(3).

100. N.J.A.C. 7:1G-6.6(c); N.J.A.C. 8:59-3.6(c). Copies of all prior trade secret determinations or references thereto must be attached to the summary. N.J.A.C. 7:1G-6.6(c); N.J.A.C. 8:59-3.6(c).

trade secret claim relates to formulae, patterns, plans, processes, data, information or compilations thereof, the employer must also state whether the knowledge is used either in the fabrication and production of a product or in research and development.[101] Moreover, the employer must identify all documents it relied upon in making the trade secret claim.[102] It may also submit any other information it deems relevant to the trade secret claim.[103]

In filing a trade secret claim, the employer must certify its truth, accuracy and completeness.[104] If the department requests additional information as to the claim, the employer must respond within 30 days unless the time period is extended by the department for good cause shown.[105] Moreover, the employer must update its claim within 60 days of receiving additional pertinent information.[106]

Upon receiving a request for disclosure of information claimed to constitute a trade secret, the relevant department must determine the validity of the trade secret claim.[107] Under the administrative regulations, a trade secret claim as to information, data, plans, formulae, or patterns will be considered valid if (1) the fact that secrecy is necessary for national defense purposes is certified by an appropriate representative of the federal government or (2) the employer establishes that the data, information or processes are not patented; are known only by the employer and selected other individuals; are used for purposes of research and development or for the production of articles or mixtures; and give the employer a competitive edge over others not possessing the knowledge.[108] Trade secret claims as to the CAS number or chemical name of a substance will be considered valid only if the substance is unknown to the competitors of the employer or is included in a process or formula meeting the criteria set forth above.[109]

Employers are notified of the department's rulings as to trade secret claims via certified mail.[110] If the claim is approved, the employer, with the exception of

101. N.J.A.C. 7:1G-6.6(b), (c); N.J.A.C. 8:59-3.6(b), (c).

102. N.J.A.C. 7:1G-6.6(f); N.J.A.C. 8:59-3.6(f).

103. N.J.A.C. 7:1G-6.6(e); N.J.A.C. 8:59-3.6(e).

104. N.J.A.C. 7:1G-6.6(g); N.J.A.C. 8:59-3.6(g).

105. N.J.A.C. 7:1G-6.6(d); N.J.A.C. 8:59-3.6(d). The department may request any information deemed relevant to its determination of the claim's validity, including information regarding the alleged competitive advantage provided by the trade secret, the harm that is alleged would result from disclosure, the amount expended in developing the trade secret information, and the extent to which the employer guards against disclosure. N.J.A.C. 7:1G-6.6(d); N.J.A.C. 8:59-3.6(d).

106. N.J.A.C. 7:1G-6.6(i); N.J.A.C. 8:59-3.6(i).

107. N.J.S.A. 34:5A-15(d); N.J.A.C. 7:1G-6.4(h); N.J.A.C. 8:59-3.4(h). Absent such a request, however, the department may consider the validity of the trade secret claims before it at any time it deems appropriate. N.J.S.A. 34:5A-15(d); N.J.A.C. 7:1G-6.4(h); N.J.A.C. 8:59-3.4(h).

108. N.J.A.C. 7:1G-6.9(a); N.J.A.C. 8:59-3.9(a).

109. N.J.A.C. 7:1G-6.9(b); N.J.A.C. 8:59-3.9(b).

those asserting a trade secret claim as to the environmental survey, must post a notice of that fact on bulletin boards readily accessible to employees.[111] If the claim is denied, the employer may request an administrative hearing before the Office of Administrative Law within 45 days of receipt of the notice.[112] Notice of such a request must be posted on bulletin boards at the facility within 15 days.[113] Subsequent OAL recommendations must be affirmed, rejected or modified by the department within 45 days of their receipt and this action shall constitute final agency action subject only to judicial review pursuant to the Rules of Court.[114] Written Notice of Appeals from such final agency action must be filed in accordance with the Rules of Court, with notice to the department within 45 days of notice of the determination.[115]

Once a trade secret claim has been denied and all avenues of appeal exhausted, the employer must modify the survey to include the information for which the trade secret claim was denied.[116] Copies of the modified survey should be filed with the appropriate department, and county and local agencies that are required by rule or regulation to receive the survey.[117] Where appropriate, the employer must also substitute the CAS number and chemical name of the substance for the trade secret registry member appearing on all labels and fact sheets.[118]

7-7:1 Access to Trade Secret Information

Written requests for the disclosure of information relating to trade secret claims may be filed with the relevant department by any person at any time.[119]

---

110. N.J.A.C. 7:1G-6.11(a); N.J.A.C. 8:59-3.11(a).

111. N.J.A.C. 8:59-3.11(a). Where Spanish speaking persons are employed, a notice in Spanish supplied by the department must also be posted; N.J.A.C. 8:59-3.11(b).

112. N.J.A.C. 7:1G-6.13(a),(c); N.J.A.C. 8:59-3.13(a),(c). The request for an administrative hearing should be filed with the Department; a copy must also be filed with the county health department, county clerk or lead agency. N.J.A.C. 8:59-3.13(b).

113. N.J.A.C. 8:59-3.13(b).

114. N.J.A.C. 7:1G-6.13(d); N.J.A.C. 8:59-3.13(d). The department must inform the employer of its determination by certified mail, return receipt requested. *Id.*

115. N.J.A.C. 7:1G-6.13(e); N.J.A.C. 8:59-3.13(e); *Rules Governing the Courts of New Jersey*, R. 2:4-1(b) (West, 1990).

116. N.J.A.C. 7:1G-6.14; N.J.A.C. 8:59-3.14.

117. *Id.*

118. *Id.*

119. N.J.A.C. 7:1G-6.10(a); N.J.A.C. 8:59-3.10(a). Requests should include the name, address, and affiliation of the requestor and may also include information as to the claim's validity. N.J.A.C. 7:1G-6.10(a); N.J.A.C. 8:59-3.10(a). Where the request is made by an employee seeking information as to trade secret information on a label or workplace survey, the name of the employee shall be kept confidential. N.J.A.C. 7:1g-6.10(a); N.J.A.C. 8:59-3.10(a).

If the claim is still pending, such a request for disclosure will prompt the department to determine its validity.[120] Where the trade secret claim has already been approved, such a request for disclosure must be accompanied by new significant information not previously submitted as to the claim's invalidity.[121] All information concerning either pending or approved trade secret claims, however, is to be treated as confidential and may only be disclosed by the department in certain limited circumstances.[122]

A physician or osteopath may obtain trade secret information from the DEPE or DOH where necessary for medical diagnosis or treatment.[123] Where feasible, the employer must be notified prior to the release of the information.[124] Similarly, an employee or officer of the state may be provided access to trade secret information upon the department's satisfaction that the request is made in connection with the requestor's official duties under a law concerning protection of the public health.[125] A state contractor or its employees may also obtain trade secret information if the department determines that the information is necessary to the completion of work contracted for in connection with the Act.[126]

All persons granted access to trade secret information under the Act must agree in writing to protect the confidentiality of the information.[127] The requirement that the agreement be signed prior to the disclosure of information, however, may be waived by the department for emergency public health or medical purposes.[128] Moreover, it is a crime of the third degree for any officer, employee, or contractor of the state, any physician or osteopath, or any employee of a county

---

120. N.J.S.A. 34:5A-15(d).

121. N.J.A.C. 7:1G-6.10(b); N.J.A.C. 8:59-3.10(b).

122. N.J.S.A. 34:5A-15(e). It should be noted that the confidentiality requirements are inapplicable to: (1) the disclosure of information required under any other act, and (2) information regarding emissions. N.J.S.A. 34:5A-15(h).

123. N.J.S.A. 34:5A-15(e); N.J.A.C. 7:1G-6.15(d); N.J.A.C. 8:59-3.15(d).

124. N.J.A.C. 7:1G-6.15(d); N.J.A.C. 8:59-3.15(d).

125. N.J.S.A. 34:5A-15(g); N.J.A.C. 7:1G-6.15(b); N.J.A.C. 8:59-3.15(b).

126. N.J.S.A. 34:5A-15(g); N.J.A.C. 7:1G-6.15(c); N.J.A.C. 8:59-3.15(c). The administrative regulations require that before being granted access to trade secret information, the contractor (1) provide evidence of adequate protection against unauthorized disclosure, (2) obtain Professional Liability Insurance or suitable indemnity insurance and Comprehensive General Liability Insurance in forms and amounts set by the department, (3) sign an agreement of confidentiality, and (4) assume responsibility for damages resulting from unauthorized disclosure. N.J.A.C. 7:1G-6.15(c); N.J.A.C. 8:59-6.15(c). Moreover, as in the case of information provided to medical personnel, the regulations provide that the employer receive advance notice of the department's intent to release the information. N.J.A.C. 7:1G-6.15(b)(2); N.J.A.C. 8:59-6.15(b)(2).

127. N.J.S.A. 34:5A-15(e); N.J.A.C. 7:1G-6.15(e); N.J.A.C. 8:59-3.15(e). In the case of physicians and osteopaths, this agreement must specifically prohibit disclosure to any other party. N.J.A.C. 7:1G-6.15(d); N.J.A.C. 8:59-3.15(d). The administrative regulations also require that certain procedures be followed by those gaining access to the information so as to insure its confidentiality. N.J.A.C. 7:1G-6.15(f); N.J.A.C. 8:59-3.15(f).

health department, county clerk, county designated lead agency, local fire department, or local police department or any other person who has access to confidential information under the Act to willingly and knowingly disclose that information to one unauthorized to receive it.[129] Similarly, unauthorized disclosure of trade secret information by a contractor, employee or agent of the department constitutes grounds for suspension, debarment, and disqualification from further contracting with the department.[130]

7-8 Public Employee Access to Information

The Act requires every public employer to maintain a central file containing the Right to Know Hazardous Substance List, the Right to Know Survey relating to the facility, and the applicable material safety data sheets and hazardous substance fact sheets.[131] The employer must also post notices alerting its employees of the availability of these materials at the facility.[132]

Employees wishing to obtain copies of these materials must make a written request upon the employer.[133] The employer must provide the requested copies at no cost to the employee within five working days of its receipt of the request.[134] Similarly, within five working days of receipt of a written request by the employee or his representative, the employer must disclose the CAS number, chemical name or trade secret-registry number of any hazardous substances and the five most predominant substances in an unlabeled container.[135] It must also disclose the name of any substance labeled by its common name.[136] If the employer cannot comply with a request for a hazardous substance fact sheet because it has not

128. N.J.A.C. 7:1G-6.15(g); N.J.A.C. 8:59-3.15(g). If the information is conveyed orally, the contents of the confidentiality agreement must be read to the recipient. N.J.A.C. 7:1G-6.15(g); N.J.A.C. 8:59-3.15(g). The requirements as to the need for written requests and notice to the employer prior to disclosure of the information may also be waived. Any person receiving trade secret information under these provisions must sign a confidentiality agreement within 72 hours. N.J.A.C. 7:1G-6.15(g)(2); N.J.A.C. 8:59-3.15(g)(2).

129. N.J.S.A. 34:5A-15(g); N.J.A.C. 7:1G-6.16(a); N.J.A.C. 8:59-3.16(a).

130. N.J.A.C. 7:1G-6.16(b); N.J.A.C. 8:59-3.16(b).

131. N.J.S.A. 34:5A-12; N.J.A.C. 8:59-7.2.

132. N.J.S.A. 34:5A-12; N.J.A.C. 8:59-7.2(b). The notice shall also state that the materials may be obtained from either the DEPE, DOH, or county health department, county clerk, or lead agency. N.J.A.C. 8:59-7.2(b). If the employer employs persons whose native language is Spanish, it must also post a notice in Spanish. N.J.S.A. 34:5A-12; N.J.A.C. 8:59-7.2(c).

133. N.J.A.C. 8:59-7.2(d); N.J.A.C. 8:59-7.5(a). The request may be made either by the employee or his representative. *Id.*

134. N.J.S.A. 34:5A-12; N.J.A.C. 8:59-7.2(d). An employee whose native language is Spanish may require the employer to provide a Spanish translation of the materials. N.J.A.C. 8:59-7.2(c).

135. N.J.A.C. 8:59-7.2(f).

136. N.J.A.C. 8:59-7.2(e).

received a sheet it has requested from the DOH, it must inform the employee of that fact in writing.[137] Similarly, if the employer has alerted the DOH that it does not know the name of a substance or component of a product, it must inform the requesting employee of that fact in writing.[138] In either case, the requesting employee should be provided the relevant material safety data sheet.[139]

7-9 Public Access to Reported Information

Under the Act, the DEPE is required to retain all completed environmental surveys it receives for a period of 30 years and to provide interested persons with copies of the document within 30 days of receipt of a written request.[140] The DOH has the identical responsibilities with respect to Right to Know Surveys and hazardous substance fact sheets filed with it.[141] Similarly, county health departments, county clerks, or designated lead agencies must make copies of surveys and fact sheets filed with them available for public inspection free of charge.[142]

7-10 Enforcement Provisions

A. Right to Inspect

Both the DEPE and DOH have the right to enter a covered facility during normal operating hours to determine compliance with the Act and relevant regulations.[143] Regulations promulgated by the DOH specifically provide that a

---

137. N.J.A.C. 8:59-7.2(h).

138. *Id.*

139. *Id.* Where a public employee's request for relevant information is not honored after five working days, the employee may refuse to work with the hazardous substance without the loss of pay or benefits until the request is honored. N.J.S.A. 34:5A-16(a); N.J.A.C. 8:59-7.5(b). However, the employee may not refuse to work with the substance if the reason the employer cannot respond to his request for a hazardous fact sheet is that the sheet has been requested but not yet been received from the DOH. N.J.A.C. 8:59-7.5(c). If the employee believes that his right to information has been violated, he may file a complaint with the Department of Health. N.J.A.C. 8:9-8.1. After administrative proceedings, the commissioner may institute a civil action by summary proceeding pursuant to the penalty enforcement law, N.J.S.A. 2A:58-1 *et seq*. The Employer may be liable to a penalty of not less than $2,500 for each violation. N.J.S.A. 34:5A-16(b).

140. N.J.S.A. 34:5A-9(a), (d).

141. N.J.S.A. 34:5A-10(d); N.J.A.C. 8:59-7.1.

A request by an employee for information relating to the facility where he is employed is to be treated as confidential by the DOH. N.J.S.A. 34:5A-10(d); N.J.A.C. 8:59-7.1(e); N.J.A.C. 8:59-7.3(d).

142. N.J.S.A. 34:5A-22; N.J.A.C. 8:59-7.3. If copies are requested, a fee equal to the cost of reproducing the documents may be imposed. N.J.S.A. 34:5A-22; N.J.A.C. 8:59-7.3.

Under the Act, local police and fire departments may not make information filed with them available to the public. N.J.S.A. 34:5A-25(a).

representative of the employer has the right to accompany the enforcement officer while conducting the inspection, unless that person's conduct interferes with the officer's ability to conduct a fair and orderly inspection.[144] However, the DOH may privately question any owner, operator, agent, employer, or public or private employee concerning matters related to the Right to Know Act.[145] In addition, the DOH may require an employer to provide copies of employee health and exposure records for the purpose of studying the effect of hazardous substances on both the worker and community populations.[146]

B. Remedies

Responsibility for enforcement is shared by the commissioners of the DEPE and DOH. Under this scheme, violations of reporting requirements associated with the environmental and ESI surveys are dealt with by the DEPE and violations of labeling, employee training, and workplace reporting requirements are handled by the DOH.[147] In either case, upon concluding that the employer has violated the Act, the department has four options available to it.[148] It may (1) issue a civil administrative order directing the employer to comply with the relevant provisions of the Act, (2) bring a civil action in the Superior Court, (3) impose an administrative penalty, or (4) commence an action for imposition of a civil penalty.[149] These options may be exercised either separately or in any combination deemed appropriate.[150]

C. Civil Administrative Orders

---

143. N.J.S.A. 34:5A-29; N.J.A.C. 8:59-8.4(a); N.J.A.C. 8:59-8.9. Similarly, county and regional health agencies that have entered interagency agreements with the DOH may enter a facility in order to conduct inspections in accordance with guidelines promulgated by the DOH. N.J.A.C. 8:59-8.4(b).

Under the regulations promulgated by the DOH, a public or private employee or employee representative may alert the department of alleged violations of the Act in his place of employment and/or request an inspection of the facility. N.J.A.C. 8:59-8.11. At his request, the employee's name will be kept confidential. N.J.A.C. 8:59-8.11(a).

144. N.J.A.C. 8:59-8.10.

145. N.J.A.C. 8:59-8.9(e).

146. N.J.S.A. 34:5A-10(c); N.J.A.C. 8:59-8.5; *see also* N.J.S.A. 26:1A-16; N.J.S.A. 26:1A-37 (granting commissioner right to enter premises for the purpose of collecting information regarding health laws). Among the records that the employer may be required to produce are those maintained pursuant to federal law. N.J.S.A. 34:5A-10(c); N.J.A.C. 8:59-8.5(a). Where the requested employee medical records reveal the name of the employee, the employer must grant the department access to the employee—either in person or by supplying his home address—so the department may request the employee's permission to review the records. N.J.A.C. 8:59-8.5(b).

147. N.J.S.A. 34:5A-31.

148. *Id.*

Administrative orders issued by the Commissioner to compel employer compliance must specifically identify the alleged violation and alert the employer of its right to an administrative hearing regarding the order.[151] Employer requests for administrative hearings must be made within 20 calendar days of receipt of the order.[152]

D. Civil Action by the Commissioners

In bringing civil actions in the Superior Court, the Commissioners may seek appropriate relief from the employer violation. This relief may include the imposition of reasonable costs incurred in the investigation leading to the discovery of the violation and in preparing and litigating the civil action.[153]

E. Civil Administrative Penalties

Under the Act, the Commissioner may impose a civil administrative penalty of up to $2,500 for each violation and an additional penalty of up to $1,000 per day for each day the violation continues after the employer's receipt of an order to cease.[154] Prior to the imposition of such a penalty, the employer must be provided with written notice setting forth the nature of the alleged violation and the amount of the administrative penalty and alerting it of its right to request an administrative hearing on the issue within 20 days.[155] If a hearing is not requested, the notice will become final.[156] Similarly, if a hearing is requested and results in the finding of a violation, the commissioner may issue a final order imposing the penalty.[157]

Both the DOH and the DEPE have promulgated regulations regarding the assessment of administrative penalties.[158] Under the DEPE's scheme, an employer

---

149. *Id.* Upon receiving a civil or administrative order or penalty, a public employer must post an unedited copy at or near the location of the alleged violation, or in such other location so as to be readily observable to all affected employees. N.J.A.C. 8:59-8.12(a). If the matter is contested, notice of that fact should be posted next to the copy of the order or penalty. N.J.A.C. 8:59-8.12(c). Such notices must remain posted for a period of three working days or until the violation is abated, whichever is later. N.J.A.C. 8:59-8.12(b).

Rather than posting such orders or penalties and notices of contest, private employees must send copies of same to their local fire department. N.J.A.C. 8:59-8.12(a),(c).

150. N.J.S.A. 34:5A-31.

151. *Id.*; N.J.A.C. 8:59-8.6.

152. N.J.S.A. 52:11B-1 *et seq.*; N.J.A.C. 8:59-8.6(c). The regulations adopted by the DOH specifically provide that if the hearing results in the finding of a violation, the Commissioner may issue a final order of compliance. N.J.A.C. 8:59-8.6(c). Moreover, if no hearing is requested by the employer within the 20 day period, the initial order will become final. N.J.A.C. 8:59-8.6(d).

153. N.J.S.A. 34:5A-31(c); N.J.A.C. 8:59-8.7.

154. N.J.S.A. 34:5A-31(d).

is assessed penalties for failing to comply with Environmental Survey reporting requirements.[159]

Administrative penalties imposed by the DOH are assessed according to a different system.[160] Under that system, violations are classified as being either "significant," "major" or "minor" and either "willful," "highly foreseeable" or "unintentional," with different point values assigned to each category.[161] The amount of the penalty is then computed as follows: (seriousness) x (type) x ($2,500) = penalty per violation.[162] Daily penalties imposed for failure to comply with an administrative order are calculated as follows: (seriousness) x (type) x ($1,000) = daily penalty.[163]

The Commissioner may compromise an administrative penalty imposed under the Act upon the employer's posting of a performance bond or upon such terms and conditions as may be established by regulation.[164]

F. Civil Actions

In addition to the administrative remedies outlined above, the Act provides that any person may institute a civil action in the Superior Court against an employer for violation of the Act or the regulations promulgated thereunder.[165] An action may also be instituted against the DOH or DEPE for failure to meet their enforcement responsibilities.[166] Such actions may be brought in law or equity and, in addition to the relief granted, the court may award costs to the prevailing party.[167]

In *Welch v. Schneider Nat'l Bulk Carriers*,[168] however, the District Court for the District of New Jersey held that this private right of action serves only to afford cit-

---

155. N.J.S.A. 34:5A-31(d); N.J.A.C. 7:1G-7.3(a); N.J.A.C. 8:59-8.2(c),(d). Such written notice may be issued separately or included within an administrative order, and must be served upon the employer personally or by certified mail. N.J.S.A. 34:5A-31(d); N.J.A.C. 7:1G-7.3(a), (b); N.J.A.C. 8:59-8.2(c).

The employer's request for an administrative hearing should be directed to either the DOH or the DEPE. N.J.S.A. 34:5A-31(d); N.J.A.C. 7:1G-7.3; N.J.A.C. 8:59-8.2(d). Moreover, DEPE regulations require that the request identify the provisions of the notice or order to which the employer objects, the basis for the objection, and proposed alternative provisions. N.J.A.C. 7:1G-7.3(d). The request should also include a statement of the relevant facts and law asserted and state the claimed legal authority and jurisdiction. *Id.*

DEPE regulations also provide that untimely requests will be denied, but, the department may grant incomplete requests on the condition that the employer correct any deficiencies within 10 days. N.J.A.C. 7:1G-7.3(e),(f).

156. N.J.S.A. 34:5A-31(d); N.J.A.C. 7:1G-7.3(h); N.J.A.C. 8:59-8.2(e).

157. N.J.S.A. 34:5A-31(d); N.J.A.C. 7:1G-7.3(h); N.J.A.C. 8:59-8.2(d). Under the regulations adopted by the DEPE and DOH, payment of civil penalties is due upon the issuance of the final order. N.J.A.C. 7:1G-7.3(i); N.J.A.C. 8:59-8.2(f). If payment is not made within a reasonable time thereafter the commissioner may file a civil action seeking the imposition of a civil penalty not to exceed $2,500 per day. N.J.S.A. 34:5A-31(e); N.J.A.C. 7:1G-7.3(i).

158. N.J.A.C. 8:59-8.2; N.J.A.C. 7:1G-7.7.

izens a method by which they may compel compliance with the Act's provisions.[169] It does not provide a basis for an employee to sue his employer in tort for money damages for personal injury sustained during the course of employment.[170]

7-11 Whistleblower Protection

Section 17 of the Act specifically provides that an employer may not discharge or otherwise discriminate against an employee for exercising his rights under the Act.[171] Employees alleging a violation of this provision may file a complaint with the Commissioner of the Department of Labor within 30 days of the violation or of learning of the violation.[172] Upon the commissioner's finding of probable cause for the complaint, the matter may be referred to the Office of Administrative Law for a hearing.[173] If there is evidence that the employee exercised a right under the Act prior to the alleged discriminatory conduct, the employer will bear the burden of justifying its conduct by clear and convincing evidence.[174] Subsequent recommendations of an OAL Judge must be adopted, rejected or modified by the commissioner within 45 days of receipt and such action will constitute final agency action subject to judicial review pursuant to the Rules of Court.[175]

---

159. N.J.A.C. 7:1G-7.7. The following table provides a summary of the appplicable penalties:

Offense	*Fine*
1. Failure to submit a Community Right to Know Survey	$1000.00
2. Failure to submit a Release and Pollution Prevention Report	$1000.00
3. Failure to report all EHS's pursuant to the Environmental Survey regulations	
a. One to ten substances	$500.00
b. More than ten substances	$1000.00
4. Failure to respond to the Department's request for clarification	$1000.00
5. Failure to submit a copy of a Community Right to Know Survey or a Release and Pollution Prevention Report	$1000.00
6. Failure to maintain or make available copies of the current Community Right to Know Survey or Release and Pollution Prevention Report	$500.00

160. N.J.A.C. 8:59-8.2.

II. DRUG TESTING

7-12 Introduction

The extent to which New Jersey law permits drug and alcohol testing of employees and applicants for employment remains unsettled. Testing by public employers is limited by the State and federal constitutional prohibitions against unreasonable searches and seizures. While that prohibition generally is not di-

---

161. N.J.A.C. 8:59-8.2. Examples of what the DOH considers to be significant and major violations are enumerated in the administrative regulations. N.J.S.A. 8:59-8.2(b).

In determining the type of violation, the DOH will assume that the employer has knowledge of all statutes and corresponding regulations applicable to its facility. Moreover, any known violation continuing for 30 days or more without the employer making an attempt to rectify it will be considered willful. N.J.A.C. 8:59-8.2(b)(3).

Point values are assigned as follows:

A. Seriousness of violations:	**Values**
(1) Significant	1.00
(2) Major	1.00 to 0.40
(3) Minor	0.40 to 0
B. Type of Violation	
(1) Willful	1.00
(2) Highly foreseeable	1.00 to 0.50
(3) Unintentional but foreseeable	0.50 to 0

N.J.A.C. 8:59-8.2(b)(4).

162. N.J.A.C. 8:59-8.2(b)(5).

163. *Id.*

164. N.J.S.A. 34:5A-31(d). Regulations adopted by the DEPE specifically provide that the Commissioner may compromise penalties assessed by the department based upon the existence of mitigating circumstances or upon any other terms and conditions he finds acceptable. N.J.A.C. 7:1G-7.4. DOH regulations similarly allow the Commissioner to compromise a penalty upon any terms and conditions he deems satisfactory. N.J.A.C. 8:59-8.2(h).

165. N.J.S.A. 34:5A-23; N.J.A.C. 8:59-8.3. *See generally Millison v. E.I. du Pont de Nemours & Co.*, 101 N.J. 161, 180-81 (1985) (describing enforcement scheme).

166. N.J.S.A. 34:5A-23; N.J.A.C. 8:59-8.3.

167. N.J.S.A. 34:5A-23; N.J.A.C. 8:59-8.3. The award of costs may include reasonable expert witness and attorneys' fees. N.J.S.A. 34:5A-23; N.J.A.C. 8:59-8.3.

168. 676 F. Supp. 571 (D.N.J. 1987).

169. *Id.* at 575.

170. *Id.* The court found that "[t]he statute is regulatory in nature, designed to monitor harmful substances in the environment and provide the public with information about these threats to their health." *Id.* It also noted that allowance of such a private cause of action under the Right to Know Act would constitute an implied repeal of the exclusive remedy provision of the Workers' Compensation Law, and stated that it could not conceive that was the legislature's intent. *Id.*

171. N.J.S.A. 34:5A-17(a); N.J.A.C. 8:59-7.2(i).

172. N.J.S.A. 34:5A-17(b).

173. *Id.*

rectly applicable to testing in the private sector, it has been found to be an expression of public policy that binds private employers under *Pierce v. Ortho Pharmaceutical Corp.*[176] This discussion is limited to New Jersey law and does not address the several federal statutory and regulatory provisions requiring and/or controlling employee drug testing in specific industries and circumstances.[177]

7-13 Public Employers

Blood and urine testing performed by the state or under its auspices constitutes a search and seizure under both the United States and New Jersey Constitutions.[178] Thus, public employers that perform such tests to detect drug and alcohol use among their employees are subject to the constitutional prohibition against unreasonable searches and seizures.[179]

In determining the reasonableness of drug testing programs under the New Jersey and United States constitutions, the courts have generally employed a balancing test, weighing the public employer's interests in detecting drug use against the privacy interests of the employees being tested.[180] Among the interests considered in this balance are: (1) the employees' expectations of privacy; (2) the intrusiveness of the testing procedure;[181] (3) the employer's interest in preventing drug use by employees; (4) the manner in which the testing is con-

---

174. *Id.*

175. *Id.*

176. 84 N.J. 58 (1980).

177. For a general view of that topic see Vol. 7, *RIA Employment Coordinator,* ¶¶EP-18, 449, *et seq.*

178. *National Treasury Employees Union v. Von Raab*, 489 U.S. 656, 665 (1989); *Skinner v. Railway Labor Executives' Ass'n*, 489 U.S. 602, 617 (1989); *N.J. Transit PBA Local 304 v. N.J. Transit Corp.*, 151 N.J. 531, 543-44 (1997); *Caldwell v. New Jersey Dept. of Corrections*, 250 N.J. Super. 592, (App. Div 1991); *Local 194A v. Burlington County Bridge Comm'n*, 240 N.J. Super. 9, 14 (App. Div.), *certif. denied*, 122 N.J. 183 (1990); *Allen v. Passaic County*, 219 N.J. Super. 352, 357 (Law Div. 1986). *Chandler v. Miller*, 117 S. Ct. 1295 (1997); *Local 304 v. New Jersey Transit Corp.*, 151 N.J. 531 (1997); *Rawlings v. Police Dep't of Jersey City*, 133 N.J. 182 (1993); *O'Keefe v. Passaic Valley Water Comm'n*, 132 N.J. 234, 242.

179. *National Treasury Employees Union v. Von Raab*, 489 U.S. 656, 665 (1989); *Skinner v. Railway Labor Executives' Ass'n*, 489 U.S. 602, 617 (1989); *N.J. Transit PBA Local 304 v. N.J. Transit Corp.*, 151 N.J. 531, 543-44 (1997); *O'Keefe v. Passaic Valley Water Commission*, 132 N.J. at 242 (1993) ("A drug test, whether administered by the government either for law enforcement purposes, is subject to the requirements of the Fourth Amendment."); *Local 194A v. Burlington County Bridge Comm'n*, 240 N.J. Super. at 14; *Allen v. Passaic County*, 219 N.J. Super. 352, 358 (Law Div. 1986). The same analysis applies where a private employer acts as an instrumentality of the state; for example, where the employer conducts testing pursuant to the mandate of state regulation. *Skinner v. Railway Labor Executives' Ass'n*, 489 U.S. 602, 614 (1989); *Chandler v. Miller*, 117 S. Ct. 1295 (1997); *Local 304*, 151 N.J. 531 (1997); *Rawlings*, 133 N.J. 182 (1993).

180. *National Treasury Employees Union v. Von Raab*, 489 U.S. 656, 665-66; *Skinner v. Railway Labor Executives' Ass'n*, 489 U.S. 602, 619; *Local 304*, 151 N.J. 531 (1997); *Local 194A v. Burlington County Bridge Comm'n*, 240 N.J. Super. at 23; *Allen v. Passaic County*, 219 N.J. Super. 352, 273-74; *Capua v. City of Plainfield*, 643 F. Supp. 1507, 1513 (D.N.J. 1986).

ducted; (5) the nature of the industry involved; and (6) the possible effects upon the public.[182]

Application of this test by New Jersey courts suggests that random tests of public employees will sometimes be allowed.[183] Testing for cause, testing in conjunction with physical examinations,[184] and government-mandated testing of employees in highly regulated industries also have been found acceptable under appropriate circumstances.[185]

Although Article 1, ¶7 of the New Jersey Constitution generally affords greater protection than the Fourth Amendment, New Jersey courts have thus far found it

---

181. *National Treasury Employees Union v. Von Raab*, 489 U.S. at 671-72; *Skinner v. Railway Labor Executives'Ass'n*, 289 U.S. at 627-29; *N.J. Transit PBA Local 304 v. N.J. Transit Corp.*, 151 N.J. 531, 559 (1997); *Capua v. City of Plainfield*, 643 F. Supp. at 1514-15; *Allen v. Passaic County*, 219 N.J. Super. at 374-75; *Local 194A v. Burlington County Bridge Comm'n*, 240 N.J. Super. at 24. In *O'Keefe v. Passaic Valley Water Comm'n*, the Court declined to rule on the constitutionality of drug testing of applicants for public employment, but nonetheless outlined the analysis that would be applied:

> An Analysis of the Fourth Amendment to the United States Constitution or article one, paragraph seven of the New Jersey Constitution initially poses the question whether an employer has a "special ...need beyond the normal need for law enforcement" to test applicants...
>
> After determining whether a special need exists, a court must then balance the applicant's or employee's privacy interests against those of the government employer in administering the drug-testing program....
>
> Yet another question is whether the employer's procedures minimize the intrusiveness of the drug testing and diminish the employee's reasonable expectation of privacy in the drug test ... Beyond that, we would be compelled to consider the significance of an employee's notice of the drug-testing requirement....
>
> With applicants, as distinguished from employees, the requirement of individualized suspicion raises a further problem because of the employer's inability to observe applicants in an office setting.... In the present case, another consideration would be whether the position of a water-meter reader is 'safety sensitive' .... Finally, we would have to consider the relevance of economic considerations, such as [the employer's] justification of the drug testing-program to decrease employee absenteeism and stabilize its work force.

132 N.J. 234, 242-44 (1993).

182. *National Treasury Employees Union v. Von Raab*, 489 U.S. at 670-72; *Skinner v. Railway Labor Executives'Ass'n*; 489 U.S. 627-29; *N.J. Transit PBA Local 304 v. N.J. Transit Corp.*, 151 N.J. 531 (1997) (upholding random tests of transit police in safety-sensitive positions in a regulated industry); *Capua v. City of Plainfield*, 643 F. Supp. at 1514-15; *Allen v. Passaic County*, 219 N.J. Super. at 374-75; *Local 194A v. Burlington County Bridge Comm'n*, 240 N.J. Super. at 24; *Egloff v. New Jersey Air National Guard*, 684 F.Supp. 1275, 1281-82 (D.N.J. 1988). *But see O'Keefe*, 132 N.J. 234 (suggesting, but not holding, that random tests in inspector positions would not be allowed); *Stanziale v. County of Monmouth*, 884 F. Supp. 140 (D.N.J. 1995) (striking down suspicionless testing of sanitary inspector whose job was determined not to be safety-sensitive).

183. *O'Keefe v. Passaic Valley Water Commission*, 253 N.J. Super. 569, 579-80 (App. Div. 1992), *aff'd on other grounds*, 132 N.J. 234 (1993) (pre-employment testing for water-meter reading positions unconstitutional); *Capua v. City of Plainfield*, 643 F. Supp. 1507 (D.N.J. 1986) (same as to fire fighters). *See Rawlings*, 133 N.J. 182 (upholding individualized reasonable suspicion drug testing; here, an attempted test of an officer arrested on suspicion of selling cocaine). *See also Drake v. County of Essex*, 275 N.J. Super. 585 (App. Div. 1994) (where work rules provided for testing upon reasonable suspicion, odor of marijuana in bathroom used by several officers sufficient; reasonable individualized suspicion is a less stringent standard than probable cause).

184. *Local 194A v. Burlington County Bridge Comm'n*, 240 N.J. Super. 9 (App. Div.), *certif. denied*, 122 N.J. 183 (1990).

unnecessary to extend the federal constitutional rule in this respect.[186] The New Jersey Supreme Court has found the United States Supreme Court opinions in *Skinner v. Railway Labor Executives' Ass'n*[187] and *National Treasury Employees Union v. Von Raab*[188] applicable in evaluating the constitutionality of employee drug tests under the state constitutional scheme as well.[189]

In *Skinner v. Railway Labor Executives' Ass'n*,[190] the United States Supreme Court upheld a Federal Railroad Administration regulation mandating drug testing of railroad employees involved in certain types of train accidents.[191] It held that, although warrantless searches conducted without probable cause or individual suspicion are generally deemed unreasonable and therefore constitutionally invalid, an exception exists where "special needs, beyond the normal need for law enforcement, make the warrant and probable-cause requirement impracticable."[192] The court further held that the government's interest in ensuring public safety through the regulation of railroad workers constituted such a "special need," which when balanced against the diminished expectations of privacy possessed by the workers and the limited intrusiveness of the tests, justified testing in the absence of individualized suspicion.[193]

---

185. *Shoemaker v. Handel*, 795 F.2d 1136 (3d Cir.), *cert. denied*, 479 U.S. 986 (1986).

186. *N.J. Transit PBA Local 304 v. N.J. Transit Corp.*, 151 N.J. 531 (1997); *Local 194A v. Burlington County Bridge Comm'n*, 240 N.J. Super. 9, 24 (App. Div.), *certif. denied*, 122 N.J. 183 (1990). *But see Caldwell v. New Jersey Dept. of Corrections*, 250 N.J. Super. 592 (App. Div. 1991), where the court noted that the New Jersey constitution provides greater protection than does the United States Constitution, but left unclear whether it was rejecting the *Local 194A* panel's conclusion that in the context of employee drug testing, a higher state standard is not required. *See* discussion *infra* at n. 207 and accompanying text.

187. 489 U.S. 602 (1989).

188. 489 U.S. 656 (1989).

189. *N.J. Transit PBA Local 304 v. N.J. Transit Corp.*, 151 N.J. 531 (1997).

190. 489 U.S. 602 (1989).

191. *Id.* at 634.

192. *Id.* at 619, quoting *Griffin v. Wisconsin*, 483 U.S. 868, 873 (1987).

193. 489 U.S. at 620, 634. While recognizing that the production of a urine sample imposed upon the privacy of the employee, the Court noted that the railroad administration regulations sought to reduce the intrusiveness of the process by providing that the sample be collected in a medical environment and by allowing the employee to produce it in private. *Id.* at 626. *See Chandler v. Miller*, 117 S. Ct. 1295 (1997). This case found that a Georgia statute requiring that candidates for state office pass a drug test did not meet the exception for suspicionless searches. The Court held that this requirement failed to demonstrate a "special need for law enforcement" important enough to override the individual's privacy interests. *Id.* at 1301-1305. *See also Stanziale v. County of Monmouth*, 884 F. Supp. 140 (D.N.J. 1995). The case emphasizes the importance of the safety-sensitive nature of the employment in applying the Fourth Amendment balancing test to suspicionless testing, and concludes that the job sanitary inspector was not safety sensitive. "Disposal of the protection afforded by the individualized suspicion requirement is justified when the targeted employee's position is such that a single misperformed duty could directly result in disastrous consequences. It is not justified, however, where the nexus between the employee's blunder and the potential injury is so attenuated as to alleviate the risk of creating irremedial consequences." *Id.*, 884 F. Supp. at 146.

Similarly, in *National Treasury Employees Union v. Von Raab*,[194] the Court held that the government's need to conduct suspicionless searches of certain customs employees to protect the public outweighed the privacy interests of those employees.[195] In so holding, it stressed that the public interest requires that employees directly involved in the interdiction of drugs not be drug users.[196] The protection of the public also requires that the government insure that employees who are issued firearms and often required to make split second decisions as to the use of those firearms are not impaired by drug use.[197] Moreover, because of the nature of the positions they hold, these employees have a diminished expectation of privacy.[198]

In *NJ Transit PBA Local 304 v. NJ Transit Corp.*, the New Jersey Supreme Court adopted the federal rule and upheld New Jersey Transit's program of random testing of weapon-carrying officers.[199] The Court found that there was a "special need" for the tests, beyond normal law-enforcement purposes, in protecting New Jersey Transit employees and the public;[200] that the procedure utilized was designed to minimize the intrusion into employee privacy;[201] and that due to the nature of their postions, the officers had a lowered expectation of privacy.[202] As a consequence, the Court found that New Jersey Transit's compelling interest in using random testing to protect the public outweighed the employees' diminished privacy expectations.[203] The Appellate Division had held similarly in *Local 194A v. Burlington County Bridge Comm'n*,[204] upholding drug testing performed without individualized suspicion, during regularly scheduled physical

---

194. 489 U.S. 656 (1989).

195. 489 U.S. at 668, 672.

196. 489 U.S. at 670.

197. 489 U.S. at 670. Because of ambiguities in the record below, the Court did not reach the issue whether the testing of customs employees who had access to classified material also passed constitutional muster. Instead, the matter was remanded to the Court of Appeals for further proceedings. *Id.* at 678-79.

198. 489 U.S. at 672. The Court noted: "Unlike most private citizens or government employees in general, employees involved in drug interdiction reasonably should expect effective inquiry into their fitness and probity." *Id.*

199. 151 N.J. 531 (1997).

200. 151 N.J. at 559. Because the transit police ride the trains and work independently at stations throughout the state, individualized suspicion testing was a practical impossibility. *Id.* at 558-59.

201. *Id.* Among other things, samples were collected in a manner so as to ensure privacy; only in limited circumstances where there was a risk of a substituted sample was a same-sex observer used; testing was limited to enumerated substances; at the employee's option, a sample testing positive could be submitted for a second test; and disclose of the results was strictly limited.

202. *Id.* at 562. The court found that the officers should have had a diminished expectation of privacy because they performed traditional police functions, carried weapons and made critical judgments.

203. *Id.* at 564-65.

204. 240 N.J. Super. 9 (App. Div.), *certif. denied*, 122 N.J. 183 (1990).

examinations, upon public bridge operators responsible for opening and closing draw bridges.[205] The court reasoned that the interest in protecting the public from the disaster that might result from the use of drugs by these employees constituted a "special need" that outweighed the employees' diminished expectations of privacy and justified the testing performed.[206] It stressed, however, that its decision was based upon the "totality of the circumstances presented."[207] Among the other factors considered important was the regularized nature of the test.[208] In fact, the court relied upon this fact to distinguish the testing from that found constitutionally invalid in *Fr. Order of Police v. City of Newark* and similar cases.[209] The Appellate Division distinguished *Local 194A v. Burlington County Bridge Comm'n* in *O'Keefe v. Passaic Valley Water Comm'n*, where it found pre-employment testing of meter-reader applicants unconstitutional for lack of a public-safety nexus.[210] Finally, a different Appellate Division panel applied a "reasonable suspicion" standard in *Caldwell v. New Jersey Dept. of Corrections*, but apparently avoided the constitutional issue by relying on a departmental procedure requiring suspicion.[211]

Random testing of employees not in safety-sensitive positions but in highly regulated industries has also been upheld. *Shoemaker v. Handel*[212] involved regulations of the New Jersey Racing Commission requiring jockeys and certain other employees to submit to alcohol breathalizer tests at the direction of the

---

205. 240 N.J. Super. at 11. Plaintiffs challenged the testing under both the Fourth Amendment to the United States Constitution and Article 1, ¶7 of the New Jersey Constitution. They also alleged that the termination of their employment based upon the results of the tests constituted a violation of the New Jersey Law Against Discrimination. *Id.* at 12.

206. 240 N.J. Super. at 24. The court further held that the decision whether to conduct drug testing of employees is a non-negotiable managerial prerogative but that the testing procedures employed are subject to negotiation between employers and employees. *Id.* at 11-12, 25. The matter was remanded to the trial court on the question whether disciplinary action taken by the employer is also negotiable. *Id.* at 25-26. Moreover, the court left open the question whether plaintiffs could assert a cause of action under the New Jersey Law Against Discrimination. *Id.* at 26. As is discussed in detail in Chapter 4, §4-14:1, the Appellate Division subsequently held, in *In re Cahill*, 245 N.J. Super. 397, 400 (App. Div 1991), that drug addiction is a handicap protected under the New Jersey Law Against Discrimination.

207. 240 N.J. Super. at 11.

208. *Id.*

209. 240 N.J. Super. at 17. The court stressed that even if the annual testing were deemed to be "random" under the circumstances, it would nevertheless be valid because of the nature of the examination. *Id.* at 23. In further commenting on the importance of the fact the testing was routinely conducted, the court stated, "the reason that drug testing during routine scheduled physicals is less objectionable than random tests is that employees have a lower expectation of privacy as to such testing, and thus the testing is only minimally intrusive." *Id.* at 17.

210. *O'Keefe v. Passaic Valley Water Comm'n*, 253 N.J. Super. 569 (App. Div 1992), *aff'd on other grounds*, 132 N.J. 234 (1993) (while the avoidance of employee absenteeism and health costs resulting from drug abuse and maintenance of a drug-free workplace are laudable goals they are insufficient to overcome Fourth Amendment protections).

State Steward.[213] The regulations also subjected employees to random urine tests to detect drug use with respect to any race.[214] Five jockeys challenged the testing on the ground that it violated the Fourth and Fourteenth Amendments to the United States Constitution and infringed upon their constitutional right of privacy.[215] At the outset, the district court found that the administrative search exemption to the warrant requirement of the Fourth Amendment extended to drug testing of persons employed in highly regulated industries.[216] As a result, testing conducted absent individualized suspicion is constitutionally valid where there is a strong state interest in performing the test and pervasive regulation of the industry has reduced the expectations of privacy possessed by those being tested. The court found each of these requirements to be satisfied with respect to the horse racing industry.[217]

The court noted the state's substantial interest in protecting the integrity of the racing industry, whose success depends heavily upon public confidence. Because the industry has been heavily regulated since its inception, the court reasoned, those employed within it have a diminished expectation of privacy. As a consequence, the court found that random testing of these workers did not violate the Fourth Amendment.[218] In addition, although the court recognized that racing industry employees have a legitimate privacy interest concerning medical informa-

---

211. 250 N.J. Super. 592, (App. Div 1991). The court stated:

> Given that our constitution has been interpreted to afford greater protection to individuals than that afforded by the federal Constitution, *see State v. Novembrino*, 105 N.J. 95, 146 (1987); *State v. Hunt,* 91 N.J. 338, 370-72 (1982); *Fraternal Order [of Police v. City of Newark]* 216 N.J. Super. at 477, and that petitioners were informed by and acknowledged receipt of the procedures which clearly stated that they would only be ordered to submit to the test if the Commissioner found there was a "reasonable individualized suspicion," we view that standard as the applicable one.

Factors considered by the court in evaluating the reasonableness of the suspicion in *Caldwell* included: (1) the nature of the tip or information; (2) the reliability of the informant; (3) the degree of corroboration; and (4) other factors contributing to the suspicion or lack of suspicion. *Id.* at 609. In *Rawlings v. Police Dep't of Jersey City,* 133 N.J. 182, 190-91 (1993), the Supreme Court upheld the termination of a police officer who had refused to submit to a drug test upon his arrest for suspected sale of cocaine. Finding that "[i]ndividualized reasonable suspicion effectively balances the Fourth Amendment rights of the officer and the interest of the police department in conducting a drug test," the Court concluded that it protected officers against arbitrary and discriminatory testing and satisfied the Fourth Amendment. The Court found that the officer's arrest and indictment gave him no special right to refuse the drug test; however, it found it unnecessary to decide whether the results of a test taken in those circumstances would be admissible in a criminal proceeding.

212. 795 F.2d 1136 (3d Cir.), *cert. denied,* 479 U.S. 986 (1986).

213. 795 F.2d at 1138.

214. 795 F.2d at 1138, 1140.

215. 795 F.2d at 1141.

216. 795 F.2d at 1142.

217. *Id.*

218. *Id.*

tion, it held that the interest was adequately protected where unauthorized disclosure of such information was prohibited.[219]

7-14 Private Employers

The constitutional prohibition against unreasonable searches and seizures is not directly applicable in the private sector. In *Hennessey v. Coastal Eagle Point Oil Co.*,[220] the Supreme Court agreed that the search and seizure provisions of the United States and New Jersey constitutions do not protect citizens from unreasonable searches by private parties. However, the Supreme Court found that those provisions, along with the inalienable rights clause of article I, paragraph 1 of the New Jersey Constitution, "give rise to a clear mandate of public policy that allows a fired employee to state a *Pierce* cause of action." The Court did not rule on whether there is a constitutional right to privacy that governs the conduct of private actors.[221] As a consequence, private employer drug tests are now subject to the public policy expressed in the constitutional provisions that are directly applicable in the public sector. However, it remains unsettled precisely what that public policy is, and whether the public policy is co-extensive with the constitutional protection, i.e., whether precisely the same standard applies in the private and public sectors. The considerations noted by the Court as relevant in the two contexts have been similar; however, the public employer may be required to make a showing of special need that is not required in the private sector.[222]

7-14:1 Testing of Prospective Employees

In *Jevic v. Coca-Cola Bottling Co. of N.Y.*,[223] the United States District Court for the District of New Jersey held that a private employer may legitimately refuse to hire prospective employees who test positive for drug use.[224] In that case, the plaintiff had been offered a position with the Coca-Cola Bottling Company conditioned upon the results of a pre-employment test for drug use.[225] Plaintiff consented to the test and provided a urine sample that was test-

---

219. 795 F.2d at 1144.

220. 129 N.J. 81 (1992).

221. *Id.* at 98-99

222. *See Hennessey*, 129 N.J. 81; *O'Keefe v. Passaic Valley Water Comm'n*, 132 N.J. 234, 242 (1993); *Rawlings v. Police Dep't of Jersey City*, 133 N.J. 182 (1993); *Hennessey v. Coastal Eagle Point Oil*, 247 N.J. Super. at 305-06; *see also, Jevic v. Coca-Cola Bottling Co. of N.Y.*, 5 IER Cases 769-70.

223. 5 IER Cases 765 (D.N.J. 1990).

224. 5 IER Cases at 766.

ed using both the enzyme-multiplied immunoassay technique and the gas chromatography/mass spectrometry technique.[226] When the results revealed that plaintiff had used marijuana, the company withdrew its conditional offer of employment.[227]

At the outset, the court found that individualized suspicion is not a prerequisite for a private employer's testing of prospective employees for drug use.[228] In addition, it stressed that under the circumstances, the Coca-Cola Company's testing was not otherwise contrary to the public policy of the state, but rather was reasonable in both design and scope.[229]

The court also noted, however, that employers conducting drug testing assume an "obligation, as a matter of public policy, to insure that its drug-testing procedures are scientifically sound," and that "an at will employee fired on the basis of a false positive, procured through second rate or negligent procedures, would surely have a cause of action based on public policy for wrongful termination."[230] The basis for this dicta is unclear since the court failed to identify any clear expression of public policy upon which such a wrongful discharge claim would need to be based. Nevertheless, pending further explanation by the courts or the legislature, it would be advisable for employers conducting drug testing to utilize scientifically sound and prudent techniques to reduce the risk of error.

7-14:2 Testing of Current Employees

The Supreme Court opinion in *Hennessey v. Coastal Eagle Point Oil Co.*,[231] substantially limits the right of private employers to conduct random drug-testing.

The *Hennessey* majority declined to decide "whether random urine testing violates either common-law or constitutional privacy rights," and repeated that it was "not finding in this opinion a constitutional right to privacy that governs the

225. 5 IER Cases at 766-67.

226. *Id.*

227. 5 IER Cases at 767.

228. 5 IER Cases at 770. *See generally, O'Keefe v. Passaic Valley Water Comm'n*, 132 N.J. 234, 243 (1993) (public sector case noting the problem of distinguishing between the privacy rights of employees and applicants and the inability of an employer to observe applicants in an office setting to develop a reasonable individualized suspicion).

229. 5 IER Cases at 771. The court also rejected plaintiff's claim that the testing violated his privacy. It reasoned that since plaintiff had consented to the testing there could be no violation of his privacy. *Id.* at 771-72. As the court stated, "one cannot intrude when one has permission." *Id.* at 771.

230. 5 IER Cases at 770.

231. 129 N.J. 81 (1992).

conduct of private actors." However, it nonetheless concluded that those constitutional provisions and common-law precedents express a public policy of privacy that may in appropriate circumstances support a *Pierce* claim. Determining when appropriate circumstances exist in the context of a drug test is a fact-intensive inquiry. Because "'a clear mandate of public policy' must be one that on balance is beneficial to the public," the employee's privacy interests cannot be considered alone:

> To constitute a 'clear mandate of public policy' supporting a wrongful-discharge cause of action, the employee's individual right (here, privacy) must outweigh the competing public interest (here, public safety) .... If the employee's duties are so fraught with hazard that his or her attempts to perform them while in a state of drug impairment would pose a threat to co-workers, to the workplace, or to the public at large, then the employer must prevail.

Applying that standard to the facts before it, the Court upheld the test of *Hennessey* and consequent discharge, noting (1) a showing of drug-use among employees; (2) the potential dangers involved in Hennessey's job assignment; and (3) the inability of the employer to detect drug use effectively through observation, due to the absence of supervision of the employees in question. On that basis, the majority concluded that "the combination of the impracticality of less-intrusive means of detecting drug use and the urgent need to ensure public safety renders urine testing a permissible method of preventing drug use among employees in safety-sensitive jobs."

At the same time, however, it instructed employers to minimize the intrusiveness of testing. Although suggesting that drug testing would be better addressed in collective bargaining agreements and legislation, the majority went on to outline specific requirements, including (1) testing procedures that allow "as much privacy and dignity as possible"; (2) notice of the program, the details of how employees will be selected, a warning to employees of the lingering effect of drugs in the system, and an explanation of how the test will be analyzed; (3) notice of the consequences of testing positive or refusing to be tested; (4) limitation of tests performed on the sample to those necessary to determine the presence of drugs; and (5) nondisclosure of the information obtained through testing.

7-15 Handicap Discrimination

Alcoholism is a handicap protected under the Law Against Discrimination (LAD).[232] The Appellate Division has held that other drug addiction—apparently even drug addiction that involves the illegal use of controlled dangerous substances—is a handicap under the LAD.[233] Recovered alcoholics and addicts—but not active drug users—are protected under the federal Americans With Disabilities Act (ADA).[234]

The requirements of the LAD with respect to handicapped employees and applicants are discussed extensively in Chapter 4, §§4-14 to 4-14:5. Employers engaged in drug testing of employees and/or applicants should carefully consider the requirements of the LAD and the federal ADA in both the conduct of testing and the administration of any sanctions therefor.

III. SMOKING IN THE WORKPLACE

7-16 Introduction

The law in New Jersey attempts to strike a balance between the individual's right to smoke and protection of the health and comfort of employees while on the job. The New Jersey Smoking Law prohibits employers from discriminating against individuals who smoke,[235] but at the same time requires employers to establish rules restricting the right to smoke in the workplace. [236]

---

232. *Clowes v. Terminix Int'l, Inc.*, 109 N.J. 575 (1988).

233. *In re Cahill*, 245 N.J. Super. 397 (App. Div 1991). *Contra N.J. Attorney General Formal Opinion No. 1-1989* (Oct. 6, 1989), 125 N.J.L.J. 100 (Jan. 11, 1990).

234. 42 U.S.C. §§12101 *et seq.* Section 510 of the ADA excludes from the definition of an "individual with a disability" an individual "who is currently engaging in the illegal use of drugs, when the covered entity acts on the basis of such use." 42 U.S.C. §12210. The ADA also amended the Rehabilitation Act of 1973 to provide, *inter alia*, that employers do not violate the Act by adopting reasonable policies or procedures, including drug testing, to ensure that individuals are no longer using drugs. Sec. 512. The EEOC's regulations under the ADA are being described by that agency as "neutral" on the question of testing. BNA, Vol. 6, No. 16 *Individual Employment Rights*, p.1 (Aug. 13, 1991). 29 U.S.C. §1630.16(b), (c). On the specific question of drug testing, the regulations provide:

> (c) *Drug testing - (1) General policy.* For purposes of this part, a test to determine the illegal use of drugs is not considered a medical examination. Thus, the administration of such drug tests by a covered entity to its job applicants or employees is not a violation of Sec. 1630.13 of this part. However, this part does not encourage, prohibit, or authorize a covered entity to conduct drug tests of job applicants or employers to determine the illegal use of drugs or to make employment decisions based on such test results.

29 C.F.R. §1630.16(c)(1). *See* 29 C.F.R. §1630.16(c)(2) regarding transportation employees.

235. N.J.S.A. 34:6B-1 *et seq.*

7-17 Prohibition of Discrimination

The New Jersey Smoking Law provides that employers may not refuse to hire or otherwise discriminate against an employee or prospective employee because the individual does or does not smoke or otherwise use tobacco products, unless the action is founded upon a rational basis reasonably related to the employment.[237] Employers violating the Act are subject to a civil penalty of up to $2,000 for the first offense and up to $5,000 for each subsequent offense.[238] The Act also provides a private right of action to aggrieved parties, who must file suit within one year of the alleged violation.[239] In such civil actions, the court may order injunctive relief and award compensatory and consequential damages.[240] The court may also award reasonable costs and attorneys fees.[241]

7-18 New Jersey Smoking Act [242]

While acknowledging that individuals have the legal right to smoke,[243] the New Jersey Smoking Act compels employers to establish policies and procedures designed to control smoking in the workplace, to protect employees from the hazards of second-hand smoke.[244] Covered employers must establish written rules regarding smoking in their places of employment which reflect a "policy and procedure to protect the health, welfare and comfort of employees from the detrimental effects of tobacco smoke."[245]

The smoking policy must provide for designated non-smoking areas and may also include designated smoking areas unless such a designation is contrary to a statute, regulation or municipal ordinance designed to prevent injury due to

---

236. N.J.S.A. 26:3D-23 *et seq.* A Bureau of National Affairs, Inc. survey in 1991 indicated that 85 percent of responding employers had workplace smoking policies, and that half of the employers without such policies planned to adopt them in 1992. Vol. 6, No. 18 BNA *Individual Employment Rights*, p.1 (Sept. 10, 1991).

237. N.J.S.A. 34:6B-1. The Act specifically provides that it does not adversely affect requirements regarding the use of tobacco during employment. N.J.S.A. 34:6B-2. Moreover, nothing in the Act would prohibit employers from charging smokers more for company health care insurance than non-smokers.

238. N.J.S.A. 34:6B-4. The penalty is collectible by the Commissioner of Labor through a summary proceeding. *Id.*

239. N.J.S.A. 34:6B-3.

240. *Id.* Injunctive relief may include the reinstatement of the employee with full seniority rights and fringe benefits. *Id.* Compensatory damages may include compensation for lost wages and benefits. *Id.*

241. *Id.*

242. N.J.S.A. 26:3D-23 *et seq.*

243. N.J.S.A. 26:3D-23.

244. N.J.S.A. 26:3D-25.

245. *Id.*

fire.[246] Each designated area provided for must also be marked with a sign indicating by either words or the appropriate international symbol whether smoking is permitted or prohibited.[247] The signs must be clearly visible to the employees and the words or symbols used must be in contrasting colors.[248] The employer is also free to adopt other rules, policies or procedures that are consistent with the provisions of the Act and to negotiate such requirements as terms or conditions of employment.[249]

To facilitate compliance, section 8 of the Act requires the State Department of Health to provide consultation services to employers who request them.[250] The Act also allows the state or its agencies and political subdivisions to provide employers with suggested guidelines for rules regarding smoking in the workplace.[251] In no case, however, may the employer's adoption of such guidelines be made mandatory.[252]

7-18:1 Covered Employers

The New Jersey Smoking Act applies to all places of employment[253] with 50 or more persons performing services pursuant to an employment relationship with or for an individual, partnership or private corporation.[254] The responsibility for meeting the provisions of the Act falls upon the "employer," defined as the proprietor of the place of employment who ultimately controls the conduct and activities at the facility.[255]

---

246. *Id.*

247. N.J.S.A. 26:3D-27.

248. N.J.S.A. 26:3D-25.

249. *Id.* Copies of the rules must be provided to employee upon request. *Id.*

250. N.J.S.A. 26:3D-30. Such services may consist of providing the employer with staff consultation or with suggested rules and/or policies. *Id.*

251. N.J.S.A. 26:3D-26(a).

252. *Id.* The Act specifically provides that it supersedes all statutes, rules, regulations and municipal ordinances regarding smoking in the workplace except those which prohibit smoking for the purpose of protecting against the risk of fire. N.J.S.A. 26:3D-26(b).

253. A place of employment is defined as any "structurally enclosed location or portion thereof which is not usually frequented by the public..." and at which employees perform the duties of their employment. N.J.S.A. 26:3D-24(b).

254. N.J.S.A. 26:3D-24(a).

255. N.J.S.A. 26:3D-24(a). Under the statute, the employer may be either an individual or a corporation. *Id.*

7-18:2 Enforcement

Enforcement of the smoking law rests with the Department of Health.[256] If the DOH suspects a violation of the Act, it must serve written notice upon the employer via certified or registered mail setting forth the alleged violation as well as its recommendations as to how the employer may bring itself into compliance.[257] Upon receipt of the notice, the employer may request a conference with the department for the purpose of facilitating compliance with the Act.[258]

Ninety days after written notice is forwarded to the employer, the Commissioner of Health may file suit in the Superior Court of New Jersey to enforce the provisions of the Act.[259] Such a suit by the Commissioner of Health is the exclusive means of enforcing employer compliance with the Act.[260] Moreover, if the employer or his agent has adopted a written smoking policy designating nonsmoking areas, it may not be subject to an action for personal injury allegedly resulting from exposure to second-hand smoke unless the action is brought by an employee pursuant to the Workers' Compensation Act.[261]

---

256. N.J.S.A. 26:3D-28(a)(1).

257. N.J.S.A. 26:3D-28(a) the DOH may present its recommendations as a series of alternative proposals. *Id.*

258. N.J.S.A. 26:3D-28 (a)(3). The conference may be held at the employer's place of business or other mutually agreed upon location.

259. N.J.S.A. 26:3D-28(b).

260. N.J.S.A. 26:3D-29.

261. *Id.*

Chapter 8

Wage and Hour

I. OVERVIEW

8-1 Scope of Chapter

This chapter examines several major areas of state regulation of employee wages and hours. The New Jersey Wage Payment Law, discussed in Part II, governs the time and manner in which wages must be paid.[1] The New Jersey Wage and Hour Law, discussed in Part III, provides for minimum wages, maximum hours, overtime pay and the like.[2] The Discrimination in Wages Law,[3] discussed in Part IV, prohibits discrimination in wages on the basis of sex and complements similar prohibitions in the New Jersey Law Against Discrimination.[4] The Prevailing Wage Act, discussed in Part V, governs wages paid to employees of contractors on public works and authorizes the establishment of minimum wage levels for such employees by craft.[5] State rules governing executions against wages are addressed in Part VI,[6] and the procedure for asserting claims through the Wage Collection Division is discussed in Part VII.[7] The Child Labor Law[8] is discussed in Part VIII.

A number of other statutes govern more particularized wage and hour concerns and are not addressed herein at length. They include the Home Work Law[9] and the Industrial Home Work Law.[10]

---

1. N.J.S.A. 34:11-4.1 *et seq.*; *see* §§8-2 to 8-3:11.
2. N.J.S.A. 34:11-56a *et seq.*; *see* §§8-4 to 8-8.
3. N.J.S.A. 34:11-56.1 *et seq.*; *see* §8-9.
4. *See* Chapter 4 for a complete discussion of the Law Against Discrimination.
5. N.J.S.A. 34:56.25 *et seq.*; *see* §§8-10 to 8-10:6.
6. *See* §§8-11 through 8-11:4.
7. §§8-12 through 8-15, *infra.*
8. N.J.S.A. 34:2-21.1 *et seq.* *See* N.J.A.C. 12:58-1.1 through 12:58-4.17.
9. N.J.S.A. 34:6-120 *et seq.*

II. WAGE PAYMENT

8-2 Time of Payment/In General

The New Jersey Wage Payment Law[11] requires that every employer[12] pay the full amount of wages due its employees[13] at least twice during the calendar month on regular paydays designated in advance.[14] "Wages" are:

> the direct monetary compensation for labor or services rendered by an employee, where the amount is determined on a time, task, piece, or commission basis excluding any form of supplementary incentives and bonuses which are calculated independently of regular wages and paid in addition thereto.[15]

Each regular payday must be no more than 10 working days after the end of the pay period for which payment is made.[16] If a regular payday falls on a non-work day, payment may be made on the next following work day,[17] unless (a) a collective bargaining agreement provides otherwise, or (b) the employer has utilized the statutory provision permitting it to wait 10 working days after the end of the pay period to make payment. In the latter case, if a regular payday falls on a non-work day, payment must be made on the preceding work day.[18]

---

10. N.J.S.A. 34:6-136.1 *et seq. See* N.J.A.C. 12:59-1.1 through 12:59-1.13.

11. N.J.S.A. 34:11-4.1, *et seq.*

12. Employer is defined as including: "any individual, partnership, association, joint stock company, trust, corporation, the administrator or executor of the estate of a deceased individual, or the receiver, trustee, or successor of any of the same, employing any person in this State." N.J.S.A. 34:11-4.1(a). The officers of a corporation, as well as any agents having the management of such corporation who knowingly permit the corporation to violate N.J.S.A. 34:11-4.2 (pertaining to the time and mode of payment of wages) or N.J.S.A. 34:11-4.3 (pertaining to the payment of wages upon suspension or termination of employment), will be deemed to be the employers of the employees of the corporation. N.J.S.A. 34:11-4.1(a). All "officers of a corporation and any agents having the management of such corporation" are now deemed to be employees, not just those who knowingly permit the corporation to violate N.J.S.A. 34:11-4.2 (pertaining to the time and mode of payment of wages) or N.J.S.A. 34:11-4.3 (pertaining to the payment of wages upon suspension or termination of employment). N.J.S.A. 34:11-4.1(a).

13. An employee is "any person suffered or permitted to work by an employer, except that independent contractors and subcontractors shall not be considered employees." N.J.S.A. 34:11-4.1(b).

14. N.J.S.A. 34:11-4.2.

15. N.J.S.A. 34:11-4.1(c). Retroactive pay benefits promised to employees in consideration of their hard work and loyalty during a reorganization were found not to be wages within the scope of this statute. *Finkler v. Elsinore Shore Assocs.*, 725 F.Supp. 828 (D.N.J. 1989).

16. N.J.S.A. 34:11-4.2.

17. *Id.*

18. *Id.*

8-2:1 Executive and Supervisory Personnel

Paydays for bona fide executive, supervisory and other "special classifications" of employees may be less frequent than twice a month.[19] But such employees must be paid in full at least once each calendar month on a regularly scheduled basis.[20]

8-2:2 Railroad Employees

Every railroad, express, car-loading and car-forwarding company authorized to do business by the laws of New Jersey must pay employees once each week.[21] Payment must be made not more than 14 days after the end of the seven-day period during which the wages were earned.[22]

8-2:3 Termination or Suspension of Employee

Whenever employment is terminated or suspended, the affected employee must be paid all wages due no later than the regular payday for the pay period during which the termination, suspension or cessation of employment took place.[23] Employees who are compensated, in full or in part, on the basis of an incentive system, shall be paid a reasonable approximation of the wages due until the exact amounts due can be calculated.[24] When an employee is suspended as a result of a labor dispute which also involves the employees who make up the payroll, the employer has an additional 10 days in which to pay the worker's wages.[25]

8-2:4 Death of Employee

If an employee dies, all wages due may be paid, without actual notice of the pendency of the probate proceedings and without requiring letters testamentary or of administration, in the following order of preference, to: (1) the decedent's

---

19. N.J.S.A. 34:11-4.2.

20. *Id.*

21. N.J.S.A. 34:11-2.

22. *Id.* For the purpose of this provision, "[w]ages means those earnings derived from basic pro rata rates of pay pursuant to a labor agreement, and shall not include incentives, bonuses, and other similar types of fringe payments." *Id.*

23. N.J.S.A. 34:11-4.3. Payment may be made through regular channels or by mail if requested by the employee. *Id.*

24. *Id.*

25. *Id.*

surviving spouse, (2) the children of decedent 18 years of age and over in equal shares, or to the guardian of children under 18 years of age, (3) the father and mother or the surviving parent of decedent, (4) the decedent's sisters and brothers, or (5) the person who pays the funeral expenses.[26]

8-3 Mode of Payment

Wages must be paid in lawful currency of the United States or with checks drawn on banks with which arrangements have been made to allow employees to cash checks without difficulty and for the full amount.[27]

An employer may not pay its employees in store goods or merchandise, or issue as payment any order or other paper unless negotiable and by its terms redeemable by the issuer for the face value in lawful United States currency.[28]

An employer who violates this rule must forfeit the amount of wages or pay for which such orders were given.[29] Such orders cannot be offset against any claims for wages, but recovery may be had for the wages in full.[30] A settlement with the employer will not bar such an action until lapse of one year after the settlement.[31]

Violation of the rule also constitutes a disorderly persons offense, punishable by fine not to exceed $500.[32]

---

26. N.J.S.A. 34:11-4.5. Payments made under this section after presentation of proof of the relationship constitute a release and discharge of the employer in the amount paid. *Id.*

27. N.J.S.A. 34:11-4.2. Direct deposit is permitted under N.J.S.A. 34:11-4.2a.

28. N.J.S.A. 34:11-17. A private individual may give orders for goods and merchandise in a store, if he has no direct or indirect interest in its profits or business. *Id.* Abuses associated with the use of "company stores" played a prominent part in New Jersey's early wage payment laws. As noted by the Appellate Division in *Dept. of Labor & Industry v. Rosen*, 44 N.J.Super. 42, 45-46 (App. Div. 1957):

> The motivating factor for the enactment of the legislation was the elimination of the practice prevalent among factory owners, particularly by owners of glass factories in southern New Jersey, of paying wages in the form of order books or scrip, redeemable only at company-owned stores. The statutes, an exercise of the police power of the State, have decided economic benefits to the employee. The assurance of payment in cash at regular intervals of wages upon which an employee is dependent for the support of himself and his family is obviously an economic and social necessity. Indeed, such a view has biblical support: "The wages of him that is hired shall not abide with thee all night until the morning," *Leviticus*, 19:13; "At his day thou shalt give him his hire, neither shall the sun go down upon it. ..." *Deuteronomy*, 24:15.

(citations omitted).

29. N.J.S.A. 34:11-18.

30. *Id.*

31. *Id.*

32. N.J.S.A. 34:11-19; N.J.S.A. 2C:1-4.

8-3:1 Withholding or Diverting of Wages/In General

As a general rule, an employer may not withhold or divert any portion of an employee's wages *unless* the employer is so required or empowered by State or federal law.[33]

8-3:2 Permissible Withholding

It is permissible to withhold or divert a portion of an employee's wages for:

1. Contributions authorized under a collective bargaining agreement, or in writing by the employee, for payment to employee welfare, insurance, hospitalization, medical and/or surgical, pension, retirement and profit-sharing plans, plans establishing annual retirement annuities, or individual retirement accounts, for the employee and/or his spouse.[34]
2. Contributions authorized under a collective bargaining agreement, or in writing by the employee, for payment into a company-operated thrift plan, or a security option or purchase plan to buy securities of the employing corporation, affiliated corporation, or other corporations, at market price or less, provided such securities are listed on a stock exchange or sold over the counter.[35]
3. Payments authorized by employees for payment into employee personal savings accounts, payments to banks for Christmas, vacation, or other savings funds. All such deductions must be employer approved.[36]
4. Payments for company products in accordance with a payment schedule contained in the original purchase agreement, if approved by the employer.[37]

---

33. N.J.S.A. 34:11-4.4(a). *See Miller v. Essex County Welfare Board*, 151 N.J. Super. 280, 285 (App. Div. 1977) (county welfare board could not withhold part of retroactive pay increase to employee/welfare recipient on ground that amount of welfare benefits paid might have been less if wage increase had been given at the outset); *Male v. Acme Markets, Inc.*, 110 N.J. Super. 9 (App. Div. 1970) (prohibition against withholding or diverting from wages except as authorized by statute barred employer from requiring cashiers to reimburse it from wages for shortages, even on day subsequent to payday); *Miller v. Director, Division of Taxation*, 6 N.J. Tax 118, 133 (1983) (interpreting contract granting an unconditional right to reduce compensation because of shortages as a franchise agreement in order to avoid illegality under N.J.S.A. 34:11-4.4(a)).

34. N.J.S.A. 34:11-4.4(b)(1).

35. N.J.S.A. 34:11-4.4(b)(2).

36. N.J.S.A. 34:11-4.4(b)(3).

37. N.J.S.A. 34:11-4.4(b)(4).

5. Payments for employer loans in accordance with a payment schedule contained in the original loan agreement, if approved by the employer.[38]
6. Payments for safety equipment, if approved by the employer.[39]
7. Payment for the purchase of United States Government bonds, if approved by the employer.[40]
8. Payments to correct payroll errors, if approved by the employer.[41]
9. Contributions authorized by employees and approved by the employer for "organized and generally recognized charities."[42]
10. Payments authorized by employees or in their collective bargaining agreements for the rental, laundering, or dry cleaning of work clothes or uniforms. Such deductions must be approved by the employer.[43]
11. Dues and initiation fees for labor organizations, and such other labor organization charges permitted by law.[44]
12. Contributions authorized in writing by employees, pursuant to a collective bargaining agreement, to a political committee and/or continuing political committee established by the employees' labor union for the purpose of aiding in the nomination, election or defeat of any candidate for public office of the State, county, municipality or school district, or the passage or defeat of any public question. Any such withholdings must comply with the specific requirements of N.J.S.A. 34:11-4.4a. [45]
13. Contributions authorized in writing by the employees to a political committee or continuing political committee other than one described in paragraph 12, for the purpose of making contributions to aid in the nomination, election or defeat of any candidate for a public office of the State, county, municipality or school district or the passage or defeat of any public question. Any such

---

38. *Id.*
39. *Id.*
40. *Id.*
41. *Id.*
42. N.J.S.A. 34:11-4.4(b)(5).
43. N.J.S.A. 34:11-4.4.(b)(6).
44. N.J.S.A. 34:11-4.4.(b)(7).

withholding must comply with the requirements of N.J.S.A. 34:11-4.4a. The employer may require the political committee to reimburse it for its administrative expenses in making the deductions.[46]

14. Payments authorized by employees for programs sponsored by the employer for group or individual purchase of insurance or annuities, if otherwise permitted by law.[47]
15. Such other contributions, deductions and payments as the Commissioner of Labor may authorize by regulation as proper and in conformity with the intent and purpose of the statute, if such deductions are employer approved.[48]

8-3:3 Employer-Owned Stores

An employer—or the agents, clerks or superintendents of the employer—who owns or controls any stores for the sale of general store goods or merchandise in connection with his manufacturing or other business, may not compel his employees to purchase goods or supplies at such stores by withholding the payment of wages beyond the usual payday.[49]

---

45. N.J.S.A. 34:11-4.4(b)(8). N.J.S.A. 34:4.4a requires that before any such withholdings are made, the following conditions must be complied with. The payroll deduction authorization must be signed by the employee and contain the following explanatory statement:

> I recognize that my/any contribution through payroll deduction is completely voluntary and in compliance with State law. It shall be unlawful for any person soliciting an employee for contribution to such a fund to fail to inform such employee of his or her right to refuse to contribute without reprisal.
>
> Any questions relative to compliance with election law may be directed to the Election Law Enforcement Commission, 28 West State Street, Trenton, New Jersey 08625, (609) 292-8700.
>
> Any political action committee or continuing political committee (hereinafter "PAC") which elects to solicit employees for such withheld contributions must file a statement of registration with the Election Law Enforcement Commission, as specified in N.J.S.A. 34:11-4.4a(b). The PAC must provide space on the payroll deduction form to allow the employee to direct his contributions to specific candidates. N.J.S.A. 34:11-4.4a(c). No employee may elect to contribute more than $5 per week by payroll deduction and no employee may have wages withheld for more than one PAC. N.J.S.A. 34:11-4.4a(d). No solicitation may be made for employee contributions on the job or in the workplace. N.J.S.A. 34:11-4.4a(e). Any PAC which solicits contributions under this provision must provide each employee participant an annual financial statement showing disbursement of funds, including administrative charges. N.J.S.A. 34:11-4.4a(f).

46. N.J.S.A. 34:11-4.4(b)(9). See footnote 45.

47. N.J.S.A. 34:11-4.4(b)(10).

48. N.J.S.A. 34:11-4.4(b)(11). *See, e.g.*, N.J.A.C. 12:55-1.3 (authorizing payroll deductions as means of providing mass transportation commuter tickets).

49. N.J.S.A. 34:11-21.

8-3:4 Payment for Medical Examinations

An employer who requests or directs any employee or prospective employee to submit to a medical examination as a condition of entering or continuing employment, by a physician designated by the employer, may not deduct from the wages or prospective wages of such individual any sum to defray the cost of such examination. [50] An employer must reimburse any employee or prospective employee who does pay for such an examination.[51]

An employer who violates this provision is liable for a penalty of $100 to be recovered by and in the name of the Department of Labor for use by the State.[52]

8-3:5 Assignment or Purchase of Wages

It is unlawful for any person to purchase or have assigned to him by an employee any pay or wages that are due or are to become due, as repayment of a loan, if the purchaser or assignee is to receive or contracts to receive, either directly or indirectly, more than the legal interest rate.[53]

Any person violating this provision is guilty of a disorderly persons offense punishable by a fine not to exceed $500.[54]

These provisions do not apply to any assignment of pay or wages for payment of the full value of goods, wares or merchandise sold to an employee, or for professional services to the employee mentioned in the assignment.[55]

---

50. N.J.S.A. 34:11-24.1. In general, an employer may not use medical examinations as a means of screening prospective employees. N.J.A.C. 13:13-2.3. However, it is not unlawful for an employer to condition an offer of employment on the results of a medical examination held subsequent to such offer provided that (1) all entering employees are subjected to such examination; and (2) the results of the examination are not used to disqualify an applicant except to the extent that any disability disclosed would, even with reasonable accommodation, preclude safe or adequate performance of the job. N.J.A.C. 13:2.4. See discussion at Chapter 4, §4-14:5.

51. N.J.S.A. 34:11-24.1.

52. N.J.S.A. 34:11-24.2.

53. N.J.S.A. 34:11-25. *See Rosenbusch v. Fry*, 5 N.J. Misc. 312 (1st Dist. Ct. of Jersey City 1927) (transaction characterized as a "purchase of wages" was in fact a loan; because rate of interest charged violated then-applicable usury laws, principal was not recoverable); *Van Vechten v. McGuire*, 70 N.J.L. 152 (Sup. Ct. 1903), *aff'd on other grounds*, 70 N.J.L. 657 (E. & A. 1904) (loan arrangement charactertized by defendant as a "contract for the purchase of unearned future pay" was subject to usury laws).

54. N.J.S.A. 34:11-26; N.J.S.A. 2C:1-4. The purchaser/assignee may also forfeit any principal or interest charges. N.J.S.A. 17:10-14,-21.

55. N.J.S.A. 34:11-26. *See also Dept. of Labor v. Asbury Metro Hotel*, 80 N.J. Super. 486 (App. Div. 1963) (upholding assignment of wages to employment agency in payment of obligations due agency by employee).

8-3:6 Other Obligations and Duties of the Employer

Employees must be told at time of hiring what their rate of pay will be, and on what day they will be regularly paid.[56]

Employees also must be told of any changes in pay rates or paydays before the changes take effect.[57]

The employer must provide each employee with a statement of deductions made under N.J.S.A. 34:11-4.4[58] for each pay period.[59]

Employers must post an abstract of the wage act furnished by the Commissioner of Labor in a place accessible to their employees; keep records as to each employee, including wage and hour records, and preserve such records for periods of time as the Commissioner shall prescribe by regulation.[60] However, an employer need not maintain records of hours worked for persons employed in a bona fide executive, administrative or professional capacity or in the capacity of an outside salesman, 18 years or older, where the wages of such persons are not determined by number of hours worked.[61]

8-3:7 Agreements for Payment of Wages

The statutory requirements for the payment of wages may not be avoided by agreement, except (1) as provided by the Wage Payment Law, (2) to pay wages at shorter intervals than as provided, or (3) to pay wages in advance.[62] Any other agreement is null and void,[63] and will not prevent the imposition of penalties against the employer.[64]

Any employee with whom such an agreement is made has a right of civil action against his employer in any court of competent jurisdiction in New Jersey for the full amount of his wages.[65]

---

56. N.J.S.A. 34:11-4.6.

57. *Id.*

58. *See* §8-3:2, *supra.*

59. N.J.S.A. 34:11-4.6.

60. *Id.* A copy of the abstract may be obtained from the Office of Wage and Hour Compliance, Room 709, CN 389, Trenton, N.J. 08625.

61. N.J.S.A. 34:11-4.6(e).

62. N.J.S.A. 34:11-4.7.

63. *Id. But see Dept. of Labor v. Asbury Metro Hotel*, 80 N.J. Super. 486 (App. Div. 1963)(upholding voluntary wage assignment agreement between employee and employment agency).

64. N.J.S.A. 34:11-4.7.

65. *Id.*

8-3:8 Dispute Over Wages

If there is a dispute over the amount of wages, the employer must pay all wages conceded by him to be due, without any conditions and within the time prescribed by the Wage Payment Law.[66] As to any balance claimed, the employee may take advantage of any remedies to which he is otherwise entitled, including those under the Wage Payment Law.[67]

An employee's acceptance of any payment does not constitute a release as to the balance of his claim.[68] Moreover, any release required by an employer as a condition of payment is a violation of the law and deemed null and void.[69]

8-3:9 Rights of Employees As Against Employer's Creditors

A creditor who seeks to remove an employer's personal property under executions, attachments or other process must first pay or cause to be paid to employees any wages then owing by the employer, not to exceed two months' wages.[70] Upon paying, or causing such wages to be paid, the creditor may proceed to execute his process.[71]

If an officer, by virtue of execution, attachment or other process, removes an employer's personal property, without first paying to employees the wages due and owing in the amount specified, then the employer's personal property cannot be sold by the officer until the wages are paid and 10 days have passed since removal.[72] However, as a preliminary step, the employees who are owed wages must give the officer notice of their claim within 10 days of the removal.[73] Notice may be served by delivery to the officer or by leaving a copy at his home.[74]

---

66. N.J.S.A. 34:11-4.8(a). *See Maldonado v. Lucca*, 636 F. Supp. 621, 624 (D.N.J. 1986) (offering wages not in dispute in exchange for a waiver of other claims violates N.J.S.A. 34:11-4.8, and conflicts directly with protections guaranteed by the federal Migrant and Seasonal Agricultural Worker Protection Act and Fair Labor Standards Act).

67. N.J.S.A. 34:11-4.8(a).

68. *Id.*

69. *Id.*

70. N.J.S.A. 34:11-31. *See State v. Rosen*, 40 N.J.Super. 363, 369-71 (Co. Ct. 1956), *rev'd on other grounds*, 44 N.J.Super. 42 (App. Div. 1957) (landlord that distrained for rent and seized property of employer subject to requirements of N.J.S.A. 34:11-31). *But see Robison-Anton Textile Co. v. Embroidery Prod. Corp.*, 97 N.J.Super. 507 (App. Div. 1967) (unperfected wage claims subordinate to lien for federal taxes).

71. N.J.S.A. 34:11-31. The creditor is entitled to recover the wages paid under this section as well as the amount due by virtue of the process. *Id.*

72. *Id.*

73. *Id.*

74. *Id.*

When a receiver takes possession of the employer's personal property, any employee to whom wages are due and owing may apply to the court appointing the receiver for the payment of his wages.[75] The court shall determine the amount of the wages due and owing and direct the receiver to sell so much of the employer's personal property as may be necessary to pay the outstanding wages, without delay and in preference to other creditors.[76]

8-3:10 Regulation And Enforcement

The Commissioner of Labor and his authorized representatives are responsible for enforcement of the Wage Payment Law.[77] They are empowered to: investigate charges of violations of this act and institute actions for penalties;[78] enter and inspect places of employment, question employees and investigate such matters as they may deem appropriate;[79] administer oaths and examine witnesses under oath, issue subpoenas, compel attendance of witnesses and production of documents, and take affidavits and depositions in any proceeding before the commissioner.[80]

The Commissioner is authorized to propose and issue rules and regulations necessary to implement the provisions of the law.[81] The proposed rules and regulations must be published and made available to the public with notice that they

---

75. N.J.S.A. 34:11-33.

76. N.J.S.A. 34:11-33. *But see In re Holly Knitwear, Inc.*, 115 N.J.Super. 564, 577-78, 581 (Co. Ct. 1971) (on assignment for benefit of creditors, unperfected claims of wage earners subordinate to rights of federal government; also, amounts owed to employees out of health and welfare fund and specified by collective bargaining agreement as not "wages" not entitled to priority), *modified on other grounds*, 140 N.J.Super. 375 (App. Div. 1976); *Robison-Anton Textile Co. v. Embroidery Prod. Corp.*, 97 N.J. Super. 507, 509 (App. Div. 1967) (federal lien taxes which had accrued and were due prior to insolvency entitled to priority over unperfected wage claims).

77. N.J.S.A. 34:11-4.9(a), 34:11-16.

78. N.J.S.A. 34:11-4.9(a). When the Commissioner of Labor finds that an employer has violated the Wage Payment Law, he may assess and collect administrative penalties up to a maximum of $250 for a first violation and up to a maximum of $500 for each subsequent violation, specified in a schedule of penalties to be promulgated as a rule or regulation in accordance with the Administrative Procedure Act. N.J.S.A. 34:11-4:10. Certain factors must be considered in setting the penalty: (1) previous violations by the employer; (2) the seriousness of the violation; (3) the good faith of the employer; and (4) the size of the employer's business. *Id.* No administrative penalty may be imposed unless the Commissioner gives the alleged violator: (1) notice of the alleged violation and the amount of the penalty by certified mail; and (2) an opportunity to request a hearing before the commissioner or his designee within 15 days of receipt of the notice. *Id.* If no hearing is requested, the notice of penalty becomes a final order at the end of the 15-day period, and payment of the penalty is due. *Id.* Any penalty which is not paid may be recovered by the Commissioner in a summary proceeding under the Penalty Enforcement Law. N.J.S.A. 2A:58-1, *et seq.*

79. N.J.S.A. 34:11-4.9(b).

80. N.J.S.A. 34:11-4.9(c). Compliance with subpoenas and the provision of testimony may be compelled in a proceeding for contempt brought by the Commissioner in Superior Court. N.J.S.A. 34:11-4.9(d).

81. N.J.S.A. 34:11-4.11. *See* N.J.A.C. 12:55.

will become effective on a specific date, but no earlier than 60 days from the date of publication.[82] Notice must also provide that a public hearing on the proposed rule or regulation will be held at a specific date, time and place, but not earlier than 15 days from the date published copies are made available to the public.[83] At the hearing, all interested parties may present testimony to be considered by the Commissioner before promulgating the final rule or regulation.[84]

8-3:11 Penalties

Any employer who knowingly and willfully violates any provision of the Wage Payment Law is guilty of a disorderly persons offense and, upon conviction, will be subject to a fine of not less than $100 nor more than $1,000. Each day during which a violation continues constitutes a separate and distinct offense.[85]

A defendant who fails to pay the amount of a judgment rendered against him, together with the incidental costs and charges, shall be jailed for a period not exceeding 100 days for the first conviction, and not exceeding 200 days for a second, subsequent or continuing violation.[86]

Any person who fails to comply with a subpoena or to testify on any matter on which he may be lawfully questioned will, on application of the Commissioner, be subject to a contempt proceeding in the Superior Court.[87]

III. WAGE AND HOUR LAW

8-4 Purpose

The New Jersey State Wage and Hour Law[88] was enacted to effectuate the public policy to provide a "minimum wage level for workers in order to safeguard

---

82. N.J.S.A. 34:11-4.11.

83. *Id.*

84. *Id.*

85. N.J.S.A. 34:11-4.10; N.J.S.A. 2C:1-4. *See also* N.J.S.A. 2A:170-90.2 (employer that knowingly and willfully fails or refuses to make payments required by collective bargaining agreement or contract with employees is a disorderly person), *aff'd*, 198 N.J. Super. 318 (App. Div. 1984); *Trustees of Local 478 Pension Fund v. Prioozzi*, 198 N.J. Super. 297 (App. Div. 1983) (no private cause of action thereunder); *O'Shea v. RCA Global Communications*, 1984 WL 49044, 117 LRRM 2880 (D.N.J. July 24, 1984) (predicting New Jersey courts would not recognize a private cause of action under N.J.S.A. 2A:170-90.2). *See also State v. Burten*, 219 N.J. Super. 239 (Law Div. 1986), *aff'd*, 219 N.J. Super. 156 (App. Div.), *certif. denied*, 107 N.J. 144 (1987) (statute pre-empted by Employee Retirement Income Security Act with respect to employee benefit plans).

86. N.J.S.A. 34:11-10.

87. N.J.S.A. 34:11-4.9(d).

88. N.J.S.A. 34:11-56a to 34:11-56a30.

their health, efficiency, and general well-being and to protect them as well as their employers from the effects of serious and unfair competition resulting from wage levels detrimental to their health, efficiency and well-being."[89] The minimum wage standard also is intended to provide compensation fairly and reasonably commensurate with the value of services rendered.[90] The employment of an individual in any occupation at an "oppressive and unreasonable" wage is contrary to public policy; any contract, agreement or understanding with respect to such employment is void.[91]

The requirements of the State Wage and Hour Law have in some respects been more stringent than those of the Fair Labor Standards Act ("FLSA"). Pursuant to §18 of the FLSA, state and local standards for minimum wages and maximum hours that provide greater protection for workers take precedence over the federal law:

> No provision of this chapter or of any order thereunder shall excuse noncompliance with any Federal or State law or municipal ordinance establishing a minimum wage higher than the minimum wage established under this chapter or a maximum workweek lower than the maximum workweek established under this chapter, and no provision of this chapter relating to the employment of child labor shall justify noncompliance with any Federal or State law or municipal ordinance establishing a higher standard than the standard established under this chapter.[92]

---

89. N.J.S.A. 34:11-56a. As noted by the Appellate Division in *Hotel Suburban System, Inc. v. Holderman*, 42 N.J.Super. 84, 89 (App. Div. 1956), the constitutionality of minimum wage laws is well-established:

> Since the decision of the United States Supreme Court in *West Coast Hotel Co. v. Parrish*, 300 U.S. 379, 57 S.Ct. 578, 81 L.Ed. 703, 108 A.L.R. 1330 (1937), it is undisputably settled that a federal or state statute fixing, or properly authorizing, an administrative agency to set minimum wages for services in private employment is a constitutional exercise of the police power which does not violate the due process clauses of the Fifth or Fourteenth Amendments to the Federal Constitution or similar provisions in State Constitutions. *Lane v. Holderman*, 40 N.J.Super. 329 (App. Div. 1956); *United States v. Darby*, 312 U.S. 100, 61 S.Ct. 451, 85 L.Ed. 609, 132 A.L.R. 1430 (1941) . . . .

The criteria identified in the Unemployment Compensation Law and interpreting case law will be used to determine if an individual is an employee or an independent contractor for the purpose of the wage and hour law. N.J.A.C. 12:56-16.1.

90. *See Council of New Jersey Hairdressers, Inc. v. Male*, 68 N.J.Super. 381, 385 (App. Div. 1961); *Lane v. Holderman*, 40 N.J.Super. 329, 341 (App. Div. 1956).

91. N.J.S.A. 34:11-56a3. An "oppressive and unreasonable wage" is one "which is both less than the fair and reasonable value of the service rendered and less than sufficient to meet the minimum cost of living necessary for health." N.J.S.A. 34:11-56a1(l).

92. 29 U.S.C. §218(a).

Section 18 of the federal law is construed broadly to reflect its purpose of ensuring "that the FLSA shall not be used to deny an employee overtime compensation he may be entitled to under local or state law."[93]

8-5 Minimum Wage Rate

As of April 1, 1992, the minimum wage rate for a 40-hour workweek[94] is $5.05 per hour.[95] When the state minimum wage is higher than that required by the federal Fair Labor Standards Act, all employers must comply with the state law.[96]

Employees engaged to perform farm labor on a piece rate must be paid for each day not less than the minimum hourly wage rate provided by this section, multiplied by the total number of hours worked.[97]

All time an employee is required to be at his place of work or on duty is counted as hours worked.[98] Employees who reside on the employer's premises and work irregular and intermittent hours that make it unfeasible to account for the hours actually on duty may be compensated for not less than eight hours per day in lieu of other applicable provisions.[99] An employee who reports for work at the employer's request must be paid for at least one hour at the applicable wage rate, except where the employer has made available to the employee the minimum number of hours agreed upon prior to commencement of work on that day.[100]

---

93. *Brennan v. State of New Jersey*, 364 F. Supp. 156, 160 (D.N.J. 1973). *See State v. Comfort Cab, Inc.*, 118 N.J. Super. 162, 170-73 (Law Div. 1972) (employees exempt from overtime under FLSA subject to New Jersey minimum wage law pursuant to 29 U.S.C. §218(a)).

94. A "workweek" is defined by regulation as follows:

> (a) A workweek shall be a regularly recurring period of 168 hours in the form of seven consecutive 24-hour periods.
>
> (b) The workweek need not be the same as the calendar week and may begin any day of the week and any hour of the day.
>
> (c) The workweek shall be designated to the employee in advance.
>
> (d) Once the beginning time of an employee's workweek is established, it remains fixed regardless of the schedule of the hours worked.
>
> (e) The beginning of the workweek may be changed if the change is intended to be permanent and is not intended to evade the overtime requirements of the act.

N.J.A.C. 12:56-5.4.

95. N.J.S.A. 34:11-56a4; N.J.A.C. 12:56-3.1.

96. 29 U.S.C. §218(a).

97. N.J.S.A. 34:11-56a4.

98. N.J.A.C. 12:56-5.2(a). An employer is not required by the act to pay an employee for hours the employee is not required to be at his place of work by reason of holidays, vacation, lunch hours, illness and similar reasons. N.J.A.C. 12:56-5.2(b).

99. N.J.A.C. 12:56-5.3.

Time spent "on-call" need not be considered hours worked where employees are not required to remain on the employer's premises and are free to engage in their own pursuits subject only to leaving word where they can be reached.[101] If such an employee does go out on an on-call assignment, only the time actually spent in making the call need be considered hours worked.[102] However, if calls are so frequent or the on-call conditions so restrictive that the employee is not free to use the time for his own benefit, he "may be considered 'engaged to wait' rather than 'waiting to be engaged,' " and the waiting time shall be considered hours worked.[103] On-call employees required to remain at home when their office is closed to receive telephone calls from customers, and enjoying long periods of leisure time to engage in normal activities, may be compensated pursuant to any reasonable agreement for determining the number of hours worked.[104] Such an agreement must count not just the actual time spent answering calls, but must also make some allowance for the restriction on freedom involved with such an arrangement.[105]

8-5:1 Overtime

Each hour of work in excess of 40 hours in any week is overtime and must be compensated at a rate of $1^1/_2$ times the employee's "regular hourly wage."[106] Overtime, as well as minimum wage pay, is computed on the basis of each workweek standing alone; hours may not be averaged over two or more workweeks.[107] There is no requirement that an employee be paid overtime for hours in excess of eight hours per day, nor for work on weekends, holidays, or other days of rest, other than the overtime required for hours in excess of 40.[108]

An employee's regular hourly wage is defined by statute as:

> the amount that an employee is regularly paid for each hour of work as determined by dividing the total hours of work during

---

100. N.J.A.C. 12:56-5.5.

101. N.J.A.C. 12:56-5.6.

102. N.J.A.C. 12:56-5.6(a).

103. N.J.A.C. 12:56-5.6(b).

104. N.J.A.C. 12:56-5.7.

105. *Id.*

106. N.J.S.A. 34:11-56a4. Employees are entitled to overtime based upon their actual wages and not the specified minimum wages. N.J.A.C. 12:56-6.3.

107. N.J.A.C. 12:56-6.2.

108. N.J.A.C. 12:56-6.4(b). This provision, of course, does not excuse employers from compliance with contractual obligations with respect to premium pay, or from compliance with other state or federal law imposing additional obligations. *Id.*

the week into the employee's total earnings for the week, exclusive of overtime premium pay.[109]

Department of Labor Regulations provide that the following items need not be included in calculating the "regular hourly wage": (1) gifts made on special occasions or as a reward for service, the amounts of which are not measured by or dependent upon hours worked, production, or efficiency; (2) payments made for periods when no work is performed, due to vacation or other similar cause; (3) payments for travel or other reimbursable expenses incurred for the employer's benefit, and not made as compensation for employment; (4) sums paid in recognition of service that are in the nature of discretionary bonuses or pursuant to a *bona fide* profit sharing type plan, as those terms are defined in the regulation; (5) irrevocable employer contributions to employee welfare or pension plans; (6) additional premium compensation paid for hours worked in excess of eight per day or for work on weekends, holidays, or regular days of rest; and (7) overtime premiums.[110]

When an employee's pay includes the value of gratuities, food or lodging, and it is not feasible to determine the regular hourly wage, the employer will be deemed to have fulfilled its obligations for overtime under the regulations if the overtime is paid in cash on the basis of an agreed hourly wage.[111] However, the premium rate so established may not be less than the applicable minimum rate.[112]

8-5:2 Exemptions From Overtime

Employees exempt from overtime include any individual employed in a bona fide executive, administrative or professional capacity; also, outside salespeople,[113] farm laborers, hotel employees,[114] employees of common carriers of passengers by motor bus,[115] limousine drivers who are employed by an employer engaged in the business of operating limousines,[116] and employees engaged in labor relative to raising or care of livestock.[117]

---

109. N.J.S.A. 34:11-56a1(e). The act does not require that employees be compensated on an hourly rate basis: "Their earnings may be determined on a piece-rate, salary, bonus, commission or other basis, but the overtime compensation due to employees shall be paid on the basis of the hourly rate derived therefrom." N.J.A.C. 12:56-6.5(b).

110. N.J.A.C. 12:56-6.6.

111. N.J.A.C. 12:56-6.7(b).

112. *Id.* Overtime premiums for these employees may not be offset by allowances for the value of food, lodging or gratuities, because those items are deemed fully accounted for by the employer in its determination of the straight-time wages paid. N.J.A.C. 12:56-6.7(a).

Department of Labor Regulations include definitions of executive, administrative and professional employees that are in large part consistent with those utilized under the FLSA. An executive under the New Jersey law is defined as an employee:

1. Whose primary duty consists of the management of the enterprise in which he or she is employed or of a customarily recognized department or subdivision thereof; and
2. Who customarily and regularly directs the work of two or more other employees therein; and
3. Who has the authority to hire or fire other employees or whose suggestions and recommendations as to the hiring and firing and as to the advancement and promotion of [*sic*; or] any other change of status of other employees will be given particular weight; and
4. Who customarily and regularly exercises discretionary powers; and
5. Who devotes less than 20 percent of his or her workweek to non-exempt work or less than 40 percent if employed by a retail or service establishment, provided that in either case he or she re-

---

113. An "outside salesperson" is defined by regulation as an employee who is employed for the purpose of being and in fact is customarily and regularly away from the employer's place or places of business, for the purpose of making sales or obtaining orders or contracts for services or facilities which will later be paid for by the customer, and whose hours of work of another nature do not exceed 20 percent of hours worked in the workweek. Work performed incidentally to sales, such as incidental deliveries, is considered exempt. Employees "who basically drive vehicles and who only incidentally or occasionally make sales shall not qualify for this exemption." N.J.A.C. 12:56-7.4. "Employees who are dispatched to perform a service and solicit performance of an additional service" are not exempt. N.J.A.C. 12:56-7.5.

114. The statutory exemption of hotel employees is not unconstitutional as arbitrary, unreasonable, or capricious. *Hotel Suburban System, Inc. v. Holderman*, 42 N.J.Super. 84, 92-95 (App. Div. 1956).

115. Taxicab drivers are not "employees of common carriers of passengers by motorbus" within the meaning of this section. *Yellow Cab Co. of Camden v. State through Director of Wage and Hour Bureau*, 126 N.J. Super. 81, 87-88 (App. Div. 1973), *certif. denied*, 64 N.J. 498 (1974); *State v. Comfort Cab, Inc.*, 118 N.J. Super. 162, 174-75 (Co. Ct. 1972).

116. N.J.S.A. 34:11-56a4. "Limousine" is defined by the statute as

> "a vehicle with a carrying capacity of not more than nine passengers, not including the driver, used in the business of carrying passengers for hire, which is hired by charter or for a particular contract, or by the day or by the hour or other fixed period, or to transport passengers to specified place, or which charges a fare or price agreed upon in advance between the operator and the passenger, or which is furnished as an accommodation for a patron in connection with some other business purpose. 'Limousine' shall not include taxicabs, hotel or airport shuttles and buses, or buses employed solely in transporting school children or teachers to and from school, or vehicles owned and operated without charge or remuneration by a business entity for its own purposes."

117. N.J.S.A. 34:11-56a4.

tains his or her role as manager and supervises two or more full time employees; and

6. Who is compensated for his or her services on a salary basis exclusive of gratuities, board, lodging or other facilities, at a rate of not less than $300 per week effective November 5, 1990, $350.00 per week effective April 1, 1991, and $400 per week effective April 1, 1992.[118]

Employees with a bona fide equity interest in the enterprise of 20 percent or more are also considered executives under the regulations.[119] Employees training to be executives and not actually performing the duties of an executive are not.[120]

An "administrative employee" is an employee:

1. Whose primary duty consists of the performance of office or non-manual work directly related to management policies or general business operations of his or her employer or his or her employer's customers; and
2. Who customarily and regularly exercises discretion and independent judgment; and
3. Who regularly and directly assists a proprietor, or an employee employed in a bona fide executive or administrative capacity; or who performs under only general supervision work along specialized or technical lines requiring special training, experience, or knowledge; or who executes under only general supervision special assignments and tasks; and
4. Who devotes less than 20 percent of his or her work to non-exempt work or less than 40 percent if employed by a retail or service establishment; and
5. Who is compensated for his or her services on a salary or fee basis, exclusive of gratuities, board, lodging or other facilities at a rate of not less than $300 per week effective November 5, 1990, $350 per week effective April 1, 1991 and $400 per week effective April 1, 1992.[121]

---

118. N.J.A.C. 12:56-7.1(a).
119. N.J.A.C. 12:56-7.1(b).
120. N.J.A.C. 12:56-7.1(c).
121. N.J.A.C. 12:56-7.2(a).

Employees whose total compensation satisfies the salary test set out above, whose primary duty consists of sales activity, and who receive at least 50 percent of their total compensation from commissions, are also deemed administrative employees under the regulations.[122]

A "professional employee" for the purpose of exemption from overtime under the Wage and Hour Law is an employee:

1. Whose primary duty consists of the performance of work:
   i. Requiring knowledge of an advanced type in a field of science or learning customarily acquired by a prolonged course of specialized intellectual instruction and study, as distinguished from a general academic education and from an apprenticeship, and from training in the performance of routine mental, manual, or physical processes; or
   ii. Which [is] original and creative in character in a recognized field of artistic endeavor (as opposed to work which can be produced by a person endowed with general manual or intellectual ability and training), and the result of which depends primarily on the invention, imagination or talent of the employee; and
2. Whose work requires the consistent exercise of discretion and judgment in its performance; and
3. Whose work is predominantly intellectual and varied in character (as opposed to routine mental, manual, mechanical or physical work) and is of such a character that the output produced or the result accomplished cannot be standardized to a given period of time; and
4. Who devotes less than 20 percent of his or her workweek to non-exempt work; and
5. Who is compensated for his or her services on a salary or fee basis, exclusive of gratuities, board, lodging or other facilities at a rate of not less than $300 per week effective November 5, 1990, $350 per week effective April 1, 1991 and $400 per week effective April 2, 1992.[123]

---

122. N.J.A.C. 12:56-7.2(b).

123. N.J.A.C. 12:56-7.3.

8-5:3 Employees Exempt From Minimum Wage Rates

The classes of employees exempt from the minimum wage rates include:

(1) Full-time students employed at a college or university at which they are enrolled, but not less than 85 percent of the effective minimum wage rate;[124]

(2) Part-time employees primarily engaged in the care and tending of children in the employer's home;[125]

(3) Salespersons of motor vehicles;[126]

(4) Persons under the age of 18 except as provided in N.J.A.C. 12:56-10 (learners, apprentices and students), 12:56-11 (first processing of farm products occupations), 12:56-13 (hotel and motel occupations), 12:56-14 (food service occupations) and 12:57 (Wage Orders for Minors);[127]

(5) Outside salesmen;[128]

(6) Persons employed in a volunteer capacity and receiving only incidental benefits at a county or other agricultural fair by a nonprofit or religious association which conducts or participates in the fair; [129]

(7) Employees of summer camps, conferences and retreats operated by nonprofit or religious corporations or associations, during the months of June, July, August and September only.[130]

(8) Student Learners enrolled in a School-To-Work Program.[131]

---

124. N.J.S.A. 34:11-56a4; N.J.A.C. 12:56-3.2 (a)(1).

125. N.J.S.A. 34:11-56a4; N.J.A.C. 12:56-3.2(a)(4).

126. N.J.S.A. 34:11-56a4; N.J.A.C. 12:56-3.2(a)(3).

127. N.J.A.C. 12:56-3.2(a)(5); N.J.S.A. 34:11-56a30. Extant Wage Orders for Minors govern employment in mercantile occupations (N.J.A.C. 12:57-3.1 to 3.13), beauty culture occupations (N.J.A.C. 12:57-4.1 to 4.11), and laundry, cleaning and dying occupations (N.J.A.C. 12:57-5.11). New Jersey's Child Labor Law is codified at N.J.S.A. 34:2-21.1 to 34:2-21.64, and is addressed in §§223-233.

128. N.J.S.A. 34:11-56a4; N.J.A.C. 12:56-3.2(a)(2).

129. N.J.S.A. 34:11-56a4.

130. N.J.S.A. 34:11-56a4.1; N.J.A.C. 12:56-3.2(a)(6).

131. N.J.A.C. 12:56-18.1-18.2. The regulators provide the appropriate definitions and conditions necessary to allow for non-paid activities of student learners. *Id.*

8-5:4 Regulation/Office of Wage and Hour Compliance

Administration of the minimum wage law is under the auspices of the Commissioner of Labor and the Office of Wage and Hour Compliance.[132]

The Commissioner, the director, and their authorized representatives have the authority to investigate and ascertain the wages of any employee; enter and inspect places of business or employment for the purpose of examining and/or copying books, registers, payrolls and any other records relevant to wages; question employees; and obtain from employers written statements, including sworn statements with respect to wages, hours and employees.[133]

The Commissioner may cause the director to investigate any occupation in order to determine whether a substantial number of employees are receiving less than a fair wage.[134] The Commissioner is obligated to so act upon the petition of 50 or more residents of the State.[135] A "fair wage" is one that is "fairly and reasonably commensurate with the value of the service or class of service rendered and sufficient to meet the minimum cost of living necessary for health."[136]

8-5:5 Creation of Wage Boards

If the Commissioner determines that any occupation is receiving less than a fair wage, he must appoint a wage board to report upon the establishment of a minimum fair wage for employees in the particular occupation.[137] The purpose of the wage board is to investigate the status of wages in the occupation, determine what wages and hours would be reasonable, and report to the Commissioner.[138]

A wage board is appointed by the Commissioner and consists of not more than three representatives of the employers in any occupation, an equal number of employee representatives, and not more than three disinterested persons representing the public.[139] The representatives of employers and the public are to be selected "as far as practicable" from nominations submitted by the employers

---

132. N.J.S.A. 34:11-56a2.

133. N.J.S.A. 34:11-56a6.

134. N.J.S.A. 34:11-56a7.

135. *Id.*

136. N.J.S.A. 34:11-56a1(k).

137. N.J.S.A. 34:11-56a8.

138. *See generally* N.J.S.A. 34:11-56a13; *J. Abbott & Son, Inc. v. Holderman*, 46 N.J.Super. 46 (App. Div. 1957). For an historical perspective, see *Lane v. Holderman*, 23 N.J. 304, 311-12 (1957).

139. N.J.S.A. 34:11-56a9. Two-thirds of the members constitute a quorum. Recommendations and reports require a vote of not less than a majority of its members. *Id.*

and employees.[140] The members of a wage board serve without pay, but may be compensated for necessary expenses.[141]

8-5:6 Powers of Wage Boards

A wage board has the power to administer oaths, issue subpoenas for witnesses and documents, cause depositions to be taken,[142] and consider evidence presented by the Commissioner or the director.[143]

The wage board recommends a minimum fair wage rate for employees in the occupation for which the board was appointed.[144] It also may recommend the establishment or modification of an overtime rate and the number of hours per week after which the overtime rate will apply.[145]

A wage board may recommend permitted charges to the employees or allowances for board, lodging, apparel, or other services or facilities customarily provided to the employees by the employer, or allowances for other special conditions or circumstances excluding gratuities.[146]

A wage board may differentiate and classify employments in any occupation and recommend appropriate minimum wage rates for different employments.[147] It also may recommend minimum fair wage rates varying with localities, and recommend a suitable scale of rates for learners and apprentices or students in any occupation.[148]

8-5:7 Procedure for Promulgation of Wage Order

A wage board must submit its report within 60 days of its organization.[149] If it does not, the Commissioner may constitute a new wage board.[150]

---

140. N.J.S.A. 34:11-56a9. The Appellate Division has found that the purpose of this requirement is to create a duty in the Commissioner to provide fair representation for diverse interests among employers. *J. Abbott & Son, Inc. v. Holderman*, 46 N.J.Super. 46, 53 (App. Div. 1957) ("In our view the statute seeks not only representation on the board for the employer bias (in contrast to the disinterestedness demanded of public members . . .), but also some balance among the various employer biases affected.").

141. N.J.S.A. 34:11-56a9.

142. N.J.S.A. 34:11-56a10. Depositions may be taken of individuals residing within and outside of New Jersey, and are conducted in the same manner as depositions in civil actions in Superior Court. *Id.*

143. N.J.S.A. 34:11-56a11. A wage board is not bound by "technical rules of evidence or procedure." N.J.S.A. 34:11-56a12.

144. N.J.S.A. 34:11-56a13.

145. *Id.*

146. *Id.*

147. *Id.*

148. *Id.*

149. N.J.S.A. 34:11-56a14.

Upon receipt of the board report, the Commissioner must confer with the director and either accept or reject the report within 10 days.[151] If the report is rejected, the matter is resubmitted to the same or a new wage board, with a statement of his reasons for the rejection.[152] If the report is accepted, it must be published within 30 days, together with such proposed administrative regulations as may be deemed necessary to supplement the report, and notice of a public hearing.[153]

Within 10 days after the public hearing, the Commissioner must approve or disapprove of the wage board's report.[154] If the Commissioner disapproves the report, the matter may be submitted to the same or a new wage board.[155] If the report is approved, the Commissioner must make a wage order defining the minimum wage rates in the occupation as recommended in the report together with such proposed administrative guidelines as he deems appropriate.[156] Provisions of the minimum wage law are applicable to wages covered by wage orders.[157]

8-5:8 Learners, Apprentices and Students

Insofar as it may be necessary to prevent the curtailment of opportunities for employment, the Commissioner may provide by regulation for the employment of learners, apprentices and students, under special certificates, and at wages lower than the applicable minimum wage.[158] The criterion utilized in determining whether a special certificate should be issued is whether "expectations for oppor-

---

150. *Id.*

151. N.J.S.A. 34:11-56a15.

152. *Id.*

153. N.J.S.A. 34:11-56a15. A failure to meet these time limitations does not render the wage board's actions invalid. "The time limitations provided in the law are clearly intended to be directory only and not jurisdictional." *New Jersey State Hotel-Motel Ass'n v. Male*, 105 N.J.Super. 174, 177 (App. Div. 1969).

154. N.J.S.A. 34:11-56a16.

155. *Id.*

156. N.J.S.A. 34:11-56a16. The order promulgated must be reasonably fit for the enforcement of the statutory policy under the circumstances of the particular employment involved. "The wage board does not have unlimited authority to make extraordinary or whimsical recommendations as to hours and wages that suit their fancy." *Council of New Jersey Hairdressers, Inc. v. Male*, 68 N.J.Super. 381, 386 (App. Div. 1961). The order will not be disturbed in the absence of an affirmative showing that it is arbitrary, capricious or unreasonable. *New Jersey Restaurant Ass'n, Inc. v. Holderman*, 24 N.J. 295, 307 (1957). Although a wage board, as an *ad hoc* administrative agency, is not accorded the same presumption of expertise as an experienced agency, it is nonetheless deferred to. *Council of New Jersey Hairdressers, Inc. v. Male*, 68 N.J.Super. 381, 390 (App. Div. 1961); *J. Abbott & Son, Inc. v. Holderman*, 46 N.J.Super. 46, 59-60 (App. Div. 1957) ("only with much reluctance and where there is manifest abuse would they set aside a wage fixed by the board, because of the excessiveness or the inadequacy of the amount").

157. N.J.S.A. 34:11-56a4.2.

158. N.J.S.A. 34:11-56a17.

tunities for employment are enhanced."[159] Application for a special certificate is made on prescribed forms to the Office of Wage and Hour Compliance.[160]

8-5:9 Handicapped Persons[161]

In occupations for which minimum wage order rates or minimum wage rates are established, employees whose earning capacities are impaired by physical or mental deficiency, may obtain a special license authorizing employment at a rate less than the minimum wage rate, and for the period of time stated in the license.[162] The criteria that may be considered in determining the necessity of a special handicap permit are:

1. The present and previous earnings of disabled employees;
2. The nature and extent of the disability;
3. The wages of non-disabled employees engaged in comparable work;
4. The types and duration of rehabilitative services;
5. The extent to which disabled persons share, through wages, in the receipts for work done;
6. The extent to which the disabled employees are learners;
7. Whether there exists any employer arrangement with customers or subcontractors which appears to be an unfair method of competition which tends to spread or perpetuate substandard wage levels; and
8. The productivity of the disabled employee.[163]

Application for handicapped employee certificates is made on prescribed forms to the Office of Wage and Hour Compliance.[164] Special blanket certificates may be issued for an entire sheltered workshop[165] or department of a sheltered workshop.[166]

---

159. N.J.A.C. 12:56-10.3.

160. N.J.A.C. 12:56-10.2.

161. The regulations define an "individual with a disability" for these purposes as "an individual whose earning capacity is impaired by a physical or mental disability and who is being served or eligible to be served in accordance with the recognized rehabilitation program of a sheltered workshop, education institution, or other program of rehabilitation approved by the commissioner." N.J.A.C. 12:56-9.1(a).

162. N.J.S.A. 34:11-56a17. *See* N.J.A.C. 12:56-9.1 to 12:56-9.5.

163. N.J.A.C. 12:56-9.3.

164. N.J.A.C. 12:56-9.2(a).

8-6 Recordkeeping

An employer must keep true and accurate records of the name and address of each employee, the employee's birth date if under the age of 18, the hours worked each day and each workweek, and the wages paid, including the regular hourly wage gross to net amounts paid with itemized deductions, and the basis upon which wages are paid.[167] This obligation does not apply to employers of outside salesmen, buyers of poultry, eggs, cream or milk in their natural or raw state, or homeworkers.[168] The employer is required to provide a sworn statement of these records on demand, and open them to the Commissioner, the director, or their delegates at any reasonable time.[169]

An employer of employees who receive gratuities must also maintain records reflecting the total gratuities received by each employee during the payroll week.[170] Employees receiving gratuities must report them to the employer on a daily or weekly basis as the employer requires.[171]

An employer who claims credit for food and lodging supplied to employees as a cash substitute must maintain records substantiating the cost of furnishing such food or lodgings.[172] The records must contain detail sufficient to enable the Commissioner to verify the nature and amount of the expenditure.[173]

In cases where additions to wages (such as gratuities, food, or lodgings) result in any workweek in an employee receiving less in cash than the minimum hourly

---

165. A "sheltered workshop" is a "charitable organization or institution conducted not for profit, but for the purpose of carrying out a recognized program of rehabilitation for individuals whose earning capacity is impaired by age, physical or mental deficiency or injury, and to provide such individuals with remunerative employment or other occupational rehabilitating activity of an educational or therapeutic nature." N.J.A.C. 12:56-9.1(b).

166. N.J.A.C. 12:56-9.2(b).

167. N.J.S.A. 34:11-56a20; N.J.A.C. 12:56-4.1. The employer may use any system of time-keeping for these records that produces a "complete, true and accurate record." N.J.A.C. 12:56-4.2. With respect to employees on a fixed working schedule from which they seldom vary, employers "may keep a record showing the exact schedule of daily and weekly work hours the employee is expected to follow and merely indicate each workweek that the schedule was followed." N.J.A.C. 12:56-4.3(a). When the employee deviates from that schedule, the employer must record the actual hours worked. N.J.A.C. 12:56-4.3(b).

168. N.J.S.A. 34:11-56a20.

169. N.J.S.A. 34:11-56a20; N.J.A.C. 12:56-4.5(c). Records must be kept at the place of employment or in a central office in New Jersey, except in unusual circumstances where it is not feasible to keep records in the state and an exception is obtained from the Commissioner. N.J.A.C. 12:56-4.5(a), (b).

170. N.J.A.C. 12:56-4.6.

171. N.J.A.C. 12:56-4.7. The employee's gratuity report must include (1) the employee's name, address, and social security number; (2) the employer's name and address; (3) the calendar day or week covered by the report; and (4) the total amount of gratuity received. N.J.A.C. 12:56-4.7. Where the report is made on a weekly or shorter basis, the Internal Revenue Service Form "Employee's Report on Tips" satisfies this requirement. N.J.A.C. 12:56-4.8.

172. N.J.A.C. 12:56-4.9(a).

wage provided in the act or in any applicable wage order, or where the employee works more than 40 hours a week, the employer must maintain records showing the additions to wages paid on a workweek basis.[174]

The records required to be maintained by this section must be retained for six years.[175]

8-7 Notice

Employers must post a summary of the minimum wage law, along with any applicable wage orders and regulations, or summaries of such wage orders and regulations, in a conspicuous and accessible place.[176]

8-8 Enforcement

An employer who willfully hinders the Commissioner in the performance of his duties in enforcement of the Wage and Hour Law or who violates the law is guilty of a disorderly persons offense and subject to a fine and/or imprisonment.[177] Each week in which an employee is paid less than the applicable rate, and each employee paid less than the applicable rate, constitutes a separate offense.[178]

An employer is guilty of a disorderly persons offense and subject to fine and administrative penalties if he discharges or otherwise discriminates against an employee because the employee (1) has made a complaint to his employer, the Commissioner of Labor, the director, or their representatives that he has not been paid wages in accordance with the Minimum Wage Law; (2) has instituted or is

---

173. N.J.A.C. 12:56-4.9(b). The regulation further requires that the records contain the data "required to compute the amount of the depreciated investment in any assets allocable to the furnishing of the lodgings, including the date of acquisition or construction, the original cost, the rate of depreciation and the total amount of accumulated depreciation of such assets." *Id.*

174. N.J.A.C. 12:56-4.10.

175. N.J.A.C. 12:56-4.4.

176. N.J.S.A. 34:11-56a21. Copies of such summaries, orders, and regulations are available to employers from the state without charge. *Id.* The New Jersey Wage and Hour Abstract may be obtained from the Office of Wage and Hour Compliance, Room 709, CN 389, Trenton, N.J. 08625.

177. N.J.S.A. 34:11-56a22. A first-time offend-er will be subject to a fine of not less than $100 nor more than $1,000, or by imprisonment for not less than 10 nor more than 90 days or by both. *Id.* Upon conviction for a second or subsequent violation, the offender will be subject to a fine of not less than $500 nor more than $1,000 or by imprisonment for not less than 10 nor more than 100 days, or both. *Id.* This is reiterated in N.J.A.C. 12:56-1.6.

178. N.J.S.A. 34:11-56a22. *See Lane v. Holderman*, 40 N.J.Super 329, 342-43 (App. Div. 1956) (upholding authority of commissioner to enter wage orders characterizing employers' acts as misdemeanors), *modified on other grounds*, 23 N.J. 304 (1957).

about to institute any proceeding under or related to that law; (3) has testified or is about to testify in any such proceeding; or (4) has served or is about to serve on a wage board.[179] Such employer will be fined, as well as required to offer reinstatement, to correct any discriminatory action, and to pay back pay.[180] An employer's failure to comply will result in initiation of a contempt proceeding.[181]

As an alternative to or in addition to other sanctions for violations of the Minimum Wage Law, the Commissioner may assess and collect administrative penalties, up to a maximum of $250 for a first violation and up to $500 for each subsequent violation, pursuant to a schedule of penalties to be promulgated as a rule or regulation in accordance with the Administrative Procedure Act.[182] No penalties will be assessed unless the Commissioner (1) provides the alleged violator with notification of the violation and the amount of the proposed penalty and (2) provides an opportunity to request a hearing within 15 days after receipt of the notice.[183] Any penalty imposed under this section may be recovered with costs in a summary proceeding under the penalty enforcement law,[184] and shall be applied toward enforcement and administration costs of the Division of Workplace Standards in the Department of Labor.[185]

The Commissioner may additionally, or alternatively, supervise the payments of wages due to employees under the Minimum Wage Law and compel employers to make payment of same directly to Commissioner, in trust for the employees.[186] A 1991 amendment to the law requires employers so ordered to pay substantial administrative fees to the Department of Labor.[187]

---

179. N.J.S.A. 34:11-56a24; N.J.A.C. 12:56-1.3. Offenders will be fined not less than $100 nor more than $1,000. N.J.S.A. 34:56a24.

180. N.J.S.A. 34:11-56a24. N.J.A.C. 12:56-1.6.

181. *Id.* N.J.A.C. 12:56-1.6

182. N.J.S.A. 34:11-56a24. The statute requires that in determining the amount of a penalty, the Commissioner "shall consider factors which include the history of previous violations by the employer, the seriousness of the violation, the good faith of the employer and the size of the employer's business." *Id.* N.J.A.C. 12:56-1.3(a)-(c).

183. N.J.S.A. 34:11-56a24, as amended by P.L. 1991, c..205. If no hearing is requested, the notice becomes a final order upon expiration of the 15-day period. *Id.* All hearings shall be held pursuant to the Administrative Procedures Act, N.J.S.A. 52:143-1 and the Uniform Administrative Procedures Rules, N.J.A.C. 1:1. The final decision of the Department is made by the Commissioner and appeals are to the Appellate Division of the Superior Court. N.J.A.C. 12:56-1.5(d),(e). After entry of a final order the penalty may be recovered in a summary proceeding by the Commissioner under the Penalty Enforcement Law. N.J.A.C. 12:56-1.5(i).

184. N.J.S.A. 2A:58-1, *et seq.*

185. N.J.S.A. 34:11-56a24.

186. N.J.S.A. 34:11-56a23.

187. *Id.* The administrative fee shall be not less than 10 percent nor more than 25 percent of any payment made to the Commissioner under this section. The statute requires that a schedule of the amounts of such fees be specified in regulations or rules promulgated in accordance with the Administrative Procedure Act. N.J.S.A. 34:11-56a23.

An employee paid less than minimum fair wage as established by statute or wage order may recover the same (less any amount actually paid) together with costs and reasonable attorney's fees in a civil action.[188] An employee may maintain an action for and on behalf of himself and other employees similarly situated.[189] At an employee's request, the Commissioner may take assignment of a wage claim in trust for an employee and institute the legal action necessary to collect the claim.[190]

An agreement between an employer and an employee to work for less than the minimum fair wage is no defense.[191] An employer may defend a charge of failure to pay minimum wages or overtime compensation under the law by pleading and proving that the act or omission complained of was in good faith conformity with and in reliance on a written regulation, order, ruling, approval or interpretation by the Commissioner or director, or any administrative practice or enforcement policy.[192] Such a defense, if established, is a complete bar to the action.[193]

IV. DISCRIMINATION IN WAGES

8-9 Prohibition Against Sex Discrimination

The sex discrimination in wages law,[194] enacted in 1952, prohibits employers[195] from discriminating in any way in the rate or method of payment of wages

---

188. N.J.S.A. 34:11-56a25. A two-year limitations period applies. N.J.S.A. 34:11-56a25.1. An action is commenced for purposes of this limitations period when either (1) a complaint is filed with the Commissioner of Labor or the Director of the Wage and Hour Bureau, and notice of such is served on the employer; or (2) where an audit by the Department of Labor discloses probable cause of action for unpaid minimum wages, unpaid overtime compensation, or other damages, and notice of such probable cause of action is served upon the employer by the Director; or (3) where a cause of action is commenced in a court of appropriate jurisdiction. *Id.*

189. N.J.S.A. 34:11-56a25. The employees may designate an agent or representative to maintain such an action on their behalf. *Id.*

190. *Id.* The employer shall be required to pay costs and attorney's fees "as may be allowed by the court." *Id.*

191. *Id.*

192. N.J.S.A. 34:11-56a25.2.

193. *Id.* Good faith has been defined in this circumstance as "honesty of intention and freedom from circumstances which ought to put the holder upon inquiry." *State v. Frech Funeral Home*, 185 N.J.Super. 385, 393-96 (Law Div. 1982) (where funeral home had a good faith and reasonable belief that its employees worked in a bona fide professional capacity—and therefore were not entitled to overtime pay—it did not matter that the belief was incorrect).

194. N.J.S.A. 34:11-56.1 *et seq.*

195. An employer includes "any person acting directly or indirectly in the interest, or as agent, of an employer in relation to an employee and further includes one or more individuals, partnerships, corporations, associations, legal representatives, trustees, trustees in bankruptcy, or receivers, *but such term shall not include nonprofit hospital associations or corporations.*" N.J.S.A. 34:11-56.1(b) (emphasis added).

to any employee[196] because of his or her sex.[197] Differentials in pay based upon a reasonable factor or factors other than sex do not constitute discrimination within the meaning of this law.[198] As observed by the Supreme Court in *Grigoletti v. Ortho Pharmaceutical Corp.*, the state's Equal Pay Act (EPA) has laid dormant since its adoption in 1952 because of the availability of other statutory provisions, particularly the Law Against Discrimination (LAD), that afford similar protection.[199]

An employer who willfully violates this act, or who discharges or discriminates against an employee asserting rights under the act is guilty of a disorderly persons offense and subject to a fine and/or imprisonment.[200]

An employer who fails to furnish records upon request, or who hinders, delays or otherwise interferes with the enforcement of the act, is guilty of a disorderly persons offense and subject to a fine.[201]

If a complaint of unlawful conduct is made to the Commissioner, or if he has reason to believe that any provision of the sex discrimination in wages law has been violated, he may give notice of the alleged violation to the employer.[202] The employer is entitled to answer the complaint and, upon request, to be heard with respect to the alleged violation.[203] All interested persons, including complainant, must be given notice of and an opportunity to attend the hearing.[204] If the alleged violation is not corrected as a result of the hearing, the Commissioner may institute suit.[205]

An employee subject to discrimination may institute a civil proceeding to recover the wages or salary due from his employer plus an additional equal amount as liquidated damages, costs of suit, and reasonable attorney's fees.[206] The Com-

---

196. An employee includes "any person, either male or female, employed by an employer, *but shall not include persons performing volunteer service for nonprofit organizations or corporations nor persons employed on a farm, or in domestic service in a private home, or in a hotel.*" N.J.S.A. 34:11-56.1(a) (emphasis added).

197. N.J.S.A. 34:11-56.2.

198. *Id.*

199. *Grigoletti v. Ortho Pharmaceutical Corp.*, 118 N.J. 89, 106 (1990).

200. N.J.S.A. 34:11-56.6. An offender may be punished by a fine of not less than $50 nor more than $200, or imprisonment for not less than 10 days nor more than 90 days, or by both fine and imprisonment. N.J.S.A. 34:11-56.6.

201. N.J.S.A. 34:11-56.7. The applicable fine is not less than $50 nor more than $200. N.J.S.A. 34:11-56.7.

202. N.J.S.A. 34:11-56.9.

203. N.J.S.A. 34:11-56.9.

204. N.J.S.A. 34:11-56.9. The statute provides that the Commissioner may promulgate regulations to govern such hearings. *Id.* No such rules have been promulgated. In any event, such hearings are now governed by the procedures set forth in the Administrative Procedure Act (APA), N.J.S.A. 52:14B-1 *et seq.*, and the Uniform Administrative Procedure Rules (UAPRs), N.J.A.C. 1:1-1.1 *et seq.*

205. N.J.S.A. 34:11-56.9, -56.8.

missioner may institute an action on assignment by the aggrieved employee and is empowered to join in one cause of action various claimants against a single employer.[207] The Commissioner, if successful, is entitled to recover the costs of the action, including a reasonable counsel fee, from the employer.[208] The employee is thus entitled to recover the double damages without deduction for counsel fees.[209]

V. WAGES ON PUBLIC WORKS

8-10 The Prevailing Wage Act

It is a matter of public policy to establish a prevailing wage level for workmen engaged in public works,[210] "to safeguard their efficiency and general well being and to protect them as well as their employers from the effects of serious and unfair competition resulting from wage levels detrimental to efficiency and well-being."[211] The Appellate Division has described the act's purpose as follows:

> The prevailing wage rate is a minimum wage rate and is unquestionably designed to protect union contractors from under-bidding on public work by their non-union competitors who conceivably would have the advantage of paying their labor non-union wages. ... Its purpose is to insure that the prevailing wage rate existing at the time of the signing of a public contract constitutes the minimum wage paid to workers under that contract.[212]

As remedial legislation, the act is entitled to liberal construction and application.[213]

---

206. N.J.S.A. 34:11-56.8. *See Dubrowsky v. Stern, Lavinthal, Norgaard, & Daly*, 922 F.Supp. 985, 996 (D.N.J. 1996) (genuine issue of material fact existed as to whether female attorney was paid less than similarly situated male attorneys). An agreement between an employer and an employee to work for a discriminatory wage or salary is no defense. *Id.*

207. *Id.*

208. *Id.*

209. *Id.*

210. N.J.S.A. 34:11-56.25. The Prevailing Wage Act was enacted in 1963. L.1963, c.150. The Act and its delegation of power to determine prevailing wage rates to the Commissioner have been upheld as constitutional. *Dept. of Labor v. Titan Const. Co.*, 102 N.J. 1, 7 (1985); *Male v. Ernest Renda Contracting Co.*, 122 N.J.Super. 526, 533 (App. Div. 1973), *aff'd*, 64 N.J. 199, *cert. denied*, 419 U.S. 839 (1974).

211. Id.

212. *Horn v. Serritella Bros., Inc.*, 190 N.J.Super. 280, 283 (App. Div. 1983), quoting *Cipparulo v. Friedland*, 139 N.J.Super. 142, 148 (App. Div. 1976). The Act reflects a legislative determination that wages paid on the performance of public works should be the same as wages paid under collective bargaining agreements negotiated between employers and labor unions representing a majority of workers engaged in a given trade. *Male v. Ernest Renda Contracting Co.*, 122 N.J.Super. at 534.

Every contract over the prevailing wage contract threshold amount[214] for a public work[215] to which any public body[216] is a party, or for public work to be done on property or premises leased or to be leased by a public body,[217] must set forth the prevailing wage rate[218] for workers[219] under the contract, and must stipulate that such workers will not be paid less than that rate.[220]

The contract also must provide that if any worker under the contract or subcontract is paid less than the prevailing rate, the public body or lessor may terminate the contractor's or subcontractor's right to proceed with the work, or such part of the work as to which there has been a failure to pay required wages, and to prosecute the work to completion or otherwise.[221] The contractor and its sureties are liable to the public body or lessor for excess costs occasioned by such a termination.[222]

---

213. *Horn v. Serritella Bros., Inc.*, 190 N.J.Super. at 283; *Quayle v. Tri-Con. Constr. of North Jersey*, 295 N.J. Super. 640, 643 (App. Div. 1996).

214. The "prevailing wage contract threshold amount" means:

a) In a public work paid for in whole or in part or performed on property or premises owned, leased or to be leased by a New Jersey municipality, the dollar amount established by the commision of labor pursuant to the authority granted by the "Administrative Procedure Act." This amount is currently $9,850 and will be adjusted every five years beginning on July 1, 1995; and

b) In any public work other than those described in paragraph a) in this subsection, the amount is $2,000.

N.J.S.A. 24:11-56:26(11).

215. " 'Public work' means construction, reconstruction, demolition, or repair work, or maintenance work, including painting and decorating, done under contract and paid for in whole or in part out of funds of a public body, except work performed under a rehabilitation program." N.J.S.A. 34:11-56.26(5).

216. A "public body" includes the State of New Jersey, any of its political subdivisions, any authority created by the state Legislature, and any instrumentality or agency of the state or any of its political subdivisions. N.J.S.A. 34:11-56.26(4).

217. Provided that not less than 55 percent of the property or premises is leased by a public body or subject to an agreement to be subsequently leased by the public body, and the portion of the property or premiums covered by the lease measures more than 20,000 square feet. N.J.S.A. 34:11-56.26(5)(a),(b).

218. The "prevailing wage" is the wage rate paid under collective bargaining agreements by employers employing a majority of workers of that craft or trade subject to collective bargaining agreements, in the locality where public work is done. N.J.S.A. 34:11-56.26(9). *See Male v. Ernest Renda Contracting Co.*, 64 N.J. 199 (1974) (upholding act as constitutional and not an impermissible delegation of legislative power), *cert. denied*, 419 U.S. 839, 42 L.Ed.2d 66 (1974).

Employer contributions for employee benefits pursuant to a bona fide collective bargaining agreement are considered an integral part of the wage rate paid by employers of any craft or trade in the locality under consideration for the purpose of determining the prevailing wage rate. N.J.S.A. 34:11-56.30. The Commissioner of Labor establishes the prevailing rate in the locality and for the craft or trade or classification, and his determination is accorded a presumption of reasonableness. *See Marr v. ABM Carpet Serv., Inc.*, 286 N.J. Super. 500, 505-06 (Law Div. 1995) (upholding decision to classify carpet installers as carpenters).

8-10:1 Procedure

A public body or lessor contracting for a public work must ascertain from the Commissioner of Labor the prevailing wage rate in the locality where the public work is to be performed and must specify in the contract what the prevailing wage rate is for each craft or trade or class of worker needed.[223] Payment of more than the prevailing wage rate is permissible.[224] The prevailing wage rate is determined and established by the Commissioner in accordance with rules and regulations.[225]

8-10:2 Employers' Obligations

Every contractor and subcontractor must keep accurate records showing the name, trade or craft, and actual hourly rate of the wages paid to each worker.[226]

---

219. "Workers" means laborers, mechanics, skilled or semiskilled, laborer and apprentices or helpers employed by any contractor or subcontractor and engaged in the performance of services directly upon a public work, regardless of whether their work becomes a component part thereof, but does not include material suppliers or their employees who do not perform services at the job site. N.J.S.A. 34:11-56.26(7). Individuals who fall within this definition will not be excluded on the ground that they are stockholders or principals of the contractor. To hold otherwise "would invite stock ownership schemes devised to frustrate the Act's purpose and defeat the uniform application intended by the Legislature." *Dept. of Labor v. Titan Const. Co.*, 102 N.J. 1, 9 (1985). In *Horn v. Serritella Bros., Inc.*, 190 N.J. Super. 280 (App. Div. 1983), "workmen" was defined to include truck drivers who carried away debris from a public project. The court found that they rendered services directly upon a public work because: "Although the drivers did no loading or lifting at the job site, they drove their trucks to the site, stood by as other workers did the loading, and drove the trucks to disposal areas." *Id.* at 284.

220. N.J.S.A. 34:11-56.27. The act is not intended to interfere with the right of workers to obtain wages higher than the minimum through the collective bargaining process.

221. *Id.*

222. *Id.*

223. N.J.S.A. 34:11-56.28. The New Jersey Administrative Code contains an extensive list of crafts, trades, and classes of workers, along with descriptions of the bases upon which those workers may be classified by task. N.J.A.C. 12:60-3.1 to 12:60-5.3.

No liability for a wage deficiency may be imposed on a public body unless there is an express contractual provision by which the public authority agrees to indemnify the contractor. *Central Constr. Co. v. Horn*, 171 N.J. Super. 152, 156 (Law Div. 1979). *See Male v. Ernest Renda Contracting Co.*, 122 N.J.Super. 526, 537 (App. Div. 1973). In *Male v. Pompton Lakes Borough Mun. Util. Auth.*, 105 N.J.Super. 348 (Ch.Div. 1969), the court had held that where a public authority did not include the prevailing wage schedules in specifications submitted to bidders and became aware of the statutory requirements before the contract was extended but concluded it was not subject to the act, the contractor was entitled to be indemnified by the public authority for any liability for a wage deficiency. The court suggested that the public authority's omission lulled the contractor into believing he was not required to comply with the Prevailing Wage Law and submitting a bid based on that assumption. That is the apparent basis upon which the Appellate Division in *Male v. Ernest Renda Contracting Co.*, found the Pompton Lakes case distinguishable. 122 N.J.Super. at 538 ("We find *Male v. Pompton Lakes Borough Mun. Util. Auth.*, 105 N.J.Super. 348 (Ch.Div. 1969), to be factually distinguishable. However, to the extent that it may appear to hold to the contrary to our holding as to the liability of a public body under the act, it is disapproved.").

224. N.J.S.A. 34:11-56.28.

225. N.J.S.A. 34:11-56.30. *See* N.J.A.C. 12:60-1.1 *et seq.*

The employer must produce those records for inspection and copying by the Commissioner or his designee, and when requested provide written sworn statements concerning wages, hours, names, addresses and other employee information.[227] Records must be preserved for two years from the date of payment.[228]

Contractors and subcontractors performing public work pursuant to a contract with a public body subject to the provisions of the act must post the prevailing wage rates in a prominent and easily accessible place.[229]

8-10:3 Obligations of the Public Body

Before the public body or lessor makes final payment, it must require the contractor and subcontractor to file written statements certifying the wages due and owing to workers, setting forth the names of persons whose wages are unpaid and the amount thereof.[230]

If a worker files a protest within three months "from the date of the occurrence of the incident complained of with the commissioner" objecting to the payment to any contractor to the extent wages are due or are to become due, the Commissioner may direct the public body or lessor to deduct from such payments the amounts admitted by the contractor in his statement to be due and owing and to pay them directly to the worker.[231]

The public body or lessor must notify the Commissioner of the name of any employer failing to pay the prevailing wage.[232] Any worker may file a protest with the Commissioner within two years of the date of the occurrence objecting to the amount of wages paid.[233]

8-10:4 Powers of the Commissioner of Labor

The Commissioner is authorized to investigate and ascertain the wages of workers employed in any public work in the State and empowered to enter and

226. N.J.S.A. 34:11-56.29.

227. N.J.S.A. 34:11-56.31(a, b); N.J.A.C. 12:60-6.1. *See* §8-10:3.

228. N.J.S.A. 34:11-56.29.

229. N.J.S.A. 34:11-56.32.

230. N.J.S.A. 34:11-56.33(a).

231. N.J.S.A. 34:11-56.33(b). The public body may also be required by the Commissioner to withhold up to 25 percent of the amount due an employer, up to a ceiling of $100,000, as a consequence of the employer's failure to provide information requested by the Commissioner. N.J.S.A. 34:11-56.31 (c), (d); N.J.A.C. 12:60-6.1(b)(1).

232. N.J.S.A. 34:11-56.34(a).

233. N.J.S.A. 34:11-56.34(b).

inspect any place of business to examine, inspect and copy records bearing on the questions of wages, hours, and conditions of employment, and to question workers.[234]

The Commissioner may require an employer to provide sworn statements respecting wages, hours, names, addresses and other information pertaining to workers, and to file any relevant records within 10 days of the receipt of a request.[235] If an employer fails to comply, the Commissioner may direct the public body to withhold up to 25 per cent of the amount (not to exceed $100,000) to be paid to the employer under the terms of the contract, until the request for records has been satisfied.[236] When the employer complies with the request for records, the Commissioner must notify the public body, which is then required to immediately release the withheld funds.[237]

The Commissioner is authorized to supervise payment of amounts due to workers under the act, and an employer may be required to make those payments to the Commissioner, who then pays the workers directly.[238] An employer required to make such payments into trust will also be required to pay the Commissioner an administrative fee equal to not less than 10 percent nor more than 25 per cent of the amount paid as due to workers.[239]

8-10:5 Enforcement

An employer who willfully hinders or delays the Commissioner in his duties in enforcement of the Prevailing Wage Act, or violates the act, regulation, or order thereunder is guilty of a disorderly persons offense and subject to a fine and/or imprisonment.[240] "Each week, in any day of which a worker is paid less than the rate applicable to him under this act and each worker so paid, shall constitute a separate offense."[241]

An employer is guilty of a disorderly persons offense if it discharges or in any manner discriminates against any worker because:

---

234. N.J.S.A. 34:11-56.31(a), (b).

235. N.J.S.A. 34:11-56.31(c), (d).

236. N.J.S.A. 34:11-56.31(c), (d); N.J.A.C. 12:60-6.1(b)(1).

237. N.J.A.C. 12:60-6.1(b)(2).

238. N.J.S.A. 34:11-56.36. N.J.A.C. 12:60-9.4 reiterates the statutory provisions.

239. N.J.S.A. 34:11-56.36. The amount of the fee is to be specified in a schedule of fees issued by rule or regulation in accordance with the Administrative Procedure Act, and will be applied toward enforcement and administration costs of the Division of Workplace Standards in the Department of Labor. *Id.* The schedule of fees appears in Table 9.4(c) to N.J.A.C. 12:60-9.4 as follows: (1) first violation - 10 percent of any amount paid to the Commissioner; (2) second violation —18 percent; and (3) third and subsequent violations —25 percent.

(1) the worker has complained to his employer, to the public body or to the Commissioner that he has not been paid wages in accordance with the provisions of the Prevailing Wage Act;

(2) the worker has instituted or is about to institute any proceeding under or related to the act; or

(3) the worker has testified in or is about to testify in any such proceeding.[242]

Any worker paid less than the prevailing wage may bring a civil action, individually or on behalf of others similarly situated, to recover the full amount of the prevailing wage less amounts already paid, plus costs and reasonable attorney's fees.[243] The Commissioner may take assignment of a wage claim in trust for the assigning worker and commence legal action to collect the claim.[244] The Commissioner has been permitted to maintain an action under this section against a general contractor whose subcontractor owed employees wages under the act.[245]

---

240. N.J.S.A 34:11-56.35; N.J.S.A. 2C:1-4. An offender is subject to a fine of not less than $100 nor more than $1,000, or imprisonment for not less than 10 nor more than 90 days, or both. N.J.S.A. 34:11-56.35. The regulations provide a nonexclusive list of specific violations:

(a) Violations of the Act shall occur when an employer:

1. Willfully hinders or delays the Commissioner in the performance of the duties of the Commissioner in the enforcement of this chapter;

2. Fails to make, keep and preserve any records as required under the provisions of this chapter;

3. Falsifies any such record;

4. Refuses to make any such record accessible to the Commissioner upon demand;

5. Refuses to furnish a sworn statement of such record or any other information required for the proper enforcement of this chapter to the Commissioner upon demand;

6. Pays or agrees to pay wages at a rate less than the prevailing rate applicable under this chapter;

7. Requests, demands, or receives, either for himself or any other person, either before or after a worker is engaged in public work at a specified rate of wages, the following:

i.That such worker forego, pay back, return, donate, contribute or give any part, or all, of his or her wages, salary or thing of value, to any person upon the statement, representation or understanding that failure to comply with such request or demand will prevent such worker from procuring or retaining employment; or

8. Otherwise violates any provision of this chapter or of any order issued under this chapter.

N.J.A.C. 12:60-9.2. *See New Jersey Dept. of Labor v. Kinder Constr.*, 95 N.J.A.R. 2d 31 (1995) (penalty of $200.00 was appropriate even though the violation was due to a misunderstanding because some salary payments were late and some emplyees received less than the prevailing wage due to a clerical error).

241. N.J.S.A. 34:11-56.35.

242. N.J.S.A. 34:11-56.39. The applicable fine is not less than $100 nor more than $1,000. N.J.A.C. 12:60-9.6 reiterates the statutory provisions

243. N.J.S.A. 34:11-56.40. An agreement between an employer and workers to work for less than the prevailing wage is no defense. *Id.*

Any person who submits a bid for a contract subject to the provisions of the Prevailing Wage Act, is not awarded the contract and is either the lowest bid or the highest ranked bid (where the contract is not awarded solely on bid amount) not selected may bring a civil action against the contractor or its subcontractors who were awarded the contract that the losing bidder alleges either violated the Act or failed to pay any contribution, tax, assessment or benefit required by law in performing the contract.[246] If the court finds that the selected bidder violated the Act or failed to fully compensate its employees as required by law and that the plaintiff's bid would have been less or more favorable than the selected bidder's bid but for the violation or failure to pay while performing the contract, the plaintiff is entitled to damages, costs and reasonable attorney's fees.[247] If the court finds the violation to be intentional, the plaintiff is entitled to treble damages.[248]

The plaintiff is not entitled to any relief if the violation was caused by the defendant's minor clerical, computer or other minor errors.[249] If the court determines that the defendant did not violate the Act or other applicable laws, the plaintiff is liable for the costs and reasonable attorney's fees of the defendant.[250]

As an alternative, or in addition to the aforesaid sanctions, the Commissioner may assess administrative penalties for violation of the act or discrimination against workers for exercising rights under the act, up to $250 for a first violation and up to $500 for each subsequent violation.[251] In determining the amount of

---

244. N.J.S.A. 34:11-56.40. *See Male v. Ernest Renda Contracting Co.*, 122 N.J.Super. 526, 535-36 (App. Div. 1973), *aff'd*, 64 N.J. 199, *cert. denied*, 419 U.S. 839 (1974) (Commissioner had implicit right to bring action to require employer to establish trust of payments due under N.J.S.A. 34:11-56.36, without obtaining assignments from employees); *Serraino v. Mar-D, Inc.*, 228 N.J.Super. 482, 490-91 (Law Div. 1988) (Commissioner not barred by the Bond Act, N.J.S.A. 2A:44-143 *et seq.*, from maintaining action for employees under N.J.S.A. 34:11-56.40).

245. *Serraino v. Mar-D, Inc.*, 228 N.J.Super. at 486-90.

246. N.J.S.A. 34:11-56.47a. If there is more than one losing bidder, a bidder who was not either the lowest or highest ranked bidder may bring the same action if he gives proper notice pursuant to this subsection of his intention to bring the action to every other losing bidder whose bid was more responsive than his. *Id.* A plaintiff may designate an agent or representative to maintain the action in appropriate circumstances. N.J.S.A. 34:11-56.47b.

247. N.J.S.A. 34:11-56.47b. Pursuant to this section, damages "include the plaintiff's costs of preparing and submitting the bid and may, if sought by the plaintiff, include profits that the court determines the plaintiff would have made if the plaintiff had been awarded the contract and complied with [the Act] and other applicable laws." N.J.S.A. 34:11-56.47c.

248. N.J.S.A. 34:11-56.47b. More than two violations by the same contractor creates a rebuttable presumption that the violation or failure to pay was not minor. *Id.*

249. N.J.S.A. 34:11-56.47b.

250. N.J.S.A. 34:11-56.47d.

251. N.J.S.A. 34:11-56.35, -56.39, as amended by L.1991, c.205. A schedule of penalties is to be promulgated by rule or regulation in accordance with the Administrative Procedure Act. *Id.* N.J.A.C. 12:60-9.3 reiterates the statutory provisions.

penalty imposed, the Commissioner is required to consider factors which include the history of previous violations by the employer, the seriousness of the violation, the good faith of the employer, and the size of the employer's business.[252] No administrative penalty may be assessed under this section unless the Commissioner gives the alleged violator notice by certified mail of the violation and amount of penalty, and provides an opportunity to request a hearing within 15 days of receipt of the notice.[253] Payment of the penalty is due when a final order is entered or the notice becomes final through lack of contest.[254]

8-10:6 Debarment

The Commissioner must maintain a debarment list of contractors and subcontractors who have failed to pay the prevailing wage, and provide that list to any public body requesting it.[255] A public body may not award a contract to, or enter a lease pursuant to which public work is to be done with any contractor or subcontractor (or to any firm, corporation or partnership in which such contractor/ subcontractor has an interest) on the debarment list until three years have elapsed from the date of listing.[256]

When the Commissioner seeks to debar a person, that person must be provided with notice of the alleged violation and his statutory rights.[257] Where the respon-

---

252. *Id.*

253. *Id.* If a hearing is requested, the Commissioner will issue an order at its conclusion; if no hearing is requested, the notice becomes final when the 15-day period expires. *Id.*

254. *Id.* Penalties imposed under this section may be recovered, with costs, in a summary proceeding by the Commissioner under the penalty enforcement law, N.J.S.A. 2A:58-1, and will be applied toward enforcement and administration costs of the Division of Workplace Standards in the Department of Labor. N.J.S.A. 34:11-56.35, -56.39.

255. N.J.S.A. 34:11-56.37; N.J.A.C. 12:60-8.1 *et seq.* The failure may be unintentional. *See Dept. of Labor and Industry, Div. of Workplace Standards v. Union Paving & Const. Co., Inc.*, 168 N.J. Super. 19, 26-28 (App. Div. 1979), *overruled on other grounds by Dept. of Labor v. Titan Const. Co.*, 102 N.J. 1 (1985).

256. N.J.S.A. 34:11-56.38; N.J.A.C. 12:60-8.4(e).

257. In *Dept. of Labor v. Titan Const. Co.*, 102 N.J. 1 (1985), the Supreme Court held that although the Commissioner had incidental power to debar those individuals in corporate and non-corporate entities who are responsible for the failure to pay prevailing wages, administrative rulemaking on the subject was prerequisite to exercise of that authority. *Id.* at 17-18. Rules governing debarment are now set forth in N.J.A.C. 12:60-8.1 to 8.5. N.J.A.C. 12:60-8.4 requires that persons subject to debarment be provided with notice stating:

1. That debarment is being considered;

2. The provisions of N.J.S.A. 34:11-56.37 and 34:11-56.38;

3. The specific details of the violations referring to employees involved by name, job classifications, dates of violations and any amount found due;

4. The public work or EDA project involved during which performance of the violations cited occurred; and

5. That the person shall have the right to hearing upon written notification to the Commissioner requesting such a hearing within 15 days of the date of the notice of intent to debar.

sible party denies a failure to pay the prevailing wage, he has the right to apply to the Commissioner for a hearing which must be given and a decision rendered within 48 hours of the request.[258] Failure to request a hearing to contest a debarment will result in automatic listing on the debarred list.[259] If the Commissioner rules against the employer, he has the right to apply for injunctive relief against the listing in the Superior Court.[260]

Department of Labor regulations provide that failure or refusal to pay the prevailing wage rate does not necessarily require debarment; that decision is made in each case at the discretion of the Commissioner, unless otherwise provided by law.[261] Factors listed by the regulation as pertinent to that determination are: (1) the record of previous violations by the person with the Office of Wage and Hour Compliance; (2) previous cases of debarment; (3) the frequency of violations by the person discovered in previous cases; (4) the significance or scale of the violations; (5) the existence of outstanding audits or failure to pay; (6) failure to respond to a request for records; and (7) submission of falsified or altered records.[262]

The regulations also provide that the Commissioner, with approval of the Attorney General, may suspend a person pending debarment action.[263] The person suspended must be provided with notice stating the fact of the suspension, its effective date, the reasons for the suspension (to the extent the Attorney General determines they properly may be disclosed), and that the suspension is temporary but may continue until legal proceedings relating to the debarment are concluded.[264]

---

258. N.J.S.A. 34:11-56.37. Individuals subject to debarment are entitled to the safeguards of procedural due process. *See Dept. of Labor v. Titan Const. Co.*, 102 N.J. at 17 ("Procedural safeguards, including notice, hearing, the right to present evidence, and the right to cross examine an adverse witness must be afforded those individuals facing debarment."), *Berlanti v. Bodman*, 780 F.2d 296, 299-300 (3d Cir. 1985) (construing *Titan Construction Co.* as holding that debarment of a corporate officer effects a deprivation of a property right). All hearings must be conducted in accordance with the Administrative Procedure Act, N.J.S.A. 52:14B-1 *et seq.*, and the Uniform Administrative Procedure Rules, N.J.A.C. 1:1. N.J.A.C. 12:60-8.4(d).

259. N.J.A.C. 12:60-8.4(b), (c). *But see Dept. of Labor v. Titan Const. Co.*, 102 N.J. at 5 (noting that the Department of Labor treated the employer's denial of a violation as a request for a hearing and on that basis transferred the matter to the Office of Administrative Law as a contested case).

260. N.J.S.A. 34:11-56.37.

261. N.J.A.C. 12:60-8.3(c).

262. *Id. See New Jersey Dept. of Labor v. V.S.P.*, 95 N.J.A.R. 2d 18 (1995) (debarment warranted for subcontractor's failure to pay prevailing wages to its employees for work on prison wastewater treatment plant where the underpayment was substantial, the subcontractor kept inadequate time sheet and payroll records, and the subcontractor required employees to sign vouchers and certifications stating that they were receiving the prevailing wage even though they were not).

263. N.J.A.C. 12:60-8.3(d). Suspension is defined as "an exclusion from contracting for future public works or EDA projects for a temporary period of time, pending the completion of debarment proceedings." N.J.S.A. 12:60-8.2.

VI. EXECUTION [265]

8-11 Judgment Creditors

When a judgment creditor is due and owed, or thereafter will be due and owed, any wages, earnings or salary (or other income) in the amount of $48 or more a week, the judgment creditor—with notice to the debtor—may apply to the court in which judgment was recovered or other court with jurisdiction. Upon satisfactory proofs, the court will enter an order directing that an execution issue against such wages, earnings or salary.[266]

On presentation of the execution, it becomes a lien and continuing levy upon the subject wages, earnings, or salary.[267]

8-11:1 Limit on Amount Garnished

The amount specified in the execution may not exceed 10 percent of wages unless debtor's income exceeds $7,500 per year. In that event, the court may order a larger percentage.[268]

8-11:2 Multiple Executions

Only one execution against wages may be satisfied at a time.[269] If more than one execution is issued, they will be satisfied in the order of priority in which they are presented to the garnishee.[270]

---

264. N.J.A.C. 12:60-8.3(d). *Cf.* N.J.S.A. 34:11-56.37, providing the right to seek injunctive relief against a debarment listing.

265. N.J.S.A. 2A:17-50 to 2A:17-56.26

266. N.J.S.A. 2A:17-50.

In *Biles v. Biles*, 163 N.J. Super. 49 (Ch. Div. 1978), the court stated that the restriction against alienation and assignment of benefits contained in the Employee Retirement Income Security Act of 1974, 29 U.S.C. §1001 *et seq.* (ERISA) prohibits voluntary transfers and involuntary transfers through garnishment and execution of monthly pension payments. The court held, however, that garnishment of pension benefits to the extent of an ex-husband's alimony obligation does not conflict with ERISA. *Id.* at 56-57. *See Western Electric Co. v. Traphagen*, 166 N.J. Super. 418 (App. Div. 1979) (same); *see also* N.J.S.A. 2A:17-56.7 *et seq.*, discussed *infra*. The reader is cautioned that the analysis of the scope of pre-emption contained in these cases is implicitly overruled by the United States Supreme Court opinion *Shaw v. Delta Air Lines, Inc.*, 463 U.S. 85 (1983). For a detailed discussion of this issue see RIA, *Pension Coordinator*, ¶26,601 *et seq.*

267. N.J.S.A. 2A:17-51.

268. N.J.S.A. 2A:17-56.

269. N.J.S.A. 2A:17-52. *See Household Finance Corp. v. Clevenger*, 141 N.J. Super. 53 (App. Div. 1976) (a wage execution and an order to pay judgment out of income cannot be satisfied at the same time in excess of the prescribed statutory limits when the source of income is the debtor's wages).

Where more than one execution is presented on the same day, and one derives from an order for support and maintenance of a wife or child[ren], the support order must be satisfied first.[271]

8-11:3 Obligations of Employer

An employer to whom a wage execution is presented, who is or will be indebted to the judgment debtor, must pay to the presenting officer the amount of indebtedness as prescribed by the execution less 5 percent, which amount constitutes compensation to the employer for expenses and services in connection with payment of the execution and which is deductible from each payment until the execution is satisfied.[272] Each payment, together with the 5 percent "service fee," is credited to the debtor's account in payment of such execution and operates as a bar to any action for such payment, including the "service fee," by the debtor.[273]

An employer who fails or refuses to make the payments is liable therefor in an action by the creditor named in the execution.[274] Any amount recovered by the creditor in such an action must be applied to the payment of the execution.[275]

8-11:4 New Jersey Support Enforcement Act[276]

Every order for alimony, maintenance or child support must include a written notice to the obligor advising that the order may be enforced by withholding income from (1) current or future wages from an employer, (2) unemployment compensation benefits, and (3) any other income, including, under appropriate circumstances defined by federal law, pension benefits.[277]

---

270. N.J.S.A. 2A:17-52. *Household Finance Corp. v. Clevenger*, 141 N.J.Super. at 57 ("the order issued first in time will prevail until the judgment upon which it was entered is satisfied").

But where the senior claimant under a wage execution informed the debtor's employer that it had entered into a separate agreement with the debtor for voluntary weekly payments and advised the employer that it did not have to make deductions from wages, and, two years later, the debt remained unpaid, a second execution claimant was entitled to priority because the senior claimant had interfered with the running of its execution and was negligent. *Family Finance Corp. v. Jenkins*, 131 N.J. Super. 336 (Dist. Ct. 1974).

271. N.J.S.A. 2A:17-52.

272. N.J.S.A. 2A:17-53.

273. *Id.*

274. N.J.S.A. 2A:17-54. The creditor may proceed by way of *ex parte* order to show cause why the employer should not be held in contempt for refusing to honor the wage execution. *Snelling & Snelling v. Goyden*, 181 N.J. Super. 479 (App. Div. 1981).

275. N.J.S.A. 2A:17-54.

276. N.J.S.A. 2A:17-56.7 *et seq.* For a detailed discussion of the enforcement of support obligations, see Skoloff & Cutler, *New Jersey Family Law Practice*, §5.7 *et seq.*

Income withholding may be initiated by a county probation department without any further court or quasi-judicial action *if* the arrearages accrue in an amount equal to the amount of support payable for 14 days.[278]

The total amount withheld cannot exceed the maximum permitted under §303(b) of the Consumer Credit Protection Act..[279] Moreover, where a wage execution is issued for both arrearages *and* current support payments, total payments cannot exceed the federal maximum.[280]

---

277. N.J.S.A. 2A:17-56.8. *See generally Western Electric Co. v. Traphagen*, 166 N.J. Super. 418 (App. Div. 1979); *Biles v. Biles*, 163 N.J. Super. 49 (Ch. Div. 1978); *Ward v. Ward*, 164 N.J. Super. 354 (Ch. Div. 1978). The reader should note that the analysis of the scope of pre-emption by the Employee Retirement Income Security Act of 1974, 29 U.S.C. §1001, *et seq.* (ERISA), contained in these cases is implicitly overruled by the United States Supreme Court opinion in *Shaw v. Delta Air Lines, Inc.*, 463 U.S. 85 (1983). For a discussion of ERISA's requirements with respect to garnishment of pension benefits to enforce a qualified domestic relations order see *RIA Pension Coordinator*, ¶26,608 *et seq.*

278. N.J.S.A. 2A:17-56.9. *See Slater v. Slater*, 223 N.J. Super. 511, 514-16 (App. Div.), *certif. denied*, 113 N.J. 338 (1988) (trial court improperly issued wage execution against husband who was consistently late in making alimony and child support payments and made payments smaller than were required, where payments were made within 14 days of date due and total arrearages were less than amount payable for 14 days).

279. N.J.S.A. 2A:17-56.9, citing the Consumer Credit Protection Act, 15 U.S.C. §1673 (b). 15 U.S.C. §1673(a) places a general ceiling on the amount of disposable earnings subject to garnishment—the lesser of either 25 percent of weekly disposable earnings or the amount by which weekly disposable earnings exceed 30 times the federal minimum hourly wage. However, 15 U.S.C. §1673(b) provides:

> (b)(1) The restrictions of subsection (a) of this section do not apply in the case of
>
> (A) any order for the support of any person issued by a court of competent jurisdiction or in accordance with an administrative procedure, which is established by State law, which affords substantial due process, and which is subject to judicial review.
>
> (B) any order of any court of the United States having jurisdiction over cases under chapter 13 of Title 11.
>
> (C) any debt due for any State or Federal tax.
>
> (2)The maximum part of the aggregate disposable earnings of an individual for any workweek which is subject to garnishment to enforce any order for the support of any person shall not exceed —
>
> (A) where such individual is supporting his spouse or dependent child (other than a spouse or child with respect to whose support such order is used), 50 per centum of such individual's disposable earnings for that week; and
>
> (B) where such individual is not supporting such a spouse or dependent child described in clause (A), 60 per centum of such individual's disposable earnings for that week;

except that, with respect to the disposable earnings of any individual for any workweek, the 50 per centum specified in clause (A) shall be deemed to be 55 per centum and the 60 per centum specified in clause (B) shall be deemed to be 65 per centum, if and to the extent that such earnings are subject to garnishment to enforce a support order with respect to a period which is prior to the 12-week period which ends with the beginning of such workweek.

280. *Burstein v. Burstein*, 182 N.J. Super. 586, 595 (App. Div. 1982); *Martinez v. Martinez*, 282 N.J. Super. 332, 334 (Ch. Div. 1995). *See also Cashin v. Cashin*, 186 N.J. Super. 183, 187-88 (Ch. Div. 1982) (husband's obligation to pay ex-wife's counsel fees was in nature of support and subject to garnishment under federal maximum).

8-11:5 Due Process

Income withholding under the Support Enforcement Act must be carried out in full compliance with the requirements of procedural due process,[281] including notice and the right to a hearing.[282]

8-11:6 Prohibition Against Discrimination

An employer who discharges or takes disciplinary action against an employee because the employee has had income withheld is a disorderly person.[283]

The aggrieved employee may bring a civil suit in Superior Court for damages and reinstatement of his employment.[284] The prevailing party may be awarded attorney's fees, but a respondent is not entitled to fees absent a showing that the action was brought in bad faith.[285]

In addition to any other relief available by law, the payor may be liable for double compensatory damages, which shall include the costs of proving discharge, out-of-pocket expenses, and lost income.[286]

VII. WAGE COLLECTION

8-12 Wage Claims

An employee may file a claim for wages against an employer in the Wage Collection Division of the Department of Labor.[287] Upon the filing of such a claim, the department will issue a summons for the appearance of the defendant, and at the time and place specified inquire in a summary way into the merits of the employee's claim and defenses of the defendant, if any.[288]

The Commissioner of Labor is authorized to investigate all such wage claims, and may summon the defendant, subpoena witnesses, administer oaths, take testimony, and make a decision or award where the sum in controversy does not ex-

---

281. N.J.S.A. 2A:17-56.9.

282. N.J.S.A. 2A:17-56.10.

283. N.J.S.A. 2A:17-56.12.

284. *Id.*

285. *Id.*

286. *Id.*

287. N.J.S.A. 34:11-59. No filing fee may be charged by the Division for accepting a wage claim. N.J.S.A. 34:11-67.

288. N.J.S.A. 34:11-59.

ceed $10,000, exclusive of costs.[289] Such decision or award shall be a judgment when a certified copy is filed with the Superior Court.[290]

The Commissioner is also authorized to supervise the payment of amounts due to employees under an award made pursuant to this section, and the employer may be required to make payments to the Commissioner to be held in a special trust account and paid directly to the employees.[291] The employer may also be required to pay an administrative fee which is equal to not less than 10 percent nor more than 25 percent of the payment made to the Commissioner.[292]

8-13 Set-off

If an employer-defendant files a set-off against an employee-plaintiff for more than $1,000, and at trial it is proved that the employer is entitled to such amount, the suit shall be dismissed unless the employer consents to accept judgment for $1,000 plus costs in full settlement of his claim.[293] The employer may not assert a counterclaim for unliquidated damages against the employee for wages in the Wage Collection Division.[294]

8-14 Appeals Procedure

Either party may appeal a judgment of the Wage Collection Division upon filing a notice of appeal with the Division within 20 days after judgment is given.[295] The Division is then required to prepare a transcript of the record to be filed in the Superior Court, which hears the appeal in a summary manner.[296]

---

289. N.J.S.A. 34:11-58; *Kopin v. Orange Products, Inc.*, 297 N.J. Super 353, 375 (App. Div. 1997), *certif. denied*, 149 N.J. 409 (1977). Process of the wage collection division runs throughout the state; service of process shall be made either by a constable or by a process server of the department. N.J.S.A. 34:11-60. N.J.A.C. 12:61-1.3.

290. N.J.S.A. 34:11-58.

291. *Id.*

292. *Id.* N.J.A.C. 12:61-1.4 provides the following schedule of fees:

(1) first violation - 10 percent of the amount due an employee;

(2) second violation - 18 percent;

(3) third and subsequent violations - 25 percent.

293. N.J.S.A. 34:11-62.

294. *Id.*

295. N.J.S.A. 34:11-63.

296. N.J.S.A. 34:11-63, 34:11-64.

On trial of the appeal, either party may, without notice, produce any witness not produced or sworn in the court below, or any documentary evidence not offered or admitted below, if otherwise legal and competent.[297]

8-15 Jury Trial

A claimant may institute an action in any court of competent jurisdiction; either the plaintiff or the defendant may demand a trial by jury.[298] A party to a proceeding in the Wage Collection Division may demand a trial by jury by paying the statutory jury fee to the Division at least two days prior to the adjourned date of hearing.[299] The Division will then file the entire record in the case in the Superior Court for trial by a judge and jury. The judgment therein is to be docketed in the Superior Court as are other judgments of the Wage Collection Division.[300]

VIII. CHILD LABOR LAWS

8-16 Purpose

It has long been the social policy of this State to protect children by limiting and regulating child labor.[301] This policy is expressed in the Child Labor Law.[302] The law sets forth in detail at what ages and under what conditions persons under 18 years of age may be employed, and carefully circumscribes the types of work they may do.[303]

It should be emphasized that in this context the term "labor" is not necessarily limited to compensatory employment.[304] Thus, the statute, which under certain conditions precludes a child from being "employed, permitted or suffered to work,"[305] is intended to protect minors irrespective of whether there is an employment relationship.[306]

---

297. N.J.S.A. 34:11-65.

298. N.J.S.A. 34:11-66.

299. *Id.*

300. *Id.*

301. *Variety Farms v. New Jersey Mfrs. Ins. Co.*, 172 N.J. Super. 10, 17 (App. Div. 1980). *See Feir v. Weil and Whitehead*, 92 N.J.L. 610 (E. & A. 1919).

302. N.J.S.A. 34:2-21.1 to -21.64

303. *Variety Farms v. New Jersey Mfrs. Ins. Co.*, 172 N.J. Super. 10, 17 (App. Div. 1980).

304. *Gabin v. Skyline Cabana Club*, 54 N.J. 550, 554-555 (1969).

305. *See, e.g.*, N.J.S.A. 34:2-21.2.

306. *Ludwig v. Kirby*, 13 N.J. Super. 116, 122 (App. Div. 1951).

8-17 Minors Under 16 Years of Age

No minor under 16 years of age can work in, about, or in connection with any gainful occupation at any time except as follows:

(1) Minors between 14 and 16 years of age may work outside school hours and during school vacations but not in or for a factory or in any other prohibited occupation;[307]

(2) Minors under 16 years of age may engage in professional employment in theatrical productions upon obtaining a permit therefor;[308]

(3) Minors under 16 years of age may engage outside of school hours and during school vacations in agricultural pursuits,[309] street trades,[310] and as newspaper carriers;[311]

(4) Minors may engage in domestic service performed outside of school hours or during school vacations with the permission of a parent or legal guardian.[312]

These restrictions do not apply to the work of a minor engaged in domestic service or agricultural pursuits performed outside of school hours or during school vacations in connection with the minor's own home and directly for his parents or legal guardian.[313]

---

307. N.J.S.A. 34:2-21.2. Minors under 16 years of age are prohibited from working in, about, or in connection with power driven machinery (*e.g.*, lawn mowers, woodworking and metal working tools) or conveyors or related equipment. N.J.A.C. 12:58-3.2, -3.3.

308. N.J.S.A. 34:2-21.2. Theatrical production means and includes stage, motion picture, and television performances and rehearsals therefor. N.J.S.A. 34:2-21.1(h). However, a minor may not take part in a statutorily defined "prohibited performance" which includes appearances as a rope or wire walker or rider, gymnast, wrestler, boxer, contortionist, acrobat, rider of a horse or other animal unless the minor is trained, rider of any vehicle other than that generally used by a minor of the same age, or appearance in any illegal, indecent or immoral exhibition, practice, or theatrical production, or in any practice, exhibition or theatrical production dangerous to the life, limb, health or morals of a minor, or appearance or exhibition of any physically deformed or mentally deficient minor. N.J.S.A. 34:2-21.57(c).

Special provisions governing the employment of minors under 16 in theatrical productions are set forth in N.J.S.A. 34:2-21.58 to -21.64.

309. Agriculture includes farming in all of its branches. N.J.S.A. 34:2-21.1(e). Minors under the age of 12 may not be employed in agricultural pursuits. N.J.S.A. 34:2-21.15.

310. Street trades include the selling, offering for sale, soliciting for, collecting for, displaying, or distributing any articles, goods, merchandise, commercial service, posters, circular, newspapers or magazines or in shining shoes on any street or other public place or from house to house. N.J.S.A. 34:2-21.15. No minor under 14 years of age may engage in any street trade. *Id.*

Minors under 16 years of age who desire to work in a street trade or agricultural pursuits at any time the schools of the district in which they reside are not in session must apply through their parent or legal guardian to the issuing officer of the school district for a special permit. N.J.S.A. 34:2-21.15. *See Ludwig v. Kirby*, 13 N.J. Super. 116 (App. Div. 1951).

311. N.J.S.A. 34:2-21.2.

Minors between the ages of 11 and 18 who desire to work as a newspaper carrier must apply through a parent or legal guardian to the publisher for a special permit. N.J.S.A. 34:2-21.15.

312. N.J.S.A. 34:2-21.2.

Except for those for whom a theatrical employment permit has been issued, no minor under 16 years of age who does not reside in this State may work in any occupation or service at any time during which the law of the state of his residence requires his attendance at school, or at any time during the hours when the public schools in the district in which employment in such occupation or services may be available are in session.[314]

8-18 Hours of Employment

No minor under 18 years of age may work in, about, or in connection with any gainful occupation more than six consecutive days in one week, or more than 40 hours in one week, or more than eight hours in one day.[315]

No minor under 16 years of age may work before 7 a.m. or after 7 p.m. of any day.[316] However, a minor who is 14 or 15 may, with the written permission of a parent or legal guardian, work until 9 p.m. in a restaurant, supermarket or other retail establishment, or in any occupation not prohibited by the law or regulations, during the period beginning on the last day of a minor's school year and ending on Labor day of each year.[317]

The hours of work of minors under 16 employed outside of school hours cannot exceed three hours in any one day when school is in session and cannot exceed in any one week when school is in session the maximum number of hours permitted for that period under the Fair Labor Standards Act of 1938,[318] and regulations promulgated pursuant to the federal act.[319]

No minor between 16 and 18 years of age may work before 6 a.m. or after 11 p.m. of any day. They may however, work after 11 p.m. during any regular vacation season and on days which do not precede a regularly scheduled school day, provided that they have written permission from a parent or legal guardian setting forth the hours they are permitted to work.[320]

---

313. *Id.*

314. *Id.*

315. N.J.S.A. 34:2-21.3. This provision is subject to exceptions set forth in N.J.S.A. 34:2-21.15 and does not apply for domestic service or messengers employed in communications companies under the supervision and control of the Federal Communications Commission. N.J.S.A. 34:2-21.3.

316. N.J.S.A. 34:2-21.3.

317. *Id.*

318. 29 U.S.C. §201 *et seq.*

319. *Id.*

320. *Id.*

Minors between 16 and 18 years of age may work in a seasonal amusement[321] or restaurant occupation after 11 p.m. and following 12:01 a.m. of the next day if that employment is a continuation of a workday which began before 11 p.m. either during any regular school vacation period, or on workdays which do not begin on a day which precedes a regularly scheduled school day provided they have written permission from a parent or legal guardian setting forth the hours they are permitted to work.[322] Under no circumstances, however, may a minor between 16 and 18 years of age work after 3 a.m. or before 6 a.m. on a day which precedes a regularly scheduled school day.[323]

Minors may be employed in a concert or theatrical performance up to 11:30 p.m.[324]

Minors who are 16 years of age or older who are attending school may be employed as pinsetters, lane attendants, or busboys in public bowling alleys up to 11:30 p.m., but may not be so employed during the school term without a special written permit from the superintendent of schools or supervising principal stating that the minor has undergone a complete physical examination and may be employed without injury to health or interference with school. Such permits are subject to renewal every three months.[325]

Minors between 16 and 18 years of age may not work after 10 p.m. during the regular school vacation periods or in a factory or in any occupation otherwise prohibited by law or regulation.[326]

None of the forgoing provisions are applicable to minors between 16 and 18 years of age who are employed during the months of June, July, August or September by a summer resident camp, conference or retreat operated by a non-profit or religious corporation or association unless the employment is primarily general maintenance work or food services activities.[327]

---

321. Seasonal amusement means any exclusively recreational or amusement establishment or business which does not operate more than seven months in any calendar year or which has received during any six consecutive months of the preceding calendar year average receipts equal to or less than 33 and $^1/_3$ percent of its average receipts for the other six months of that year. It includes but is not limited to amusement rides and amusement device ticket sales, and operations of games. It does not include retail, eating or drinking concessions, camps, beach and swimming facilities, movie theaters, theatrical productions, athletic events, professional entertainment, pool and billiard parlors, circuses and outdoor shows, sport activities or centers, country club athletic facilities, bowling alleys, race tracks and like facilities which are not part of a diversified amusement enterprise. N.J.S.A. 34:2-21.1(i).

322. N.J.S.A. 34:2-21.3.

323. *Id.*

324. N.J.S.A. 34:2-21.3.

325. *Id.*

326. *Id.*

327. *Id.*

A newspaper carrier between the ages of 11 and 14 may deliver, solicit, sell and collect for newspapers on routes in residential neighborhoods between the hours of 6 a.m. and 7 p.m. A newspaper carrier 14 years of age and older may work between the hours of 5:30 a.m. and 8 p.m. However, no newspaper carrier under 18 may work beyond the period of time wherein the combined hours devoted to his duties as a newspaper carrier and the hours in school exceed a total of 40 hours per week and not more than eight hours in any one day.[328]

No minor engaged in agricultural pursuits may work more than 10 hours per day.[329]

8-19 Prohibited Employments

No minor under the age of 16 may work in, about, or in connection with power-driven machinery.[330]

No minor under the age of 18 may work in, about, or in connection with the following:

(1) The manufacture or packing of paints, colors, white or red lead;[331]

(2) The handling of dangerous or poisonous acids or dyes, or injurious quantities of toxic or noxious dust, gases, vapors or fumes;[332]

(3) Work involving exposure to benzol or any benzol compound which is volatile or which can penetrate the skin;[333]

(4) The manufacture, transportation or use of explosives or highly inflammable substances;[334]

---

328. N.J.S.A. 34:2-21.15.

329. *Id.*

330. N.J.S.A. 34:2-21.17; N.J.A.C. 12:58-3.2(a). Power-driven machinery includes power tools, including but not limited to power lawn mowers, power woodworking and metalworking tools. N.J.A.C. 12:58-3.2(b). It does not include standard office-type machines; standard domestic-type machines or appliances when used in domestic or business establishments; agricultural machines when used on farms, *e.g.*, standard-type poultry feeders, egg washers, egg coolers, milking machines; and attended or unattended standard-type passenger elevators. N.J.A.C. 12:58-3.2(c).

A minor under the age of 18 may not work with cornpickers, power-driven hay balers, or power field choppers. N.J.A.C. 12:58.4.3(a).

331. N.J.S.A. 34:2-21.17.

332. *Id.*; N.J.A.C. 12:58-4.9(a). A toxic or hazardous substance means any material exceeding a threshold limit value listed in the tables of § 1910.1000 of Subpart Z of 29 C.F.R. Part 1910. N.J.A.C. 12:58-4.9(b).

333. N.J.S.A. 34:2-21.17. *See* N.J.A.C. 12:58-4.8 (prohibiting minors from performing work which may expose them to carcinogenic substances).

(5) Oiling, wiping, or cleaning machinery in motion or assisting therein;[335]

(6) Operation or helping in the operation of power-driven woodworking machinery; however, apprentices operating under conditions of bona fide apprenticeship may operate such machines with competent instruction and supervision;[336]

(7) Grinding, abrasive, polishing or buffing machines; however, apprentices operating under conditions of bona fide apprenticeship may grind their own tools;[337]

(8) Punch presses or stamping machines if the clearance between the ram and dye or the stripper exceeds $^1/_4$ inch;[338]

(9) Cutting machines having a guillotine action;[339]

(10) Corrugating, crimping, or embossing machines;[340]

(11) Paper lace machines;[341]

(12) Dough breaks or mixing machines in bakeries, or cracker machinery;[342]

(13) Calendar rolls or mixing rolls in rubber manufacturing;[343]

(14) Centrifugal extractors, or mangles in laundries or dry cleaning establishments;[344]

(15) Ore reduction works, smelters, hot rolling mills, furnaces, foundries, forging shops, or any other place in which the heating, melting, or heat treatment of metals is carried on;[345]

(16) Mines or quarries;[346]

---

334. N.J.S.A. 34:2-21.17; N.J.A.C. 12:58-4.6(a). Any employment certificate authorizing the employment of a minor under 18 in any gasoline service station or garage must be stamped with the following warning: "The certificate does not in any way affect any prohibition contained in the Child Labor Act concerning power-driven or hazardous machinery or hazardous occupations." N.J.A.C. 12:58-4.6(b).

335. N.J.S.A. 34:2-21.17.

336. *Id.*; N.J.A.C. 12:58-4.11.

337. N.J.S.A. 34:2-21.17.

338. *Id.*

339. *Id.*; N.J.A.C. 12:58-4.11.

340. N.J.S.A. 34:2-21.17.

341. *Id.*

342. *Id.*

343. *Id.*

344. *Id.*

345. *Id.*

346. *Id.*

(17) Steam boilers carrying a pressure in excess of 15 pounds;[347]

(18) All construction work[348] except the construction of affordable housing as a volunteer for a nonprofit organization;[349]

(19) Fabrication or assembly of ships;[350]

(20) Operation or repair of elevators or other hoisting apparatus;[351]

(21) The transportation of payrolls other than within the employer's premises;[352]

(22) An establishment where alcoholic beverages are distilled, rectified, compounded, brewed, manufactured, bottled, or are sold for consumption on the premises, or in a pool or billiard room;[353]

(23) A junk or scrap metal yard;[354]

(24) A disorderly house;[355]

(25) Compactors;[356]

---

347. *Id.*

348. *Id.*; N.J.A.C. 12:58-4.2(a). Construction work means "the erection, alteration, repair, renovation, demolition or removal of any building or structure; the excavation, filling and grading of sites; the excavation, renovation, repair or paving of roads and highways; and any function performed within 30 feet of the above operations." N.J.A.C. 12:58-4.2(b). It does not include the repair or painting of fences, buildings and structures not exceeding 12 feet in height. N.J.A.C. 12:58-4.2(c).

349. N.J.S.A. 34:2-21.17d; N.J.A.C. 12:58-4.2(d). The affordable housing/nonprofit organization exception is available only to children between the age of 14 and 17. N.J.S.A. 34:2-21.17d. Any work done under this exception must be under the direct supervision of an adult. N.J.S.A. 34:2-21.17d(d). The exception also requires that no minors work in connection in any way with power-driven machinery, are exposed to hazardous substances, work on any excavation, scaffolding, or roofing, or work hours prescribed by this section. N.J.S.A. 34:2-21.17d(b),(e-g). The nonprofit organization must carry sufficient amounts of liability insurance, N.J.S.A. 34:2-21.17(k). A minor working under this section is not an employee for Workers' Compensation purposes. N.J.S.A. 34:2-21.17e.

350. N.J.S.A. 34:2-21.17.

351. *Id.*

352. *Id.*

353. *Id.*; *see* N.J.A.C. 12:58-4.17 (prohibiting the serving of beverages by a minor out of any bar service area). These prohibitions do not apply to minors 16 or over employed as pinsetters, lane attendants or busboys in public bowling alleys or to minors employed in theatrical productions where alcoholic beverages are sold on the premises, or to minors 16 and over employed in a restaurant, or in executive offices, maintenance departments, or pool or beach areas of a hotel, motel or guesthouse. N.J.S.A. 34:2-21.17. However, no minor may engage in the preparation, sale or serving of alcoholic beverages, nor in the preparation of photographs, nor in any dancing or theatrical exhibition or performance which is not part of a theatrical production where alcoholic beverages are sold on premises. *Id.* A minor may be permitted to engage in the clearing of alcoholic beverages provided that he is closely supervised. *Id.*

354. N.J.A.C. 12:58-4.4(a). A junk or scrap metal yard is "any place where old iron, metal, paper, cordage and other refuse may be collected and deposited or both and sold or may be treated so as to be used again in some form or discarded or where automobiles or machines are demolished for the purpose of salvaging of metal or parts." N.J.A.C. 12:58-4.4(b).

355. N.J.A.C. 12:58-4.5(a). A disorderly house is a brothel or a gambling place. N.J.A.C. 12:58-4.5(b).

(26) Radioactive substances and ionizing radiation;[357]
(27) Carcinogenic substances;[358]
(28) Slaughtering and meat packing establishments, and rendering plants;[359]
(29) Servicing of single piece or multi-piece rim wheels;[360]
(30) Any place of employment, or at any occupation hazardous or injurious to the life, safety, or welfare of such minor, as may be determined and declared by the Commissioner of Labor, after a public hearing thereon and after such notice as the commissioner by regulation may prescribe.[361]

8-20 Lunch Periods

No minor under 18 years of age may be employed or allowed to work for more than five continuous hours without an interval of at least 30 minutes for a lunch break. No period of less than 30 minutes shall be deemed to interrupt a continuous period of work.[362]

8-21 Posting Requirements

Every employer must post and keep conspicuously posted in the workplace where any minor under 18 is working a printed abstract of this act and a list of prohibited occupations provided by the Department of Labor.[363]

Every such employer also must post a schedule of hours containing the name of each minor under 18, the maximum number of hours he can work during each day of the week, the total hours per week, the time of beginning and stopping work each day, and the time for beginning and ending the daily meal period.[364]

---

356. N.J.A.C. 12:58-4.10(a). A compactor is a power-operated device designed to join or pack closely together, consolidate or condense material. It does not include residential compactors or compacting type garbage trucks if minors aged 16-17 ride inside the cab of the truck. *Id.*

357. N.J.A.C. 12:58-4.7(a).

358. N.J.A.C. 12:58-4.8(a). Carcinogenic substance includes any material classified as carcinogenic by 29 C.F.R. Part 1910 Subpart Z.

359. N.J.A.C. 12:58-4.12. This prohibition, which also applies to wholesale, retail or service establishments, is directed to a variety of occupations fully described in N.J.A.C. 12:58-4.12 (a)(1-7).

360. N.J.A.C. 12:58-4.16.

361. N.J.S.A. 34:2-21.17.

362. N.J.S.A. 34:2-21.4.

363. N.J.S.A. 34:2-21.5. A copy may be obtained from the Office of Wage and Hour Compliance, Division of Workplace Standards, Department of Labor, CN 389, Trenton, N.J. 08625-0389.

The schedule is to be on a form provided by the Department of Labor and remains the property of the Department.[365]

An employer may allow a minor to start work later than the time provided on the schedule and to stop before the time for ending work as stated on the schedule. Otherwise, a minor may not work except as stated on the schedule.[366]

For each employee under 19 years of age, an employer must keep a record, in a form approved by the Department of Labor, which states the name, date of birth and address of the minor employee, the number of hours worked by such person on each day of the week, the hours of beginning and ending such work, the hours of beginning and ending meal periods, the amount of wages paid, and such other information as the Department may require. These records must be kept on file for at least one year after entry of the record and are subject to inspection by the Department of Labor, attendance officers, and police officers.[367] These provisions do not apply to the employment of minors in agricultural pursuits or in domestic service in private homes, or as newspaper carriers.[368]

8-22 Employment Certificates

No minor under 18 years of age[369] may work in, about, or in connection with any gainful occupation unless and until the person employing such minor procures and keeps on file an employment certificate or special permit issued by the issuing officer of the school district in which the child resides, or of the district in which the child has obtained a promise of employment if the child is not a resident of this State.[370]

No certificate or special permit is required:

(1) For any child 16 or over employed in agricultural pursuits;

(2) For any child 14 or over employed at any agricultural fair, horse, dog, or farm show which does not last more than 10 days, and at such times as the schools of his district are not in session;

(3) In the first 14 days of employment for any minor 15 or over employed in seasonal amusement, food service, restaurant or retail occupations, at such times

364. N.J.S.A. 34:2-21.5.

365. *Id.*

366. *Id.*

367. N.J.S.A. 34:2-21.6.

368. N.J.S.A. 34:2-21.5, 21.6.

369. Except as provided in N.J.S.A. 34:2-21.15.

370. N.J.S.A. 34:2-21.7(a).

as the schools of his district are not in session provided that no minor under 16 years of age may be permitted to operate, service, or work in, about, or in connection with power-driven machinery.[371]

There are rules governing the procurement of employment certificates and special permits.[372]

8-23 Non-Commercial Recycling Centers

Minors between the ages of 12 and 17 may work as volunteers at non-commercial recycling centers operated by a municipality or community service organization authorized by the municipality to operate the facility,[373] subject to the following:

(1) The recycling centers must handle only those waste products normally included in the municipal waste stream, *e.g.*, newspapers and glass and metal beverage containers;[374]

(2) The minor cannot work in a community recycling center that is in any way associated with a profit-making commercial enterprise other than to sell the recyclable products referred to above;[375]

(3) No minor may operate, perform maintenance, clean, inspect, work in, about, or in connection with any power-driven machinery involved in the recycling process;[376]

(4) No minor may work without the safety equipment required by law;[377]

(5) No minor may work except under the direct supervision of an adult;[378]

(6) No minor may handle or be exposed to hazardous-waste products or other hazardous substances;[379] and

---

371. N.J.S.A. 34:2-21.7(a).

372. N.J.S.A. 34:2-21.7 to -21.16

373. Such a minor working voluntarily at a recycling center is not deemed an employee under N.J.S.A. 34:15-36.

374. N.J.S.A. 34:2-21.17b(a).

375. N.J.S.A. 34:2-21.17b(b).

376. N.J.S.A. 34:2-21.17b(c).

377. N.J.S.A. 34:2-21.17b(d).

378. N.J.S.A. 34:2-21.17b(e).

379. N.J.S.A. 34:2-21.17b(f).

(7) The municipality which operates the center or authorizes the operation of the center by the community service organization has secured adequate liability insurance to provide compensation for injuries sustained by minors working as volunteers.[380]

8-24 Enforcement

Enforcement of the child labor laws is the duty of the Department of Labor and includes the filing of complaints against violators and prosecution of same.[381]

The Commissioner of Labor and any inspector or other authorized person acting under him, persons employed by law to compel attendance of children at school, and officers and agents of any duly incorporated society for the protection of children from cruelty and neglect, are authorized to enter and inspect at any time any place or establishment covered by the act, and to have access to employment certificates or special permits kept on file by employers and such other records as may aid in enforcement.[382]

8-25 Penalties

Any person who employs or permits or suffers any minor to be employed or to work in violation of the act or of any order or ruling issued under its provisions, or obstructs the Department of Labor, its officers or agents, or any other authorized person to inspect places of employment, or any person, having custody or control of a minor, permits or suffers him to be employed or work in violation of the act, is guilty of an offense.[383] Where the defendant acts knowingly, it is a crime of the fourth degree; otherwise it is a disorderly persons offense.[384]

Each day during which any violation of this act continues constitutes a separate and distinct offense.[385] The employment of any minor in violation of this act constitutes a separate and distinct offense with respect to each minor so employed.[386]

---

380. N.J.S.A. 34:2-21.17b(g). A minor working voluntarily at a recycling center is not deemed an employee for the purposes of the Workers' Compensation Act. N.J.S.A. 34:2-21.17c.

381. N.J.S.A. 34:2-21.18.

382. *Id.*

383. N.J.S.A. 34:2-21.19.

384. *Id. See* N.J.S.A. 2C:43-3 and -6. Punishment for the disorderly persons offense shall be a fine of not less than $100 nor more than $1,000. N.J.S.A. 34:2-21.19.

385. N.J.S.A. 34:2-21.19.

386. *Id.*

As an alternative to, or in addition to, other sanctions for violation of the Child Labor Law, the Commissioner may assess and collect administrative penalties, up to a maximum of $250 for a first offense and up to $500 for each subsequent offense.[387] When determining the amount of penalty, the Commissioner must consider (1) the history of previous violations by the employer; (2) the seriousness of the violation; (3) the good faith of the employer; and (3) the size of the employer's business.[388]

Before any penalty is imposed, the alleged offender must be given notice by certified mail of the violation and proposed penalty and an opportunity to request a hearing before the Commissioner or his designee within 15 days of receipt of the notice.[389] If no hearing is requested, the notice of penalty becomes a final order upon expiration of the 15-day period and must be paid.[390] If it is not paid, it may be collected in a summary proceeding under the Penalty Enforcement Law.[391] The Commissioner shall make the final decision of the Department and appeals therefrom are to the Appellate Division of the Superior Court.[392]

8-26 Workers' Compensation and Civil Liability

Unlike adult employees, employees under the age of 18 are not subject to the exclusive remedy bar of workers' compensation. The Workers' Compensation Act provides:

> Nothing in this chapter contained shall deprive an infant under the age of 18 years of the right or rights now existing to recover damages in a common law or other appropriate action or proceeding for injuries received by reason of the negligence of his or her master.[393]

Thus, a minor who suffers a work-related injury may elect to accept workers' compensation benefits or pursue a tort remedy in a civil action against his em-

387. N.J.S.A. 34:2-21.19; N.J.A.C. 12:58-5.3.

388. Id.

389. N.J.S.A. 34:2-21.19; N.J.A.C. 12:58-5.4.

390. Id.

391. N.J.S.A. 2A:58-1, et seq.

392. N.J.A.C. 12:58-5.4(c), (d).

393. N.J.S.A. 34:15-10.

ployer.[394] Both remedies are not available. Recovery in one proceeding is a complete bar to recovery in the other.[395]

Of course, if a minor chooses to pursue a common law tort action, the potentially higher recovery is conditioned on proof of the employer's fault or other misconduct, and proximate causation—elements not necessary in a workers' compensation proceeding.[396]

Moreover, where a minor is illegally employed in violation of the child labor laws, defenses of contributory negligence and assumption of the risk are not available to the employer, even if the illegal employment is the result of fraud, misrepresentation or mistake as to the minor's age.[397]

---

394. *Terlingo v. Belz-Parr, Inc.*, 106 N.J.L. 221 (E. & A. 1929); *Kristiansen v. Morgan*, 153 N.J. 298, 312 (1998); *Mohan v. Exxon Corp.*, 307 N.J. Super. 516, 519, n.1 (App. Div 1998); *Chubb Group v. Trenton Bd. of Educ.*, 304 N.J. Super. 10, 16 (App. Div.), *certif. denied*, 152 N.J. 188 (1997).

395. *Damato v. De Lucia*, 110 N.J.L. 380, 381 (E. & A. 1933); *Variety Farms v. New Jersey Mfrs. Ins. Co.*, 172 N.J. Super. 10, 18 (App. Div. 1980); *Balogh v. Landanye*, 59 N.J. Super. 132, 133 (App. Div. 1960); *Watson v. Stagg*, 108 N.J.L. 444, 446 (Sup. Ct. 1932); *Goetaski v. California Packing Corp.*, 19 N.J. Super. 460, 464 (Law Div. 1952). A minor injured in a work-related accident may also pursue a common law remedy against a co-employee. *Thompson v. Family Godfather, Inc.*, 212 N.J. Super. 270 (Law Div. 1986).

396. *La Pollo v. Hospital Service Plan of New Jersey*, 113 N.J. 611, 614 (1989). Violation of the provisions of the child labor law prohibiting operation of power-driven machinery (N.J.S.A. 34:2-21.17) constitutes negligence *per se* if the violation is the proximate cause of the injury. *Gabin v. Skyline Cabana Club*, 54 N.J. 550, 554 (1969); *Variety Farms v. New Jersey Mfrs. Ins. Co.*, 172 N.J. Super. 10, 21 (App. Div. 1980); *Cernadas v. Supermarkets General*, 192 N.J. Super. 500, 503-504 (Law Div. 1983). *Cf. Dubiel v. Laneco, Inc.*, 161 N.J. Super. 360 (Law Div. 1978) (employer who allowed 17-year-old to operate cardboard box baling machine did not violate statute because machine was not specified in statute as prohibited).

397. *Miller v. American Cyanamid Co.*, 61 F.2d 389, 390-91 (3d Cir. 1932) (applying New Jersey law); *E. Heller & Bros. v. Dillon*, 96 N.J. Eq. 334, 336-37 (E. & A. 1924); *Volpe v. Hammersley Mfg. Co.*, 96 N.J.L. 489, 491-92 (E. & A. 1921); *Chipman v. Cramer*, 16 N.J. Misc. 178, 180 (Sup. Ct. 1938); *Lesko v. Liondale Bleach, Dye & Print Works*, 93 N.J.L. 4, 6 (Sup. Ct. 1919). An unlawfully employed minor who elects to pursue a remedy under the Workers' Compensation Act is entitled to recover benefits double the amount payable under the schedules provided in N.J.S.A. 34:15-12 and -13. N.J.S.A. 34:15-10. This provision does not apply to minors who are members of a junior fireman's auxiliary established pursuant to N.J.S.A. 40:47-30.6 *et seq.*, employees of summer camps operated by religious or charitable organizations, student-learners employed in a cooperative vocational education program approved by the State Board of Education, or participants in volunteer programs under the supervision of the Palisades Interstate Park Commission with respect to that part of Palisades Interstate Park located in New Jersey.

Chapter 9

Unemployment Compensation

I. INTRODUCTION

9-1 Generally

The Unemployment Compensation Law (the "UC Law") is set forth in N.J.S.A. 43:21-1 to -24.[1] Its remedial objective is to protect the welfare of the people by providing a cushion against the shocks and rigors of unemployment.[2] It is designed to provide some income for a worker who through no fault or act of his own is earning nothing, until such time as he can find work, or the period provided by statute expires.[3] Because it is social legislation, the UC Law is accorded liberal construction.[4] However, that result may not be accomplished by extending application of the statute to factual situations not covered by its provisions.[5] "The basic policy of the law is advanced as well when benefits are denied in improper cases as when they are allowed in proper cases."[6] The purpose of the law is not only to protect the unemployed, but also the public.[7]

---

1. It was enacted to form an integral part of the unemployment insurance system established by the federal Social Security Act of 1935, U.S.C. 49 *Stat.* 620, ch. 531. Tax provisions of the federal act were incorporated into the Internal Revenue Code of 1939 and became known as the Federal Unemployment Tax Act, 26 U.S.C. §§1600-1611, now 26 U.S.C. §§3301 to 3311. *Pioneer Potato Co. v. Div. of Employment Sec.*, 17 N.J. 543, 546-7 (1955).

2. N.J.S.A. 43:21-2. *See Brady v. Bd. of Review*, 152 N.J. 197, 211-212 (1997); *Provident Inst. for Sav. in Jersey City v. Div. of Unemployment Sec.*, 32 N.J. 585, 590 (1960); *Bogue Elec. Co. v. Bd. of Review*, 21 N.J. 431, 435 (1956).

3. *Battaglia v. Bd. of Review*, 14 N.J.Super. 24, 27 (App. Div. 1951) (not every case of unemployment warrants benefits, only those where employee lost work through no fault of his own); *Yardville Supply Co. v. Bd. of Review*, 114 N.J. 371, 375 (1989) (reiterating same).

4. *Brady v. Bd. of Review*, 152 N.J. 197, 212 (1997); *Teichler v. Curtiss-Wright Corp.*, 24 N.J. 585, 592 (1957); *Trauma Nurses, Inc. v. Bd. of Review*, 242 N.J.Super. 135, 142 (App. Div.1990).

5. *Hancock v. Bd. of Review*, 46 N.J.Super. 418, 421 (App. Div. 1957).

6. *Yardville Supply Co. v. Bd. of Review*, 114 N.J. 371, 374 (1989) (holding that truck driver who lost his license for driving while intoxicated was disqualified from benefits because he "left work voluntarily without good cause"); *Krauss v. A. & M. Karagheusian*, 13 N.J. 447, 455-56 (1953); *Schock v. Bd. of Review*, 89 N.J.Super. 118, 125 (App. Div. 1965), *aff'd*, 48 N.J. 121 (1966).

9-2 Employment Status

The test of employment status is broad and liberally construed; "the relation of employer and employee may be deemed to exist under circumstances which would not lead to that determination under the common-law classification."[8] "Employment" within the scope of the UC Law is defined as "services... performed for remuneration[9] or under any contract for hire, written or oral, express or implied."[10] A joint venture in which one member of the venture receives the proceeds and distributes them among the other members is not an "employment" relationship between the recipient and the other members.[11] Services for remuneration will be excluded from "employment" only if they fall within the scope of a specific statutory exception, or if the three-part test of N.J.S.A. 43:21-19(i)(6) is met:

a) The individual has been and will continue to be free from control or direction over the performance of such service, both under his contract of service and in fact; and

b) Such service is either outside the usual course of business for which such service is performed, or that such service is performed outside of all the places of business of the enterprise for which such service is performed; and

c) Such individual is customarily engaged in an independently established trade, occupation, profession or business.[12]

Unless all three prongs of this "A, B, C" test are met, the service will be considered employment under the UC Law.[13] Executive officers of corporations charged with running the business are normally considered employees under this test.[14]

---

7. *Brady v. Bd. of Review*, 152 N.J. 197, 212 (1997).

8. *Provident Inst. for Sav. in Jersey City v. Div. of Unemployment Sec.*, 32 N.J. 585, 590 (1960), *quoting Gilchrist v. Div. of Employment Sec.*, 48 N.J.Super. 147, 153 (App. Div. 1957).

9. "Remuneration" is defined as "all compensation for personal services, including commission and bonuses and the cash value of all compensation in any medium other than cash." N.J.S.A. 43:21-19(p).

10. N.J.S.A. 43:21-19(i)(1)(A). "'Contract for hire' need not be given a technical meaning ... for the act must be construed to effectuate the declared public policy of providing security against unemployment which the Legislature has declared to be the 'greatest hazard of our economic life.' " *Provident Inst. for Sav. in Jersey City v. Div. of Unemployment Sec.*, 32 N.J. 585, 593 (1960).

11. *Koza v. N.J. Dep't of Labor*, 307 N.J. Super. 439, 443-444 (App. Div. 1998) (reversing determination that musicians who played together and with others were employees of individual who obtained bookings and received and distributed payments because the recipient/distributor of the funds was merely a conduit for the putative employer).

Provided they are also exempt under the Federal Unemployment Tax Act (FUTA), or that contributions with respect to same are not required to be paid into a state unemployment fund as a condition for a tax offset credit against the tax imposed by FUTA, the following services for remuneration are excluded from "employment" under the UC Law:[15]

(1) Agricultural labor that is performed for (a) an entity that is not an "employer" under the UC Law, or (b) an employing unit that during the current and preceding calender years has paid less than $20,000 a quarter in gross wages to individuals engaged in agricultural labor; or (c) an employing unit that employs fewer than 10 employees for a portion of a day in each of 20 different calendar weeks in the current or preceding calendar year.[16]

(2) Domestic service in a private home unless performed in the private home of an employing unit that paid cash remuneration of

---

12. To meet this test, it must be established that the "trade, occupation, profession or business" referred to was established independently of the alleged employer and the personal service at issue:

> The fact that a salesman who works on commission must rely on his efforts and ability to secure orders to make a livelihood does not necessarily mean that he is working for himself as an entrepreneur or businessman, within the intendment of test C. The double requirement that an individual must be 'customarily engaged' and 'independently established' calls for an enterprise that exists and can continue to exist independently of and apart from the particular service relationship. The enterprise must be one that is stable and lasting—one that will survive the termination of the relationship.

Gilchrist v. Div. of Employment Sec., 48 N.J.Super. 147, 158 (App. Div. 1957). *See LBK Computer Assocs. Corp. v. N.J. Dep't of Labor*, 95 N.J.A.R.2d (LBR) 13 (1995) (computer consultant was not independent contractor because "none of the indicia of an independent business such as independent trade names, incorporation, commercial premises, federal income tax identification numbers, yellow page listings, business telephones, advertisements, and liability insurances were evident on the record."). *But see Koza v. N.J. Dep't of Labor*, 307 N.J. Super. 439, 443-444 (App. Div. 1998) (ABC test need not be applied where relationship between musician workers was as a joint venture rather than as "employment.").

13. *Carpet Remnant Warehouse, Inc. v. Dept. of Labor*, 125 N.J. 567, 581 (1991); *Provident Inst. for Sav. in Jersey City v. Div. of Unemployment Sec.*, 32 N.J. 585, 591 (1960); *Trauma Nurses, Inc. v. Bd. of Review*, 242 N.J.Super. 135, 143 (App. Div. 1990); *Gilchrist v. Div. of Employment Sec.*, 48 N.J.Super. 147, 157 (App. Div. 1957) (collecting cases).

14. *See Provident Inst. for Sav. in Jersey City v. Div. of Unemployment Sec.*, 32 N.J. at 592-94 (members of executive committee of bank employees under UC Law); *Paramus Bathing Beach v. Div. of Employment Sec.*, 31 N.J.Super. 128, 132-33 (App. Div. 1954) (officers of corporation employees under UC Law: "The intimation that the relationship of employer and employee cannot exist between a corporation and its officers is unrealistic").

15. N.J.S.A. 43:21-19(i)(7). Individuals who participate in workfare in return for public assistance are ineligible for unemployment compensation under N.J.S.A. 43:21-19(i)(1)(D)(V). That statutory exclusion is rationally related to the State's interest in preserving the unemployment compensation fund and is not unconstitutional. *Costello v. Board of Review*, 273 N.J. Super. 536 (App. Div. 1994).

16. N.J.S.A. 43:21-19(i)(7)(A)(ii). The Department of Labor publication, *New Jersey's Unemployment & Disability Insurance Programs*, p.11 (January 1991), instructs employers that the exemption applies to them if they employ fewer than 10 employees for any portion of a day in each of 20 weeks in a calendar year.

$1,000 or more for such domestic service in any calendar quarter of the current or preceding year.[17]

(3) Service performed in the employ of one's son, daughter, or spouse; or service performed by a child under the age of 18 in the employ of his parent;[18]

(4) Service performed in the employ of another state or local government or instrumentality, to the extent that entity is, with respect to such service, exempt under the United States Constitution from the tax imposed under FUTA, except as provided in N.J.S.A. 43:21-19(i)(1)(B).[19]

(5) Service performed in the employ of the United States government or instrumentality thereof, except as otherwise provided by federal law.[20]

(6) Service in the employ of fraternal beneficiary societies, orders, or associations operating under the lodge system or for the exclusive benefit of the member of a fraternity itself operating under the lodge system and providing for the payment of life, sick, accident, or other benefits to the members of the society or their dependents.[21]

(7) Service performed as a member of the board of directors, trustees, managers, or committee of a bank, building and loan, or savings and loan association, where such services do not constitute the principal employment of the individual.[22]

(8) Service with respect to which unemployment is payable under a federal unemployment insurance program.[23]

(9) Service performed by agents of mutual fund brokers or dealers in the sale of mutual funds or other securities, or by agents of insurance companies (exclusive of industrial insurance companies), or by agents of investment companies, who are compensated wholly on a commission basis.[24]

---

17. N.J.S.A. 43:21-19(i)(7)(B).
18. N.J.S.A. 43:21-19(i)(7)(C).
19. N.J.S.A. 43:21-19(i)(7)(E).
20. N.J.S.A. 43:21-19(i)(7)(F).
21. N.J.S.A. 43:21-19(i)(7)(G).
22. N.J.S.A. 43:21-19(i)(7)(H).
23. N.J.S.A. 43:21-19(i)(7)(I).

(10) Service by real estate salespersons or brokers who are compensated wholly on a commission basis.[25]

(11) Service for a theater, music hall, or other place of entertainment, not in excess of 10 weeks per year, by any band leader, musician, entertainer, vaudeville artist, actor, actress, singer, or other entertainer.[26]

(12) Service for a union local as a committee member reimbursed by the union for time lost from regular employment, or as a part-time officer of a union local paid less than $1,000 per year.[27]

(13) Service in the sale or distribution of merchandise by home-to-home salespersons or in-home demonstrators whose remuneration consists solely of commissions or commissions and bonuses.[28]

(14) Service for a foreign government,[29] certain service for instrumentalities of foreign governments,[30] and service for an international organization entitled to protection under the International Organizations Immunities Act.[31]

(15) Service covered by an election approved by an agency charged with enforcement of another state or federal unemployment law, in accordance with N.J.S.A. 43:21-21.[32]

(16) Service in the employ of a school, college or university, by certain full-time students and their spouses.[33]

(17) Service by a student in a full-time program at a public or non-profit educational institution that combines academic instruction with work experience, if the service is an integral part of the pro-

---

24. N.J.S.A. 43:21-19(i)(7)(J).

25. N.J.S.A. 43:21-19(i)(7)(K).

26. N.J.S.A. 43:21-19(i)(7)(M). The Department of Labor states in its booklet, *New Jersey Unemployment Compensation & Temporary Disability Benefits*, p.3 that this exception does not apply to "house bands."

27. N.J.S.A. 43:21-19(i)(7)(N).

28. N.J.S.A. 43:21-19(i)(7)(O).

29. N.J.S.A. 43:21-19(i)(7)(P).

30. N.J.S.A. 43:21-19(i)(7)(Q).

31. N.J.S.A. 43:21-19(i)(7)(R).

32. N.J.S.A. 43:21-19(i)(7)(S).

33. N.J.S.A. 43:21-19(i)(7)(T). The student must be enrolled on a full-time basis in an educational program or completing such educational program leading to a degree. Service by the spouse of such an employee may be exempt if the spouse is advised at the start of employment that (1) the employment is part of a program of financial aid, and (2) the employment will not be covered by any unemployment insurance. *Id.*

gram and the educational institution has so certified to the employer.[34]

(18) Service in the employ of a hospital by a patient, student nurse, nurse trainee, or medical intern.[35]

(19) Service by agents of mutual benefit associations if paid wholly on a commission basis.[36]

(20) Service by operators of motor vehicles weighing 18,000 pounds or more, licensed for commercial use and used for the highway movement of motor freight, who own their own equipment or lease or finance it from an entity other than the entity for whom they are performing services, and who are compensated by a percentage of the gross revenue generated by the move or by a schedule of payment based upon the distance and weight of the move.[37]

(21) Service by a certified shorthand reporter who is referred by another reporter or a reporter service on a freelance basis, and who is compensated on the basis of a fee per transcript page, flat attendance fee, other flat attendance fee, or combination thereof.[38]

(22) Service performed by certain owners of limousine franchises.[39]

(23) Services performed by an "outside travel agent," who acts as an independent contractor, is paid on a commission basis, sets his or her own work schedule, and receives no benefits, sick leave, vacation, or other leave from the travel agent owning the facility the outside travel agent uses.[40]

---

34. N.J.S.A. 43:21-19(i)(7)(U). The educational institution must normally maintain a regular faculty and curriculum and normally have a regularly organized body of students at the place where its educational activities are carried on. The exception does not apply to service performed in a program established for or on behalf of an employer or group of employers. *Id.*

35. N.J.S.A. 43:21-19(i)(7)(V).

36. N.J.S.A. 43:21-19(i)(7)(W).

37. N.J.S.A. 43:21-19(i)(7)(X).

38. N.J.S.A. 43:21-19(i)(7)(Y).

39. N.J.S.A. 43:21-19(i)(9). To be entitled to exemption, the limousine franchise must be incorporated; the franchise must be subject to regulation by the Interstate Commerce Commission; the franchise must exist pursuant to a written franchise agreement; and the franchisee must be registered with the Department of Labor and receive an employer registration number. *Id.*

40. N.J.S.A. 43:21-19(i)(7)(Z).

II. BENEFITS

9-3 Measure of Benefit

For benefit years[41] commencing after September 30, 1984, the weekly benefit rate is 60 percent of an eligible claimant's average weekly wage, subject to a maximum of 56 and 2/3 percent of the Statewide average weekly remuneration paid to workers by employers subject to the Law, as determined and promulgated by the Commissioner of Labor.[42] The "average weekly wage" is computed on the basis of the most recent employer with whom claimant was employed for 20 or more weeks.[43] If there is no such employer, the average weekly wage is computed as if all wages were received from one employer.[44]

The weekly benefit is increased by 7 percent for the first dependent, and 4 percent each for the next two dependents (up to a maximum of 3 dependents).[45] However, the weekly benefit including dependency benefits still cannot exceed the statutory maximum of 56 and 2/3 percent of the statewide average.[46]

One may not claim dependency benefits for a spouse who is employed during the week the initial claim for benefits is filed. If both spouses establish claims for benefits, only one can obtain dependency benefits.[47] Remuneration from self-

---

41. "Benefit year" refers to the 364 consecutive calendar days beginning with the day on, or as of which, an individual first files a valid claim for benefits, and thereafter beginning with the day on, or as of which, the individual next files a valid claim for benefits after the termination of his last preceding benefit year. N.J.S.A. 43:21-19(d).

42. N.J.S.A. 43:21-3(c)(1). For 1991, the maximum weekly rate was $291 per week for unemployment compensation, and $272 per week under the Temporary Disability Benefits Law. For 1998, the maximum weekly rate is $390 per week for unemployment compensation and $364 per week under the Temporary Disability Law. N.J.A.C. 12:15-1.2.

43. The average weekly wage is the amount derived by dividing an individual's total wages received during his base year base weeks from the most recent base-year employer with whom he established at least 20 base weeks, by the number of base weeks in which such wages were earned. N.J.S.A. 43:21-19(u). Under appropriate circumstances severance pay will be treated as wages earned during the base year. *See, e.g., Dingleberry v. Bd. of Review*, 154 N.J.Super. 415, 418-19 (App. Div. 1977). Gratuities are included as "wages" for this purpose only when reported to the employer. N.J.S.A. 43:21-19(o); *Masterson v. Board of Review*, 284 N.J. Super. 561 (App. Div. 1995).

44. *See* N.J.S.A. 43:21-19(u); *Mortimer v. Bd. of Review*, 99 N.J. 393, 398-401 (1985).

45. N.J.S.A. 43:21-3(c)(2)(A). A dependent is an individual's unemployed spouse or an unmarried unemployed child under the age of 19 (including an adopted or step child), or an unmarried unemployed child under the age of 22 who is attending school full-time. N.J.S.A. 43:21-3(c)(2)(B). *Cf.* N.J.A.C. 12:17-7.2 (spouse is a person to whom claimant is legally married and a dependent unmarried child includes legally adopted stepchildren who are either under 19 or under 22 and attending an educational institution as defined in N.J.S.A. 43:21-19(4)).

46. N.J.S.A. 43:21-3(c)(2)(A). If an individual is barred by the cap of N.J.S.A. 43:21-3(c)(1) from collecting the dependency allowance, his spouse may declare those dependents on her claim. N.J.A.C. 12:17-7.3(c).

47. N.J.S.A. 43:21-3(c)(2)(B); N.J.A.C. 12:17-7.3(b).

employment to one receiving a self-employment assistance allowance is deducted from the weekly benefit rate.[48]

9-4 Maximum Total Benefits

Eligible individuals are entitled to receive total benefits equal to $^3/_4$ of the individual's base weeks[49] with all employers in the base year [50] multiplied by the individual's weekly benefit rate.[51]

However, no individual is entitled to receive benefits in excess of 26 times his weekly benefit rate in any benefit year.[52]

Except as provided by N.J.S.A. 43:21-7(c)(1) (future rates based on benefit experience), benefits so paid shall be charged to the accounts of the individual's base year employers as follows: each week of benefits paid shall be charged against each base year employer's account in the same proportion that the wages

48. N.J.S.A. 43:21-3(b).

49. "Base week" for a benefit year commencing on or after October 1, 1985 and before January 1, 1996 means any calendar week of an individual's base year during which the individual earned in employment at least 20 per cent of the statewide average weekly remuneration. N.J.S.A. 43:21-19(t)(1). That amount is calculated annually. For benefit years commencing after January 1, 1996, benefit weeks means any calendar week of an individual's base year during which the individual earned in employment at least 20 per cent of the statewide average weekly remuneration, or any calendar week of the base year during which the individual earned in employment at least 20 times the minimum wage (as provided in N.J.S.A. 34:11-56a4) in effect on October 1 of the calendar year preceding the calendar year in which the benefit year commences. N.J.S.A. 43:21-19(t)(2). In any calendar week an individual is employed for more than one employer, the individual may in that week establish a base week with respect to each such employer.

The base week amount calculated based on the statewide average for 1998 is $128. N.J.A.C. 12:15-1.5. The base week amount calculated based on the state minimum wage is $101. *Id.*

50. "Base year" with respect to benefit years commencing on or after July 1, 1986, means the first four of the last five completed calendar quarters immediately preceding the benefit year. For benefits years commencing on or after July 1, 1995, if an individual does not have sufficient qualifying weeks or wages in his base year to qualify for benefits, the individual may designate the "alternative base year" as the individual's base year. The alternative base year is the last four completed calendar quarters immediately preceding the benefit year, except that for benefit years commencing after October 1, 1995, alternative base year means the last three completed calendar quarters immediately preceding his benefit year. The division must inform the individual of the individual's options in this regard, and may base the determination of eligibility on the individual's affidavit, supported by payroll documentation if available, if the requisite information is not otherwise available. N.J.S.A. 43:21-19(c)(1). There is no express time limit for exercising this option. N.J.S.A. 43:21-19(c)(2); *Gilliland v. Board of Review*, 298 N.J. Super. 349, 353 (App. Div. 1997). The division must provide a reasonable time limit for claimants to choose an alternative base year calculation. *Id.*

51. N.J.S.A. 43:21-3(d)(1)(B)(i). This formula is applicable to benefit years commencing on or after July 1, 1986. "Benefit year" with respect to any individual means the 364 consecutive calendar days beginning with the day on, or as of, which the individual first files a valid claim for benefits. Thereafter, the benefit year begins with the day on which or as of which the claimant next files a valid claim for benefits after the termination of his last preceding benefit year. A claim is considered valid for the purpose of this definition if (1) the claimant is unemployed for the week in which or as of which the claim is filed; and (2) he has fulfilled the conditions imposed by N.J.S.A. 43:21-4(e) [established 20 base weeks or satisfied the alternative earnings requirement, which was $8,300 in 1998]. N.J.S.A. 43:21-19(d); N.J.A.C. 12:15-1.6.

52. N.J.S.A. 43:21-3(d)(2).

paid by each employer to the individual during the base year bear to the wages paid by all employers to that individual during the base year.[53]

9-5 "Unemployment" for Entitlement Purposes

Unemployment, for the purpose of entitlement to benefits, occurs in "any week during which [the claimant] is not engaged in full-time work *and* with respect to which his remuneration is less than his weekly benefit rate...." [54] Weeks during which an employee is on involuntary vacation without pay are included.[55] However, an officer of a corporation and any person with a five percent equitable or debt interest in a corporation will not be deemed unemployed from such corporation in any week during his term of office or ownership.[56] Although both prongs of the definition must be met, the meaning of "full-time" employment is based upon the amount of remuneration earned and not necessarily upon the number of hours worked.[57]

9-6 Eligibility/General

To be eligible for benefits, an individual generally must (1) file a claim; (2) be able to work; (3) be actively seeking work; (4) be available for work; (5) satisfy a one-week waiting period; and (6) satisfy an earnings requirement.[58]

---

53. N.J.S.A. 43:21-3(d)(1)(B)(ii).

54. N.J.S.A. 43:21-19(m)(1).

55. *Id.*

56. *Id.* This provision does not violate the Due Process or Equal Protection clauses of the United States Constitution because it is rationally related to legitimate state purposes.

> The legislature rationally could have concluded that corporate officers and stockholders ordinarily control the terms of their own employment and therefore would be able to manipulate the system to obtain benefits if they qualified for unemployment compensation. The legislature also rationally could have concluded that corporate officers and stockholders are ordinarily better suited financially than most other employees and therefore have a lesser need for benefits if they become unemployed.

Buckwald v. Board of Review, 267 N.J. Super. 617, 621-22 (App. Div. 1993) (holding that lounge manager who owned more than 5 percent of the employer and who was negotiating with insurers while lounge was closed temporarily because of fire damage was disqualified from benefits).

57. *See Borromeo v. Bd. of Review*, 196 N.J.Super. 576, 579 (App. Div. 1984); *Caldwell v. Div. of Unemployment and Disability Ins.*, 145 N.J.Super. 206, 208-09 (App. Div. 1976) (claimant who received back-pay award for period he was not working, in settlement of grievance with employer, was not "unemployed" during that period).

58. *See generally* N.J.S.A. 43.21-4.

9-6:1 Filing a Claim

To be eligible for benefits, an individual must file a claim at a claims office and thereafter continue to report to a service or claims office as directed, in mail or in person, in accordance with regulations.[59] A claim for benefits must be made in accordance with the procedures set forth in N.J.S.A. 43:21-6(a) and regulations thereunder.

An individual who wants to claim benefits must report to an unemployment claims office in person to file a new claim for benefits, unless the Division requires otherwise.[60] Except as otherwise prescribed by regulation, a week of unemployment commences only after a claim has been so filed.[61] The effective date of the claim is the Sunday of the week in which it is filed; the effective date, in turn, establishes the period of time during which wages can be used for determining the monetary entitlement.[62]

To maintain eligibility for unemployment benefits, claimants must report on the date, at the time and place, and in the manner (in person, by telephone, by mail, or otherwise) prescribed by the Division.[63] A claimant who fails to report as directed will be ineligible for benefits unless it is determined that the individual had "good cause" for the failure to comply.[64]

9-6:2 Able To Work

An individual is eligible for benefits only if he is physically and mentally able to work.[65] He must also be legally able to work.[66]

---

59. N.J.S.A. 43:21-4(a). The regulations may in certain cases waive or alter these requirements. *Id.*

60. N.J.A.C. 12:17-4.2(a).

61. N.J.S.A. 43:21-19(m)(3).

62. N.J.A.C. 12:17-4.2(a).

63. N.J.A.C. 12:17-4.1(c).

64. N.J.A.C. 12:17-4.1(b). "Good cause" is determined in a fact finding hearing and is defined as "any situation over which the claimant did not have control and which was so compelling as to prevent the claimant from reporting as required by the Division." *Id.*

65. N.J.S.A. 43:21-4(c); *Krauss v. A. & M. Karagheusian*, 24 N.J.Super. 277, 283 (App. Div.), *rev'd on other grounds*, 13 N.J. 447 (1953).

66. *Brambila v. Bd. of Review*, 124 N.J. 425 (1991) (aliens); *Pinilla v. Bd. of Review, Dept. of Labor and Indus.*, 155 N.J. Super. 307 (App. Div. 1978)(same); *See* N.J.S.A. 43:21-4(i) (codifying rules for aliens).

9-6:3 Actively Seeking Work

A claimant must be "actively seeking work."[67] This requires more than being passively available for work.[68] One should make some effort to obtain employment, going out within a reasonable distance of one's home in search of work, and not rely entirely on an employment service, word of mouth, or reading want ads.[69]

However, after termination, an unemployed individual may utilize an interim period to look for work in the craft or trade in which he has experience before he is obligated to seek general unskilled work.[70]

9-6:4 Available for Work

A claimant must be "available for work."[71] He must be willing, able and ready to accept suitable work that he does not have good cause to refuse; *i.e.*, he must be "genuinely attached to the labor market."[72]

An individual may accept work in another state without jeopardizing his rights under the New Jersey Act during the benefit year if he loses his position in the other state before becoming eligible to collect in that state.[73]

Advanced age does not of itself conclusively establish that a claimant is unavailable for work. It is properly a consideration upon the issue of his availability for work only as it relates to his ability to work or to restrictions that materially limit his capacity to work.[74]

A claimant who moves from an area in which a job market exists to one in which there is a high level of unemployment is not "available for work" and is ineligible for benefits.[75]

---

67. N.J.S.A. 43:21-4(c).

68. *Worsnop v. Bd. of Review*, 92 N.J.Super. 260, 265 (App. Div. 1966).

69. *Calamusa v. Bd. of Review*, 164 N.J.Super. 325, 329-30 (App. Div. 1978); *Breskin v. Bd. of Review*, 46 N.J.Super. 338, 343 (App. Div. 1957); *Boyer v. Bd. of Review*, 4 N.J.Super. 143, 146 (App. Div. 1949).

70. *Breskin v. Bd. of Review*, 46 N.J.Super. 338, 344 (App. Div. 1957) (however, claimant in that case so limited her job search that she failed to comply with actively seeking work requirement). *But cf. De Rose v. Bd. of Review*, 6 N.J.Super. 164 (App. Div. 1950) (claimant who was unwilling to accept job as cashier that paid less than her previous pay of $37/week, although usual starting pay for cashier was closer to $28-30/week, precluded from collecting additional compensation).

71. N.J.S.A. 43:21-4(c).

72. *Vasquez v. Bd. of Review, Dept. of Labor and Indus.*, 127 N.J.Super. 431, 434 (App. Div.), *certif. denied*, 65 N.J. 559 (1974).

73. *Eagle Truck Transport Inc. v. Bd. of Review*, 29 N.J. 280 (1959).

74. *Krauss v. A. & M. Karagheusian*, 13 N.J. 447, 462 (1953); *Campbell Soup Co. v. Bd. of Review*, 13 N.J. 431, 438 (1953).

75. *Vasquez v. Bd. of Review, Dept. of Labor and Indus.*, 127 N.J.Super. 431 (App. Div.), *certif. denied*, 65 N.J. 559 (1974); *see Gonzalez v. Bell Laboratories*, 132 N.J.Super. 330 (App. Div. 1975).

If a claimant is working full time before losing his job, and thereafter restricts his availability to part-time work, he is not "available for work" and is ineligible for benefits.[76] However, an individual who had been working part time during a substantial portion of the previous year and thereafter limits his or her availability to part-time work may be eligible for benefits if: 1) there is good cause for the limitation; 2) there is sufficient part-time work in the individual's general labor market to justify the limitation; and 3) the individual is available for a sufficient number of hours weekly to be able to earn at least the individual's weekly benefit sum.[77] It also has been held that under some circumstances, a claimant who limits her availability to a particular shift to care for her young children during the day is not ineligible.[78]

An otherwise eligible individual is not deemed ineligible or unavailable for work because he is involuntarily on vacation without pay, *e.g.*, as the result of a collective bargaining agreement.[79] Moreover, as long as the individual is ready, willing and able to work, it is of no consequence that he knows in advance that there will be a shut-down period.[80]

An individual is not deemed unavailable for work if he is attending a training program approved for the individual by the division to enhance his employability, or because he has failed or refused to accept work while attending such program.[81]

A claimant is not unavailable for work during the period he is serving on a jury,[82] or if he is attending the funeral of an immediate family member (parent, parent-in-law, grandparent, child, grandchild, spouse, foster child, sibling, or any relatives residing in the claimant's household)—provided the duration of the attendance is not more than two days.[83]

An otherwise eligible individual is not ineligible because the individual fails or refuses to accept work while participating full-time in self-employment assistance activities.[84] However, an individual determined, based on information ob-

---

76. *Edmundson v. Bd. of Review*, 71 N.J.Super. 127, 134 (App. Div. 1961).

77. N.J.A.C. 12:17-12.7. "Substantial portion" is defined in the regulations as "earning sufficient wage credits in part-time employment to establish a claim of benefits." N.J.A.C. 12:17-12.7(a)(1). "Good cause" is defined in this context as "compelling circumstances which prevent the individual from accepting full-time employment." N.J.A.C. 12:17-12.7(a)(2).

78. *Tung-Sol Elec. v. Bd. of Review*, 35 N.J.Super. 397, 404 (App. Div. 1955).

79. N.J.S.A. 43:21-4(c)(3). *O'Rourke v. Bd. of Review*, 24 N.J. 607, 611-12 (1957).

80. *Teichler v. Curtiss-Wright Corp.*, 24 N.J. 585, 596-98 (1957); *Watson v. U.S. Rubber Co.*, 24 N.J. 598, 602-03 (1957); *John A. Roebling's Corp. v. Bodrog*, 24 N.J. 604, 607 (1957).

81. N.J.S.A. 43:21-4(c)(4).

82. N.J.S.A. 43:21-4(c)(5).

83. N.J.S.A. 43:21-4(c)(6).

tained by the worker profiling system, to be likely to exhaust regular benefits and need reemployment services is ineligible unless that individual participates in available reemployment services (unless the individual has completed the services or has justifiable cause for failure to participate).[85]

9-6:5 Waiting Period

To be eligible for benefits, an individual must be totally or partially unemployed for a waiting period of one week in the benefit year which included that week.[86] A week may not be counted as a week of unemployment if

(1) benefits have been paid or are payable in that week;[87]

(2) it counts as a waiting period under the Temporary Disability Benefits Law, N.J.S.A. 43:21-25, *et seq.*;[88]

(3) the individual has not filed a claim and/or is not able and available for work and seeking same;[89] or

(4) the claimant is disqualified for benefits because his unemployment is due to a stoppage of work arising from a labor dispute.[90]

9-6:6 Earnings Requirement

To be eligible for benefits a claimant must have earned at least 12 times the statewide average weekly remuneration[91] during his base year.[92]

The relevance of this section is to determine eligibility; it is not to be used as a basis for computing the average weekly wage to determine the amount of benefits to which a claimant is entitled.[93]

---

84. N.J.S.A. 43:21-4 (c)(7)

85. N.J.S.A. 43:21-4(c)(8)

86. N.J.S.A. 43:21-4(d). When benefits become payable with respect to the third consecutive week following the waiting period, the individual is eligible to collect benefits for the waiting period. *Id.*

87. N.J.S.A. 43:21-4(d)(1).

88. N.J.S.A. 43:21-4(d)(2).

89. That is, he fulfills the requirements of 43:21-4(a) and (c). N.J.S.A. 43:21-4(d)(3).

90. N.J.S.A. 43:21-4(d)(4). *See* 43:21-5(d).

91. "Remuneration" under this section has been held to include a monthly displacement allowance given to the claimant under the Regional Rail Reorganization Act. *Bilankov v. Bd. of Review*, 190 N.J.Super. 370 (App. Div. 1983). Similarly, a claimant has been held entitled to have her severance pay attributable to her 11th year of service included in a calculation of her base year earnings. *Dingleberry v. Bd. of Review*, 154 N.J.Super. 415 (App. Div. 1977).

9-6:7 Total Disability

An individual may be eligible for benefits if he has suffered any accident or sickness not compensable as Worker's Compensation that results in total disability to perform any work for pay, and if he would be eligible for benefits except for the inability to work, and has furnished notice and proof of his claim and payment is not precluded by N.J.S.A. 43:21-3(d).[94] However, no benefits are so payable for any period during which the claimant is not under the care of a licensed physician, dentist, optometrist, chiropractor, psychologist or podiatrist;[95] for any period of disability due to a willfully and intentionally self-inflicted injury, or to injuries sustained in the commission of a crime of the first, second, or third degree;[96] for any week in which the individual is seeking benefits under the unemployment compensation or disability laws of another state or of the United States, unless it is determined that he is ineligible for such benefits;[97] for any week or part of which he has received or is seeking temporary disability benefits;[98] or, for any period of disability commencing while the individual is a "covered individual" under the Temporary Disability Benefits Law.[99]

---

92. N.J.S.A. 43:21-4(e)(1). This is the rule for benefit years commencing on or after October 1, 1984. Somewhat different rules apply to farm workers. N.J.S.A. 43:21-4(e)(3).

Prior to October 1, 1984, claimant had to establish at least 20 base weeks or, if not, show earnings of $2,200. N.J.S.A. 43:21-4(e)(1).

Under the old rule, where an employee was still employed during a one-year pregnancy leave without pay, and informed during the year that she would not be asked to return after leave ended, the base period for computing her eligibility was the year preceding termination of leave and not the year preceding the day she stopped working. *Halenar v. Sayreville Bd. of Educ.*, 177 N.J.Super. 157 (App. Div. 1981). For the purpose of unemployment benefits, leave of absence connotes continuity of employment. *Id.*

Where claimant's employer was a successor to his former employer, and there was no interruption in operations, employment was continuous for purposes of eligibility. *Marcello v. Bd. of Review*, 90 N.J.Super. 332, 334 (App. Div. 1966).

93. *See* N.J.S.A. 43:21-19(u) and *Unemployment & Disability Ins. Div. v. Bd. of Review*, 188 N.J.Super. 71, 75-77 (App. Div. 1983), *approved in Mortimer v. Bd. of Review*, 99 N.J. 393 (1985).

For benefit years commencing after July 1, 1986, the "average weekly wage" is the amount derived by dividing an individual's total base year wages by the number of base weeks worked by the individual during the base year. The maximum number of base weeks is 52. N.J.S.A. 43:21-19(u).

94. N.J.S.A. 43:21-4(f). *See* N.J.A.C. 12:17-17.5. Under N.J.S.A. 43:21-3(d)(2), no individual is entitled to receive benefits in excess of 26 times his weekly benefit rate in any benefit year under this subsection or N.J.S.A. 43:21-4(c). If any individual qualifies for benefits under both subsections during any benefit year, the maximum total of benefits payable under the combined subsections is one and one-half times the maximum amount of benefits payable under one of said subsections.

95. N.J.S.A. 43:21-4(f)(1)(A).

96. N.J.S.A. 43:21-4(f)(1)(C).

97. N.J.S.A. 43:21-4(f)(1)(D).

98. N.J.S.A. 43:21-4(f)(1)(E).

99. N.J.S.A. 43:21-4(f)(1)(F), referring to the Temporary Disability Benefits Law, N.J.S.A. 43:21-25 *et seq.*

Benefit payments under this provision are charged to and paid by the State disability benefits fund established by the Temporary Disability Law and are not charged to any employer account in computing the employer's experience rate for contributions payable under this chapter.[100]

An employee seeking benefits under this provision must file a notice of disability and proof of claim with the Division within 30 days of commencement of the period of disability.[101] The notice must set forth the claimant's full name, address and Social Security account number, as well as the date on which the claimant was too sick (or disabled) to work.[102] The filing of Form DS-1 (Proof of Claim for Disability Benefits) along with a certification of the claimant's health care professional is sufficient to constitute notice of disability.[103]

9-6:8 Part-Time Employees

A part-time employee is eligible for benefits if he can show good cause for working part time, if there exists in his locality a sufficient amount of suitable work to justify such limitation, and if he is available for enough weekly hours of work or amount of work to earn remuneration equivalent to his weekly benefit amount.[104]

9-6:9 Rules for Employees of Educational Institutions

Federal law mandates that benefits are to be denied during vacation periods between academic years or between terms to any individual employed in an instructional, research or principal administrative capacity for an educational institution (even while in the employ of an educational service agency) if such individual works in the first of such academic years or terms and if there is a contract or a reasonable assurance that he will work in the same capacity in the second of such academic years or terms.[105] The same rule applies to weeks of

---

100. N.J.S.A. 43:21-4(f)(2).

101. N.J.S.A. 43:21-4(f)(1); N.J.A.C. 12:17-17.1(a). Failure to file a notice of disability or proof of claim will not make a claim invalid if the Division determines that there was good cause for the late filing. N.J.A.C. 12:17-17.1(c).

102. N.J.A.C. 12:17-17.1(a).

103. *Id.*

104. N.J.S.A. 43:21-20.1. *See Levine v. Universal Furniture Indus.*, 146 N.J. Super. 326 (App. Div. 1977) *see also* N.J.A.C. 12:17-12.7.

105. N.J.S.A. 43:21-4(g)(1),(4). A nonprofit preschool/day care facility is not an "educational institution" within the scope of N.J.S.A. 43:21-4(g)(1) or N.J.S.A. 43:21-4(g)(2). Therefore, a claimant teacher laid off during the summer was not disqualified from benefits, even though she had a reasonable expectation of returning to her job. *In the Matter of J.S.R.*, 95 N.J.A.R.2d (UCC) 14 (1994).

unemployment commencing after September 3, 1982 for *any* employee of an educational institution.[106]

Benefits similarly are not payable for any week that commences during periods between academic years or terms and during established vacation and holiday periods, if the employee has *reasonable assurance* of continued employment in any such capacity in the net academic year or term or after the vacation holiday.[107] If a non-professional school employee is denied benefits only because the individual had reasonable assurance of return to work and is then not allowed to return to work, the individual may collect benefits retroactively if: 1) the claimant complied with the continued claim reporting requirements outlined in N.J.A.C. 12:17-4; and 2) the individual is not otherwise disqualified from receiving benefits.[108]

9-6:10 Rules for Professional Athletes

An individual may not seek benefits on the basis of work that substantially or entirely consists of participating in sports or athletic events or training or preparing to so participate, with respect to weeks that commence during the period between two successive sports seasons, if he performed such services in the first of such seasons and there is a reasonable assurance that he will perform such services in the latter of such seasons.[109]

9-6:11 Extended Benefits

Extended benefits are available to those individuals who have exhausted benefits under their regular claims. Generally, extended benefits are available during periods of high unemployment.[110]

---

106. N.J.S.A. 43:21-4(g)(2).

107. N.J.A.C. 12:17-12.4(a). "Reasonable assurance" is defined by the regulations as "a written, oral, or other implied agreement that the employee shall perform services in any such capacity during the next academic year, term, or remainder of a term." N.J.A.C. 12:17-12.4(a)(1). "Any such capacity" is defined as "the same or similar capacity and refers to the type of services provided" in a professional or non-professional capacity. *Id.*

108. N.J.A.C. 12:17-12.4(d).

109. N.J.S.A. 43:21-4(h).

110. N.J.S.A. 43:21-24.11 to -24.19.

9-7 Disqualification

Individuals may be disqualified from benefits for a variety of reasons, including: (1) voluntary termination of employment; (2) misconduct; (3) failure to apply for or to accept suitable work; (4) involvement in a labor dispute; (5) receipt of remuneration in lieu of notice; (6) receipt of other benefits; (7) fraud; and (8) participation in a training program.

9-7:1 Voluntary Termination of Employment

An individual is disqualified for benefits for the week in which he has left work voluntarily without good cause attributable to the work, and for each week thereafter until the individual becomes reemployed, works for four weeks, and earns at least six times his weekly benefit rate.[111] The purpose of this provision is to distinguish between (1) a voluntary quit with good cause attributable to the work; and (2) a voluntary quit without good cause attributable to the work, with the latter being deemed a disqualifying "voluntary departure without good cause related to work."[112] It has been held that disqualification under this section is reserved for cases where it was the intent of the employee to quit, and not those cases where an employee merely walks out without intending to resign:

> Employees frequently leave work temporarily for some fleeting physical or mental irritation, or "in a huff" occasioned by one or more of the frustrations attending commercial life, without intending to quit. Although such an individual may be said to have left work voluntarily and without good cause attributable to the work, thus engaging in conduct which might justify a discharge by the employer, nevertheless such a party may not be said to

---

111. N.J.S.A. 43:21-5(a). *But see Goodman v. Bd. of Review,* 245 N.J.Super. 551 (App. Div. 1991) (claimant who voluntarily quit unsuitable part-time job because it interfered with search for suitable employment not disqualified from receiving benefits). *Combs v. Board of Review,* 269 N.J. Super. 616, 621-22 (App. Div. 1994) (employee forced to resign due to alleged physical inability to perform job tasks is not a "voluntary" quit; however, if refusal to perform job duties is not warranted, employee may be considered terminated for cause).

The wages needed to be earned in order to remove disqualification need not be earned within New Jersey. *Eagle Truck Transport Inc. v. Bd. of Review,* 29 N.J. 280 (1959).

112. *Self v. Bd. of Review,* 91 N.J. 453, 457 (1982). "Good cause attributable to such work" is defined in the regulations as "a reason related directly to the individual's employment, which was so compelling as to give the individual no choice but to leave the employment." N.J.A.C. 12:17-9.1(b). The claimant bears the burden of proving "good cause." N.J.A.C. 12:17-9.1(c). Before 1961, the UC Law did not disqualify claimants who "left work voluntarily for good cause," regardless of whether the good cause was personal or work related. In 1961, the Legislature amended N.J.S.A. 43:21-5(a) to require the disqualification of any individual who "has left work voluntarily without good cause attributable to such work." L. 1961, ch.43, §3. *See Yardville Supply Co. v. Bd. of Review,* 114 N.J. 371, 374-75 (1989).

> have "left work" in the meaning of having severed his employment relationship with an intent not to return.[113]

If an employee has multiple reasons for leaving work, and at least one of the reasons constitutes good cause attributable to such work, the employee shall not be disqualified for benefits.[114]

In *Yardville Supply Co. v. Bd. of Review*,[115] the Supreme Court held that a truck driver who was terminated by his employer after he lost his drivers' license as a consequence of a driving while intoxicated conviction had left work *voluntarily* without good cause attributable to the work.[116] The Court described the test of voluntariness broadly:

> Where it is reasonably foreseeable that an employee's voluntary conduct will render him unemployable, and his actions actually do lead to the loss of a prerequisite of employment, the employee leaves work voluntarily without good cause attributable to such work under N.J.S.A. 43:21-5(a).[117]

The test for "good cause" is whether there is cause sufficient to justify an employee's voluntarily leaving the ranks of the employed to join the ranks of the un-

---

113. *Savastano v. State Bd. of Review*, 99 N.J.Super. 397, 400 (App. Div. 1968). *See Garcia v. Bd. of Review*, 191 N.J.Super. 602, 608-09 (App. Div. 1983). An individual who is absent from work for five or more work days without notice is deemed to have left work voluntarily and is subject to disqualification from benefits where the absence was not for good cause. N.J.A.C. 12:17-9.10(a).

114. N.J.A.C. 12:17-9.1(d).

115. 114 N.J. 371 (1989).

116. *See* N.J.A.C. 12:17-9.9(a) (codifying *Yardville*). If an individual fails to apply for or renew a license necessary to job performance and is then separated from work because of this failure, the separation is deemed voluntary and the individual is disqualified from benefits. N.J.A.C. 12:17-9.9(b). The separation is deemed a discharge. N.J.A.C. 12:17-9.9(c).

117. *Id.* at 377. In a dissent joined by Justice Handler, Justice O'Hern questioned the majority's reasoning, and whether the Court's reaction to the particular nature of offense there at issue was translatable into a general rule:

> Although it may be tempting to decide this case against Sparks on the narrow ground that he committed a serious criminal violation, I search for an organizing principle of the majority opinion. Is it creating a "constructive voluntary quit" doctrine? *See Steinberg v. California Unemployment Ins. Appeals Bd.*, 151 Cal. Rptr. 133, 87 Cal. App. 3d 582 (1978) (outlining the requirements for such a doctrine). How far does the Court's policy go? Is it the voluntariness of the offense? Would speeding that causes a loss of license disqualify a worker from unemployment benefits? Would engaging in a touch football game that causes a driver to break his hand be disqualifying? Or is it the stigmatic nature of the offense? If so, what sort of misconduct outside of work disqualifies one from benefits?

114 N.J. 371, 378, 381 (O'Hern, J., dissenting). *See also Fennel v. Board of Review*, 297 N.J. Super. 319, 324 (App. Div.), *certif. denied*, 151 N.J. 464 (1997) (claimant who was terminated as a result of inability to attend work because of incarceration is denied unemployment benefits because his actions are deemed voluntary and without good cause attributable to work); *Pagan v. Board of Review*, 296 N.J. Super. 539, 542 (App. Div.) *certif. denied*, 150 N.J. 24 (1997) (woman who left work because of an abusive spouse did so voluntarily and without good cause attributable to such work).

employed.[118] Thus, if an individual voluntarily leaves his job under circumstances reasonably regarded as having compelled him to do so, then the termination is involuntary.[119] His reasons must be real, substantial and reasonable, not imaginary, trifling or whimsical.[120]

The issue of voluntariness may also have a bearing on a claimant's availability for work[121] to the extent his quitting permits the inference of an intention to withdraw from the job market.[122]

The reason for leaving must be attributable to the work itself.[123] If the reason is purely personal and not directly related to work, good cause will not be found.[124]

Good cause will be found where an individual terminates his employment because of dangerous or unhealthy working conditions.[125] Good cause also will be found when an employee terminates his employment rather than act illegally or immorally.[126]

---

118. *Brady v. Bd. of Review,* 152 N.J. 197, 214 (1997); *Inside Radio/Radio Only, Inc. v. Bd. of Review,* 204 N.J.Super. 296, 299 (App. Div. 1985); *Stonco Elec. Products Co. v. Bd. of Review,* 106 N.J.Super. 6 (App. Div. 1969). The test for determining "good cause" is one of "ordinary common sense and prudence." *Brady,* 152 N.J. at 214 (citation omitted).

119. *See Breskin v. Bd. of Review,* 46 N.J.Super 338, 342 (App. Div. 1957). *See Combs v. Board of Review,* 269 N.J. Super. 616, 622 (App. Div. 1994) (forced resignation is not "voluntary").

120. *Domenico v. Bd. of Review,* 192 N.J.Super. 284 (App. Div. 1983).

121. *See* N.J.S.A. 43:21-4(c)(1) and *supra* §9-6:4.

122. *See Krauss v. A. & M. Karagheusian,* 13 N.J. 447, 458 (1953). Provisions governing an employee's voluntarily leaving a second job after qualifying for benefits after separation from a full time job are outlined in N.J.A.C. 12:17-9.2.

123. *Self v. Bd. of Review,* 91 N.J. 453, 457 (1982).

124. *See, e.g., Self v. Bd. of Review,* 91 N.J. 453 (1982) (termination was voluntary and not for a good cause related to work, where it was due to claimant's inability to get to work because of lack of transportation); *Rider College v. Bd. of Review,* 167 N.J.Super. 42 (App. Div. 1979) (claimant who quit job because housing near workplace was too expensive and more affordable housing would have necessitated long commute left voluntarily without good cause related to work); *Roche v. Bd. of Review,* 156 N.J.Super. 63 (App. Div. 1978) (claimant who left work to find a new place to live disqualified); *Morgan v. Bd. of Review,* 77 N.J.Super. 209 (App. Div. 1962) (holding that commuting is merely a condition of employment; quitting a job because of excessive commute is not for good cause related to the work).

125. N.J.A.C. 12:17-9.4. *See Sanchez v. Bd. of Review,* 206 N.J.Super. 617 (App. Div. 1986) (case remanded where claimant alleged unhealthy working conditions due to employer's failure to provide work gloves, knee pads or boots for farm laborer; also, although claimant subject to collective bargaining agreement, not required to seek adjustment of grievances regarding work conditions before quitting); *Stonco Elec. Products Co. v. Bd. of Review,* 106 N.J.Super. 6 (App. Div. 1969) (work too heavy and work area too cold); *Domenico v. Bd. of Review,* 192 N.J.Super. 284 (App. Div. 1983) (fear of imminent physical harm to employee in state psychiatric hospital after two assaults, one requiring hospitalization); *Condo v. Bd. of Review,* 158 N.J.Super. 172 (App. Div. 1978) (threats of physical violence by co-employee). Although an employee has the responsibility to do whatever is necessary and reasonable to remain employed, he need not do "everything possible to maintain intact the employer-employee relationship." *Id.* at 175. *See also Coombs v. Bd. of Review,* 269 N.J. Super. 623 (App. Div. 1994) (employee who is medically disabled from performing her job due to work-related conditions has "good cause" for a "voluntary" quit).

To the extent an individual purports to resign because of medical reasons, his claim must be supported by sufficient credible evidence.[127] An individual will not be disqualified from receiving unemployment benefits for leaving work because of a disability with a work-connected origin, if there was no other suitable job available that the claimant could have performed within the bounds of the disability.[128]

An individual also will not be disqualified from receiving unemployment benefits for leaving work because of a physical and/or mental health condition or state of health not caused by work if the condition was aggravated by the working conditions and there was no other suitable job available that the claimant could have performed within the bounds of the disability.[129] If an employee claims that he was forced to resign because of the aggravation of a pre-existing condition, he must be prepared to show that the aggravation is related to his work.[130] Evidence that the work "may" have aggravated an employee's pre-existing medical problem is insufficient to establish good cause.[131] When the health condition that causes the individual to leave work is not work-related, the individual will be disqualified from benefits for voluntarily leaving work.[132]

However, a failure to report to work because of illness not attributable to the work is not a voluntary quit that disqualifies the employee, if he takes steps reasonably calculated to protect his employment and seeks to return to the job after the illness.[133]

---

126. *Casciano v. Board of Review*, 300 N.J. Super. 570, 577 (App. Div. 1997) (employee who leaves employment rather than over bill customers is qualified to receive unemployment benefits).

127. *Inside Radio/Radio Only, Inc. v. Bd. of Review*, 204 N.J.Super. 296 (App. Div. 1985) (employee who was forced to work 60-80 hours per week, forego meals and obtain medical care for fatigue, nutritional problems and a mild depression had good cause related to her work for resigning: "the job pressures imposed by the employer were so compelling and so onerous as to leave [claimant] with no reasonable alternative to leaving"). Where health hazards are not apparent, medical proofs will be required. N.J.A.C. 12:17-9.3(d). *See Sanchez v. Bd. of Review*, 206 N.J.Super. 617, 624 (App. Div. 1986); *Gerber v. Bd. of Review*, 313 N.J. Super. 37 (App. Div. 1998) (on the job stress insufficient to amount to good cause attributable to such work where no medical documentation was presented to establish the severity of the stress or its causal connection with plaintiff's job functions); *Coombs vs. Bd. of Review*, 269 N.J. Super. 623 (App. Div. 1994) (employee bears the burden of demonstrating medical condition and its impact on her ability to perform the job).

128. N.J.A.C. 12:17-9.3(a).

129. N.J.A.C. 12:17-9.3(b).

130. *Stauhs v. Bd. of Review*, 93 N.J.Super. 451 (App. Div. 1967). *See also Israel v. Bally's Park Place, Inc.*, 283 N.J. Super. 1 (App. Div. 1995), *certif. denied*, 143 N.J. 326 (1996) (claimant not required to show that illness was caused by job, but rather that environment of job aggravated illness or will impair continued recovery; where claimant can show by medical evidence that claimant is a recovering alcoholic and that recovery is impaired by pervading presence of alcohol at workplace, claimant is not disqualified from receiving benefits).

131. *Wojcik v. Bd. of Review*, 58 N.J. 341, 343-44 (1971).

132. N.J.A.C. 12:17-9.3(b).

Dissatisfaction with the terms or conditions of employment generally does not justify its termination.[134] If, however, a condition or term of employment is unlawful, an employee has good cause to voluntarily resign, even if the law provides other remedies to correct the unlawful condition.[135] Thus, good cause will be found where an employee is subject to intentional harassment by a supervisor.[136]

An attempt to cancel a resignation after voluntarily quitting without good cause will not qualify claimant for benefits where the employer has refused to allow the claimant to continue to work.[137] However, even if an employee voluntarily quits without good cause after securing replacement employment, if her former employer subsequently eliminates her replacement opportunity the resulting unemployment is deemed involuntary.[138]

Where an employee is terminated because he is no longer deemed to be qualified for the job, the termination is not voluntary.[139]

An employee who loses his job because of a provision in a collective bargaining agreement negotiated by a union of which he is a member does not leave his

---

133. N.J.A.C. 12:17-9.3(c). "A reasonable effort is evidenced by the employee's notification to the employer, requesting a leave of absence or having taken other steps to protect his or her employment." *Id. See also DeLorenzo v. Bd. of Review*, 54 N.J. 361 (1969). The employee will be disqualified upon a finding that he, in fact, decided to quit because his work was detrimental to a preexisting medical condition. *Id.* The question is one of intent. *Garcia v. Bd. of Review*, 191 N.J.Super. 602, 606-07 (App. Div. 1983).

134. *See Heulitt v. Board of Review*, 300 N.J. Super. 407, 414 (App. Div. 1997) (an employee who quit his job because he worked long hours, was required to drive a company car, and did not receive overtime pay does not have good cause to do so); *Zielenski v. Bd. of Review*, 85 N.J.Super. 46 (App. Div. 1964) (quitting job because work unsteady and employee only worked one or two days per week did not constitute good cause; claimant disqualified when he gives up parttime employment for none at all); *DeSantis v. Bd. of Review*, 149 N.J.Super. 35 (App. Div. 1977) (resignation after not being given hoped for raise where employer not contractually obligated to give any raise); *Spatola v. Bd. of Review*, 72 N.J.Super. 483 (App. Div. 1962) (employee who quit job immediately after being offered 30-day trial period in which to improve his work did not have good cause).

135. *See Sanchez v. Bd. of Review*, 206 N.J.Super. 617, 621 (App. Div. 1986) (hearing examiner should have explored migrant worker's claim that deductions were made from his wages that resulted in his receiving less than the minimum wage; "we find no bar to an employee raising this issue in an unemployment compensation case by way of a claim that underpayment motivated his quitting").

136. *See Doering v. Bd. of Review*, 203 N.J.Super. 241, 245 (App. Div. 1985) ("claimant had good cause for voluntarily leaving work by reason of the continued sexual harassment, gender biased and racially prejudicial comments, and threats of physical harm made to her by her supervisor"); *Associated Utility Services, Inc. v. Bd. of Review*, 131 N.J.Super. 584, 587 (App. Div. 1974) (claimant's supervisor subjected her to undue scoldings and called her at home to "give her hell").

137. N.J.A.C. 12:17-9.6(a). *See also Nicholas v. Bd. of Review*, 171 N.J.Super. 36 (App. Div. 1979). However, where a claimant resigned her position for good cause, her reapplication for the same job, although she did not really want it, held insufficient to find that she resigned voluntarily without good cause where she demonstrated that she reapplied because she thought it was necessary to remain on the list for other state jobs. *Domenico v. Bd. of Review*, 192 N.J.Super. 284, 290 (App. Div. 1983).

138. *Gerber v. Bd. of Review*, 313 N.J. Super. 37 (App. Div. 1998) (unemployment as the result of a previous employer's threat of litigation to enforce a restrictive covenant against the employee's future employer is deemed attributable to the work because the employee "joined the ranks of the unemployed" without fault).

job voluntarily.[140] Similarly, an employee who quits because his employer has breached a collective bargaining agreement is entitled to benefits.[141] But where an employee voluntarily leaves work in violation of a collective bargaining agreement, he is disqualified from collecting benefits.[142]

An employee who leaves his job voluntarily because of a subjective belief based on objective facts that (1) his position was subject to "imminent layoff" and (2) he would suffer substantial economic loss as a result is entitled to collect benefits.[143] For a layoff or discharge to be "imminent," it must separate the employee from employment within four weeks.[144]

---

139. *See Means v. Hamilton Hospital*, 172 N.J.Super. 465 (App. Div.) (nurse discharged by hospital after failing to pass state-mandated licensing examination), *certif. denied*, 84 N.J. 451 (1980). *But cf. Yardville Supply Co. v. Bd. of Review*, 114 N.J. 371 (1989) (truck driver who lost job after license was suspended for DWI held to have left work voluntarily without good cause; claimant's unemployment "traceable directly to conduct for which he is responsible").

140. *See Watson v. U.S. Rubber Co.*, 24 N.J. 598 (1957) (vacation shutdown); *Campbell Soup Co. v. Bd. of Review*, 13 N.J. 431, 436-37 (1953) (forced retirement at age 65); *Myerson v. Bd. of Review*, 43 N.J.Super. 196 (App. Div. 1957) (forced pregnancy leave). *Cf. Krauss v. A. & M. Karagheusian*, 13 N.J. 447 (1953) (employee who had option of retiring and taking pension or continuing in his employment with the consent of the union and the employer, and who chose to take retirement, voluntarily left work without good cause and denied benefits); *Bateman v. Bd. of Review*, 163 N.J.Super. 518 (App. Div. 1978) (employee whose termination of his employment was motivated by desire to retire and not by disadvantageous commute disqualified from receiving benefits).

141. *Bd. of Review v. Kearfott Mfg. Corp.*, 46 N.J.Super. 39 (App. Div. 1957).

142. *Bd. of Review v. Bogue Elec. Co.*, 37 N.J.Super. 535 (App. Div. 1955), *modified on other grounds*, 21 N.J. 431 (1956). *See also* N.J.A.C. 12:17-9.7.

143. *Brady v. Bd. of Review*, 152 N.J. 197, 215 (1997). In *Brady*, the New Jersey Supreme Court held that claimants who had elected early retirement when their employer announced that their plant would be closing had done so "without good cause attributable to such work." *Id.* at 221. The Court found that the layoff was not "impending" because of the extensive amount of time it would have taken for the plant to close, the lack of a definite closing date, and the claimants level of seniority. *Id.* at 218-219. The Court also found that the claimants suffered no substantial economic loss by taking early retirement because they would have been better off financially if they were laid off than they would have been had they been allowed to collect unemployment benefits. *Id.* at 220-221. *See also Trupo v. Bd. of Review*, 268 N.J. Super. 54, 60-61 (App. Div. 1993) (affirming disqualification due to lack of proofs below); *Fernandez v. Bd. of Review*, 304 N.J. Super. 603, 605-606 (App. Div. 1997) (general letter to all employers stating that there would be more employees in their division after reorganization does not create a "real imminent and substantial risk" of job loss. "Mere speculation about job stability is insufficient to establish good cause. Rather the surrounding circumstances at the time of voluntarily resigning must demonstrate a lack of suitable continuing work ... together with statements or actions of the employer showing a very strong likelihood of imminent layoff.").

144. N.J.A.C. 12:17-9.5(a). "An individual who leaves due to an imminent layoff or discharge shall be considered to have withheld his or her services from the employer and shall be deemed unavailable for work and ineligible for benefits for such period." N.J.A.C. 12:17-9.5(b).

9-7:2 Misconduct

An employee may not recover benefits for the week in which he has been suspended or discharged for misconduct connected with the work[145] and for the five weeks immediately following (in addition to the waiting period).[146]

Misconduct must be "improper, intentional, connected with one's work, malicious, within the individual's control, a deliberate violation of the employer's rules, or a disregard of standards of behavior which the employer has the right to expect of an employee."[147] Inadvertent, unintentional or negligent conduct not amounting to wanton disregard of consequences does not constitute "misconduct." [148]

An absence from work constitutes misconduct if the individual did not have good cause for the absence or was unjustified in failing to properly notify the employer of the absence and the reasons for the absence.[149] In this context "good cause" means "any compelling personal circumstance, including illness, which would normally prevent a reasonable person under the same conditions from reporting for work."[150]

An employee will be guilty of misconduct if he or she lies on an employment application or other record required by the employer or omitted information

---

145. *See Yardville Supply Co. v. Bd. of Review*, 222 N.J.Super. 201 (App. Div. 1988) (truck driver's loss of license for non job-related DWI conviction not misconduct connected with work), *rev'd on other grounds*, 114 N.J. 371 (1989); *Connell v. Bd. of Review*, 216 N.J.Super. 403 (App. Div. 1987) (off-duty police officer convicted for death by auto was discharged for misconduct connected with work since police officer is deemed to be on duty at all times); *Broderick v. Bd. of Review*, 133 N.J.Super. 30 (App. Div. 1975) (employee's refusal to comply with employer's reasonable requests that she not wear transistor radio earplug and not proselytize during work constituted work-connected misconduct).

146. N.J.S.A. 43:21-5(b); N.J.A.C. 12:17-10.1(a). Before 1974, the statutory exception referred only to discharge (and not suspension or discharge), although a divided Court in 1966 affirmed an Appellate Division decision interpreting it as applicable to both. *Schock v. Bd. of Review*, 89 N.J.Super. 118, 124-25 (App. Div. 1965), *aff'd per curiam*, 48 N.J. 121 (1966). That interpretation was codified by L.1974, c.86, §3.

147. N.J.A.C. 12:17-10.2(a). "Connected with the work" includes actions outside working hours that adversely affect the employer or the individual's ability to perform his or her job duties. N.J.A.C. 12:17-10.2(c). *See also Beaunit Mills v. Bd. of Review*, 43 N.J.Super. 172, 183 (App. Div. 1956), *certif. denied*, 23 N.J. 579 (1957). A hospital employee who left a tray of food for a patient scheduled for surgery and thereby jeopardized the health and safety of that patient was terminated for misconduct and properly disqualified from benefits. *Smith v. Board of Review*, 281 N.J. Super. 426 (App. Div. 1995). In the health care field where the risk of injury to patients is involved, even a single, inadvertent violation of work rules may be sufficient to constitute misconduct. *Id.* at 430-33.

148. *Demech v. Bd. of Review*, 167 N.J.Super. 35 (App. Div. 1979). In *Demech*, the claimant was discharged after throwing a 25-pound roast at a coemployee after the latter's persistent verbal and physical abuse. The Appellate Division found that this "single episode of spontaneous minor violence made in response to clearly provocative conduct cannot be considered misconduct in an unemployment compensation context." *Id.* at 40. *Cf. Schock v. Bd. of Review*, 89 N.J.Super. 118 (App. Div. 1965), *aff'd per curium*, 48 N.J. 121 (1966) (employee who left public service truck unattended on a public street, with the motor running, while he was drinking beer in a tavern, in violation of work rules, was engaged in misconduct within scope of statute).

149. N.J.A.C. 12:17-10.3(a).

which created a material misrepresentation about the individual's suitability or qualifications to perform the job.[151] Failing or refusing to take a bona fide employer drug test will constitute misconduct where a drug-free work place is a prerequisite of employment and the employer has a written drug test policy that has been conveyed to its employees.[152]

An illegal work stoppage in violation of a collective bargaining agreement constitutes misconduct.[153] But employees who were discharged after engaging in a work stoppage not expressly prohibited by their collective bargaining agreement were not guilty of misconduct.[154]

It also is misconduct where an individual: 1) refuses to comply with lawful and reasonable employer instructions that are within the individual's job duties; 2) acts beyond the scope of express or implied authority granted by the employer; or 3) violates a reasonable rule of the employer which the individual knows or should have known is in effect.[155] Violating the employer's reasonable safety standards is misconduct even if the violation did not endanger anyone.[156]

This provision does not apply if the discharge is rescinded by the employer unless the final discharge is changed to a suspension for misconduct connected with the work.[157] But if the individual is restored to employment with back pay, he must return any benefits received for any week of unemployment for which he is subsequently compensated by the employer.[158]

If the discharge is for gross misconduct connected with the work because of the commission of a crime of the first, second, third or fourth degree under the

---

150. N.J.A.C. 12:17-10.3(b). Tardiness will constitute misconduct where it is chronic or excessive and repeated after employer warnings and is without reasonable excuse or could have been foreseen by the individual and the individual failed to take the proper steps necessary to notify the employer. N.J.A.C. 12:17-10.4(a).

151. N.J.A.C. 12:17-10.5.

152. N.J.A.C. 12:17-10.9.

153. *See Bogue Elec. Co. v. Bd. of Review*, 21 N.J. 431 (1956).

154. *See Beaunit Mills v. Bd. of Review*, 43 N.J.Super. 172, 182 (App. Div.), *certif. denied*, 23 N.J. 579 (1957) (breach of collective bargaining agreement by employee does not *per se* constitute misconduct under UC Law).

155. N.J.A.C. 12:17-10.6. Failing to meet the employer's reasonable standards for quantity or quality of work is also misconduct if the individual's failure was deliberate. N.J.S.A. 12:17-10.7.

156. N.J.A.C. 12:17-10.8.

157. N.J.A.C. 12:17-10.1(b). *See also Beaunit Mills v. Bd. of Review*, 43 N.J. Super. 172, 182 (App. Div.), *certif. denied*, 23 N.J. 579 (1957).

158. N.J.S.A. 43:21-5(b); N.J.A.C. 12:17-10.1(b). An employee indicted on criminal charges was given a mandatory leave of absence and thereafter collected unemployment benefits. After the employee was acquitted on the criminal charges, the arbitrator awarded back pay exclusive of unemployment benefits paid. Held, the employee did not have to repay the benefits received. However, his employer was regarded as constructive trustee of money representing such benefits in favor of the beneficiary, the state fund. *Dept. of Labor and Industry v. Smalls*, 153 N.J.Super. 411 (App. Div. 1977).

New Jersey Criminal Code, an employee is disqualified in the same manner as if he voluntarily left his job without good cause.[159]

9-7:3 Failure to Apply For or Accept Suitable Work

An employee cannot collect benefits for the week in which he fails, without good cause, either to apply for available, suitable work when so directed by the employment office or the director, or to accept suitable work when it is offered, or to return to his customary self-employment, if any, when so directed by the director, and for the three weeks immediately following (in addition to the waiting period).[160]

A determination of the suitability of a particular job takes into account the degree of risk to health, safety, morals, physical fitness and prior training, experience, prior earnings and employee benefits, length of unemployment and prospects for finding work in the individual's usual occupation, and the distance of the work to his residence.[161]

Work is not deemed suitable and benefits cannot be denied to an otherwise eligible individual if he refuses to accept work if the position offered is vacant due to a strike, lockout, or other labor dispute;[162] if the pay, hours or working conditions are substantially less favorable to the individual than those prevailing for similar work in his locality;[163] or if the individual will be required to join a company union or to resign from a union or refrain from joining any bona fide labor organization as a condition of employment.[164]

---

159. N.J.A.C. 12:17-10.1(c); *Dept. of Labor and Industry v. Smalls*, 153 N.J. Super. 411 (App. Div. 1977). *See* N.J.S.A. 43:21-5(b) and §9-7:1, *supra* .

160. N.J.S.A. 43:21-5(c); N.J.A.C. 12:17-11.1.

161. N.J.S.A. 43:21-5(c)(1); N.J.A.C. 12:17-11.2(a). *See Krauss v. A. & M. Karagheusian*, 24 N.J.Super. 277 (App. Div.), *rev'd on other grounds*, 13 N.J. 447 (1953).

162. N.J.S.A. 43:21-5(c)(2); N.J.A.C. 12:17-11.2(b)(1).

163. *Id*; N.J.A.C. 12:17-11.2(b)(2).

A claimant is not required to accept work that is unsuitable. *Wojcik v. Bd. of Review*, 58 N.J. 341 (1971). An employee laid off from his position and offered a less skilled job by his employer that paid a substantially lower wage did not refuse "suitable" work. *Johns-Manville Products Corp. v. Bd. of Review*, 122 N.J.Super. 366 (App. Div. 1973). *See Wojcik, supra* (factory work deemed unsuitable where it involved substantial reduction in prior earnings and was incompatible with claimant's training and experience); *Campbell Soup Co. v. Bd. of Review*, 13 N.J. 431 (1953) (claimant not detached from labor market where particular kind of common labor he did for former employer was not available with anyone else although other types of common labor work were available). Conversely, a claimant cannot restrict his availability for work to a particular employer or job. *See Ludwigsen v. N.J. Dept. of Labor and Industry*, 12 N.J. 64 (1953); *Worsnop v. Bd. of Review*, 92 N.J.Super. 260 (App. Div. 1966); *Muraski v. Bd. of Review*, 136 N.J.L. 472 (Sup. Ct. 1948); *W.T. Grant Co. v. Bd. of Review*, 129 N.J.L. 402 (Sup. Ct. 1943).

164. N.J.S.A. 43:21-5(c)(2); N.J.A.C. 12:17-11.2(b)(3). *See Cointreau, Ltd. v. Bd. of Review*, 171 N.J.Super. 407 (App. Div. 1979). *But see Ludwigsen v. N.J. Dept. of Labor and Industry*, 12 N.J. 64 (1953)(lack of sympathy of new operator of business for union did not justify claimant's refusal to work for him).

An individual will not be denied benefits for refusing to accept suitable work unless there was a bona fide offer of work or referral to work that the individual refused.[165] For there to be a "bona fide offer or referral" it must be shown that: 1) there was a specific job offer containing job details such as duties, rate of pay, and hours of work, and 2) the offer was made in writing or orally to the individual.[166]

Finally, an individual will not be denied benefits if he or she has good cause to refuse a bona fide offer or referral of suitable work.[167] "To establish good cause, the claimant must have made a reasonable attempt to remove the restrictions pertaining to the refusal."[168]

9-7:4 Involvement in Labor Dispute

An employee cannot collect benefits if his unemployment is due to a work stoppage[169] arising from a labor dispute,[170] unless the individual is not participating in or financing or directly interested in the labor dispute in question; and he does not belong to a grade or class of workers of which, immediately before the work stoppage, there were members employed at the premises at which the stoppage occurs, any of whom are participating in or financing or directly interested in the dispute.[171]

The purpose of this provision is to place the State in a neutral position regarding labor disputes.[172] The United States Supreme Court has upheld a similar disqualification provision as not implicitly preempted by Section 7 of the National Labor Relations Act.[173]

---

165. N.J.A.C. 12:17-11.3(a).

166. N.J.A.C. 12:17-11.3(a)(1).

167. N.J.S.A. 43:21-5(c); N.J.A.C. 12:17-11.1. "Good cause" is defined as "any situation over which the claimant did not have control or which was so compelling as to prevent the claimant from accepting work." N.J.A.C 12:17-11.4.

168. N.J.A.C. 12:17-11.4.

169. A "stoppage of work" is a "substantial curtailment of work which is due to a labor dispute." N.J.A.C. 12:17-12.2(a)(2). The work stoppage will be sufficiently substantial if 80 percent or less of the normal production of goods and services is being produced. *Id.* "[T]he employer too must experience the impact of inactivity on account of the labor dispute." *Sweeney v. Board of Review*, 43 N.J. 535, 539 (1965). Thus, if an employer is able to resume normal business operations notwithstanding the continuation of a labor dispute, there is no longer a work stoppage and the striking employees will not be disqualified. *Radice v. New Jersey Department of Labor and Industry*, 4 N.J.Super. 364 (App. Div. 1949); *see Ablondi v. Board of Review*, 8 N.J.Super. 71 (App. Div. 1950). Conversely, a work stoppage need not be complete and it will suffice if there has been a substantial curtailment of operations. *Mortensen v. Bd. of Review*, 21 N.J. 242, 244-245 (1956); *Ablondi v. Board of Review*, 8 N.J. at 77. *Cf. Great A & P Tea Co. v. New Jersey Dept. of Labor*, 29 N.J.Super. 26 (App. Div. 1953) (employer's decision to terminate business operations brought work stoppage to an end, thereby removing disqualification).

170. A "labor dispute" is any controversy concerning wages, hours, working conditions or terms of employment between an employer and a bargaining unit or a group of employees." N.J.A.C. 12:17-12.2(a)(1).

9-7:5 Remuneration in Lieu of Notice

Benefits are not recoverable for any week in which an individual is receiving remuneration in lieu of notice.[174] However, this exclusion does not apply to severance pay received after layoff.[175]

---

171. N.J.S.A. 43:21-5(d). N.J.A.C. 12:17-12.2(c).

A "labor dispute" includes not only a strike, but also a work stoppage caused by a decrease in the employer's volume of business because of an imminent strike, even if the strike never materializes. *See Mortensen v. Bd. of Review*, 21 N.J. 242 (1956). It also includes a lockout by the employer precipitated by a strike threat. N.J.A.C. 12:17-12.2(e); *Basso v. News Syndicate Co.*, 90 N.J.Super. 150 (App. Div. 1966); *Sweeney v. Board of Review*, 81 N.J.Super. 90 (App. Div. 1964), *aff'd*, 43 N.J. 535 (1965); *Schoenwiesner v. Bd. of Review*, 44 N.J.Super. 377 (App. Div. 1957). *See Ablondi v. Board of Review*, 8 N.J.Super. 71 (App. Div. 1950).

A refusal to cross a picket line because of solidarity with another union will disqualify a claimant from benefits. *See Basso v. News Syndicate Co.*, 90 N.J.Super. 150 (App. Div. 1966); *Soricelli v. Bd. of Review*, 46 N.J.Super. 299 (App. Div. 1957); *Aitken v. Bd. of Review*, 136 N.J.L. 372 (Sup. Ct. 1948). However, a claimant who can establish that his refusal to cross a picket line was due to a reasonable and genuine fear of harm is not subject to disqualification. *See Marczi v. Bd. of Review*, 63 N.J.Super. 75 (App. Div. 1960); *Schooley v. Bd. of Review*, 43 N.J.Super. 381 (App. Div. 1957).

Financing of labor dispute: Where members of first local went out on strike which caused work stoppage, members of second local were disqualified from benefits where both locals were part of an international union and dues of second local members were used to finance strike. *Burgoon v. Bd. of Review*, 100 N.J.Super. 569 (App. Div. 1968); *see Soricelli v. Bd. of Review*, 46 N.J.Super. 299 (App. Div. 1957).

Where a claimant is a member of the union that stands to benefit by the labor dispute, he generally is deemed to be "directly interested" in the dispute, even if he is not a participant in it. *See Burgoon v. Bd. of Review*, 100 N.J.Super. 569 (App. Div. 1968); *Gerber v. Bd. of Review*, 36 N.J.Super. 322 (App. Div. 1955), *aff'd* 20 N.J. 561 (1956); *Wasyluk v. Mack Mfg. Corp.*, 4 N.J. Super. 559 (App. Div. 1949).

Common employment of claimants with striking workers does not place claimants in the same "grade or class" of workers involved in dispute. *Haley v. Bd. of Review*, 106 N.J.Super. 420 (App. Div. 1969). Members of different locals which both belong to same international union are deemed to be within the same grade or class, particularly where operations performed by the two groups are closely integrated so that they essentially are part of a unified production. *Burgoon v. Bd. of Review*, 100 N.J.Super. 569 (App. Div. 1968); *see also Amico v. Bd. of Review*, 49 N.J. 159 (1967) (workers engaged in production on integrated assembly line and represented by same union as striking welders considered to be of same class and disqualified for benefits—claimant is member of class if any of its members are directly interested in or participate in the dispute or finance it); *Gerber v. Bd. of Review*, 20 N.J. 561 (1956) (employees represented by same union are in same grade or class).

Single Establishment: A plant in New Jersey forced to close because of a strike at a Michigan plant was not considered part of the same establishment, notwithstanding that the production at each was integrated into a single system centered in Michigan. Disqualification held limited to those employed at the place where the labor dispute is itself situated, notwithstanding functional integration with work done at other location. *Ford Motor Co. v. Dept. of Labor & Industry*, 5 N.J. 494 (1950). *Cf. Ablondi v. Board of Review*, 8 N.J.Super. 71 (App. Div. 1950) (unemployment due to labor negotiations taking place in NYC involving work at N.J. factory; labor dispute deemed to take place at N.J. factory).

172. *See Sweeney v. Board of Review*, 43 N.J. 535, 539 (1965); *Febbi v. Bd. of Review*, 35 N.J. 601, 606 (1961); *Cointreau, Ltd. v. Bd. of Review*, 171 N.J.Super. 407 (App. Div. 1979).

173. *Baker v. General Motors Corp.*, 478 U.S. 621 (1986).

9-7:6 Other Benefits

Benefits will not be paid to an individual for any week in which he is seeking or collecting benefits under an unemployment compensation law of the United States or any other state. But if it is finally determined that he is not entitled to such benefits, the disqualification will not apply.[176]

9-7:7 Fraud

Benefits will not be paid for a period of one year from the date the division discovers that an individual has illegally received or attempted to receive benefits as the result of any false or fraudulent misrepresentation.[177] Such a disqualification may be appealed; but a conviction in a New Jersey state court for the offense is conclusive upon the appeals tribunal and the board of review.[178]

Such a disqualification does not preclude the prosecution of the individual pursuant to N.J.S.A.43:21-16 in any civil, criminal or administrative action to collect penalties or recover amounts collected as benefits, where the individual obtains or attempts to obtain money by theft, robbery, or false statements or representations, or to recover money erroneously or illegally obtained.[179]

9-7:8 Participation in Training Program

Notwithstanding any other provisions of the Act, an otherwise eligible individual cannot be denied benefits for any week because he is in training approved under the Trade Act,[180] or because he has left work to enter such training if the work from which he left was not suitable employment.[181]

The Workforce Development Partnership Program ("WDPP") was enacted in 1992 to provide additional unemployment options to displaced employees while they are in training or receiving education in order to acquire marketable skills.[182] The purpose of the WDPP is to extend unemployment benefits as need-

---

174. N.J.S.A. 43:21-5(e).

175. *Western Electric Co. v. Hussey*, 35 N.J. 250, 258 (1961); *Dingleberry v. Bd. of Review*, 154 N.J.Super. 415 (App. Div. 1977).

176. N.J.S.A. 43:21-5(f). *See Nikolajewski v. Bd. of Review*, 56 N.J. 91 (1970) (disability benefits from VA); *McLaughlin v. Bd. of Review*, 7 N.J.Super. 12 (App. Div. 1950) (benefits paid in New York).

177. N.J.S.A. 43:21-5(g)(1).

178. *Id.*

179. N.J.S.A. 43:21-5(g)(2).

180. 19 U.S.C. §2296

181. N.J.S.A. 43:21-5(h)(1). *Cf.* N.J.S.A. 43:21-4(c)(4).

ed to provide training and education for positions in occupations where there are demonstrated long-term shortages of skilled labor.[183]

9-7:9 Attending School Full Time

Benefits will not be paid for any week in which an individual is a student in full time attendance at an educational institution, unless either (1) he is attending a job-training program, or (2) during his base year, he earned sufficient wages, while attending an educational institution, during periods other than established and customary vacation periods or holiday recesses from the educational institution.[184]

9-7:10 Employees on Leave of Absence

Employees on voluntary and mutually agreed upon leaves of absences from their employer are not unemployed and therefore unentitled to workers' compensation benefits.[185] Failure by the employer to allow or suggest a personal leave of absence for other than the individual's health does not establish good cause attributable to the work for the individual to leave such employment if the denial does not violate the state or federal leave laws.[186]

9-8 Offsets for Pension and Retirement Benefits

The amount of benefits payable in any week that begins during a period when a claimant is receiving a governmental or other pension, retirement pay, annuity or other similar periodic payment from a plan maintained by a base period or other chargeable employer[187] based on previous work of the claimant is subject to

---

182. *See* N.J.S.A. 43:21-57 to 43:21-66. *See also Bose v. Board of Review*, 303 N.J. Super 570 (App. Div. 1997).

183. N.J.S.A. 43:21-57(i). The statute defines a "labor demand occupation" as: "an occupation for which there is or is likely to be an excess of demand over supply for adequately trained workers, including, but not limited to, an occupation designated as a labor demand occupation by the [N.J.O.I.C.C.] pursuant to [N.J.S.A. 34:1A-79]. N.J.S.A. 43:21-58.

184. N.J.S.A. 43:21-5(i); N.J.A.C. 12:17-12.6. *See also Singer v. Board of Review*, 273 N.J. Super. 72 (App. Div. 1994) (employee who worked "full time" and attended school "full time" was not disqualified because he met income levels and was employed while school was in session). The requirements for "full time" status are outlined in N.J.A.C. 12:17-12.6(a)(1-3).

185. N.J.A.C. 12:17-12.3(a). An exception to this rule exists for individuals whose leave of absence was granted at least partially due to a disability or projected disability. *Id.* Any request for a leave of absence due to a medical condition must be supported by competent medical evidence. N.J.A.C. 12:17-12.3(c).

186. N.J.A.C. 12:17-12.3(b).

187. N.J.S.A. 43:21-5a(a); N.J.A.C. 12:17-8. *See Trupo v. Board of Review*, 268 N.J. Super. 54, 62-63 (App. Div. 1993).

offset.[188] Where the payment is being made from a plan to which claimant did not make a contribution, the offset is in an amount equal to the amount of such pension, etc., but not less than zero.[189] If the payment is made from a plan to which the employer and claimant contributed, the offset is in an amount equal to 50 percent of the pension, retirement, annuity or other payment.[190] If the payment is made from a plan to which the individual contributed 100 percent, there shall be no deduction.[191]

If an employee whose employment is terminated before the employee may retire with full pension, and the employee receives a lump sum distribution in lieu of retirement benefits, unemployment benefits are reduced only in the week the employee received the lump sum.[192]

9-9 Deductions for Child Support

Amounts owing for child support may be deducted from unemployment compensation benefits.[193]

III. PROCEDURES

9-10 Claims for Benefits

Claims for benefits are made in accordance with the regulations promulgated by the Director of the Division of Unemployment and Temporary Disability In-

---

188. N.J.S.A. 43:21-5a; N.J.A.C. 12:17-8.2(a)(1). *See, e.g.*, *Schuenemann v. Bd. of Review*, 208 N.J.Super. 48, 52-53 (App. Div. 1986) (benefits reduced by lump-sum payment for 3-month period following claimant's layoff which constituted pension payment).

The constitutionality of this provision was upheld in *McKay v. Horn*, 529 F.Supp. 847 (D.N.J. 1981). *See Moyer v. Bd. of Review*, 183 N.J.Super. 543 (App. Div. 1982). The Commissioner of Labor must have "maximum flexibility" and discretion in this area to conform to the dictates of federal law so employers and the State Department of Labor do not suffer the loss of credits that flows from noncompliance with the Federal Unemployment Tax Act. *Schuenemann v. Bd. of Review*, 208 N.J.Super. at 51-52.

This provision is not inconsistent with the Employment Retirement Income Security Act of 1974 (ERISA), 29 U.S.C. §1001 *et seq. Cf. Alessi v. Raybestos-Manhattan, Inc.*, 451 U.S. 504 (1981) (pension plan allowing for offset or reduction in retirement benefits by the amount of a workers' compensation award held lawful under ERISA).

189. N.J.S.A. 43:21-5a. *See Trupo*, 268 N.J. Super. at 63.

190. N.J.A.C. 12:17-8.2(a)(2).

191. N.J.A.C. 12:17-8.2(a)(4).

192. N.J.S.A. 43:21-5a.

193. N.J.S.A. 43:21-6.1. *See generally In the Matter of E.C.B.*, 94 N.J.A.R.2d (UCC) 15 (1994) (discussing authority for deducting child support from unemployment compensation and temporary disability benefits).

surance of the Department of Labor.[194] The burden is upon the claimant to show his entitlement to benefits.[195]

Employers must issue Form BC-10, "Instructions for Claiming Unemployment Benefits," to all employees expected to be separated for seven days or more.[196] That form provides the local unemployment insurance office with the correct name, address, and New Jersey Employer Registration Number of the separating employer.[197]

9-10:1 Initial Determinations[198]

A claim is examined by a "deputy" who notifies the claimant's most recent employer and, successively as needed, each other employer in inverse chronological order during the base year.[199] The notification includes a request for information from the employer to furnish such information as is necessary to determine the claimant's eligibility and rights with respect to the employer in question.[200] Form BC-3E.1, "Request for Separation Information," asks for facts about the claimant's separation.[201] The Division requires return of that form only if:

1. The claimant was separated for reasons other than lack of work; or
2. The claimant is receiving a company pension; or
3. The claimant received wages for a period after the last day of work; or
4. The claimant's separation is temporary with a definite date of recall.[202]

---

194. N.J.S.A. 43:21-6(a). *See* N.J.A.C. 12:17-3.1 *et seq.*

195. *See Rider College v. Bd. of Review*, 167 N.J.Super. 42, 47 (App. Div. 1979); *Patrick v. Bd. of Review*, 171 N.J.Super. 424, 426 (App. Div. 1978).

196. N.J.A.C. 12:17-3.1(a). *See Employer Handbook, New Jersey's Unemployment & Disability Insurance Programs*, p.3 (Dept. Labor, Jan. 1991) ("*Employer Handbook*") Copies of the form may be obtained from local unemployment compensation offices.

197. N.J.A.C. 12:17-3.1(a).

198. "Initial determination" is a determination of benefit rights as measured by eligible individual's base year employment with a single employer covering all periods of employment with that employer during the base year. N.J.S.A. 43:21-19(v).

199. N.J.S.A. 43:21-6(b)(1). The employer is notified of claimant's potential monetary eligibility by way of Form BC-3E, "Notice to Employer of Potential Liability." *Employer Handbook* at 29.

200. N.J.S.A. 43:21-6(b)(1).

201. *Employer Handbook* at 29. Employers that are the most recent employer, but not a base year employer, are sent Form BC-28 instead. *Id.* at 11.

202. *Employer Handbook, New Jersey's Unemployment & Disability Insurance Programs*, pp. 10-11 (Dept. Labor, Jan. 1991).

If an employer fails to respond to an information request within 10 days, the deputy will rely entirely on other sources including the claimant's affidavit as to the wages earned and the time worked.[203] No penalty is imposed on the claimant if his information is incorrect except in the event of fraud.[204]

The claimant and the affected employers are promptly notified of the initial determination which is based on the information available.[205] The initial determination shows the amount of the weekly benefit payable, the maximum duration of benefits with respect to the employer to whom the determination relates, and the ratio of benefits chargeable to the employer's account.[206]

If an employer fails to respond to a request for information, he cannot contest the initial determination and any subsequent determinations[207] as to those benefits paid—and charged to his account—prior to the close of the calendar week in which his reply is received.[208] Thereafter, the initial determination will be altered in accordance with the information supplied by the employer.[209]

9-10:2 Time for Appeal of Initial Determination

The deputy issues a separate initial benefit determination to each of claimant's base year employers. If any employer other than the first chargeable base year employer (the last employer worked for) appeals the determination, the appeal will be limited to the following issues: (1) the correctness of the benefit payments authorized; (2) any fraud committed in connection with the claim; (3) the claimant's refusal of suitable work; and, (4) gross misconduct.[210]

An appeal by either the claimant or an employer must be filed within seven calendar days after delivery of the notification of initial determination or within 10 days after the notification is mailed to the last-known address.[211] Otherwise, the decision is final and benefits will be paid accordingly.[212] Failure to appeal within the prescribed time period acts as a jurisdictional bar to a further appeal to Superior Court.[213]

---

203. N.J.S.A. 43:21-6(b)(1).

204. *Id.*

205. *Id.*

206. *Id.*

207. In the course of a benefit year, a deputy will make subsequent determinations in accordance with any initial determinations allowing benefits under which benefits have not been exhausted. The allowance or denial of benefits is appealable in the same manner and under the same restrictions as provided for initial determinations. N.J.S.A. 43:21-6(b)(3).

208. N.J.S.A. 43:21-6(b)(1).

209. *Id.*

210. *Id.*

The appeal must be in writing and may be filed in person at the local claims office or by mail.[214] An appeal is considered filed on the date it is postmarked, or if the postmark is missing, on the date of receipt by an office or employee of the Division of Employment Security authorized to accept appeals.[215] Appeals filed by mail should include the claimant's Social Security number and refer to the specific decision being appealed.[216] However, any written statement filed within the time provided by law, "which sets forth the fact that a party to a determination made by the [D]ivision [of Employment Security] is aggrieved thereby or dissatisfied therewith shall be deemed to be an appeal."[217] In cases involving a large number of claimants, a blanket notice of appeal may be filed; however, no case will be scheduled for hearing until an individual appeal on the prescribed form has been filed.[218]

---

211. N.J.S.A. 43:21-6(b)(1). A notation on an office copy showing the date of delivery of the Notice of Determination creates a rebuttable presumption that the notice was delivered on that date so as to start running the time for bringing an appeal. *Bamburgh v. Bd. of Review*, 48 N.J.Super. 472, 474-75 (App. Div. 1958). *But cf. Borgia v. Bd. of Review*, 21 N.J.Super. 462 (App. Div. 1952) (notation on copy of Notice indicating date of mailing insufficient proof of mailing in absence of evidence as to who made the notation, the circumstances of its making, and evidence of office custom).

212. N.J.S.A. 43:21-6(b)(1). Generally, a determination is not final if the division fails to give sufficient notice to the claimant or any other interested party. *See General Bowling Corp. v. Bd. of Review*, 166 N.J.Super. 58 (App. Div. 1979) (notice to employer which failed to state that employee could collect benefits after a 3-week disqualification period was deficient and tolled period for bringing appeal). *But cf. Alfonso v. Bd. of Review*, 89 N.J. 41, *cert. denied*, 459 U.S. 806, 103 S. Ct. 30, 74 L.Ed.2d 45 (1982) (notice written in English to woman who neither spoke nor read English held sufficient; moreover, failure to provide bilingual notice did not constitute violation of due process under the Fourteenth Amendment or violation of Civil Rights Act of 1964).

213. *See Lowden v. Bd. of Review*, 78 N.J.Super. 467 (App. Div. 1963). *See In the Matter of C.R.*, 95 N.J.A.R. 2d (UCC) 15 (1995) (late filing of appeal excused; claimant showed good cause in that his conversations with Division personnel led him to believe that he had already appealed).

214. Notice of appeal filed in a local office is transmitted immediately to the appeal tribunal. N.J.A.C. 12:20-3.1(g).

215. N.J.A.C. 12:20-3.1(d).

216. State of New Jersey, Department of Labor, Division of Unemployment & Disability Insurance, *The Appeals Process* (January 1990).

217. N.J.A.C. 12:20-3.1(a).

218. N.J.A.C. 12:20-3.1(e). The blanket notice should list the full names and social security numbers of the claimants. A "reasonable time" after filing of the blanket appeal will be allowed for filing the individual appeals. *Id.*

9-10:3 Benefits During Pendency of Appeal

Benefits that are payable while an appeal is pending are paid as they accrue.[219] If the appeal is from a determination that the claimant is disqualified under N.J.S.A. 43:21-5,[220] benefits pending determination of the appeal are withheld only for the disqualification period provided under N.J.S.A. 43:21-5.[221] If there are two determinations of entitlement, benefits are paid regardless of any appeal taken thereafter, but no employer's account is charged with benefits paid if the decision is ultimately reversed.[222]

9-10:4 Appeal Tribunals

When an appeal of an initial determination is filed, all documents relating thereto are forwarded to the appeal tribunal and a hearing scheduled with notice to interested parties.[223] Absent a showing of good cause for a closed hearing, the proceeding shall be open to the public.[224] The examiner opens the hearing by ascertaining and summarizing the issues.[225] The parties, their representatives and attorneys may examine or cross-examine witnesses, inspect documents, and explain or rebut any evidence.[226] The appeal tribunal may examine the parties and witnesses as it deems necessary, and shall allow all parties the opportunity to present argument.[227] All oral testimony is under oath or affirmation and is re-

---

219. N.J.S.A. 43:21-6(b)(1). The Division of Unemployment and Disability Insurance emphasizes that: "Once the appeal is filed, the claimant must CONTINUE TO MAIL IN THE MAIL CERTIFICATE WORK SEARCH RECORD AND THE PENDED CONTINUED CLAIM FOR UNEMPLOYMENT BENEFITS on the dates designated by the claims office personnel." State of New Jersey, Department of Labor, Division of Unemployment & Disability Insurance, *The Appeals Process* (Jan. 1990).

220. *See* §§9-7 to 9-7:1, *supra* .

221. N.J.S.A. 43:21-6(b)(1).

222. N.J.S.A. 43:21-6(b)(1). This section requires that two separate administrative tribunals make independent determinations that the claimant is both eligible and not disqualified. *Bocchino v. Bd. of Review*, 202 N.J.Super. 469, 472 (App. Div. 1985):

> The purpose seems to be to relieve a claimant who, in good faith, accepts and spends benefits sanctioned by two different administrative tribunals and who should, therefore, not have repayment added to the already heavy burden of unemployment. Because the two-determination rule rests on the concurrence of two tribunals on the matter of entitlement, their determinations must be independent and must encompass both essential factors of eligibility and nondisqualification.

Id.

223. State of New Jersey, Department of Labor, Division of Unemployment & Disability Insurance, *The Appeals Process* (Jan. 1990) (*The Appeals Process*).

224. N.J.A.C. 1:12-14.1.

225. N.J.A.C. 1:12-14.2(b).

226. N.J.A.C. 1;12-14.2(b). With the consent of the appeal tribunal, the parties may stipulate to the facts involved. N.J.A.C. 1:12-15.2. In that event, the appeal tribunal may render a decision on the stipulation or take evidence as it deems necessary. *Id.*

corded.[228] The opportunity for a fair hearing is a matter of procedural due process.[229] Subpoenas to compel the attendance of witnesses and the production of records may be issued by the appeal tribunal upon a showing of necessity by the party applying therefor.[230]

After so affording the parties a reasonable opportunity for a fair hearing, an appeal tribunal must affirm or modify the findings of fact and the determination.[231] Its decision will be in the form set forth in N.J.A.C. 12:20-3.4(b).

The decision of the appeal tribunal is deemed a final decision of the Board of Review unless a further appeal is initiated within 10 days after the parties are notified of the decision.[232]

9-10:5 Action by the Board of Review

The Board of Review[233] may on its own motion affirm, modify or set aside the decision of the appeal tribunal on the basis of previously admitted or additional

227. *Id.* "Where a party is not represented, the tribunal shall give every assistance that does not interfere with the impartial discharge of its official duties."

228. *Id.* The appeal tribunal may take further evidence after the original hearing, provided proper notice of the time and place of the supplemental hearing is provided to the parties. N.J.A.C. 1:12-14.2(c).

229. *Agresta v. Bd. of Review*, 232 N.J.Super. 56, 63 (App. Div. 1989) (basic requirements of due process are (1) adequate notice; (2) opportunity for a fair hearing; and (3) availability of ultimate review). *See also Bastas v. Bd. of Review*, 155 N.J.Super. 312 (App. Div. 1978) (hearing is in the nature of a civil proceeding; adverse inference drawn from claimant's refusal to testify did not offend her Fifth Amendment right against self-incrimination or due process and equal protection rights).

230. N.J.A.C. 1:12-11.1. When a matter is pending before the Board of Review, a member of the Board may issue a subpoena upon the requisite showing of need. *Id.*

231. N.J.S.A. 43:21-6(c). The appeal tribunal consists of a salaried body of examiners under the supervision of the Chief Appeals Examiner, all of whom are appointed pursuant to the provisions of Title 11 of the Revised Statutes, Civil Service and other applicable statutes. N.J.S.A. 43:21-6(d); N.J.A.C. 12:20-2.1.

232. N.J.S.A. 43:21-6(c). *But cf. Hopkins v. Bd. of Review*, 249 N.J.Super. 84 (App. Div. 1991) (notwithstanding claimant's failure to make timely appeal, Division was estopped from recovering unemployment benefits to which it improperly determined claimant was not entitled).

233. The Board of Review consists of three members appointed by the Assistant Commissioner responsible for the administration of the Unemployment Compensation Law subject to the provisions of the Civil Service Act, from Department of Personnel eligible lists. N.J.A.C. 12:20-1.1.

evidence.[234] To the extent the Board has such power, it must exercise it within the time prescribed in N.J.S.A. 43:21-6(c) for bringing an appeal, *i.e.*, 10 days.[235]

The Board also may permit the parties to initiate further appeals before it in any case; where the decision of the appeal tribunal is not unanimous, or where a determination has been overruled or modified by the appeal tribunal, appeals of the parties must be permitted.[236] The Board of Review also may remove to itself or transfer to another appeal tribunal proceedings on any claim pending before an appeal tribunal.[237]

Notice of appeal to the Board of Review must be filed within 10 days of the date of notification or mailing of the decision appealed from.[238] Appellant must file in triplicate at the office where the claim was filed or with the Board of Review.[239] All testimony must be recorded, but need not be transcribed unless the claim is further appealed.[240]

---

234. N.J.S.A. 43:21-6(e). The Board has inherent power to reconsider, rehear, and revise prior determinations without offending principles of res judicata or collateral estoppel. *Castellucci v. Bd. of Review*, 168 N.J.Super. 301 (App. Div. 1979), *Supplemental op.*, 174 N.J.Super. 289 (App. Div. 1980). Every decision of an appeal tribunal is transmitted to the executive secretary of the Board of Review upon issuance, and presented to the Board for consideration. N.J.A.C. 1:12-18.1(c). The Board may, by majority vote, set aside any decision of an appeal tribunal, remand it to the same or another tribunal, or withdraw the case for its own review. N.J.A.C. 1:12-14.8(a). *See also* N.J.A.C. 1:12-14.3(a)-(d). When the Board withdraws a case for decision itself, it may either (a) decide the case on the existing record; (b) remand the case to an appeal tribunal for the taking of additional evidence upon which the Board may act; or (c) hold a new hearing itself. *Id.* Any such additional hearing may be held only on five days notice to the parties and in the manner prescribed for hearings before the Board. N.J.A.C. 1:12-14.8(b).

235. *See Charles Headwear, Inc. v. Bd. of Review*, 11 N.J. 321 Sup. (App. Div. 1951); *Kaske v. State*, 34 N.J.Super. 222 (App. Div. 1955) (word "appeal" construed as including action taken on Board's own motion).

236. N.J.S.A. 43:21-6(e). The Board need not conduct a full hearing if one was conducted before the appeal tribunal. A hearing is required only when the Board removes to itself a claim pending before the appeal tribunal. *Marczi v. Bd. of Review*, 63 N.J.Super. 75 (App. Div. 1960); *see* N.J.A.C. 1:12-14.3, 14.8. *Cf. Softexture Yarns v. Bd. of Review*, 59 N.J.Super. 57 (App. Div. 1960) (upon failure of Board to advise party that it would conduct hearing, it should have, consistent with administrative rules, adjourned the matter and allowed party to prepare properly).

The Board must undertake an analysis of the evidence and make specific findings of fact supportive of its conclusion. *Savastano v. State Bd. of Review*, 99 N.J.Super. 397 (App. Div. 1968). The Board has the power to consider each claim for benefits and not merely those ruled on by the appeal tribunal. *Ludwigsen v. N.J. Dept. of Labor and Industry*, 12 N.J. 64 (1953).

237. N.J.S.A. 43:21-6(e). "Any proceedings so removed to the board of review shall be heard by a quorum thereof in accordance with the requirements of [N.J.S.A. 43:21-6(c)]."

238. N.J.A.C. 12:20-4.1(a). The date of filing is the date of the postmark, or if the postmark is missing, the date of receipt by an office or employee of the Division of Employment Security authorized to accept appeals. N.J.A.C. 12:20-4.1(c).

239. N.J.A.C. 12:20-4.1(d). An appeal filed with a local office is transmitted immediately to the Executive Secretary of the Board of Review. N.J.A.C. 12:20-4.1(e).

240. N.J.S.A. 43:21-6(f).

9-10:6 Judicial Review

The decision of the Board of Review is final as to any party upon the mailing of a copy to him or his attorney.[241]

The Division of Unemployment or any party may secure judicial review of such final decision.[242] Any party not joining in the appeal is made a defendant thereto.[243] Any party in interest must be made a party to the appeal.[244]

9-10:7 Failure to Give Notice

The failure of a public officer or employee to give notice in accordance with N.J.S.A. 43:21-6(b), (c), and (e) does not relieve an employer's account of any charge because of benefits that are paid unless and until employer can prove to the satisfaction of the director of the division that the benefits, in whole or in part, would not have been charged or chargeable to his account if notice had been given.[245] The director's determination is subject to judicial review.[246]

IV. CONTRIBUTIONS

9-11 By Employers

Employers (other than governmental entities or nonprofit organizations) must pay contributions to the controller of the Unemployment Compensation Fund.[247] Contributions accrue and become payable for each calendar year.[248] Such con-

---

241. N.J.S.A. 43:21-6(h).

242. *Id.* The Appellate Division must defer to the findings of the Board. *Domenico v. Bd. of Review*, 192 N.J.Super. 284 (App. Div. 1983); *Johns-Manville Products Corp. v. Bd. of Review*, 122 N.J.Super. 366 (App. Div. 1973). The test is whether the conclusion of the fact finder is reasonable based upon the proofs. *Medwick v. Bd. of Review*, 69 N.J.Super. 338 (App. Div. 1961). But a failure of the Board to include in the record its reasons for its determination is grounds for reversal. *Castellucci v. Bd. of Review*, 174 N.J.Super. 289 (App. Div. 1980).

243. N.J.S.A 43:21-6(h).

244. *Amico v. Bd. of Review*, 49 N.J. 159 (1967).

245. N.J.S.A. 43:21-6(i). Where an employer was not prejudiced by the lack of notice, a failure to give notice of the benefits paid after the employer's failure to provide the commission with requested information was not an unconstitutional denial of due process. *Horsman Dolls v. Unemployment Compensation Comm'n*, 7 N.J. 541 (1951), *app'l dismissed and cert. denied*, 342 U.S. 890, 72 S.Ct. 201, 96 L.Ed. 667 (1951).

246. N.J.S.A. 43:21-6(i).

247. N.J.S.A. 43:21-7. The Unemployment Compensation Fund is administered by the Department of Labor. N.J.S.A. 43:21-9.

A subsidiary not liable for contributions where the employee is hired and paid by the parent corporation. *MBL Holding Corp. v. State*, 215 N.J. Super. 418 (App. Div. 1987).

248. N.J.S.A. 43:21-7(a)(1).

tributions are in the nature of taxes.[249] A detailed analysis of the tax aspects of the unemployment compensation system is beyond the scope of this treatise.[250]

A separate account is maintained for each employer and credited with contributions made.[251] Benefits paid are charged against the account of the employer to whom the determination relates up to a maximum of 50 percent of the total base year, base week wages paid to an individual claimant by that employer.[252]

The rates of contributions for employers are set forth in N.J.S.A 43:21-7(b) and (c). New employers are assigned a contribution rate of 2.8 percent to 3.4 percent of the taxable wage base,[253] depending on the financial condition of the employment trust fund at the time the employer came into existence.[254] Currently, (as of June 30, 1991) the new employer rates are 2.8 percent for unemployment compensation, and .5 percent for temporary disability.[255] Initial rates apply for the first year assigned, and the next three following years.[256] They are subject to adjustment on the July 1 of the fourth year and periodically thereafter, based upon (1) the overall solvency of the employer trust fund; (2) the amount of money contributed in the past by the employer; (3) the amount of unemployment benefits the employer paid to former employees ("Benefits Charged"); and (4) the average size of its annual taxable payroll.[257] An employer can minimize its tax rates by making timely payments and "voluntary" (early) contributions to its unemployment account.[258]

---

249. *State of N.J. v. Witrak*, 194 N.J. Super. 526 (App. Div. 1984).

250. *See generally* 392-2nd *Tax Management Portfolio*, Withholding, Social Security and Unemployment Taxes on Compensation.

251. N.J.S.A. 43:21-7(c)(1).

252. *Id.*

253. The taxable wage base is recalculated annually, and was $19,300 during the calendar year 1998. N.J.S.A. 43:21-7(b)(3); N.J.A.C. 12:15-1.3.

For purposes of determining employer contributions, the term "wages" includes sick leave payments (except where payments are considered "benefits" under the regulations), most forms of fringe benefits (such as vacation pay and personal use of a company car), payments made to benefit plans under Section 125 (cafeteria plan), Section 129 (dependent care assistance) and Section 401(K) plans, to the extent that the employee could have elected to receive cash in lieu of the contribution; compensation for services as an officer of a corporation; tips and other incentive pay; back pay, where accompanied by reinstatement and awarded "where the discharge from employment was held invalid;" and certain payments in kind for personal services. N.J.A.C. 12:16-4.2 thru 4.14.

254. N.J.S.A. 43:21-7(b)(4). The Department of Labor controller determines the "Unemployment Trust Fund Reserve Ratio" prior to July 1 each year, by dividing the balance of the unemployment trust fund as of the prior March 31 by the total taxable wages reported by employers by March 31, for the preceding calendar year. N.J.S.A. 43:21-7(c)(5)(A).

255. *Employer Handbook*, New Jersey's Unemployment & Disability Insurance Programs, p. 18 (Dept. Labor, Jan. 1991) ("Employer Handbook").

256. N.J.S.A. 43:21-7(c)(4); *Employer Handbook* at 20.

257. *See* N.J.S.A. 43:21-7(c)(4)-(6); *Employer Handbook* at 20. The process for determining temporary disability tax rates is essentially the same. *Employer Handbook* at 23; *see* N.J.S.A. 43:21-7(e).

Upon the transfer of the "organization, trade or business, or substantially all the assets" of the employer to a successor in interest, the employment experience of the predecessor is transferred to the successor if it is determined that the employment experience of the predecessor is indicative of the future employment experience of the successor.[259] Unless the predecessor was owned directly or indirectly by the successor, or both were owned, directly or indirectly, by the same interest, the transfer of employment experience will not be effective if within four months of the date of transfer, the successor files a written notice of protest.[260] If there is a transfer of only a part of the employer's business, that portion of his employment experience attributable to the part transferred may be transferred to the successor.[261]

An employer also must contribute to the State Disability Benefits Fund unless excused from doing so under N.J.S.A. 43:21-27(a) or unless its workers are covered under an approved private plan.[262]

9-12 By Nonprofit Organizations and Governmental Entities

Nonprofit organizations may elect between making contributions or making payments to the fund equal to the amount of regular benefits and one-half of the extended benefits paid attributable to base year service in the employ of such organization.[263] A governmental entity may also elect to make payments in lieu of contributions.[264]

9-13 By Employees

The contributions of employees are subject to the rates prescribed by statute.[265]

---

258. *Employer Handbook* at 22; *see* N.J.S.A. 43:21-7(c)(6); N.J.S.A. 43:21-14(a)(1).

259. N.J.S.A. 43:21-7(c)(7)(A). *See Morristown Elec. Supply Co. v. State Dept. of Labor and Indus.*, 4 N.J. Super. 216 (App. Div. 1949), where partnership operated three separate businesses and, as partnership, had 0.9 percent contribution rate, a division of the separate businesses among two partners did not qualify either to benefit of prior employment experience as neither acquired the "organization, trade or business, or substantially all the assets" of the partnership).

260. N.J.S.A. 43:21-7(c)(7)(A).

261. N.J.S.A. 43:21-7(c)(7)(B).

262. N.J.S.A. 43:21-7(e).

263. N.J.S.A. 43:21-7.2.

264. N.J.S.A. 43:21-7.3.

265. *See* N.J.S.A. 43:21-7(d)(1).

Workers' contributions are withheld in trust by their employer and transmitted to the controller. If the employer fails to deduct the contributions, it alone will be liable thereafter for such contributions.[266]

9-14 Collection/Employer Obligations

An employer is required to file with the controller periodic contribution reports setting forth the employer's liability for contributions.[267] Failure to file a report will subject the employer to a penalty that may be waived by the controller if he is satisfied that the employer's failure was not intentional or the result of fraud.[268] If the employer fails to pay its contributions on or before the due date, it must pay interest from the due date until the date of payment at the rate of 1.25 percent per month.[269] The employer may apply in writing for an extension not to exceed 30 days which the controller may grant on a showing of good cause shown.[270]

An employer must file quarterly reports within 30 days from the end of each quarter, listing the name, social security number, and wages paid to each employee, and the number of base weeks each employee has worked during the quarter.[271]

The employer must pay a fine for each employee not included in the report or for whom the required information is not accurate.[272]

---

266. N.J.S.A. 43:21-7(d)(1)(E). *See State of N.J. v. Pilot Mfg. Co.*, 83 N.J.Super. 177 (Law Div. 1964)(trustee relationship imposed on employer with regard to employee contributions).

A claimant whose employer erroneously reported her commissions as earnings was not entitled to benefits notwithstanding that the claimant's contributions had been deducted from her "wages" by employer. Although the claimant was required to refund benefits received, she also was entitled to a credit for her contributions. *Fischer v. Bd. of Review*, 123 N.J.Super. 263 (App. Div. 1973).

267. N.J.S.A. 43:21-14(a)(1).

268. *Id.*

269. N.J.S.A. 43:21-14(a)(1). Employer's contributions shall be paid and contribution reports filed on a quarterly basis as follows, unless the controller authorizes more frequent reports and payments:

Quarter ending	Due Date
March 31	April 30
June 30	July 30
September 30	October 30
December 31	January 30

N.J.A.C. 12:16-5.2.

270. N.J.S.A. 43:21-14(a)(1).

271. N.J.S.A. 43:21-14(a)(2).

272. *Id.*

9-14:1 Personal Liability of the Employer

Upon an employer's failure to file any required report, the controller may estimate the employer's liability and assess the employer accordingly for contributions, penalties and interest.[273]

The contributions, penalties and interest due from any employer become a personal debt of the employer to the State of New Jersey from the time they become due, recoverable in a civil action in any court of competent jurisdiction.[274]

As an additional remedy, the controller can issue to the Clerk of the Superior Court a certificate setting forth the amount of the employer's indebtedness and liability.[275] Thereupon, the Clerk must enter the certificate as a docketed judgment and duly enter same.[276] From the time of such docketing, the certificate will have the same force and effect as a judgment entered in the Superior Court.[277] The controller then has available to him all of the remedies of any judgment creditor.[278] The debt becomes a lien on the employer and his property.[279]

9-14:2 Limitations Period for Action Against an Employer

An employer is not liable for contributions, penalties or interest, except in the event of fraud, unless contribution reports have been filed or assessments have been made before four years have elapsed from the last day of the calendar year within which such contributions become payable.[280]

If contribution reports were filed or assessments made within the four-year period, no civil action can be instituted or certificate issued to the Superior Court Clerk[281] after six years have elapsed from the last day of the calendar year in which payments became payable.[282]

---

273. N.J.S.A. 43:21-14(c).

274. N.J.S.A. 43:21-14(b); *see State of N.J. v. Witrak*, 194 N.J.Super. 526 (App. Div. 1984).

275. N.J.S.A. 43:21-14(e).

276. *Id.*

277. *Id.*

278. *Id.*

279. *Id.* Where all reasonable efforts to collect amounts owed have been exhausted, or in order to avoid litigation, the Department of Labor, with concurrence of the State Treasurer, may reduce the amount of liability except that which represents employee contributions.

280. N.J.S.A 43:21-14(a)(2).

281. *See* N.J.S.A. 43:21-14(c).

282. N.J.S.A. 43:21-14(b).

9-14:3 Rights of the Employer

The employer or any other party with interest in his property subject to the lien may deposit the amount claimed with the Clerk of the Superior Court together with 10 percent to cover interest and court costs, or give a bond in lieu thereof.[283] Thereafter, the employer or the other party may, after exhausting the available administrative remedies, secure judicial review of the validity or legality of the indebtedness or the amount thereof.[284]

All proceedings on the "judgment" are stayed pending final disposition. However, the money deposited will be used to satisfy the amount of the lien together with interest and costs.[285]

9-14:4 Refunds

An employee or an employer may request a refund or credit for contributions money erroneously paid, voluntarily or involuntarily, if an application is made no later than two years after the calendar year in which the money was paid or collected.[286] A credit or refund may be made on the initiative of the controller within the same period.[287]

V. RIGHTS AND BENEFITS

9-15 Protection of Claimants

An agreement by any individual to waive, release or commute his right to benefits is void.[288] An agreement by any individual to pay all or any portion of his employer's contribution is not valid.[289] Similarly, an employer cannot make or require any deduction from an employee's wages to finance the employer's contribution.[290]

---

283. N.J.S.A. 43:21-14(e).

284. *Id.*

285. *Id.*

286. N.J.S.A. 43:21-14(f).

287. *Id. See Fischer v. Bd. of Review,* 123 N.J.Super. 263 (App. Div. 1973).

288. N.J.S.A. 43:21-15(a). *See, e.g., Johns-Manville Products Corp. v. Bd. of Review,* 122 N.J.Super. 366 (App. Div. 1973) (collective bargaining agreement held void where it provided that employee refusing transfer forfeits right to unemployment benefits).

289. N.J.S.A. 43:21-15(a).

290. *Id.*

Any employer who violates these provisions is subject to a fine of $100 to $1000 and/or imprisonment of up to six months.[291]

A claimant cannot be charged fees of any kind in any proceeding to collect benefits.[292] Any claimant appearing before the Board of Review or a court may be represented by counsel.[293] However, counsel may not charge or receive any fee except as approved by the Board.[294]

Any assignment of benefits is void.[295] Moreover, a right to benefits is exempt from levy, execution, attachment, or any other remedy for the collection of debts as are the benefits themselves if not mingled with other funds of the recipient.[296] An exception exists for debts incurred for necessities furnished to an individual or his spouse or dependents during the period such individual is unemployed.[297] Unemployment benefits are subject to federal income tax. [298]

VI. PENALTIES

9-16 Penalties for Claimants

Any person who knowingly makes a false statement or knowingly fails to disclose a material fact in order to obtain or attempt to obtain an increase in benefits, for himself or another, is liable to pay a fine of $20 or 25 percent of the amount fraudulently obtained, whichever is greater, recoverable in an action at law.[299]

If it is determined that an individual who received benefits was for any reason not otherwise entitled to them, he must repay those benefits.[300] The sum may be paid directly by the individual or deducted from any future benefits payable.[301]

---

291. *Id.*

292. N.J.S.A. 43:21-15(b). *See, e.g., Sweeney v. Board of Review,* 81 N.J.Super. 90, 95-96 (App. Div. 1963) (assessment of fee for transcript of proceedings before Board, necessary to pursue appeal, was improper), *aff'd in part,* 43 N.J. 535 (1965).

293. In a proceeding before the Division, Board of Review, or appeal tribunal, a claimant or an employer may appear *pro se* or be represented by an attorney or nonattorney. N.J.S.A. 43:21-17(b).

294. N.J.S.A. 43:21-15(b). *See Stein and Kurland, P.C. v. Bd. of Review,* 181 N.J.Super. 269 (App. Div. 1981) (nature of case and type of services rendered should be taken into account in determining fee), *certif. denied,* 89 N.J. 401 (1982).

295. N.J.S.A. 43:21-15(c).

296. *Id.*

297. *Id.*

298. N.J.S.A. 43:21-15(d). The individual making the claim for benefits must be informed by the Division of his or her federal income tax rights and obligations. *Id.*

299. N.J.S.A 43:21-16(a). The penalty is considered civil rather than criminal. *Malady v. Bd. of Review,* 166 N.J.Super. 523 (App. Div. 1979).

The sum is collectible in any manner provided by law including the filing of a certificate of debt with the Superior Court Clerk.[302]

Except in the case of fraud, a four year limitations period applies.[303]

Any determination is final unless the individual files an appeal within seven calendar days after the delivery of such determination, or within 10 calendar days after notification is mailed to his last known address.[304]

Any person who aids and abets another to obtain benefits to which he is not entitled or to a larger amount than to which he is entitled, is subject upon conviction to a fine of $1,000 and/or imprisonment of 90 days.[305]

9-17 Penalties for Employers

An employer or its agent or any other person who knowingly makes a false statement, or knowingly fails to disclose a material fact in order to prevent or reduce the amount of benefits payable to an individual, or to avoid becoming or remaining subject to the Act, or to avoid or reduce its contribution or other payment, or to avoid producing or permitting inspection of records, is liable to pay a fine of $100 recoverable in an action at law.[306]

Any employer or officer or agent of the employing unit (if the officer or agent is directly or indirectly responsible for filing required reports or remitting contributions) who fails to remit required contributions or who files or causes to be

---

300. N.J.S.A. 43:21-16(d). The authority to order repayment rests exclusively with the director (or his representative) of the Division of Unemployment. The Board of Review cannot order repayment. *Howard v. Bd. of Review*, 173 N.J.Super. 196 (App. Div. 1980).

The director may waive repayment if the claimant did not misrepresent or withhold any material fact in obtaining benefits *and* the claimant is deceased or permanently disabled and unable to work. N.J.A.C. 12:17-10.2. *See Hopkins v. Bd. of Review*, 249 N.J.Super. 84, 90 (App. Div. 1991).

The fact that recipient may have acted in good faith does not excuse her liability for repaying benefits to which she was not entitled. *Fischer v. Bd. of Review*, 123 N.J.Super. 263 (App. Div. 1973). *See also Bannan v. Bd. of Review*, 299 N.J. Super. 671, 674 (App. Div. 1997) (retiree who received unemployment benefits while working full time must repay them in full even though the agency was responsible for the overpayment); *Kugel v. Bd. of Review*, 66 N.J.Super. 547 (App. Div. 1961) (claimant obligated to repay overpayment notwithstanding it was result of erroneous determination).

Before a refund of benefits can be ordered, due process requires that party liable be given proper notice and hearing. *See Agresta v. Bd. of Review*, 232 N.J.Super. 56 (App. Div. 1989); *Howard v. Bd. of Review*, 173 N.J.Super. 196 (App. Div. 1980); *Malady v. Bd. of Review*, 166 N.J.Super. 523 (App. Div. 1979).

301. N.J.S.A. 43:21-16(d).

302. *Id.*

303. *Id.*

304. *Id.*

305. N.J.S.A. 43:21-16(f).

306. N.J.S.A. 43:21-16(b).

filed a false or fraudulent report is subject upon conviction to a fine of $1000 and/or 90 days imprisonment.[307]

Any employer or officer or agent of the employing unit who knowingly makes a false statement, or knowingly fails to disclose a material fact to reduce benefit charges to the employing unit is liable to pay a fine of $1,000 recoverable in an action at law.[308]

---

307. N.J.S.A. 43:21-16(e). This liability, which is quasi-criminal in nature, attaches only for acts which are intentional, willful or fraudulent. *State of N.J. v. A.J. Emers, Inc.*, 220 N.J. Super. 503 (App. Div. 1987); *State of N.J. v. Witrak* 194 N.J. Super. 526 (App. Div. 1987).

308. N.J.S.A. 43:21-16(h).

Chapter 10

Temporary Disability

I. INTRODUCTION

10-1 Generally

New Jersey is one of only a very few states that provide compulsory health and accident insurance for workers.[1] Employers subject to the Temporary Disability Benefits Law (TDB Law)[2] are automatically included in a state plan of disability benefits, which is financed through employer and employee contributions.[3] In lieu of participating in the state plan, employers may establish private plans, provided through insurance, self-insurance, or an agreement with a union, or other employee group or association.[4] However, any such private plan must be approved by the Division of Employment Security and provide benefits equal to or better than those available under the state plan.[5]

The TDB Law was enacted to fill a gap for workers who had been left unprotected between the Unemployment Compensation Law and the Workers' Compensation Act.[6] Unemployment compensation benefits are intended to provide payments to replace wage loss where the individual is involuntarily unemployed but able to, and available for, work. The TDB Law is intended to protect against wage loss caused by an inability to work because of non-occupational illness or accident.[7] It is not intended to cover those who become disabled and unable to

---

1. According to the Department of Labor, the only other states providing similar protection are Rhode Island, California, New York, and Hawaii. Dept of Labor, *New Jersey's Temporary Disability Insurance Program*, p.1 (1990) (N.J.'s TDB Insurance Program).

2. The Temporary Disability Benefits Law is set forth in N.J.S.A. 43:21-25 to 43:21-56. All employers subject to the Unemployment Compensation Law, except certain governmental entities, are subject to the TDB Law.

3. *Snedeker v. Bd. of Review*, 139 N.J.Super. 394, 400 (App. Div. 1976).

4. *Id.*

5. *Id.*

6. *Potts v. Barrett Div., Allied Chemical & Dye Corp.*, 48 N.J.Super. 554, 559-60 (App. Div. 1958).

work while unemployed.[8] The TDB Law is remedial legislation which should be liberally construed.[9]

For purposes of the Temporary Disability Benefits Law, a disability occurs where a covered individual[10] suffers an accident or illness not arising out and in the course of his employment or not otherwise compensable under the workers' compensation law.[11]

II. BENEFITS

10-2 Entitlement to Benefits

To be eligible for disability benefits, a claimant must have either (1) established 20 base weeks of New Jersey covered employment within the 52 calendar weeks preceding the week in which his disability began or, (2) earned 12 times the statewide average weekly remuneration as determined under N.J.S.A. 43:21-3(c).[12]

If an otherwise eligible individual dies prior to filing a claim, a claim may be filed by a surviving spouse or other legally entitled person.[13]

---

7. N.J.S.A. 43:21-26. *See Snedeker v. Bd. of Review*, 139 N.J. Super. 394, 400 (App. Div. 1976); Dept. of Labor, *Employer Handbook—New Jersey's Unemployment & Disability Insurance Programs*, p. 34 (1991) (*Employer Handbook*) ("The primary purpose of the Temporary Disability Benefits Law is to provide protection against wage loss suffered because of inability to perform the duties of a job due to illness.").

8. *See Butler v. Bakelite Co.*, 32 N.J. 154, 162 (1960). Disability during unemployment is covered by the Unemployment Compensation Law. N.J.S.A. 43:21-4(f); N.J.A.C. 12:17-8.4. *See* Chapter 9, §9-6:7.

9. *Baker v. Dept. of Labor & Industry*, 183 N.J.Super. 29, 34 (App. Div. 1982).

10. "Covered individual" means any person who is in employment as defined in N.J.S.A. 43:21-19 (Unemployment Compensation Law; *see* discussion at Chapter 9, §9-2), for which he is entitled to remuneration from a covered employer, or who has been out of such employment for less than two weeks. A state employee cannot become a covered individual until he has exhausted all accumulated sick leave. N.J.S.A. 43:21-27(b). *See Butler v. Bakelite Co.*, 32 N.J. at 163 (employee should be working, or kept on payroll in readiness for work, or on paid vacation or leave for a definite period at the end of which he is to return to work; employee who is permanently terminated is not an employee during the period he receives payment for unused vacation time).

11. N.J.S.A. 43:21-29.

12. N.J.S.A. 43:21-41(d). A base week is a calendar week in the base year, in which the employee earned at least 20 per cent of the statewide average weekly wage. N.J.S.A. 43:21-27(i)(2); Dept. of Labor, *Employer Handbook—New Jersey's Unemployment & Disability Insurance Programs*, p. 35 (1991) (*Employer Handbook*). The statewide average weekly wage is recalculated annually; in 1991 it was $515. *Id.*

For purposes of the TDB Law, "wages" means "all compensation payable by covered employers to covered individuals for personal services, including commissions and bonuses and the cash value of all compensation payable in any medium other than cash." N.J.S.A. 43:21-27(h). An individual's earnings may include the monetary value of sick days and vacation days earned. *Baker v. Dept. of Labor & Industry*, 183 N.J. Super. 29, 34-35 (App. Div. 1982) (value of sick and vacation days contractually earned during relevant period included in determining whether plaintiff satisfied wage minimum). "The weekly wage may include overtime pay, tips and/or the cash value of remuneration other than cash." *Employer Handbook* at 35.

13. N.J.S.A 43:21-42(b).

If an infant or minor under 21 years of age is entitled to receive disability benefits, his parent or natural guardian is authorized and empowered to receive such money to the same extent as a court-appointed guardian.[14] The release or discharge of such parent or natural guardian is a full and complete discharge of all claims or demands of the infant or minor.[15]

10-3 Duration of Benefits

Benefits are payable from the eighth consecutive day of disability and for each day thereafter that the disability continues, up to a maximum of 26 weeks.[16] If benefits are payable for three consecutive weeks, then benefits become payable for the first seven days of the disability.[17] Total benefits payable under the state plan for each period of disability is the lesser of either 26 times the weekly benefit or one third of total wages in the base year.[18]

10-4 Maximum Amount of Benefits

An individual's weekly benefit is two-thirds of his average weekly wage,[19] up to a maximum of 53 percent of the statewide average weekly remuneration as determined under N.J.S.A. 43:21-3(c).[20] The amount of benefits payable for each day of disability is one-seventh of the corresponding weekly benefit amount.[21]

---

14. N.J.S.A. 43:21-42(c).

15. *Id.* The Director has the power to appoint a representative to act for the person who may be entitled to receive benefits. N.J.S.A. 43:21-42(d).

16. N.J.S.A. 43:21-38.

17. *Id.* Benefits for the first week are payable if the disability extends into any day or days of the third week. *Continental Casualty Co. v. Knuckles*, 142 N.J.Super. 162, 166 (App. Div. 1976). The disability need not continue for three full weeks. *Id.*

18. N.J.S.A. 43:21-38.

19. The average weekly wage under the TDB Law is calculated differently from the average weekly wage under the Unemployment Compensation Law. *See* Chapter 9, §9-3. Under the TDB Law, the average weekly wage is generally calculated on the basis of total wages earned from the most recent covered employer during the base weeks in the eight calendar weeks immediately preceding the week in which the disability began. N.J.S.A. 43:21-27(j). However, if the amount so derived is less than the individual's weekly earnings in employment as calculated under the Unemployment Compensation Law (see Chapter 9, §9-3) with *all* covered employers during the base weeks in the eight calendar weeks, then the average weekly wage is to be calculated "on the basis of earnings from all covered employers during the eight base weeks immediately preceding the week in which the disability commenced." N.J.S.A. 43:21-27(j).

20. N.J.S.A. 43:21-40. In 1991, 53 percent of the average weekly wage was $272. Dept. of Labor, *Employer Handbook—New Jersey's Unemployment & Disability Insurance Programs*, p. 35 (1991).

21. *Id.*

10-5 Limitation of Benefits

No benefits are payable to any person under the state plan:

(1) For the first seven consecutive days of each period of disability (the "waiting week") unless benefits become payable for three consecutive weeks; then benefits will be paid for the waiting week.[22]

(2) For more than 26 weeks with respect to any one period of disability.[23]

(3) For any period of disability that commenced when the claimant was not a "covered individual."[24]

(4) For any period claimant is not under the care of a licensed physician, dentist, optometrist, podiatrist, psychologist or chiropractor.[25]

(5) For any period of disability caused by a willfully and intentionally self-inflicted injury,[26] or by an injury sustained during the commission of a crime of the first, second or third degree.[27]

(6) For any period the claimant is working for remuneration or profit.[28]

---

22. N.J.S.A. 43:21-39(a). The three weeks is measured from the first day of disability. *Continental Casualty Co. v. Knuckles*, 142 N.J. Super. 162, 166 (App. Div. 1976).

23. N.J.S.A. 43:21-39(b).

24. N.J.S.A. 43:21-39(c). A covered individual is one who is employed by a covered employer when the disability began, or who has been out of such employment for less than two weeks. *Employer Handbook* at 35.

25. N.J.S.A. 43:21-39(d). *Cf. Thomas v. Carlton Hosiery Mills*, 14 N.J. Super. 44, 49 (App. Div. 1951) (construing prior version of section as including chiropodists); *Ross v. Bd. of Review*, 212 N.J.Super. 467, 469 and 470 n.2. (App. Div. 1984) (construing prior version of section as excluding psychologist; and providing history of certification requirements under TDB and UC Laws).

Where an employer's private plan required employees to be under the "treatment" of a licensed physician, and the term "treatment" was deemed more restrictive than the term "care," the statutory provision was controlling. *Bogda v. Chevrolet-Bloomfield Div., General Motors Corp.*, 8 N.J. Super. 172 (App. Div. 1950).

26. In *Pasetti v. Bd. of Review*, 156 N.J.Super. 296 (App. Div. 1978), the court held that a self-inflicted gunshot wound to the head was not intentionally or willfully inflicted within the meaning of the statute because the claimant was severely depressed at the time and there was uncontradicted psychiatric testimony that he "did not have any awareness of the consequences of his actions. His actions were impulsive, decisive and final in their nature, but without thought of purpose or outcome in relation either to himself or to his family." *Id.* at 298. *See generally Potts v. Barrett Div., Allied Chemical & Dye Corp.*, 48 N.J.Super. 554 (App. Div. 1958) (employee who killed a woman and then shot himself in the eye in an apparent suicide attempt, disqualified from benefits under private plan even though private plan failed to incorporate statutory exclusion of self-inflicted wounds).

27. N.J.S.A. 43:21-39(f). *See Mayoros v. Bd. of Review*, 136 N.J.Super. 421 (App. Div. 1975) (benefits not payable for disability due to heroin addiction because the addiction was sustained in the perpetration of a high misdemeanor, *i.e.*, possession of heroin).

(7) In a weekly amount which, when added to any remuneration he continues to receive from his employer, exceeds his regular weekly wages immediately prior to the disability.[29]

(8) For any period the individual would be disqualified for unemployment compensation benefits under N.J.S.A. 43:21-5 for participation in a labor dispute, unless the disability began prior to such disqualification and there is no other cause of disqualification or ineligibility to collect temporary disability benefits.[30]

Until 1980, temporary disability benefits for pregnancy and childbirth were limited to the four weeks immediately preceding the expected birth of the child and the four weeks immediately following termination of the pregnancy.[31] That limitation was deleted following an Attorney General opinion that it was inconsistent with pregnancy disability amendments to Title VII of the federal Civil Rights Act of 1964.[32]

10-6 Non-duplication of Benefits

No benefits are payable for any period in which benefits are paid or payable under any unemployment compensation law, or any disability or cash sickness benefit or similar law, of this or any state or of the federal government.[33]

No benefits are payable for any period in which benefits are paid or payable on account of disability; compensable under any workers' compensation law, occupational disease law, or other similar legislation, except benefits for permanent partial or permanent total disability previously incurred.[34]

---

28. N.J.S.A. 43:21-39(g). *See Kazala v. Prudential Ins. Co. of America*, 12 N.J. 75 (1953) (provision held to relate to physical ability to perform work; employee who engaged in substantial activities as real estate salesman could not collect benefits although he received no remuneration or profit).

29. N.J.S.A. 43:21-39(h).

30. N.J.S.A. 43:21-39(i). For a discussion of N.J.S.A. 43:21-5 and labor disputes, *see* Chapter 9, §9-7:4.

31. N.J.S.A. 43:21-39(e) (deleted by amendment, P.L. 1980, c.90). Regarding the validity of the prior limitation, *see N.J. Attorney General Formal Opinion No. 1-1975* (Jan. 6, 1975). *See also N.J. Attorney General Formal Opinion No. 4-1976* (Jan. 23, 1986).

32. P.L. 1980, c.90; *N.J. Attorney General Formal Opinion No. 2-1979* (Feb. 9, 1979).

33. N.J.S.A. 43:21-30. *See Thomas v. Bd. of Review*, 43 N.J. 549 (1965); *Seatrain Lines, Inc. v. Medina*, 39 N.J. 222, 234 (1963) (seaman's benefits for maintenance and cure are within intendment of N.J.S.A. 43:21-30; non-duplication rule not limited to funds acquired under statutory enactment). Social Security permanent disability benefits are within the scope of this section. Dept. of Labor, *Employer Handbook, New Jersey's Unemployment & Disability Insurance Programs*, p. 36 (1991) (*Employer Handbook*).

34. N.J.S.A. 43:21-30; *Sperling v. Board of Review*, 301 N.J. Super. 1, 5 (App. Div. 1997), *aff'd* 156 N.J. 466 (1998) (lump sum settlement of appellant's workers' compensation claim barred him from obtaining temporary disability benefits for the same injury).

However, where a claim under the Workers' Compensation Act is contested and thereby delayed, a claimant is eligible for temporary disability benefits until and unless he receives workers' compensation benefits.[35] If he receives workers' compensation benefits retroactive for the weeks he has already collected temporary disability benefits, the state fund or private plan, if he is so covered, is subrogated to the claimant's rights in the workers' compensation award to the extent of temporary disability benefits paid.[36]

Benefits otherwise payable are reduced by the amount paid concurrently under any government or private retirement, pension or permanent disability plan to which the claimant's most recent employer contributed on his behalf.[37] However, Social Security retirement benefits do not reduce state plan disability benefits.[38]

A private plan may not preclude simultaneous or concurrent coverage by reason of an individual's employment with two or more employers.[39] If an employee is in concurrent employment and only one employer has a private plan, then the employee shall be entitled to receive benefits under that private plan.[40] However, the benefits paid from the private plan must be at least as much as the employee would have received from the state plan.[41] No benefits shall be payable under the State plan for disability commencing while he is covered under the private plan.[42]

If an employee is in concurrent employment with two or more employers, each of whom has a private plan, each plan is required to pay not less than the full amount the employee would be entitled to if covered under the state plan.[43] The

---

35. *Id*; *Brinkerhoff v. CNA Ins. Co.*, 263 N.J. Super. 1 (App. Div. 1993) (disabled workers were entitled to benefits under temporary disability law after workers compensation benefits were terminated in dispute over continued entitlement to same). However, a claimant is not entitled to TDB during a period where workers compensation benefits were stopped based on the claimant's refusal to submit to a medical examination. *Matter of Patterson*, 298 N.J. Super. 333, 337-38 (App. Div. 1997).

36. *Id*; *see Janovsky v. American Motorists Ins. Co.*, 17 N.J. Super. 57 (Ch. Div. 1951), *aff'd*, 11 N.J. 1 (1952).

37. N.J.S.A. 43:21-30. *See Nikolajewski v. Bd. of Review*, 56 N.J. 91 (1970).

38. *Employer Handbook* at 36.

39. N.J.A.C. 12:18-2.10(a). An individual is in concurrent employment under this section if he is in employment with two or more employers during the last calendar day of employment immediately preceding the period of disability. N.J.A.C. 12:18-2.10(b).

40. N.J.A.C. 12:18-2.10(c).

41. *Id.*; *Snedeker v. Bd. of Review*, 139 N.J.Super. 394 (App. Div. 1976) (regulation furthers the legislative intent that employees covered by a private plan not be entitled to benefits from the state plan, and violates neither due process nor equal protection; the employee in that case was entitled to $81 per week under the state plan and $34 per week under the terms of a private plan; the private plan was held liable under N.J.A.C. 12:18-2.10(c) to pay $81 per week).

42. N.J.A.C. 12:18-2.10(c).

benefits payable may be apportioned among the plans in the same proportion as the employee's wages during the eight weeks preceding his disability, but in no event may benefits be less than those available under the most favorable plan, as to both weekly amount and duration.[44]

III. PRIVATE PLANS

10-7 Establishment of Private Plans

An employer may establish a private plan[45] for the payment of temporary disability benefits to be provided by a contract of insurance or by an agreement between the employer and a union, or by the employer as self-insurer.[46] Such a plan must be approved by the Division of Employment Security[47] and must provide that:

> (1) All employees are covered for any disability commencing while the plan is in effect, except as provided elsewhere in the regulations.[48]
>
> (2) Eligibility requirements for benefits are no more restrictive than those under the state plan.[49]
>
> (3) Weekly benefits under the private plan are at least equal to those payable under the state plan and the total number of weeks

---

43. N.J.A.C. 12:18-2.10(d).

44. *Id.*

45. *See generally* N.J.A.C. 12:18-1.1, *et seq.* Any covered individual not covered by a private plan is entitled to benefits under the state plan. N.J.S.A. 43:21-37.

46. N.J.S.A. 43:21-32.

47. Division of Unemployment and Disability Insurance regulations provide that an employer who fails to obtain approval of a private plan shall be deemed to be a participant in the state plan and shall be liable for the deduction of workers' contributions and payment of workers' and employers' contributions to the fund until such time as a private plan is effective. N.J.A.C. 12:18-2.1(c). Employees excluded from a private plan are covered under the state plan, and the employer is liable for deduction and payment of workers' contributions and employer's contributions as required by N.J.S.A. 43:21-7. N.J.A.C. 12:18-2.1(b). An employer may provide TDB through a multi-benefit plan, but the multi-benefit plan must also comply with all provisions of the NJ TDB law. N.J.A.C. 12:18-2.9(b).

48. N.J.S.A. 43:21-32(a); N.J.A.C. 12:18-2.9(a)1. A private plan may exclude a class or classes of employees, if (1) the exclusion is approved by the Division; (2) the classes are not determined by the age, sex, or race of the employees; (3) the classes are not based upon the wages of the employees; and (4) in the opinion of the Division, the exclusion will not result in a substantial selection of risk adverse to the state plan. N.J.S.A. 43:21-32(f); N.J.A.C. 12:18-2.1(a).

49. N.J.S.A. 43:21-32(b); N.J.A.C. 12:18-2.9(a)2. Private plans may be more liberal in their allowance of benefits. *See Potts v. Barrett Div., Allied Chemical & Dye Corp.*, 48 N.J.Super. 554, 557-58 (App. Div. 1958) (private plan included only five of eight statutory exclusions; however, public policy mandated denial of benefits for self-inflicted wound by sane person, despite omission of that exclusion from the private plan).

of disability for which benefits are payable is at least equal to the total number of weeks for which benefits are payable under the state plan.[50]

(4) Employees are not required to contribute more to the private plan than they would be required to contribute to the state plan.[51]

(5) Coverage is continued under the plan as long as the employee is "covered" but not after the employee may become employed by another employer following termination of the employment to which the plan relates.[52]

(6) A majority of the employees to be covered by the private plan agree to the plan if they are required to contribute to its cost.[53]

When a private plan is approved, the Division issues a Certificate of Approval of private plan," and the plan takes effect on the first day of the calendar quarter next following the approval date.[54] The Division may grant an employer's request for a plan to become effective at an earlier date only upon finding that the plan: (1) is the result of an agreement contained in a labor-management contract; or (2) covers a newly formed subsidiary of an employer with an existing plan; or (3) is the result of a succession from an employer with an existing private plan.[55]

---

50. N.J.S.A. 43:21-32(c); N.J.A.C. 12:18-2.9(a)3.

If an employee is employed by two employers, only one of which has a private plan, the employee will be eligible to receive benefits only under the private plan and not under the state plan. *Snedeker v. Bd. of Review*, 139 N.J. Super. 394 (App. Div. 1976).

51. N.J.S.A. 43:21-32(d).

52. N.J.S.A. 43:21-32(e).

53. N.J.S.A. 43:21-32(f) and 43:21-33. If employees must contribute to a private plan, the employer must submit to them a brief written summary of the provisions of the plan, including the weekly benefit rate, the maximum amount and duration of benefits and the contribution required from employees for the benefits thereunder. N.J.A.C. 12:18-2.11. A majority of employees must agree to the plan, including the workers' contribution, by written election, and evidence of that consent must be provided on the application for approval. *Id.*; N.J.A.C. 12:18-2.12. Amendments to a private plan affecting these items must similarly be approved by the employees.

54. N.J.A.C. 12:18-2.13.

55. N.J.A.C. 12:18-2.13(b). As defined in the regulations, which refer to the Unemployment Compensation Law definition set forth in N.J.S.A. 43:21-7(c)(7)(A), "a successor in interest is an entity that acquires the organization, trade, or business, or substantially all the assets of an employer, whether by merger, consolidation, sale, transfer, descent, or otherwise." N.J.A.C. 12:18-2.13(b)3.

10-8 Benefits Under Private Plans

Private plans must set forth the eligibility requirements for benefits and the amounts of benefits payable.[56] Benefits must be paid to employees at the same intervals at which they are paid wages, unless otherwise approved by the Division.[57] No employee is entitled to benefits from the state plan with respect to any period of disability commencing while he is covered under a private plan.[58] Nor shall an employee be paid benefits for disability during unemployment under the Unemployment Compensation Law with respect to any period of disability that commenced while he was in employment, as defined by the TDB Law.[59] If an employee applies for benefits under the state plan or the Unemployment Compensation disability during unemployment program, and it is determined that the claim should have been made under a private plan, the employee will not be disqualified for failure to give timely notice and proof of disability provided that:

1. The application to the state plan would have been timely notice to the private plan if made then; and
2. Proof of disability is furnished under the private plan within either the period required thereunder or 30 days after the employee has notice that his claim should have been made to the private plan and not the state plan.[60]

A private plan may not reduce the amount or duration of benefits, or increase the rate of employee contributions, without prior approval of the Division.[61] The Division will approve such changes if it finds that, after amendment, the plan continues to meet the requirements of the TDB Law and regulations.[62] If the amendment requires an increase in employee contributions, it will not be approved unless a majority of employees covered by the plan agreed to the amendment by written election.[63] Private plans should give the Division prompt notice

---

56. N.J.A.C. 12:18-2.2(c). Employees must be given notice of the benefits provided by the private plan, either by individual certificates or other direct notification at the time of coverage, or by posting in the workplace. N.J.A.C. 12:18-2.3. The notice should indicate current rates, eligibility requirements, benefit entitlements, and appeal rights. *Id.* A copy of the notice should be available for inspection at the worksite and submitted annually to the Division. *Id.*

57. N.J.A.C. 12:18-2.2(g).

58. N.J.A.C. 12:18-2.2(a).

59. N.J.A.C. 12:18-2.2(b). Benefits paid to an employee under either the state plan or a private plan may not be deducted from the amount of benefits the employee may be entitled to as an unemployed claimant for a subsequent period of disability. N.J.A.C. 12:18-2.2(e).

60. N.J.A.C. 12:18-2.2(d).

61. N.J.A.C. 12:18-2.2(h).

62. *Id.*

of other changes, which do not require approval.[64] No employer, union, or other association representing employees may administer or apply the provisions of a private plan so as to derive any profit therefrom.[65]

10-9 Termination of Private Plan

A private plan may be discontinued by an employer, or by election in writing by a majority of covered employees.[66] If 10 percent of the employees covered by a private plan sign a petition, the Division will order an election after 30 days written notice to the employer, and will supervise the election if necessary.[67] The Division may also withdraw its approval of a private plan for good cause shown, upon notice and opportunity for a hearing,[68] if it finds that:

1. There is danger that benefits will not be paid; or
2. Security for payment is insufficient; or
3. There has been a failure to comply with the terms and conditions of the plan; or
4. There has been a failure to pay benefits to eligible claimants promptly; or
5. The insurance company (in the case of an insured plan) has given notice of cancellation of the policy of insurance thereunder; or
6. The employer, the employer's agent, the union, or other association representing the employees is deriving a profit from the plan; or
7. The employer, insurer, or other party responsible for the payment of benefits has failed to comply with the TDB Law or regulations; or
8. Other good cause.[69]

---

63. *Id.*

64. *Id.*

65. N.J.A.C. 12:18-2.5.

66. N.J.S.A. 43:21-35; N.J.A.C. 12:18-2.20.

67. N.J.A.C. 12:18-2.15. Elections will not be held more often than once in any 12 consecutive months. *Id.* An employee must be employed as of the date of the election and covered by the plan to be eligible to vote. *Id.* Election procedures are set forth in N.J.A.C. 12:18-2.17 to -2.19.

68. N.J.S.A. 43:21-35.

The termination of a private plan will not affect payment of benefits to those employees whose period of disability commenced before the date of termination.[70]

After the effective date of termination, the employer is liable for the deduction of workers' contributions and the payment of workers' and employers' contributions to the state plan.[71] A form notice of the withdrawal of approval must be posted for not less than 30 days.[72]

10-10 Supplementary Plans

An employer may establish without approval a supplementary plan for payment to employees or to any class or classes of employees benefits over and above those payable under a private plan. The employer may also collect additional voluntary contributions from employees toward the cost of additional benefits.[73]

IV. OBTAINING BENEFITS

10-11 Filing a Claim Under the State Plan

On the ninth day of disability of an employee under the state plan, the employer must issue notices to the employee and to the Division, on forms provided by the Division, that contain the name, address, social security number, and wage information as to the individual and the name, address and ID number of the employer.[74] The employee must also be provided with a copy of the Division's benefit instructions.[75]

Within 30 days of the commencement of disability, a written *notice* of same must be provided to the Division, by or on behalf of the person claiming benefits.[76] The notice need not be on a prescribed form,[77] but must provide claimant's full name, address and social security number and the date on which he was too

---

69. N.J.A.C. 12:18-2.14(a). The withdrawal may be made effective as of the date of the act or omission upon which it is based or at any subsequent date determined by the Division. N.J.A.C. 12:18-2.14(b). All interested parties must be given notice and an opportunity for a hearing. *Id.*

70. N.J.A.C. 43:21-35.

71. N.J.A.C. 12:18-2.21(a).

72. N.J.A.C. 12:18-2.21(b).

73. N.J.S.A. 43:21-36. *See O'Boyle v. Prudential Ins. Co. of America*, 241 N.J. Super. 503 (App. Div. 1990).

74. N.J.S.A. 43:21-49(a).

75. *Id.*

disabled to work.[78] *Proof* of disability must also be furnished within 30 days of the commencement of disability, by any claimant who is or expects to be totally unable to perform his employment for eight or more consecutive days, and is under the care of a legally licensed medical practioner.[79] Benefits may be paid for three weeks, but not more, pending receipt of medical proof.[80]

Proof of disability should be provided on the Division's Form DS-1 (Proof and Claim for Disability Benefits) and should be accompanied by a certification of the licensed medical practitioner.[81] Failure to furnish written notice or proof of disability in the time and manner required will not reduce or invalidate any claim if claimant complies within a reasonable time and shows that it was not reasonably possible for him to comply within the specified time.[82] Tolling is not limited to cases where claimant was physically unable to file a claim.[83] An employer must respond to a Division request for information within ten days of its mail-

---

76. N.J.A.C. 12:18-3.2(a). All claims and related documents may be filed by mail except where the claimant is notified by the Division that a personal appearance or examination will be required. N.J.A.C. 12:18-3.3(a). Filing is deemed complete upon mailing. *Id.*

77. Form DS-1, "Proof and Claim for Disability Benefits," accompanied by a certification of the attending licensed medical practitioner will suffice. N.J.A.C. 12:18-3.2(a), (b). The form is generally available, from local unemployment claims offices, the Disability Insurance Service in Trenton, employers, unions, and some doctors and hospitals. Dept. of Labor, *Employer Handbook—New Jersey's Unemployment & Disability Ins. Programs*, p. 35 (1991) (*Employer Handbook*).

78. N.J.A.C. 12:18-3.2(a).

79. N.J.S.A. 43:21-49(a); N.J.A.C. 12:18-3.2(b). This may be done by claimant's authorized representative. *Id.*

80. N.J.S.A. 43:21-49(a).

81. N.J.S.A. 43:21-49(a); N.J.A.C. 12:18-3.2(b). A continued claim form on which the claimant must provide additional medical information in order to continue receiving benefits should be filed as proof of continued disability, when requested by the Division. N.J.A.C. 12:18-3.2(b).

A "period of disability" is payable from the first day of disability if the claimant receives medical care by a licensed medical practitioner within 10 days of the first day of disability. N.J.A.C. 12:18-3.2(c). If the claimant fails to furnish such proof, benefits shall be payable from the first day of medical care. *Id.*

82. N.J.S.A. 43:21-49(a); N.J.A.C. 12:18-3.2(c). If claimant fails to make the required showing, benefits will be limited to the period commencing 30 days before receipt of the notice or proof of disability, the first seven days of which will not be compensable unless the three weeks immediately thereafter are. *Id.*

83. In *Mazzarella v. Bd. of Review*, 172 N.J.Super. 459, 463 (App. Div. 1980), the Appellate Division held that the standard of "not reasonably possible" encompasses "those situations wherein the claimant has been prevented from filing by the totality of relevant factors rather than by physical incapability alone." *Id.* at 464. In that case, claimant's failure was excused as justified by his employer's failure to provide notice as required by N.J.S.A. 43:21-49(a), his union's provision of erroneous information, and his union insurance carrier's delay in rejecting his claim. *Id.* at 462. *See also Toppi v. Prudential Ins. Co. of America*, 153 N.J.Super. 445, 450 (Dist.Ct. 1977) (where insured has failed to file a claim for TDB, insurer who has primary responsibility for payment to insured may file in his name to recoup applicable portion of claim paid).

ing.[84] An employer failing to respond to a request for information within the prescribed time period is subject to penalties provided under N.J.S.A. 43:21-55(b).

Both the claimant and his employer will be given notice of the decision on a claim and the reason for any denial of a claim.[85] Within two working days of receipt of a determination of eligibility, the employer must furnish the Division with any known information bearing on the eligibility of the claimant or duration of benefits to be paid.[86]

The claimant or employer must file an appeal within seven calendar days of delivery of a decision or notification thereof, or within 10 calendar days of mailing of same to his last known address or else the determination shall be final.[87] The rules of the board of review govern appeals under the state plan.[88]

The claimant must, at the Division's request, submit to a relevant examination, but not more than once per week.[89] Refusal to submit to an examination will disqualify the claimant from all future benefits for the disability in question.[90]

10-12 Hearings

If an individual covered under a private plan cannot agree with his employer or the insurer as to the amount of benefits to which he is entitled, he may, within one year after the beginning of the period for which benefits are claimed, file a written complaint with the Division.[91]

---

84. N.J.A.C. 12:18-3.7(a). If the employer fails to respond, the Division will rely entirely on information from other sources, including an affidavit from claimant as to wages and time worked. N.J.A.C. 12:18-3.7(b). Except in the case of fraud, no penalty will be imposed upon a claimant for providing erroneous information in such an affidavit. *Id.*

85. N.J.A.C. 12:18-3.6. A copy of the decision of eligibility stating the claimant's weekly benefit rate and probable duration of benefits will be mailed or delivered to the employer or employers by whom claimant was employed at the commencement of disability. N.J.A.C. 12:18-3.6(c).

86. N.J.A.C. 12:18-3.7(d). An employer who thereafter obtains information which would render claimant ineligible or reduce his benefits should immediately forward that information to the Division. N.J.A.C. 12:18-3.7(e).

87. N.J.A.C. 12:18-3.8.

88. N.J.S.A. 43:21-50(b); N.J.A.C. 12:18-3.9. The review and hearing procedures under the Unemployment Compensation Law which are applicable to claims against the state plan under the TDB Law, are discussed in Chapter 9, §9-10:5.

89. N.J.S.A. 43:21-49(b).

90. *Id.* The Department of Labor states as follows:

> The claimant may be required to submit to a physical examination by a state-appointed physician in order to medically substantiate his/her claim. In addition, the employer may request an independent medical examination if there is good cause to suspect that the employee is not disabled. There is no cost to the employee or the employer for the examination. Failure to submit to an examination is cause for the denial of benefits.

Employer Handbook at 36.

Upon receipt of a complaint, the Division will conduct such investigation and informal hearings as may be necessary to determine the facts and settle issues.[92] If the issues are not settled, a formal hearing will be scheduled upon due notice to all parties.[93] The hearing officer will open the hearing by ascertaining the facts and summarizing the issues on the record.[94] Evidence other than *ex parte* affidavits may be produced by any party, and the hearing officer is not bound by the Rules of Evidence.[95] Any individual may appear for himself or may be represented by an attorney or a non-attorney pursuant to N.J.S.A. 43:21-17.[96] The parties and their representatives may examine and cross-examine witnesses, inspect documents, and explain or rebut evidence.[97] All testimony must be under oath or affirmation and recorded; however, it need not be transcribed unless the order is to be reviewed.[98] If a party fails to appear for a hearing after due notice, the issues may be decided on the evidence available, the complaint may be dismissed, or evidence may be taken and the matter disposed of in accordance with same.[99]

Upon completion of any hearing, the hearing officer shall promptly make a determination of facts and an order in writing, which shall be final and binding.[100] Any appeal of the order shall be in accordance with the Rules of the Court.[101] An

---

91. N.J.S.A. 43:21-50(a); N.J.A.C. 12:18-2.6(b), (c). The complaint will be considered filed on the day it is delivered to the office of the Division of Temporary Disability Insurance, Labor Building, PO Box 957, John Fitch Plaza, Trenton, N.J. 08625-0957, or if mailed, on the date a properly addressed and stamped envelope is postmarked. N.J.A.C. 12:18-2.6(f).

92. N.J.A.C. 1:12A-9.1; N.J.A.C. 12:18-2.6(e).

93. N.J.S.A. 43:21-50(a); N.J.A.C. 1:12A-9.2(a). Written notice must be provided at least five days before the hearing unless a shorter notice is not prejudicial to the parties. N.J.A.C. 1.12A-9.2(b). Notice may be served personally or by certified or registered mail or by telegram upon a party or his duly authorized representative. N.J.A.C. 1:12A-9.2(a).

94. N.J.A.C. 1:12A-14.1(c).

95. N.J.A.C. 1:12-14.1(b).

96. N.J.A.C. 1:12A-5.1.

97. N.J.A.C. 1.12A-14.1. The hearing officer may also examine witnesses as he deems necessary. *Id.* He may take additional evidence, upon notice to the parties of the time and place of the hearing. N.J.A.C. 1:12A-14.1(g). The matter may also be submitted to the hearing officer upon stipulated facts. N.J.A.C. 12:18-2.43(i).

The hearing officer has power to administer oaths, take depositions, and issue subpoenas to compel the attendance of witnesses and the production of documents. N.J.A.C. 12:18-2.48(a). However, subpoenas to compel the attendance of witnesses or the production of documents shall issue only upon a showing of need. N.J.A.C. 1:12A-14.1(h).

98. N.J.A.C. 1:12A-14.1(f).

99. N.J.A.C. 1.12A-14.2. Any complaint dismissed for failure to appear or failure to prosecute may be reconsidered, provided good cause for the failure is shown and an application for reopening is made within ten days after mailing or notification of the order of dismissal. N.J.A.C. 1:12A-14.2(b).

100. N.J.S.A. 43:21-50(a); N.J.A.C. 1:12A-15.1(a). The order must set forth a statement of the facts involved, the reasons for the order, and the order. N.J.A.C. 1:12A-15.1(a). It must be served upon each of the parties, by registered mail, to his last known address. N.J.A.C. 1:12A-15.1(b).

101. N.J.S.A. 43:21-50(a); N.J.A.C. 1:12A-15.1(d) .

individual covered by the state plan is entitled to a review and hearing as provided in the provisions governing unemployment compensation hearings.[102]

If an award of benefits is made to an employee, the hearing officer may allow a reasonable attorney's fee, not to exceed 20 percent of the award, payable by the employer or insurer; he may also allow a reasonable appearance fee to any medical witnesses, which may be assessed in whole or in part against any party.[103] Except as so provided, it is unlawful for any attorney to charge for services in securing or attempting to secure benefits under the TDB Law, or for a medical witness to charge for appearance at a hearing.[104]

V. RECORDS

10-13 Records of Employers Under the State Plan

An employer must keep accurate employment records and make them available for inspection by the Division or its authorized representative during ordinary business hours.[105] An employer must furnish the Division with any requested information regarding the eligibility of claimant within 10 days of the mailing of the request.

10-14 Records of Employers Under Private Plans

Employers who provide private plans, as well as the insurers of private plans, must provide such reports and information as may be required.[106]

Self insurers, unions and insurance companies must provide semi-annual reports on forms prescribed by the Division on or before the 30th day following the end of the respective six month period showing, *inter alia*, (1) the number of claims received during the six month period; (2) the number of claims accepted during the six month period; and (3) the amount of benefits paid during the six month period.[107]

---

102. N.J.S.A. 43:21-50(b). *See* Chapter 9, §§ 9-10:1 to9-10:5.

103. N.J.S.A. 43:21-51.

104. *Id.*

105. N.J.S.A. 43:21-52(a).

106. N.J.S.A. 43:21-52(b); N.J.A.C. 12:18-2.29 to 12:18-2.32.

107. N.J.A.C. 12:18-2.30(a). Reports required to be filed by self-insurers are set forth in N.J.A.C. 12:18-2.29; reports by unions and other benefit payers in N.J.A.C. 12:18-2.30; and reports by insurance companies in N.J.A.C. 12:18-2.31.

Annual reports to be filed by self-insurers and unions, on forms provided by the Division, are required to show, *inter alia*, (1) the funds available at the beginning of the year for the payment of disability benefits; (2) the amount contributed to benefits that year; (3) the amount of disability benefits paid that year; (4) direct costs of administration; and (5) the number of employees covered by the plan as of December 31.[108] Annual reports to be filed by insurance companies, on forms provided by the Division, are required to show: (1) premiums earned during that year with respect to the private plan; (2) dividends to holders of policies providing the benefits of such private plans; (3) benefit losses incurred under the private plan; and (4) expenses incurred with respect to the private plan.[109] Employers maintaining two or more plans must also file semi-annual reports.[110]

VI. PROTECTION OF CLAIMANTS

10-15 Benefits Protected

Benefits payable under a private plan have the same preference against an employer's assets as claims for unpaid wages.[111]

The TDB Law provides that benefits under the state plan and for any disability during unemployment[112] or under an approved private plan are not assignable or subject to levy, execution, attachment or other process for the satisfaction of debts.[113] Nonetheless, the Review Board has held that the Division is authorized to withhold child support payments from temporary disability benefits, because the TDB Law was enacted as a supplement to the Unemployment Compensation Law and, therefore, should be subject to the same rules, regulations and practices. *In Re E.C.B.*[114] The Unemployment Compensation Law includes a provision expressly allowing the Division to deduct child support payments.[115] *See also In re J.T.S.*[116] (reinstating and enforcing employee's agreement to repay TDB benefits if she was awarded workers' compensation, despite the fact that the workers' compensation judge, in approving the employer's settlement, found the

108. N.J.A.C. 12:18-2.29(b) (self-insurers); N.J.A.C. 12:18-2.30(b) (unions).
109. N.J.A.C. 12:18-2.31(b).
110. N.J.A.C. 12:18-2.32.
111. N.J.S.A. 43:21-53. *See* discussion of unpaid wage claims in Chapter 8, §8-12.
112. *See* N.J.S.A. 43:21-4(f).
113. N.J.S.A. 43:21-53.
114. 94 N.J.A.R. 2d (UCC) 15 (1994)
115. *Id.* at 17
116. 95 N.J.A.R.2d 18 (UCC) (1995)

employee's injuries not work-related and on that basis purported to void the agreement to repay TDB).

VII. PENALTIES

10-16 Penalties for Claimants

If it is determined that an individual who received benefits was for any reason not otherwise entitled to them, he must repay those benefits.[117] The sum that the individual is liable to repay shall be deducted from future benefits payable to the individual under the Act or shall be repaid by the individual to the Division, the employer or the insurer.[118]

In addition, an individual who knowingly makes a false statement or fails to disclose a material fact to obtain or increase benefits under the state or a private plan, either for himself or for another, is subject to a $20 fine which may be recovered in a civil action.[119] Each such statement or failure to disclose constitutes a separate offense.[120]

10-17 Penalties for Employers

An employer or its agent or any other person who knowingly makes a false statement or knowingly fails to disclose a material fact in order to prevent or reduce the amount of benefits payable to an individual, or to avoid becoming or remaining subject to the act, or to avoid or reduce its contribution or other payment, or to avoid producing or permitting inspection of records is subject to a $20 fine which may be recovered in a civil action.[121]

---

117. N.J.S.A. 43:21-55(a). *See generally In re J.T.S.*, 95 N.J.A.R.2d 18 (UCC) (1995) (reinstating and enforcing employee's agreement to repay TDB benefits if she was awarded workers' compensation, despite the fact that the workers' compensation judge, in approving the employer's settlement, found the employee's injuries not work-related and on that basis purported to void her agreement to repay TDB).

118. *Id.*

119. N.J.S.A. 43:21-55(a).

120. *Id.*

121. N.J.S.A. 43:21-55(b).

10-18 Penalty for Fraud

Any person who acts with the intent to defraud the Division, in addition to the other penalties, will be liable upon conviction in a judicial proceeding to payment of a fine of up to $250 and imprisonment of up to 90 days.[122]

122. N.J.S.A. 43:21-55(d).

Chapter 11

Insurance Coverage For Employees

I. GROUP LIFE INSURANCE

11-1 Introduction

This chapter reviews various provisions of New Jersey insurance law that govern group life and group health insurance policies issued to employers, unions and trustees. This is not intended as an exhaustive analysis of insurance law, but rather, as an outline of provisions that are required by state law to be included in all group life and health insurance policies issued to these entities.

Readers are cautioned to bear in mind the impact of federal laws governing employer-provided health and welfare benefits on state regulation of insurance policies. For example, employers subject to the Consolidated Omnibus Budget Reconciliation Act of 1985 (COBRA), must comply with that statute's specific requirements as to the continuation of individual health insurance benefits after group coverage ends.[1] And employers maintaining plans subject to the Employee Retirement Income Security Act of 1974 (ERISA), must of course design and administer them in compliance therewith.[2] Although ERISA broadly pre-empts all state laws relating to employee benefit plans regulated thereunder,[3] the statutory provisions discussed herein, which govern only the terms of group insurance policies, are likely to be found saved from pre-emption under an exception for state laws regulating insurance.[4]

---

1. P.L. 99-272 (April 7, 1986), as amended by the Tax Reform Act of 1986, P.L. 99-514 (Oct. 22, 1986), the Technical and Miscellaneous Revenue Act of 1988, P.L. 100-647 (Nov. 11, 1988), and the Omnibus Budget Reconciliation Act of 1989, P.L. 101-239 (Dec. 19, 1989). For a detailed and extensive analysis of the requirements of these statutes, see Paul M. Hamburger, *Employer's Handbook—Mandated Health Benefits* (1990); Jeffrey D. Mamorsky, *Employee Benefits Handbook*, 36.05, *et seq.* (3d ed. 1992).

2. 29 U.S.C.A. §§1001, *et seq.*

11-2 Requirements for Individual Employers

A group life insurance policy may be issued to an employer or to the trustees of a fund established by the employer to insure employees for the benefit of persons other than the employer.[5]

The employees eligible under such a policy must be all the employees of the employer or all of any class or classes of employees determined by conditions relating to their employment or by a combination of such conditions and conditions relating to their family status.[6]

The term "employees" may be defined to include the employees of one or more subsidiary corporations and the employees, individual proprietors and partners

---

3. *See, e.g., New York State Conference of Blue Cross and Blue Shield Plans v. Travelers Ins.*, 514 U.S. 645 (1995) (a N.Y. statute which required hospitals to collect surcharges from patients covered by ERISA–governed health care plans, and from HMOs that derive fees from ERISA plans but not from Blue Cross and Blue Shield Plans held not pre–empted; the purpose of pre–emption was "to avoid a multiplicity of regulation in order to permit the nationally uniform administration of employee benefit plans"; the "indirect economic influence" that results from the surcharges "does not bind plan administrators to any particular choice and thus function as a regulation of an ERISA plan itself .... Nor does [it] ... preclude uniform administrative practice or the provision of a uniform interstate benefit package"); *Metropolitan Life Ins. Co. v. Taylor*, 481 U.S. 58 (1987) (common law contract claims pre-empted); *Fort Halifax Packing Co. v. Coyne*, 482 U.S. 1 (1987) (Maine statute requiring one-time severance payment upon plant closing not pre-empted); *Metropolitan Life Ins. Co. v. Commonwealth of Massachusetts*, 471 U.S. 724 (1985) (Mass. statute requiring insurance policies to provide specified minimum benefits not pre-empted); *Shaw v. Delta Air Lines, Inc.*, 463 U.S. 85, 96-97 (1983) (state law pre-empted "if it has a connection with or a reference to" an ERISA plan); *Alessi v. Raybestos-Manhattan, Inc.*, 451 U.S. 504 (1981) (N.J. statute prohibiting integration of workers' compensation and pension benefits pre-empted).

4. ERISA Section 514 provides in pertinent part:

> (a)Except as provided in subsection (b) of this section, the provisions of this subchapter and subchapter III of this chapter shall supersede any and all State laws insofar as they may now or hereafter relate to any employee benefit plan described in section 1003 (a) of this title.
>
> ****
>
> (b)(2)(A) Except as provided in subparagraph (B), nothing in this subchapter shall be construed to exempt or relieve any person from any law of any State which regulates insurance, banking, or securities.
>
> (B)Neither an employee benefit plan described in section 1003 (a) of this title, which is not exempt under section 1003 (b) of this title (other than a plan established primarily for the purpose of providing death benefits), nor any trust established under such a plan, shall be deemed to be an insurance company or other insurer, bank, trust company, or investment company or to be engaged in the business of insurance or banking for purposes of any law of any State purporting to regulate insurance companies, insurance contracts, banks, trust companies, or investment companies.

29 U.S.C. §1144. *See Pas v. Travelers Ins. Co.*, 7 F.3d 349 (3d Cir. 1993) (N.J.S.A. 17B:30-12(d), prohibiting discrimination in insurance policies, was not pre-empted by ERISA); *Cassidy v. Welfare and Pension Fund*, 580 F.Supp. 175, 178-79 (E.D. Pa. 1983) (N.J.S.A. 17B:27-51.12 applicable only to policies of insurance, and not to self-funded benefits; to the extent it is suggested the statute applies to self-funded benefits, it is pre-empted by ERISA). For a discussion of ERISA pre-emption see Bruce, *Pension Claims: Rights and Obligations*, p. 361, 299-300 (1988).

5. N.J.S.A. 17B:27-2.

6. N.J.S.A. 17B:27-2(a).

of one or more affiliated corporations, proprietorships or partnerships if the business of such affiliated companies and the employer is under common control through stock ownership, contract or otherwise.[7] However, no director of a corporate employer will be eligible under the policy unless such person is a bona fide employee of the corporation—that is, he performs duties other than those usually performed by a director.[8]

"Employees" may also include an individual proprietor or partners if the employer is an individual proprietorship or partnership, provided that the individual proprietor or partner is actively engaged in and devotes a substantial amount of time to the conduct of the business.[9]

"Employees" may include retired employees.[10]

In the case of a fund established by the employer, "employees" may include the trustees and/or their employees if their duties are principally connected to the trusteeship.[11]

The employer or trustee is deemed the policyholder.[12] The policy must cover at least 10 employees at the date of issue.[13] Premiums are paid by the policyholder entirely from the employer's funds or funds contributed by him, or partly from such funds and those contributed by insured employees.[14] No policy may issue on which the entire premium is to be borne by the insured employees.[15]

A policy with respect to which part of the premium is to be paid by employee contributions may issue only if at least 75 percent of the eligible employees elect to make the required contributions.[16] A policy for which no portion of the premium is to be funded by contributions from insured employees must insure all eligible employees except any as to whom evidence of individual insurability is not satisfactory to the insurer.[17]

The amounts of insurance under the policy must be based upon some plan precluding individual selection either by the policyholder or the employees.[18]

---

7. *Id.*
8. N.J.S.A. 17B:27-2(a).
9. *Id.*
10. *Id.*
11. *Id.*
12. N.J.S.A. 17B:27-2.
13. N.J.S.A. 17B:27-2(c).
14. N.J.S.A. 17B:27-2(b).
15. N.J.S.A. 17B:27-2(a).
16. N.J.S.A. 17B:27-2(b). Employees whose evidence of individual insurability is unsatisfactory to the insurer are excluded from this calculation. *Id.*
17. *Id.*
18. N.J.S.A. 17B:27-2(d).

11-3 Requirements for Labor Unions

A policy may be issued to a labor union as policyholder to insure union members for the benefit of persons other than the union, its officers, representatives or agents.[19]

Individuals eligible under such a policy must include all union members, or all of any class or classes of members determined by conditions relating to their employment or membership in the union or both, or a combination of such conditions and conditions pertaining to members' family status.[20]

The policy must cover at least 10 members at the date of issue.[21] Premiums must be paid by the policyholder either entirely from union funds or partly from such funds and partly from funds contributed by the insured members specifically for that purpose.[22] The entire premium cannot be funded solely by contributions from the insured members.[23]

A policy in which part of the premium is to be funded by insured members specifically for their insurance may issue only if at least 75 percent of the eligible members elect to make the required contributions.[24] A policy for which no portion of the premium is to be derived from members' contributions specifically for their insurance must insure all eligible members except any as to whom evidence of individual insurability is not satisfactory to the insurer.[25]

The amounts of insurance under the policy must be based upon some plan precluding individual selection either by the policyholder or the members.[26]

11-4 Requirements for Trustee Groups

A policy may be issued to the trustees of a fund established by two or more employers in the same or related industries, or by one or more labor unions, or by one or more employers and one or more labor unions.[27] The trustees of such a

19. N.J.S.A. 17B:27-4.

20. N.J.S.A. 17B:27-4(a).

21. N.J.S.A. 17B:27-4(c).

22. N.J.S.A. 17B:27-4(b). Presumably, contributions by members "specifically for their insurance" are to be distinguished from general membership dues.

23. N.J.S.A. 17B:27-4(b).

24. N.J.S.A. 17B:27-4(b). Members whose evidence of individual insurability is unsatisfactory to the insurer are excluded from this calculation. *Id.*

25. N.J.S.A. 17B:27-4(b).

26. N.J.S.A. 17B:27-4(d).

27. N.J.S.A. 17B:27-5.

fund are deemed the policyholder for the purpose of insuring employees of the employer or members of the union for the benefit of individuals other than the employers or the unions.[28]

Persons eligible under such a policy must include all of the employees of the employer or all the members of the unions, or all or any classes of employees or union members determined by conditions relating to their employment or union membership or by a combination of such conditions and conditions relating to family status.[29]

The term "employees" may include retired employees.[30] "Employees" may also include individual proprietors or partners if the employer is an individual proprietor or partnership and provided such proprietor or partners are actively engaged in and devote a substantial amount of their time to the conduct of the business.[31]

A director of a corporate employer is eligible for coverage under the policy only if he qualifies as an otherwise eligible employee of the corporation by performing duties other than those usually performed by a director.[32]

Employees covered by the policy may also include the trustees and/or their employees, if their duties are principally related to the trusteeship.[33] Similarly, if the fund is established by members of an association of employers, "employees" may include association employees.[34]

The policy must cover at least 100 persons at the date of issue.[35] The policy also must cover an average of not less than three persons per employer unit unless (1) the policy is issued to the trustees of a fund established by employers that have assumed obligations under a collective bargaining agreement and are participating in the fund pursuant to such obligations with respect to one or more classes of employees that are covered by the collective bargaining agreement or as a method of providing insurance benefits for other classes of their employees; or (2) the policy is issued to the trustees of a fund established by one or more unions.[36]

---

28. *Id. See Tulipano v. U.S. Life Ins. Co. in City of New York*, 57 N.J. Super. 269 (App. Div. 1959) (employer, designated as beneficiary of deceased employee under policy issued to welfare fund created under collective bargaining agreement and funded entirely by employer, not entitled to recover on policy).

29. N.J.S.A. 17B:27-5(a).

30. *Id.*

31. *Id.*

32. *Id.*

33. *Id.*

34. *Id.*

35. N.J.S.A. 17B:27-5(c).

The amounts of insurance under the policy must be based upon some plan precluding individual selection either by the policyholder, the insured, the employers or the unions.[37]

11-5 Dependents of Employees

The coverage under a policy issued to employers, employer groups, labor unions, or funds established for the purpose of providing life insurance may be broadened to insure employees and members against loss due to the death of a spouse or dependent or minor children.[38]

Premiums for such insurance must be paid by the policyholder, from the employer's or union funds and/or from funds contributed by the insureds.[39] Where any part of the premium is to be derived from contributions by the insured employees or members, the insurance coverage for dependents may issue only if at least 75 percent of the then-eligible employees or members elect to make the required contributions.[40] If no part of the premium is to be funded by employee or member contributions, then all eligible employees and members must be insured with respect to their dependent spouses and children, excluding those whose family members' evidence of insurability is not acceptable to the insurer.[41]

The amounts of insurance must be based upon some plan precluding individual selection by either the insured, policyholder, employer or union.[42] The amount of insurance for spouses and children cannot exceed 50 percent of the insurance on the life of the employee or $5,000, whichever is less.[43] Moreover, the amount of insurance for a child less than 6 months of age at the time of death may not exceed $100.[44]

Upon the termination of the employee's or member's employment or membership in the class or classes eligible for coverage, or upon his death, insurance coverage for the employee's or member's spouse may terminate. In such a case, the insurer must issue to the spouse, without evidence of insurability, an individual

---

36. N.J.S.A. 17B:27-5(c).

37. N.J.S.A. 17B:27-5(d).

38. N.J.S.A. 17B:27-9.

39. N.J.S.A. 17B:27-9(a).

40. *Id.* Employees whose family members' evidence of individual insurability is unsatisfactory to the insurer are excluded from the calculation. *Id.*

41. *Id.*

42. *Id.*

43. *Id.*

44. *Id.*

policy of life insurance, without disability or supplementary benefits, provided that within 31 days of the termination of the principal policy,[45] the spouse (1) applies for the policy, and (2) pays the first premium to the insurer.[46]

If the group policy is terminated or amended so as to terminate the coverage of any employee or member and such employee or member is entitled to have issued an individual policy under N.J.S.A. 17B:27-20,[47] then the spouse also shall be so entitled subject to certain conditions and limitations.[48]

If the spouse dies within the time period in which he or she is entitled to be issued an individual policy and before such policy becomes effective, the amount of insurance to which the spouse would have been entitled under the individual policy is payable as a claim against the group policy, even if the spouse failed to apply therefore or make the first premium payment.[49]

11-6 Standard Provisions Applicable to Group Policies

No policy of group life insurance may issue in this State unless it contains in substance certain provisions required by statute or provisions at least as favorable to the insured.[50] These include provisions governing grace periods for payments of premiums,[51] contesting the validity of the policy,[52] applications and statements made therein,[53] evidence of insurability,[54] adjustments of premiums

---

45. Subject to the provisions of N.J.S.A. 17B:27-19(a), (b), and (c). *See* §11-7, *infra.*

46. N.J.S.A. 17B:27-9(c).

47. *See* §11-8, *infra.*

48. N.J.S.A. 17B:27-9(c), -20. Application must be made and the first premium paid within 31 days of termination of coverage under the group policy. N.J.S.A. 17B:27-9(c). The group policy may provide that the individual policy may not exceed the lesser of (1) the amount of life insurance under the terminating coverage minus the amount of insurance obtained under another group policy within 31 days; and (2) $2,000. N.J.S.A. 17B:27-20.

49. N.J.S.A. 17B:27-9(c).

50. N.J.S.A. 17B:27-10.

51. N.J.S.A. 17B:27-11. There must be a provision that the policyholder has a 31-day grace period for the payment of any but the first premium. During the grace period, the death benefit coverage continues in force, unless the policyholder gave advance written notice of termination. The policy may require payment of a pro-rata premium for time the policy was in effect during the grace period. *Id.*

52. N.J.S.A. 17B:27-12. There must be a provision that after the policy has been in effect for two years, its validity may not be contested except for non-payment of premiums. No statement by an insured with respect to his insurability may be used in contesting the insurance as to which the statement was made unless (1) the insurance was in effect less than 2 years prior to the contest during the person's lifetime, and (2) the statement is in a written instrument signed by the insured. *Id.*

53. N.J.S.A. 17B:27-13. There must be a provision that a copy of any policyholder's application will be attached to the policy when issued; that all statements by the policyholder or insured are deemed representations and not warranties; and that no statement by an insured will be used in a contest unless a copy of the instrument containing the statement is or has been furnished to the insured or his beneficiary. *Id.*

or benefits because of a misstatement as to the age of the insured,[55] participating policies,[56] payments to the beneficiary,[57] and certificates of insurance.[58]

11-7 Conversion on Termination of Employment or Membership[59]

A group policy must also provide that if an insured ceases to be covered because of the termination of his employment[60] or his membership in the class or classes eligible for coverage, the insurer must issue to him, without evidence of insurability, an individual policy, without disability or supplemental benefits, provided that within 31 days of the termination, the individual applies for the policy and pays the first premium.[61]

---

54. N.J.S.A. 17B:27-14. "There shall be a provision setting forth the conditions, if any, under which the insurer reserves the right to require a person eligible for insurance to furnish evidence of individual insurability satisfactory to the insurer as a condition to part or all of his coverage." *Id.*

55. N.J.S.A. 17B:27-15. In all policies except those where premiums are not based upon age, there must be a provision "specifying an equitable adjustment of premiums or of benefits or of both to be made in the event the age of a person insured has been misstated, such provision to contain a clear statement of the method of adjustment to be used." *Id.*

56. N.J.S.A. 17B:27-16. Participating policies must contain a provision that the policy will participate in the divisible surplus of the insurer as determined annually by the insurer. It must also provide that the policyholder has the right to have the dividend paid in cash unless another option contained in the policy was elected. *Id.*

57. N.J.S.A. 17B:27-17. The policy must include a provision that any money due because of death of the insured will be payable to the designated beneficiary except where the policy contains conditions pertaining to family status. It must further provide that:

> the beneficiary may be the family member specified by the policy terms, subject to the provisions of the policy in the event there is no such designated or specified beneficiary, as to all or any part of the insurance payable, living at the death of the person insured, and subject to any right reserved by the insurer in the policy and set forth in the certificate to pay at its option a part of such sum not exceeding $500 to any person appearing to the insurer to be equitably entitled thereto by reason of having incurred funeral or other expenses incident to the last illness or death of the person insured.

Id.

58. N.J.S.A. 17B:27-18. The policy must provide that the insurer will issue certificates to the policyholder for delivery to the insureds, and that the certificates will set forth: (1) the insurance to which the individual is entitled; (2) to whom the insurance benefits are payable; and (3) the rights and conditions set forth in N.J.S.A. 17B:27-19, -20, and -21 (pertaining to conversion). *Id.*

59. N.J.S.A.17B:27-19.

60. "Termination of employment" includes retirement. *Wells v. Wilbur B. Driver Co.*, 121 N.J. Super. 185 (Law Div. 1972). Notice of termination of employment must be given before the conversion period begins to run. *McKenna v. Prudential Ins. Co.*, 224 N.J. Super. 172 (App. Div. 1988). Accidental death and dismemberment benefits are not covered by the statute. *Gamino v. General Am. Life Ins. Co.*, 288 N.J. super. 125 (App. Div. 1996).

11-8 Conversion on Termination or Amendment of Policy [62]

A group policy must provide that if it terminates or is amended so as to terminate the coverage of any class of insured, every person so affected who has been insured for at least five years prior to the date of termination is entitled to obtain from the insurer an individual insurance policy subject to the conditions and limitations contained in N.J.S.A. 17B:27-19.[63]

11-8:1 Death Within the Conversion Period [64]

A group policy must provide that if an insured dies during the period within which he would have been entitled to have issued to him an individual policy under N.J.S.A. 17B:27-19 or -20,[65] and before such a policy becomes effective, the amount of life insurance to which he would be entitled under the individual policy shall be payable as a claim against the group policy, even if he did not apply for the individual policy or pay the first premium therefor.[66]

11-8:2 Notice of Conversion Rights

An individual insured under a group policy who becomes entitled to have an individual policy issued to him without evidence of insurability, subject to applying and paying the first premium therefor within the specified period, must be given notice of his conversion rights at least 15 days before expiration of the period.[67] If such notice is not given, then the individual has additional time within

---

61. At the option of the individual, the individual policy so issued must be on any one of the forms, except term insurance, customarily issued by the insurer at the age and for the amount applied for. N.J.S.A. 17B:27-19, subsection a. The amount of the individual policy cannot exceed the amount ceasing under the group policy minus the amount of insurance the individual becomes eligible for under another group policy within 31 days; however, any amount of insurance which has become payable as an endowment to the insured on or before the date of termination, is not to be included in the amount considered to be ceasing. *Id.*, subsection b. The premium on the individual policy must be at the insurer's customary rate applicable to the type and amount of the policy relative to the insured's age and class of risk. *Id.*, subsection c.

62. N.J.S.A. 17B:27-20.

63. *See* §11-12 (a), *infra.* However, the group policy may provide that the amount of the individual policy cannot exceed the lesser of (a) the amount of the individual's life insurance coverage ceasing because of termination or amendment of the group policy less the amount of any insurance for which he is or becomes eligible under a group policy issued or reinstated by the same or another insurer within 31 days of the termination, or (b) $2,000. N.J.S.A. 17B:27-20.

64. N.J.S.A. 17B:27-21.

65. *See* §§11-7 and 11-8, *supra.*

66. N.J.S.A. 17B:27-21. Accidental death and dismemberment benefits are not covered by the statutes which require conversion privileges on employment termination, and thus no benefits are due under N.J.S.A. 17B:27-21 if the insured dies during what would otherwise be the continuation period. *Gamino v. General Am. Life Ins. Co.*, 288 N.J. super. 125 (App. Div. 1996).

which to exercise that right[68] —at least 15 days after the individual is given notice, but no more than 60 days after the expiration of the initial period.[69]

The notice requirement is satisfied by written notice presented to the individual, or mailed by the policyholder to the individual's last known address.[70]

II. GROUP HEALTH INSURANCE

11-9 General Requirements

A group health insurance policy may be issued to an employer, to the trustees of a fund established by one or more employers, to a labor union, to an association formed for reasons other than obtaining such insurance, or to the trustees of a fund established by one or more labor unions or by one or more employers and one or more labor unions, for the purpose of insuring employees and union members.[71]

The term "employees" may be defined in the policy to include as employees of a single employer the employees of one or more subsidiary corporations, and the employees, individual proprietors and partners of affiliated corporations, individual proprietorships, and partnerships, if their business and the business of the principal employer is under common control.[72]

The term "employees" may also be defined to include the individual proprietor or partners of an individual proprietorship or partnership.[73]

"Employees" may include retired employees.[74]

A policy issued to the trustees of a fund may define "employees" to include the trustees and their employees or both, if their duties are principally connected to

---

67. N.J.S.A. 17B:27-24.

68. The additional time under this section is solely for the purpose of exercising the right to convert. It does not continue coverage. "[N]othing herein shall be construed to continue any insurance under the policy beyond the period provided in the policy." N.J.S.A. 17B:27-24. *See Wells v. Wilbur B. Driver Co.*, 121 N.J. Super. 185, 196-202 (Law Div. 1972) (benefits continue for the 31-day period set forth in the then-equivalent of N.J.S.A. 17B:27-21, and not for the period under N.J.S.A. 17B:27-24; however, where employee did not receive notice of the date of termination of employment or of the fact that insurance premiums on his behalf had ceased, employee continued as insured under policy).

69. N.J.S.A. 17B:27-24.

70. The 31-day period begins to run from the date an employee is notified of the termination of his employment, not of his right to convert. *McKenna v. Prudential Ins. Co.*, 224 N.J. Super. 172 (App. Div. 1988).

71. N.J.S.A. 17B:27-27.

72. N.J.S.A. 17B:27-31.

73. *Id. Cf.* N.J.S.A. 17B:27-2(a) (providing that an individual proprietor or partners may be considered employees under group life insurance only if they are actively engaged in and devote a substantial amount of time to the business).

74. N.J.S.A. 17B:27-31.

the trusteeship.[75] A policy issued to trustees of a fund established by the members of an employers' association may define "employees" to include association employees.[76]

An insurer may not consider a person's eligibility for medical assistance pursuant to P.L.1968, c. 413 (C. 30:40D-1 *et seq.*), or the equivalent in another state, in determining eligibility for a policy providing hospital or medical benefits.[77]

Every group policy must provide benefits for treatment of cancer by dose-intensive chemotherapy/autologous bone marrow transplants and peripheral blood stem cell transplants to the same extent as for any other illness under the policy.[78] If a policy provides maternity benefits, it must provide at least 48 hours of in-patient care following a vaginal delivery and 96 hours of in-patient care following a cesarean section for the mother and newly born child, so long as the such care is medically necessary or requested by the mother.[79] Written notice of this requirement must be provided.[80] Certain diabetes treatment, self-management education, equipment, and supplies must be provided by every group health insurance policy.[81] Expenses insured in conducting a Pap smear must also be covered by group health insurance policies providing benefits for groups of greater than 49 persons.[82]

11-10 Dependents

A policy may provide for payment of benefits on behalf of family members or dependents of insured employees.[83] Any such policy must provide that in the event of the death of the insured employee, covered family members or dependents will continue to have coverage for at least an additional 180 days, subject to the payment of the necessary premium, and subject to the policy provision governing termination of coverage for reasons other than the death of the insured employee.[84]

---

75. *Id.*
76. *Id.*
77. N.J.S.A. 17B:27-36.1.
78. N.J.S.A. 17B:27-46.1j.
79. N.J.S.A. 17B:27-46.1k.
80. *Id.*
81. N.J.S.A. 17B:27-46.1m.
82. N.J.S.A. 17B:27-46.1n.
83. N.J.S.A. 17B:27-30.
84. N.J.S.A. 17B:27-30

Coverage of a family member or other dependent of an insured employee may terminate upon his or her attainment of a specific age. However, coverage may not terminate with respect to any such family member or dependent who, prior to the age of 19, becomes incapable of self-sustaining employment because of mental retardation or physical handicap and is chiefly dependent upon the employee for support and maintenance.[85] Coverage must continue while the employee's insurance remains in force and the family member or dependent remains in that condition.[86] The employee must submit proof of the dependent's incapacity within 31 days of the dependent reaching the termination age.[87]

If dependent coverage is available for hospital or medical expenses, coverage of children may not be denied on grounds of the child's birth out of wedlock, failure to be claimed on insured's federal tax return, or failure to reside with the insured.[88] If a child has coverage through a noncustodial parent, the insurer must provide adequate information to the custodial parent as is necessary for the child to obtain benefits, permit the custodial parent to submit claims without the approval of the non-custodial parent, and make payments on claims directly to the custodial parent, provider, or state agency, as appropriate.[89]

When a parent/insured is eligible for dependent coverage and is required by court or administrative order to provide health insurance for the child, the insurer must allow the child to enroll regardless of enrollment season restrictions, permit the child's other parent (or the state) to enroll the child if the parent/insured fails to do so, and not terminate the child's coverage unless the parent/insured provides written evidence that the order is no longer in effect or that the child will be enrolled in comparable benefits plan.[90]

Certain blood lead and child immunizations must be covered by all group health insurance policies providing hospital or medical expense benefits for group of more than 49 members.[91]

---

85. *Id.*

86. *Id.*

87. *Id.* The provisions of this section do "not require an insurer to insure a dependent who is a mentally retarded or physically handicapped child of an employee or other member of the insured group where such dependent does not satisfy the conditions of the group policy as to any requirements for evidence of insurability or other provisions as may be stated in the group policy required for coverage thereunder to take effect. In any such case the terms of the policy shall apply with regard to the coverage or exclusion from coverage of such dependent."

88. N.J.S.A. 17B:27-30.1(a); N.J.S.A. 17B:27-30.3(a).

89. N.J.S.A. 17B:27-30.1(b); N.J.S.A. 17B:27-30.3(a).

90. N.J.S.A. 17B:27-30.1(c); N.J.S.A. 17B:27-30.3(a).

91. N.J.S.A. 17B:27-46.11.

11-11 Standard Provisions

No policy of group health insurance may issue in this State unless it contains in substance certain provisions required by statute[92] or provisions at least as favorable.[93] These include provisions governing applications and statements made therein,[94] policy changes,[95] new entrants,[96] premium payments,[97] certificates of insurance,[98] age limits,[99] written notice of sickness or loss,[100] written proof of loss of time for disability,[101] forms for proof of loss,[102] examinations and autopsy,[103] time for payment of benefits,[104] beneficiaries and assignment of benefits,[105] and time limits for commencing civil actions.[106] There are also required provisions regarding benefits for alcoholism,[107] reconstructive breast surgery,[108] second and third surgical opinions,[109] hemophilia,[110] mammograms,[111] benefits for the treatment of cancer by dose–intensive chemotherapy/autologous bone

---

92. N.J.S.A. 17B:27-34 to -46.

93. N.J.S.A. 17B:27-23 and 17B:27-47.

94. N.J.S.A. 17B:27-34.

95. N.J.S.A. 17B:27-35.

96. N.J.S.A. 17B:27-36. New entrants may not be excluded or have their rates changed because of actual or expected health conditions or on the basis of genetic characteristic. N.J.S.A 17B:27-36.2. A "Genetic Characteristic" is any inherited gene or chromosome, or alteration thereof, that is scientifically or medically believed to predispose an individual to a disease, disorder or syndrome, or to be associated with statistically increased risk of development of a disease, disorder or syndrome. Id.

97. N.J.S.A. 17B:27-37.

98. N.J.S.A. 17B:27-38.

99. N.J.S.A. 17B:27-39.

100. N.J.S.A. 17B:27-40.

101. N.J.S.A. 17B:27-41.

102. N.J.S.A. 17B:27-42.

103. N.J.S.A. 17B:27-43.

104. N.J.S.A. 17B:27-44.

105. N.J.S.A. 17B:27-45.

106. N.J.S.A. 17B:27-46.

107. All group and individual contracts of insurance providing hospital or medical expense benefits must provide benefits for expenses incurred in connection with the treatment of alcoholism when the treatment is prescribed by a doctor of medicine. N.J.S.A. 17B:27-46.1. Benefits shall be provided to the same extent as for any other sickness under the contract. *Id.* Every contract must provide benefits for (a) inpatient or out-patient care at a licensed hospital; (b) treatment at a licensed detoxification facility; (c) confinement as an inpatient or out-patient at a licensed, certified, or state-approved residential treatment facility, under a program that meets minimum standards of care equivalent to those set by the Joint Commission on Hospital Accreditation. *Id.*

108. N.J.S.A. 17B:27-46.1a. All group health insurance policies providing hospital or medical expense benefits must provide benefits for reconstructive breast surgery, including but not limited to: (1) costs of prostheses; (2) following a single or double mastectomy, surgery to restore and achieve symmetry; and (3) under any policy providing outpatient x-ray or radiation therapy, the costs of outpatient chemotherapy following surgical procedures for the treatment of breast cancer. *Id.*

109. N.J.S.A. 17B:27-46.2 through -46.9.

marrow transplants and peripheral blood stem cell transplants when performed by institutions approved by the National Cancer Institute or pursuant to protocols consistent with the guidelines of the American Society of Clinical Oncologists, and pre-existing conditions.[112] Of particular note is the requirement that maternity benefits be made available to women without regard to their marital status, and that the extent of benefits for pregnancy and childbirth be the same as for other covered illnesses.[113]

11-12 Continuation Upon Total Disability

(a) General Requirements

A group policy that insures employees and their dependents for hospital, surgical or major medical insurance on an expense incurred or service basis, other than policies limited to specific diseases or accidental injuries, must provide that an employee whose insurance would otherwise terminate because of termination of employment due to the total disability of the employee is entitled to continue his coverage under the group policy, for himself and his dependents.[114]

Continuation is available only to those employees who have been continuously insured under the group policy during the entire 3-month period ending with the termination.[115]

An employee is entitled to continuation notwithstanding his eligibility or coverage under Medicare, subject to provisions in the group policy governing non-duplication of benefits.[116]

Continuation applies to other benefits provided by the group policy, including dental, eye care, or prescriptions.[117]

An employee electing to continue under the group policy must pay each month, in advance, the amount of contribution required by the employer or policyholder, but not more than the group rate.[118] An employee must give written

110. N.J.S.A. 17B:27-46.1c. Policies that provide benefits for the treatment of hemophilia must also provide benefits for expenses for home treatment of bleeding episodes, including the purchase of blood products and blood infusion equipment. *Id.*

111. N.J.S.A. 178:27-46.1f.

112. N.J.S.A. 17B:27-46.1d, -46.1j.

113. N.J.S.A. 17B:27-46.1b.

114. N.J.S.A. 17B:27-51.12.

115. N.J.S.A. 17B:27-51.12(a).

116. N.J.S.A. 17B:27-51.12(b).

117. N.J.S.A. 17B:27-51.12(c).

118. N.J.S.A. 17B:27-51.12(d).

notice of his election and pay the first month's contribution, within 31 days of the date his insurance would otherwise terminate.[119]

11-12:1 Termination of Continued Insurance

Continuation of insurance will terminate if:

1. The former employee fails to make timely payment of the required contribution. Coverage will continue through the period for which contributions were made.[120]
2. The employee becomes employed and eligible for benefits under another group policy of health insurance; in the case of a qualified dependent, if the dependent becomes employed and eligible for such benefits.[121]
3. The group policy is terminated or the employer terminates participation in the group policy.[122] However, the employee has the right to coverage under any new group policy obtained by the employer for as long as he would have remained covered under the old policy if it had not terminated.[123] The minimum level of benefits available under the new policy must be the applicable level of benefits under the old policy reduced by any benefits payable under that policy.[124]

The old policy must continue to provide benefits to the extent of liabilities and extension of benefits already accrued as if it continued in force.[125]

11-12:2 Notification

Notification of the privilege of continuation must be included in each certificate of coverage.[126]

---

119. *Id.*
120. N.J.S.A. 17B:27-51.12(e)(1).
121. N.J.S.A. 17B:27-51.12(e)(2).
122. N.J.S.A. 17B:27-51.12(e)(3).
123. N.J.S.A. 17B:27-51.12(e)(3)(a).
124. N.J.S.A. 17B:27-51.12(e)(3)(b).
125. N.J.S.A. 17B:27-51.12(e)(3)(c).
126. N.J.S.A. 17B:27-51.12 (f).

Chapter 12

Successor Liability

12-1 Introduction

Whether a company that assumes the business or assets of another also assumes its liabilities is determined by principles of successor liability.[1] Traditionally, successor liability has been determined by strict rules dependent on the form of the transfer and rigidly applied criteria. These rules increasingly have given way to case-by-case balancing of relevant policies and factors.[2]

New Jersey courts have not yet articulated in a reported decision the approach to successor liability to be followed in a case involving liability arising out of the employer-employee relationship. It is likely, however, that New Jersey law will be construed to require some continuity of identity between the predecessor and successor employers, extending beyond merely the continuation of business operations, before imposing such liability on the successor. This approach would be consistent with New Jersey successor liability law as applied in tort cases other than those involving strict liability, with the successor liability analysis applied under federal law in labor and employment cases, and with the analogous alter ego analysis applied by the New Jersey Supreme Court in cases arising under anti-discrimination laws.

12-2 Traditional Rules in New Jersey

Under New Jersey law, corporate successor liability generally depends on the structure of the acquisition: If a corporation is acquired through statutory merger

---

1. *See generally* 15 *Fletcher Cyclopedia Corp.* §§7102 *et seq.* (1990 rev.).

2. *See generally id.* §7122.60, at p. 261, and Blumberg, *The Law of Corporate Groups, Statutory Law-General*, §14.07, at pp. 510-11 (1989) (both discussing successor liability for employment discrimination).

or consolidation,[3] the successor corporation becomes liable for all obligations and liabilities of the predecessor or purchased corporation.[4]

Subject to certain exceptions, however, the purchaser of business assets does not become liable for the debts and liabilities of the seller.[5] Under traditional rules, the purchaser assumes the seller's debts and liabilities only if one of four exceptions is met: "(1) the purchaser expressly or impliedly agrees to assume such debts and liabilities; (2) the transaction amounts to a consolidation or merger of the seller and purchaser; (3) the purchasing corporation is merely a continuance of the selling corporation; or (4) the transaction is entered into fraudulently in order to escape liability for such debts" or is not supported by adequate consideration.[6]

The exceptions to nonliability in the cases of a *de facto* merger and a continuance of the selling corporation focus on whether there is an identity of ownership and management of the predecessor and successor corporations. A *de facto* merger is characterized by a "transfer or sale of all assets, exchange of stocks, change of ownership whereby stockholders, officers and creditors go to the surviving corporation, and assumption of a variety of liabilities pursuant to previously negotiated agreements."[7] A continuance of the selling corporation giving rise to successor liability is characterized by "use of the same name, at the same location, with the same employees and common identity of stockholders and directors."[8] The requirements for each exception traditionally have been applied strictly. Neither the purchase of all tangible and intangible assets, nor the continuation of the transferor's operations, nor both together, is sufficient to support successor liability in the absence of continuity of ownership and management.[9] "For liability to attach, the purchasing corporation must represent merely a 'new hat' for the seller."[10]

---

3. *See* N.J.S.A. 14A:10-1 *et seq.*

4. N.J.S.A. 14A:10-6(e); *New Jersey Dept. of Environmental Protection v. Ventron Corp.*, 94 N.J. 473, 503 (1983). *See generally Brotherton v. Celotex Corp.*, 202 N.J. Super. 148, 153-154 (Law Div. 1985); *Dept. of Transportation v. PSC Resources, Inc.*, 175 N.J. Super. 447, 453 (Law Div. 1980).

5. *Jackson v. New Jersey Mfrs. Ins. Co.*, 166 N.J. Super. 448, 454 (App. Div.), *certif. denied*, 81 N.J. 330 (1979) (citing cases).

6. *Jackson v. New Jersey Mfrs. Ins. Co.*, 166 N.J. Super. 448, 454-55 (App.Div.), *certif. denied*, 81 N.J. 330 (1979). *See also Dept. of Transportation v. PSC Resources, Inc.*, 175 N.J. Super. at 453; *McKee v. Harris Seybold Co.*, 109 N.J. Super. 555, 561-562 (Law Div. 1970), *aff'd on other grounds*, 118 N.J. Super. 480 (App. Div. 1972).

7. *Wilson v. Fare Well Corp.*, 140 N.J. Super. 476, 485 (Law Div. 1976).

8. *Id.* at 485-86.

9. *McKee v. Harris Seybold Co.*, 109 N.J. Super. 555, 566-67, 570 (Law Div. 1970), *aff'd on other grounds*, 118 N.J. Super. 480 (App. Div. 1972).

10. *Id.* at 570.

Reacting to a perceived unfairness of traditional successor liability rules as applied to the tort plaintiff, the court in *Wilson v. Fare Well Corp.* adopted a "more modern approach" to successor liability in product liability cases—the "continuation test":

> [T]he most relevant factor is the degree to which the predecessor's business entity remains intact. The more a corporation physically resembles its predecessor, the more reasonable it is to hold the successor fully responsible. In this way, the innocent, injured consumer is protected without the possibility of being left without a remedy due to the subsequent corporate history of the manufacturer.[11]

This approach essentially entails balancing the policies supporting providing relief to the injured plaintiff with considerations of fairness to the successor corporation. Under this approach, successor liability requires sufficient similarities between the predecessor and successor corporations that the one may be fairly identified with the other.[12] The sufficiency of the similarities is to be determined on a case-by-case basis.[13] The rationale of the approach is that "a corporate entity which enjoys all the benefits of an ongoing concern also should assume its burdens" if the predecessor concern is rendered defunct by the transfer.[14]

In *Ramirez v. Amsted Industries, Inc.*[15] and *Nieves v. Bruno Sherman Corp.*,[16] decided on the same day, the New Jersey Supreme Court went one step further. The Court rejected any requirement of corporate identity between the predecessor and successor corporations to hold the successor strictly liable in tort for a defective product manufactured by a company that was rendered defunct by the transfer of its manufacturing assets.[17] Extending the policies underlying strict tort liability, the Court adopted a "product line" test of successor liability.[18] This test focuses exclusively on the successor's continuation of the "actual manufacturing operation" without regard to commonality of ownership or management.[19] An analogous standard has been applied respecting strict liability for environmental torts,[20] and suggested in the context of strict liability for defective

---

11. *Wilson v. Fare Well Corp.*, 140 N.J. Super. at 490. *See Brotherton v. Celotex Corp.*, 202 N.J. Super. 148, 157 (Law Div. 1985); *Dept. of Transportation v. PSC Resources, Inc.*, 175 N.J. Super. 447, 457 (Law Div. 1980).

12. *Brotherton v. Celotex Corp.*, 202 N.J. Super. 148, 156 (Law Div. 1985).

13. *Id.* at 159.

14. *Id.* at 157.

15. 86 N.J. 332 (1981).

16. 86 N.J. 361 (1981).

business premises.[21] In *Mettinger v. Globe Slicing Mach. Co. Inc.*,[22] the Court reaffirmed the successor liability standard as set forth in *Ramirez* and *Nieves*, and further extended the product-line exception to include a distributor and retailer's right to seek indemnification from successor corporations.[23]

The successor liability standard adopted in *Ramirez* and *Nieves* is not always applicable. It may make sense to reject the corporate identity requirement completely when the underlying basis of liability is strict liability in tort, in which the focus is on the condition of a product or property rather than on the predecessor's conduct. When liability is based on negligence or other culpable conduct of the predecessor, and particularly when the predecessor's *mens rea* is relevant, some identity between the predecessor and successor should still be required to justify holding the successor liable. Thus, considering the liability of a successor for punitive tort damages, the court in *Brotherton v. Celotex Corp.*,[24] distinguished

---

17. When the predecessor corporation remains viable, the justification for imposing strict liability on the successor corporation is nullified. *See LaPollo v. General Electric Co.*, 664 F. Supp. 178, 184 (D.N.J. 1987) (applying New Jersey law); *Wilkerson v. C.O. Porter Machinery*, 237 N.J. Super. 282, 290 n.8 (Law Div. 1989); *Holloway v. Slate*, 237 N.J. Super. 71 (Law Div. 1989). In *Alloway v. General Marine Indus., L.P.*, 288 N.J. Super. 479, 490 (App. Div. 1996), *rev'd*, 149 N.J. 620 (1997), the court rejected the argument that *Ramirez* is limited to suits involving personal injury to plaintiffs. However, the New Jersey Supreme Court reversed the Appellate Division, holding that tort principles, such as strict liability and negligence, are better suited to claims for personal injury or property damage, while contract principles should be applied to claims for economic loss. *See Alloway v. General Marine Inds.*, 149 N.J. 620, 627 (1997). The Court specifically stated that it need not reach the issue of successor liability under *Ramirez*. *See id.* at 643.

18. *Ramirez v. Amsted Industries, Inc.*, 86 N.J. 332, 347-348 (1981).

19. *Id.* at 347-348. *See also Velasquez v. Franz*, 123 N.J. 498, 529 (1991) (Stein, J. dissenting). In *Ramirez v. Amsted Indus., Inc.*, 86 N.J. 332 (1981), the New Jersey Supreme Court identified the "virtual destruction of the plaintiff's remedies against the original manufacturer caused by the successor's acquisition of the business" as part of the rationale for imposing successor liability. *Id.* at 349. Nonetheless, other courts subsequently dispensed with any requirement of such a causal relationship between the asset transfer and the predecessor's demise:

> It is the fact of nonviability that supports the imposition of liability. Any discussion with regard to the reasons for the demise of the predecessor is irrelevant.

Pacius v. Thermtroll Corp., 259 N.J. Super. 51, 56 (Law Div. 1992). *Accord Bussell v. DeWalt Products Corp.*, 259 N.J. Super. 499, 519 (App. Div. 1992). *Cf. Goncalves v. Wire Technology*, 253 N.J. Super. 327, 330-34 (Ch. Div. 1991). These courts relied on the risk-spreading rationale underlying the New Jersey Supreme Court's approach to successor liability in *Ramirez* and *Nieves v. Bruno Sherman Corp.*, 86 N.J. 361 (1981). Therefore, their holdings are logically limited to defining the scope of successor liability in strict liability contexts. *But see Saez v. S&S Corrugated Paper Mach. Co. Inc.*, 302 N.J. Super. 545, 558 (App. Div. 1997) (noting that *Pacius*' expansion of the successor liability standard was very expansive, and that "So broad a test would be no test at all.")

20. *Dept. of Transportation v. PSC Resources, Inc.*, 175 N.J. Super. 447, 461-462, 470 (Law Div. 1980).

21. *Brown v. Racquet Club of Bricktown*, 95 N.J. 280, 300 (1984) (Schreiber, J., concurring in part and dissenting in part).

22. 153 N.J. 371 (1998).

23. *See id.* at 385. ("Consequently, we hold that, absent an agreement to the contrary, distributors and retailers may use the product-line exception to seek indemnification from corporations that purchased all or substantially all of the original manufacturer's assets and undertook essentially the same manufacturing operation as that corporation.")

Ramirez.[25] The court applied instead the "continuation test" as adopted in *Wilson v. Fare Well Corp.*[26] Although *Wilson* had involved strict liability in tort, the court in *Brotherton* reasoned that the continuation test's requirement of a sufficient degree of identity struck "a fair balance between an individual's recovery and a corporation's liability in situations where the actual wrongdoer no longer exists and the successor is sufficiently connected to the culpable conduct."[27]

12-3 Successor Liability for Employment Practices

New Jersey courts have not yet addressed the standard for successor liability for the employment practices of a predecessor.[28] Where that standard lies in the spectrum between traditional rules and the principles announced in *Ramirez*[29] is not altogether clear. While the traditional rules of successor liability may no longer apply in strict liability tort cases under common law, liability for employment practices often is statutory and, even when under common law, is not uniquely based in either tort or contract.[30]

Further, unlike strict liability for a defective product, liability for employment practices generally focuses on an employer's conduct and requires some element of *mens rea*, such as discriminatory intent. Also, unlike the plaintiff in a product liability case who may never have had the opportunity to seek relief against the predecessor corporation because the injury may not have been suffered until long after the predecessor's business was acquired, the plaintiff who complains of adverse employment actions by a predecessor corporation more likely will have

---

24. 202 N.J. Super. 148 (Law Div. 1985).

25. *Id.* at 157-59.

26. 140 N.J. Super. 476 (Law Div. 1976).

27. 202 N.J. Super. at 157. *See also id.* at 159.

28. The question of successor employer liability is addressed expressly under New Jersey law in at least one respect. N.J.A.C. 12:18-2.36 provides a broad standard of successor employer responsibility for a predecessor's liability under the Unemployment Compensation Law, N.J.S.A. 43:21-1 *et seq.*, for assessments for refunds to workers of contributions to the Unemployment Compensation Fund, for the Disability Benefits Fund, and for administration costs:

> Any employer who acquires the organization, trade, assets or business, in whole or in part, whether by merger, consolidation, sale, transfer, descent or otherwise, from an employer liable for any assessment made under N.J.S.A. 43:21-7(d)(3), N.J.S.A. 43:21-46 and N.J.S.A. 43:21-48 shall likewise be liable for such assessment.

29. *Ramirez v. Amsted Industries, Inc.*, 86 N.J. 332 (1981).

30. *See Pierce v. Ortho Pharmaceutical Corp.*, 84 N.J. 58, 72 (1980) (a common law cause of action for wrongful discharge in violation of public policy may be stated in tort, contract or both); *EEOC v. Vucitech*, 842 F.2d 936, 945 (7th Cir. 1988) (suggesting that successor liability for an unfair labor practice or employment discrimination—"a tort in a labor context"—is a "mixed case" not clearly subject to the successor liability doctrine as developed in either tort or labor contract contexts).

had the opportunity to seek relief against that corporation. But the policies favoring successor liability may be strong. New Jersey courts have emphasized, for example, that the public policy underlying its anti-discrimination laws should not be frustrated by changes in corporate form or other devices, "whether innocent or subtly purposeful."[31]

The question of successor employer liability has been addressed by the federal courts. The successor analysis first developed in federal labor law actions[32] has been applied also to determine successor liability for employment discrimination.[33] Under this analysis, the court considers several indicia of continuity:

1. Whether there has been a substantial continuity of the same business operation;
2. Whether the new employer uses the same plant or equipment;
3. Whether the same or substantially the same work force is employed;
4. Whether the same jobs exist under the same working conditions;
5. Whether the same supervisors are employed;
6. Whether the same machinery, equipment, and methods of production are used; and
7. Whether the same product is manufactured or the same service is offered.[34]

---

31. *Jones v. Haridor Realty Corp.*, 37 N.J. 384, 395-96 (1962). *See Frank v. Ivy Club*, 120 N.J. 73 (1990) ("All facts must be carefully reviewed so that '[no] device, whether innocent or subtly purposeful, can be permitted to frustrate the legislative determination to prevent discrimination.' "), *cert. denied*, 498 U.S. 1073 (1991). *Jackson v. Concord Co.*, 101 N.J. Super. 126, 130 (App. Div. 1968) (individual owners and officers of corporation that had refused housing on the basis of race were held to have been properly subject to orders of the Division of Civil Rights enjoining further discrimination: "Effective implementation of the Division's orders required that the individuals concerned be included in the findings and orders. Otherwise a new corporate shield could be formed to evade the Division's rulings."), *aff'd in relevant part and rev'd on other grounds*, 54 N.J. 113, 121 (1969). *But cf. American Bell, Inc. v. Federation of Tel. Workers*, 736 F.2d 879, 886-87 (3d Cir. 1984) (federal labor policy does not require a less demanding standard for piercing the corporate veil to hold a transferee corporation bound by the collective bargaining agreement signed by the transferor, although both were subsidiaries of a common corporate parent).

32. *I.e.*, under §301 of the Labor Management Relations Act, 1947, 29 U.S.C. 185, and under the National Labor Relations Act, 29 U.S.C. §§151 *et seq.* Successor liability under federal labor law is discussed at length in Hardin, 1 *The Developing Labor Law*, ch. 15 (3d ed. 1992 & Supp. 1997).

33. *See Rojas v. TK Communications, Inc.*, 87 F.3d 745, 749 (5th Cir. 1996); *EEOC v. MacMillan Bloedel Containers, Inc.*, 503 F.2d 1086, 1093-94 (6th Cir. 1974). *See also Criswell v. Delta Air Lines, Inc.*, 869 F.2d 449, 450 (9th Cir. 1989); *Wheeler v. Snyder Buick, Inc.*, 794 F.2d 1228, 1236 (7th Cir. 1986); *Trujillo v. Longhorn Mfg. Co.*, 694 F.2d 221, 224-25 (10th Cir. 1982); *Dominquez v. Bartenders Local 64*, 674 F.2d 732, 733-34 (8th Cir. 1982). *See generally* Schlei & Grossman, *Employment Discrimination Law*, pp. 1102-03 (2d ed. 1983), and five year cum. supp. at p. 418 (1988); 15 *Fletcher Cyclopedia Corp.* §7122.60, p.261 (990 rev.); Kevin W. Brown, Annotation, *Liability Under Title VII of Civil Rights Act of 1964 (42 USCS §§2000e et seq.) Of Employer, As Successor Employers, For Discriminatory Employment Practices of Predecessor*, 67 A.L.R. Fed. 806 (1984).

In addition, courts in employment discrimination cases have considered the ability of the predecessor to provide relief and whether the successor had notice of the administrative charge, if any, filed against the predecessor company.[35] The gist of the analysis is whether there is a "continuity of enterprise"[36] or "substantial continuity of identity"[37] between the successor and predecessor corporations, rather than a mere continuation of business operations.

Accordingly, "[n]o one of these factors is controlling; the court must look at all of them along with any others that present themselves in the case before it, and it must make its decision by balancing the interests of the plaintiff and the national policy of abhorrence toward employment discrimination against the interests of the successor...."[38] But the Fifth Circuit has stated that whether the successor company had notice and whether the predecessor company has the ability to provide relief are "critical." "The remaining seven [factors] simply 'provide a foundation for analyzing the larger question of whether there is a continuity in operations and the work force of the successor and predecessor employers.' "[39]

In the development of law under the State's Law Against Discrimination (LAD), New Jersey courts previously have looked to analogous developments under federal anti-discrimination laws.[40] Other considerations also suggest that New Jersey courts would look to the federal successor liability analysis for guidance in formulating standards of successor liability under the LAD or otherwise in the context of employment law.

The factors considered under the federal successor liability analysis are similar to those considered by the New Jersey Supreme Court to determine the interdependence of ostensibly separate entities or operations for jurisdictional purposes under the LAD.[41] Similarly, discussing the possible effect of a labor agreement

---

34. *Systems Mgmt., Inc. v. NLRB*, 901 F.2d 297, 303-04 (3d Cir. 1990). *See Stardyne, Inc. v. NLRB*, 41 F.3d 141, 145 (3d Cir. 1994) (applying *Systems Management Inc. v. NLRB* standard in finding successorship status).

35. *E.g.*, *Kolosky v. Anchor Hocking Co.*, 585 F. Supp. 746, 748-49 (W.D. Pa. 1983) (holding that jurisdiction over successor corporation was warranted to enable award of prospective relief under Title VII). *Rojas v. TK Communications, Inc.*, 87 F.3d 745, 750 (5th Cir. 1996) (setting forth all nine factors); *EEOC v. G-K-G*, Inc., 39 F.3d 740, 747-48 (7th Cir. 1994) (finding that a plaintiff may hold a successor corporation liable for a violation of federal rights if the successor had notice of the claim before the acquisition, if there is "substantial continuity in the operation of the business before and after the sale, and...if no major changes are made in that operation.").

36. *Systems Mgmt., Inc. v. NLRB*, 901 F.2d at 303. *See Stardyne*, 41 F.3d at 145 (applying *Systems Management Inc.* standard in finding successorship status).

37. *Kolosky v. Anchor Hocking Co.*, 585 F. Supp. at 749.

38. *Id.* quoting *Brown v. Evening News Assoc.*, 473 F. Supp. 1242, 1245 (E.D. Mich. 1979).

39. *Rojas v. TK Communications, Inc.*, 87 F.3d 745, 750 (5th Cir. 1990).

40. *See Peper v. Princeton Univ. Bd. of Trustees*, 77 N.J. 55, 81 (1978) (adopting under the LAD the standards of proof of discrimination developed by federal courts under Title VII); Chapter 4, §4-32.

on an alleged alter ego of the signing employer, the Court described the federal law of successor employer liability as "[c]onsistent with" New Jersey law concerning the potential disregard of separate corporate forms.[42]

Further, the successor liability analysis developed by the federal courts in the labor and employment contexts appears to approximate that contemplated under the "continuation theory" adopted and applied by the New Jersey courts in *Wilson v. Fare Well Corp.*[43] and *Brotherton v. Celotex Corp.*[44]

It thus appears likely that the New Jersey courts would adopt a successor employer liability analysis similar to that articulated by the federal courts in labor and employment cases. While the standard for successor liability under such an analysis would not be as strict as under traditional successor liability rules, it would not be satisfied by a continuation only of business operations. Rather, it would require sufficient continuity "that it may be fairly inferred that the successor and predecessor reasonably expected that the successor would be bound" by the predecessor's employment practices.[45]

---

41. *See Frank v. Ivy Club*, 120 N.J. 73, 102-104, 110 (1990), *cert. denied*, 498 U.S. 1073, 111 S.Ct. 799, 112 L.Ed. 20 860 (1991) (holding that "functional interdependence" of defendant private clubs and university deprived those clubs of their private status); *Fraser v. Robin Dee Day Camp*, 44 N.J. 480, 489-90 (1965) (finding that day camp, private school and nursery facilities "were so interdependent and intermingled that they were in effect one unitary operation" subject in their entirety to the LAD).

42. *See Laborers' Local Union v. Interstate Curb & Sidewalk*, 90 N.J. 456, 464-65 (1982).

This similarity parallels that between the federal "continuity of identity" analysis and the federal "single employer" analysis, developed to determine when separate operations may be treated as unitary for jurisdictional or liability purposes under federal labor and anti-discrimination laws. For applications of the "single employer" analysis under Title VII and the ADEA, *see Lusk v. Foxmeyer Health Corp.*, 129 F.3d 773, 777 (5th Cir.. 1997) (applying single employer test under the ADEA); *Switalski v. International Ass'n of Bridge, Structural & Ornamental Iron Workers*, 881 F.Supp. 205, 207 (W.D. Pa. 1995) (applying single entity test under Title VII). *Chaiffetz v. Robertson Research Holding Ltd.*, 798 F.2d 731, 735 (5th Cir. 1986) (Title VII); *Mas Marques v. Digital Equipment Corp.*, 637 F.2d 24, 27 (1st Cir. 1980) (Title VII); *Saulsberry v. Atlantic Richfield Co.*, 673 F. Supp. 811, 815 (N.D. Miss. 1987) (Title VII); *Beckwith v. International Mill Services*, 617 F. Supp. 187, 189 (E.D. Pa. 1985) (ADEA); *Nation v. Winn-Dixie Stores, Inc.*, 567 F. Supp. 997, 1010-11, *judgment reaffirmed*, 570 F. Supp. 1473 (N.D. Ga. 1983) (Title VII).

43. 140 N.J. Super. 476 (Law Div. 1976).

44. 202 N.J. Super. 148 (Law Div. 1985). *But see Baker v. Nat'l State Bank*, 312 N.J. 268 (App. Div.), *certif. granted*, 156 N.J. 425 (1998), in which the court held that a successor corporation could be liable for punitive damages of its predecessor. The court relied on the legislature's statement of intent that damages be available to all persons protected by the LAD, as well as N.J.S.A. 14A:10-6(e), which provides that when merger or consolidation of two corporations becomes effective, the new corporation shall be liable for all the obligations and liabilities of the prior corporations, and that "any claim existing or action or proceeding pending by or against any of such corporations may be enforced as if such merger or consolidation had not taken place." *Id.* at 292.

45. 15 *Fletcher Cyc. Corp.*, §7122.60, at p. 261 (1990 rev.).

Table of Cases

Citation Abbreviations

A.L.R. (2nd, 3d)	American Law Reports Annotated (Second, Third)
A. (A.2d)	Atlantic Reporter (2d Series)
Cal App. 3d	California Appellate Reports, Third Series
Cal. Rptr.	California Reporter
EBC	Employee Benefits Cases
Ed. Law Rep.	Education Law Reporter
E.P.D.	Employment Practice Decisions
F. (F.2d)	Federal Reporter (2d Series)
FEP	Fair Employment Practice Cases
F.R.D.	Federal Rules Decisions
Fed. R. Evid. Serv.	Federal Rules of Evidence Service
Fed R. Serv (2d, 3d)	Federal Rules Service (Second, Third Series)
F. Supp	Federal Supplement
IER	Individual Employment Rights Cases
Lexis	LEXIS
L.C.	Labor Cases
L.Ed	U.S. Supreme Court Reports, Lawyers' Edition
L.R.R.M.	Labor Relations Reference Manual
N.J.A.R. (2d)	New Jersey Administrative Reports (Second Edition)
N.J.	New Jersey Reports
N.J.Eq.	New Jersey Equity Reports
N.J. Super	New Jersey Superior Court Reports
N.J.L.	New Jersey Law Reports
N.J. Tax	New Jersey Tax Court Reports
P.(2d)	Pacific Reporter, 2d Series
Pa.	Pennsylvania State Reports
S.Ct	Supreme Court Reports
Trade Cases	Trade Cases
U.S.	United States Reports
Wash. 2d	Washington Reports, 2d Series
W & H	Wage & Hour Cases
WL	WESTLAW

Index

EMPLOYEES, INSURANCE FOR

EMPLOYERS

EMPLOYMENT, NATURE OF RELATIONSHIP

EMPLOYMENT, OUTSIDE

EMPLOYMENT, TERMINATION OF (*see* TERMINATION OF EMPLOYMENT; WRONGFUL DISCHARGE)

EMPLOYMENT ADVERTISING

EMPLOYMENT AGENCIES

EMPLOYMENT CONTRACT, 1-1

EMPLOYMENT PRACTICES, UNLAWFUL

ENFORCEMENT

UNION COUNTY COLLEGE
3 9354 00137023 4